The Mounted Police and Prairie Society, 1873-1919

The Mounted Police and Prairie Society, 1873-1919

edited by William M. Baker

Canadian Plains Research Center
University of Regina
1998

Copyright © Canadian Plains Research Center 1998

Copyright Notice

All rights reserved. No part of this work covered by the copyrights hereon may be reproduced in any form or by any means — graphic, electronic or mechanical — without the prior written permission of the publisher. Any request for photocopying, recording, taping or information storage and retrieval systems of any part of this book shall be directed in writing to the Canadian Reprography Collective.

Canadian Plains Research Center
University of Regina
Regina, Saskatchewan S4S 0A2
Canada

Since this page cannot accommodate all the copyright notices, page 363 constitutes an extension of the copyright page.

Note: Every possible effort has been made to contact copyright holders. Any copyright holders who could not be reached are urged to contact the publisher.

Canadian Cataloguing in Publication Data

Main entry under title:

The Mounted Police and prairie society, 1873-1919
(Canadian plains studies, ISSN 0317-6290 ; 36)

Includes bibliographical references.
ISBN 0-88977-103-0

1. Royal North West Mounted Police (Canada) – History.
2. Northwest, Canadian – History – 1870-1905.*
3. Prairie Provinces – History – 1905-1945.*
4. Frontier and pioneer life – Prairie Provinces.
I. Baker, William M. (William Melville), 1943-
II. University of Regina. Canadian Plains Research Center.
III. Series.

FC3216.2.M68 1998   363.2'09712   C98-920101-5   F1060.9.M68 1998

Cover Design: Alexander Angelov, Ishtar Publishing and Design
(ishtar@cableregina.com)
Cover photograph courtesy of the Royal Canadian Mounted Police Museum, Regina, Saskatchewan.

Printed and bound in Canada by
Hignell Printing Limited, Winnipeg, Manitoba.
Printed on acid-free paper.

Contents

Introduction
Twenty-five Years After: Mounted Police Historiography Since the 1973-74 Centennial of the Force
William M. Baker vii

Section A: First Nations
1. Cavalry or Police: Keeping the Peace on Two Adjacent Frontiers, 1870-1900
Desmond Morton 3
2. The Interlude: The North-West Mounted Police and the Blackfoot Peoples, 1874-1877
B.J. Mayfield 17
3. Policemen and Poachers: Indian Relations on the Ranching Frontier
John Jennings 41
4. Horse Stealing and the Borderline: The NWMP and the Control of Indian Movement, 1874-1900
Brian Hubner 53
5. The Wild Ones
H.A. Dempsey 71

Section B: Law Enforcement
6. Crime and Criminals in the North-West Territories, 1873-1905
R.C. Macleod 85
7. Mob Law Could Not Prevail
William Beahen 101
8. Tar and Feathers: The Mounted Police and Frontier Justice
Anna-Maria Mavromichalis 109

Section C: Social Issues
9. The NWMP and Minority Groups
R.C. Macleod 119
10. The Miners and the Mounties: The Royal North-West Mounted Police and the 1906 Lethbridge Strike
William M. Baker 137
11. The (Royal) North-West Mounted Police and Prostitution on the Canadian Prairies
S.W. Horrall 173
12. Abortion and Infanticide in Western Canada 1874 to 1916: A Criminal Case Study
William Beahen 193

Section D: Characteristics of the Force
13. Pioneers and Police on the Canadian Prairies, 1885-1914
Carl Betke 209

14. Fort Battleford and the Architecture of the North-West Mounted Police
Walter Hildebrandt. 231
15. Captain R. Burton Deane and Theatre on the Prairies, 1883-1901
William M. Baker 243
16. Character
Keith Walden 263

Section E: Crisis and Change

17. Malczewski's List: A Case Study of Royal North-West Mounted Police-Immigrant Relations
Steve Hewitt 297
18. The Royal North-West Mounted Police and Labour Unrest in Western Canda, 1919
S.W. Horrall. 307
19. The Surveillance State: The Origins of Domestic Intelligence and Counter-subversion in Canada, 1914-1921
Gregory S. Kealey. 325

Epilogue

From RNWMP to RCMP: The Power of Myth and the Reality of Transformation
S.R. Hewitt 351

INTRODUCTION

Twenty-five Years After: Mounted Police Historiography Since the 1973-74 Centennial of the Force

William M. Baker

The Mounted Police have long been a potent symbol of Canada and Canadians. Dedicated, upright, long-suffering, resourceful, determined, and effective, these modest superheroes are projected as model Canadians, the best the country has to offer.

On the other hand, the constable who stops us for speeding does not seem all that heroic. And we are familiar with the accusations of the dirty trick activities of the Mounties. We've listened to the complaints against the force by striking workers, Quebec separatists, aboriginal groups, ethnic minorities, and on and on. Moreover, we have all seen or heard the skits on television, radio, or live theatre where the Mounties are scorned, ridiculed, made to appear nothing short of ludicrous.

It seems that the Mounted Police arouse strong emotions, whether positive or negative. Yet the force, and its personnel, deserve to be heaped with neither plaudits nor abuse (nor mockery for that matter). There were moments of triumph and times of failure in the history of the Mounted Police. But even the actions viewed as a success at the time can become tarnished over the years as standards of judgement change. Take, for example, the role played by the Mounted Police in restricting the movement of the First Nations of the Plains in the last quarter of the nineteenth century. At the time it seemed like a good idea to most white Canadians; today it seems domineering at best and genocidal to a culture at worst.

Given the status of the Mounties as a Canadian icon, and given the conflicting and changing evaluations of their actions and policies, the historical examination of the force is of considerable importance. The collection that follows presents a variety of scholarly explorations of the nature and role of the Mounties on the Prairies from the formation of the North West Mounted Police in 1873-74 to its transformation into the Royal Canadian Mounted Police in 1919-20. Indeed, taken together, these articles demonstrate the involvement of the Mounted Police in virtually all facets of Prairie society throughout the period. The history of the Mounties opens doors to the exploration of an almost unlimited array of topics concerning the so-called pioneering era of the Canadian Plains. Thus, while the collection will not provide definitive answers to all questions about the virtues and vices of the Mounties, at the very least it will substantially expand the reader's knowledge about the force, its activities, and the development of prairie society.

On the occasion of the Mounted Police centennial there was a proliferation of celebrations, displays, and publications.[1] Many of the publications were reprints.[2] And while the new works removed many of the overtones of racial supremacy and British imperialism that characterized earlier writings about the force, none provided comprehensive and substantial new insight. The most substantial and best general history produced at the time of the centennial, Stan Horrall's *The Pictorial History of the Royal Canadian Mounted Police*,[3] mapped little new territory but was a useful popular history that may still be consulted to advantage. Indeed, when one views the potboilers on the Mounties available at airport bookstores today, one wishes it had remained in print. Still, as C.P. Stacey put it, "The centenary of the Royal Canadian Mounted Police came and went in 1973 without producing the thorough and scholarly history of the force which is so much needed."[4]

---

1   For an analysis of the official centennial celebrations see J.M.F. Dawson, "Re-weaving the Tapestry of Order: The Royal Canadian Mounted Police's 1973 Centennial and the Renovation of Historical Narrative," M.A. thesis, Queen's University, 1995. See also Dawson's new book based on the thesis, *The Mountie from Dime Novel to Disney* (Toronto: Between the Lines, 1998).

2   At the time the publishing arm of Coles Bookstores had an active program of republishing out-of-print Canadian materials in its Coles Canadiana Collection. For the Mounted Police centennial it reprinted old histories, such as E.J. Chambers' first book-length history of the force, *The Royal North-West Mounted Police: A Corps History* (Montreal: Mortimer, 1906), and memoirs, such as R.B. Deane, *Mounted Police Life in Canada: A Record of Thirty-one Years' Service* (London: Cassell and Co., 1916), J.G. Donkin, *Trooper and Redskin in the Far Northwest...* (London: Sampson Low, Marston, Searle, & Rivington, 1889), and S.B. Steele, *Forty Years in Canada: Reminiscences of the Great North-West...* (New York: Dodd Mead & Co., 1915). Even more impressive in showing the depth of Coles' commitment to preserving and promoting the history of the Mounties for the centennial was the printing in four volumes of the first fifteen years of the annual reports of the Mounted Police which had appeared in the Sessional Papers of the Parliament of Canada (*Opening Up The West... 1874-1881, Settlers and Rebels... 1882-1885, Law and Order... 1886-1887,* and *The New West 1888-1889* — the report for 1875 was not printed in the Sessional Papers and therefore did not appear in the first of the Coles Canadiana volumes; it was, however, printed by the Historical Society of Alberta in 1975 under the title *A Chronicle of the Canadian West...*). Coles was not the only publisher with a Canadiana facsimile reprint series. Hurtig, for example, reprinted A.L. Haydon's *The Riders of the Plains* (London: A. Melrose, 1910) in 1971, thus getting a jump on the market for the centennial. Hurtig also collaborated with the Glenbow-Alberta Institute in the 1973 publication *William Parker: Mounted Policeman*, a collection of Parker's letters and recollections, edited by Hugh Dempsey. Another effort of Dempsey as editor and the Glenbow as co-publisher, this time with McClelland and Stewart West, was the 1974 work *A Winter at Fort Macleod* based on the letters, sketches and paintings of R.B. Nevitt who provided medical services to the force during the first winter of 1874-75. Mika Publishers reprinted Jean D'Artigue's *Six Years in the Canadian North-West* (translated from the French by L.C. Corbett and S. Smith; Toronto: Hunter, Rose, 1882); while Dent (Canada) brought out a second edition of Cecil Denny's *The Law Marches West* (Toronto: J.M. Dent and Sons (Canada), 1939). Thus if nothing else, scholars have reason to be grateful that the centennial provided an opportunity to bring both primary sources and classic works into print.

3   Published by McGraw-Hill Ryerson Ltd., 1973.

4   In the *Canadian Historical Review* 56, no. 4 (December 1975): 461. Stacey was reviewing Horrall's *Pictorial History* and N. and W. Kelly, *The Royal Canadian Mounted Police: A Century of History* (Edmonton: Hurtig Publishers, 1973). Stacey considered these two as being the most worthy of notice amongst the publications occasioned by the centennial, but he had few words of praise for either. R. Atkin, *Maintain the Right: The Early History of the North West Mounted Police, 1873-1900* (New York:

For the most part, pre-centennial writing on the history of the force could be described as episodic, nostalgic, eulogistic, antiquarian, non-scholarly, romantic, and heroic historiography.⁵ This literature was almost formulaic in its emphasis on the Mounties as a frontier force, with a concentration on the pre-settlement era on the Prairies and then switching the focus to the Yukon and the far north. These accounts favoured a chronological rather than a thematic approach and gave much greater emphasis to the nineteenth than the twentieth century. Equally evident is that there were favourite episodes to be presented, such as the Trek West, Sitting Bull and Walsh, the Almighty Voice incident, the Klondike Gold Rush, the so-called Lost Patrol in the north, and so forth. In virtually all these accounts the Mounties always came out smelling like roses. The Trek West, for instance, could have been viewed as a monumental fiasco of poor planning, ignorance, incompetence, and cruelty to men and beasts. In the received interpretation, however, the Trek exemplified courage, determination, and the building of character and strength in the face of formidable odds.⁶

In a very real sense, the historical literature on the Mounties up to the centennial was little more than an extension of the public image the force was at great pains to develop and maintain. For example, one of the most thorough works on the Mounties, J.P. Turner's 1950 publication *The North-West Mounted Police 1873-1893* in two volumes, is little more than a synopsis of the official reports of the police published annually in the Sessional Papers of the Canadian Parliament. Even the previously mentioned *Pictorial History* was prepared by the RCMP Staff Historian, Stan Horrall. The volume expressed Horrall's opinions, not officially those of the RCMP

John Day Co., 1973), though not a comprehensive survey, was an equally noteworthy publication for the popular audience.

5   In addition to the items cited in note 2, the following books were standard references on Mounted Police history: L.C. Douthwaite, *The Royal Canadian Mounted Police* (Toronto: Ryerson Press, 1939); R.C. Fetherstonhaugh, *The Royal Canadian Mounted Police* (New York: Garden City Publishing Co., 1940); T.M. Longstreth, *The Silent Force: Scenes From the Life of the Mounted Police of Canada* (New York: The Century Co., 1927); R.G. MacBeth, *Policing the Plains: Being the Real-Life Record of the Famous North-West Mounted Police* (London: Hodder and Stoughton, 1921). There were also dozens of articles that appeared in everything from the *Canadian Illustrated News* of July 1881 (by R.B. Nevitt) to the *Canada Year Book 1957-58* (by L.H. Nicholson). There is no single, comprehensive bibliography on the Mounted Police. The most useful guides to publications are located in V. Arora, *Royal Canadian Mounted Police: A Bibliography* (Regina: Bibliographic Services Division, Provincial Library, 1973); B.A. Drew, *Lawmen in Scarlet: An Annotated Guide to Royal Canadian Mounted Police in Print and Performance* (Metuchen, NJ: The Scarecrow Press, Inc., 1990); C.D. Shearing et al., *Policing in Canada: A Bibliography* (Ottawa: Solicitor General Canada, Research Division, 1979); the books by Macleod and Walden cited elsewhere in this volume; and the Klassen article and the end bibliography in *Men in Scarlet* cited in note 9. In addition to the various listings I have compiled for course purposes at the University of Lethbridge, probably the most comprehensive list of sources, both non-fiction and fiction, is that of the library of the avid collector and former Mounted Policeman, Al Lund, #21313 (Retired).

6   The most recent account of the March, *The Great Adventure: How the Mounties Conquered the West* by David Cruise and Alison Griffiths (Toronto: Viking, 1996), does not minimize the ineptitude of the force, but it still is a descriptive, sensationalist account rather than an analytical evaluation. As the dust jacket trumpets: "This is our *Lonesome Dove* — gripping, shocking, hilarious, sad, glorious — and true." Keith Walden has explored the legend of the Trek in "The Great March of the Mounted Police in Popular Literature, 1873-1973," Canadian Historical Association, *Historical Papers 1980*, 33-56. A recent statement of the traditional interpretation of Mounted Police history appeared in the *Royal Bank Letter* 79, no. 2 (Spring 1998) under the title "Canada and the Mounties."

although the copyright was held by the RCMP, but naturally his position imbued his views with a positive impression of the history of the force.

By 1973-74 academic historians were beginning to evaluate the history of the Mounted Police. Horrall himself had left the force to pursue academic credentials in history right up to the graduate level before returning many years later to become its official historian. In 1972 his article "Sir John A. Macdonald and the Mounted Police Force for the Northwest Territories," was published in the *Canadian Historical Review*. Stan Hanson had published an article about policing along the 49th parallel in Saskatchewan.[7] E.C. Morgan had completed an M.A. thesis and published an article revealing the troubles inside the force and the public complaints about it during the first decade of the existence of the Mounties. The most impressive collection of essays produced by the centennial itself was the outgrowth of a conference at the University of Lethbridge. The papers, published under the title, *Men in Scarlet*,[8] were prepared by such senior scholars as George Stanley and Hugh Dempsey (who edited the volume), and by young, newly established historians such as David Breen and Rod Macleod, who had just completed an admirable Ph.D. dissertation about the Mounted Police to 1905. Within the Canadian historical profession, then in the midst of a golden age of expansion and innovation, new priorities and emphases were being established. Historical studies related to ethnicity, race, class, family, gender, disease, mobility, lifestyle, *mentalité*, social control, social disorder, Native peoples, recreation, sexuality, and a host of other themes under the general rubric of social history were emerging. Writings on the history of the Mounties began to reflect that shift. In *Men in Scarlet*, for example, John Jennings and Bill Morrison provided far more acute analyses of the relationship between the Mounted Police and Native groups, while George Stanley, Dick Harrison, and Henry Klassen all explored aspects of how the image of the Mounted Police had been created.[9]

The centennial publication that differed most radically from its predecessors was *An Unauthorized History of the RCMP*[10] by Lorne and Caroline Brown, at the time a lecturer in political science at the Regina campus and a researcher for CBC respectively. Not only was it highly critical of the Mounties but also it breezed through the pre-1919 history of the force and concentrated on more recent activities. The response of mainstream academics to the *Unauthorized History* was dismissive, asserting that the authors' leftist and presentist political agenda had resulted in an extremist diatribe against the Mounties. Still, the Browns demonstrated that the history of the force could be viewed as the story of the physical arm of the state oppressing minorities, workers, radicals and reformers in support of a social and economic elite.

---

7   S. Hanson, "Policing the International Boundary Area In Saskatchewan, 1890-1910," *Saskatchewan History* 19 (1966): 61-73.

8   Published by Historical Society of Alberta/McClelland and Stewart West, n.d. [1975?].

9   The articles published in *Men in Scarlet* by the aforementioned scholars are as follows: G.F.G. Stanley, "The Man Who Sketched the Great March"; H.A. Dempsey, "Writing-On-Stone and the Boundary Detachment"; R.C. Macleod, "The Mounted Police and Politics"; D.H. Breen, "The Mounted Police and the Ranching Frontier"; D. Harrison, "The Mounted Police in Fiction"; and H. Klassen, "The Mounties and the Historians."

10 Published by James Lewis & Samuel, 1973.

The changing trends in historical scholarship on the Mounted Police which were glimpsed during the centennial have been steadily extended over the past twenty-five years. Samples of that literature are presented in this collection. The essays demonstrate the greater depth of analysis and expanded breadth of coverage of Mounted Police historiography since the centennial. Five general themes are presented.

First we have studies exploring a variety of aspects of the relationship of the Mounted Police and the aboriginal inhabitants of the Plains. Chapter 1, by the prolific Canadian historian, Desmond Morton, is an overview of the origins and first quarter century of the North West Mounted Police. It provides a continental context for the early years of the Mounted Police, for what happened south of the 49th parallel was crucial to the formation and operation of the force. There were important distinctions in circumstances, in historical pattern, and in political ideology on the two sides of the border, but Morton notes that the negative result for First Nations people was similar. The second chapter, part of a Master's thesis by B.J. Mayfield, gives detailed analysis of the relationship between the Blackfoot peoples and the Mounted Police in the crucial period leading to the signing of Treaty 7 in 1877. It clearly indicates that people of the First Nations were not naive, gullible primitives in awe of the Mounties and eternally grateful to them for ending the trade in devil whiskey, but that their stance was based on a rational calculation about how best to defend their interests. As a result, it is fruitful to view Native expressions of confidence in the Mounties as flattery in order to win support from the force. Mayfield's analysis of the negotiations leading to Treaty 7 and its contents also indicates the basis for the emergence of a sense of betrayal by Native people.[11] Chapter 3, written by John Jennings, is one of the early attempts to provide a more even-handed approach than the pre-Centennial accounts which had asserted, in essence, that the Mounted Police had assisted and protected the indigenous people of the Canadian Plains, and, as a result, had been revered as friends. Jennings indicates that the relationship was infinitely more complex. Each party had multiple pressures on it. By the 1880s, for example, the threat of starvation hovered over Native bands. At the same time, the NWMP had the interests of the white ranching community to consider. Jennings makes the case that the tameness of the Canadian ranching frontier, which followed the buffalo days but preceded the farmer/settler era, was in large part due to the presence of the Mounted Police. The chapter also makes the important point that the Department of Indian Affairs and the NWMP were often at loggerheads in their approaches to Native people. Evidence of this conflict also emerges in the fourth chapter, written by Brian Hubner, but its main concern is to demonstrate how Canadian officialdom collaborated to restrict Native people to reserves, in spite of treaty promises to the contrary. Certainly, the Mounted Police were crucial factors in the physical curtailment of First Nations on the Canadian Prairies and one key element in this restriction was the prevention of cross-border horse theft. The concluding chapter in the section was prepared by Hugh Dempsey. For decades Dempsey has given exceptional service to the archival and historical communities of western Canada. Two topics he has turned to over and over again have been the history of the Mounted Police and the history of the Blackfoot people. The activities

---

11 For a recent evaluation of Treaty 7 from the Native perspective see Treaty 7 Elders and Tribal Council with Walter Hildebrandt, Dorothy First Rider, and Sarah Carter, *The True Spirit and Original Intent of Treaty 7* (Montreal: McGill-Queen's University Press, 1996).

related in the evocative episode included in this chapter demonstrate that Police-Blackfoot relations remained as complex as ever, even after the supposed watershed of the 1885 violence known in our history texts as the North-West Rebellion. It also shows the continued ability of Native peoples to resist total domination by white society. Finally, the reputed efficiency of the Mounties is brought down to earth by the details of their performance presented in this tale.

In Section B, the nature of Mounted Police law enforcement in reality — not the shibboleth of the Mountie always getting his man — is investigated. An excerpt from Rod Macleod's book, *The NWMP and Law Enforcement 1873-1905*, leads off. That volume was a trailbreaking publication which immediately raised the academic study of the Mounted Police to a new plateau. It remains the best single book on the North West Mounted Police and deserves to be brought back into print. Macleod assessed the focus of Mounted Police activity in the suppression of crime and determined that crimes which threatened to undermine the orderly development of Anglo-Canadian society on the Prairies were the ones given top priority by the force. At times, the views of important elements of Territorial society differed from those of the Mounted Police, as can be seen in chapter 7, Bill Beahen's account of a comic opera episode in Calgary. Beahen emphasizes that in the early days the Mounties felt obligated to step in, even in urban settings where municipal police forces existed, when order was threatened. On the other hand, the next chapter, by A.-M. Mavromichalis, about a tarring and feathering case in Lethbridge demonstrates that when social order and stability was not really challenged the Mounties were both unenthused about and unable to enforce the law. In fact, there are many examples — particularly for the so-called social vices such as liquor, gambling and prostitution — of the Mounted Police foregoing enforcement of the law if order was not threatened.

Section C probes the interaction of the force with various social groups, along with questions of morality, particularly as related to the Mounties' enforcement of laws prohibiting prostitution and abortion. The first chapter in this section, written by Rod Macleod, provides an overview of the attitudes and interactions of the Mounties with a variety of social groups whether ethnic, religious, or occupational. Chapter 10, a contribution by the editor, adopts a case-study approach to explore the relationship of the Mounted Police and striking coalminers. In the final two chapters in this section, two staff historians with the RCMP, Horrall and Beahen, examine, respectively, the "social evils" of prostitution and abortion/infanticide. Aside from providing fascinating information about the Police handling of these groups and activities, this section also demonstrates the wealth of information contained in the manuscript materials of the force. All four chapters also show that in attitude and approach to both minority groups and moral issues, the Mounted Police generally shared the stance of the dominant Anglo-Canadian middle class, but that their perceptions and actions were also shaped by the reality of face-to-face contact with minorities and by practical difficulties of enforcing moral laws on a hypocritical society.

Under Section D, the nature, cultural impact, and image of the force is analyzed. In his effort to understand why the force became so popular with residents of the Prairies, Carl Betke (chapter 13) examined the day-to-day duties of the force and found that the real strength of public support for the force was built on such seemingly mundane, unheroic activities as providing relief, enforcement of quarantine regulations, and visiting immigrant settlements. Certainly, the usual day of the typical Mountie, as is the case with most policemen most of the time, was filled not with exciting action but with boring routine. Indeed, the (Royal) North West

Mounted Policeman may have had more in common with constables elsewhere than the received version would suggest. Perhaps the Mounties were not such an elite force after all. Such issues interest Greg Marquis, a prominent historian of Canadian police history. Indeed, in a fine forthcoming article Marquis compares the Mounted Police with the Royal Irish Constabulary which was, supposedly, the model for the Mounties.[12] The Mounted Police did not merely import policing techniques to the Prairies, they also brought much cultural baggage. Architectural forms are an important symbol of a culture and, as Walter Hildebrandt points out in chapter 14, Mounted Police buildings are about the first physical representations of Anglo-Canadian culture to be erected on the Canadian Prairies. Sports, music, organization of fraternal associations, painting, flower and vegetable gardening, and a multitude of other activities were also practiced and promoted by members of the force as part of the spread of Anglo-Canadian culture to prairie Canada. Drama was one such activity as demonstrated in chapter 15 on Superintendent Deane's involvement in theatre. Concluding the section is a portion of Keith Walden's fascinating study of the literature, both fiction and non-fiction, on the Mounted Police. The excerpt examines what characteristics constituted the basis for the heroic status of Mounted Policemen, as seen in the writings on the force, and why these attributes fulfilled deep needs within English- speaking society.

In the final section the transformation of the Mounted Police during and immediately after the First World War is subject to debate by three historians. Hewitt's writing on accusations made against Mounties raises the possibility that all members of the force had not been squeaky clean. Indeed, any detailed examination of the history of the Mounted Police provides numerous examples of the misdemeanours, or worse, of members.[13] This chapter also shows that the duties of the force had been greatly transformed by the war. Things did not return to the pre-war situation in 1919. Rather, it seemed that a new war had begun. Horrall's chapter on the 1919 labour upheaval may defend the role of the force in moderating anti-communist hysteria but it certainly shows how the Winnipeg General Strike and other labour troubles were instrumental in creating the new body, the Royal Canadian Mounted Police. Finally, a contribution by Greg Kealey, a prolific historian who has been at the forefront of the campaign to make available and utilize RCMP materials for the post-1919 era, provides a detailed study of the process of transformation and makes the argument that the force emerged as a spy agency working on behalf of a capitalist state.

The Epilogue, written especially for the volume by Steve Hewitt, not only makes the case that the force was dramatically changed after 1919-20, but also that the new organization cashed in heavily on the positive image created by the old force.

The collection has both a geographic and temporal focus. The essays concern the Prairies, not the North. Consequently, the stimulating work of Bill Morrison and Thomas Stone on the Mounted Police in the Yukon and far north has not been

---

12   G. Marquis, "Policing Two Imperial Frontiers: The Royal Irish Constabulary and the North-West Mounted Police," in L. Knafla and J. Swainger, eds., *Essays in the History of Canadian Law. The Middle Kingdom: The Northwest Territories and the Prairie Provinces, 1670-1945* (Toronto: University of Toronto Press for the Osgoode Society for Legal History, forthcoming).

13   See, for example, the sordid tale told in Lois Simmie's *The Secret Lives of Sgt. John Wilson: A True Story of Love & Murder* (Vancouver: Greystone Books, 1995).

included.[14] As far as restricting the selection to the pre-1920 period when the force was the North West Mounted Police (after 1904, the Royal NWMP) is concerned, the decision was a matter of both practicality and interpretation. In the first place, the length of the volume had to be kept within bounds. On the second count, the RCMP was dramatically different in size, function, operation, and location compared to the (R)NWMP. After 1919 the RCMP's greatly increased manpower covered the entire country, did no ordinary policing (except in the North) and did not return to that function even in Saskatchewan and Alberta for a decade, and concerned itself heavily with surveillance and security duties. Moreover, it was largely mechanized, the "mounted" part of its name becoming more and more a matter of mere show and of trading on the good reputation of the old force. In short, the RCMP simply was not the (R)NWMP unless one believes that a plane is a bird because both have wings. What this means, however, is the exclusion of some very exhilarating publications and presentations on the post-1919 RCMP era by such scholars as Paul Axelrod, Michael Butt, Mike Dawson, Larry Hannant, Greg Kealey, David Kimmel, Gary Kinsman, Michael Lonardo, Daniel Robinson, Christabelle Sethna, Wesley Wark, and Reg Whitaker.[15] These authors do not concentrate on Mounted Police activities on the Prairies, but the 1919 cut-off date also means omitting studies specific to the Prairies prepared by such an individual as Glen Makahonuk, and much of the work of Steve Hewitt.[16] In spite of these necessary omissions, the essays printed in this

---

14   See W.R. Morrison, *Showing the Flag: The Mounted Police and Canadian Sovereignty in the North, 1894-1925* (Vancouver: University of British Columbia Press, 1985); and T. Stone, *Miners' Justice: Migration, Law and Order on the Alaska-Yukon Frontier, 1873-1902* (New York: Peter Lang Publishing, 1988). In addition, both authors have published a variety of articles of relevance to the history of the Mounted Police.

15   Sample works of these scholars are: P. Axelrod, "Spying on the Young in Depression and War: Students, Youth Groups and the RCMP," *Labour/Le Travail (L/LT)* 35 (Spring 1995): 43-63; M. Butt, "RCMP 'O' Division Surveillance of the Communist Party of Canada's Attempts to Mobilize Toronto Unemployed, 1929-1931," paper presented to the Canadian Historical Association conference, St. Catherines, June 1996; M. Dawson, "Marching to Maturity and Riding to Respect: The Emergence of the Mountie as a Canadian Symbol," paper presented to the "Imperial Canada" conference, Edinburgh, May 1995; L. Hannant, *The Infernal Machine: Investigating the Loyalty of Canada's Citizens* (Toronto: University of Toronto Press, 1995); G.S. Kealey, "The Early Years of State Surveillance of Labour and the Left in Canada: The Institutional Framework of the Royal Canadian Mounted Police Security and Intelligence Apparatus, 1918-26," in W.K. Wark, ed., *Espionage: Past, Present, Future?* (Ilford, Essex: Frank Cass & Co., 1994), 129-48; D.J. Robinson and D. Kimmel, "The Queer Career of Homosexual Security Vetting in Cold War Canada," *Canadian Historical Review* 74 (1994): 319-45; G. Kinsman, "'Character Weaknesses' and 'Fruit Machines': Towards an Analysis of the Anti-Homosexual Security Campaign in the Canadian Civil Service," *L/LT* 35 (Spring 1995): 133-61; M. Lonardo, "Under a Watchful Eye: A Case Study of Police Surveillance During the 1930s," *L/LT* 35 (Spring 1995): 11-41; D. Robinson, "Planning for the 'Most Serious Contingency': Alien Internment, Arbitrary Detention, and the Canadian State 1938-39," *Journal of Canadian Studies* 28, no. 2 (Summer 1993): 5-20; C. Sethna, "High School Confidential: RCMP Surveillance of Secondary School Activists," paper presented to the Canadian Historical Association conference, Ottawa, June 1, 1998; W.K. Wark, "Security Intelligence in Canada, 1864-1945: The History of a 'National Insecurity State'," in K. Neilson and B.J.C. McKercher, eds., *Go Spy the Land: Military Intelligence in History* (Westport, CT: Praeger Publishers, 1992), 153-78; and R. Whitaker, "Apprehended Insurrection? RCMP Intelligence and the October Crisis," *Queen's Quarterly* 100, no. 2 (Summer 1993): 383-406. Many of these scholars have many more books, articles and presentations to their credit. Kealey and Whitaker have been the driving force behind the ongoing publication of the multi-volumed RCMP Security Bulletins (1919-1945).

volume include the work of numerous leading scholars and bring together in one place many of the most important of the post-centennial writings on the history of the force. Readers will draw different interpretive conclusions about the role and function of the force from these articles. Collectively, however, they demonstrate the significant deepening of understanding of the pre-1920 history of the Mounted Police that has taken place over the last twenty-five years.

Although the scholarly examination of the history of the Mounties in the post-1919 era has scarcely begun, there is plenty remaining to be done on the earlier period.[17] For example, Rod Macleod's excellent breakthrough book, *The North-West Mounted Police and Law Enforcement 1873-1905*, does not include the age of massive immigration and settlement in the new provinces of Saskatchewan and Alberta. The topic of gender relations as seen both through the case files, reports, letters and diaries of the Mounties, and through the masculine and feminine stereotypes projected in Mounted Police literature would be fascinating to pursue.[18] A pioneer society's treatment of the indigent, the infirm, the diseased, the mentally and physically challenged, and the other unfortunates, as seen through the records of the force, would also be a fruitful subject of study. An examination of the visual representation of the Mounted Police in photographs, paintings, sketches, advertisements, and cartoons could prove as valuable in comprehending the image of the Mounties as have the studies of Mounted Police literature by Dick Harrison, Robert Thacker and Keith Walden.[19] At various levels of sophistication for different audiences, the history of the Mounted Police should remain an endless source of fascination for decades to come. For scholars of Canada, the force has been so important in the history of the country on so many levels that continuing examination

---

16 G. Makahonuk, "The Saskatoon Relief Camp Workers' Riot of May 8, 1933: An Expression of Class Conflict," *Saskatchewan History* 37, no. 2 (Spring 1984): 55-72; S. Hewitt, "September 1931: A Re-interpretation of the Royal Canadian Mounted Police's Handling of the 1931 Estevan Strike and Riot," *L/LT* 39 (Spring 1997): 159-78; Hewitt, "Spying 101: The RCMP's Secret Activities at the University of Saskatchewan, 1920-1971," *Saskatchewan History* 47, no. 2 (1995): 35-44; and Hewitt, "'We Are Sitting at the Edge of a Volcano': Winnipeg During the On-to-Ottawa Trek," *Prairie Forum* 19, no. 1 (1994): 51-64.

17 The detailed new publication convering the years when L.W. Herchmer was commissioner, *Red Coats on the Prairies: The North-West Mounted Police 1886-1900*, by William Beahen and Stan Horrall (Regina: Centax Books/Print West Publishing Services, 1998), provides a good sample of the range of themes involved in historical studies of the Mounted Police.

18 A start on this theme has been made by several scholars. Early relations between the Mounted Police and aboriginal women have been examined in S. Carter, *Capturing Women: The Manipulation of Cultural Imagery in Canada's Prairie West* (Montreal and Kingston: McGill-Queen's University Press, 1997). L.R. Baskier-Miller is currently engaged in a Ph.D. at the University of Alberta on "R.C.M.P. and Women in the West 1875-1950." See also M. Dawson, "'That Nice Red Coat Goes To My Head Like Champagne': Popular Images of the Mountie, 1880-1960," *Journal of Canadian Studies*, forthcoming; and S. Hewitt, "The Masculine Mountie: The Royal Canadian Mounted Police as a Male Institution, 1914-1939," *Journal of the Canadian Historical Association* (1996): 153-74.

19 An excerpt of Walden's fine book is included in this volume. For Harrison, aside from the item cited in note 9, see his "Introduction: Selling a Birth-Rite For a Mass of Plottage," in the collection he edited, *Best Mounted Police Stories* (Edmonton: University of Alberta Press, 1978). See also R. Thacker, "Canada's Mounted: The Evolution of a Legend," *Journal of Popular Culture* 14, no. 2 (Fall 1980): 298-312; and R. Thacker, "Mountie Versus Outlaw: Inventing the Western Hero," *Journal of Canadian Studies* 20, no. 1 (Spring 1985): 161-69.

of the Mounted Police will no doubt necessitate a similar volume another quarter-century hence.

The essays in this collection were prepared by scholars. Most were professional historians, some working for the RCMP, some for Parks Canada, some for academic institutions. Several of the authors were students also working in an academic environment. With few exceptions — the excerpt from Mayfield's dissertation, the Introduction, and the Epilogue — all items have been previously published. For the most part the content and stylistic preferences of the original publication have been retained. Except for Hildebrandt's article on architecture, illustrations have been omitted. The editor thanks all publishers and authors for their willingness to allow re-publication in this volume. Thanks as well to Steve Hewitt for preparing such a fitting Epilogue. I also wish to express my apprecia- tion to Corrine Lenfesty, Charlene Sawatsky and Bhagwan Dua for their invaluable assistance in the preparation of this collection. Finally, the volume is dedicated to my students at the University of Lethbridge, past, present, and future, particularly those in History 4070: The Mounted Police and Western Canada, 1873-1919. Thanks for all your support over the years.

SECTION A

First Nations

ONE

Cavalry or Police:
Keeping the Peace on Two Adjacent Frontiers, 1870-1900

Desmond Morton

In an article in the *Pacific Historical Review* for 1955, Professor Paul F. Sharp renewed Frederick Jackson Turner's invitation to test the famous frontier thesis in other settings. Sharp had done so in his own pioneering book on the Canadian-American West, finding the differences more significant than the similarities.[1] In the article, he went on to contrast relations between the Canadian government and the aboriginal people of the Northwest with comparable developments in the United States and Australia: "Against a background of violence and hatred south of the forty-ninth parallel, the Canadian government conceived and executed an orderly, well-planned and honorable policy."[2]

The tribute was overly generous. A century of Indian policy has left the Canadian native people in much the same state of poverty and dependence as their brothers south of the border.[3] Sharp's contrast between Canadian order and American violence may be questioned in detail although north of the forty-ninth parallel it is established as one of those self-congratulatory myths which bind a nation together.[4] While Americans, reputedly, were electing sheriffs, summoning the U.S. Cavalry and filling the graves on Boot Hill, Canadians were establishing law and order with the aid of a few hundred men of the North West Mounted Police.[5] According to Russell

---

1   Paul F. Sharp, *Whoop-up Country: The Canadian-American West 1865-1885* (Minneapolis, 1955, 2 vols.).

2   Paul F. Sharp, "Three Frontiers: Some Comparative Studies of Canadian, American and Australian Settlement," *Pacific Historical Review*, XXIV, 1955, p. 373.

3   See Roy W. Meyer, "The Canadian Sioux: Refugees from Minnesota" in Roger L. Nichols and George R. Adams (eds.), *The American Indian: Past and Present* (Waltham, Mass., 1971), for a generous account. On Canadian Indians, see G.F.G. Stanley, "The Indian Background of Canadian History," Canadian Historical Association, *Historical Papers*, 1952; Heather Robertson, *Reservations are for Indians* (Toronto, 1970); Harold Cardinal, *The Unjust Society: The Tragedy of Canadian Indians* (Edmonton, 1971).

4   See, for example, the essays in William Kilbourn (ed.), *Canada: The Peaceable Kingdom* (Toronto, 1971).

5   See, for example, S.W. Horrall, "Sir John A. Macdonald and the Mounted Police Force for the Northwest Territories," *Canadian Historical Review*, LIII, 1972, pp. 179-80. To illustrate, see D.G.

F. Weigley, there were 943 military engagements in the American West between 1866 and 1895; in the Canadian Northwest, there were only six or seven comparable clashes, almost all of them associated with the North-West Campaign of 1885.[6]

Why were the adjacent frontiers apparently so different? Since whites, not Indians, are found at the root of most trouble in the West, Sharp agreed with most American historians that a ten-year lag in settlement had allowed the Canadian tribes and the police to adjust to new patterns of existence.[7] Robert M. Utley, the major historian of the United States Army during the Indian wars, conceded that police methods might sometimes have been more effective than conventional military tactics but he also concluded that the Canadian approach succeeded only "because the sparsity of settlement prevented serious competition between whites and Indians for the lands and resources of the Northwest Territories."[8] However, friction between white and native people was not simply a function of numbers but of law, policy and political philosophy as well.[9] "The fact that the Police arrived before settlement," a young Canadian historian has commented, "is not nearly so significant as what they did when they got there."[10] The predominantly conservative political values of post-Confederation Canada allowed the use of both law and authoritarian structures to protect minority rights. In his recent study of the Mounted Police, R.C. Macleod has argued that the force succeeded because, in contrast to British and American practice, it combined judicial and administrative functions in a kind of benevolent despotism moderated, at least until 1905, by the presumption that it would be no more than a temporary expedient.[11]

In the United States, prevailing interpretations of liberty and democracy and a recurrent suspicion of militarism repeatedly undermined the Army's attempts to resume control of Indian policy after 1849.[12] Congress usually preferred the sometimes

---

Creighton, *Dominion of the North* (Toronto, 1957, rev. ed.), p. 360 or Douglas Hill, *The Opening of the Canadian West* (London, 1967), p. 133. A perceptive study of one of the most celebrated police-Indian encounters, Inspector James Walsh and Sitting Bull, is C. Frank Turner, *Across the Medicine Line* (Toronto, 1973).

6   Russell F. Weigley, *History of the United States Army* (New York, 1967), p. 267. (Canadian engagements would include Duck Lake, Fish Creek, Cut Knife Hill, Batoche and Frenchman's Butte, all in 1885, with perhaps the battle with Almighty Voice in 1897 as a final conflict.)

7   Sharp, "Three Frontiers," p. 373.

8   Robert M. Utley, *Frontier Regulars: The United States Army and the Indian, 1866-1891* (New York, 1973), pp. 55-6. The sparsity was certainly striking. In 1880, the Dakotas boasted 133,147 people while the 1881 census found only 6,974 whites and Metis in the entire Canadian North-West. See G.F.G. Stanley, *The Birth of Western Canada: A History of the Riel Rebellions* (Toronto, 1961, rev. ed.), p. 187. The significance of the Metis as a mediating force in white-Indian relations also appears to have little United States counterpart.

9   See, for example, President Jackson's response to the decision in Worcester v. Georgia, 1832. On American Indian policy, see Francis P. Prucha, *American Indian Policy in the Formative Years* (Cambridge, Mass., 1962); Lorring Benson Priest, *Uncle Sam's Stepchildren* (New Brunswick, N.J., 1942; Lincoln, Neb., 1969).

10   John Jennings, "The Plains Indians and the Law" in Hugh A. Dempsey (ed.), *Men in Scarlet* (Calgary [1974]), pp. 50, 54.

11   R.C. Macleod, *The North-West Mounted Police and Law Enforcement, 1873-1905* (Toronto, 1976), pp. 4-6 and passim.

12   On the U.S. Army officers and Indian-white relations, see, for example, Robert G. Alhearn, "War Paint against Brass; The Army and the Plains Indians," *Montana: The Magazine of Western History*, VI,

inept and frequently corrupt agencies of the Department of the Interior. In Canada, one finds only the palest reflection of the ideal of possessive individualism which, in turn, inspired the doctrine of severalty as the ultimate solution of the Indian problem. For good or ill, Canada produced no equivalent to the Dawes Act of 1887.[13] Western Indians on Canadian reserves continued to hold land in common.

Canadian politicians of the Confederation era were preoccupied with avoiding what they considered to be "excesses" in the United States constitution.[14] The concern was bipartisan. "Our chiefest care," insisted Richard Cartwright, a Liberal, "must be to train the majority to respect the rights of the minority, to prevent the claims of the few from being trampled under foot by the caprice or passion of the many."[15] That minority could, of course, be the rich;[16] it could also be the French Canadians, the Catholics, English-speaking Protestants in Quebec — or it could be the Indians.[17] Influential Canadians saw the American West as a manifestation of the dangers of democracy and materialism; they wished no imitation on their side of the border. Visiting Edmonton in 1895, that feminist virago, Lady Aberdeen, noted with satisfaction that most of the newcomers were "heartily glad" to become British subjects but "there is a remnant who would like to introduce American ideas as to what conduct in the West should be. These must be dealt with ruthlessly, & the magistrates & N.W. Mounted Police are determined that this shall be the case if they can manage it."[18]

Canadians may explain the contrast between the frontiers by differing ideologies while Americans point to delayed settlement; both must recognize the role of accident and of defence considerations. Far from learning from American experience and planning a judicious interval between the despatch of a police force and the advent of white settlers, the Canadian government planned that the costly burden of law enforcement would be assumed only as settlement advanced.[19] Macdonald and his cabinet endured years of well-authenticated reports of murder, violence and illegal whiskey trading without displaying any of the purported Canadian devotion to law and order. What moved the prime minister was a consideration which can hardly have disturbed his Washington counterparts: the threat posed by an expansive and powerful neighbour.

Canadians of Macdonald's generation were obsessed by the American claim of "Manifest Destiny." Sir John both shared the fears and also used them shrewdly for

---

    1956; Priest, *Uncle Sam's Stepchildren*, ch. 11; Robert M. Utley, "The Celebrated Peace Policy of General Grant," *North Dakota History*, XX, July, 1953.

13   On the Dawes Act, see Priest, *Uncle Sam's Stepchildren*, chs. XIII-XIX; William T. Hagan, *American Indians*, pp. 139-48.

14   On Canadian political attitudes, see, for example, Bruce W. Hodgins, "Democracy and the Ontario Fathers of Confederation" in *Profiles of a Province* (Toronto, 1967), pp. 83-91.

15   Cited in R.C. Brown, "Canadian Opinion after Confederation" in S.F. Wise and R.C. Brown (eds.), *Canada Views the United States: Nineteenth Century Political Attitudes* (Seattle, 1967), p. 113.

16   "The rights of the minority must be protected, and the rich are always fewer in number than the poor" (Macdonald's comment on the proposed Canadian senate, April 6, 1865, *Confederation Debates*).

17   Jennings, "Indians and the Law," p. 51.

18   Journal of Lady Aberdeen. August 5, 1895, Public Archives of Canada, Aberdeen Papers.

19   Horrall, "A Mounted Police Force," pp. 185-8.

political advantage. A prime goal of British North American confederation 1867 had been to safeguard the huge, empty territories of the Northwest from American expansion. If Canadians trampled on the feelings of Red River settlers in their haste to possess the Hudson's Bay Company territories in 1869, they remembered how the Company's weakness had cost them the rich Oregon Territory in 1846.[20] After the Civil War, the risk of overt aggression from the United States faded. The British military withdrawal of 1869-71, and the Treaty of Washington in 1871 served notice that Whitehall would never contemplate a re-match of the War of 1812.[21] The international boundary had been delineated in principle at all but a few points. By 1872, a joint commission was surveying its location on the prairies. An American threat remained only if the young Dominion failed to sustain its own authority. A breakdown in internal order, a movement for secession, a failure to restrain marauding Indian bands might provoke official or unofficial intervention from below the border. Whatever revisionists may believe, most imperial expansion in the 19th Century owed less to capitalist greed or missionary fervor than to disorder or lawlessness of the frontier. When slave-trading flourished, murder went unpunished and plundering tribesmen found easy sanctuary; the Victorian era found little reprehensible in the forcible extension of government and social order. As the dominant power in the Western Hemisphere, the United States had demonstrated its willingness to enforce its view of international law on Mexico during the Nineteenth Century. Specifically, Indian wars drew retaliatory U.S. military expeditions deep into Mexican territory in the 1870s.[22]

S.W. Horrall, the official historian of Royal Canadian Mounted Police, has emphasized Macdonald's view that Canada also could not afford an American-style West: "He feared that a repetition of the American experience would involve the dominion in a series of costly Indian wars, retard development in the Northwest and strain the country's resources."[23] Just as important, Canadian authority had to be firmly imposed so that Americans or their local sympathisers would have no excuse to disrupt the national destiny of a British North America *a mare usque ad marem.* To Edward Watkin, the British railway magnate, Macdonald confessed: "I would be quite willing, personally, to leave that whole country a wilderness for the next half-century but I fear if Englishmen do not go there, Yankees will..."[24]

How could peace and order be imposed on a huge and potentially turbulent territory at a cost that Canadian taxpayers would suffer? The Americans had solved their problem with a mixture of absent-mindedness and the brilliant inspiration of John C. Calhoun as War Secretary by deploying a tiny regular army on the forward edge of settlement and beyond. The 19th Century saw a growing distinction between

---

20 See, for example, A.C. Gluek, *Minnesota and the Manifest Destiny of the Canadian North West* (Toronto, 1965).

21 On the implications of the British withdrawal, see C.P. Stacey, *Canada and the British Army, 1846-1871* (Toronto, 1963, rev. ed.) and J.M. Hitsman, *Safeguarding Canada, 1763-1871*, ch. X.

22 Utley, *Frontier Regulars*, ch. VIII, esp. p. 355.

23 Horrall, "A Mounted Police Force," pp. 180-1. The $20 million spent annually on Indian wars by Congress was comparable to Canada's entire federal budget. Macleod, *Mounted Police*, p. 3.

24 Cited by P.B Waite, *The Life and Times of Confederation* (Toronto, 1962), p. 307. The most thorough treatment of defence considerations in Canada's policy in the Northwest remains C.P. Stacey's "The Military Aspect of Canada's Winning of the West, 1870-1885," *Canadian Historical Review*, XXI, 1940, pp. 1-24.

police and military functions in English-speaking countries. To the north, the Hudson's Bay Company had joyfully combined the roles when they occasionally wheedled detachments of British troops from the War Office: "If we succeed in getting a garrison established at Red River," wrote Sir George Simpson in 1845, "we shall be able to put down the illicit trade and keep the settlers in order."[25] However, when Canada acquired the Northwest, it had no standing army apart from the small remaining British garrison, and not the slightest desire to acquire one. To manage its vast new territory, Ottawa proposed to appoint a lieutenant governor and council, backed by a 250-man police force. "It seems to me," Macdonald wrote to the proposed commander, "that the best Force would be *Mounted Riflemen*, trained to act as cavalry, but also instructed in the Rifle exercises. They should also be instructed, as certain of the Line are, in the use of artillery. This body should not be expressly Military but should be styled *Police* and have the military bearing of the Irish Constabulary."[26] An order-in-council allowed 50 men to be recruited in the East (15 of them to be French-speaking) and 200 more in the West, where they would reflect the ethnic balance of the population. In short, the prime minister had conceived of a force capable of anything, from firing a cannon to achieving racial harmony, all for a dollar a day and a three-year enlistment.

Macdonald's plan was the genesis for the North West Mounted Police but the realization was postponed by the first Riel rebellion of 1869-70. To pacify the Metis, Canada was obliged to grant a premature provincial status to Manitoba; for its own peace of mind, it felt compelled to maintain a "provisional" garrison. The few hundred men of the Manitoba Force swallowed the appropriations which the government might otherwise have spent to police the rest of the Northwest. Constitutionally, Manitoba's provincial status prevented Ottawa from creating its proposed "Mounted Police" but Macdonald could retain troops under federal control.[27]

Louis Riel's challenge to Ottawa and his association with W.B. O'Donoghue, Fenian agitator and unofficial U.S. agent, had forcibly reminded Canadians of the vulnerability of their Northwest to the Americans.[28] So had American attempts to prevent Colonel Garnet Wolseley from getting his British-Canadian military expedition through the canals at the Soo.[29] As the winter of 1871 approached, Ottawa again felt compelled to send troops hurrying over the Dawson Trail to meet a reported Fenian threat on the Manitoba border.[30] The militia arrived only to find that the Fenians had been seized at Pembina by a detachment of United States troops. Unfortunately, when Captain Lloyd Wheaton also proclaimed that the little Hudson's Bay post was on American soil, he illustrated the danger of allowing American soldiers to cope with frontier law and order. In due course, the International Boundary Commission

---

25 E.E. Rich, *Hudson's Bay Company, vol. III, 1821-1870* (Toronto, 1960), p. 542. See also A.S. Morton, *A History of the Canadian West to 1870-71* (Toronto, 1973, 2nd ed.), p. 809; A.C. Gluek, "Imperial Protection for the Trading Interests of the Hudson's Bay Company,1857-1861," *Canadian Historical Review*, XXXVII, 1956, pp. 119-40.

26 Horrall, "Mounted Police Force," p. 181. See also Macleod, *Mounted Police*, pp. 8-11.

27 On the Manitoba Force, see Stacey, "Military Aspect," pp. 15-18.

28 Stanley, *Western Canada*, pp. 164-6.

29 Ibid., ch. VI.

30 See C.P. Stacey, "The Second Red River Expedition, 1871," *Canadian Defense Quarterly*, January, 1931, p. 1 ff.

restored Pembina to Canada; equally, a Minnesota jury refused to condemn Fenians for looting Canadian property.[31]

The comic-opera Fenian threat proved the loyalty of Manitoba half-breeds to the Canadian regime. However, a militia garrison remained at Winnipeg, largely because winter and the Pre-Cambrian shield left Manitoba isolated from the rest of Canada for six months of the year. The American route was hardly trustworthy in a crisis. More immediately, as lieutenant governors soon discovered, negotiation of treaties and land surrenders with Indian bands went more smoothly in the presence of a military escort.[32]

This was no help for the vast regions beyond Manitoba and the Northwest Angle. Far from being threatened by crowds of land-hungry settlers, it was their emptiness that brought trouble. Reports in 1871 by Lieutenant W.F. Butler and in 1873 by the Adjutant-General of the Canadian Militia, Colonel Patrick Robertson Ross, both emphasized the need for policing, preferably by small bodies of mounted troops. Successive governors of Manitoba revived the idea of a mounted police.[33] However, the emptiness of the Great Lone Land, as Butler called it, generated no political pressure. Only the Prime Minister could act and, beset by illness, family problems and innumerable more immediate political crises, Macdonald was unmoved.[34] Not until the end of March 1873 did he invite Parliament to pass enabling legislation for a mounted police force. "They are to be a purely civil, not a military body," he assured the House of Commons, "with as little gold lace, fuss and fine feathers as possible; not a crack cavalry regiment, but an efficient police force for the rough and ready — particularly ready — enforcement of law and justice."[35] Still they did not exist.

It was Governor Alexander Morris, backed by sensational reports of the massacre of a party of Assiniboines in the Cypress Hills, plus urgings from the American secretary of state, Hamilton Fish, who finally got Macdonald to move.[36] Although the responsibility for the deaths lay with American and Canadian wolf hunters from Fort Benton, Montana, Ottawa was left with a confused impression that, somehow, American whiskey traders from the notorious Fort Whoop-up were to blame.[37] "It

---

31 See Return to Parliament, 1884, Public Archives of Canada, Macdonald Papers, vol. 329, pp. 148570-2. On the raid, see J.P. Pritchett, "The Origin of the So-called Fenian Raid on Manitoba in 1871," *Canadian Historical Review*, X, 1929; Stacey, "Military Aspect," pp. 12-14.

32 J.L. Taylor, "The Development of an Indian Policy for the Canadian North West, 1869-79" (Ph.D. dissertation, Queen's University, Kingston, 1976), p. 56 and passim. See Alexander Morris, *The Treaties of Canada with the Indians* (Toronto, 1880), p. 32 ("Military display has always a great effect on savages, and the presence, even of a few troops, will have a good tendency," in A.G. Archibald's report on Treaty No. 2).

33 See W.F. Butler, *The Great Lone Land* (London, 1872); Edward McCourt, *Remember Butler: The Story of Sir William Butler* (London, 1967), ch. VI; Colonel Patrick Robertson Ross, "Reconnaissance of the North West Provinces and Indian Territories of the Dominion of Canada...," Canada, *Sessional Papers*, 1873, no. 9, pp. cvii-cxxvii.

34 On Macdonald in this period, see D.G. Creighton, *John A. Macdonald: The Old Chieftain* (Toronto, 1955), pp. 111-79. The Prime Minister's best known nickname, "Old Tomorrow," was given by Commissioner A.G. Irvine of the NWMP in 1881.

35 Canada, House of Commons, *Debates* (reported in the *Toronto Globe*), May 3, 1873. See also ibid., March 31, 1873.

36 Horrall, "Mounted Police Force," pp. 192-3.

37 Ibid., pp. 192-4; Taylor, "Indian Policy," pp. 88-114.

would not be well for us to take the responsibility of slighting Morris' repeated and urgent entreaties," Macdonald advised the Governor General, Lord Dufferin. "If anything went wrong, the blame would lie at our door."[38] On this courageous note, the North West Mounted Police was born. A draft of 150 recruits was assembled and despatched via the Dawson Trail to Winnipeg. In the spring of 1874, a second contingent travelled by way of Chicago to Fargo, North Dakota, where they donned their scarlet tunics, mounted nervous horses and set off on the first leg of what would be the Mounted Police's epic "March West."[39]

At least two popular myths about the well-known Force deserve to be exploded. The first is that the police wore red coats because the Indians had special confidence in the traditional British uniform. The only British redcoats to serve in the West were 300 men of the 6th Foot at Fort Garry from 1846 to 1848. Other British and Canadian troops had worn dark green or more bizarre local costumes. The idea of scarlet tunics came from Governor Morris and, more insistently, from Colonel Robertson Ross, a noted devotee of military finery.[40] Despite the Prime Minister's promise about fuss and feathers, the Mounted Police full dress soon resembled British dragoon guards. The uniform was elaborate, expensive and, in the eyes of competent military critics, highly unsuitable.[41] A second myth surrounds the alleged alteration of the title of the force from Mounted Rifles to Mounted Police, presumably to soothe American anxieties about a military expedition along their northern border. The susceptibilities belonged to Sir John A. Macdonald, not the Americans. By 1874, when the NWMP was at last in existence, the Conservative leader was out of office. His successor, Alexander Mackenzie, was a dull, honest man with a major's commission in the militia. Frankly, he would have preferred a military force and a military expedition. Hewitt Bernard, the deputy minister of justice and Macdonald's brother-in-law, had prepared the detailed scheme for the mounted police force and he refused to allow the project to be so cavalierly altered. The new Minister of Justice, A.A. Dorion wanted the police patronage for his department, and, as one of the few experienced members of the new government, he proved a formidable ally. The "mounted police" concept survived.[42]

The new Prime Minister also had to be talked out of an even more dangerous notion. Any major expedition, argued Mackenzie, should be conducted jointly with the Americans. They had the experience and the resources. Problems of law enforcement were their concern too. A shocked Lord Dufferin headed off any such venture into internationalism. Not only would Canadian pride be flattered by a national expedition but: "in the next place, we should appear upon the scene, not as the Americans have done, for the purpose of restraining and controlling the Indian tribes, but with a view of avenging injuries inflicted on the red man."[43] The Governor

---

38 Macdonald to Dufferin, September 24, 1873, Public Archives of Canada, Macdonald Papers, v. 523.

39 On the trek, see S.W. Horrall, "The March West" in Dempsey, *Men in Scarlet*, pp. 13-26, reviewing the literature.

40 On Robertson Ross, see D.P. Morton, *Ministers and Generals: Politics and the Canadian Militia, 1868-1904* (Toronto, 1970), pp. 25-6. See also Morris to Macdonald, January 17, 1873, Macdonald Papers, vol. 252.

41 See Middleton to Duke of Cambridge, July 31, 1885, Royal Archives, Windsor, Cambridge Papers.

42 Horrall, "Mounted Police Force," pp. 198-9.

43 Dufferin to Kimberley, December 24, 1873, Public Record Office, London, Kimberley Papers.

General was right on both counts. Thanks to inexperience and inadequate reconnaissance, the "March West" was a near-disaster but it immediately established the Mounted Police as a Canadian legend. Perhaps more important for its effectiveness in the ensuing ten years, the NWMP proved that it was not simply another regiment of U.S. cavalry. Scarlet jackets may have been inappropriate for hard service on the prairies but they helped to establish a symbolic distinction between the force and its American counterpart in the eyes of western Canadians, white and Indian alike.

Uniforms and names would not have signified much to the plains Indians if they had not symbolized more substantive differences in the role and outlook of the Mounted Police and their U.S. counterparts. American cavalrymen and Canadian policemen had much in common. Pay was meagre and often in arrears. Traders at military and police posts were equally rapacious. Barracks were often temporary shacks, ill-constructed, frigid in winter and sometimes unsanitary. Arms and equipment was sometimes obsolete and often inappropriate for western conditions. Political influence in both countries pervaded every sphere of administration, from forage contracts to promotions. Officers in the NWMP often owed their commissions to party patronage and men in the ranks were by no means always the muscular, adventurous paragons of popular imagery.[44] In 1885, after a few months in the Northwest, General Fred Middleton reported to the Duke of Cambridge: "... among them are some of the greatest scamps in the country, broken-down gentlemen who in many cases are called here inebriates, being sent here by their friends because no liquor is admitted in these territories." Since an important duty of the force was prevention of whiskey smuggling, it might be disturbing to learn from Middleton that it had "by no means a good character for sobriety."[45]

There were excellent officers and men in both the American and the Canadian forces in the West. Frontier conditions, hardship and danger weeded out misfits and chronic failures. Veterans of the Mounted Police played a leading role in many western Canadian communities and their contribution to the economy of the ranching frontier has only begun to be explored.[46] Presumably comparable work is underway for officers and men discharged from the U.S. Army. However, the similarity in the strengths and deficiencies of the two organizations indicates that differences cannot be explained by special qualities in the officers and men nor by exemplary leadership and administration. If the Canadian and the American West developed differently, the sources of divergence must be found in time, law and society.

By the time the North West Mounted Police took up its station in 1874, the outcome of the Indian struggle was really no longer in question. Bravado or gross miscalculation, as at the Little Big Horn, would be sharply punished. Able leadership and tactical skill would allow Chief Joseph and the Nez Perces to inflict setbacks on American military columns. However, most Canadian Indians, even the warlike Blackfoot Confederacy, could sense their relative safety on the north side of the Medicine Line. The NWMP was not very successful in capturing white exploiters of

---

44 Ronald Atkin, *Maintain the Right: The Early History of the North West Mounted Police, 1873-1900* (London, 1973), pp. 124-36, 257-69, giving the best brief review of conditions of service. See also J.P. Turner, *The North West Mounted Police* (Ottawa, 1950, 2 vols.), passim, together with many personal memoirs of service in the Force. On patronage and politics, see MacLeod, *Mounted Police*, ch. VII.

45 Middleton to Cambridge, July 31, 1885, Cambridge Papers.

46 D.H. Breen, "The Mounted Police and the Ranching Frontier" in Dempsey, *Men in Scarlet*, pp. 115-37.

the Indian — they, too, could find immunity across an international frontier — but at least the force was eager to chase them away. The development of railroads, the concomitant increase in American military effectiveness and the remorseless annihilation of the buffalo were settling the fate of the native people. By the time the Mounted Police arrived, the Indians of the Great Plains were looking for terms, not triumphs. Sent to administer and to accommodate, the police did not adopt the aggressive mode normal to soldiers nor did minor clashes inevitably produce a warlike response. Proudly military in style, the NWMP was a police force in tactics and attitude.[47]

In contrast to the United States, Canada's political system reinforced the power of the Mounted Police to provide satisfactory terms to the native people. While some American army officers sympathised with the Indians in their plight and sought to offer a paternal protection against white traders, ranchers and land speculators, they could count on little support in Washington. The anti-militarism of most Americans, both pro- and anti-Indian, almost guaranteed sympathy for any self-professed victim of military tyranny. Far from condemning civilians for the misery inflicted on the Indian, the vocal humanitarians of the "Friends of the Indian" organizations in the East were prone to blame the Army. "The soldiers demoralize the Indian men by whiskey and cards and debauch the women," claimed former Indian agent Alfred B. Meacham in his famous series, "Abolish the Army," "and the officers insult the chiefs by their arrogant assumptions of superior power and authority."[48]

On the relatively rare occasions when Canadian politicians considered Indian affairs in this period, such sentiments might be echoed. George Landerkin, an Ontario Liberal, suggested benignly that the Indians might soon become civilized "if they were not menaced day by day by the force."[49] He was one of a minority of opposition members who kept insisting that the Mounted Police had been a temporary expedient, to be disbanded when white settlement began in earnest. Significantly, only a very few Canadian politicians and journalists, almost all of them in the East, ever condemned the enormous power confided in the NWMP;[50] the usual criticism was the annual cost of the force.

In the United States, eastern humanitarians and western expansionists might at least find common ground in condemning the tyranny or the inefficiency of the Army and its officers. Western interests were vehemently argued in state and territorial assemblies and in Congress. In Canada, the price of a tranquil West was apparently a benevolent police despotism, with the officers of the force sitting in judgement on charges laid by their men against white and Indian alike. Not until 1887 were the first members of an independent judiciary appointed for the Territories. In that year, the territorial council was transformed into an elected assembly; a further ten years would pass before the assembly won the cherished powers of responsible government. Paid and administered from Ottawa, the Mounted Police remained largely immune from

---

47 See Macleod, *Mounted Police*, ch. VIII.
48 See Arthur A. Ekirch Jr., *The Civilian and the Military: A History of American Anti-Militarist Tradition* (Colorado Springs, 1972), p. 115, See also Francis P. Prucha, *Americanizing the American Indian: Writings by the "Friends of the Indian," 1880-1900* (Cambridge, Mass., 1973).
49 Canada, House of Commons, *Debates*, September 1, 1891, p. 4820.
50 R.C. Macleod, "The Mounted Police and Politics," in Dempsey, *Men in Scarlet*, pp. 101-5.

local pressures and, as long as Sir John A. Macdonald was alive, it could depend on a powerful guardian against attempts to subvert its authority or discipline for political ends.[51] Settler hostility to the NWMP as a "whiskey police" or, during the 1885 campaign, as "gophers" was at least comparable to American criticism of the Army on the frontier: it did not substantially influence government policy. When Commissioner L.W. Herchmer was under remorseless fire from a swarm of angry western newspapers, an earnest suitor for his position was assured: "Sir John always stands by and defends an 'official' and makes every allowance for peculiarities of temper and disposition — and I may say even unpopularity, provided the results of an official's actions are satisfactory."[52] However, even Macdonald's support might not have saved the force from united western anger. Instead, nowhere was it more vehemently defended.

In the decade between its arrival and the grim years before the 1885 outbreak, the NWMP could help the Indians adjust to the constraints of the treaty system with only occasional concern for the impact of white settlement. The early years, when the buffalo were still plentiful, the tribal structure still had resilience and the police were sufficiently trusted that a couple of constables could make an arrest in the heart of an Indian camp, could not last. While Canadians had been suitably apprehensive about the arrival of Sitting Bull and his band of Sioux in the aftermath of the Little Big Horn, the ensuing relations between the Indians and Superintendent James Walsh rapidly became part of a self-congratulatory mythology for both Canadians and the NWMP.[53]

If Ottawa had shown some inventiveness in creating the NWMP, other features of its western policy bear a dreary resemblance to American practice. Canadian dealings with the Indian, with treaties, land surrenders, annuities, agents and land reserves, bore a close family resemblance to American methods, if only because both were a heritage of pre-Revolutionary British administration.[54] Like the American Indian administration, the Canadian department was not immune from political patronage, speculation by minor officials and ill-informed penny-pinching by remote bureaucrats like the notorious Lawrence Vankoughnet, Deputy Superintendent of Indian Affairs.[55] Faced with the enormous and unfamiliar responsibility for feeding the Indians following the failure of the buffalo, Ottawa and most of its agents were unequal to the task. The best of them, Cecil Denny, a former NWMP inspector, resigned in disgust. Pressed to reduce public spending, Ottawa officials found logical economics by reducing rations, substituting bacon for beef on the Blackfoot reserves and dismissing junior employees.[56]

---

51   Jennings, "Indians and the Law," pp. 57-65.

52   Fred White to Colonel W.D. Otter, May 18, 1890, cited in Desmond Morton, *The Canadian General: Sir William Otter* (Toronto, 1974), p. 139.

53   Turner, *Medicine Line*, op. cit.; "Sitting Bull Tests the Mettle of the Redcoats" in Dempsey, *Men in Scarlet*, pp. 67-76. See also S.W. Horrall, *The Pictorial History of the Royal Canadian Mounted Police* (Toronto, 1973), pp. 70-4; Macleod, *Mounted Police*, pp. 30-2.

54   Taylor, "Indian Policy," pp. 19-22; Morris, *Treaties*, pp. 4-12, 16.

55   See Stanley, Western Canada, ch. XIII; Hugh A. Dempsey, *Crowfoot: Chief of the Blackfeet* (Edmonton, 1972), pp. 108-45.

56   C.E. Denny, *The Law Marches West* (Toronto, 1972, 2nd ed.), pp. 204-5; Dempsey, *Crowfoot*, pp. 161-2.

The era of starvation more than the advent of white settlement cost the NWMP its former standing with the native people. Obliged to defend insensitive and sometimes incompetent officials from the wrath of starving Indians, the Force no longer appeared as an even-handed dispenser of justice. The influence of the chiefs, enormously elevated by the police to provide a convenient authority system, plummeted with the waning of the buffalo. By 1883, making an arrest required a small military operation. The arrival of the Canadian Pacific Railway and of speculators in the vast grazing lands suddenly opened by the government only aggravated a problem already created by destitution.[57]

In 1885 came the explosion. Still, the uprising was essentially a Metis rebellion, not an Indian war. Support for Louis Riel was concentrated in halfbreed settlements near Prince Albert. Only in the Cree bands of Poundmaker and Big Bear were more than a minority of Indians involved. It was the white settlers, panic-stricken by memories of the Minnesota massacres or the Sioux wars of the 1870s, who fled to the police forts and who spread their terror by telegraph as far as Winnipeg. Only at Frog Lake, where nine whites and halfbreeds were murdered, was the terror justified. Few Indians joined Louis Riel at Batoche; most pillaged whatever the settlers had abandoned and then waited nervously for a retribution they knew would follow. Within three months of the outbreak, the campaign was over with the loss of about eighty lives.[58]

For the NWMP, expanded to a thousand men on the eve of the outbreak, the 1885 operations brought little glory. Most of the force, hurriedly concentrated in the troubled district, spent the campaign waiting for orders and protecting the white settlement at Prince Albert. At Fort Pitt, a timid Inspector Francis Dickens allowed civilian men, women and children to surrender to the Indians and then loaded his men on a barge and fled downstream. At Battleford, in a fort jammed with able-bodied men, Inspector W.S. Morris used his telegraph wire to send piteous appeals for help. More redoubtable officers, like Superintendent Herchmer and Inspector Sam Steele, demonstrated unusual fortitude and leadership.[59] However, it is hard to disagree with General Middleton, the British officer responsible for bringing the campaign to an early conclusion that, when good, well-trained troops were needed, the Mounted Police did not qualify.[60]

Middleton's solution was to transform the force into mounted infantry, clad in workmanlike Khaki and firmly under military discipline. Instead, it was as apparent to Canadians as it was to Americans that the era of Indian wars was over. In Parliament, there was now discernible pressure for the elimination of the Mounted Police, a possibility brought to a head in 1889 when the government proposed long-service

---

57   Atkin, *Maintain the Right*, pp. 196-211. See *Settlers and Rebels: Official Reports of the North-West Mounted Police, 1882-1881* (facsimile edition, Toronto, 1973), passim.

58   On the campaign, see Stanley, *Western Canada*, pp. 327-80; Desmond Morton, The *Last War Drum: The North West Campaign of 1885* (Toronto, 1972) and, from the viewpoint of a contemporary participant, C.A. Boulton, *Reminiscences of the North-West Rebellions* (Toronto, 1886).

59   See Atkin, *Maintain the Right*, pp. 217-53.

60   On Middleton and the NWMP during the 1885 campaign see Middleton to Caron, May 2, 1885, Public Archives of Canada, Caron Papers, vol. 199. See also Canada, Department of Militia and Defence, *Report upon the Suppression of the Rebellion in the North West Territories and Matters in Connection Therewith in 1885* (Canada, Sessional Papers, 1886, no. 6a, p. 5); Desmond Morton and R.H. Roy (eds.), *Telegrams of the North-West Campaign, 1885* (Toronto, 1972), pp. lxxxi, xcii, 230, 357.

pensions for members of the Force.[61] Indians planted disconsolately on their reserves, the tide of white settlement began to have political consequences for the NWMP. Liquor prohibition became the bitterest issue until licensing triumphed in 1892. "Why any Mounted Police Officer should dictate to any Canadian Citizen as to what and when he should drink is more than any fellow can tell," complained the Fort Macleod *Gazette* in 1887;[62] most westerners would have agreed. A constable, posted in full uniform to watch a notorious Prince Albert saloon, was arrested and fined $25 by a locally-appointed magistrate. Another magistrate insisted that he had no proof that liquor was an intoxicant and turned Calgary into a wide-open town.[63] Since the Force's own records indicate that some of its own senior officers were notoriously heavy drinkers, the struggle to keep the Canadian West dry was almost hopeless until the triumph of women's suffrage in 1916 brought a new army into the fray.[64]

Although the liquor issue provoked continual conflict within the NWMP and between the Force and civilians, the prestige of the Mounted Police grew steadily. Exaggerated accounts of its prowess brought recruits from all corners of the British Empire and it became the beneficiary of the sentimental adulation that marked the late heyday of British imperialism. Commissioner L.W. Herchmer, appointed in 1886, may have been loathed by officers and men but he restored discipline, improved training, equipment and welfare, and out-fought most of his critics.[65] Of these, the most remorseless was Nicholas Flood Davin, poet, editor and, after 1882, member of parliament for Assiniboia West. Davin's grievance began when Herchmer's brother fined him $50 for bringing liquor into the Territories,[66] but it easily encompassed the entire family and reached a climax in a sensational judicial investigation of 137 separate charges against the commissioner. Herchmer emerged with both honour and reputation intact. What is significant about the Davin charges is that the editor-politician felt obliged, for the sake of his political career, to accompany his assault on Herchmer with the most fulsome praise of the NWMP as a whole. Moreover, despite his claim that the commissioner was a tyrant, hated across the West, not a single western member of either party supported Davin.[67] One suspects that Davin would have found more friends if he had sat in the U.S. Congress attacking an army general.

The fundamental critics of the Force, R.C. Macleod has argued, tended to come from western Ontario and to be heirs of the Clear Grit tradition with its clear links to American democratic ideology. The most articulate of them was David Mills, a former Liberal cabinet minister who had attempted in 1877 to negotiate Sitting Bull's return to the United States. Mills' philosophy was in evidence when he attacked the

---

61 Canada, House of Commons, *Debates*, March 21, 1889; April 15, 1889. See Macleod, "Mounted Police and Politics," pp. 103-4.

62 *Fort Macleod Gazette*, February 21, 1887.

63 Atkin, *Maintain the Right*, pp. 274-7.

64 On the later history of the issue and correction of the notion of a quiet, law-abiding Canadian West, see J.H. Gray, *Booze: The Impact of Whiskey on the Prairie West* (Toronto, 1972) and *Red Lights on the Prairies* (Toronto, 1971). See Macleod, *Mounted Police*, ch. X.

65 Atkin, *Maintain the Right*, pp. 257-73; R.B. Deane, *Mounted Police Life in Canada: A Record of Thirty-One Years Service, 1883-1914* (London, 1916), pp. 30-42.

66 On Davin, see Macleod, "Mounted Police and Politics," pp. 99-105.

67 The Davin debate may be found in Canada, House of Commons, *Debates*, March 31, 1890, pp. 2674-99.

proposed police pension bill in 1889; "I say that a man who has served fifteen years and, much more, twenty-five years in the force, would be utterly unfit for any other pursuit in life afterwards. The hon. gentleman knows that a man who has served a great many years in the idle life of a soldier or policeman becomes, so far as industrial pursuits are concerned, a poor member of the community."[68] Later, Mills argued that interposing the police between the whites and the Indians and providing for their welfare frustrated the natural law of the survival of the fittest. The Americans, he insisted, had managed their Indians more wisely.[69]

Such a commitment to Social Darwinism, common enough in American debate on Indian policy, was rare in Canada. Indeed, there was relatively little debate in Parliament or elsewhere beyond the time-honoured propositions that economies could be made and that officials would be more prudent and successful if they were only chosen from the party not currently in power. The Indian as an equal citizen was hardly conceived save by idealists or radicals. In 1885, as part of an ingenious extension of the franchise, Macdonald proposed to include all Indians in the electorate. With a rebellion about to begin, the proposal could hardly have come at a less propitious moment and the absurdity of votes for Indians (as well as for certain categories of women) provided the Opposition with ammunition for a largely successful filibuster. However, it was apparent that Macdonald, like his critics, expected the native people to march to the polls not as independent yeomen but under the guidance of dependable Conservative agents and officials.[70]

When the Liberals finally returned to power in 1896, both the reserves policy and the Mounted Police survived the transition. In the aggressive campaign to attract immigrants to the Canadian West from the United States, Britain and Europe, the presence of the firm, kindly authority of the Force became a major selling point. Older settlers were reassured that the Mounted Police would guarantee that newcomers would rapidly appreciate and respect the principles of British justice. Discovery of gold in the Klondike gave the NWMP a new frontier just as the old one was running out. Canadians could soon take appropriate pride in the relative order and respectability of Dawson in the Yukon in contrast to the sordid regime of "Soapy" Smith at Skagway.[71]

Pressed by jeering Tories in 1897 to state whether power had indeed changed his party's attitude to the Mounted Police, the new Liberal prime minister rose to the bait. He was, Sir Wilfrid Laurier confessed, "inclined to be rather conservative with regard to this force."[72] So were most Canadians. Perhaps the Mounted Police deserved only incidental credit for avoiding Indian wars in Canada: it was the U.S. Army that demonstrated the invincibility of white weapons. It was easier to mediate the contact of white and Indian when the settlers came in a trickle, not an expected flood.

---

68 Ibid., March 21, 1889, p. 770.

69 Ibid., May 16, 1892, p. 2688.

70 On the Indian franchise, see J.E. Chamberlin, *The Harrowing of Eden: White Attitudes Toward North American Natives* (Toronto, 1975), pp. 200-2 and passim; Morris Davis and Joseph Krauter, *The Other Canadians* (Toronto, 1971), pp. 12-14. (The Indian franchise was withdrawn by the Liberals in 1898.)

71 Atkin, *Maintain the Right*, pp. 298-359. A personal account with appropriate flourishes is S.B. Steele, *Forty Years in Canada: Reminiscences of the Great North-West* (London, 1915), pp. 288-337.

72 Canada, House of Commons, *Debates*, May 10, 1897, p. 2039.

Examined closely there was little to choose between the blue-clad soldiers below the border and the red-coated Canadian policemen. Both were shabbily treated by government; both could furnish ample evidence of human frailty; both lived at odds with the surrounding communities, white and Indian.

Many nations are in love with their army; fondness for a police force is so rare as almost to be a perversion. For Canadians, the excuse must be that, almost absent-mindedly, they had created a national institution in a country that has very few. By the turn of the century, Canadians took extraordinary pride in offering the world the "last, best West." They could be excused for believing that their Mounted Police had made it so.[73]

NOTE

A paper prepared for the Seventh Military History Symposium at the USAF Academy, Colorado Springs, September 1976. This article was first published in *Journal of Canadian Studies* 12, no. 2 (spring 1977): 27-37.

---

73   Macleod, "Mounted Police and Politics," p. 113.

TWO

The Interlude: The North-West Mounted Police and the Blackfoot Peoples, 1874-1877

B.J. Mayfield

For the Blackfoot peoples, the expedient creation of the North-West Mounted Police in the late fall of 1873 was a first step in official Dominion-Blackfoot relations. From the Dominion Government's perspective the primary purpose of the Force was to conciliate the native inhabitants and contain potential Indian-White conflict through enforcing law and order. In this manner the Mounted Police would provide a peaceful interlude until the Government's own priorities or the expanding settlement frontier necessitated formal treaties. During the winter of 1873-74 news of further "Indian unrest" following the Cypress Hills Massacre reconfirmed this rationale and caused the NWMP expeditionary Force to proceed towards the Blackfoot territory.

Initially, the Blackfoot peoples responded to the arrival of the NWMP on a basis of cooperative co-existence. The imposition of law and order was mutually beneficial; the demoralizing whiskey traffic ended while the Dominion peacefully asserted her sovereignty. Yet British-Canadian justice also heightened inter-tribal hostilities which were already exacerbated by the diminishing supply of buffalo. Increasingly after the winter of 1874-1875 NWMP and Blackfoot coexistence was undermined. Despite these tensions, however, Treaty Number Seven was concluded in the fall of 1877.

*****

Throughout the winter of 1873-74, Lieutenant-Governor Alexander Morris continued his campaign to persuade the Dominion Government to re-adjust its over-all plan for national expansion. His urgent entreaties had resulted in the arrival of the North-West Mounted Police at Lower Fort Garry prior to the original schedule for the spring of 1874. Now, Morris pressed the Government to proceed with signing treaties with Indian peoples at Fort Ellice and further west, and to authorize the Mounted Police to proceed from Lower Fort Garry into the Territories. From the Lieutenant-Governor's perspective, recurring reports of "Indian unrest" made both of these actions essential before the actual advance of settlement would be possible. As Morris pointed out to the new Prime Minister, Alexander Mackenzie:

> We have now a Police Force, which I hope to see increased, and, with this, and the small Battalion now here [Fort Garry] it may be possible to maintain order, though I do not believe the Privy Council have yet fully recognized the magnitude of the task

that lies before them, in the creation of the institution of civilization in the North
West, in the suppression of crime there, and in the maintenance of peaceful relations
with the fierce tribes of the vast prairies beyond Manitoba.[1]

The Prime Minister's reply epitomized Ottawa's superficial comprehension of both the nature of pre-existing Indian-White relations in the North-West and the subsequent impact of the Dominion Government's perpetual indecision regarding treaty negotiations. Mackenzie informed Morris: "We have on several occasions discussed the Indian question. I never doubted that our true policy was to make friends of them even at a considerable cost, as anything is cheaper than an Indian War."[2] Echoing Prime Minister Macdonald's attitude, Mackenzie recognized the value of expedient appeasement. Similarly, his government did not authorize that any immediate action be taken.

Morris's anxiety stemmed from additional correspondence he had received describing the state of inter-tribal and Indian-White relations in the western and south-western regions of the Territories. On August 24, 1873, Edward McKay had reported to the Lieutenant-Governor that as a result of the Cypress Hills Massacre, the Crees, Assiniboines and Saulteaux who lived along the south side of the Saskatchewan River, were maintaining their traditional, defensive alliance.[3] Of equal importance, McKay stressed that these Indians regarded him as their agent and were expecting him "to carry an answer to them about the treaty ... They [were] anxious to know whether the Government intended to take away this land without paying them for it, as they fear."[4] Subsequently, in mid-October, 1873, a message from an Indian trader named "Kitchewassis" [sic] notified Morris that war had broken out between the Crees and the Blackfoot peoples.[5]

For the Lieutenant-Governor this continuation of traditional inter-tribal warfare had wider significance. As a part of his December 4, 1873, communication to Prime Minister Mackenzie, Morris relayed "positive information,"

> that there are no less than six forts of United States traders (any one of which is as large as the H.B. Coy's posts at Carlton or Pitt) fully armed and equipped, in our territory, and the question we have to solve is, how to deal with the matter, and avoid an Indian War, which may at any moment, burst out, and involve the Dominion in enormous expense, and expose the people of the Territories and this Province, to the fearful atrocities which overwhelmed Minnesota a few years ago.[6]

Later, in February, reports that Americans at Bow River had once again made a number of Assiniboine drunk and had killed 55 of them,[7] added to the Lieutenant-Governor's alarm. When, by April 25, 1874, Prime Minister Mackenzie had not yet

---

1   Public Archives of Manitoba (PAM), Morris Papers, Ketcheson Collection, Morris to Mackenzie, December 4, 1873.
2   Ibid., Mackenzie to Morris, December 6, 1873.
3   Ibid., Lieutenant-Governor's Collection, enclosure from Edward McKay, August 24, 1873. McKay reported that: "The Chiefs [had] sent tobacco to the various tribes directing them to keep together, in view of a probable attack from the Americans."
4   Ibid.
5   Ibid., Ketcheson Collection, Morris to Campbell, October 15, 1873. This message may also have been a diversion created by the Metis to protect their traditional fur trade interests from their Indian rivals.
6   Ibid., Morris to Mackenzie, December 4, 1873.
7   Ibid., Telegram Book No. 2, Morris to A.A. Dorion, May 26, 1874.

taken any direct action to send the NWMP further west, Morris emphatically wrote that "the lowest estimate of the number of men who could be safely sent on an expeditionary force, has uniformly been 500 men."[8] In his opinion, that number would be needed to restore order and to control the "numerous and well-armed Indians." The Lieutenant-Governor also suggested that a "messenger should go in advance of the Boundary Commission and the Police Force to explain their objects."[9] The Dominion Government's eventual response to Morris's analysis of Indian-White relations was clearly summarized by the Governor-General, Lord Dufferin. Focussing on British-Canada's priorities, the Governor-General encouraged the Prime Minister to authorize a mounted expeditionary force specifically aimed at suppressing the illicit whiskey trade established by the American forts. Implicitly, Dufferin articulated Ottawa's view of Canada's relationship to the Indian peoples of the North-West:

> Even though the expense might be considerable, an expedition organized by Canada itself would have its advantages. In the first place the mere fact of putting forth her strength for the purpose of asserting her jurisdiction and repressing outrage in those wild districts, would flatter in a very legitimate manner the national pride of the Dominion ... In the next place we should appear upon the scene, not as the Americans have done, for the purpose of restraining and controlling the Indian tribes, but with the view of avenging injuries inflicted on the red man by the white.[10]

In addition to enhancing the Dominion's diplomatic prestige, the presence of the NWMP would appear to accommodate the Indian peoples' interests.

Following this rationale, on May 20, 1874, Minister of Justice A.A. Dorion carried out Morris's request that a messenger be sent in advance of the NWMP. In order to appease the native inhabitants, Dorion advised that the Hudson's Bay Company Chief Factors at Fort Ellice and Edmonton be asked to open communication "of a friendly nature ... with the Blackfoot and other tribes ... by means of personal interviews" and the distribution of presents.[11] Dorion then addressed the immediate issues enumerated in Lieutenant-Governor Morris's correspondence. Primarily, the Indian peoples were to understand that the object of sending the NWMP was the preservation of British-Canadian law and order in the North-West Territories. The Force would prevent "lawless American Traders" from interfering "with the ordinary usages and pursuits of the Indians," and would suppress the traffic in "intoxicating liquor." As representatives of Canada's sovereignty, the Mounted Police would maintain the principles of justice which were consistent with the values and priorities of the settlement frontier. For this reason, the Chief Factors of the Company were asked to use their knowledge of the native inhabitants "to secure their goodwill and sympathy" for the Force and to convince them of the Queen's intent to promote "harmony and happiness among Her people in the North-West."[12]

More specifically, with regard to official Indian-White interaction, Dorion instructed the Hudson's Bay Company's representatives to make it clear "that the

---

8   Ibid., Ketcheson Collection, Morris to Mackenzie, April 25, 1874.

9   Ibid., Telegram Book No. 2, Morris to Dorion, May 26, 1874.

10   Kimberley Papers, Dufferin to Kimberley, 24 Dec. 1873, as cited in S.W. Horrall, "Sir John A. Macdonald and the Mounted Police Force for the Northwest Territories," *Canadian Historical Review*, Vol. 53, 1972, p. 198.

11   PAM, Morris Papers, Lieutenant-Governor's Collection, A.A. Dorion to Morris, May 20, 1874.

12   Ibid.

cooperation of the Indians is not in any way desired or sought in any action which the Mounted Police may find it necessary to take."[13] The NWMP were a separate, distinct authority and the native peoples were not to consider themselves to be allies. Similarly, the presents to be distributed to the Indian peoples were meant to conciliate and were not intended as an expression of political or social equality. This conception of Indian-White relations was strongly reminiscent of the position of wardship assigned to the native inhabitants of Eastern Canada. Further, the Dominion Government had not re-assessed its decision during the summer of 1873 not to proceed with further treatying. Neither the Hudson's Bay Company advance messenger nor the Mounted Police were authorized to promise treaty negotiations.[14] Instead, the NWMP, by enforcing law and order, were to reinstate "the moral influence exercised by the Hudson's Bay [sic] over the Indians."[15] From Ottawa's perspective, therefore, the NWMP would carry forward the law and order considered a part of frontier settlement and necessary for containing Indian-White conflict.

On the basis of this limited comprehension, the Mounted Police were to quell the "Indian unrest" and establish, in practice, Canada's sovereign interests in the North-West Territories. Yet two years earlier, reports sent in by Lieutenant W.F. Butler and Colonel Robertson-Ross had already informed the Dominion officials that the "Indian Question" rested with the Blackfoot peoples and the Plains Cree. These peoples would not accept White encroachers who did not recognize and accommodate themselves to the values and priorities of the Blackfoot or Plains Cree societies.[16] More particularly, as a part of his observations, Ross had inadvertently recorded the Blackfoot peoples' specific terms. First, commenting on the illicit whiskey traffic, Ross had noted that "for the peace of the country and welfare of the Indians ... a Custom House [built] on the Belly River near the Porcupine Hills, with a military guard of about 150 soldiers" was highly advisable. Furthermore, this post would also aid in "stopping the horse stealing expeditions carried on by hostile Indians from south of the line into Dominion Territory..." Summarizing both of these factors from the Blackfoot peoples' perspective, Ross had concluded:

> Indeed it may now be said with truth, that to put a stop to horse-stealing and the sale of spirits to Indians, is to put a stop altogether to Indian wars in the North West. The importance of the Porcupine Hill in a strategical point of view is very great, commanding as it does the entrance of both the Kootenay Passes towards the West, and the route from Benton into the Saskatchewan territory on the south and east; the country can be seen from it for immense distances all round. Although hostile to citizens of the United States it is believed that the Blackfeet Indians would gladly welcome any Dominion Military Force sent to protect them from the incursions of other tribes, and to stop the horse-stealing which has for so long been carried on. With excellent judgment they have pointed out the southern end of the Porcupine Hill as the proper place for a Military Post.[17]

---

13 Ibid.
14 Ibid.
15 Ibid.
16 Public Archives of Canada (PAC), Macdonald Papers, Vol. 518/594-595, Macdonald to Hincks, April 14, 1871. Also cited in J.L. Taylor, "Development of an Indian Policy for the Canadian North West, 1869-79" (Ph.D. thesis, Queen's University, Kingston, 1976), p. 91.
17 Canada. *Sessional Papers*, Vol. V, No. 9, Annual Report of the State of the Militia for 1872, p. CXXIII.

Ross's report articulated the Blackfoot peoples' comprehension of the "Indian unrest" and presented their solution which was mutually beneficial to themselves and to the Dominion. Rather than confronting British-Canada with its failure to officially recognize their own sovereign interests, the Blackfoot peoples chose to counteract any causes for direct reprisal, and to maintain and consolidate their own position. From this standpoint the NWMP, with their policy of appeasement through the imposition of law and order, would superficially meet the Blackfoot terms for cooperative coexistence.

*****

Carrying forward British-Canada's principles of justice and Indian policy, the NWMP expeditionary Force under their first Commissioner, Colonel G. A. French, finally departed from Dufferin, Manitoba, on July 8, 1874. French was ordered "to move by way of Fort Ellice towards the Belly and Bow Rivers."[18] To enforce law and order, the Force's first objective was to chastise the American whiskey traders. At the same time, to appease the native inhabitants, the Mounted Police were to set forth the Dominion's "goodwill and assurances that [Blackfoot] lands will not be taken from them without treaties being made to their satisfaction..."[19]

On August 13, 1874, Commissioner French recorded the first contact with the native population:

> A Sioux Indian came into camp this morning ...They [the Sioux] want to know why we are coming this way; and grunted out their satisfaction when I told them that the White Mother had heard that the American outlaws had killed some of her red children, and that she sent me, with these braves, to capture the men who did it. I impressed upon them the fact that we did not want their land...[20]

Three weeks later, on September 4, French met up with the Sioux a second time:

> Seven Sioux came into camp this evening. It appears they were with some half-breeds when our advanced guard passed, and seeing no carts they put us down as Blackfoot. After passing they crept up a ravine till they crossed our trail, they caught up with the rear guard about 2 p.m., and as a precautionary measure loaded their guns. Our people seeing this extended in skirmishing order, but a Sioux who could speak French came forward unarmed and explained matters. We gave them some tea, buffalo meat, biscuits, and ammunition, which apparently much pleased them. A few small presents go a long way in showing the Indians that we come as friends...[21]

In neither instance did the Commissioner show any understanding of the traditional inter-tribal relations or the contemporary forces at work among the Indian population. Whether or not the Sioux actually mistook the Police for Blackfoot, French did not acknowledge that the NWMP were considered interlopers. In addition, the presence of the Sioux ought to have verified for the Commissioner the "Indian unrest" which Morris's informants had reported. Instead, adhering strictly to his instructions, French remained blind to Indian grievances. His report of the peaceful resolution of the confrontation merely provided its own answer to the Commissioner's

---

18   PAM, Morris Papers, Telegram Book No. 2, H. Bernard to Morris, June 22, 1874.
19   Ibid., Ketcheson Collection, Campbell to Morris, August 14, 1873.
20   Annual Report of the North-West Mounted Police, 1874, Appendix A, Diary, p. 41.
21   Ibid., p. 45.

limited knowledge. This answer seemed to support the validity of the Dominion Government's attitude and policy.

If Commissioner French failed to recognize the "Indian unrest" of Morris's correspondence, equally his first report upon reaching the vicinity of the Bow and Belly Rivers undermined the official reasons for sending the Force. French noted that when in the Cypress Hills he too had been told of "500 Americans working all summer at their forts at the fork of the Bow and Belly Rivers, making underground galleries and etc [sic]..."[22] In fact, however, when the Commissioner arrived on the Bow, he discoved that "the Forts" were log shanties in which trappers or traders passed the winter. These log huts were usually burnt down when the trappers left, "as was the case with the one in the Cypress Hills, where the Assiniboines were murdered in the spring of 1873."[23] Most of the traders came from Fort Benton, in Montana Territory, with "Whoop-Up" being the only fort having inhabitants as well as a name.

Commissioner French went on to clarify that reports from the region of the Bow and Belly Rivers were vague and riddled with errors because: "The Country beyond the Cypress Hills [was] not alone arid and sterile, but it [was] the war-path of the Blackfeet, Assiniboines, Crees, and Sioux. [Consequently], no half breeds [would] venture there except in large brigades."[24] In fact, Assistant Commissioner James F. Macleod, upon inquiry, had reported that only two such half-breeds were known to have travelled into the region. French himself had discovered that one of his guides was an imposter, while the other, who claimed a knowledge of the Blackfoot language, promptly became lost once beyond the Cypress Hills.[25]

As for the "savage and warlike" Blackfoot peoples, Commissioner French reported that the Force had not seen any of the member tribes. When the Commissioner proceeded to Fort Benton, Montana Territory, to purchase supplies he was given a partial explanation. A "Trader" informed him that the elusive Blackfoot had already announced the arrival of the Force, stating that "...white men were *as thick as ants on a hill at Bow River.*"[26] Despite this failure to establish immediate contact, French on September 28, 1874, notified Ottawa:

> Force on way back — state of affairs on Bow and Belly Rivers has been greatly exaggerated. I leave a large force in that vicinity under Major Macleod. I hope to have the laws relating to liquor effectually enforced this winter.[27]

As the Commissioner's report implied, the NWMP would proceed to enforce the determined policy of maintaining law and order while appeasing the native inhabitants. Indeed, even though there was no thriving, garrisoned whiskey trade, nor a potential Indian war, Assistant Commissioner James F. Macleod persisted in seeing the situation in these British-Canadian terms.[28] As early as December 4, 1874, he noted:

---

22   Ibid., 1874, p. 22.

23   Ibid., Appendix A, Diary, p. 47.

24   Ibid., p. 22.

25   Ibid.

26   Ibid.

27   PAM, Morris Papers, Telegram Book No. 2, French to Morris, September 24, 1874.

28   For a consideration of the North-West Mounted Police as an expression of the social values which accepted and regarded the administration of justice as a vital element of Canada's westward expansion, see Roderick C. Macleod, "The North West Mounted Police 1873-1905: Law Enforcement and the Social Order in the Canadian North-West" (Ph.D. thesis, Duke University, 1972).

I am happy to be able to report *the complete stoppage of the whisky trade throughout the whole of this section of the country*, and that the drunken riots, which in former years were almost of a daily occurrence, are now entirely at an end; in fact a more peaceable community than this, with a very large number of Indians camped along the river, could not be found anywhere ... People never lock their doors at night, and have no fear of anything being stolen, which is left lying about outside, whereas; just before our arrival gates and doors were all fastened at night, and nothing could be left out of sight.[29]

On December 15 the Assistant Commissioner commented further on the ease with which the NWMP had not only established the new order but had gained Blackfoot support. A number of traders had been circulating rumors to the effect that the Mounted Police would remain in the area only for the winter, leaving again in the spring. Recording his response to the Indians' inquiries, Macleod noted: "All [Indians] that have come to see me invariably ask how long are we going to stay. Their delight is unbounded when I tell them that I expect to remain with them always."[30]

Assistant Commissioner Macleod's interpretation of these first encounters with the Blackfoot peoples assumed that the Indians' "unbounded delight" was directly attributable to the efficacy of law and order. Yet from the Blackfoot peoples' perspective, this peaceful situation was not just the first stage in containing "Indian unrest," or in implementing British-Canada's traditional approach towards Indian-White relations. Through imposing law and order, the NWMP not only ended the degrading liquor traffic, but established a basis for Indian-White interaction which did not conflict with Blackfoot self-determination. The mutual benefits allowed for the development of cooperative coexistence.

The Blackfoot leaders' concern not to compromise the interests of their people had caused them at first to give the Mounted Police a wide berth. Not until October 30, 1874, had Three Bulls approached the Police specifically to test their professed intentions. He reported to Macleod that a colored man by the name of William Bond had a trading post at Pine Coulee, located fifty miles away. Bond had traded "a couple gallons of Whisky" for two of Three Bulls' horses. With the assistance of Jerry Potts,[31] Blackfoot emissary and official interpreter and guide of the NWMP, Assistant Commissioner Macleod had succeeded in arresting Bond, thereby proving the worth of the NWMP in the eyes of the Blackfoot. Two days after the arrest of Bond, Macleod had recorded that he had "now had interviews with chiefs of all three branches of the Blackfeet Tribe, viz, Bloods, Peigans, and Blackfeet."[32] The Blackfoot had informed him that they had heard that "[the NWMP] were their friends, but desired to be assured of this before they came to see me."[33]

During these first interviews, the Blackfoot leaders had also started to assert their policy for cooperative coexistence as the basis for Indian-White relations. From

---

29 Annual Report of the NWMP, 1874, p. 62.

30 Ibid., p. 67.

31 "Jerry Potts was a Scottish-Blood frontiersman who was engaged by Colonel Macleod at Fort Benton during the March West ... He remained as scout and interpreter for the Police until his death in 1896." See Hugh A. Dempsey (ed.), *A Winter at Fort Macleod* (Calgary: McClelland and Stewart West, 1974), p. 125.

32 Annual Report of the NWMP, 1874, p. 64.

33 Ibid.

Assistant Commissioner Macleod's point of view, however, the interviews had followed an expected pattern. Relying upon Jerry Potts to bring "the chiefs and two or three of their chief warriors" to the meeting, Macleod had made the following notes:

> Upon being introduced they all shake hands and invariably express their delight at meeting me. They then sit down, and my interpreter [Potts] lights and hands the chief a pipe, which he smokes for a few seconds, and then passes to the others, and all remain silent to hear what I have got to say. I then explain to them what the Government has sent this Force into the country for, and endeavour to give them a general idea of the laws which will be enforced, telling them they need not fear being punished for doing what they do not know is wrong. I then tell them also that we have not come to take their land from them (an intimation they all receive with great pleasure), but that when the Government wants to speak to them about this matter, their great men will know the intentions of the Government before anything is done.[34]

Similarly, the Assistant Commissioner had observed that the Indian chiefs for their part generally responded with a speech merely summing up the social and moral degradation which had resulted from the whiskey traffic, the resulting economic loss in buffalo robes and horses, and concluding, "that all this was now changed, as one old chief expressed, suiting the action to his words, 'before you came the Indian crept along, now he is not afraid to walk erect'."[35] Revealing his superficial understanding of the Blackfoot peoples' presentations, Macleod summarized these statements as auguring well for British-Canada's future expansion. He commented that "[the Blackfoot] ... have all the name of being extremely hospitable to strangers, and from what I can learn have no objection to white men settling in their country."[36]

The Blackfoot peoples' ready acceptance of British-Canadian law and order, therefore, apparently offered no conflict with the Dominion Government's priorities for expansion. This circumstance allowed the Force to compliment itself. Indeed, Macleod concluded his report with the observation:

> The only difficulty that I apprehend at present is, the meeting of some of their war parties with each other. A war party consists of a dozen or so, bent upon a horse-stealing expedition. If I hear of any of these war parties, I shall endeavour to meet them, and warn them of the consequences, before any collision between them.[37]

Although the Assistant Commissioner's decision was consistent with the policy to appease and to contain "Indian unrest," it ran directly counter to the Blackfoot peoples' concept of coexistence. To end the Indians' horse-stealing expeditions had far greater ramifications than simply securing peace. With the horse as a determinant of economic and social status, not only were these expeditions integral to the Plains Indian culture and way of life,[38] but the expeditions themselves set forth and maintained each Peoples' territorial rights. This was the reason why the country beyond the Cypress Hills had remained a common fighting ground for the Blackfoot, Cree, Assiniboine and Sioux. In maintaining appeasement through law and order,

---

34 Ibid.
35 Ibid.
36 Ibid., p. 65.
37 Ibid.
38 See John C. Ewers, *The Horse in Blackfoot Indian Culture* (Washington: 1955, Bureau of American Ethnology, Bulletin 159), particularly pp. 212-218, 240-253.

Macleod's limited knowledge of inter-tribal relations supported a policy which would only benefit the Blackfoot insofar as controlling lawless White encroachment.

The full impact of Assistant Commissioner Macleod's decision to "maintain the right" of British-Canadian law and order, and control inter-tribal hostilities was not felt by the Blackfoot during the first winter of 1874-75. Particularly noting the horse trade, Macleod himself wrote on December 15, 1874:

> I am happy to say that a large number of horses are now being imported. Immediately before our arrival, large bands of them were being continually sent the other way — proceeds of the whisky trade. Now a horse can't be got from an Indian, and they wish to buy more than the traders have to sell.[39]

The NWMP also benefited from this re-adjustment of trade.[40] Throughout the winter, Macleod had the majority of the Force's horses and cattle herded at Sun River, Montana Territory. The traditional wintering region of the Blood and Peigan, Sun River was also a central location for the inter-tribal horse trade. Under the guidance of Jerry Potts and under the command of Inspector Walsh, the Force's livestock was taken south by way of the Mountain Road.[41] In the following spring the herd was replenished with "Mexican and Spanish ponies" deemed to be "a terror for chasing whisky traders."[42]

Similarly, throughout the winter months, the NWMP and the Blackfoot peoples mingled socially. One of the few remaining records of the first months at Fort Macleod, the diary of Assistant Surgeon R.B. Nevitt, reveals the extent to which the Mounted Police shared in some of the activities of the Indian community. On February 9, 1875, Nevitt noted:

> Well, last night Col. Macleod, Capt. Jackson, Allen, Denny, and myself went for Conrad and took him over to the squaw dance. It was in a lodge; no light save that of the fire in the centre. The people all sat round the lodge on the sleeping bunks, the men on one side, the squaws and children on the other. The orchestra, consisting of three drums like tambourines without bells, kept up an incessant tomtom and the voices of the men and women kept time with the dancers and tom toms in a melancholic, monotonous chant. Every now and then a chap would become very much excited and start up in the circle dancing around the fire and dance in a most excited manner. Their dancing consists in a simple bending of the knees, keeping their feet close together and keeping time with the music. The dancer may vary his dance by numerous absurd and grotesque attitudes or movements and must keep continually singing...
>
> Now and again while the band was resting some buck would get up and make a speech, telling of the wonderful and doughty deeds he had done. The squaws would dance up to the one they wished to dance with them and pull him out from his seat. If they wished and were allowed they could kiss you, after which you were expected to give them a blanket. Denny, Jackson, and the Col. were each pulled out and made

---

39 Annual Report of the NWMP, 1874, p. 67.

40 See John C. Ewers, *The Horse in Blackfoot Indian Culture*, pp. 216-220. Also John C. Ewers, *Indian Life on the Upper Missouri* (Norman: University of Oklahoma Press, 1968), pp. 14-44.

41 See John C. Ewers, *The Horse in Blackfoot Indian Culture*, pp. 299-336; John C. Ewers, *The Blackfeet: Raiders on the Northwestern Plains* (Norman: University of Oklahoma Press, 1958), pp. 196-204; Dennis Lloyd Rinn, "Territorial Diffusion of the European Horse among the Blackfoot Tribes and Sarcee" (M.A. thesis, University of Manitoba, 1975).

42 Winnipeg *Daily Free Press*, March 8, 1875.

to dance. They felt too much respect for me so I was allowed to sit in dignified quietness.[43]

Five months later, however, in June, 1875, a letter from Assistant Surgeon Nevitt, published in the Winnipeg *Daily Free Press*, observed a significant change in the Fort Macleod community. "There are at present about twenty lodges of half-breeds encamped in the vicinity of the Fort [Macleod], who I believe intend settling there. They were however, too late to try farming this year and I suppose must content themselves with hunting for the present."[44] Only nine months previously Colonel French had despaired over the half-breed guides' ignorance of the territory beyond the Cypress Hills. Continual warfare between the Cree, Assiniboine, Sioux and Blackfoot peoples had traditionally secured the Blackfoot country from such half-breed encroachment. Now, Assistant Commissioner Macleod's decision to end inter-tribal horse-stealing, and to maintain peace through law and order, had removed this important safeguard for the Blackfoot. Indeed, the arrival of the half-breed families marked the beginning of a major transition in the nature of inter-tribal and Indian-White relations within the Blackfoot peoples' homeland. The apparent peace and security promoted by British-Canadian law and order threatened Blackfoot initiative in determining inter-tribal alliances. This, in turn, would disturb the equilibrium of their current coexistence with the Mounted Police.

In May, 1875, the *Manitoba Free Press* published another letter which indicated that the new half-breed settlement near Fort Macleod was but the first in a wave of prospective settlers:

> The police are doing good work out North, and by another year will make the North territories one of the most desirable to live in north of the Missouri River. By the strictness with which they enforce the laws, property, life and everything else will be more secure under your government than ours [Montana Territory], which will cause an emigration to Fort Macleod and its vicinity. Several of our large stock dealers and farmers would move over now if they were assured that the police force would remain any length of time, for without them they are afforded no protection out there.[45]

As a partial answer to this observation, during the fall of 1875 the NWMP permanently established Forts Calgary and Macleod, while the Hudson's Bay Company also moved its post into the valley of the Bow River, locating at the mouth of the Ghost River.[46] This Company post was the second attempt to establish trade in the heart of the Blackfoot peoples' country. Forty-three years earlier Piegan Post or Old Bow Fort had been built at the confluence of Old Fort Creek and Bow River. In 1834, the post had been forced to close because of Blackfoot hostility.[47] Now, with the apparent stability created by the presence of the NWMP, John Shaw laid the foundation for the future cattle industry by bringing from the Columbia Lakes, 700 head of cattle for stock-raising purposes.[48]

---

43 Hugh A. Dempsey (ed.), *A Winter at Fort Macleod* (Calgary: McClelland and Stewart West, 1974), pp. 49-50.
44 Letter of June 15, 1875, published in the Winnipeg *Daily Free Press*, July 10, 1875.
45 *Manitoba Free Press*, May 24, 1875.
46 John McDougall, *Opening the Great West* (Calgary: Glenbow-Alberta Institute, 1970), p. 14.
47 Ibid., see footnote 2, p. 14.
48 Ibid., p. 26.

These developments were directly contrary to the policy which Assistant Commissioner Macleod had espoused during the first interviews in the late fall of 1874. In addition to establishing a regime of law and order, Macleod had informed the Blackfoot peoples that their leaders would be told "the intentions of the Government before anything is done,"[49] and that the NWMP had "not come to take their land from them."[50] Yet the prevailing peace had justified the Mounted Police in building permanent posts without consulting the Blackfoot. Moreover, this action was further encouragement to White settlement. The Force's success in appeasing the native inhabitants through maintaining justice disregarded the Blackfoot peoples' perspective. In so doing, the NWMP confirmed the Dominion Government's priorities for expansion, but, with this same limited comprehension, they undermined the basis of their coexistence with the Blackfoot.

*****

Faced with these changing circumstances, the Blackfoot peoples persisted in asserting their own interests. This was apparent in their response to the arrival of Major-General Selby-Smith in the late summer of 1875. The Major-General had been authorized to conduct a tour of inspection across the Territories and into British Columbia.[51] Upon reaching the Bow River area, he recorded that he was met by "a band of about 200 Blackfeet, who received him cordially";[52] among the chiefs present was Crowfoot, "considered paramount chief of the Blackfoot." According to the interview, as translated, at a Council meeting the Indians "expressed their great pleasure at meeting the General in their country, and promised to have a better road for him before he returned. They spoke in high terms of the Mounted Police, and the security and good order their presence had established through the country."[53] In relation to the Dominion Government the Blackfoot leaders once again had defined their position of cooperative coexistence. The thrust of the Major-General's report expressed the Blackfoot peoples' recognition of the mutual benefits resulting from the NWMP and their ability to adapt to the process of British-Canadian expansion.

This open offer of cooperation with the Dominion Government, however, was but one facet of Blackfoot self-determination. At approximately the same time as this interview, the Wesleyan missionary at nearby Morleyville, John McDougall, recorded in his memoirs that the politically astute head chief of the Blackfoot, named

> Crowfoot ... paid us a visit. He was full of questions regarding the future. I took time to explain to him the history of Canada's dealing with its Indian peoples thus far and assured him that I expected in due time treaties would be made and a settled condition created in this country wherein justice would be given to all concerned. The chief expressed himself as delighted with what I had told him and said that he

---

49 Annual Report of the NWMP, 1874, p. 64.
50 Ibid.
51 Annual Report of the State of the Militia for 1875, Report of Major-General Selby-Smith, "Reconnaisance of the North West Provinces and Indian Territories of the Dominion of Canada, and Narrative of Journey Across the Continent through Canadian Territory to British Columbia and Vancouver Island," pp. cvii-cxxvii.
52 Winnipeg *Daily Free Press*, October 2, 1875.
53 Ibid.

was much pleased with the change that the coming of the Mounted Police had brought in all the West. He also told me that he would depend upon me to inform him of anything in the future that would be of interest to him and his people. He also assured me of his friendship and thanked me for our past experiences.[54]

Chief Crowfoot's caution was more than a safeguarding of Blackfoot interests. His turning to McDougall, as an informant independent of the Mounted Police, exemplified the tension resulting from the ambivalent worth of British-Canadian law and order. Over the short term this protection afforded the Indian peoples an alternative to the social and moral degradation created by an illegal liquor trade. But, in the long term this protection was synonymous with White, and native, encroachment. Law enforcement, and its accompanying principle of equality before the law, carried with it social and cultural ramifications which greatly qualified the sovereignty of the Blackfoot peoples. In this regard, in 1875, the Reverend John McDougall noted two factors which specifically indicated the full impact of the NWMP regime on the native inhabitants. Referring to the permanent establishment of Fort Macleod, McDougall noted: "[The Indians] are quite indignant that another post was being placed, as they said, right in the path of the buffalo. This would entail hunger and possibly starvation to the Indians." Furthermore, McDougall continued, the Blackfoot peoples question the British-Canadian assumption of proprietorship: "What right had the white man at this time to establish centres without the government conferring first about it with the Indians?"[55] Both the threat to the already diminishing buffalo herds and the absence of treaty negotiations were as much a part of the "new order in the West" as the termination of the whiskey traffic.

Events throughout the summer and fall of 1876 crystallized this tension, pointing out the tenuous balance in the relationship between the Mounted Police Force and the Blackfoot peoples. A crucial factor was the Dominion Government's continuing attitude towards treaty negotiations. Still unwilling to break free of its own priorities regarding the settlement frontier, the Government pursued its policy of containing possible Indian-White conflict through the expedience of law and order. Ottawa officials presumed that this approach would be sufficient to appease the interests of the native inhabitants.

Lieutenant-Governor Alexander Morris's correspondence concerning the preliminary arrangements for the signing of Treaty Six with the Cree indicated the current state of affairs in Blackfoot territory. Morris enclosed in his despatch to the Secretary of State for July 11, 1876, "a copy of a letter ... received from the Chiefs of the Blackfeet Indians, with regard to a Treaty, from which, it is evident, that negotiations cannot much longer be delayed."[56] The Indian intermediary Kassowaysis [*sic*] had also brought a message from the Blackfoot saying "that they desired a Treaty, and thanked me for keeping out the Fire Water, and sending the Police Force."[57] Recognizing the significance of these messages, the Lieutenant-Governor held that, although there was insufficient time to prepare properly for treaty negotiations with the Blackfoot in the current year, nevertheless authorization "to send Messengers to

---

54   John McDougall, *Opening the Great West*, p. 15.
55   Ibid., p. 17.
56   PAM, Morris Papers, Ketcheson Collection, Morris to Secretary of State, July 11, 1876.
57   Ibid.

them to fit a period next year for the making of a Treaty [was] ... essential, as the Treaty with the Crees who now hunt on their grounds [made] it necessary, if there were no other considerations suggesting it."[58] Morris's request summarized the influence of British-Canadian law and order on current Blackfoot-Dominion relations.

Ottawa's initial response to the Lieutenant-Governor's telegram rigidly followed their previous policy towards signing treaties west of the immediate areas of settlement in Manitoba. On July 25, 1876, Secretary of State R.W. Scott notified Morris: "Treaty with Blackfeet under consideration. Government indisposed to make any promises."[59] The next day Lieutenant-Governor Morris wired Ottawa that the treaty Commissioners already present at Fort Pitt were anticipating the arrival of "two Blackfeet, who spoke Cree." He requested "authority to give assurances if they [the Commissioners] deem necessary that Blackfeet will be treated with next year."[60] Three days later Morris re-emphasized: "Commissioners request authority to promise Treaty to Blackfeet you cannot avoid this accept my advice and appreciation of position..."[61] Reacting to this pressure, Prime Minister Mackenzie finally replied: "may if really necessary notify Blackfeet we will treaty with them next year, but we desire to save years [sic] expenses."[62]

Lieutenant-Governor Morris's requests echoed his initial entreaties to have the NWMP sent west. Similarly, Mackenzie's reply confirmed a policy of appeasement and underlined the Government's hesitancy for further commitment. Indeed, the over-riding economic consideration restated Ottawa's persistence in viewing treaties as inextricably joined with the process of settlement expansion.

A letter written by Reverend Constantine Scollen, during the negotiations for Treaty Number Six at Fort Pitt, outlined the nature of prevailing Indian-White relations and the Blackfoot peoples' comprehension of the situation. Stating that initially the arrival of the NWMP had been a "great boon" to the Blackfoot, Scollen pointed out that now

> although they are externally so friendly, to the Police and other strangers who now inhabit their country, yet underneath this friendship remains hidden some of that dread which they have always had of the white man's intention to cheat them.[63]

Supporting this suspicion, British-Canadian "equality before the law" had enabled Cree, half-breeds and White men to enter a country where they were never before allowed. Further, the settlements around Fort Macleod and Fort Calgary had driven the buffalo away from the traditional hunting grounds. Consequently, the Blackfoot opinion was "that the Police were in the country not only to keep out whiskey traders, but also to protect white people against them [the Blackfoot], and that [the] country [would] be gradually taken from them without any ceremony."[64] As Scollen's letter revealed, the Blackfoot peoples directly addressed the long-term implications of the

---

58 Ibid.
59 Ibid., Telegram Book No. 2, R.W. Scott to Morris, July 25, 1876.
60 Ibid., Morris to Mackenzie, July 26, 1876.
61 Ibid., Morris to Mackenzie, July 28, 1876.
62 Ibid., Mackenzie to Morris.
63 The Hon. Alexander Morris, P.C., *The Treaties of Canada with the Indians of Manitoba and the North West Territories* (Toronto: Belford, Clarke & Co., 1881), pp. 248-249.
64 Ibid., p. 249.

Dominion Government's priorities. Without official recognition of their interests, the mutual benefits derived from the NWMP regime were of little value to the Blackfoot. Instead, the Mounted Police were simply an additional factor precipitating the final destruction of Blackfoot cultural and economic independence.

In essence, Reverend Scollen's presentation of the Blackfoot peoples' perspective summarized the basis for the "Indian unrest" which had existed since the decision not to carry out the 1872 Order-in-Council authorizing a formal land cession with the Cree and Blackfoot.[65] As early as July 19, 1875, Commissioner French of the NWMP had reacted to the ascendancy of this unrest among the native inhabitants. Looking to local initiative, French had written that "he intended pressing the subject [preservation of the buffalo] on the new Council of the North-West Territories as soon as it assembled. He would ask for an export duty on buffalo robes and pemmican, a closed season for hunting, and penalties for killing buffalo and taking less than half the meat."[66] Following British-Canadian custom, the Commissioner ironically presumed to redress through legislation a situation already exacerbated for the Indian peoples by NWMP law and order. Indeed, this proposal embodied the ambivalence of Indian-White relations. Eight months later, on March 26, 1876, John C. Schultz, member for Lisgar, carried the question to the House of Commons. He expressed the issue in a manner consistent with the Dominion Government's concern to appease frontier Indian-White interaction:

> So long as the buffalo were numerous ... there was little danger of difficulty with the Plains tribes of Indians with whom we are now being brought into contact. When these were extinct we must expect to deal with a race of paupers rendered dangerous by want of food.[67]

Schultz recommended that a law be passed to forbid buffalo hunting from November 1st to May 1st and to prohibit, during any season, the killing of calves. One year later, however, in March of 1877, the Dominion Government had not yet passed any legislation. When Schultz repeated his enquiry and recommendations, the Minister of the Interior, David Mills, reported "that the Government had given the matter serious consideration but was of the opinion that the Council of the North-West Territories was more able to deal with the matter."[68] This decision to defer the question to the territorial Council was in itself a year late.

For the Blackfoot peoples the further deterioration of economic conditions compounded the inefficacy of this protracted discussion. As the Winnipeg *Daily Free Press* observed on September 29, 1876: "Immense herds of buffalo were passed on the other side of the Qu'Appelle, heading eastward. Last winter there were none hunted in the immediate proximity of Fort McLeod, though buffalo were very abundant the previous seasons."[69] The full impact of this eastward migration was reported to the Ottawa *Free Press* on October 12, 1876:

> the more easterly Indian has laid by ample supplies [of the buffalo meat] for his present and subsequent requirements. The advance of the buffalo in this direction

---

65   See Chapter III, p. 18, this thesis.
66   PAC, RG 18 133, vol. 46, French to Jarvis, July 19, 1875, as cited in J.L. Taylor, "Development of an Indian Policy," p. 238.
67   Canada, House of Commons, *Debates*, March 20, 1876, p. 730.
68   Ibid., p. 933.
69   Winnipeg *Daily Free Press*, September 29, 1876.

has, however, left the plains of the Blackfeet almost deserted, and I have been informed that these people have actually been killing their horses for food. That tribe of red men are very numerous, and hence the prospect is that they will spend the winter on the 'ragged edge' of starvation.[70]

Traditionally, the underlying principle of the Blackfoot peoples' concept of co-operative coexistence had been preservation of their economic independence. Now the prevailing deprivation deepened the tensions caused by the social and cultural inroads of British-Canadian law and order and the lack of treaty negotiations.

*****

In the annual report of the NWMP for 1876, Comptroller Frederick White noted that "the country ... which has hitherto been claimed by the Blackfeet as their hunting ground, has this year been encroached upon by other Indians and Half-breeds, causing much irritation among the Blackfeet ... [who say] that if they were not restrained by the presence of the Police, they would make war upon the intruders."[71] The Comptroller's remarks reflected more than an official awareness of the changing conditions of 1875-76 in Blackfoot territory. During December, 1876, the arrival of refugee American Sioux at Wood Mountain gave new significance to White's observation. The immediate arrivals numbered "about 500 men, 1,000 women, and 1,400 children, with about 3,500 horses."[72] Later in March, 1877, Four Horns, head of the Teton Sioux, arrived with 57 lodges, and in May, Sitting Bull along with 135 lodges, also crossed the border.[73] From the Dominion Government's perspective, this occurrence added the diplomatic pressures of international relations with the United States Government to the question of future treaty negotiations in the Territories.[74] For the Blackfoot peoples, this arrival not only posed problems with inter-tribal relations, but also made the question of economic independence absolutely crucial.

Earlier, in 1876, when the Dominion Government had adhered to its own economic concerns in refusing a Treaty with the Blackfoot peoples, the Blackfoot had also asserted their own economic priorities. The reality of starvation had required a reassessment of their cooperative coexistence with the Mounted Police. Accordingly, the Blackfoot leaders had chosen to address the long-term implications of British-Canadian encroachment with a declaration of mutual obligation. The political activity of the Sioux was the catalyst for this strategy. As a correspondent from the Toronto *Globe* had reported:

> There is at present a large gathering of Indians at Cypress Hills — North and South Peigans, Blackfeet, Bloods, Assiniboines, beside Gros Ventres, Crows, and Sioux from the American side, in all about 3,000 lodges. What this great meeting of Indians, all heretofore enemies, may portend I am unable to say, but it is reported, and generally believed here, that the Sioux who planned and carried out this meeting of the different tribes, will attempt to sow the seeds of dissension and distrust amongst the other Indians with a view to a general rising hereafter against the whites. Major Irvine,

---

70   Published in Winnipeg *Daily Free Press*, October 12, 1876.
71   Annual Report of the NWMP, 1876, p. 23.
72   Ibid., 1877, p. 20.
73   Ibid. For further details see Gary Pennanen, "Sitting Bull: Indian Without a Country," *Canadian Historical Review*, Vol. 51, 1970, pp. 123-140.
74   See Pennanen, "Sitting Bull."

with one officer and a detachment of ten men left here [Fort Macleod] on the 13th for Cypress Hills, to be present at this Indian gathering and to learn, if possible, what takes place in their councils.[75]

On July 8, 1876, Sub-Inspector C.E. Denny reported on the Blackfoot leadership's response to this inter-tribal council. Noting that he was "detained [in the Blackfoot] camp by a council called by the principal Blackfeet Chiefs, who invited me to their meeting," Denny recorded that one month earlier the Sioux had "sent a message to the Blackfoot Camp with a piece of Tobacco, signifying a proposed alliance." The Sioux had asked the Blackfoot to join them in war against other enemy tribes and the Americans, in return for which the Sioux would give the Blackfoot "plenty of horses and mules they had captured from the Americans." The Sioux had "also told the Blackfeet that if they would come to help them against the Americans, that after they had killed all the Whites they would come over and join the Blackfeet to exterminate the Whites on this side."[76] Shortly before Denny's arrival the Blackfoot council had sent a reply to the Sioux "to the effect that they would not smoke their tobacco on such terms, and that they were not willing to make peace with the understanding of helping them to fight the Whites, as they were their friends and they would not fight against them."[77] As Denny indicated, the Blackfoot were confirming their decision of the late 1860s[78] to consolidate their homeland by clearly delineating their position regarding Indian-White conflict south of the forty-ninth parallel.

Yet the full reasoning behind this rejection of the proposed Sioux alliance was revealed by Chief Crowfoot:

> We all see that the day is coming when the buffalo will all be killed, and we shall have nothing more to live on, and then you will come into our camp and see the poor Blackfeet starving. I know ... that the heart of the White soldier will be sorry for us, and they will all tell the great mother who will not let her children starve ... We are getting shut in, the Crees are coming into our country from the north, and the White men from the south and east, and they are all destroying our means of living; but still, although we plainly see these days coming we will not join the Sioux against the Whites, but will depend upon you to help us.[79]

Chief Crowfoot's re-assertion of the Blackfoot peoples' coexistence with the NWMP underlined the necessity of mutual benefits with the requirement of mutual responsibility, particularly with regard to economic well-being. Although an expression of expedience in the face of immediate circumstances, Crowfoot's attitude made self-determination and future adaptation the continuing core of Blackfoot existence. The absence of a Treaty, the reduction of the buffalo herds and the disadvantage of British-Canadian law and order did not modify this concern.

Whether the full import of Chief Crowfoot's pact with the Mounted Police in 1876 was realized is debatable. Sub-Inspector Denny's report stressed that the Blackfoot, like the NWMP, were mainly intent upon preventing tribal warfare. According to Denny, Chief Crowfoot had asked "whether in case they were attacked by the Sioux without themselves being the aggressors, and called upon us, for the Mounted Police,

---

75 Winnipeg *Daily Free Press*, July 31, 1876.
76 Annual Report of the NWMP, 1876, p. 22.
77 Ibid.
78 See Chapter I, this thesis.
79 Annual Report of the NWMP, 1876, p. 22.

to help them, we would do so."[80] Denny had replied that if the Blackfoot peoples were attacked in such a manner British-Canadian justice guaranteed the Blackfoot "the right of protection as well as any other subjects." Yet Denny also clarified the terms governing the Blackfoot claim to equality within the law. He qualified his promise of NWMP support with the statement "that as long as they [the Blackfoot] were quiet and peaceable they would always find us their friends and willing to do anything for their good."[81] This reply was in keeping with the Dominion Government's aim to use the application of justice as a way to appease the native inhabitants, and contain Indian-White conflict. Further, these priorities limited Sub-Inspector Denny's comprehension of the Blackfoot pact for a policy of mutual obligation.

From these two different perspectives the NWMP and the Blackfoot peoples dealt with the continuing influx of refugee Sioux in 1877 and the preparations for concluding Treaty Number Seven. In May, 1877, Commissioner James F. Macleod reported: "The Blackfeet I know are anxious about the invasion of their country. They say that before our arrival they were always able to keep them out, but that they now wish to be friends, so long as they [the Sioux] keep away." Because the Blackfoot showed no opposition to the Force, the Commissioner interpreted the Blackfoot position as simply the establishment of a stronger alliance with the NWMP against the Cree and Sioux. Similarly in August, one month prior to the formal Treaty signing, he stated that the Blackfoot had once again "expressed their unaltered loyalty to the British Crown, and repeated their willingness to fight in its defence, if they were ever required to do so."[82] In neither of these instances did the Commissioner indicate any understanding of the Blackfoot intent to nurture a reciprocal recognition of interests.

As a partial explanation of Commissioner Macleod's viewpoint, on July 5, 1877, the Winnipeg *Daily Free Press* had voiced the commonly accepted interpretation of the professed loyalty of the Blackfoot peoples:

> The different results of the very different kinds of policy adopted towards the aborigines of the United States and Canada respectively afford a convincing proof of the superior wisdom of the system of justice and humanity not only professed but carried out by the Canadian Government. The Americans are never wholly without an Indian war on their hands, and probably the contest between the races will intermittently continue until the red man is finally driven off every inch of territory covered by the star-spangled banner. In British North America, on the contrary, the Indians are permitted to enjoy their existence under the protection of the laws, and, if they do not prove very industrious or productive members of the commonwealth, they are at any rate law-abiding and peaceful citizens, whose loyal and not unimportant aid might be reckoned on with confidence should the Dominion ever be threatened with hostile invasion. The basis of this happy state of the relations between the white and red population of Canada is undoubtedly the treatment in good faith of the weaker race.[83]

---

80   Ibid.
81   Ibid.
82   Ibid., 1877, p. 21.
83   Winnipeg *Daily Free Press*, July 5, 1877. The British-Canadian conception of western expansion asserted the validity of law and order as intrinsic to future settlement. Correspondingly, the British-Canadian perception of Indian-White relations in the Territories merged the native peoples with these values, implying their ready acceptance. This pattern of comprehension influenced policy

Prompted by the seemingly peaceful coalescence of the Blackfoot, Cree and Sioux peoples in the Territories, this popular analysis expressed the British-Canadian belief that frontier stability was synonymous with the principles of justice. From a national perspective the Blackfoot peoples were the benefactors of NWMP law and order; their alliance with the NWMP was sufficient proof. Furthermore, the absence of open conflict justified this interpretation and belittled the validity of the Blackfoot grievances. As the Winnipeg *Daily Free Press* pointed out, just prior to the negotiation of Treaty Number Seven:

> the chief difficulty of consummating an arrangement lies in the probability that excessive demands will be made by the Indians for compensation for the extinction of the buffalo, which they foresee must happen as white immigration progresses. The condition that they will also desire to import with reference to the total exclusion of other Indians and half-breeds from the Blackfeet hunting grounds is another difficult point to arrange.[84]

In emphasizing the two key factors resulting from White encroachment, and essential for maintaining the balance of Blackfoot-Dominion coexistence, this article clearly focussed the underlying tension in Blackfoot territory. Yet at the same time, this insight overlooked the intent of the Blackfoot leaders' pact of 1876 which determined a policy to carry forward self-interest on the basis of cooperative interchange rather than confrontation. The actual negotiation of Treaty Number Seven was to reflect a similar divergence in the British-Canadian and Blackfoot conception of Indian-White relations.

*****

Commenting on the background of Dominion-Blackfoot relations, Minister of the Interior, the Hon. David Mills, noted: "[The Blackfoot] have for years past been anxiously expecting to be treated with, and have been much disappointed at the delay of negotiations."[85] After this brief recognition of the tensions which had marked Blackfoot-NWMP relations since 1875-76, Mills went on to stress "the benefits [which the Blackfoot had] ... derived from the presence of the Mounted Police, the prohibition of liquor, and the establishment of law and order in the North-West Territories, under Canadian rule."[86] In keeping with the Dominion Government's priorities, these judicious steps had brought "the cessation of warfare between the various tribes, which was before of constant occurrence." In fact, as one "intelligent Ojibbeway [*sic*] Indian trader" had observed: "Before the Queen's Government came, we were never safe, and now I can sleep in my tent anywhere, and have no fear. I can go [to] the Blackfeet, and Cree Camps, and they treat me as a friend."[87] The Minister of the Interior's example epitomized the central issue of the Blackfoot peoples'

---

formation in response to the native inhabitants of the North-West. See Douglas Robb Owram, "White Savagery: Some Canadian Reactions to American Indian Policy, 1867-1885" (M.A. thesis, Queen's University, 1971), particularly Chapters III and IV; and Douglas Robb Owram, "The Great North West: The Canadian Expansionist Movement and the Image of the West in the Nineteenth Century" (Ph.D. thesis, University of Toronto, 1976), particularly pp. 327-329.

84 Winnipeg *Daily Free Press*, September 13, 1877.
85 Morris, *The Treaties of Canada*, p. 245.
86 Ibid., p. 247.
87 Ibid.

discontent. Mills adhered to an approach which foresaw law and order as a means to appease Indian-White interaction; this containment of potential conflict equated inter-tribal relations with the ideal of frontier stability and national expansion.

From this vantage point, on September 17, 1877, Ottawa authorized formal negotiations for treating with the Blackfoot. The Government commissioned David Laird, the new Lieutenant-Governor of the North-West Territories, and Commissioner James F. Macleod of the NWMP as the Queen's special representatives.[88] Macleod's presence was considered essential to assure a good rapport between the Dominion Officials and the Blackfoot peoples. In addition, he was accompanied by "an escort, consisting of 108 police, 119 horses and two 9-pounder guns."[89]

The Lieutenant-Governor's opening remarks to the Blackfoot leaders echoed those of Lieutenant-Governor Archibald at Lower Fort Garry in August of 1871. Drawing an analogy with Indian-White relations as they existed in Eastern Canada, Laird informed the Blackfoot:

> The Great Spirit has made all things — the sun, the moon, and the stars, the earth, the forests, and the swift running rivers. It is by the Great Spirit that the Queen rules over this great country and other great countries. The Great Spirit has made the white man and the red man brothers, and we should take each other by the hand. The Great Mother loves all her children, white and red man alike; she wishes to do them all good...
>
> Many years ago our Great Mother made a treaty with the Indians far away by the great waters in the east. A few years ago she made a treaty with those beyond the Touchwood Hills and the Woody Mountains. Last year a treaty was made with the Crees along the Saskatchewan, and now the Queen has sent Col. McLeod and myself to ask you to make a treaty ... She wishes you to allow her white children to come and live on your land and raise cattle, and should you agree to this she will assist you to raise cattle and grain, and thus give you the means of living when the buffalo are no more.[90]

The Lieutenant-Governor went on to advise the Blackfoot that in regard to the means of living, "the other Indians wanted farming implements, but these you do not require, as your lands are more adapted to raising cattle, and cattle, perhaps, would be better for you. The Commissioners will give you your choice, whether cattle or farming implements."[91]

Laird's introductory proposal carried forward the basic outline of British-Canada's pre-Confederation policy for civilizing the Indian peoples. Although a modification of the Eastern Canadian approach, the pastoralist programme,[92] as an alternative to

---

88   Ibid., p. 245.
89   Annual Report of the NWMP, 1877, p. 21.
90   Morris, *The Treaties of Canada*, pp. 267-268.
91   Ibid., p. 268.
92   In a letter of July 26, 1877, to the Hon. D. Mills, Minister of the Interior, Commissioner James F. Macleod recommended that the Blackfoot be supplied with cattle as the country was "admirably adapted to stock raising." The Indians could then "be induced gradually to lead pastoral lives and by imitating the example of white settlers who have already commenced farming in this neighbourhood, to go into agricultural pursuits on their own account." (RG 10 Vol. 3651 File 8576.)
Similarly, on August 1, 1877, in his letter of instructions to the Commissioners for Treaty Number Seven negotiations, the Hon. D. Mills pointed out:

> *The Commissioners will do well to bear in mind that there is a large tract of country within the unsurrendered*

sedentary agriculture, was consistent with the Government's on-going objective. As with the creation of an Indian Fund in 1845,[93] the Dominion Government remained determined to promote economic self-sufficiency among the Indian peoples of Manitoba and the North-West. To this extent, Laird's opening comments foreshadowed the approach to Indian-White relations which Treaty Number Seven represented.

At the same time, the Lieutenant-Governor was cognizant of the value which the Indian people attached to their lands, despite their traditional disinterest in tilling the soil. On January 22, 1877, he had observed "that to the Indian the land question far transcends all others..."[94] Accordingly, during the first of his interviews with the Blackfoot Council, the Lieutenant-Governor clearly set forth that a reserve of land would be set aside for themselves and their cattle, "upon which none others [would] be permitted to encroach."[95] The actual size of the reservation followed the pre-Confederation format; "for every five persons one square mile [would] be allotted ... on which they [could] cut the trees and brush for firewood and other purposes."[96] Three days later, just prior to hearing the Indian leaders' response to the Treaty terms, Laird again stressed the sanctity of their lands. In accordance with the official definition of Indian-White relations as declared in the special Indian legislation of 1857, he stated:

> The Queen's officers will permit no white man or Half-breed to build or cut the timber on your reserves. If required roads will be cut through them ... it is your privilege to hunt all over the prairies, and that should you desire to sell any portion of your land, or any coal or timber from off your reserves, the Government will see that you receive just and fair prices...[97]

In these general terms the Lieutenant-Governor defined the nature of the Treaty and its implications for the Blackfoot peoples in relation to British-Canadian society. To establish the spirit in which the terms were offered, Laird asserted that "by the past conduct of the Police towards you, you can judge of the future;" "just as the NWMP 'speak and act straight,' so too the terms of the treaty will be fulfilled."[98]

For the Blackfoot peoples, the Lieutenant-Governor's statement meant that the mixed blessing of British-Canadian law and order would now be complicated by the Dominion's vague Treaty. From this perspective, Laird's underlining of the terms by invoking the superficial trust apparent in the NWMP-Blackfoot relationship, served

---

territory of a somewhat arid character and unsuited for settlement, but over which it is said the buffalo are found to roam; and it would perhaps be well if the Reserves were selected from the fertile lands found at places within this territory, or at least in its vicinity, where the Indians would be near and have easy access to their hunting grounds, where settlement would not be likely to take place at a very early period, and where the bands could, if they chose, keep cattle and engage in pastoral pursuits. (RG 10/3650)

For a discussion of the Blackfoot peoples as pastoralists, see John C. Ewers, *The Horse in Blackfoot Indian Culture*, pp. 123-129.

93 See Chapter II, this thesis.
94 Winnipeg *Daily Free Press*, January 22, 1877.
95 Morris, *The Treaties of Canada*, p. 268.
96 Ibid.
97 Ibid., p. 269.
98 Ibid., p. 270.

only to emphasize the one-sided policy which was eroding Blackfoot sovereignty. Medicine Calf, otherwise known as Button Chief, expressed this view as a rebuttal to Laird's re-affirmation of the Treaty terms. Having been present at the first treaty signing between the Blackfoot peoples and the American Government in 1855, Button Chief's statement showed an awareness of the full implications of White encroachment, whether American or British-Canadian. Clearly setting forth the political sovereignty of the Blackfoot peoples, Button Chief established:

> The Great Spirit sent the white man across the great waters to carry out His (the Great Spirits) ends. The Great Spirit, and not the Great Mother, gave us this land. The Great Mother sent Stamixotokan (Col. McLeod) and the Police to put an end to the traffic in fire-water. I can sleep now safely ... The Great Mother sent you to this country, and we hope she will be good to us for many years. I hope and expect to get plenty; we think we will not get so much as the Indians receive from the Americans on the other side; they get large presents of flour, sugar, tea and blankets. The Americans gave at first large bags of flour, sugar, and many blankets; the next year it was only half the quantity and the following years it grew less and less, and now they give only a handful of flour. We want to get fifty dollars for the Chiefs and thirty dollars each for all the others, men, women, and children and we want the same every year for the future.[99]

Button Chief's monetary demands greatly exceeded those provided for in the Treaty. Lieutenant-Governor Laird had stipulated that as a gratuity "every man, woman and child [would] get twelve dollars each"; and, as an annuity, to be paid in perpetuity, every man, woman and child would receive five dollars.[100] While these terms represented an increase over the three to four dollars per capita allotment originally advised by Secretary of State Joseph Howe in 1871,[101] the financial commitment at Treaty Number Seven represented the upper limit.[102] From Ottawa's perspective the annuity payment was an expense which only settlement and development of resources would justify. Yet Button Chief's terms were part of a rationale, the long term aim of which was not entirely dissimilar from that professed by the Dominion Government. His claim for thirty to fifty dollars per capita annually was closely tied to his demand that the Blackfoot peoples "be paid for all the timber the Police and whites have used since they first came to our country. If it continues to be used as it is, there will soon be no firewood left for the Indians."[103] If the Treaty was to provide adequate means to make possible a new existence, its terms would have to provide resources equivalent to those the native inhabitants had surrendered with the passing of their traditional way of life. The Treaty would have to enable cooperative coexistence.

---

99   Ibid.

100 Ibid., p. 268.

101 See Chapter III, this thesis.

102 J.L. Taylor in "Development of an Indian Policy," pp. 267-278, argues that the Dominion Government was forced to adjust the financial terms of the treaties in order to maintain peaceful Indian-White relations.

103 Morris, *The Treaties of Canada*, p. 270. On November 18, 1876, the Winnipeg *Daily Free Press* had noted a report from Fort Macleod stating: "...2,000 pine logs arrived there safely from the mountains on the15th of Sept. They were driven by a gang of the Force, numbering five men, a distance of 150 miles down Old Man's River to that post. Four days after their arrival they were all landed on the bank, and the Government mill was in full swing. Extra buildings were in course of construction..."

Lieutenant-Governor Laird's argument in response to Button Chief's terms articulated the cultural and social implications of British-Canadian expansion. Maintaining that the "Chief is asking too much," Laird held up the past record of the NWMP:

> [Button Chief] has told us of the great good the Police have done for him and his tribe and throughout the country by driving away the whiskey traders, and now he wants us to pay the Chiefs fifty dollars and others thirty dollars per head, and to pay him for the timber that has been used. Why, you Indians ought to pay us rather, for sending these traders in fire water away and giving you security and peace, rather than we pay you for the timber used ... We cannot do you good and pay you too for our protection ... Button Chief wishes to get the same every year as this year; this we cannot promise. We cannot make a treaty with you every year. We will give you something to eat each year but not so much as you will receive now. He says the Americans at first gave the Indians many large sacks of flour, and now they only receive a handful. From us you receive money to purchase what you may see fit; and as your children increase yearly you will get the more money in the future, as you are paid so much per head.[104]

The Lieutenant-Governor's pronouncement precluded any radical re-adjustment of the Treaty terms. The essence of the Dominion Government's approach was the provision of basic necessities as a means towards achieving a new way of life. The philosophy behind the policy carried with it no guarantee as to the Indian peoples' future standard of living; this was left to the individual's own efforts. This attitude did not recognize that the Treaty terms represented the Blackfoot peoples' homeland and their continuing social and cultural identity. As with the activities of the NWMP, Laird's reply assumed British-Canadian sovereignty. This assumption caused the Lieutenant-Governor to view Button Chief's demands as unjustified.

Throughout the week-long negotiations, Button Chief's opposition was the only open rejection of Treaty terms. His sentiment, however, was supported by the actions of the Blackfoot Council. Crowfoot, head chief of the Blackfoot tribe, refused to accept the food supplies provided by the Dominion officials during the negotiations, until he was assured that acceptance of the rations did not involve an automatic obligation to accept the Government's terms. The Blood tribe did not arrive at Blackfoot Crossing until the day before the official negotiations ended. Until their arrival, the Blackfoot Council refused to make a final decision.

Faced with the vague, uncertain exchange offered by the Dominion Government for their lands, the Blackfoot Council ultimately chose to accept Treaty Number Seven on the same basis as their 1876 pact between Sub-Inspector C.E. Denny and Chief Crowfoot. As spokesman for the Blackfoot Council, Crowfoot implicitly recognized the inevitability of British-Canadian encroachment and the eventual extinction of the buffalo herds. He, therefore, reiterated the Blackfoot determination to adapt through maintaining a cooperative relationship with the NWMP as representatives not only of Canada, but as a party to a mutual trust. Through this trust the Blackfoot peoples would address the basic requirements needed to ensure adequate means for the continuation of both individual and cultural integrity. In his opening address Lieutenant-Governor Laird had stated:

> The good Indian has nothing to fear from the Queen or her officers. You Indians know this to be true. When bad white men brought you whiskey, robbed you, and

---

104   Ibid., p. 271.

made you poor, and, through whiskey, quarrel amongst yourselves, she sent the Police to put an end to it. You know how they stopped this and punished the offenders, and how much good this had done. I have to tell you how much pleased the Queen is that you have taken the Police by the hands and helped them, and obeyed her laws since the arrival of the Police. She hopes that you will continue to do so, and you will always find the Police on your side if you keep the Queen's laws.[105]

The Blackfoot Council accommodated this perspective in choosing to negotiate on the grounds of Laird's guarantee that they would always find the Police on their side if they kept the Queen's laws. As Crowfoot stated:

I hope you look upon the Blackfeet, Bloods and Sarcees as your children now, and that you will be indulgent and charitable to them. They all expect me to speak now for them, and I trust the Great Spirit will put into their breasts to be a good people — into the minds of the men, women and children, and their future generations. The advice given me and my people has been very good. If the Police had not come to the country, where would we all be now? Bad men and whiskey were killing us so fast that very few, indeed, of us would have been left today. The Police have protected us as the feathers of the bird protect it from the frosts of winter. I wish them all good, and trust that all our hearts will increase in goodness from this time forward ... I will sign the treaty.[106]

Accordingly, Button Chief acceded, stating, "I must say what all the people say, and I agree with what they say. I cannot make new laws. I will sign."[107] Similarly, Red Crow, head chief of the Bloods, restated the basis upon which the Blackfoot peoples would enter into an official relationship with the Dominion Government:

Three years ago, when the Police first came to the country, I met and shook hands with Stamixotokon (Col. McLeod) at Pelly [sic] River. Since that time he made me many promises. He kept them all — not one of them was ever broken. Everything that the police have done has been good. I entirely trust Stamixotokon, and will leave everything to him. I will sign with Crowfoot.[108]

Crowfoot's and Red Crow's statements were equally as general as the terms which Lieutenant-Governor Laird had stipulated. Temporarily ignoring the problems caused by the imposition of law and order in Blackfoot Territory, both leaders addressed the principle of justice as a cornerstone of the Treaty. Throughout the actual negotiations the Government officials had interpreted the Blackfoot position as a trusting, naive acceptance of the benefits of British-Canadian law and order. The Blackfoot Council, however, had acquiesed in Treaty Number Seven knowing the potential for future economic deprivation. As a part of this realization, the Blackfoot addressed the necessity of perpetuating a strong liaison with the NWMP as the immediate representatives of the Dominion Government. Only on this basis would the Treaty function as a commitment to the Blackfoot peoples.

The period from 1874 to 1877 marked an interlude during which NWMP law and order and the Blackfoot concept of cooperative coexistence had satisfied the Dominion Government's desire for frontier stability. From British-Canada's perspective, this interlude had furthered the progress of national expansion by laying the foundation

---

105 Ibid., p. 267.
106 Ibid., p. 272.
107 Ibid., p. 273.
108 Ibid.

for successfully concluding Treaty Number Seven. Yet for the Blackfoot peoples the signing of the Treaty was the first step in a process which would redefine their existence according to the Dominion Government's conception of Indian-White relations. Indeed, by an act of Parliament in 1876, the Indian legislation of 1857 had been extended to include the Indian peoples of the North-West. The policy accompanying this legislation would also complicate future NWMP-Blackfoot relations.

NOTE

This chapter was previously presented as Chapter 4 of Barbara Joan Mayfield, "The North-West Mounted Police and the Blackfoot Peoples 1874-1884" (M.A. dissertation, University of Victoria, 1979), 97-149.

THREE

Policemen and Poachers: Indian Relations on the Ranching Frontier

John Jennings

The calm of the Canadian West has become a cliché. There are no major horrors to be exposed by revisionists or gross injustices to Indians which might surface. The white settlement of southern Alberta, and the Canadian West in general, was peaceful and comparatively enlightened. The relations between the Indians and the ranchers, who pre-empted their hunting grounds, were surprisingly benign. There seemed to be little of the racial friction between Indians and ranchers which had erupted into major Indian wars south of the border.

The obvious explanation for this difference is the presence of the Mounted Police. But perhaps there were fundamental differences in frontier attitudes which resulted in greater racial harmony. The Macleod *Gazette,* the early journal of the ranching community of southern Alberta, demonstrated its journalistic sagacity in an editorial in 1883:

> It has just come to this, these Indians must be kept on their reserves, else the indignant stockmen will some day catch the red rascals and make such an example of them that the noble red man will think h-ll's a poppin, besides a probable attack of kink in the back of the neck [hanging] and we can't say that we should greatly blame them either. That a lot of dirty, thieving, lazy ruffians should be allowed to go where they will, carrying the latest improved weapons, when there is no game in the country, seems absurd.[1]

A footnote was added two months later when the *Gazette* stated, "If we are obliged to fight these Indians to stop their depredations, let the entertainment commence..."[2]

The Calgary *Herald*, by 1887, had become even more violent than the *Gazette* in its attitude toward Indians. Several editorials, one entitled the "Indian Pest," advocated a policy of removing the Indians from the path of white settlement. The implications of these editorials are chilling, for in both language and sentiment they echoed the American Indian removal policy of the 1830's, one of the worst blights on that country's history.[3]

---

1 Macleod *Gazette*, May 14, 1883.
2 Ibid., July 14, 1883. See also *Gazette,* June 26, 1890.
3 See Calgary *Herald*, May 20, 1887 and Sept. 9, 1887.

It could easily be concluded from the vitriolic tone in southern Alberta's early newspapers and the continual barrage of letters from ranchers both to the newspapers and to the Mounted Police complaining about Indians, that the Indians were causing much friction. The sad fact is that western Canada's much-lauded history of peaceful and enlightened Indian relations did not rest on the tolerance and understanding of early settlers. In the newspapers and in the complaints from ranchers to the Mounted Police were all the ingredients for trouble which were also found in the American West. If it had not been for the influence of the Mounted Police it is hard to avoid the conclusion that Indian wars would have broken out in the Canadian West.

In fairness to these early ranchers it must be pointed out that most of the violently anti-Indian attitudes were found in towns like Calgary and not in the ranching community. Many of the ranchers had very good relations with the Indians and defended them against those who accused them of tampering with most of the livestock in the country. It is difficult to prove that these good relations existed because, for the most part, proof is found in chance remarks in diaries and other reminiscences, while proof to the contrary is all too obvious in newspapers and letters of complaint to the Mounted Police.

F.W. Stimson, manager of the North-West Cattle Company, and Captain Stewart, of the Stewart Ranche Company, two of the largest ranches in the territory, both expressed deep sympathy and understanding for their Indian neighbours. In an article in the Calgary *Herald* in 1885 they accused the government of starving the Stonies and stated that, although they had not heard of the Stonies killing cattle, they would not blame them if they did.[4]

Fred Ings, owner of the Rio Alto ranch in the Highwood, described the Stonies in his part of the country as "decent, well behaved and fairly friendly," but added that the Blackfoot and Bloods were "a constant source of annoyance."[5] On the other hand, Harold Mayne Daly, writing about the Bar U ranch, recalled that the Blackfoot had the run of the house and were perfectly honest, but when the Stonies arrived all the doors were locked.[6]

There were many ranchers who lived in genuine harmony with their Indian neighbours. For instance, E.H. Maunsell was made an honorary chief by the Peigan Indians, the same Indians who had earlier forced him to leave the country with the remnants of his herd in the starvation years at the end of the 1870's.[7] He did not hold it against the Indians that they had killed half his herd to survive, and returned to the Canadian range as soon as the Indians were on reserves and provided for by the government.

---

4   Calgary *Herald*, Feb. 12, 1885. Stimson described the Stonies as the best Indians in the territory and warned that if the government did not feed them better they would either starve or kill more cattle. Stimson was considered a great friend of the Indians and often treated them better than he did his cowboys. Glenbow Archives, Reminiscences of W.E.M. Holmes in Eleanor Luxton, History of Ranching in Alberta.
5   Glenbow, Fred Ings Papers, Tales from the Midway Ranch.
6   Glenbow, J.D. Higinbotham Papers.
7   Ibid. Maunsell was one of the early members of the NWMP, serving from 1874 to 1877. He started ranching in 1878, one of the first on the Canadian frontier.

H.M. Hatfield was a close neighbour of both the Blood reserve and the Cochrane ranch, whose owner was continually complaining of Indians killing cattle. In a very detailed diary during the 1890's Hatfield complains constantly of wolves, gophers, and cutworms, but not about Indians.[8]

The conclusion which can be drawn from numerous ranching diaries and reminiscences is that relations with the Indians were often friendly, but usually distant and condescending. Many ranchers make no mention whatever of Indians in their diaries, while others refer to them in a most casual way.[9] A picture emerges of two cultures widely separated by custom and development, but more fundamentally by government policy. The regulations of the Mounted Police and the Indian Affairs Department produced a gulf between rancher and Indian which resulted in some lack of understanding, but on the other hand led also to a lack of friction.

A tentative conclusion can be drawn from these diaries concerning Indian poachers. Those who spoke well of the Indian did not refer to cattle killing. A few, who were continually complaining of Indian depredations, such as General Thomas Bland Strange of the Military Colonization Company, had some rather harsh things to say about Indians. Either those in Strange's category developed a hardened view toward Indians because the Indians were killing their cattle or, perhaps more likely, the Indians picked on those who treated them with disdain.

Among ranchers who were not bothered by cattle losses to Indians there is much evidence of real friendship. The wife of one rancher was given the name White Angel by the Blackfoot because she drove many miles to the Blackfoot reserve to nurse an Indian girl.[10] Joe Fisher, a rancher near Millarville, often had Indians camped near his ranch, and his children were asked by the Indians to stay for dinner. They took one horrified look at Indian cooking and fled home. When their father discovered what had happened he promptly sent them back to the Indian camp to apologize. The Fishers were often visited by Indians, particularly in later years when they acquired a phonograph.[11]

Another Millarville pioneer, Jack Stagg, remembered seeing a group of Stony Indians swimming the Sheep River and hanging onto their horses by the tails in order to join the ranchers for the church service.[12] It is perhaps significant that these ranchers who accepted the Indians as friends and knelt with them on Sunday morning did not complain of cattle killing.

The two ranchers who complained most loudly about Indians killing cattle were General Strange and W.F. Cochrane. In both their cases there were possible reasons why they were singled out for special attention by the Indians. General Strange often had Chief Crowfoot as a guest in his house and had a great admiration for the chief, comparing him on one occasion to the Duke of Wellington. But the rank and file of

---

8 Glenbow, Diaries of H.M Hatfield, 1893-1900. On May 17, 1895, Hatfield stated in his diary a typical ranching sentiment: "Some Stonies came last night and wanted Grub. I did not give them any as they are little better than tramps and I wish the Government would keep them on their reserve."

9 See Glenbow, Henry Sharples Papers; Frank White diary; A. Stavely Hill, From Home to Home; John McHugh, Reminiscences of H2 Jack; A.E. Cross Papers; Letterbook of Stair Ranch, 1890-1893.

10 Glenbow, Kenneth Coppock Papers, p. 109.

11 Glenbow, Sheilagh Jameson, Biographies of Pioneers.

12 Ibid.

Indians, as he called them, were not invited into his house.[13] This would obviously offend the Indian sense of democracy. Strange blamed the Mounted Police and the courts for being too soft with the Indians and added, "with all savages, leniency has no meaning but cowardice, and is followed by contempt."[14]

In the case of the Cochrane Ranch, there was a steady pressure on the Mounted Police to give them better protection because of cattle losses to Indians. However the Cochrane Ranch letterbook shows clearly that many of the Cochrane cattle had strayed on to the Blood reserve and were devouring Indian pasture. There were no more complaints from W.F. Cochrane after he paid the Blood chiefs to winter his cattle on the reserve.[15]

There is clear evidence of cattle killing by Indians in the writings of early ranchers, but in hardly any of them is found the frenzied attitudes of the newspapers toward the Indians. Ranchers expected to lose some stock to Indians, but at the same time realized that their losses would have been far greater except for the Mounted Police. Actually, the ranchers seemed more concerned about white horse stealing which required a sophistication with a branding iron which Indians did not possess.

It would be unfair to accuse most ranchers of antagonism toward their Indian neighbours or of a desire to possess their land, but this, to a degree, was also an unfair accusation of the rancher in the American West. It took only a small minority in the American West to guarantee turmoil. That same turmoil could easily have been created in the Canadian West if there had not been a different concept of law.

Armed with the steady flow of newspaper accounts of Indian depredations, one would expect to find stout files in the Mounted Police records concerned with Indian horse-stealing and cattle-killing. These are conspicuously lacking. The Mounted Police records show that in the early stages of relations between the Police and the Indians, the Indians showed an incredible restraint toward cattle.

Even during the worst years at the end of the 1870's, when the buffalo officially disappeared from the Canadian plains and many Indians were hovering on starvation, the Mounted Police reports express both admiration and surprise at Indian behaviour.[16] Some ranchers in 1878 and 1879 took their herds back to Montana, claiming that Indian cattle-killing forced them to do so.[17] Certainly there was some truth to this but there were many extenuating circumstances. In the first place the Indian Affairs Department only began to function systematically in the West in 1879. Until the early 1880's there were large numbers of Indians who were totally dislocated and without food in the face of the buffalo's extinction.

---

13 Thomas Bland Strange, *Gunner Jingo's Jubilee* (London: Remington, 1893), pp. 386-7.
14 Ibid., p. 401.
15 Glenbow, Cochrane Ranch Letter Book, 1884-1885. On Jan. 28, 1885, Cochrane wrote to J.M. Browning that he had paid seven chiefs ten dollars each for the right to graze the cattle on the reserve.
16 Canadian Sessional Papers, Annual Report of the North West Mounted Police, 1879, p. 3. Colonel Macleod, the commissioner, stated: "It is undoubtedly the case that they [Indians] killed some, but nothing like the numbers claimed. It is the opinion of many respectable stockmen that whites had more to do with it than the Indians."
17 D.H. Breen, "The Cattle Compact: The Ranch Community in Southern Alberta, 1881-1896" (Unpublished M.A. thesis, The University of Calgary, 1969), p. 8.

Cattle looked similar to buffalo and tasted much the same. Undoubtedly many Indians minimized the difference and began to hunt this new source of meat which, through providence, had been left largely unattended. But the striking fact of this period is not that cattle, left to roam at will, were occasionally killed, but that thousands of Indians, literally dying of starvation, existed on their own horses and dogs and even whatever gophers could be snared, rather than touch the white man's cattle.[18]

A surprising aspect of Indian history during the period of the cattle frontier from the late 1870's to the mid-1890's is the very low rate of Indian crime. Mounted Police crime statistics show unequivocally that the Indian population had a much lower crime rate than did the white.[19] The Police expressed astonishment at the fact that the Indians, faced with starvation, were showing extraordinary restraint toward cattle. It is also evident that in this early period the Mounted Police were more lenient toward the Indians than they were toward whites. During the 1880's the Indians, with a much larger population than the whites, had fewer total convictions than did whites for liquor offences alone.[20] However, the two offences that Indians were most frequently arrested for were horse-stealing and cattle-killing. The early cattlemen, whose stock largely wandered an open range, had a very real cause for anxiety.

Fortunately there was little thought on the part of the ranchers of taking the law into their own hands. Occasionally their complaints to the Mounted Police became rather strident, but the great majority of them realized how fortunate they were, in contrast to their American counterparts, in having strong protection. The vitriolic tone of the newspapers probably did not accurately represent the attitudes of ranchers, for whom the newspapers professed to be speaking.

In several instances, an informal vigilance committee of ranchers would pay a visit to someone strongly suspected of putting his brand on other men's cattle, and he would be escorted across the border. But there was never any real threat of violence or lynching, nor was this type of informal justice extended to the Indians.[21]

Throughout the period of the ranching frontier there is only one recorded incident of a rancher shooting an Indian, and that was done in self-defence. A man named Thompson followed a party of three Blackfoot who had broken into his house and stolen a few articles. When he found their camp he and a friend were attacked, and in the shoot-out that followed one of the Indians was wounded. This incident is significant because the wounded Indian, Trembling Man, later died, and for a time his band was in a great state of excitement. There was much talk among the Indians of killing Thompson, and the Mounted Police had great difficulty in soothing these passions.[22] The importance of this incident is clear to anyone who has read American Indian history. It was exactly this sort of situation south of the border which, in the absence of effective police action, so often escalated into a major Indian war.

---

18 C.S.P., 1881, Report of NWMP, Report of Major Walsh for 1880.

19 John Jennings, "The Plains Indians and the Law" in *Men in Scarlet* (McClelland and Stewart, 1974), pp. 61-63.

20 Detailed crime reports are listed in the back of each annual report of the NWMP.

21 D.H. Breen, "The Canadian West and the Ranching Frontier, 1875-1922" (Unpublished Ph.D. thesis, University of Alberta, 1972), p. 174.

22 Public Archives of Canada, Record Group 18 (Mounted Police Papers), Vol. 1085, 1887, file 544.

Undoubtedly there would have been far more friction between ranchers and Indians than there was, except for two main factors of police control. The Mounted Police, through very tough liquor laws, were able to eliminate almost entirely the liquor trade to the Indians. The other main contribution to orderly development was a very thorough patrol system which reached its maximum effectiveness after Lawrence W. Herchmer became commissioner in 1886. This patrol system included a network of rather primitive posts, and it is significant that each of the four largest ranches in the Canadian West had a Police post situated within a few miles of the home buildings. It is doubtful that any other ranching community has ever had the sort of protection that the Mounted Police gave to Alberta ranchers.[23]

This was an enthusiastic protection, partly because there were very strong links between the Police and the ranchers. The ranch owners and the Mounted Police, particularly the officers, shared much the same social values and had a mutual respect for each other. The bonds went very deep, for ex-Mounted Police formed the core of the ranching industry after 1877 and were a dominant element in ranching society. Many Mounted Police had originally been attracted to the Force by the promise of free land after three years' service. The Mounted Police files for 1893 give a list of the occupations of former policemen in which fifty-four are listed as ranchers in southern Alberta and many more are associated with the ranching community.[24] Their influence in ranching society undoubtedly had a large influence on attitudes toward law generally and toward Indians specifically.

All of these early Mounted Policemen who became ranchers had been fortunate enough to fall under the influence of Colonel Macleod, who was commissioner at one of the most crucial moments in Mounted Police history. There have been few to equal his influence in Mounted Police history; certainly none have surpassed it. Perhaps his most important legacy was the establishment of precedents in dealing with Indians which, though eroded in later years, formed the core of successful control of the Canadian frontier. Under Colonel Macleod's tutelage the Indians were given time to understand white laws and came to look on the Mounted Police as their protectors, not their persecutors.

One of Colonel Macleod's most important accomplishments was his ability to gain the friendship and confidence of Indian chiefs, particularly Crowfoot. This confidence to some extent sifted down through Indian ranks, and even led in many cases to Indians turning themselves in to the police and quite cheerfully admitting their crimes, confident that they would be treated fairly.[25] The friendship of chiefs was crucial to effective law enforcement because in most cases it was virtually impossible for the Police to capture Indians without Indian help.[26] There were many instances in which an Indian gave himself up to the Police for horse-stealing or cattle-killing because a chief convinced him that he should do so.[27] But, as the influence of the

---

23 Breen, "Canadian West," p. 174.
24 PAC, RG 18 (Mounted Police), Vol. 80, 1893, file 262.
25 See early annual reports of the NWMP.
26 Indian scouts were responsible for making many arrests and in the notable case of the arrest of the murderer Charcoal, it is unlikely that he would have been captured without massive Indian support.
27 On numerous occasions Chief Crowfoot, particularly, aided the Police in making arrests. References to the help of chiefs in making arrests are scattered through the Mounted Police annual reports. In 1889 Crowfoot was given a reward by the Government for helping in the arrest of the notorious

chiefs waned, due to the policy of the Indian Affairs Department, the Mounted Police found it increasingly difficult to make Indian arrests.

In convincing the Indians that it was better not to steal horses the Police were tackling a major tenet of their cultural values. The horse formed the basis of their entire monetary and social system. Before the arrival of the white man it was the ultimate goal to borrow as many horses as possible from enemies. This was the road to social prominence and to acquiring an attractive and useful wife.[28]

The Mounted Police found it impossible to control horse stealing in southern Alberta due to the proximity of the border. Horses belonging to Alberta ranchers were hardly touched by Canadian Indians, but a fair number were stolen by American Indians who were basically after the Canadian Indians' horses. Many horses belonging to American ranchers were also lost in the same way. Indians on both sides of the border soon learned that the "medicine line" gave them a large degree of immunity from the law. But they also learned very quickly that it was foolish to steal branded stock.

Alberta ranchers were largely immune from Indian horse-stealing because brands could be very quickly traced. American sheriffs were notoriously unhelpful to Canadian authorities in tracing stolen horses, but the American army and the Mounted Police had extremely good relations with each other and with the advent of the telegraph it was not uncommon for Indians to be apprehended in their raids across the border before they reached their reserves. The Indian departments in both countries aided this procedure by notifying the authorities if a number of Indians did not turn up for their rations. In this way the Police were often able to apprehend potential horse-stealing parties shortly after they left their reserve.[29]

The dwindling of horse-stealing among the Plains tribes poignantly marked inevitable acceptance of their new condition as total dependents of the Canadian government. When, with considerable government prodding, they gave in to the policy of trading their horses for equal numbers of government cows, their nomadic heritage was flickering on the point of extinction.

Many of them lashed out against the inevitability of reservation life by continuing to steal horses, though by the 1890's the odds were against them and many ended behind bars.[30] But cattle-killing was a different matter. With ranchers' cattle scattered over a vast range it was relatively easy for Indians to kill individual animals without being caught. It was pure luck when these Indians were detected either by the Mounted Police or by cowboys. Even if detected, it was usually quite simple to outrun the pursuers and evaporate into the foothills. There was a steady stream of complaints to the Police about cattle-killing, but the Police could do little.

By the early 1880's the Indians were beginning to realize the fatal impact of the

---

    Indian runner Deerfoot, who was continually in trouble with the Police. PAC, RG 18, Vol. 33 (1889), file 350.

28   See Frank Gilbert Roe, *The Indian and the Horse* (Norman: University of Oklahoma Press, 1955), and John C. Ewers, *The Horse in Blackfoot Indian Culture* (Washington: U.S. Government Printing Office, 1955).

29   PAC, RG 18, Vol. 39 (1890), file 137. One Indian, Trembling Man, who was caught red handed with eight Cree horses, testified in court, "I took them all right enough, but nobody saw me do it."

30   See crime reports in the annual reports of the Mounted Police.

reserve system. The threat of starvation was replaced by a new blow. Within an incredibly short time, a decade or less, the entire way of life of the Plains Indians was revolutionized and disoriented, leaving the Indians in a state of anxiety, and ultimately, torpor.

In essence, the Indians became Canada's first welfare recipients. The extinction of the buffalo forced the Canadian government to take over completely the feeding of the Indians after 1880. This, of course, erased the momentary problem of starvation, but introduced one that was more serious. There was now nothing to compel the Indians to do anything. There was not even enough work to be done on the reserves to justify a policy of food in return for work. Thus the Indians began in the early 1880's to accept and even demand that the government would take care of them completely. Herein lay one of the most fundamental reasons for the disintegration of Indian society.

At the same time, partly through the pressure of cattlemen, the government introduced a policy of not allowing Indians to leave their reserves without a pass signed by the Indian Agent.[31] The purpose of this policy was to prevent Indians loitering around towns like Calgary for immoral purposes, and also to control the parties of Indians who were wandering over the cattle ranges. These Indians were allegedly on hunting trips, but there was virtually nothing left to hunt except cattle. This pass system was not really necessary to control Indians in towns because the vagrancy laws were adequate for this. Its primary purpose was to prevent Indian horse-stealing raids into the U.S. and to keep Indians off ranch land. It was also designed to ensure that Indians were weaned of their roving habits so that they could become good farmers.

The pass system represented, in fact, a total reversal of the early philosophy of the federal government and the Mounted Police toward the Indians. It had no validity in law and ran directly counter to the promises made to the Indians in Treaty Seven that they would still be free to roam the plains. It came dangerously close to a policy of apartheid.

It became the duty of the Mounted Police to uphold this system. This law put them in a rather awkward position since the system was not legal and they felt they would lose much of their credibility with the Indians if they enforced it too strictly and the Indians refused to comply. Indians could not be prosecuted for being off reserves without passes but there were still very compelling reasons for obeying the regulation. Indian agents had the power, and often used it, of cutting off annuities and rations to Indians who refused to comply.[32]

The Mounted Police took an equivocal attitude toward passes. Some officers complained of their inequity and injustice, while others like Sam Steele were much

---

31 First mention of passes, or the permit system as it was first called, is found in the annual report of the Department of Indian Affairs for 1882. A report to the Privy Council from the Governor General in Council dated 24 April, 1882, advocated this policy so that Indians would settle on reserves and discontinue their border raids.

32 Annual report of Indian Affairs Dept., 1889, report of Hayter Reed, Indian commissioner for North West Territories, p. 167. This method was also used to "persuade" Indians to become monogamous and send their children to school. See also PAC, RG 18, Vol. 1100 (1888), file 134, and Vol. 56 (1891), file 696.

in favour of them.³³ Generally the officers saw the pass system as a necessity to avoid friction between Indians and ranchers. But at the same time they were all too aware of the potential for violence in its enforcement. Although most ranchers had sense enough not to take the law into their own hands, it took only a small minority to start a major conflict. The pass system did at least have the virtue of enforcing tranquility and, by separating the races, ensuring that Indians would be insulated from some of the worst aspects of white society. To those who accused the Indians of an assortment of depredations, the Mounted Police and the Indian Affairs Department could answer that the great majority of Indians were quietly working on their reserves and bothering no one.

The situation was, however, not so simple. By taking over the feeding of the Indians, the government was now faced with the problem of trying to make them self-supporting. Quite naturally the Indians saw no virtue in working if they could be supported in leisure. Furthermore, the Indians of Treaty Seven made reluctant farmers, partly because their land was generally unsuited for crops. The success of the government's farming policy on reserves in Treaty Four and Treaty Six was conspicuously lacking in Treaty Seven.³⁴ This meant that the government policy of cutting back rations on reserves in an effort to make the Indians industrious and self-supporting was not a success in Treaty Seven. The Indians complained that they were not given enough to eat, and the ranchers complained that starving Indians were killing their cattle.

The situation came to a head in the mid 1890's. A group of Blood Indians finally went to the Mounted Police at Fort Macleod, admitted that they were killing cattle, but stressed the necessity of their doing so because rations had been cut by the Indian Department, leaving them in their present half-starving state. They admitted that the Bloods alone were killing from twenty-five to thirty head per month and that the killing was done at night on the same day as beef rations were issued so that they could not be detected.³⁵

Sam Steele, who commanded the Mounted Police post at Fort Macleod, initiated night patrols, but at the same time wrote to the commissioner that three times the number of police would have no effect on the cattle-killing. He also felt that the Indian scouts, who in many cases had been very effective, were useless in this situation because their sympathies were totally with their people.

The situation became intense at the time of the annual roundup and branding. During this period most of the cattle on the range were closely bunched and guarded, making it almost impossible for Indians to kill them. The Mounted Police now feared serious trouble because the Indians' safety valve of cattle-killing was closed.³⁶

The commissioner of the Mounted Police immediately wired the Indian Affairs Department warning of serious trouble if rations in Treaty Seven were not

---

33   PAC, RG 18, Vol. 84 (1893), file 505, Steele to Commissioner, June 9, 1893.
34   Annual reports of the Department of Indian Affairs, 1884, p. xlviii; 1887, p. lix; 1889, pp. 82-4; 1890, p. 62; 1892, p. 47; 1894, pp. 85-91; 1895, pp. 73-5.
35   PAC, RG 18, Vol. 101 (1895), file 38. Superintendent Steele to Commissioner of Mounted Police, June 9, 1894.
36   Ibid., Vol. 1295 (1894), file 82, part II. Commissioner of Mounted Police to assistant commissioner of Indian Affairs, July 8, 1894.

increased.[37] This Mounted Police interference in Indian Affairs policy set off a minor explosion in relations between the Police and the Indian Department which had been simmering below the surface for years. The Blood agent accused the Police of listening to the "groundless complaints of unreliable Indians," even though the chief of the Bloods, Red Crow, and a number of other Blood chiefs had led the delegation to the Police. The official investigation by the Indian Department concluded that the Indians were killing cattle out of "pure devilment" and were better fed than the Mounted Police.[38] At the same time the commissioner of the Mounted Police was directed by the commissioner of Indian Affairs to see to it that the Police "be no longer permitted to interfere in matters which properly belong to the Indian Department."

The attitude of the Indian Department prompted the commissioner of the Mounted Police to send a plea to the Lieutenant-Governor:

> You are aware, Sir, that outside the rations actually issued by the Government to the Bloods, they have absolutely no lawful means of support; there is positively no game in the district, and unless the Government rations are sufficient to sustain life, the Indians must resort to cattle-killing for subsistence, as, even if they could work, there is very little available. The temptation to kill cattle grazing on the Reserve for which the Indians receive no compensation from the owners thereof, is very great ... the peace and safety of these Territories have been placed in my charge, and as these hinge in a very great measure on the Indian question, I think it is my duty to report whenever in my opinion the Indians have been badly treated.[39]

Despite the assertions of the Indian Department, it is clear from the annual reports of the Department that rations in the 1890's were being cut back as a conscious policy of forcing Indians to become self-supporting. Indian Department officials were very concerned that reserve policy would foster laziness and lack of purpose unless the Indians were goaded into supporting themselves.[40]

The Indians of Treaty Seven were caught between the policy of the Indian Department, whose philosophy it was to force them to alter drastically their way of life; and the policy of the Mounted Police and ranchers who wanted the Indians to be well fed and contented on their reserves, insulated by a full stomach from thoughts of roaming the plains and shooting their dinner. The Indians of Treaty Seven became little more than pawns in the policies of the government agencies which saw to their well-being.

For the Indian both policies meant enforced compliance and even pure compulsion. They were compelled by the Police to stay away from cattle ranges; they were compelled by Indian agents, through the threat of the loss of their rations, to work at the occupation of farming for which both they and the land were not suited; they were compelled to send their children to school which they did not like; they were compelled to remain on their reserves unless given a pass by the agent.

This was the price of harmony in the Canadian West. The ranchers of Alberta

---

37 Ibid., July 8, 1894.
38 Ibid., Vol. 101 (1894), file 38. Report of T.P. Wadsworth to Indian Department, July 27, 1894.
39 Ibid., Aug. 27, 1894.
40 Annual reports of the Department of Indian Affairs, 1883, p. x; 1891, p. x and p. 190; 1892, p. xii and p. 47.

were almost completely insulated by these policies and by the effectiveness of the Mounted Police from negative contact with the Indians. There was enough cattle-killing by Indians to create a frontier atmosphere, but not enough to cause serious friction.

The rights of the Indians guaranteed by Treaty Seven were sacrificed for peace. Because of this the relations between the Indians and the ranchers were, on the whole, very good. The majority of the ranchers showed the Indians both sympathy and understanding. But they could afford to have these attitudes, for rebellious elements in Indian society had been defused and the ranchers dealt with Indians completely on white terms. Beneath this surface calm there were still the threats of the newspapers to remind one that bigotry could easily rise to the surface to destroy the harmony with the Indians which had been so carefully nurtured by the Mounted Police.

NOTE

This chapter was previously published in A.W. Rasporich and H.C. Klassen, eds., *Frontier Calgary: Town, City, and Region 1875-1914* (Calgary, University of Calgary/McClelland and Stewart West, 1975), pp. 87-99 and 284-86.

FOUR

Horse Stealing and the Borderline: The NWMP and the Control of Indian Movement, 1874-1900

Brian Hubner

Within a span of only twenty years, 1870-90, the nomadic way of life of the Indians of western Canada came to an end with their forced confinement to a series of reserves. A decade later, most of the remaining structures intended to create "brown white people" out of these Indians were in place. A key instrument in this process of "Canadianization" was the North West Mounted Police (NWMP), a paramilitary force created in 1873 for the express purpose of bringing law and order to the West. In the 1880s, the NWMP imposed Canadian law on the prairie tribes, and specifically targeted Native horse stealing as a crime that could be used to circumscribe Indian movement and restrict Indian men to their reserves, symbolically crushing their way of life. The NWMP was less concerned with the actual thefts, many of which involved "Canadian" Indians stealing from tribes south of the border, than with ending the "wild" and free life of the Indians. The police helped secure Canadian control of the western hinterland so the land and its inhabitants could be integrated into the new world of industrial capitalism. By the turn of the century, horse theft and Indians crossing the border in an uncontrolled fashion were things of the past. Many Indians who had hunted buffalo only a few years before were on the way to finding a place in the new economy as wage labourers, although the final stage of this process of assimilation was never completed.

Several fairly recent attempts have been made to place this "Canadianization" of the Native people within the theoretical concept of class struggle. Ron Bourgeault, writing in 1983, argued that Native society was gradually transformed by capitalism, with class divisions closely following along racial splits.[1] In the West, he speculated that this process began as the fur trade extended west from Hudson Bay. Bourgeault believed the mercantile capitalist system transformed the nomadic Cree Indians into serf-like dependents of the local factor. It is accepted that a modern capitalist system had begun to penetrate the West in 1810 with the introduction of modern business methods in the Hudson's Bay Company (HBC), consolidated by the appointment of

---

1 Ron G. Bourgeault, "The Indian, the Métis and the Fur Trade: Class, Sexism and Racism in the Transition from 'Communism' to Capitalism," *Studies in Political Economy* 12 (Fall 1983): 46-47.

George Simpson as HBC administrator in 1830.[2] In 1870, when the Canadian government purchased Rupert's Land from the HBC, the area was formally linked to the markets of eastern Canada and the rest of the world. The Plains tribes, who lived communally and still hunted buffalo, for the most part remained outside this system.[3] Bourgeault's views were concerned mainly with the Métis. David Leadbeater's study of the political economy of Alberta dealt with some of the specifics of the integration of the Plains tribes into the new world of capitalist accumulation.[4] The critical instrument implementing government policy in this early period of economic transition was the NWMP. For Leadbeater, the NWMP's suppression of crime committed by Indians, Treaties 6 and 7, and the Indian Act of 1876 were linked to changing patterns of "socio-economic development" of the Prairies.[5] This development required that the Indians be moved off valuable land to allow for European settlement, and then concentrated on reserves to provide the arriving settlers with a ready pool of low-wage labour.

Within such a class-conscious view it has been theorized that those who control the means of production, the dominant capitalist classes, will give law-making and law-enforcement bodies the power to act in their interests.[6] Several authors have attempted to define specifically the nature of crime within such a theory. Richard Quinney represents an extreme pole of a class approach to crime. Quinney believed that all crime was the result of class conflict: either crimes of resistance or crimes of control.[7] A somewhat more moderate approach is "Claus Offe's Theory of Welfare and Justice under Capitalism" as outlined by Ian Taylor. According to this view: "The state's function is in creating the *conditions* in which the process of [capitalist] accumulation can occur." Threats that might upset this include "kinds of behaviour that are considered incompatible with the orderly pursuit of surplus value production."[8] It is these kinds of behaviour which must be controlled and are defined as criminal by the law-enforcement and judicial agencies who wield power for the capitalists.

A quick glance at the criminal cases dealt with by the NWMP, in 1879-89, will reveal that three crimes were predominantly associated with Indians: cattle killing, horse stealing, and bringing stolen property (horses) into Canada[9] (see Table 1). In the late 1880s, a fourth crime — drunkenness — crept into the records with increasing frequency. On the one hand, cattle killing was rare, and almost exclusively an Indian activity. Cases involving horse theft, on the other hand, were much more common.

---

2   John E. Foster, "The Plains Metis," in R. Bruce Morrison and C. Roderick Wilson, eds., *Native Peoples: The Canadian Experience* (Toronto: McClelland and Stewart, 1986), 387-88.

3   Bourgeault, "The Indian, the Métis," 64.

4   David Leadbeater, "An Outline of Capitalist Development in Alberta," in Leadbeater, ed., *Essays on the Political Economy of Alberta* (Toronto: Hogtown Press, 1984), 3-5.

5   Ibid., 5-6.

6   Ronald Hinch, "Cultural Deviance and Conflict Theories," in Rick Linden, ed., *Criminology: A Canadian Perspective* (Toronto: Holt, Rinehart and Winston, 1987), 189-90.

7   Richard Quinney, *Criminology*, 2nd ed. (Boston: Little and Brown, 1979), 400.

8   Ian Taylor, *Crime, Capitalism and Community: Three Essays in Socialist Criminology* (Toronto: Butterworths, 1983), 133-34.

9   William Waiser, *The North-West Mounted Police, in 1874-1889: A Statistical Study* (Ottawa: Parks Canada, 1979), 32-33. (Research Bulletin No. 117.)

Table 1 Summary of Indian Horse Stealing Cases in the NWT, 1879-1889			
Year	Indian Horse Stealing/ Total Cases Horse Stealing	Indian Horse Stealing/ Total Cases of Indian Crime	Indian Crime/ Total Cases of Crime
1879	3/5 = 60.0%	3/26 = 11.5%	26/82 = 31.7%
1880	3/13 = 23.1%	3/24 = 12.5%	24/98 = 24.5%
1881	7/12 = 58.3%	7/19 = 36.8%	19/84 = 22.6%
1882	10/16 = 62.5%	10/59 = 16.9%	59/278 = 21.2%
1883	5/12 = 41.7%	5/44 = 11.4%	44/386 = 11.4%
1884	5/31 = 16.1%	5/52 = 9.6%	52/596 = 8.7%
1885	29/48 = 60.4%	29/194 = 14.9%	194/612 = 31.7%
1886	5/12 = 41.7%	5/15 = 33.3%	15/602 = 2.5%
1887	3/9 = 33.3%	3/47 = 6.4%	47/422 = 11.1%
1888	4/17 = 23.5%	4/41 = 9.8%	41/417 = 9.8%
1889	15/21 = 71.4%*	15/95 = 15.8%	95/660 = 14.4%

* Waiser appears to be in error here. The author's examination of the *Sessional Report* for 1889 puts the figure at 5/14 = 35.1%. This would also put the figures of the next two columns into doubt.

Source: Waiser, William A., *The North-West Mounted Police, in 1874-1889: A Statistical Study* (Ottawa: Parks Canada, 1979), 24-26. Research Bulletin No. 117.

Bill Waiser, in summarizing these cases from the Parliament of Canada's *Sessional Reports* found that Indians were involved in about half of the horse thefts from 1879-89.[10] An examination of the cases, in a similar period, involving stolen property brought into Canada revealed that they, as well as can be determined, all involved Indians bringing horses, stolen from American tribes across the international line. It is clear that in the 1880s the NWMP successfully "clamped down" on this behaviour and ended cross-border horse-stealing raids. Since most of this activity involved Indians as both victims and perpetrators (something that one would not think the police would be overly concerned with), the question must be asked — why did this crime attract NWMP attention? The answer may be found in an examination of the NWMP's attitude and reaction to Native horse stealing which emphasizes the class conflict of the Leadbeater/Taylor model. Horse stealing across the border was given special emphasis by the police because it most clearly symbolized the Indian's free nomadic lifestyle, and eliminating it was the most obvious way to reduce their autonomy and control of their lives. Donald Swainson, commenting specifically on a single tribe, identified the process that was occurring: "In bringing effective federal rule to southern Alberta they [the NWMP] abetted the termination of the international aspect of Blackfoot life. This breakdown of regional international societies was part of the process of Canadianization."[11] This "civilizing" or "Canadianization" of the West continued the process of bringing a preindustrial people and their land, into the capitalist economy, and the suppression of cross- border horse theft was an important part of this process.[12]

---

10   Ibid.
11   Donald Swainson, "Canada Annexes the West: Colonial Status Confirmed," in R. Douglas Francis and Howard Palmer, eds., *The Prairie West: Historical Readings* (Edmonton: Pica Pica Press, 1985), 135.
12   David McCrady observed that Canadian historians have concluded that although this process was

The NWMP, formed as a paramilitary organization modelled on the Royal Irish Constabulary, was intended to enforce Canadian law and carry out government policy in the West. The bill that created the Mounted Police, dated 23 May 1873, placed the federal government securely in control of the new police.[13] The NWMP were a key instrument in connecting the West to eastern Canada, by establishing law and order and overseeing the peaceful settlement of the region. The police continued the task of incorporating the Plains Indian people into the legal system, a process that had begun at Red River in the previous decades. This was clearly justice on an Anglo-Canadian model, as R.C. Macleod wrote: "Much of the machinery of justice, including the courts and their officials, procedures, and the law itself, was transferred to the west without significant change."[14] The NWMP was closely integrated with the courts — the act which created the force made all officers "stipendiary magistrates" and *ex officio* justices of the peace, up until the creation of regular courts in 1886, even after which their judicial power remained considerable.[15] NWMP justice gained a reputation for swiftness, and the police's effectiveness was, in part, due to the certainty of punishment.[16]

The NWMP was well suited to administer justice in the interests of eastern Canadian capitalists. The officers were products of the elite of Upper Canadian society, or British-born, and they proceeded to recreate the emerging society of the West in the image of the one they had left behind. The police stressed the values of order and control, and established the legitimacy of a hierarchical social order.[17] Race was an additional element in this process: "Race was a factor to be considered because it correlated with the class ideas which were so important to the force."[18] This was not a situation unique to the western Plains. From the 1850s to the 1880s, the dominant classes created professional police forces all over North America to control subordinate groups and integrate them into a social and economic structure. This was done in a climate of crisis, such as the "lawless" West typified by the "Cypress Hills Massacre," which justified the raising of such forces to the general public.

---

coercive it was less violent than in the United States. He believed this was because, to some extent, prairie Natives "welcomed" the Canadians and the NWMP out of a greater fear of the Americans. See McCrady, "Stopping the Americans: A Comment on Indian Warfare in Western Canada, 1850-1885," *Journal of the West* 32, no. 4 (1993): 48-49.

13   S.W. Horrall, "Sir John A. Macdonald and the Mounted Police Force for the Northwest Territories," *Canadian Historical Review* 53, no. 2 (1972) : 180-90.

14   Roderick C. Macleod, "The Problem of Law and Order in the Canadian West, 1870-1905," in Lewis G. Thomas, gen. ed., *The Prairie West to 1905: A Canadian Sourcebook* (Toronto: Oxford University Press, 1975), 132.

15   Hayter Reed, Acting Assistant Indian Commissioner for Manitoba and the North-West Territories, once requested that two DIA officials also be made "stipendiary magistrates" of the NWMP to combat horse stealing because the Indian Act was too restrictive. See National Archives of Canada (NA), MG 26, vol. 212, Macdonald Papers, letter from Hayter Reed to E. Dewdney, 15 February 1884, pp. 90045-47.

16   Macleod, "Problem of Law and Order," 136.

17   Roderick C. Macleod, "The North-West Mounted Police 1873-1905: Law Enforcement and the Social Order in the Canadian North-West" (Ph.D. dissertation, Duke University, 1972), 52-53.

18   John L. Tobias, "Protection, Civilization, Assimilation: An Outline History of Canada's Indian Policy," *Western Canadian Journal of Anthropology* 6, no. 2 (1976): 17-19; and R.J. Surtees, "The Development of an Indian Reserve Policy in Canada," in J.K. Johnson, ed., *Historical Essays on Upper Canada* (Toronto: McClelland and Stewart, 1975), 273-74.

The NWMP was very important in implementing Canadian Indian policy in the North-West Territories (NWT). Macleod has outlined how the NWMP assisted the government with its Indian policy which he divided into three periods: the cession of Indian lands, the restriction of Indians to reserves, and the assimilation of Indians into Canadian society.[19] By the 1870s this policy was anchored in the reserve system, started in Upper Canada in the 1830s: "The reserve system ... was to be the keystone of Canada's Indian Policy."[20] NWMP influence was important in influencing the major chiefs to sign the Prairie treaties such as Treaty 7. The Indian Act of 1876, revised and amended many times (for example, 1880 and 1914) created the modern Department of Indian Affairs (DIA) and established legislation to govern and control the Indians and keep them on the reserves.[21] The police assisted in the implementation of the policies contained within the act.

The prairie tribes that the NWMP encountered, the Cree, Blackfoot and Peigan, Assiniboine, Dakota, Gros Ventre and others, had somewhat different notions of justice. They did not view horse stealing, when conducted against an enemy tribe, as a crime at all. To them it was a form of small-scale warfare, similar to a dangerous sport or game. In this context, horse stealing was a demonstration of male virility conducted for "economic security and social advancement," undertaken mainly by young men seeking to acquire wealth or advance themselves socially.[22] Prairie tribes, such as the Cree, viewed horses as a measure of wealth and status, and from the time of the acquisition of the horse to the mid-nineteenth century, horse theft was generally tribal in nature, although it had become more individualistic by 1870.[23] Horse stealing was but a step from full-scale tribal warfare and could lead to such, but in any case it was often very bloody and retaliation and counterretaliation were often in order. In the summer of 1880, the Cree chief Pasqua, despite the opposition from the local Indian agent Captain Allen McDonald, left his reserve at Upper Fishing Lake (Fort Qu'Appelle), on a horse-stealing expedition to the United States. The raid eventually resulted in a battle between American Indians of the Gros Ventre and Mandan against some Assiniboine and Saulteaux that killed or wounded thirty-one Indians.[24] In the 1880s and 1890s, horse stealing seems to have replaced warfare on a larger scale as an important expression of Native autonomy. The NWMP realized the place that horse stealing had in Indian culture and believed it was an activity which had to be stopped before the tribes would settle down on the reserves. In 1889, while at Fort Macleod, Superintendent Sam Steele commented: "Old warriors take this occasion [a Sun Dance] of relating their scalps and giving the numbers of horses

---

19 Derek G. Smith, "The Indian Act, 1876," in Smith, ed., *Canadian Indians and the Law: Selected Documents, 1663-1972* (Toronto: McClelland and Stewart, 1975), 86-114; and F. Laurie Barron, "A Summary of Federal Indian Policy in the Canadian West, 1867-1984," *Native Studies Review* 1, no. 1 (1984): 28.

20 Macleod, "North-West Mounted Police," 8.

21 Roderick C. Macleod, *The NWMP and Law Enforcement, 1873-1905* (Toronto: University of Toronto Press, 1976), 149.

22 John C. Ewers, *The Horse in Blackfoot Indian Culture* (Washington, DC: Smithsonian Institution Press, 1955), 176-77.

23 John Milloy, *The Plains Cree: Trade Diplomacy and War, 1790 to 1870* (Winnipeg: University of Manitoba Press, 1988), 80-81.

24 Bruce Peel, "The Last Indian Battle," *The Beaver* (Winter 1966): 12-13.

they were successful in stealing. This has a pernicious effect on the young men; it makes them unsettled and anxious to emulate the deeds of their forefathers."[25]

Several authors, including Macleod and John Jennings, have examined the pattern of NWMP activities as they related to the prairie tribes, and placed horse stealing in the context of law enforcement in the NWT. Macleod saw the period 1874-85 as one of mutual respect and cooperation between the Native peoples and the NWMP: "Up to this point [1885] they [Indians] had been the primary concern of the police."[26] The second period began with the arrival of the railway and large numbers of settlers and continued until 1900. In the first period the police slowly educated the Indians about the new way of things, generally preferring to recover property rather than to arrest.[27] Macleod noted that it was not until 1884, when organized gangs of non-Native horse thieves began operating, that such criminal activity attracted police attention.[28] Macleod found that after the 1885 Rebellion, Indian horse stealing became the most serious external difficulty the police faced. It emerged as a problem because the tribes discovered that they could use the border as a shield; it did not attract a lot of police attention.[29]

Jennings presented a somewhat different view of Indian crime and horse stealing. He also identified an early period when the NWMP was lenient with such crime, but believed that this changed in the early 1880s when the DIA became more involved in creating Indian policy.[30] Jennings found that in 1880 the crime rate rose slightly, and in 1881 more Indians were convicted, the formerly light sentences replaced by two- to five-year terms. Although some prisoners were also let off for lack of evidence, stiff sentences were handed down to repeat offenders. In 1882, non-Native crime increased as the CPR started to move West, but there was also a sharp rise in Indian crime. Jennings believed that the Indian crime rate remained static for the next three years, but noted that many Indians were involved in horse raids across the border.[31]

Jennings identified two major trends in the NWMP approach to horse stealing: an initial period of leniency, and a "crack-down" that started in 1880-81. Jennings seems to have believed that the DIA was mainly responsible for this change. This was a factor, but the NWMP pursuit of Indian horse thieves should be seen within a broader context. In 1879, the last major buffalo herds disappeared from the Canadian Prairies, eliminating the most critical element which could have maintained Indians as independent people. The NWMP and the DIA were then able to impose stricter measures, further restricting the Indians to their reserves. With the CPR on the way it was understood that the West must be quickly prepared for settlement. The implementation of these policies was helped along by the replacement of Colonel

---

25 North West Mounted Police (NWMP), Annual Report, Canada, *Sessional Papers*, 1889, p. 65.
26 Macleod, *NWMP and Law Enforcement*, 144.
27 Macleod, "North-West Mounted Police," 52-53.
28 Ibid.; and Macleod, *NWMP and Law Enforcement*, 44. Horses stolen in Canada were traded in the United States and possibly even as far south as Mexico.
29 Macleod, *NWMP and Law Enforcement*, 44-45.
30 John Jennings, "The North West Mounted Police and Indian Policy after the 1885 Rebellion," in F. Laurie Barron and James B. Waldram, eds., *1885 and After: Native Society in Transition* (Regina: Canadian Plains Research Center, 1986), 225.
31 John Jennings, "The Plains Indian and the Law," in Hugh A. Dempsey, ed., *Men in Scarlet* (Calgary: Historical Society of Alberta/McClelland and Stewart West, 1974), 62.

James F. Macleod, as commissioner of the force, by the more pliable A.G. Irvine.[32] The "wild" life of the Plains Indians was not compatible with the plan the government had for the West.

The whole process was closely tied to events in the United States, which introduced additional factors. The disappearance of the buffalo herds from the Prairies forced many Canadian Indians to hunt south of the line, where the buffalo remained plentiful until 1883, and which led to increased cross-border horse stealing, which seemed to peak in 1884-85.[33] This was not welcomed by American authorities, and was a problem the NWMP believed could develop into something more serious. Throughout the decade the NWMP was under pressure from ranchers, both in the United States and Canada, to end Indian interference in their operations. By 1880, the NWMP's period of initiation was over and the penalties for horse stealing quickly became harsher. Within ten years, the Indians, confined to reserves, were discovering their place in the capitalist economy evolving in the West.

Horse stealing (and to a lesser extent cattle killing) was the Indian crime that the NWMP directed attention against because it most obviously represented the elements of the prairie Indian lifestyle that were incompatible with the emerging new world. This was echoed many times in the reports of the NWMP — the goal was to break the Indians of their "wild" and "lawless" habits, the most obvious manifestations of which were horse stealing and cattle killing.[34] In December 1880, Superintendent L.N.F. Crozier, at Wood Mountain, summed up these sentiments well: "I very much fear that killing and stealing will increase to such an extent that the country along the border will be scarcely habitable ... [if they are punished for] ... horse stealing other Indian outrages along the border will cease."[35]

The Canadian prairie tribes stole horses whenever the opportunity arose, and from anyone — neighbouring Indian groups with whom they were not allied, settlers and ranchers, and even the police themselves. As a general rule, however, after the arrival of the NWMP horse stealing by Canadian Indians was directed increasingly against tribes south of the border. Conversely, Indians from Montana and Dakota Territories, when they had the opportunity, stole from tribes across the Canadian line. Large numbers of horses could be taken in a single raid. NWMP Superintendent Sam Steele reported that in April and May of 1889, Bloods and Peigans from southern Alberta stole a hundred horses from the Crow Reservation in Montana.[36] Canadian Indians who were on the way to take horses from enemy tribes often took or killed livestock that belonged to American Indian agents, ranchers and settlers.

In the late 1870s, neither Canadian nor American law was prepared to deal with this sort of cross-border activity. No extradition treaty existed between the two nations, although the NWMP repeatedly called for some type of agreement.[37] In

---

32 A.B. McCullough, *Papers Relating to the North-West Mounted Police and Fort Walsh* (Ottawa: Parks Canada, 1977), 55-56. (National Historic Parks and Sites Branch Manuscript Report No. 213.)

33 Anthony McGinnis, *Counting Coup and Cutting Horses: Intertribal Warfare on the Northern Plains, 1738-1889* (Evergreen, CO: Cordillera Press, 1990), 180.

34 NWMP, *Annual Report*, 1881, p. 12. Report of A.G. Irvine, 1 September 1882.

35 Ibid., 1880, p. 33.

36 Ibid., 1889, pp. 65-66.

37 Ibid., 1880, pp. 15-16.

Canada, a Canadian Indian could not be arrested for a theft which had occurred in the United States, unless the plaintiff went north to press charges — a trip that was often impossible because of the expense involved — although the stolen property could be confiscated.[38] This was the same in American law. Because of this the NWMP increasingly resorted to arresting Indians for bringing stolen horses into Canada, a law that did not exist in the United States. Indians could be punished for possession of stolen property as if they had been caught stealing in Canada.[39] Not only was American law weaker in this regard but initially American authorities, especially the civilian law enforcement officials, were indifferent concerning the recovery of Canadian horses, or were even hostile to the NWMP itself. This was true, for example, of J.J. Healy, a founder of the illegal whiskey trading post Fort Whoop-Up, who was sheriff of Chouteau County (Fort Benton area) in the late 1870s. The American military was more willing to cooperate, but technically was unable to act except in cases that involved army property.[40]

This lack of action contrasted sharply with the activities of the NWMP. They appeared to have made every effort to return and recover American horses for both civilians and the military. In May 1879, the NWMP recovered a group of horses for the United States Army, and eleven horses and a mule for two American civilians, going as far as paying Indians cash to retrieve them. The operation received the personal attention of Fort Walsh Superintendent, J.M. Walsh; A.G. Irvine, the NWMP commissioner; and the deputy Minister of the Interior.[41]

It is evident that the NWMP were not just interested in stolen horses; they needed to appear to the Americans to be in control of Canadian territory and able to deal with any problems that occurred, especially those which concerned Indians. There was always a fear that Indians north of the 49th parallel would use Canada as a base of operations against the United States Army, perhaps provoking the Americans to stage a punitive military expedition, or that a full-scale tribal war would result from these horse-stealing raids.[42] Control of the border had to be maintained, and Forts Macleod and Walsh were built with that in mind: "The massing of the Force at these posts near the frontier has no doubt secured tranquility in that section of the Territory and prevented the American Indians from using Canadian soil as a base of operations for prosecuting the war with the United States."[43]

The possibility that Canada might be used as a base to fight the "Long Knives" did not materialize until the disappearance of the buffalo in 1879. From the spring of 1879, until the last wild buffaloes were killed in Montana's Judith Basin in the mid-1880s, Indians based in Canada went south to hunt, and in conjunction with these hunting expeditions horses were stolen and cattle were killed. These Indians were often escorted or driven back across the border by the United States Army. The

---

38 Hugh A. Dempsey, ed., "Final Treaty of Peace," *Alberta Historical Review* 10, no.1 (1962): 8.
39 NA, RG 2-1, O/C P.C., No. 859E, "Privy Council Minutes 21 April-3 May 1882, Approved 24 April 1882." The relevant law was 32-33 Victoria, c. 21, s. 112 and 113. See also RG 10, "Indian Affairs Black Series," vol. 3790, file 28, 748-1, memo of E. Dewdney, April 1883.
40 NWMP, *Annual Report*, 1884, p. 17.
41 NA, RG18, Series B3, vol. 2232, "Commanding Officer's Letterbooks, Fort Walsh"; and NWMP, *Annual Report*, 1879, p. 13.
42 NWMP, *Annual Report*, 1880, p. 33.
43 Ibid., 1876, p. 21.

most famous incident occurred during the 1876-81 exile of the Dakota Sioux in Canada. In early 1879, Sitting Bull's people went south in search of the herds, but in midsummer were forced back by troops under General Nelson A. Miles, after a skirmish south of the Milk River.[44] That same year groups of Canadian Cree and Assiniboine went south, to the Milk and Missouri Rivers, to hunt. Along the way the Cree stole horses and killed ranchers' cattle. These Indians returned before the end of 1879, but more went south in the spring of 1880. Such intrusions were not appreciated by the American Army, or by the Crow and Peigan who threatened to fight the Canadian Indians and break their American treaties if the government did not protect the buffalo ranges. The United States military in Montana, on 14 September 1881, issued orders to the commanding officer of Fort Assinniboine (the United States Army insisted on spelling the name of their fort "Assinniboine," as opposed to the generally accepted "Assiniboine," and I have retained their orthography) to use soldiers if necessary to force the "return north of any who may cross to South of the line."[45] In 1881, Cree chief Big Bear again went south, and with some Blackfoot, raided the Crow. This time they were confronted by the United States Army and ranchers organized into *ad hoc* militia regiments, and the Indians were forced to return to Canada.[46] The NWMP and DIA officials increasingly believed that these movements south were actually intended to steal horses or "lift scalps" and would soon result in more serious incidents with the United States military.[47] This was an important factor in the decision to refuse several Indian bands, including those under Big Bear and Piapot, reserves in the Cypress Hills in 1881-83, as one author commented:

> The Government was nervous about having large numbers of Indians located close to the boundary with the United States; it wanted to minimize contact, especially horse-stealing raids, between Canadian and American Indians for fear they should lead to serious disputes between the two nations.[48]

The movement south of Canadian Indians was also not appreciated by American ranchers or businessmen, and these people were not shy in protesting to the Canadian government or to the NWMP about the situation. The DIA *Annual Report* for 1881 mentioned that Montana ranchers, concerned about Canadian Indians stealing their horses and killing their cattle, approached United States authorities about the matter. American officials eventually brought this to the attention of Prime Minister John A. Macdonald, as superintendent general of Indian Affairs, and to the governor general.[49] Montana-based businessmen like I.G. Baker, who also had extensive operations in Canada, were quick to inform the NWMP of the loss of some of their property due to the actions of Canadian Indians. Such was the case when Canadian Cree took forty horses from Indians on the Marias River, and killed nine cattle and several horses belonging to Baker.[50] Montana newspapers like J.J. Healy's

---

44 Robert M. Utley, *Frontier Regulars: The United States Army and the Indian* (New York: Macmillan, 1973), 287; and NWMP, *Annual Report*, 1879, pp. 13-14.

45 Fort Assinniboine Preservation Association (courtesy of James S. Magera), Correspondence of Fort Assinniboine, Fort Assinniboine Letters, file 48.

46 John L. Tobias, "Canada's Subjugation of the Plains Cree, 1879-1885," *Canadian Historical Review* 64, no. 4 (1983): 525-29.

47 Jennings, "North West Mounted Police," 228.

48 David Lee, "Foremost Man, and his Band," *Saskatchewan History* 36, no. 3 (1983): 96.

49 DIA, *Annual Report*, 1881, pp. vii-lxii.

50 Fort Assinniboine Letters, file 69.

Fort Benton *Record* were eager to support these ranchers and businessmen, and always quick to criticize the NWMP and label their efforts to stop this activity as feeble or calculating.[51]

In the early 1880s, the NWMP began in earnest to put a stop to Indian horse thefts. The most important measure they adopted was the selective use of considerably more severe sentences for horse theft and the possession of stolen horses in Canada. These measures could not have been successful had they not occurred in conjunction with the expansion of the patrol system and the NWMP outpost network. The police were also aided by the United States military who, by the mid-1880s, were more willing and able to cooperate in ending the international connections of the Plains tribes.

In 1880, the NWMP attitude towards Indian horse thieves changed. Before this date (though it must be remembered that records are incomplete) there is but one case in the NWT of an Indian being convicted and sentenced (three months with hard labour) for horse theft. In the years 1880-82, eight Indians received sentences ranging from two to five years of hard labour in Stoney Mountain Penitentiary (Manitoba), and several others received sentences of two to three years. As A.B. McCullough correctly noted in a history of Fort Walsh, the apparent increase in the number of thefts was not the result of increased activity, "it was the result of an increased severity in sentencing."[52] At first these measures were directed mainly at Indians stealing on Canadian soil, rather than at combatting cross-border theft. The NWMP were particularly tough on repeat offenders. Little Fisher, who had been convicted of larceny the year before, on 11 October 1880, received a sentence of six months with hard labour in the Fort Walsh jail, for horse theft.[53] Despite escaping at least once from the "temporary prisoner's room," because a careless policeman on "provost duty" had left an ax there, Little Fisher served out his sentence and was released. However, when he appeared in court again charged with horse stealing, in May of 1881, he was sentenced to five years in prison.[54]

In his 1881 report, Superintendent Crozier, commanding officer of Fort Walsh, commented that bringing stolen horses into the country had previously not been "considered by them [the Indians] as an offence," and that the courts had dealt leniently with this sort of activity.[55] This state of affairs had certainly ended by the time of Crozier's report and the transportation and possession of stolen animals was being dealt with harshly. The assumption appears to have been that the persons who were involved in such activity were always the actual thieves. In September 1880, four Indians were sentenced to fourteen days each for the transportation of stolen property.[56] In 1882, a year that also saw an increase in non-Native horse theft because of the arrival of the CPR in the West, an Indian was sentenced at Fort Macleod to two years in prison.[57]

---

51 NWMP, *Annual Report*, 1880, p. 39.
52 McCullough, *Papers*, 55.
53 NWMP, *Annual Report*, 1880, p. 19.
54 Ibid., 1881, p. 35; and NA, RG 18, Series B3, vol. 2185, "Commissioner's Office Letterbooks, A.C. Irvine, Fort Walsh, 8 November 1880-31 March 1881," letter of A.G. Irvine to F. White, 8 December 1880.
55 NWMP, *Annual Report*, 1881, p. 16.
56 Ibid., 1880, pp. 18-19.
57 Ibid., 1882, p. 36.

The NWMP "crackdown" on the transportation of stolen horses into Canada reached a peak in the following two years. When thirty-four horses were stolen from I.G. Baker in Montana, and reported to be in Canada, the police from the Maple Creek division acted swiftly — they found all but three of the stolen horses and returned them to him. In May 1883, eleven Indians were sent to Stoney Mountain for two years each on the charge of transporting stolen property across the border. Irvine commented with satisfaction: "So far as our Indians were concerned, this summary justice had the effect of putting an end to their raiding expeditions."[58] Other arrests, both involving horse stealing and transportation of stolen property, followed that summer in the Cypress Hills. They all resulted in convictions, with sentences ranging from two to five years with hard labour. According to Irvine these had the "most beneficial results."[59] Two more Indians were convicted at Fort Macleod for horse theft: one received six months at hard labour, the other four years. The convictions and harsh sentences continued in 1884: seven Cree were convicted at Regina for transporting stolen property, and received sentences from one month to two years; and, on 15 November, two Bloods and one Peigan were given two years each at Fort Macleod for horse stealing.[60]

These arrests occurred within the context of efforts to remove bands under Big Bear, Piapot, Little Pine, Lucky Man and Foremost Man from the Cypress Hills; indeed, it appears the arrests were part of DIA and police strategy.[61] In March 1883, acting assistant commissioner of the DIA, Hayter Reed, under orders from Indian commissioner for Manitoba and the North-West Territories, Edgar Dewdney, was despatched to Fort Walsh to accomplish this. Over the next three months, with the full cooperation of the police, Reed made promises and cut off rations in order to get the Indians to move.[62] A special tactic was to assure the Native leaders that fifteen Indians, arrested in the Cypress Hills that summer for horse stealing and currently incarcerated in disease-ridden Stoney Mountain Penitentiary, would receive reduced sentences if they complied with the wishes of the government. By the end of summer the chiefs and headmen had led their people to the north and west, out of the Cypress Hills, but to the consternation of the Indians no prisoners had been released. Apparently they had believed that Reed had meant immediate release, and not simply a reduction of their prison sentences.[63] Under pressure from the Native leaders, Dewdney finally had these Indians freed on 14 March 1884, ordering the warden of Stoney Mountain to release the prisoners and allow members of DIA to conduct them to their reserves.[64] (See Table 2.)

By 1885, Irvine was able to report there was "a falling off" of horse stealing by

---

58   Ibid., 1883, pp. 18, 28.
59   Ibid., p. 36.
60   Ibid., 1884, pp. 44, 51.
61   Hugh A. Dempsey, *Big Bear: The End of Freedom* (Vancouver: Douglas and McIntyre, 1982), 112.
62   Brian E. Titley, "Hayter Reed and Indian Administration in the West," in R.C. Macleod, ed., *Swords and Ploughshares* (Edmonton: University of Alberta Press, 1993), 113.
63   NA, MG 26, vol. 212, Macdonald Papers, p. 90041, letter of Edgar Dewdney to J.A. Macdonald, 16 February 1884.
64   NA, RG 10, "Indian Affairs Black Series," vol. 3770, file 33,972, "From the Manitoba Penetentiary — Release of Indian prisoners arrested at Cypress Hills for horse stealing, 1884."

Table 2
Names of Indian Prisoners Released on 14 March 1884 from Stoney Mountain Penitentiary

Name of Prisoner	Band (all Cree)	Sentence
Wa-kee-ew	Big Bear	Two years
The Lonesome Man	Nepu-es (also named "like a Dead Man")	Five years
Mis-as-quat	Pie Pot	Five years
Cut Foot	Pie Pot	Five years
The Wolf	Pie Pot	Five years
Old Moccasin	Pie Pot	Two years
Sitting Horse	No band	Two years
The Strong Body	Little Horse	Two years
Pigs Fat	Big Bear	Two years
Little Calf	Pie Pot	Two years
The Flying Quill	No band	Two years
Fawn Standing	Me nah ne cos sis	Two years
Lo-pa-is-ta-o	Me nah ne cos sis	Two years
Wa-cho-kum	The wise man	Two years
Ne-pay-ya-chi	Big Bear	Two years

Source: Based on a list in NA, RG 10, vol. 3770, file 33, 972, "From the Manitoba Penitentiary — Release of the Indian Prisoners arrested at Cypress Hills for horse stealing, 1884."

Indians.[65] Paradoxically the 1885 statistics represent the high point of convictions of Indians for crimes related to horse theft. However, it is evident that the eleven Indians sentenced in Regina, in November 1885, to one to four months in jail, and the five Indians who received from two to six years for horse theft or illegal possession of horses, at Battleford in September, were actually being punished for their part in the North-West Rebellion of 1885. This, in itself, illustrates the way the police were able to effectively use these laws to punish Indians for unlawful behaviour.[66]

After 1885, the number of convictions of Indians for horse stealing and related crimes gradually diminished, but penalties often remained harsh, and officers of the force seemed more eager than ever to advocate strict measures to end the problem. In December 1886, Superintendent J.H. McIllree, commanding officer of "A" Division (Maple Creek) went just short of advocating that horse thieves be shot on sight, and concluded: "I have advised several times that severe measures should be used with these Indian horse thieves."[67] A year later, at Fort Macleod, Sam Steele believed that officers of the force should retain enough power, in light of the judicial changes in the NWT, to "inflict severe punishment on [Indian] horse thieves." Steele, who was an admirer of American-style "summary justice" and who recommended it for Canada, said that the Bloods and Peigans were turning stolen horses over to their chiefs for fear of punishment.[68] The new commissioner of the force, Lawrence W.

---

65   NWMP, *Annual Report*, 1885, p. 10.
66   Ibid., pp. 105, 115-16.
67   Ibid., 1886, p. 27.
68   For justice, see ibid., 1887, p. 62; for punishment, see ibid., 1889, p. 66.

Herchmer, understood these feelings, and in his report for 1889 promised that the police would act with "speedy justice" to make our territories dangerous to those "bringing stolen horses into Canada."[69] Penalties remained heavy for convicted Indians, especially when compared to the many non-Native prisoners who were released.[70] In May 1887, two Bloods, The Dog and Big Rib, were convicted of stealing horses from non-Natives at Medicine Hat, and received five years each at hard labour, but the pair never went to jail because they managed to escape.[71]

The NWMP could not have achieved the results that they did in the suppression of horse stealing, especially related to cross-border activities, without the improvement and the expansion of the patrol system and the system of outposts. These were the organizational changes which insured that Indian thieves would face justice, or at least lose their horses. The police had always utilized patrols and outposts, but after 1885 Herchmer instituted a system of systematic patrols which eventually covered the police's entire jurisdiction, concentrating on the border areas. Herchmer's initial motivation to do this may well have been the gangs of non-Native horse thieves from Montana who started to operate in the border regions in 1884.[72] The patrol system was very effective and many, including contemporaries such as Herchmer, and Indian agent William Pocklington, and historians such as R.C. Macleod, have credited it with ending horse stealing.[73] A good example of police efficiency in patrolling the border occurred in April 1889, when Superintendent Richard Burton Deane, commanding the Lethbridge division, was informed that Canadian Indians had left for the United States to steal horses. Deane warned Colonel Otis, his counterpart at Fort Assinniboine, who wired back that the thieves were returning to Canada through the Sweet Grass Hills with Gros Ventre horses. Deane, who had fifty-six men patrolling night and day, found the Indians with a "flying patrol," and although the criminals escaped, many of the horses were recovered.[74]

The network of NWMP outposts went hand in hand with the patrol system to increase police effectiveness in dealing with horse thieves. The expansion of the number of outposts after 1885 was especially important in protecting ranchers from the Indians. NWMP outposts had existed since the force had been in the West and they had been recognized as being effective against horse stealing since the early 1880s.[75] From 1886 to 1889, Herchmer established many more outposts in the NWT such as Writing-on-Stone, a post on the Milk River in southern Alberta, which was built to stop Blackfoot, Assiniboine and Gros Ventre "raids across the border."[76] As

---

69 Ibid., 1887, report of Sam Steele, p. 62 and report of Herchmer, pp. 7-8.

70 Rider, a Blood Indian, was sentenced to two years in prison, see ibid., 1886, p. 148 and ibid., 1887, pp. 129-32.

71 Ibid., 1887, pp. 7, 148.

72 Macleod, "North-West Mounted Police," 84-86; and Carl Betke, "Pioneers and Police on the Canadian Prairies, 1885-1914," in R.C. Macleod, ed., *Lawful Authority: Readings on the History of Criminal Justice in Canada* (Toronto: Copp Clark Pitman, 1988), 99.

73 NWMP, *Annual Report*, 1888, p. 9; ibid., 1889, pp. 1-2; Macleod, "North-West Mounted Police," 86; and DIA, *Annual Report*, 1891, p. 82.

74 NWMP, *Annual Report*, 1888, pp. 42-43.

75 Ibid., 1883, p. 10.

76 Gary Adams, Michael R.A. Forsman and Sheila J. Minni, *Archaeological Investigations: Writing-On-Stone N.W.M.P. Post* (Edmonton: Historical Resources Division, Alberta Culture, 1977), 6-7. (Historic Sites Service Occasional Paper No. 4.)

ranching took hold in southern Alberta, the police extended special protection to the ranchers' livestock.[77] A few ranchers vocally complained about Indians, mainly American, interfering with their stock.[78] Some, like Senator W.F. Cochrane, owner of the Cochrane Ranche, had influential voices. In a letter sent to his father on 4 January 1885, Cochrane told of how the NWMP were tardy in placing men at the old Standoff Post near his property, and that he considered going to their superiors. This sort of pressure evidently worked, and by 1889 the NWMP had a system of outposts within a few miles of the home ranch of the four major ranching operations in Alberta, including the Cochrane Ranche and the Walrond Ranche.[79]

Despite some initial problems, the NWMP were always eager to establish good, cooperative relationships with the United States military and Indian agents to stop cross-border horse stealing.[80] It is clear that events south of the border were important in the NWMP successes against the horse thieves. This is understandable, as American authorities were involved in exactly the same process as the police. The establishment of the NWMP's system of forts, in 1874-75, was followed by the American Army's defeat of the Dakota Sioux and their occupation of the northern Plains with a series of new military installations: Forts Keogh, Custer and Missoula (1877); Fort Assinniboine, which replaced the old fur trade post Fort Benton (1879); and Fort Maginnis (1880).[81] Fort Assinniboine, acting in conjunction with its sister — Fort Buford (1868) — was particularly important in dealing with cross-border horse stealing as it was expressly built to stop Indians from coming across the Canadian border. Soldiers from Fort Assinniboine were involved in roundups of Canadian Cree in 1881, 1883, 1884, 1885, and in the two "anti-Cree campaigns" of 1895 and 1896.[82]

The NWMP developed an effective working relationship with the officers of Fort Assinniboine, who, by 1883 seemed to have been willing to go well beyond official regulations to cooperate with the police. Critical to this cooperation was the use of the telegraph system which came West with the railroad. Army or police officials on either side of the border could relay accurate descriptions of horses to each other before the culprits had even crossed the border. On 3 October 1883, the quartermaster of Fort Assinniboine was able to supply the commanding officer of the Maple Creek division with full descriptions of stolen horses — within days of the

---

77 David H. Breen, "The Turner Thesis and the Canadian West: A Closer Look at the Ranching Frontier," in Lewis H. Thomas, *Essays on Western History* (Edmonton: University of Alberta Press, 1976), 217.

78 John Jennings, "Policemen and Poachers: Indian Relations on the Ranching Frontier," in A.W. Rasporich and H.C. Klassen, eds., *Frontier Calgary: Town, City, and Region 1875-1914* (Calgary: McClelland and Stewart West, 1975), 88-89, 94.

79 David H. Breen, *The Canadian Prairie West and the Ranching Frontier, 1874-1924* (Toronto: University of Toronto Press, 1983), 82-85.

80 The NWMP were eager to establish a relationship with the American authorities. See NA, RG 18, Series B3, vol. 2185, "Commissioner's Office Letterbooks, A.C. Irvine, Fort Walsh, 8 November 1880-31 March 1881," letter of A.G. Irvine to the Minister of the Interior, 8 December 1880. The differences which separated the two sides are outlined in RG 10, vol. 3740, file 28, 748-1, 1881-1883.

81 Robert M. Utley, "War Houses in Sioux Country," in Paul L. Hedren, ed., *The Great Sioux War, 1876-77* (Helena: Montana Historical Society Press, 1991), 253-62; and Francis Paul Prucha, *Atlas of American Indian Affairs* (Lincoln: University of Nebraska Press, 1990), 168-71.

82 Nicholas P. Hardeman, "Brick Stronghold of the Border: Fort Assinniboine, 1879-1911," *Montana: The Magazine of Western History* 24, no. 2 (1979): 56-61.

crime.[83] The relationship the police developed with the United States military frequently bore fruit, as in late August 1883 when Colonel Jacob Kline of Fort Assinniboine returned fifty-three horses stolen from British subjects on the Bow River. The suspect, Dragon Fly, was turned over to the NWMP at Fort Walsh crossing at noon on 25 August.[84]

This spirit of cooperation also extended to the DIA. In the mid-1880s they began to cooperate with American Indian agents to encourage their respective charges to remain on their proper side of the border; the agents often kept track of the Indians by recording who showed up for rations. In 1887, the enterprising Canadian Indian agent, William Pocklington of the Blood Agency, accompanied the NWMP, scout Jerry Potts, and Chief Red Crow, to arrange a "peace conference" at Fort Assinniboine between his Bloods and the American Gros Ventres, with the cooperation of United States Indian agent Major Field. This was the result of the theft, in May 1887, of eighty horses from the Assiniboine and Gros Ventre, in retaliation for six Bloods killed in the Sweet Grass Hills the year before.[85] In 1894, Pocklington and Captain L.W. Cooke, agent at the Blackfeet Agency, Montana, arranged a system for their respective reserve and reservation, which consisted of keeping careful track of those able to draw rations and then expelling foreigners. If such an Indian was caught without a pass he was arrested and returned home; a second time meant a spell of hard labour and a police escort to the border — on foot. There were no third time repeaters.[86] Pocklington declared that these arrangements prevented the "roaming between the two countries" of the Blackfoot and Peigan Indians.[87]

By the late 1880s, the police were full of praise for the United States Army's help in suppressing horse stealing; Superintendent W.D. Antrobus, at Maple Creek, singled out Colonel Otis, commanding officer of Fort Assinniboine, for his great assistance with such matters. The feeling in Montana was mutual. In 1888, Granville Stuart, leader of Montana's lynching movement, and head of the Montana Stock Association, lauded the NWMP for the swiftness of their justice.[88]

As the DIA came more and more to the fore in dealing with Indians, the NWMP's role was gradually restricted to enforcing government policy towards Indians. One such policy seems to have been initially intended to stop horse stealing but soon had much wider applications. This was the introduction of the "pass law" in 1885. The first mention of the institution of a system of border passes was in 1882 when Prime Minister Macdonald suggested to the Privy Council it might be used to end raiding by both Canadian and American Indians. It was thought that such a system would discourage crossing of the border by Indians and that they would then "abandon their nomadic habits and settle down on reservations provided for them."[89] It was not

---

83 Fort Assinniboine Letters, Letter 6.
84 At least, this is what was planned. The author assumes it occurred as the matter does not come up again in the literature. See ibid., file 81, 20 August 1883.
85 Dempsey, "Final Treaty of Peace," 8.
86 *Annual Report of the Commissioner of Indian Affairs* (United States), 1894, p. 87.
87 DIA, *Annual Report*, 1894, p. 87.
88 For Otis, see NWMP, *Annual Report*, 1888, p. 119; and for Granville Stuart, see ibid., pp. 7-8.
89 NA, RG 2-1, O/C P.C. 859.E, "Privy Council Minutes — Copy of the Privy Council Committee Report, 24 April 1882." See also DIA, *Annual Report*, 1882, x-xi; and John Leslie and Ron Maguire, eds., *The*

implemented at that time because it was believed that vigorous application of the vagrancy laws was sufficient. The pass system was next mentioned in Commissioner A.G. Irvine's 1884 annual report when he referred to the suggestion of Lawrence Vankoughnet, the deputy superintendent general for Indian Affairs, that such passes would stop Indians from loitering in settled areas. Irvine had doubts about the legality of such a "permit" system, a doubt that the police were to voice in the following decades.[90]

In 1885, the pass system was put into place by Lawrence Vankoughnet and Hayter Reed, after Major General Frederick Middleton had instituted it as a temporary measure during the North-West Rebellion. Reed primarily wanted to stop Indians from leaving the reserves and straying into the towns, but the system was also supported by the strong cattle lobby led by Senator Cochrane.[91] The "pass law" was added as an amendment to the Indian Act, and made the Indian agent a local justice of the peace able to enforce the Criminal Code with regard to vagrancy and loitering laws. The system required that an Indian have a pass signed by an Indian agent in order to leave the reserve. It was generally only effective when rations were withheld as a punishment. The NWMP, the DIA, and the federal government all knew the "pass law" had no legal basis and violated the promises of Treaty 7 — promises that the Indians would not be confined to the reserves. Yet the police, according to Macleod, "co-operated with the Indian Department in enforcing it as a matter of mutual convenience."[92]

In the 1880s and 1890s, the NWMP had a difficult time enforcing the pass system. Superintendent Deane, at Lethbridge, reported that the Blood Indians ignored it as they knew it had no valid basis in law.[93] In May 1893, Commissioner Herchmer, after he was told by his legal advisors that the system was illegal, decided to end NWMP enforcement of the system, but this stop appears to have been only temporary. The force remained involved in enforcing of the "pass law," but they were again doubting its legality in 1904.[94] The DIA still continued to issue passes in the 1930s and 1940s, even though, by the mid-1890s, the belief that passes could keep Indians on the reserve had already largely been abandoned. All requests for passes were now to be granted and used only to obtain "a knowledge of their [Indian] movements."[95] By this time the pass system was hardly needed — other laws and measures had been enacted to erode the traditional life of the Plains Indians, such as the measures intended to end the Sun Dance.[96] The pass system only had a minor role in ending horse stealing, but the idea behind it was the same as the NWMP efforts to end cross-border raids. As historian Sarah Carter wrote in reference to the system:

Historical Development of the Indian Act, 2nd ed. (Ottawa: Treaties and Historical Research Centre, Indian and Northern Affairs Canada, 1978), 84.

90 Jennings, "North West Mounted Police," 228-30; and NWMP, *Annual Report*, 1884, p. 6.

91 F. Laurie Barron, "The Indian Pass System in the Canadian West, 1882-1935," *Prairie Forum* 13, no. 1 (1988): 28-38.

92 Macleod, *NWMP and Law Enforcement*, 146.

93 NWMP, *Annual Report*, 1888, p. 68.

94 Sarah Carter, "Controlling Indian Movement: The Pass System," *NeWest Review* 11 (May 1985): 8-9.

95 Hayter Reed quoted in Barron, "Indian Pass System," 37.

96 Ibid., 38.

"Prospective settlers also had to be assured that they had nothing to fear from Indians if they homesteaded on an isolated part of the prairie."[97]

If the pass system presented a problem for the NWMP the police found the "Act Respecting ... Public Morals" — the vagrancy law — a most useful tool and it was used in a limited way against horse thieves. In 1884, Irvine commented: "In connection with horse stealing, no less than in other crimes the Vagrant Act has been found, in the West, to be efficacious."[98] In the following decades, the vagrancy law was employed extensively to remove undesirable Indians from wherever the authorities did not want them.[99]

In 1888, the NWMP reported that Indian theft of horses was no longer a very serious problem.[100] This view was being increasingly confirmed by the reports of local Indian agents. Blood Indian agent William Pocklington wrote to the commissioner of Indian Affairs, Edgar Dewdney on 18 July 1889, that " there have been fewer war parties travelling round the country" in the last twelve months, and fewer rancher complaints.[101] Indeed, a year later, Pocklington noted that Chief Red Crow turned in some Indians who had been attempting to bring stolen property into Canada.[102] By then, the NWMP were also greatly assisted by the formation of Indian police forces.[103] In 1890, Pocklington reported "not an instance of a single horse having been stolen from the south."[104] Indian agents like Pocklington began replacing their reports of horse stealing with glowing reports of the progress Indians were making in the wage economy: cutting hay, mining coal, cutting and freighting lumber. Initially much of this work was done for the agents themselves or the local NWMP division at Fort Macleod, but in the Lethbridge area the Indians were soon mining coal for settlers or "working out" for non-Native farmers in the district.[105] In 1895, the new agent on the Blood reserve, James Wilson, reported: "The others, seeing their success, soon followed and thus we now have a large body of good working men."[106] NWMP crime reports for 1895 do not include any Indians accused of horse theft or the transportation of stolen property into Canada. By this time, the police and the Indian agents were identifying drunkenness and prostitution as the major Indian crimes. Horse stealing was almost a thing of the past. As Wilson said of the Indians: "their proximity to the international boundary line made it much harder in former years to gain any control over them because upon the least attempt at restraint they immediately crossed the line."[107] In his 1898 report, Commissioner Herchmer said

---

97   Carter, "Controlling Indian Movement," 9.

98   NWMP, *Annual Report*, 1884, p. 19.

99   T. Thorner, "The Not-So-Peaceable Kingdom: Crime and Criminal Justice in Frontier Calgary," in Rasporich and Klassen, eds., *Frontier Calgary*, 101.

100 NWMP, *Annual Report*, 1880, p. 7.

101 DIA, *Annual Report*, 1889, p. 83.

102 Ibid., 1890, p. 60.

103 On 1 June 1887, Indian police helped the NWMP in returning a stolen horse, see NWMP, *Annual Report*, 1887, p. 51. See also McGinnis, *Counting Coup and Cutting Horses*, 187. In 1887 the United States also established Indian police forces in Montana.

104 DIA, *Annual Report*, 1891, p. 82.

105 Ibid., 1893, pp. 84-85; ibid., 1894, p. 87; and ibid., 1896, p. 156.

106 Ibid., 1895, p. 75.

107 Ibid., p. 154.

much the same thing — there were few cases of horse stealing in the West and the Indians were now no trouble; indeed they had a "growing inclination to make money, fostered by the Indian Department."[108]

The NWMP had been instrumental in achieving this satisfactory state of affairs by imposing harsher sentences on Indians, and utilizing their effective patrol and outpost system to catch offenders and return horses. The police were aided in these endeavours by the American military, and the Mounted Police in turn assisted the Canadian DIA in circumscribing Indian movement. This was not surprising as all these groups had the same goal in mind — the restriction of the tribes to the reserve lands that the non-Natives had set aside for them, in preparation for the Indians to be absorbed into the capitalist economy. Horse stealing was the most prominent manifestation of continuing, albeit feeble, Native independence and it had to be suppressed. These historical events fit very well into a model of class conflict, like that proposed by Leadbeater and Taylor. This process, however, was not fully completed: the Indians on the reserves were never completely integrated into the new wage economy, despite the overly optimistic reports of Indian agents. In part, this was an unwanted result of the initial success of government policy — the confinement and then isolation of the tribes to the reserves, for the reserves were crucial elements in the ultimate survival of traditional Indian culture on the Prairies.[109] There Indians were able to develop other forms of resistance in relative isolation and neglect on the very reserves which were intended as the crucibles of their assimilation.[110]

NOTE

This chapter was previously published in *Prairie Forum*, 20, no. 2 (fall 1995), 281-300.

---

108 NWMP, *Annual Report*, 1898, p. 3.

109 The best treatment of the Indian experience in Canada remains J.R. Miller's *Skyscrapers Hide the Heavens: A History of Indian-White Relations in Canada* (Toronto: University of Toronto Press, 1989). See especially chapter 11 — "The Policy of the Bible and the Plough," 189-210.

110 Vic Satzewich and Terry Wotherspoon, *First Nations: Race, Class and Gender Relations* (Scarborough, ON: Nelson Canada, 1993), 44-46.

FIVE

The Wild Ones

H.A. Dempsey

This was no life for a real Indian. Seven years earlier when there had been buffalo, the tribes had been free of the white man's yoke. Now only the ration house stood between them and starvation; only the crumbs from the white man's table kept them alive.

The year was 1887, six years after the Bloods had drifted onto their reserve from the buffaloless plains to the south. Now their leather tepees were tattered and log cabins dotted the camps in the bottomlands of the Belly River. The old days were over, gone with the buffalo whose disappearance had so suddenly taken away their freedom and independence.

O'mukopi'kis, or Big Rib, and *Imitah'*, The Dog, had missed the days of glory, for in 1887 Big Rib had just turned twenty-one, while his companion was twenty-three. But they knew about those thrilling times and were not to be denied their chance for adventure and fame. The boys were cousins from the Many Children Band, one of the most warlike families in the tribe. Big Rib was a son of the chief, Running Wolf, and was married to a daughter of White Bull of the Peigans. In the eyes of the Indians he was a good man but to the Indian agent he was "one of the worst characters on the reserve."[1] This meant that he scorned farming, clung to his Native religion, and displayed the arrogant independence for which his family had become famous.

The Dog, on the other hand, was something of a dandy. A son of Bad Horses, he had gained considerable fame in the camps a year earlier when he courted and won an attractive woman who had been married to a white trader. To accomplish such a deed was almost as good as counting a victory on the warpath, so The Dog was hailed and praised by his comrades. Like his cousin, he was no favorite of the Indian agent, who described him as "the ringleader of all the stealing parties,"[2] and as keeper of the war drums, he helped to encourage the warlike traditions of his tribe.

These budding warriors wanted no part of scratching the earth to grow turnips and potatoes. They scorned those who humbled themselves before the Indian agent,

---

1 Letter, Indian agent William Pocklington to Indian comissioner, August 4, 1891. Blood Reserve letter-book.

2 Letter, Indian agent Pocklington to Indian commissioner, May 18, 1887. Blood Reserve letter-book.

but found it hard to keep their independence in the face of hunger and privation. In 1884 Big Rib had been caught stealing a white man's trousers when he was short of clothing, and the following year his name was linked with a horse theft. But not until the spring of 1887 did he and his cousin decide to really strike out on their own. They would prove that the Bloods were "the cream of creation."[3]

Many young men were ready for war that spring, all because six Bloods had been killed a few months earlier by Assiniboine Indians from the United States. They had been ambushed while trying to recover stolen horses in Montana in October of 1886, but before the Bloods could get revenge, winter was upon them. By the time spring arrived, the older and wiser chiefs were preparing to make a peace treaty with the offending tribe, so the young men now had to find another enemy. Big Rib and The Dog decided to raid the Gros Ventres; they were age-old foes who shared a Montana reservation with the hated Assiniboines.

Late in April, the pair organized a small war party to make the raid. Led by Big Rib and The Dog, it consisted of Rainy Chief, Real Man's Shirt, Coming Singer, and Small Eyes.[4] Most of them were teenagers on their first expedition. Slipping away from the Many Children camp, the party eluded Mounted Police patrols and were free at last from the confines of their reserve. Traveling cautiously on foot, they carried their trusty Winchester rifles and a few other essentials for the trail. As they crossed the barren plains towards the Cypress Hills, they kept a wary eye peeled for police patrols but all they saw were a few scattered herds of cattle.

When far out on the prairie, they killed a cow that was wandering on the range and spent the next few days feasting and drying the meat. They took only what they could carry and traveled until they came to the upper reaches of Seven Persons Creek. By this time it was raining, but the temperature turned cold and soon the heavy snowfall forced them to stop. The war party found a small grove of trees and built a war lodge — a tepeelike structure made of logs and branches. The blizzard lasted for ten days, and when it was over, the war party had run out of food, except for some tea. They killed another cow, dried more meat, then circled past Badwater Lake, heading southeast towards the Gros Ventre camps in Montana.

They had just crossed the Milk River when one of their keen-eyed scouts noticed the tracks of unshod ponies cutting across their trail in a north-easterly direction. The only Indians heading in that way would be another war party, either Cypress Hills Crees returning from a raid or Gros Ventres heading to steal horses from the Cree camps. Either way, the horsemen were enemies.

At the direction of Big Rib and The Dog, the party swung north and followed the trail, their scout riding ahead and watching for signs of campfires or other evidence that their enemies were close. That evening they found the Indians encamped for the night and succeeded in running off their entire herd of twelve horses. They never did find out if they were Crees or Gros Ventres, but it didn't really matter.

From there the victorious Bloods went to the Bull's Head, a grassy promontory

---

3   Observation by Mounted Police superintendent R. Burton Deane in *Report of the Commissioner of the North-West Mounted Police Force, 1889* (Ottawa: Queen's Printer, 1890), 42.

4   Rainy Chief was also known as Swan Shout, and Real Man's Shirt as Mike Snake Eater; Small Eyes was later baptized Paul Little Walker, and Coming Singer was also known as Dead Before.

that marked the western edge of the Cypress Hills. This had been a favorite summer camping ground of the Bloods for generations. Two decades earlier, a thousand Indians would have been camped within its shadows and the buffalo so thick that they carpeted the prairie with their mass of bodies. Now there was only a lonesome prairie wolf, a hawk circling the blue skies, and bleached bones that marked the demise of the mighty monarch.

The war party hid all the following day in case the raiders tried to pursue them but when no one came near them, they relaxed. They killed another cow, loaded the meat on their horses, and were on their way to a distant coulee when someone pointed out to Small Eyes that he had lost his meat. He went back and was just repacking it on his horse when he was suddenly attacked by a Cree war party. These men were well armed and were not the same ones the Bloods had unseated. Small Eyes dropped his meat and opened fire on the closest attacker. When the others pulled back, he jumped on his horse and dashed away to warn his friends. They took shelter in a grove of trees where they were quickly surrounded by their enemies. Desperately, they dug shallow foxholes to protect themselves from the rapid gunfire. One of the Bloods was grazed by a bullet but their protective position kept the Crees at bay.

The war party lay surrounded all day, and during the night the Crees lit fires to prevent them from escaping. The Dog, leader of the war party, sent a scout to search for an escape route. Meanwhile, each of the men prayed to his spirit protector and made vows. One promised to join a secret society; another said he would dance with the Horn Society staff; and Small Eyes vowed to go through the self-torture ritual at the Sun Dance if they successfully escaped.

A short time later, the scout reported that he had discovered a narrow coulee leading down to a nearby creek. Quietly, the Bloods slithered down the path and when they reached the valley, they walked all night; as soon as the first streaks of light began to color the eastern sky, they went into hiding. They had made their escape, but they were again without horses.

Traveling east, the Bloods entered the Cypress Hills; Big Rib and The Dog had decided they should raid one of the Cree camps rather than make the long trip south to the Gros Ventres. However, after prowling through the eastern slopes of the hills, the Bloods learned that they had come too late. Other war parties had been there before them. Now the Crees were so cautious that their herds were driven into makeshift corrals for the night and were heavily guarded during the day. A raid under such conditions would not be brave; it would be stupid.

Not wishing to suffer the indignity of returning home empty-handed, Big Rib and The Dog announced that they would check out the local ranchers. This immediately led to an argument with Real Man's Shirt, who insisted that they stay away from white settlements. He knew that Indians could show up with a herd of stolen Indian ponies and hardly a word was said, yet if even one branded horse of a white man was brought to the reserve, the whole country would be in an uproar. But Big Rib and The Dog were adamant; they would raid a ranch. Reluctantly, the other Indians followed as the two leaders traveled northward out of the hills until they reached the main line of the Canadian Pacific Railway. There they turned west, following the railway line until they came to the siding of Irvine. A short distance away, they scouted a small ranch owned by Abram Adsit and noted with satisfaction some good saddle horses in the corral. Unlike the Crees, the rancher seemed to have taken no precautions against a Blackfoot attack. Why should he? Everyone knew that Indians raided only Indians.

That night, April 27, 1887, Big Rib, The Dog, and the others quietly crept to the edge of the corral. The Indians were ready to swing the gate open and ride off with their booty but to their surprise the horses were gone; the corral was empty. Puzzled, they checked the outbuildings and finally discovered that the stock had been put in the barn. The door had no lock so it had been tied shut. Muttering under his breath at the delay, Big Rib pulled out his double-bladed knife and began to saw at the cords, hoping that the slight creaking noise would not be enough to wake the dogs.

It wasn't, but the owner's son was a light sleeper and the strange noise outside disturbed him. Clad only in his nightshirt, he picked up his rifle and opened the cabin door just as the Indian had finished cutting the rope. The rancher yelled aloud and fired wildly into the night as the raiders dashed for cover. One of the bullets went through Small Eyes's coat, but he was not wounded. A short time later, The Dog returned, angrily firing two shots at the ranchhouse and threatening to kill the occupants.

Real Man's Shirt had had enough. He refused to pursue the madness of the leaders so the war party split, Man's Shirt taking one of the young Bloods back home while the others continued their raid. The two leaders were determined to prove to everyone, including themselves, that they were fit to be warriors just like their fathers and uncles before them.

When it was reported to the North-West Mounted Police that unknown Indians had fired on a rancher, the telegraph lines were soon humming between headquarters in Regina and the political offices in Ottawa. At dawn, a patrol under Corporal Birtle set out from Maple Creek to search for the miscreants, fanning out from the ranch and following the trail into the hills. From a bushy knoll, the Bloods saw the patrol approaching. Had they stayed hidden, the police would have passed them by. But these men were warriors so they boldly showed themselves and defiantly fired several shots in the direction of the patrol. The corporal, not knowing the size of the war party, wisely retreated to his detachment. From there he sent out a general alarm: Indians were on the warpath!

The following day, a heavily armed patrol of fifteen men under Inspector Mills left Maple Creek to search for the Bloods. Another force under Inspector Moodie set out from Medicine Hat, and Sergeant Major Lake with twenty-five men formed a flying patrol from Lethbridge to head off the Indians in case they were withdrawing back to their reserve.

But retreat was not part of the warriors' plans. Neither knowing nor caring about the sensation they were creating, the warriors realized only that they still were empty-handed. After Birtle's patrol had fled, the Indians hid in the neighborhood until nightfall, then followed a dry coulee westward. From there, they traveled towards the railway town of Medicine Hat, and when they reached Seven Persons Coulee, they saw three Cree tents with five horses grazing nearby.

Because it was a cloudless night, the moon cast an eerie light over the prairie and there was no place to hide once the Bloods began moving in on the enemy camp. They waited until they were sure that the Crees had settled down, then the warriors crept forward and picked their horses. During the raid, one of the men became frightened and was almost left behind, but a friend went back for him and soon the war party was riding south, into a protective coulee between two ridges. There they stayed for the next two days.

But Big Rib and The Dog still weren't satisfied. They set out again, coming closer to Medicine Hat and were almost on the outskirts of the town before they found what they were looking for: two horses in the unguarded corral of rancher Robert Watson. Silently and efficiently they led the animals away from the buildings and then, satisfied and jubilant, they set out for home. However, they had traveled only a short distance along the trail when they unexpectedly met a man on foot. Recognizing him as a Cree Indian, they fired several shots at him before galloping away with their captured horses. The Cree, frightened but unhurt, carried the electrifying news to the townspeople of Medicine Hat that a raid had taken place almost in their back yards.

Elated, the Bloods rode back to their reserve. Wise to the old war trails, they easily eluded the police patrols and entered the Many Children camp with their faces painted black as a sign of victory and singing their war songs. The stolen horses, decorated with feathers, were paraded through the camp to prove that the old days were not dead.

Some of the older Bloods did not appreciate the efforts of the raiders in attacking white man's ranches. They still remembered how their relatives, the Peigans, had been massacred in Montana when a white rancher was killed several years earlier. Maybe it was different in Canada with the Mounted Police, but maybe it wasn't. Quietly, word of the triumphant return was passed along to the redcoats and a patrol was sent out from Fort Macleod to arrest the raiders. They were interested only in Big Rib and The Dog, the two ringleaders. However, as soon as the police appeared, the wanted men were nowhere to be found.

Realizing that they had little hope of catching the warriors when they were being watched by almost every young man in the camp, Inspector Gilbert Sanders withdrew his patrol to the nearby Standoff detachment for the night. Then, long after sunset, he was guided through the darkness by a half-breed scout until he and his men came to the camp of the Many Children Band. There, at three o'clock on the morning of May 13, they swooped down on the sleeping raiders and had Big Rib and The Dog in handcuffs before anyone was fully awake.

Excitement and anger swept through the camp, with one old warrior even going so far as to urge the younger men to attack the redcoats. But the police held their ground and by sunrise the two raiders were in the Fort Macleod guardhouse.

Four days later, when they were brought before Magistrate James F. Macleod, the two Indians were charged only with horse stealing; no mention was made of their potshots at the police and citizens. The news of the single charge was greeted with some relief by the prisoners, for in the past judges had recognized that horse stealing was an integral part of Indian life and usually imposed a nominal sentence of two months in the guardhouse. Confidently, the two Bloods pleaded guilty but were shocked when each was sentenced to five years in Stony Mountain Penitentiary. Although the shooting charges had not been laid because of a lack of evidence, the Bloods immediately realized that these were the crimes for which they were being punished. To steal Indian cayuses was one thing but to shoot at the police and take the white man's horses was an entirely different matter.

The news grieved and distressed the Indians who had gathered for the trial. A long term in penitentiary in the far-off province of Manitoba was like a death sentence, for many Indians could not survive the cold dank cells and died there of tuberculosis. As the prisoners were led from the courtroom, women wailed and tried to grasp the men's arms, hoping to restrain them. One old woman even tried to stab them so they would not suffer in prison. Amid all the cries of anguish and mourning,

Big Rib and The Dog remained stoic to the end, singing their war songs as they were led away.

Next morning, Sheriff Duncan Campbell and two police officers collected the prisoners and escorted them to the nearest railway point at Lethbridge, thirty-five miles away. Upon arrival, they learned that the local train wasn't running so they continued their journey another 110 miles (177 km) to Dunmore, just a few miles from where the original raid had taken place. There, at Dunmore station, the sheriff's bad luck continued, for regular service on the main line of the Canadian Pacific had been canceled and the next train was not due until the following day.

By this time, all fight seemed to have gone out of the prisoners. As they were escorted to the nearby Ford Hotel and chained together in the second floor corridor, they told Campbell they accepted their fate and knew they would die in jail. This should have warned the sheriff that he was dealing with two desperate men who felt they had nothing to lose; instead, he was relieved to find them docile and subdued. When he went to bed, he left them chained in the corridor with police downstairs guarding the only exit.

That night, about one o'clock, a terrific crash shattered the stillness of the warm spring night. Rushing to the corridor, Campbell discovered that the Bloods had jumped through the glass window from the second story and he could hear the clinking of their shackles as they dashed to freedom through the darkness. Running as a team, and holding the chains loosely between them, Big Rib and The Dog did not waste any time to rest or congratulate themselves for a successful escape. By the time red streaks of sunlight began to paint the eastern sky, they had reached the rolling hills far from the law's searching eyes.

Shortly after sunrise, they found a small ranch and, muffling their chains, they crawled through the prairie grass until they reached some outbuildings. There they slipped into the first shack and, as luck would have it, they found a rusty old file. Gleefully, they grasped this key to freedom and disappeared back into the hills. A few hours later, after some hard labor, the shackles were removed and the last vestige of captivity was cast aside.

Within two or three days, the men were back in their home camps where they were greeted as heroes. To the younger Bloods they were great warriors who had made fools of the white man and his laws. Maybe the buffalo were gone, maybe the Bloods were forced to eat white man's food, but they still were men and not cattle to be put into iron corrals. Even the old men were glad to see the boys back home; they may not have agreed with their wild ways, but they did not want to see them die in jail.

For the next few weeks Big Rib and The Dog wandered freely through the Many Children village, for the Mounted Police usually stayed away from the troublesome band unless they were on routine patrols. Not until July 20 — over two months later — did Inspector Sanders learn that the wanted men were in the camp. He thought they had fled to the safety of Montana. A patrol was sent to search The Dog's lodge but the warrior was gone. Three weeks later another patrol was told where to find the fugitive, but again he was tipped off by his friends and slipped out of sight. It seemed as though the men were taunting the police, as probably they were.

Not until September 11, almost four months after the escape, did the police sight one of the men. The officers were told that Big Rib was in the bushes near his house drinking beer with some of his buddies. Sergeant Williams and two constables were sent to the spot, and this time they succeeded in grabbing the wanted Indian before he could dash away. Just as the sergeant started to fasten the handcuffs, a number of Bloods, led by minor chief Eagle Ribs, were upon him. In the melee, Constable Gilmore fired a shot that killed an Indian horse, and in the wild confusion, Big Rib disappeared. A few days later, Eagle Ribs was given three months for obstructing the police, while Calf Tail and Lizard Hips were let off with a warning. Constable Gilmore, who appeared before a police enquiry, was fined forty dollars for shooting the horse, the money going to its owner, Yellow Horn.

With those exciting events, 1887 passed into history. The two Bloods continued to enjoy their freedom, and although the police received reports from time to time, there was never enough information to warrant a search. By now, Big Rib and The Dog were considered to be the leaders of the young men, and although some of the elders may have preferred more docile heroes, they were powerless to interfere. As the months passed, the possibility of recapture seemed more and more remote. Then, one day in September of 1888, in sheer bravado, The Dog decided to visit the Mounted Police in their own town of Fort Macleod.

The wanted man and four other Bloods rode into the village unnoticed, made a few purchases in a local store, and almost succeeded in their audacious enterprise. Then, just as they were riding away, The Dog was recognized by an alert police officer who tried to make an arrest. The other Bloods quickly came to their comrade's assistance, and as the officer drew his revolver, he was pulled to the ground. Just then, another officer arrived and shot twice at the fugitive as he prepared to flee. The first bullet, fired at close quarters, would have hit the warrior but his horse plunged at that instant and took the shot instead. The second veered off wildly as The Dog and his wounded steed raced for the safety of the Blood Reserve.

This was the final insult. Within a few days the Mounted Police had placed a fifty-dollar reward on each man's head. It was a lot of money for the destitute Bloods but there were no takers. Instead, Big Rib and The Dog continued to move openly within their camps, joining the religious gatherings and attending rituals of their warrior and age-grade societies. As the months passed, the freedom of the two men seemed to symbolize the independent spirit of the tribe.

Two years later, at the beginning of 1890, the men were still at large. During the intervening months, the Indian agent had received several unconfirmed rumors about them. One was that they had gone to Montana where, with some admiring comrades, they had built a cabin by St. Mary's Lakes, not far from the Canadian border. There, according to the agent, "they had lots of cartridges and if the police wanted them, to go and take them, as they were ready for them."[5] These were brave words from a pair of fugitives who, according to another rumor, had stood off a patrol of United States Indian police who had tried to arrest them.

But the days of glory and freedom for Big Rib and The Dog were almost at an end. No police officer had been able to catch them and no scout had been able to trap them. Yet their presence was becoming a painful reminder of the past. Their chiefs had grown weary of the police patrols and the accusations that the Bloods couldn't be trusted. So in the end, the pride of the tribe was at stake.

---

5   Letter, Indian agent Pocklington to Indian commissioner, January 31, 1890. Blood Reserve letterbook.

Red Crow, the head chief, considered Big Rib to be like a grandson, so he wanted to resolve the problem in the fairest way possible. Since the original conviction, both men had been guilty of a number of crimes, including escape from custody and resisting arrest. If the judge threw the book at them, they would either die in jail or be old men when they got out. However, Red Crow spoke to the authorities in Fort Macleod and received their assurances that if the two men surrendered no further charges would be laid. Besides, conditions had improved at Stony Mountain and more and more Indians were surviving their confinement.

Red Crow met with Running Wolf, leader of the Many Children, who agreed that his son and his cousin must give themselves up to the police. Red Crow himself escorted The Dog into the barracks and two days later Big Rib was sent in by his father. True to their promise, the police reimposed the original sentences without further charges, and the two men were admitted to the penitentiary late in March of 1890.

The sentences proved to be much shorter than anyone expected. Both men were model prisoners and had served only fourteen months when they were released with time off for good behavior. When they returned, a reporter noted that they wore "fashionable clothes and white shirts with high collars and cuffs, talk English fluently and possess other equally useful attributes of civilization acquired at Stony Mountain."[6] They said they had enjoyed themselves, had plenty to eat, and were well treated.

After they parted and went to their separate homes, the two cousins never again worked as a team. They had fought for and won the right to be warriors. They had flaunted the white man's laws, taken his horses, and successfully eluded capture for many months. As a pair they had been the wild ones on the reserve, and although others tried to imitate them, none ever succeeded.

They were no longer reckless youngsters when they returned from prison; Big Rib was twenty-four and The Dog twenty-seven. As the elder of the two, The Dog was interested only in settling down. Using his newly gained knowledge of English, he applied for a job as scout for the North-West Mounted Police. When he was accepted, he was posted to the St. Mary's detachment at the east side of the reserve. From there he went on patrols, interpreted, and did general duties. His tepee was pitched nearby and his wife helped by doing washing for the men.

But it didn't last. In September of 1893, a drunken constable tried to molest The Dog's wife and all the Indian's warlike fury returned with a vengeance. Angrily he drew his knife and when the fracas was over, the officer lay wounded and bleeding on the floor.

When he appeared in court, The Dog testified that he had acted to defend his wife. He claimed he was on his way to the detachment with her when he saw the police officer looking out the window. "I told my woman to go home, they were drunk," he said. "I saw Currie running after us and [he] caught the two of us. He caught my woman on the chest by the blanket and brought us back to the Detachment."[7] Then followed an argument in which the officer struck both the scout and his wife. At that point, The Dog pulled his knife and stabbed the drunken man, first in the arm and then in the head.

---

6   *Macleod Gazette*, May 21, 1891.

7   Fort Macleod Judicial Notebooks, Fort Macleod Town Hall Records, Book 6, 48. Microfilm in Glenbow Archives.

The Dog protested his innocence, but the police said the attack had been unprovoked. In the end, the word of an ex-con did not carry much weight with the courts. He was found guilty of assault causing grievous bodily harm, sentenced to two years in Stony Mountain, and this time he stayed there for the full term. When he was released, he was suffering the ravages of tuberculosis and died the following spring.

Meanwhile, Big Rib continued his wild ways on the wrong side of the law. He hung around with a hard-drinking bunch that always seemed to be getting into fights and trouble. In May of 1893 he was accused of raping a girl named Takes a Gun Woman during a drinking party, but was found not guilty for lack of evidence. He was also involved in a number of "women scrapes," and of the troublemakers on the reserve, Indian agent Wilson considered him to be " the worst among the whole lot."[8]

During this time, inadequate rations continued to be a vexing problem for the Bloods. Among the old people, actual starvation was a reality, while few people ever had a decent meal. The chiefs complained, the missionaries wrote letters, Mounted Police officers prepared reports, and local citizens expressed their concern, but nothing was done to improve the situation.

Some of the young men turned to Big Rib for leadership. Flattered by the attention and always ready to flout the law, he joined with Black Rabbit — a man who had once stood off the police with a gun — to systematically kill and butcher the cattle of nearby ranchers. No one knows whether they did it for excitement, glory, or the benefit of the tribe, but they were eminently successful.

Young boys were shown how to go out late in the day to scout the neighborhood southwest of the reserve and to find stray cattle. These usually belonged to one of the larger ranches, such as the Cochrane, and roamed at will. At night, a team of Bloods, sometimes under the leadership of Big Rib or Black Rabbit, would kill the chosen animal, butcher it, and carry the meat back to the reserve. They were so audacious that some of the killings took place within a mile of the Big Bend police detachment. By 1894, Superintendent Sam Steele estimated the Bloods were killing 350 cattle a year in this fashion.

The Mounted Police and their scouts could never apprehend the cattle killers, but then the young men started fighting among themselves and growing jealous of each other's success. It was only a matter of time until someone in their anger went to the police and informed on the whole lot. Based on the information, the Mounted Police descended on the Blood camps in August of 1894 and arrested eighteen Indians, with Big Rib among them.

It seemed as though the Indian's checkered life was at last tumbling down in ruins. The evidence was strong and it looked as if the ex-convict would soon be following the lonely trail back to Stony Mountain. But Big Rib had learned about law and justice the hard way, so he and Black Rabbit turned Queen's evidence, told the full story to the police, and were released.

Indian agent Wilson was incensed. "It is a strange thing," he fumed, "that two of the worst men among the whole lot who had anything to do with this cattle killing are allowed free. I am told they are Queen's evidence men but from their past records

---

8   Letter, Indian agent Wilson to Indian commissioner, August 4, 1894. Blood Reserve letter-book.

and from what appears on the face of the committal papers, there is little doubt in my mind that the two principal ring leaders are to be allowed to go free, while a number of young men and lads are likely to be punished for offences into which they have been in a great measure drawn by these two men."[9]

At the trial, Big Rib and Black Rabbit gave evidence that sent six of their fellow Bloods to jail for two years, two for six months, and two for a month, the rest receiving suspended sentences.[10] Not surprisingly, Big Rib was roundly condemned for his actions, but those who knew him weren't surprised. He didn't care what anyone thought, Indian or white. He simply did what he wanted.

Two years later, Big Rib joined the Mounted Police as a scout, demanding and receiving their highest possible salary, twenty dollars a month. From then until the end of the century, his wildness was channeled into arresting law breakers, practicing Native religion, and providing a spirited opposition to the dictates of the Indian agent.

Like many other Bloods, he detested Agent James Wilson. Most other agents were bureaucratic, but at least they seemed to have had the interests of the people at heart. Within the limits of budgets and legal restraints, they tried to make life bearable for the tribe. Wilson, on the other hand, was single-minded about his desire to suppress the Sun Dance and other religious practices. He defended and helped maintain the status quo in the inadequate rationing system, and he seldom questioned the dictates from headquarters, even when he knew they were foolish.

Big Rib soon discovered that the Mounted Police had no more love for the officious Indian agent than had the Bloods. So the wily scout learned to pit one against the other, with the hope that the Indians might be the winners for a change.

During the 1890s, Big Rib's father, Running Wolf, was one of the leading figures in the religious life of the reserve. He was active in the Sun Dance, owned and transferred medicine bundles, and belonged to several secret societies. To him, religion was essential to the tribe and it was a feeling shared by his son.

In 1898, a number of Bloods decided to rebel against the agent's efforts to suppress Native rituals. Wilson had already squelched the Sun Dance for three years, offering the Indians a sports day as a substitute. When Running Wolf announced that he intended to put on a medicine pipe dance, his son joined with him in defiance of the Indian Department. For four days the Many Children camp was alive and excited as the rituals took place and feasts were held, despite the meager rations. Horses, blankets, and other gifts were presented during the religious event.

When Agent Wilson heard about it, he laid charges against Running Wolf, Big Rib, and the wife of White Man, another Mounted Police scout, citing the Indian Act provision that prohibited giveaway dances. The Mounted Police, however, saw the dance as a religious event, so Inspector Davidson simply told the accused not to break the law, and released them.

Heartened by their success, Big Rib and his father decided to tackle the Sun

---

9 Ibid.

10 Those receiving two years were Never Ties his Shoe Laces, Wolf Child, Tough Bread, Nibs, Short Man, and Longtime Squirrel; six months went to Slap Face and Many Different Axes; and one month to Melting Tallow and Carries Something.

Dance. Together with Red Crow, they visited Superintendent R.B. Deane in Fort Macleod and asked the Mounted Police for permission to resume holding the summer religious festival. The officer told them there was nothing illegal about gathering for religious purposes as long as they refrained from giving away gifts at the time.

Excitedly, the chiefs spread the word that they should assemble in a large camp so that some of the societies could perform their rituals. It was too late for a Sun Dance, as no tongues had been prepared for the sacrament, but at least they would have a gathering. Agent Wilson was furious about police interference and particularly complained about Big Rib. "I hear he is telling that he has been promised a Sun Dance," he chided Deane, "and have no doubt he will try to get one up. He is a Police Scout and ought to be the last to break the law."[11]

A year later, another gathering was held but there was still no formal Sun Dance. Finally, in 1900, Red Crow, Running Wolf, and the other leaders decided they had had enough of Agent Wilson. Red Crow announced plans for a full Sun Dance, with the wife of Eagle Child taking the role of holy woman. With Big Rib's help, tongues were taken as rations by the Mounted Police scouts and turned over to her for the ritual. Agent Wilson had always prevented this sacrament from being performed by cutting any tongues in half before they were issued as rations; he knew that only whole tongues could be used in the ceremony.

When summer came, Big Rib and the other scouts scoured the reserve, rousting people out of bed and bringing them in from the fields to go to the ceremony. By the time the Sun Dance started, the Bloods had their biggest camp in years and the power of the agent was broken.

Big Rib resigned from the Mounted Police the same year. By this time he had become so involved with the Sun Dance that he decided to devote his entire attention to religious life. When he died in 1907, he was recognized as a religious leader who had won the admiration and grudging respect of everyone around him.

During their first years on the reserve, the Bloods had been starved, suppressed, humiliated, and repressed, but their pride could not be destroyed. People like Big Rib and The Dog wouldn't let it happen.

NOTE

This chapter was previously published in H.A. Dempsey, *The Amazing Death of Calf Shirt and Other Blackfoot Stories: Three Hundred Years of Blackfoot History* (Saskatoon: Fifth House Publishers, 1994), pp. 104-118 and 240. The illustration in the original has been omitted.

---

11   Letter, Indian agent Wilson to NWMP Supt. Deane, July 5, 1898. Blood Reserve letter-book.

SECTION B

Law Enforcement

SIX

Crime and Criminals in the North-West Territories, 1873-1905

R.C. Macleod

Crime, like beauty, is in the eye of the beholder. Every society in every age works out its own definition of anti-social and therefore proscribed behaviour. In the last century and a half, however, this truism has acquired new complexities which have made the relationship between legislation and the maintenance of social order much less straightforward than before. The idea of a graduated system of punishments tailored to the seriousness of the offence is one of the most important of these new developments. In theory the police are merely the agents of society in identifying and apprehending offenders to whom the courts then apply the appropriate punishment. In fact the police play a mediating role in determining which offences will be taken most seriously. There are many areas of ambiguity in the law which leave enforcement open to interpretation. An almost infinite variety of situations arise which come under the heading of extenuating circumstances. Legislators have a habit of trying from time to time to outlaw basic human appetites which all may agree should be curbed but which few really wish to see effectively diminished. All these factors help ensure that the police play a dominant part in determining the quality of life in any society.

This kind of selective perception and enforcement of the law is apparent in the history of the North-West Mounted Police. The police had very definite ideas about which crimes were more dangerous than others. Sometimes this ranking corresponded with the degree of seriousness implied in the penalty provided by law, but this was not always the case. The police operated on the assumption that their first duty at all times was the maintenance of peace and order. This meant that crimes of violence were always accorded top priority. Illegally carrying a firearm, for example, carried no greater penalty than some contraventions of the liquor laws, but the police enforced gun laws rigidly although this was not always true of the liquor laws. Crimes against property occupied second place in the hierarchy. Many of these were considered of minor importance but some offences against property could threaten the orderly conduct of life and were dealt with accordingly. Moral offences such as gambling, prostitution, and the like received much more sporadic and superficial attention. One category of moral offence, violation of the liquor laws, was an exception to this rule and is discussed separately in a later chapter.

The least serious offence involving violence to concern the police was assault. In some respects the North-West Territories may have been peaceful but they were not without their share of this kind of violence. The police records are crammed with assault cases of varying degrees of severity. Even the smaller divisions reported at least two or three cases a month. Punishments awarded ranged all the way from a fine of fifty cents to two months in jail.[1] The great majority of assault cases resulted in small fines of between one and ten dollars. Such minor cases were seldom reported in detail and it is difficult to know exactly who was involved and what was the nature of the offence. The small size of the fines and the fact that very many cases were dismissed or given suspended sentences seems to indicate that in most cases minor community quarrels were involved. The police accepted such small incidents as inevitable and tried whenever possible to act as arbiters. This interpretation is supported by a statement of Inspector Joseph Howe in 1897 who complained about "The immense amount of work entailed upon the Police in connection with the most trivial cases (the outcome most often of mere spite and jealousy)..."[2] In another case Superintendent Deane described such an incident. "The afternoon of the 24th was somewhat uselessly consumed in hearing a charge of assault preferred by Mrs. Davis, a livery stable keeper's wife, against Mrs. Keys, a blacksmith's wife, and the expressions of endearment etc., used by the respective ladies led to Mrs. Keys heaving clods of earth over the garden fence at her neighbour."[3]

If a cowboy got drunk and started a fight in a bar he could expect fast action and a light penalty from the police. If he chose to make an issue of it he could expect to spend some time behind bars. One J. Donohue assaulted a Mounted Police constable in Calgary in 1902 and received a month in jail. The judge who awarded the sentence, Chief Justice McGuire, said that the prisoner had got off lightly only because of his ill health. "He further impressed upon all present that as the N.W.M. Police was very small in comparison with the population in and about Calgary he intended to back up all members of the force as long as they in no way exceeded their authority."[4] Violence which had the effect of leading to further violence or which undermined respect for the law was not taken lightly. The police recognized that to prevent all fights and quarrels was not humanly possible; their concern was to prevent the public from accepting violence as a normal way of life.

The police knew that if tempers were lost in a fight it could end in injury or death. The loser of a barroom fight in 1902 ended it by drawing a revolver and killing his opponent.[5] The second line of defence against such occurrences was to try to limit the availability of deadly weapons. The police accordingly enforced laws against the carrying of firearms as strictly as possible. (It should be noted that the shooting just referred to occurred in Calgary, which had its own municipal police. The Mounted Police were not called into the case until some hours after it happened.) Stiff punishments were imposed when the police felt that public order was threatened. Fines of a hundred dollars and jail sentences of up to twenty-one days are recorded.[6]

---

1   Public Archives of Canada (PAC), RG 18, A-1, vol. 18, no. 225, Ft Saskatchewan Monthly Reports for January and December 1888.

2   PAC, RG 18, A-1, vol. 126, no. 2, Regina Monthly Report for March 1897.

3   PAC, RG 18, A-1, vol. 49, no. 192, Lethbridge Monthly Report for April 1891.

4   PAC, RG 18, A-1, vol. 239, no. 672, Calgary Crime Reports, 1902.

5   PAC, RG 18, A-1, vol. 230, no. 159, Calgary Monthly Report for March 1902.

6   PAC, RG 18, A-1, vol. 18, no. 255, Ft Saskatchewan Monthly Report for January 1888; and vol. 49, no. 140, Regina Monthly Report for December 1891.

In other cases the police recognized that no serious danger was involved and penalties were light, as when Inspector Joseph Howe remarked: "The dime novel reader was to the fore in the cases of two lads carrying concealed revolvers."[7] In another case a dude travelling west on the CPR announced his arrival by stepping off the train at a small stop in Saskatchewan and firing his gun into the night air. A Mounted Police inspector who happened to be on the train took his revolver away and ordered him back on the train. The would-be desperado went meekly.[8]

In one instance at least the police sympathized with the offender in a firearms case. Superintendent Deane reported sending Inspector W.H. Irwin to Cardston to try a case:

> A man named Donaldson living there had made some filthy remark in connection with the name of a Miss Mary Macleod, sister of the ex-editor of Cardston *Record*. The young lady compelled Mr. Donaldson at the muzzle of her revolver to make her an abject public apology which I understand he did in haste.[9]

A small fine was imposed for this display of righteous indignation. By limiting the immediate availability of deadly weapons the police prevented most of the random and casual violence which tended to occur when tempers were lost, as in the case of the Regina man in 1896 who shot an acquaintance for refusing to drink with him.[10] The police were both fascinated and repelled by the number of shooting incidents in United States border towns. Their attitude towards the practice of carrying guns was based to a large extent on a determination not to let the same sort of thing happen on their side of the border.

Murder, the ultimate crime of violence, was treated by the police with all the seriousness that it deserved. Except for a handful of cases murderers caused the police little trouble and were apprehended with surprising ease. Most murders were unpremeditated crimes of passion, committed on the spur of the moment. The murderer was usually too stunned by what had happened even to think about getting away. In one case the police were notified of a murder at 8:30 AM and the prisoner was arrested and awaiting trial before noon.[11] Murderers who did have the presence of mind to escape rarely remained at large for periods of more than a few days, even if they managed to get out of the North-West Territories. For example, the perpetrator of the barroom shooting at Calgary in 1902, mentioned earlier, got away but was captured within three days.[12] The police communications network was simply too well organized for the average man to escape.

In most murder cases, assembling the evidence, guarding the prisoner, and attending the trial absorbed far more of the energies of the police than the actual capture of the suspect. One fairly typical murder case occupied 'B' Division at Regina from 22 June 1893 to 10 February 1894. It began with the discovery by some CPR

---

7   PAC, RG 18, A-1, vol. 126, no. 2, Regina Monthly Report for June 1897.
8   PAC, RG 18, A-1, vol. 121, no. 270, Inspector A.C. Macdonell to Superintendent Perry, 9 April 1896.
9   PAC, RG 18, A-1, vol. 181, no. 163, Ft Macleod Monthly Report for June 1900.
10   PAC, RG 18, A-1, vol. 113, no. 8, Regina Monthly Report for December 1896.
11   PAC, RG 18, A-1, vol. 65, no. 313, Superintendent Steele to Herchmer, 2 April 1892. Similar cases may be found in vol. 88, no. 729; vol. 93, no. 200; vol. 105, no. 147; vol. 114, no, 24; and vol. 124, no. 480.
12   PAC, RG 18, A-1, vol. 230, no. 159, Calgary Monthly Report for March 1902. Similar cases may be found in vol. 74, no. 63; vol. 93, no. 215; vol, 127, no. 20; and vol. 143, no. 17.

section men of a body under a pile of railway ties near Grenfell on the main line of the railway. The body was decomposed beyond recognition but it was possible to see that the back of the skull had been crushed by a heavy blow or blows. Questioning the CPR employees who had been working along the section of line where the body was found, the police discovered the dead man had been seen in the company of two others near where the section men had found him. This had been on 10 June, twelve days earlier. Further investigation revealed that the dead man was an itinerant Italian scissors grinder by the name of Giovanni Petterali.

Petterali had been seen in the company of the other two, also Italians, before 10 June but after that date his companions were only seen by themselves. Descriptions of the two men were sent out and they were arrested by the Winnipeg police on 26 June. Inspector Charles Constantine and Sergeant C. Brown spent a week investigating the case, and by the time of the preliminary hearing, 3 July, had ample evidence to send the two suspects, Antonio D'Edigio and Antonio Luciano, to trial. The trial did not take place until the following January (1894) in order that the defence could have time to obtain character references for the accused from Italy. When the trial began it occupied eighteen days during which, in addition to those men testifying, the police had a sergeant and seven constables assigned to guarding the prisoners and looking after the jury. The prisoners were found guilty although they were defended very ably by a lawyer described by Superintendent Perry as having the largest criminal practice in western Canada.[13]

Two other individual murder cases deserve mention here, not because they were typical, but for the opposite reason. They were unusual and provoked a very strong reaction from the police because they represented the two developments the force most wished to avoid. One was the case of the Cree murderer Almighty Voice (1895-7). In October 1895 Almighty Voice, who had been jailed for cattle killing, escaped and then killed a police sergeant, C.C. Colebrook, who tried to recapture him. Almighty Voice managed to elude the police for a year and a half with the help of other members of his tribe, a fact which the police considered the most disturbing aspect of the case. The incident showed signs for a time of developing into a third western Canadian rebellion. Almighty Voice was finally discovered and cornered with two other Indians in May 1897. Two more policemen were wounded and three killed trying to capture him. Finally the police surrounded the patch of bush in which Almighty Voice was hiding and shelled it with two field guns, bringing an end to the whole tragedy.[14]

The only other case which caused as much concern and public excitement was that of Ernest Cashel in 1903 and 1904. Cashel's origins are uncertain. Before he came to Canada he was reputed to have been a member of Butch Cassidy's gang in Wyoming, but it is impossible to check this story. In any case Cashel was arrested by the Calgary police on a charge of forgery in October 1902. He escaped and took refuge with a settler east of Lacombe by the name of Isaac Rufus Felt whom he shortly murdered and dumped in the Red Deer River attached to a large rock. When the Mounted Police caught up with Cashel west of Calgary in January 1903 they suspected the murder but could not prove it without the body. Cashel was tried and sentenced on several charges of theft. A few months later a rancher discovered the body of the

---

13   PAC, RG 18, A-1, vol. 93, no. 215, Superintendent Perry to Herchmer, 17 February 1894.
14   PAC, RG 18, A-1, vol. 126, no. 2, Regina Monthly Report for May 1897.

unfortunate Belt and it was easy for the police to prove that he had been killed with the revolver which Cashel had in his possession when he was arrested. Cashel was tried and convicted of the murder. He was awaiting execution at the police post at Calgary in December 1903 when his brother managed to smuggle a gun to the condemned man.

After escaping on 10 December Cashel remained at large for over a month. He was the subject of the most intense manhunt in the history of the police to that point. Every other division was denuded of men to help in the search. Public hysteria threatened in the Calgary area with dozens of false reports that the escaped killer had been sighted. The fugitive was finally discovered only a few miles from Calgary and was recaptured when the police burned down the shack in which he was hiding in order to flush him out. He was executed the following month.[15] What Cashel represented to the police and public alike was the kind of professional criminal who did not hesitate to kill anyone who got in his way. This sort of murderer was a new phenomenon in the North-West Territories and the police were determined to spare no effort to make an example of him.

Mob action was considered by the police to be the most potentially dangerous of all manifestations of violence. Reporting on one such incident, Superintendent Griesbach wrote:

> You are no doubt aware that in this District during the last 14 years on three occasions mobs have assembled and on two of them, to my own knowledge, bearing arms. I consider that in a well-governed country such exhibitions of mob law should be strongly repressed, otherwise sooner or later serious consequences will ensue.[16]

The superintendent suited his actions to his words in this case. A dispute had arisen between two settlers over the ownership of some homestead land at St Albert near Edmonton. The case was being adjudicated by the Dominion Lands Commissioner but not fast enough to suit one of the claimants. This man, Octave Mogeon, collected a group of his friends and proceeded to destroy the buildings erected by the other claimant. The police rounded up no less than fifty-six men and had them tried on charges of creating a riot.[17]

The reaction of the police to anti-Chinese riots in Calgary in 1892 also illustrates their concern about any form of mob violence. By 1892 relations between the Mounted Police and the municipal authorities in Calgary had been strained for some time. The mayor of Calgary and the chief of police harboured an intense dislike for the Mounted Police. This situation was due largely to disputes over enforcement of the liquor laws. In any case it was police policy to stay out of municipal law enforcement if possible and the force was normally very reluctant to interfere in any way with events in Calgary. In July 1892, however, a serious outbreak of smallpox took place in the city. The disease made its appearance first in a Chinese laundry and when this fact became known a mob collected and began ransacking Chinese dwellings. The

---

15 The Cashel case is reported in several places: PAC, RG 18, A-1, vol. 270, no. 240, Calgary Monthly Reports for 1904; Glenbow Alberta Archives (GAI), G.E. Sanders Papers and the Reminiscences of A.C. Bury. There is also an article on the case by a former policeman, Constable T.E.G. Shaw, "The Cashel Case," *Alberta Historical Review* VIII (Winter 1960) 17.

16 PAC, RG 18, A-1, vol. 123, no. 441, Griesbach to Herchmer, 7 August 1896.

17 PAC, RG 18, A-1, vol. 114, no. 26, Ft Saskatchewan Monthly Report for August 1896.

mayor happened to be away at the time and the Mounted Police moved in at the request of "several respectable citizens..."[18] Most of the Chinese community took shelter at the Mounted Police barracks and the mob was easily dispersed. No further trouble occurred in spite of the arrival on the scene of an anti-Chinese agitator by the name of Locksley Lucas who, with the mayor acting as chairman, gave several speeches trying to stir up the populace against the Chinese.[19]

At this point the Calgary Police Committee requested that the municipal police be replaced by a town detachment of the Mounted Police. Inspector A.R. Cuthbert reported:

> It is difficult to determine how the whole thing will end, the feeling is bitter between sections of the town, the respectable portion with a majority of the town council are for law and order, the remainder under the mayor are in favour of letting the mob have its way and no police protection. There is no doubt that at the present time should it become known that the Mounted Police would not interfere, life and property in Calgary would be at the mercy of a drunken mob.[20]

Herchmer favoured the establishment of a town detachment also but the proposal was eventually rejected although the Calgary authorities were given to understand that the force would intervene on similar occasions should they arise in future.[21] The significance of the affair lies not in the fact that a detachment for Calgary was refused. The significance of the police reaction is that no other crime or series of crimes could have made them attempt to reverse such a well-established policy. Disorders of this kind, the police believed, threatened the very basis of law enforcement and could not be allowed to occur.

Minor incidents of mob action, especially those in which public sympathy and that of the police was on the side of the offenders, were more difficult to handle than obvious riots. Such a case occurred in Lethbridge in 1895. One James Donaldson seduced the wife of a man at whose house he was boarding. The man became despondent for this and other reasons and committed suicide. Donaldson then had the effrontery to appear at the funeral as chief mourner. This was too much for the local citizenry, some of whom turned out that evening and applied what Superintendent Deane described as, "a rather mild daub of tar and feathers..."[22] Donaldson at first refused to lay charges against his tormentors because public opinion was running so strongly against him. "The entire population including ministers of religion are of the opinion that Donaldson was well served, and the only pity is that it was not kept out of the newspapers."[23] Commissioner Herchmer was not pleased, reprimanded Deane for not preventing the affair in the first place, and insisted that charges be laid by the police. With some difficulty, since he had hurriedly left town, Donaldson was located and persuaded to give evidence. The members of the mob were subsequently acquitted although the trial was held at Ft Macleod in order to obtain a more impartial jury. At the trial it came out that Sergeant Hare of the

---

18   PAC, RG 18, A-1, vol. 69, no. 615, Inspector A.R. Cuthbert to Herchmer, 3 August 1892.
19   PAC, RG 18, A-1, vol. 68, no. 521, Cuthbert to Herchmer, 19 August 1892.
20   PAC, RG 18, A-1, vol. 69, no. 615, Cuthbert to Herchmer, 9 August 1892.
21   PAC, RG 18, A-1, vol. 70, no. 664, White to Herchmer, 26 August 1892.
22   PAC, RG 18, A-1, vol. 104, no. 131, Lethbridge Monthly Report for February 1895.
23   Ibid.

Mounted Police had been a member, if not the leader of the tar and feather gang. He deserted immediately to the United States.[24]

The next time a similar situation showed signs of developing Deane handled it differently. This time a CPR brakeman came to Deane and complained that his wife intended to run off with Archibald McKay, a tailor and ex-Mounted Police constable.

> I had heard of this liaison and some feeling in town was arising in consequence. Some 5 or 6 men, sympathizers with the husband, looked for A. McKay and would probably have handled him roughly if they had been able to find him. I suggested to the aggrieved husband that he should forbid the stage driver to carry his wife, and this he did, for later on in the morning she came to me. I referred her to her husband and instructed Constable Lewis to tell A. McKay that if he remained in town evil might befall him which I might be unable to prevent. This MacKay is a tailor, working for Mr. E.J. Hill and the message brought up that gentleman and the Methodist Minister, apparently to convert me to the Doctrine that the mob law, which he thought meritorious in the case of James Donaldson and his tar and feathers, became quite reverse when brought in conflict with E.J. Hill's business interests. Mr. Hill asked if A. McKay could not have police protection, and I replied "certainly" but that I had not enough men to guarantee his not being tied up for instance to a telephone pole and given a sound flogging. I should probably not hear of the circumstances until after the occurrence and one had to look for a similar public sympathy in such a case as was accorded the tar and feather gang. Mr. Goard, the Parson, I think agreed with me. A. MacKay left town for British Columbia on the 28th instant, and the brakeman and his wife, who is still here, have concluded a sort of armed truce.[25]

There were no further attempts at private enforcement of public morality in Lethbridge. Superintendent Deane's actions in this case amounted to a recognition that legal proceedings would be futile where public opinion was unanimously in favour of those who broke the law. To handle the situation informally was the only effective approach.

Most crimes against property were regarded by the police as a routine part of their work. Small thefts and the occasional burglary were investigated and solved if possible. But since such cases were difficult to prove and impossible to anticipate they caused the police few sleepless nights. The police paid special attention to theft and burglary only if they showed signs of being the work of organized professionals, which was rare, or if they involved violence or large amounts of money, which was rarer still. Until about the turn of the century a year could pass in any given division with only a few minor thefts or even none at all. When two cases of theft occurred in the town of Boucher, Saskatchewan, in two years it looked like a crime wave to the inhabitants. They applied for a permanent police detachment but were refused, the police pointing out that in both cases the offenders had been arrested and convicted.[26] After 1900 thefts increased considerably and a special Detective Branch came into being to help deal with the problem.

Curiously enough two of the larger robberies which occurred in this period were thefts from Mounted Police posts. In 1890 about $1700.00 was stolen from the safe

---

24 Ibid., Lethbridge Monthly Reports for June and July 1895.
25 PAC, RG 18, A-1, vol. 114, no. 25, Lethbridge Monthly Report for December 1896.
26 PAC, RG 18, A-1, vol. 107, no. 218, D.H. MacDowall, MP, to Mackenzie Bowell, 16 February 1895 and Inspector D'Arcy Strickland to Herchmer, 4 March 1895.

in the orderly room of the police post at Ft Macleod. The thieves, a constable and an ex-constable of the force, were caught but only a small portion of the money was recovered.[27] Six years later at Calgary some $600.00 disappeared from the police safe. The mystery in this case was never solved. Some of the evidence seemed to indicate that the commanding officer at Calgary, Superintendent Joseph Howe, had taken the money home rather than leave it in the safe over the weekend but nothing conclusive was ever established.[28]

It would appear that the police went to considerable lengths to deal with cases of fraud and embezzlement but there were so few of these that it is impossible to draw any general conclusions. Most of the cases which fall into this category involved the Post Office.[29] If the offender was successful he usually fled the country. The police would go to some lengths to get such people back. In 1893 the postmaster of Whitewood, Assiniboia, took his fellow townsmen for about $2500.00 and escaped to the United States. Inspector Charles Constantine spent a month looking for him in Chicago and Pittsburgh. Constantine was unsuccessful but made arrangements to have the man arrested if he came to the attention of the police in those cities. The Chicago police picked him up a few months later.[30]

A more enterprising group of confidence men a few years later sold the manager of Molson's Bank at Calgary over $11,000.00 worth of phony gold bricks, alleged to have come from the gold diggings of the Yukon. The bricks turned out to be copper but the fraud was not discovered for several days, by which time the swindlers had long since departed. The Mounted Police traced them as far as Seattle but there the trail disappeared.[31]

Some mention has already been made of the problems created for the police by stock theft around the turn of the century. If there were enough policemen to make the patrol system operate properly stock theft could be kept under control. This ceased to be the case after 1897 and the difficulties inherent in this type of criminal activity began to assert themselves. Horse and cattle stealing was hard to detect and harder to prove because of the numbers of animals and the problem of identifying individual beasts. The police compiled files running to hundreds of pages on cases which involved a few head of livestock. In many such cases it was almost impossible to prove either original ownership or intent to commit theft. The usual argument was that the cattle or horses in question had strayed in amongst another herd and had not been recognized. Some of the difficulties were removed in 1897 when the Criminal Code was amended to make brands *prima facie* evidence of ownership.[32] Many small farmers did not bother with brands, however, or failed to register them. Many cases therefore depended upon the ability to prove the age of a given animal. Each side would produce expert witnesses who would give lengthy and diametrically opposite testimony. The result was usually acquittal for the accused.[33]

---

27 PAC, RG 18, A-1, vol. 47, no. 34, Superintendent John Cotton to Herchmer 10 May 1890.

28 PAC, RG 18, A-1, vol. 130, no. 76, Herchmer to White, 29 November 1896.

29 PAC, RG 18, A-1, vol. 44, no. 775; vol. 98, no. 671; and vol. 107, no. 220.

30 The postmaster, Campbell by name, fled in March 1893 and was arrested in Chicago 29 September of the same year. PAC, RG 18, A-1, vol. 98, no. 671.

31 PAC, RG 18, A-1, vol. 140, no. 493.

32 PAC, RG 18, A-1, vol. 147, no. 549.

33 PAC, RG 18, A-1, vol. 214, no. 452, Superintendent G.E. Sanders to Herchmer, 5 May 1899.

Stock theft was more serious than an equivalent amount of ordinary theft because it tended to exacerbate an element of class conflict already present. In areas where the homesteaders were beginning to encroach upon the large ranches there was hostility between farmers and ranchers. In this situation one of the easiest ways to get back at a neighbour for offences real or imagined was to make off with a few of his cattle when the opportunity presented itself. Superintendent Deane described the situation in 1901 with his usual insight. "The little men 'smuggle' a calf when and how they conveniently can. The big men (or some of them) want to have the entire range to themselves and be free to do as they like."[34] Both parties complained frequently to the police but their complaints were always general. Whenever the police investigated specific incidents no one could be found who was willing to give evidence. In a summary of many reports from the field, Commissioner Perry wrote:

> The large ranchers in the West are very jealous of the settlers who are crowding them out. They believe that these settlers are fattening at their expense. Around Calgary there is a great reluctance on the part of the ranchers to have their names mixed up with any complaint. Why I do not know. Some of them doubt even the men in their own employ and almost expect the police to protect them from their employees.[35]

The reluctance of both ranchers and farmers to become involved is understandable. It is one thing to report a theft or burglary committed by persons unknown to the police and quite another to accuse a neighbour who is in all other respects a reputable citizen. The social penalties for such an accusation if it is not substantiated were too great to make it worth the risk.

The result of this situation was general frustration and some dark mutterings about vigilantes and lynch law. The Calgary *Herald* complained in an editorial that the Mounted Police had been reduced so much that cattle stealing was now commonplace. So far, the editor continued, the North-West Territories had been free of vigilante justice, "but the stockmen are becoming so incensed at the repeated depredations of the cattle 'rustlers' that one of these fine days we will wake up and find that Judge Lynch has set up his court here."[36] The police dismissed such predictions as idle talk.[37] Nevertheless some action seemed imperative and the police responded by hiring special stock detectives to work exclusively on such cases. The Western Stock Grower's Association also employed one and after 1901 the problem became less serious.[38]

Professional criminals who operated on a large scale were not common in the North-West Territories in the period to 1905 although the police occasionally professed to believe otherwise. Inspector Charles Constantine in 1887 advanced the rather peculiar theory that the Territories were the repository of all the more expert

---

34 PAC, RG 18, A-1, vol. 217, no. 723, Deane to Perry, 24 August 1901.

35 Ibid., Perry to White, 20 August 1901. The same complaint was voiced by Inspector A.R. Cuthbert, vol. 207, no. 210, Prince Albert Monthly Report for October 1901.

36 Calgary *Herald*, 27 June 1901. See also the Moose Jaw *Times*, 24 October 1902 and Superintendent Deane's comments on cattle rustling in PAC, RG 18 A-1, vol. 183, no. 202, Lethbridge Monthly Report for January 1900.

37 PAC, RG 18, A-1, vol. 216, no. 651, Perry to White, 4 July 1901.

38 PAC, RG 18, A-1, vol. 273, no. 315, Perry to White, 28 August 1901; and vol. 300, no. 510, Perry to White, 12 June 1905.

criminals driven out of other parts of Canada and the United States.[39] There is no evidence in the police records or anywhere else to support this idea. In fact the reverse seems to have been the case. The North-West was too thoroughly policed to present an attractive prospect for criminals and until about the turn of the century there was neither enough wealth in the area to support a professional criminal nor a sufficient density of population to provide the necessary cover. Before 1900 there were occasional rumours of gangs being organized to rob trains or systematically rustle cattle but when investigated they always failed to materialize.[40] When the professional criminal did begin to make his appearance in the first few years of the century the indications were much less dramatic; a general increase in the number and size of thefts and the occasional safe expertly blown.[41] The police responded with their own experts, the men of the Detective Branch, and Commissioner Perry's reorganization of the reporting system. With only a few exceptions the criminals encountered by the North-West Mounted Police in their first thirty years were amateurs, part-time offenders who spent most of their time in more or less honest pursuits.

The duty which aroused the least enthusiasm in the breast of the average Mounted Policemen was the enforcement of those laws designed to protect the moral well being of the inhabitants of the North-West Territories. The police were very much aware that vigorous efforts to eliminate such things as gambling and prostitution were futile. They would inevitably fail, for one thing, and for another, no matter how much energy was expended, no one would be completely satisfied. Those who happened to enjoy these pursuits would feel persecuted, while the puritanically-minded would never be satisfied that enforcement was strict enough. The response of the police was therefore to enforce these laws as infrequently as they could. If offenders were too blatant in their operations or if public pressure was exerted, the police acted. The same was true if moral offences seemed to be connected with more serious crimes. On the whole, however, the police preferred to control rather than eradicate. A vice which took place at a known location and within unwritten but strict limitations was much to be preferred to one driven underground and therefore out of reach.

Gambling and violations of the laws relating to amusements on the Sabbath were almost entirely ignored by the police. There is no single case in the police records to 1905 in which the police moved to enforce Sunday observance except as the result of a complaint. Such complaints were infrequent, occurring perhaps once or twice a year in the whole of the North-West Territories. Gambling offences appear even less frequently in the police files. In 1888 the managers of the Fall Race Meeting at Calgary requested that the police allow games of chance to be held. White replied that it would not be possible to alter police duties imposed by statute.[42] The tone of the letter made it clear that, in spite of the refusal, White did not regard gambling as a very serious offence. On one other occasion Commissioner Herchmer reported that he had been obliged to place a detachment in Calgary because gambling, along

---

39   PAC, RG 18, A-1, vol. 22, no. 383, Constantine to Herchmer, 14 August 1887.

40   For the former see PAC, RG 18, A-1, vol. 114, no. 24, Calgary Monthly Report for October 1896; and vol. 125, no. 586. For the latter see vol. 91, no. 148, Lethbridge Monthly Reports for April and May 1894.

41   PAC, RG 18, A-1, vol. 249, no. 154, Calgary Monthly Report for February 1903; and vol. 271, no. 241, Calgary Monthly Report for July 1904.

42   PAC, RG 18, A-1, vol. 24, no. 711.

with the illegal sale of liquor, had "reached a stage which necessitates active steps to suppress it."[43] Beyond these few instances the Mounted Police were content to let the individual do battle on his own with the gods of chance.

Traffic in narcotics, mainly opium, took place on a surprisingly large scale over the international boundary in the late nineteenth century. There are frequent references to it in the police records. From the point of view of the present the attitude of the police toward drug trafficking and addiction seems astonishingly casual. Narcotics cases were treated as rather less serious matters than liquor law violations. In 1896 an opium addict at the urging of his friends asked the police to lock him up for a few months so that he could kick the habit. But when the time came to actually go into the cell he changed his mind. The police awarded him a suspended sentence on a charge of intoxication and let him go.[44] When a prostitute at Calgary was found dead of an overdose of morphine a few years later, the discovery provoked neither surprise nor any particular interest on the part of the police.[45] Drugs were simply not a social problem of any importance since the numbers of people affected were so few.

The police did, of course, confiscate drugs which came to their attention. A shipment of one hundred and forty-one pounds of opium was seized at Swift Current in 1891.[46] The traffic in drugs appears to have been largely one way, from Canada to the United States. Most drugs were smuggled in by employees of the CPR who worked on the company's steamers which travelled to Asian ports. The police made some effort to keep the traffic under surveillance, as the following report indicates:

> I have the honour to state that Donald McLean, better known as "Little Danny" or "Opium Dan" is not occupying lands in Township 23, Range 2, west of the 3rd Meridian. McLean rented these lands to one Naismith who left this Fall for Maple Creek. McLean is working on a Pacific Steamer, as cook or steward, but I suspect he is doing this to work his trade in opium. McLean is worth at least $15,000.00 in cash.[47]

On one occasion a saloon in Sweet Grass, Montana, known to be a depot for smuggled opium, was closed down by the American authorities after Mounted Police reports were forwarded to them through diplomatic channels.[48] It should be noted that in this case it was not primarily the opium which bothered the police. They considered the saloon to be a haven for both Canadian and American horse thieves and other undesirables and generally a centre of disorder which spilled over onto Canadian jurisdiction.

Next to liquor law violations, the most widespread moral offence by far was prostitution. It was illegal both to be a prostitute and to patronize one but these two laws were evaded more often than any others in the Criminal Code. The police attitude toward prostitution was generally the same as for other manifestations of public immorality as defined by law; they preferred to have it more or less in the open

---

43　PAC, RG 18, A-1, vol. 43, no. 660, Herchmer to White, 1 September 1890.
44　PAC, RG 18, A-1, vol. 104, no. 25, Lethbridge Monthly Report for February 1896.
45　GAI, Diaries of Sergeant S. Hetherington, 1 June 1899.
46　PAC, RG 18, A-1, vol. 52, no. 369.
47　PAC, RG 18, A-1, vol. 128, no. 44, Constable A.F. Glend to Superintendent Perry, 29 December 1896.
48　PAC, RG 18, A-1, vol. 58, no. 37, Superintendent Deane to Herchmer, 22 October 1891 and Sir Julian Pauncefote to Lord Stanley, 5 January 1892.

where they could keep an eye on it. An occasional prosecution was all that was necessary to demonstrate that the police retained the upper hand. Thus when a sentence handed out by Superintendent Deane for frequenting a house of ill fame was appealed, he asked leave to argue the case before the higher court, explaining his reasoning as follows:

> As Police Officer in charge of the District and responsible for order therein, I am very much interested in the eventual decision, because there are a few persons in town, pimps, etc., who are at the bottom of most of the rows that take place and I am bent on making them understand that when they get a Police hint to behave themselves or leave town they must comply forthwith.[49]

Significantly what Deane asked for and got from the higher court was a suspended sentence on the charge.

Normally the police attitude toward prostitution was even more favourable than the case described above would indicate. In 1894 Deane reported that he was being pressured by the town's clergymen to stamp out prostitution completely in Lethbridge. The request annoyed the superintendent.

> If they would turn their attention to the juvenile depravity and promiscuous fornication that is going on under their own eyes and in their own congregations, they would be kept so busy that they would have no time to think of the professional ladies, who at all events are orderly, clean, and on the whole not bad looking.

> Not long ago the two ministers above mentioned formed themselves into a delegation and interviewed the Town Council in public session convened and talked about the "soiled doves" etc. The whole town was there to see and hear. The "doves" had a lawyer present to watch the case for them and I was told that the whole business was great fun. The Reverend gentlemen got no satisfaction from the Council and retired covered with ridicule.[50]

Deane's attitude was not a personal idiosyncracy. A few years after the incident mentioned above, the Lethbridge Town Council fell temporarily under the sway of respectability and passed a resolution asking the Mounted Police to close up all houses of prostitution in the municipality. As it happened, Superintendent Deane was on leave at the time and the division was under the command of Inspector A.R. Cuthbert, who recorded his reaction to the request:

> I informed the Town Council for obvious reasons, that should houses of ill fame be removed from the municipality, they would not be allowed to exist in the District and outside the Municipality; whereupon a Council meeting was held, their previous actions reconsidered and the latter left to the discretion of the Police. It is needless to add that the best course is to leave them within the Municipality where they can be under a certain amount of control without more than the usual Police supervision.[51]

The same attitude prevailed in other areas and approaches differed only slightly. Some police officers preferred to stage an occasional raid to satisfy that part of the public which felt something should be done.[52] This approach was not without its pitfalls either since one raid turned up two members of the force among the clientele. These two worthies claimed to be investigating on their own time but the commissioner,

---

49   PAC, RG 18, A-1, vol. 74, no. 73, Lethbridge Monthly Report for October 1893.
50   PAC, RG 18, A-1, vol. 91, no. 148, Lethbridge Monthly Report for July 1894.
51   PAC, RG 18, A-1, vol. 143, no. 17, Lethbridge Monthly Report for September 1898.
52   PAC, RG 18, A-1, vol. 167, no. 215, Calgary Monthly Report for January 1899.

unimpressed by their zeal, felt compelled to bring charges against them under the Police Act.[53]

Crime, like other human activities, tends to reflect the predominant social ideas of the era in which it occurs. In the case of the nineteenth-century Canadian West, crime was very closely tied to class and to popular concepts of class. Respectability was the dominant virtue of the middle and upper classes, which meant that criminal activites were associated in the public mind with lower classes. A middle class individual who was discovered in some serious violation of the law became almost automatically a social outcaste. Everyone expected that the lower orders would break the law. It was one measure of their inferiority. Many of these attitudes prevail still but in a much diluted form. They were a good deal more pronounced a century ago.

This fact helps explain a number of more or less puzzling aspects of both criminal activity and police attitudes to that activity. The reluctance of rustling victims to become involved in aiding the police is one example. The police explained this phenomenon by the theory that such people feared retaliation. This does not seem a very plausible explanation. The victims had already suffered losses and they would continue to do so. The large ranchers certainly did not fear violent retaliation from the small farmers. What they did fear was the social pressure which would have been exerted on a man who accused someone of his own class or social level. Few were willing to run the risk of falsely accusing a respectable citizen, especially since stock theft was so difficult to prove. In 1905, to give one example of the hazards involved, the police arrested a prominent citizen of Calgary on a charge of horse stealing which they were subsequently unable to prove. The force was censured in an editorial in the Calgary *Herald* and Inspector D.M. Howard, who had been in charge of the case, was immediately ordered to duty in the far North.[54]

Much the same set of attitudes explains the reluctance of the police to strictly enforce the laws governing such moral offences as prostitution. The public liked to believe that the offence of frequenting houses of ill fame was almost the sole prerogative of the lower classes. So long as houses of prostitution remained quiet and did not impinge upon the sphere of the respectable class they were not molested. If the laws were strictly enforced there was always a good chance that raids would turn up a respectable citizen or two. This would have meant only trouble for the enforcers and town authorities were thus anxious to transfer this unpopular duty to the Mounted Police whereas the police were equally anxious to avoid it.[55] Styles in criminal activity change and so does the relationship between evader and enforcer of the law. So-called "white collar" crime is a characteristic of our own day as lower class crime was of the nineteenth century. The successful criminal no longer has an identifiable life style of his own as he did a century ago.

---

53   PAC, RG 18, A-1, vol. 279, no. 579, Perry to Inspector J.V Begin, 11 June 1904.
54   Calgary *Herald*, 6 February 1905; and PAC, RG 18, A-1, vol. 297, no. 323, White to Perry, 21 March 1905.
55   In 1894, for example, the Regina Town Council applied for a Mounted Police detachment, "To maintain law and order and especially enforce those by-laws pertaining to licences, gambling, and the suppression of vice and immorality." PAC, RG 18, A-1, vol. 94, no. 258, John Secord (Regina Town Clerk) to Herchmer, 28 February 1894. The request was refused by the police. White to Herchmer, 10 March 1894.

The attitudes of the police toward the relationship between class and crime is nowhere more clearly illustrated than in their approach to the problem of vagrancy. Every summer the North-West Territories was inundated by a flood of transients. Some of these were genuine tramps; dropouts from society who lived the life of the hobo by choice. Most of them, however, were young men in search of work. They represented an unacknowledged social problem of the day, unemployment, for which there were no conventional solutions. The employed labourer had his place in the social scheme, the man without a job did not. He was at the mercy of the construction companies and farmers who might give him work for a few months or weeks from time to time. As soon as the job ended he became, in the eyes of the police and public alike, a crime looking for a place to happen. The police term for this group was "the floating population," a phrase which was invariably used in the context of a threat to the social order.

The penalties imposed for vagrancy were severe. The law provided a very wide range of sentences for vagrancy; from small fines to six months in jail. Substantial jail sentences were awarded much more frequently than the lesser penalties.[56] Many vagrants were simply ordered to move on within twenty-four or forty-eight hours.[57] Others were given suspended sentences to let them know that the police were watching them and would tolerate no misbehaviour.[58] If jobs could be found for vagrants enjoying the hospitality of the police guardrooms, they were sometimes released before their sentences had expired.[59] On the whole, however, the system bore harshly on transients. The police treated them as a problem to be dealt with by whatever means were available rather than as citizens temporarily down on their luck. There is little evidence in the police records to indicate that transients were any more prone to break the law than that part of the population which was more or less permanently employed. The source of the police attitude was rather an uneasy feeling that those without roots in a particular community had less to lose than permanent residents and would therefore be more likely to break the law.

One of the most widely held public assumptions, then as now, is that the crime rate is directly related to the state of the economy. The proposition is that since poverty presumably breeds crime the crime rate will be higher in bad times, lower when there is general prosperity. The experience of the Mounted Police indicates that no simple, direct relationship exists. If anything, in the period under study, the crime rate tended to be higher when the economy of the North-West Territories was booming and lower when it was depressed. Usually in the police papers complaints of increases in crime accompanied reports of good crops, full employment, and general prosperity.[60] Reports of destitution, the distribution of relief, and hard times tend to be found alongside comments about the absence of criminal activity.[61] The

---

56 See, for example, PAC, RG 18, A-1, vol. 131, no. 202, Regina Monthly Reports for 1899, in which sentences for vagrancy range from a fine of one dollar to three months in jail.

57 PAC, RG 18, A-1, vol. 112, no. 190, Calgary Monthly Report for June 1894.

58 PAC, RG 18, A-1, vol. 49, no. 192, Lethbridge Monthly Report for April 1891.

59 PAC, RG 18, A-1, vol. 126, no. 2, Regina Monthly Report for April 1897.

60 For example see, PAC, RG 18, A-1, vol. 229, no. 156, Prince Albert Monthly Reports, 1902; and vol. 247, no. 101, Regina Monthly Reports, 1903.

61 PAC, RG 18, A-1, vol. 107, no. 215, Ft Saskatchewan Monthly Reports for 1895; and vol. 143, no. 20, Prince Albert Monthly Reports for 1898.

police were filled with apprehension at the prospect of large numbers of seasonal workers being idle in the winter but their predictions were seldom borne out by actual increases in crime.[62]

Some of the more perceptive individuals of the force noted this discrepancy between expectations and events and commented. During a bad winter at Regina, Superintendent Perry wrote: "I anticipated that, owing to the straitened circumstance of many people, thieving could be prevalent but such has not been the case. Fewer cases have been reported than for many previous months."[63] The obvious explanation in this case was that there was little of value around to attract the thief. Superintendent Deane in 1889 observed: "This district has generally been very quiet — business is dull — the mines work only half time — money is scarce, and whiskey much the same."[64] But such a theory does not help account for the fact that all types of crime, including assaults and other crimes of violence, tended to increase when times were good economically. So many possible causes exist for fluctuations in the crime rate that any attempt to establish a relationship on the basis of this single situation would be unproductive. What the evidence does seem to indicate is that the rapid changes engendered by periods of fast economic growth had a general unsettling effect on the population which found expression in crimes of violence as well as crimes against property.

It will be evident from this brief survey of criminal activity in the North-West Territories that the Mounted Police were generally successful in enforcing the law. They kept a firm hand on those areas of delinquency which they considered to be important. The police view of what was important usually coincided with that of the public; an important element in maintaining their reputation. Enforcement of the law also emerges as a factor of the utmost importance in the maintenance of social stability. Without an enlightened and humane approach to its application, the best legal code imaginable would be useless. A good police force, on the other hand, can do much to moderate the bad influence of harsh and unjust laws.

The attitudes toward crime discussed in this chapter also have an important bearing on the myth of the orderly character of Canadian society. Obviously there was a good deal of violence in the North-West Territories and equally obviously both police and public expected it to occur. The point is that they expected it to be confined to the lower classes and it generally was. The thing that shocked Canadian observers of life in the American West was not violence per se, but the fact that it sometimes occurred among social and economic groups which in Canada would have fallen into the category of the respectable middle class. What conditioned the Canadian view of the United States was not so much hypocrisy, although there was undoubtedly an element of that, as a different view of the relationship between crime and class.

NOTE

This chapter was first published in R.C. Macleod, *The NWMP and Law Enforcement 1873-1905* (Toronto: University of Toronto Press, 1976), pp. 114-130 and 189-192.

---

62   PAC, RG 18, A-1, vol. 247, no. 101, Regina Monthly Report for October 1903.

63   PAC, RG 18, A-1, vol. 102, no. 54, Regina Monthly Report for January 1895.

64   PAC, RG 18, A-1, vol. 30, no. 130, Lethbridge Monthly Report for April 1889.

SEVEN

Mob Law Could Not Prevail

William Beahen

Municipal government and law enforcement in the North-West Territories were in their infancy when a smallpox outbreak and anti-Chinese riot occurred in Calgary in the summer of 1892. Town authorities experienced difficulties in coping with this crisis and turned to a more experienced authority, the North-West Mounted Police. Although the police were wary of cooperation because of previous clashes with town officials, especially the police chief, they did act, recognizing the necessity of protecting the country from spread of disease and of preserving law and order when threatened by mob violence. Inspector A.R. Cuthbert, commander of E Division, reasoned that "mob law could not be allowed to prevail in the N.W.T. even in a Municipality."[1]

When the NWMP first arrived at Calgary in 1875, they had sole responsibility for policing the area. But, with the creation of the urban municipality of Calgary in 1884, came the power for the local council to pass bylaws to regulate the order and morality of the town and to appoint policemen to enforce them.[2] Thus, the following year, 1885, the Calgary Police Department was established. The North-West Mounted Police continued to exercise authority for enforcement of federal statutes and N.W.T. ordinances in the town.[3] But in practice they withdrew from acting within the municipality except in cooperation with town police or when a serious crime obviously violated more than a municipal bylaw.[4] In this way town council used its four man police force to determine the balance of vice and morality to be allowed in the frontier community and to collect revenue from the imposition of fines. The larger 70 man force of Mounted Police stationed at Calgary was left free to patrol the outlying district. But after the appointment of a new Chief of Police, Tom English, in 1890,[5] a conflict arose with the Mounted Police over the degree of licence to be

---

1   Public Archives of Canada (PAC), RCMP Records, RG 18, V. 1255, File 365, Part I, Aug. 3, 1892, Inspector A.R. Cuthbert to Commissioner L.W. Herchmer.

2   Ordinance No. 2 entitled "An Ordinance Respecting Municipalities" in Ordinances of the North-West Territories, Regina, 1883, Sections 25 and 47.

3   PAC, RG 18, V. 1255, File 338-92, various documents.

4   Canada, Sessional Papers, *Annual Report of the Commissioner of the North-West Mounted Police*, 1892, 128. (Hereafter referred to as *NWMP Annual Report*). Calgary *Tribune*, Aug. 10, 1892.

5   M. Gilkes and M. Symons, *Calgary's Finest: A History of the City Police Force*, Century Calgary Publications, Calgary, 1975, 282.

allowed in the community. By reports, Chief English was a big, brawling man with a dominant personality and not inclined to a severe imposition of law and order.[6] This approach may have been a realistic appraisal of the wants and needs of the Calgary's 4,000 citizens, but it began to have a detrimental effect on the internal discipline of E Division, the district unit of the Mounted Police.

For example, Lottie Carkeek, alias Dutch Lottie, alias Lottie Diamond, alias Lottie Sargent, a keeper of a house of ill fame, helped to ruin the careers of a Mounted Police sergeant and a sergeant-major, the former being reduced to constable before quitting the Force and the latter having his personal life reduced to a shambles. When the Mounted Police tried to gain the cooperation of the town police in putting Lottie out of business, Chief of Police English was reluctant to do anything "for some reason best known to himself."[7] The pressure for action continued until the madam was arrested and fined for keeping a house of ill fame, but the nominal fine of $50 was no real deterrent.

The Mounted Police had failed in their attempt to drive Lottie Carkeek out of business.[8] What had been accomplished was to create enmity between Chief Tom English and the Mounted Police, with the former said to be considering suing Cuthbert for libel for accusing him of protecting a prostitute.[9] The suit was not made, but English got a measure of revenge on the NWMP by inspiring a story in the Calgary *Tribune* that an officious Mounted Policeman had almost trampled a mentally deficient lad at a local athletic association games. The article commented editorially:

> It would be far better, indeed, if the mounted police were kept to their legitimate duties. There was not the slightest necessity of their presence at the games yesterday to maintain order and in future the town police, who are paid for doing town duty should be required to perform that duty.[10]

It turned out that the boy had been interfering with runners in a race and had been accidently knocked down by a Mounted Policeman who was trying to clear him from the course at the request of the organizers.[11] The editor of the newspaper apologized privately to Inspector Cuthbert for the article explaining that it had been placed in the newspaper without his knowledge by a reporter acting for Chief English.[12]

On June 30, 1892, a Chinese man working at a laundry on Stephen Avenue was found to be suffering from smallpox. Considerable feeling against the Chinese was aroused among the citizenry for having introduced this disease in their midst. The

---

6   James H. Gray, *Red Lights on the Prairies*, Macmillan of Canada, Toronto, 1971, 129.

7   PAC, RG 18, V. 3339, File 878, Part I, June 1, 1892, Hooper to Cuthbert.

8   Lonie Carkeek, or Dutch Lottie, remained in Calgary at least into 1893, and continued to corrupt members of the Mounted Police, to the consternation of the Comptroller. "Her house has been out of bounds for a long time, but despite the embargo and the fact that she is old and withered in appearance, it is apparently impossible to keep the Mounted Police entirely out of her house." (PAC, RG 18, Vol. 86, File 656-93, Nov. 13, 1893, White to W.B. Ives.)

9   PAC, RG 18, File 616-92, July 15, 1892, Herchmer to White.

10   Calgary *Tribune*, July 6, 1892.

11   Ibid, July 9, 1892.

12   PAC, RG 18, V. 1256, File 362-92, July 19, 1892, Cuthbert to Herchmer. Cuthbert believed that English was also deliberately fostering public opinion against the NWMP because he might soon face a jury trial for assaulting a Mounted Policeman. PAC, RG 18, V. 1255, File 356, Part I, July 10, 1892, Cuthbert to Herchmer.

municipal board of health acted quickly by setting up a quarantine camp across Nose Creek for the patient and for the other occupants of the house and by burning the building and its contents. Mayor Alexander Lucas then appealed to the Mounted Police to guard the camp both to keep the Chinese inside and others away. When he pointed out that the quarantine was in the national interest as well as that of the locality, Cuthbert immediately complied.[13]

This precautionary arrangement was soon threatened by the friction existing between the town authorities and the Mounted Police. The agreed procedure for supplying the camp was that the town authorities would deliver goods to a point outside the quarantine grounds but within reach of camp attendants, thus ensuring that no contact would be made. But on the evening of July 4, Chief English drove a wagon load of supplies straight into camp and proceeded to visit with those detained there.[14] Then, when English tried to leave, he was stopped by Sgt. Dee of the NWMP acting on orders that anyone having unnecessary contact with those infected were to be kept in quarantine. English was not persuaded by this argument and responded with a string of curses and the claim that there were not enough Mounted Police in the country to hold him. The chief then assaulted Sgt. Dee and had to be restrained by force. Inspector Cuthbert was notified and he authorized the release of English when Mayor Lucas agreed in writing to assume responsibility for him.[15]

The Mounted Police then had Chief English charged with assault, but the Crown prosecutor said he would not press the case because "he did not wish to make an enemy of English."[16] And although the mayor assured Cuthbert that English would be severely dealt with, he doubted the outcome because municipal authorities had shown "little backbone" in dealing with the policeman.[17] The trial began on July 12, with the chief pleading not guilty, and it was immediately postponed because two of the defence witnesses were inmates of the quarantine camp.[18]

The incident caused the Mounted Police to consider withdrawing from their role in enforcement of the quarantine. Three days after the assault, Inspector Cuthbert notified Mayor Lucas that he would recall the Mounted Policemen from guard duty at the quarantine grounds as soon as the town could provide substitutes.[19] Lucas responded that in his view the responsibility for dealing with the disease lay with the federal government and not the town because the smallpox was brought in from the coast. He said that the Mounted Police services were appreciated by Calgarians and must continue.[20]

The question of governmental responsibility was confused because quarantine had not been proclaimed under the provisions of the N.W.T. Infectious Diseases

---

13 Ibid, July 1, 1892, Cuthbert to Herchmer.
14 One historian of Calgary contends that English was visiting "one of his interned lady friends" but this author has found no evidence of this. Max Foran, *Calgary: An Illustrated History*, James Lorimer and Co., National Museum of Man, Toronto, 1978, 44.
15 PAC, RG 18, V. 1255, File 256, Part I, July 5, 1892, Cuthbert to Herchmer.
16 Ibid, July 7, 1892, Cuthbert to Herchmer.
17 Ibid, July 10, 1892, Cuthbert to Herchmer.
18 Calgary *Herald*, July 13, 1892.
19 PAC, RG 18, V. 1255, File 365, Part I, July 7, 1892, Cuthbert to Herchmer.
20 Ibid, July 9, 1892, Mayor Alexander Lucas to Cuthbert.

Ordinance. Arrangements for the quarantine had been made by the municipal board of health as a local precaution.[21] As a result the Mounted Police had no official role in controlling the outbreak. But finally by July 22, as the disease spread in Calgary, town authorities were forced to publicly admit to the infection, and the lieutenant-governor set up a territorial health district to deal with it. Under this regulation any peace officer was authorized to enforce the quarantine and so the Mounted Police were more officially committed to act.[22]

The first case of smallpox had appeared in a man who had just arrived from China in April. His illness had not been reported to the authorities for a month, and by that time a second man in the household had been infected. Three days after the cases were discovered, a white man who had his washing done at the laundry was found to have contracted the disease. After the incident with Chief English, no new cases were reported until mid-July when suddenly there were three more, one a white woman just arrived from British Columbia.

The spread of the disease engendered considerable anxiety in Calgary, manifesting itself in part by outbursts of hostility towards the town's Chinese residents. The Chinese were not very popular with whites in Canada, who regarded them as bearers of disease and source of every sort of vice from gambling to drugs to enslavement of white girls for prostitution. These attitudes were reinforced by the knowledge that smallpox was imported from China and was occurring not only in Calgary but in British Columbia and other parts of the Territory.[23]

In Calgary, the initial reaction from citizens was to run the Chinese out of town, but this attitude abated when the quarantine was established. In fact, there was no publicity about the disease in Calgary newspapers for the first two weeks, probably because a growing town does not like to advertise its shortcomings. This changed in mid-July when the three fresh cases were reported. Rabid anti-Chinese sentiments began to be expressed and the first ominous warning of the violence came on July 19, when the Calgary *Herald* warned the town's health committee to consult with citizens about what to do with the Chinese when they were to be released from quarantine. "The local feeling is strong against the race, and it is well for the authorities to recognize the fact. If the Chinamen now at the quarantine be sent back into town there will be trouble."[24]

The reaction of some of Calgary's citizens to the appearance of smallpox in their midst was to take temporary leave of the town. Inspector Cuthbert characterized these departures as "a great exodus."[25] The Winnipeg Industrial Exhibition was being held at this time and large numbers of Calgarians took the opportunity to visit it.

---

21   Ibid, July 10, 1892, Cuthbert to Herchmer.

22   Ordinance No. 6 entitled "An Ordinance Respecting Infectious Diseases" in *The Revised Ordinances of the North-West Territories*, Regina, 1888, 41-42. PAC, RG 18, V. 1255, File 365, Part I, July 22, 1892, Cuthbert to Herchmer.

23   W. Peter Ward, *White Canada Forever: Popular Attitudes and Public Policy Towards Orientals in British Columbia*, McGill-Queen's University Press, Montreal, 1978, 22 and 50-51. J. Brian Dawson, "The Chinese Experience in Frontier Calgary, 1885-1910" in A.W. Rasporich and H.C. Klassen, eds., *Frontier Calgary: Town City and Region, 1875-1914*, University of Calgary, M. & S. West, 1975, 124 to 140.

24   Calgary *Herald*, July 19, 1892.

25   PAC, RG 18, V. 1255, File 365, Part I, July 20, 1892, Cuthbert to Herchmer.

Among the holiday-makers was the unco-operative Chief of Police, Tom English. The chief left Calgary on July 23,[26] originally for one week in Winnipeg, but he found private business to attend to and gained an extension of his leave,[27] not returning until Aug. 9.[28] It was most curious and inopportune of Calgary's Chief of Police to take his holidays at such a critical juncture in the town's history.

There was a hiatus in the spread of the disease but the end of July saw the sudden appearance of three more cases, two in the quarantine camp and one a woman in the CPR community of Shepherd. Nine more people were brought into the Calgary quarantine grounds from Shepherd, and a separate health district set up at that place, policed by the NWMP.[29] Three people died, a mother and her newly-born infant, and a pregnant woman who also suffered a miscarriage after contracting the disease.[30]

As the Calgary *Herald* had warned, the release of several Chinese from quarantine on Aug. 2, triggered a riot among white Calgarians. The trouble started at a banquet after a cricket match between two local clubs. Excessive drinking was followed by a decision to demonstrate against the return of the Chinese. A mob of about 200 gathered in the streets of Calgary by about 11 p.m. The mob then descended on the Chinese district, destroying property, assaulting several Chinese residents and by some reports stealing money. From the outset, no attempt was made by the town's two constables, nor any other municipal authority, to stop the riot.[31]

Anticipating trouble, Cuthbert earlier had notified the council of the release of the Chinese from quarantine and Mayor Lucas had promptly left town. When the rioting did break out he was nowhere to be found. Cuthbert believed this was a deliberate act by Lucas who was in league with the mob leaders.[32] Several respectable citizens, however, including town councillor W.H. Cushing, who was also a member of the police commission, asked the Mounted Police to act. Cuthbert was prepared to move on the town anyway citing violations of federal statutes, but this request gave a semblance of local support as well. Cuthbert gave shelter to Chinese fleeing the violence that night, then took a squad of police to town. At the approach of the small force, the ringleaders disappeared, and the police picked up three quarrelsome men from the mob which then dispersed. The police continued in town on patrol until 4 a.m.[33]

Cuthbert at first thought that the dispersal of the riot would stave off any further trouble.[34] But he was wrong. The Chinese continued to receive threats that unless they left town their properties would be burned, and they would receive personal injury. The editor of the Calgary *Tribune* who was considered to favour the Chinese

---

26 Ibid, July 23, 1892.
27 Calgary *Tribune*, Aug. 10, 1892.
28 Calgary *Herald*, Aug. 9, 1892.
29 Ibid, Aug. 9, 1892, Supt. McIllree to White.
30 Calgary *Herald*, Aug. 16, 1892.
31 PAC, RG 18, V. 1255, File 365, Part I, Aug. 3, 1892, Cuthbert to Herchmer. Calgary *Herald*, Aug. 3, 1892.
32 PAC, RG 18, V. 70, File 664-92, Aug. 12, 1892, Cuthbert to Herchmer. *NWMP Annual Report*, 1892, 127-128.
33 PAC, RG 18, V. 1255, File 365, Part I, Aug. 3, 1892, Cuthbert to Herchmer.
34 Ibid, Aug. 4, 1892, Cuthbert to Herchmer.

was also warned his building would be burned. Under pressure from some more broad-minded elements of the community, the council asked the Mounted Police to shelter the Chinese and then patrol the town, but their own sentiments were clearly with the mob.[35] Town officials refused to prosecute the three men arrested the night of the riot[36] and to seek out the leaders of the mob.[37] Later, Mayor Lucas confessed that he understood the feelings of the rioters against the Chinese because by secretly sheltering a smallpox victim they had endangered the whole community. "He thought that the whites had some rights as well as Chinamen."[38] When several clergymen petitioned town council to denounce the actions of the rioters, council would not comply.[39]

As requested, both unofficially by respectable members of the community and officially by town council, the NWMP began to patrol Calgary regularly on Aug. 5. Reinforcements were rushed to E Division, and mounted and dismounted patrols were in town day and night.[40] Cuthbert was concerned that cowmen might be brought in from the country and plied with whiskey and that a mob could turn the stones on Calgary's streets into formidable weapons.[41] To counter this threat Cuthbert organized a special squad composed of NCO's and old cavalry men armed with swords and side-arms which would hopefully disperse rioters without giving them a chance to fire.[42]

No further confrontations occurred, although Cuthbert was informed of another planned attack on the Chinese quarter.[43] There also was a flurry of excitement in town over a rumour that a man had died of smallpox and was buried under the Chinese laundry. The area was excavated, but no body was discovered.[44] The termination of the quarantine on Aug. 17, eased the tensions somewhat, and the NWMP reduced patrols in town on Aug. 19, withdrawing them entirely two days later.[45] This change was marred by a final incident on Aug. 20, when several rowdies made a brief attack on a Chinese laundry, kicking in the door and heaving in some stones. No damage or injuries were reported.[46]

The lingering racial resentment which continued in Calgary concentrated briefly on a visiting orator, Locksley Lucas. A professional public speaker, he had been successful in Vancouver in turning bitterness against the Chinese into an organization called the Anti-Chinese League. He arrived in Calgary to organize a local chapter, offering a free lecture the first evening and charging for subsequent talks.

---

35 Ibid, Aug. 5, 1892, Cuthbert to Herchmer.
36 PAC, RG 18, V. 1244, File 215-92, Aug 3, 1892, Cuthbert to Herchmer.
37 Calgary *Tribune*, Aug. 6, 1892.
38 Ibid, Aug. 10, 1892.
39 Ibid, Aug. 24, 1892.
40 PAC, RG 18, V. 1244, File 215-92.
41 PAC, RG 18, V. 1255, File 365, Part I, Aug. 5, 1892, Cuthbert to Herchmer.
42 Ibid, Aug. 7, 1892, Cuthbert to Herchmer.
43 Ibid, Aug. 19, 1892, Cuthbert to Herchmer.
44 Ibid, Aug. 9, 1892, Cuthbert to Herchmer. Calgary *Herald* and Calgary *Tribune*, Aug. 9, 1892.
45 PAC, RG 18, V. 1244, File 215-92.
46 Calgary *Tribune*, Aug. 24, 1892.

Locksley Lucas's first meeting held on Aug. 17 was a great success. He told lurid tales of the great lust of the Chinese and their methods of enslaving young white girls through drugs and using them as prostitutes. The Chinese were said also to be habitual gamblers who drew young whites into games and ruined their lives. For those who claimed that the Chinese were peaceable citizens, Lucas countered that 28 percent of the criminals in New Westminister jail were of that race. The crowd was convinced. Mayor Alexander Lucas (no relation to the orator), who was in attendance, "showed that he was not at all favourable to the presence of the Mongolian in this quarter."[47] The mayor and town councillors Orr and Freeze agreed to serve on a provisional committee for a local branch of the Anti-Chinese League. Councillor Wesley Orr was also moved to offer free property to any white people who would set up a laundry in Calgary to drive the Chinese out of business.[48]

The atmosphere of dangerous hostility was somewhat dissipated by a farcical ending to the campaign of Locksley Lucas. Apparently when Lucas arrived in Calgary, he had sent his dirty clothes out to be cleaned at a Chinese laundry.[49] This became known and harmed the credibility of a man who advocated no employment of Chinese labour. Morose at the public ridicule, Lucas bought a small dose of morphine from a local druggist, claiming it was needed to ease a toothache. He then consumed the drug in his hotel room leaving a suicide note for a sympathizer. Lucas was found and revived by a doctor who said that the dosage was not sufficient to kill and a staged attempt was suspected. A charge of attempted suicide was laid, but the orator was acquitted in a brief trial before Mayor Lucas, doubling as a magistrate.[50] The whole affair was apparently now regarded as a great joke to be exceeded a few days later only by the escape and recapture of a pet bear kept by a local restauranteur.[51]

The NWMP's effective response to this crisis of law and order in Calgary was finally recognized by town council. A motion was passed on Aug. 10, instructing its police committee to determine if the Mounted Police would take over the policing of Calgary on a permanent basis.[52] The committee asked the Mounted Police to replace the town police, assume responsibility for the maintenance of law and order, and enforce municipal bylaws including collection of taxes and licence fees. In commenting on this request, the Calgary *Tribune* warned the town council to insist that any Mounted Police town detachment be under the absolute control of municipal authorities.[53] This factor of control and the inappropriateness of federal police enforcing local bylaws convinced the NWMP to turn down the request. As Fred White, the Comptroller and Deputy Minister responsible for the Mounted Police, commented: "such an arrangement would lead to the clashing of authority between the Officers of the Force, to whom the Police would be responsible, and the officials of the Town, and the result would be unsatisfactory to all parties interested."[54] But, White continued,

---

47 Calgary *Herald*, Aug. 17, 1892.
48 Calgary *Tribune*, Aug. 19, 1892.
49 Ibid, Aug. 18, 1892.
50 Ibid, Aug. 19 and 23, 1892.
51 Calgary *Herald*, Aug. 20 and 23, 1892.
52 Calgary *Tribune*, Aug 10, 1892.
53 Ibid, Aug. 12, 1892.
54 PAC, RG 18, V. 1255, File 365, Part I, Aug. 26, 1892, White to Herchmer, and Sept. 15, 1892, White to Herchmer.

the Mounted Police at Calgary would always be available to suppress any serious disturbance in town.

The smallpox incident in Calgary is evidence of the continuance of federal authority exercised by the Mounted Police in the West during the territorial period. In the latter part of the 19th century, federal departments, especially Agriculture, Interior and Indian Affairs, virtually programmed the development of the West. At that time, the responsibility of policing the departmental programs usually fell to the NWMP. As a result, the authority of the Force was pervasive, creating habits of dependence among the Indians and the settlers. Even the larger urban centres, like Regina, Calgary and Edmonton, were reluctant to assume full responsibility for law enforcement long after developing other municipal institutions.

NOTE

This chapter was previously published in *Alberta History*, 29, no. 3 (summer 1981), 1-7. Illustrations in the original have been omitted. The author is Staff Historian for the RCMP in Ottawa.

EIGHT

Tar and Feathers:
The Mounted Police and Frontier Justice

Anna-Maria Mavromichalis

"Maintain the Right" — the North-West Mounted Police could not have chosen a more appropriate motto. For the pioneer policemen themselves, "Maintain the Right" had a meaning all its own, which often had little to do with either politics or the law. These were the men charged with the maintenance of what their bureaucratic superiors idealistically called "law and order." Through their experiences, the Mounties came to understand that the real often differed from the ideal, and that law and order were not necessarily synonymous concepts. The cases which the Mounties tackled were varied, often complex, and seldom black-and-white.

The tarring and feathering of James Donaldson in Lethbridge in 1895 exemplifies the conflict between the law and moral justice. The case caused a public sensation on the local and even national level, being the topic of newspaper columns across the country.[1] In order to fully understand the reasons for the public outrage, one must begin with a separate but related case, the suicide of Charles Gillies.

Charles Gillies shot himself in the head on February 13th, 1895. The coroner's jury determined the cause of death to be "suicide while being under mental depression caused by domestic troubles."[2] A long and unhappy sequence of events had brought Gillies to the point of overwhelming desperation. He had been in charge of the North West Coal and Navigation Company's stables until alcoholism had cost him his job. Thereafter, his only income came from a lodger in his house named James Donaldson.[3]

Donaldson had been having an affair with Gillies' wife for a number of years. Gillies was well aware of this and had frequently quarrelled with his wife over the matter. About three weeks before Gillies' death, Donaldson had thrown him out of his own house when Gillies had discovered the lodger in bed with his wife.

---

1   R. Burton Deane, Special Report on the Suicide of Charles Gillies (hereinafter cited as "Special Report"), February 16, 1895. National Archives of Canada (NAC) RG 18, 106, 191-95; and letter, Samuel Donaldson to Deane, May 27, 1895. NAC, RG 18, 1325, 55-95.
2   Deane, Special Report, op. cit., February 16, 1895.
3   R. Burton Deane, Annual Report, 1895, in *Pioneer Policing in Southern Alberta, 1888-1914: Deane of the Mounties*. William Baker, editor. Calgary: Historical Society of Alberta, 1993, 68.

Charles Gillies was not a man to keep his problems private, especially when drink loosened his tongue, and he repeatedly complained to others about his domestic troubles. Consequently, his situation was well known among the townspeople, "and not a little indignation had been aroused by the treatment which the husband complained of having received."[4] In the end, his frustrations with his wife, with Donaldson, and with his creditors had finally driven him over the edge. "I'll end this," he said; he sought out his Winchester carbine, placed the barrel into his mouth and pulled the trigger.[5]

The funeral was held on February 15th, at which time Donaldson committed what the townsfolk saw as the final outrage: he attended the last rites as chief mourner. In his special report to the Commissioner, Superintendent R. Burton Deane of the North-West Mounted Police in Lethbridge had already stated that "there has been an unusual amount of indignation aroused by the manner in which he [ie. Donaldson] has treated the deceased."[6] The entire town had known Gillies' lot well, and the gall displayed by Donaldson in this final insult had fired their righteous indignation. In fact, Deane reports that "there is a general expression of wonder that he [Gillies] did not kill the other man instead."[7] Retribution was clearly on the town's agenda.

What Superintendent Deane referred to as "an unprecedented occurrence of lynch law" took place the night of Gillies' funeral.[8] Plans had been made earlier in the day, and the self-appointed avengers set out for Donaldson's home around midnight.[9] It was, as they say, "a dark and stormy night," with the wind howling and the snow flying.[10] After the shooting, James Donaldson had moved in with his brother Maxwell. The Donaldson brothers had retired at about the same time the gang left town. Some time later, the pair were startled by the front door smashing in. According to Maxwell Donaldson, "a gang of masked men rushed in with firearms and ordered us to throw up our hands or we should be shot — covering us with the firearms at the same time."[11] The gang, which numbered about seven or eight, dispersed itself through the house, with one man in the kitchen, another in the kitchen doorway, and the remainder in the front room where the Donaldsons had been sleeping. James was pulled from the bed onto the floor, and his light was extinguished. The masked men, said James, "stripped off my drawers, but not my shirt, rolled me on the floor, and put tar and feathers on me from my waist downwards, on my head and face and on my arms and hands."[12] Maxwell Donaldson had been blindfolded and remained on the bed at gun point.

The attackers became violent. When the tarring and feathering was done, the

---

4   Deane, in *Pioneer Policing...*, 68.
5   Deane, Special Report, op. cit., February 14, 1895.
6   Ibid.
7   Ibid.
8   Deane, in *Pioneer Policing...*, 68.
9   Statutory Declaration of James Alexander Donaldson, Deane to Commissioner, Schedule A, February 7, 1895. NAC, RG 18, 1325, 55-95, 1.
10 Testimony of Peter Smith, Court Transcripts, Preliminary Examination, Queen vs Warren (hereinafter cited as Court Transcripts). Provincial Archives of Alberta (PAA), Acc. 78.235/306-307, 19.
11 Testimony of Maxwell Donaldson, Court Transcripts... op. cit., 21.
12 Ibid., 2.

lamp was relighted and James, still lying on the floor, was hit in the head, and a rope with a slip knot was placed around his neck. The attackers then dragged him by the rope into the kitchen and told him they were going to take him outside; he was given his clothes and ordered to dress. They then dragged James out the door, lifted him to his feet, and began walking toward the Lethbridge House. He was warned not to yell or he would be gagged.

The procession made its way along the dark, snowblown streets into town, and was met along the way by three men — William Henderson, Peter Smith, and Donald Fraser. Their sworn testimonies state that they had no involvement in the tarring and feathering; yet, their presence on the streets at such a late hour and in such bad weather is, at the very least, suspicious.[13] The leader of the gang, who had been giving all the orders, commanded Smith, Henderson, and Fraser to "fall in line," which they did.

Meanwhile, the gang continued their attack on Donaldson. The rope around his neck was tightened enough to choke him, apparently to prevent him from saying anything to the approaching men. According to Donaldson, "the man who was on my left hand, struck me with his fist on the corner of the left eye: the wound bled freely. The blow to the head knocked me down — they dragged me a piece and kicked me, then I got on my feet again and we went on."[14]

The procession reached the Lethbridge House without further incident, and approached the front door. Donaldson was thrown into the barroom, and the doors were barred from the outside to prevent him from going back out. According to Charles Bulger, who was tending bar at the time, the rope around Donaldson's neck became caught in the door, and Donaldson asked the bartender to help him. Bulger removed the rope from his neck and, after pulling at the door for some time, managed to get it open. "The bartender ... says J. Donaldson complained of having been knocked about a good deal but that beyond a little blood on his face he did not show any marks of violence."[15]

The gang had dispersed by the time Donaldson came out again. There was nothing left for him to do but go home, and "some parties who met him on the way mistook him for an Indian with war paint on";[16] he did, however, reach home without further harassment.

Maxwell Donaldson had been told by the leader of the gang before he left that two armed guards would remain to make sure he did not move from his bed for at least twenty minutes; thus, Maxwell was unable to reach Superintendent Deane until 1:15 a.m. Deane called Sergeant James Hare at the town police station and discovered that James Donaldson had already gone home. The incident was over and the perpetrators had disappeared before the police were even made aware of what had happened.

Deane knew that the circumstances of the case would make it virtually impossible

---

13 Testimonies of Peter Smith, p. 20, Donald Fraser, p. 46, William Henderson, p. 1, Court Transcripts ... op. cit.
14 Statutory Declaration of James Donaldson, op. cit., 3.
15 Deane, Special Report, op. cit.
16 *Lethbridge News*, February 20, 1895.

to prosecute. First, "there was no chance of catching the perpetrators redhanded"; Maxwell Donaldson had remained in his house for about twenty minutes after his brother had left, and it did not take twenty minutes for the gang with James to reach the Lethbridge House.[17] Thus, the masked gang was long gone before Maxwell could even leave home. Second, the weather conditions had made patrolling that night impossible. On the surface, it seemed that the police had no way of learning about the incident while it was happening. However, they *did* have foreknowledge of it, making Deane's initial exoneration of the Mounties at the very least questionable. The day before the tarring and feathering, Deane wrote: "Tar and feathers have been mentioned in connection with Donaldson's name, for there has been an unusual amount of indignation aroused [against him]..."[18] Deane either did not take the threat very seriously or did not want to involve the police at that early stage; this may be taken as further validation that Deane's real sympathies lay with the perpetrators. In any case, the Mounties neither prevented the incident nor were they able to catch the men in the act. Finally, James and Maxwell Donaldson, the only sources of information regarding the incident, were reluctant to give any details which might be useful for prosecution. Besides, their attackers had been masked and could not easily be identified. Deane concluded that "it is clear we can get no information worth mentioning from the Donaldsons family and it is very unlikely that a prosecution will succeed."[19]

Deane's suspicions were confirmed. James Donaldson got the message that his presence in Lethbridge was most certainly not welcome. He refused to file a complaint against his attackers and left Lethbridge three days after he was tarred and feathered. A noisy crowd turned up at the station for his departure, and "hooted and jeered as the train pulled out."[20]

Historian R.C. Macleod has made the observation that "minor incidents of mob action," particularly those where the offenders had gained public sympathy, were difficult for the NWMP to handle.[21] The tarring and feathering of James Donaldson provides an especially good illustration of the extent to which public sympathy could cause difficulties for the NWMP in enforcing the law.

Superintendent Deane was fully aware of the connection between the suicide of Charles Gillies and the attack on James Donaldson. Two days after the tarring and feathering, he wrote:

> I have recently learned what was the immediate cause of this attack on Donaldson ... it seems to have been brought about by his going to Gillies's funeral as chief mourner. I was told "the boys" could not stand this Pharisaic proceeding.[22]

The attack on Donaldson became an instant public sensation; the words "public sympathy" do not begin to convey the extent to which the local community supported

---

17   Letter, Deane to Commissioner, February 23, 1895. NAC, RG 18, 1325, 55-95.
18   Deane, Special Report, op. cit.
19   Report, Deane to Commissioner, Tar & Feathering Case, February 18, 1895. NAC, RG 18, 1324, 55-95, 2.
20   *Lethbridge News*, February 20, 1895.
21   R.C. Macleod, *The NWMP and Law Enforcement, 1873-1905*. Toronto: University of Toronto Press, 1976, 120.
22   Deane to Commissioner, Tar & Feathering Case, op. cit., February 17, 1895.

the attackers. Even Deane, who had been in Lethbridge for some time, was impressed by "the extraordinary expression of public approval that was evoked by the act."[23]

The verdict among the citizens of Lethbridge was vocal and absolutely unanimous: James Donaldson deserved what he got and the men who tarred and feathered him had done well. Deane was not the only one who remarked on the complete absence of any condemnation of the attack. William Hutton said, "I came up town the next day and every person I met talked about this business [ie. the tarring and feathering]. Every person seemed to think it was a good thing..."[24] Henry Howard went to the Lethbridge House the next morning, and "heard a great many talking about what had taken place — there were perhaps 20 people in the Lethbridge House laughing about it — they seemed to think it was rather a good thing to have done."[25] Walter Whitney said that "I have never heard any one single body say that it was an outrage."[26] Nor was anyone particularly shocked that such a thing had happened; Donaldson's treatment of Gillies was well known and viewed with great public contempt. The tarring and feathering of Donaldson was a subject of conversation both before and after it occurred.

Faced with such massive repugnance, it is not surprising that James Donaldson should have wanted to leave town as quickly as he did. In fact, his departure had been the intended end of the attack — he had literally been "Treated to a Coat and told to 'Git'."[27] Superintendent Deane, who spoke to Donaldson before his departure, commented on his situation:

> James is afraid of his life to stay in the place [ie. Lethbridge], or to go out in the daytime, and wants to leave for eastern Canada tonight. He says he is shunned by everyone, and no one will speak to him, not even members of a fraternal society to which he belongs.[28]

The ostracism James Donaldson experienced could not have been more complete. In fact, he was so utterly ostracized that even those he considered his friends condemned him! Walter Whitney, on Donaldson's departure, remarked that "Donaldson shook hands with me the night he was leaving and said I was the best friend he had in the country ... I think he deserved what he got. It didn't hurt him any that I seen."[29] Even the town's ministers thought the attack on Donaldson had been a good thing:

> Ministers of religion, while deprecating mob law, are of opinion that Donaldson was well served and the pity is that it was not kept out of the newspapers.[30]

The universal contempt felt for Donaldson precluded any immediate attempts to bring the offenders to justice. Superintendent Deane wrote: "It is difficult for

---

23 Deane, in *Pioneer Policing...*, 68.
24 Testimony of William Hutton, Court Transcripts, op. cit., 13.
25 Testimony of Henry Howard, Court Transcripts, op. cit., 8.
26 Testimony of Walter Whitney, Court Transcripts, op. cit., 38. Later evidence revealed that Howard and Whitney were among the men who had perpetrated the act. This may have influenced their expressions of approval somewhat.
27 *Lethbridge News*, February 20, 1895.
28 Deane to Commissioner, Tar & Feathering Case, op. cit.
29 Testimony of Walter Whitney, Court Transcripts, op. cit.
30 Deane, monthly report, February 1895. NAC, RG 18, 104, 131-95, 3.

outsiders to understand the state of feeling in this place on this question. A few nights ago I was told that I was not supposed to be very keen on bringing the perpetrators to justice…"[31] A local merchant, when told he may have to testify in the case, said he would tell the truth, "whereupon the suggestion was made that he should be tarred and feathered (for not consenting to commit perjury!)."[32] The preliminary examination of the case revealed this local bias with glowing clarity. Deane, who heard the preliminary examination, was convinced that

> it would be impossible to find in this town even six men who would convict the prisoner or any other person concerned, for this offence, even though the strongest possible evidence were presented … I am also satisfied that it would be impossible for the Crown to obtain a fair and impartial trial in this case before a Lethbridge jury.[33]

A man named Charles Warren was identified in the preliminary examination by Maxwell Donaldson as the leader of the tar and feather gang. He was arrested, charged with burglary and riot, and a change of venue was granted to have him tried in Macleod. The trial was held in the first week of July.

Initially, James Donaldson had been so terrified of retaliation that he refused to file charges against his attackers. There would have been no case at all, but for outside forces which made themselves felt. Commissioner L.W. Herchmer was not happy at all about the incident and rebuked Deane for having done nothing to prevent the tarring and feathering. He demanded that the police lay charges. In addition, James Donaldson's father wrote to Deane and "insisted on the offenders being brought to justice if possible."[34] Deane had no choice but to press charges.

The problem of lack of evidence was effectively solved by a surprising turn of events. Sergeant Hare, the Mountie assigned to the town police station, "turned Queen's evidence on promise of immunity."[35] The onus of bringing the case to trial was on Deane, and he managed to extract Hare's confession:

> I must say here that I had at the time [ie. before the Macleod trial] sufficient evidence to convict Sergeant Hare under the Police Act. It was in my power to prove that he was seen immediately at the dispersion of the gang, masked and disguised … he was offered the choice between telling what he knew and taking his medicine. He chose the former alterative.[36]

To obtain Hare's confession, Deane had "promised to shield him so far as lay in my power from any penal consequences."[37] He had no intention of placing Hare on the stand, being convinced that, were it known in Lethbridge that Hare was a "turncoat," his life would be in danger. However, the Counsel for the Crown, C.F.P Conybeare, "had some reason to suspect that Sergt. Hare knew all about the business at least, told me that he had determined to put Hare in the box."[38] Conybeare convinced Deane to let him speak to Hare, and after receiving reassurance from Conybeare, Hare finally agreed to testify.

---

31 Deane to Commissioner, July 8, 1895. NAC, RG 18, 1325, 55-95, 4.
32 Ibid., 3-4.
33 Deane, Affidavit, Queen vs Warren, Court Transcripts, op. cit., 2.
34 Deane, in *Pioneer Policing…*, 69.
35 Deane to Commissioner, July 8, 1895, op. cit., 1.
36 Deane, in *Pioneer Policing…*, 70.
37 Deane to Commissioner, July 8, 1895, op. cit.
38 Ibid.

Sergeant Hare took the stand in Macleod and created a sensation: not only did he report all the missing details of the case, but admitted that he had taken part in the tarring and feathering and was one of the leaders. Hare identified all the members of the gang: Henry Howard, David Whitney, Matthew Goldsmith, William Thompson, Daniel McIntosh, and finally Charles Warren, the accused, as the leader. Warren had been asked to captain the mob because he supposedly had had past experience in similar situations, and because there was less chance of him being recognized, as he was from out of town. The others in the gang used false voices during the incident, but Warren had not, hence he was the only one who could be directly implicated in the act. Maxwell Donaldson had identified Warren by the sound of his voice, a conclusion now confirmed by Sergeant Hare. As for the other members of the gang, two had left the country before the trial; the others testified and committed perjury.

James Donaldson was supposed to testify. In fact, it was his promise to take the stand in Macleod that had, in part, convinced Deane to bring the case to trial in the first place. To Deane's disappointment and disgust, however, "James Alexander Donaldson was cur enough to 'wilt' at the last moment and dare not face the music in the witness box."[39]

Testimony was concluded and the jury began its deliberations. They were out for two hours, then returned to announce that there was no possibility that they could agree on a verdict. The jury was disbanded, and a new trial called for July 10th.

It was at this juncture that the case fell apart. The two key witnesses for the prosecution disappeared. Sergeant Hare escaped to the United States. Matthew Goldsmith also "slipped out." The case was called, but the witnesses did not appear. The trial was finally postponed until the next court (that winter) and Warren was released on bail. He decided to take advantage of his freedom and follow Hare south, so when he failed to appear at his trial on November 16th, the case was dismissed. The whole affair had undoubtedly disgusted and frustrated Deane from beginning to end. He had been forced to acknowledge Hare's disregard for his oath of office and had also been forced, against his better judgement, to bring local heroes to trial. Against overwhelming popular sentiment, he had managed to build a solid case against Charles Warren and felt that "the result of the trial seemed to be a foregone conclusion."[40] Though Deane could not have been very surprised by the outcome, he was nevertheless disgusted: "it was a marvel how any men having any respect for the oath which they had taken 'true verdict to give according to the evidence' could have failed to convict the prisoner."[41] However, Deane consoled himself when it was all over, saying "the prosecution has had its effect, and it is quite likely that there will be no further experiments here with lynch law."[42]

The tarring and feathering of James Donaldson is an example of the least serious type of violent crime — assault. The crime was a one-shot deal, and did not undermine the law in any serious manner or lead to further uprisings. One target — James Donaldson — was specific, as was the goal — to run him out of town. Minor incidents such as this were fairly common in frontier towns; thus the Mounties "accepted

---

39 Ibid.
40 Deane, in *Pioneer Policing...*, 70.
41 Deane to Commissioner, July 8, 1895, op. cit.
42 Deane, in *Pioneer Policing...*, 71.

[them] as inevitable and tried whenever possible to act as arbiters."[43] After all, their main concern was to maintain peace and order and, so far as it was possible, to ensure that no one esteem violence as an acceptable course of action.

Superintendent R. Burton Deane and his handling of the tar and feather case is a perfect illustration of how the Mounties dealt with cases involving the ever-present human factor. It must be noted that Deane had been in Lethbridge for seven years at the time of the incident. He was experienced, and knew the local community well. Yet, Deane and his men had to maintain some distance between themselves and the townspeople. In other words, they had to be in, but not of, the community.

This position, held by the Mounted Police in Lethbridge, ensured that anything which was known within the community would most likely be known to them. An awareness of this led Deane to blame Sergeant Hare for not preventing the tarring and feathering. However, it is apparent that both Hare and Deane had foreknowledge of the incident, so close was the Mounties' tie with the local community.

It is fascinating to realize that a Mounted Policeman could have taken part in "frontier justice," for it was the goal of every Mountie to maintain a certain professional distance from those in his jurisdiction. However, it may be relevant that Sergeant Hare had been in charge of the town police station for some time before the incident. It is possible that he may have closed some of the distance between himself and the locals, and thus became "of" the community, as well as being "in" it. In his report on the suicide of Charles Gillies, Deane mentioned that "Sergeant Hare had occasion to see him [Gillies] and talk to him in the afternoon [that he committed suicide] and noticed nothing unusual in him."[44] Possibly Hare felt some guilt over Gillies' death and had tried to absolve it by taking part in the tarring and feathering of James Donaldson. Based on the evidence, however, any conclusions about Sergeant Hare's motives are pure speculation.

Most of the time, "the police view of what was important coincided with that of the public."[45] In this case, whether or not the Mounties agreed with the public, they were forced to prosecute, and the manner in which they handled it was in itself revealing. It showed that the Mounties attempted to maintain both law and order as much as possible, and worked in a spirit of compromise to make the best of situations where this was not possible. Knowing all too well the harsh realities of pioneer life, they tried to make their lives, and the lives of those around them, as peaceable as possible. Where morality was concerned, the police were often reluctant to enforce the law, and often compromised in favour of maintaining order. Indeed, "selective perception and enforcement is apparent in [the entire] history of the North-West Mounted Police."[46]

NOTE

This chapter was first published in *Alberta History* 43, no. 2 (spring 1995), 16-24. Illustrations in the original have been omitted. The author wishes to acknowledge the assistance of Professor William M. Baker, University of Lethbridge, in editing this manuscript.

---

43   Macleod, 1976, 115.
44   Deane to Commissioner, February 14, 1895, op. cit.
45   Macleod, 1976, 129.
46   Ibid, 114.

SECTION C

Social Issues

NINE

The NWMP and Minority Groups

R.C. Macleod

One of the most important criteria for assessing the claims of a society to have established social justice is the way in which it treats its minorities. If there is justice for those who lack the power to demand it effectively there is justice for all. If some are oppressed by others the entire social fabric is weakened. Not all minorities are powerless, of course. The rich, as Sir John A. Macdonald pointed out during the Confederation debates, are also a minority. But the rich normally have little trouble protecting their own interests. Other minority groups vary widely in their ability to manipulate the institutions of society and government to their own advantage. In nineteenth-century Canada minority groups ranged all the way from the native peoples who were virtually defenceless to the settler from the United States who was almost indistinguishable from his Canadian counterpart.

The first question which arises in considering minority groups in the North-West Territories in the last third of the nineteenth century is, which groups fall into this category? Even settlers from eastern Canada were not a majority in numerical terms. On the other hand the Canadian element in the population thought of themselves as a majority and with good reason since the North-West, however isolated, was only part of a larger whole. The settler from the United Kingdom was much the same, acting always on the assumption that the Canadian North-West was his birthright, an assumption shared by the Canadian government, which regarded British settlers and those from eastern Canada as equally desirable. The American settler, although on the whole even better adapted to life in the Canadian West than the British immigrant, does not qualify as part of the majority. What made the Americans a minority group was their political outlook, or at least what Canadians generally assumed that outlook to be. In the view of the authorities American settlers needed to undergo a process of Canadianization before they were fully acceptable.

Immigrants from continental European countries were clearly minorities, readily identifiable as such by their language and customs. Like the Americans they were officially regarded as good settler material, able to take their place with the majority after a period of tutelage. Indians and Métis were a minority group after about 1885 and were even more easily identifiable than the Europeans but much less amenable to assimilation. The final important minority group in the North-West in this period was organized labour, obviously a different kind of group from the others but at least as foreign to the generality of the rural population and in many ways the least powerful segment of the population.

The police treated all these minorities differently from the rest of the population, indeed there was a different approach for every group. This did not mean that the ideal of equality before the law was abandoned, nor did it mean that the powerless suffered from official discrimination. Differential treatment was based in part on the recognition that some minorities had disabilities and was intended rather to protect them than oppress them. In part also differential treatment grew out of the primary preoccupation of the Mounted Police with the maintenance of order and compliance with the law. Not to have recognized that outsiders had different concepts of the citizen and his relationship with the state would not only have been unrealistic but would have operated to the disadvantage of most minorities. The police tried to ensure that in the long run social stability in the North-West would be the product of a concensus on Canadian ideas of law and order.

The native peoples of the North-West Territories, Indians and Métis, became a minority in the years following the completion of the Canadian Pacific Railway in 1885. Up to this point they had been the primary concern of the police. Once they ceased to be a major threat to the advance of settlement there was a subtle shift in the attitude of the police which gave rise to some changes in policy. The relationship after 1885 was no longer the old one of mutual respect as exemplified by Colonel Macleod and Chief Crowfoot. Now the relationship was paternal, with the Indians protected and pitied but not respected.[1] There was less emphasis on persuasion and co-operation and more on coercion. A sign of the times was a General Order issued in 1890 which instructed all detachments not to allow Indian prisoners out of the guardroom without ball and chain.[2] This precaution was reiterated in the 1895 edition of *General Orders for the North-West Mounted Police,* along with instructions to avoid feeding Indian prisoners at hotels and restaurants if at all possible.[3]

The police were also more willing to go along with the occasionally rather high-handed methods of the Indian agents. In 1888 Herchmer wrote to the commissioner of Indian affairs asking for stricter controls on Indians leaving reservations near Calgary. "If the same stringent rules administered to the Northern Indians about leaving their Reservations were issued by your Department in the South, the NWMP are now in a position to rigidly enforce them without danger to the general peace of the country."[4] In 1903 the agent on the Peigan reserve sentenced a recalcitrant brave to two months' imprisonment. This action was technically illegal since the agent only had the authority to commit for trial. The police continued to hold the prisoner at the request of the Indian Department while the agent altered the documents in the case.[5]

This changed approach represented a concession on the part of the police to popular prejudices against the Indians. There can be no doubt that most settlers, and indeed many members of the police, regarded Indians as inferior beings to be tolerated only as long as they stayed out of the way. A freighter by the name of William

---

1   This phenomenon in the relations between whites and non-whites in the British Empire generally is explored at length in Christine Bolt, *Victorian Attitudes to Race* (Toronto 1971).
2   Public Archives of Canada (PAC), RG 18, B-4, vol. 7, General Order No. 4640 (new series), 21 January 1890.
3   RCMP Museum, Regina, *Revised General Orders for the North-West Mounted Police,* 1895, 17.
4   PAC, RG 18, A-1, vol. 25, no. 900, Herchmer to Commissioner of Indian Affairs, 12 November 1888.
5   PAC, RG 18, A-1, vol. 256, no. 410.

Wallace Clarke, snowbound in the Touchwood Hills in the winter of 1875, had the leisure to record his feelings about the Indians. "There is horror and loathing in the very thought that the miserable, ragged, filthy, crawling wretch of an Indian papoose or even its parent should sit in the same heaven with us."[6] In 1888 Constable Simons of the Mounted Police was accused of giving some iodine to an Indian woman who drank it and died from the effects. In his report on the case, Simons's commanding officer wrote: "Simons has retained Mr Haultain for his defence, but I do not think any Western jury will convict him."[7]

In another case Superintendent Deane dismissed charges of intoxication brought against a constable by an Indian scout. He explained his reasons for doing so to the commissioner. "Ever since Mr F.W. Haultain told me of the true circumstances attending the conviction of John Bush here in 1884, I, in common with others, have hesitated to convict a white man on the unsupported testimony of an Indian."[8] Colonel Macleod as magistrate had once ruled it illegal to arrest Indians at a sun dance, on the analogy of a church.[9] A few years later Superintendent Steele made the following report on the same subject.

> I regret very much to say that permission has been granted to the Bloods and Piegans to hold a Sun Dance. It is a relic of barbarism that should be stamped out once and forever. I am convinced that the present generation of Indians have absorbed sufficient civilization and Christianity to render the ceremonies accompanying the Sun Dance a burlesque. It still, however, has power to excite the Indians and takes them away from their legitimate occupations of farming and inflames the young bucks with a desire for glory that can no longer be gratified, but finds vent in cattle killing and horse stealing.[10]

Logic was never one of Sam Steele's strong points but his report gives an indication of the shift in attitudes.

Examples of popular prejudice against the Indian could be multiplied many times. It is scarcely surprising that the attitudes of the police should have moved in the same direction. What is more significant is how few changes actually took place in relations between the police and the Indians. A strong element of sympathy along with the responsibility to uphold the law ensured that the force would maintain its role as protector of the tribes against the harsher manifestations of white civilization. The Indian Department in an effort to control the movements of their charges had made use of a system of passes issued by agents for Indians who wished to leave the reserve to visit the towns. The pass system was without legal foundation but the police had co-operated with the Indian Department in enforcing it as a matter of mutual convenience. In 1892, however, the subject came up in a conversation between Commissioner Herchmer and some of the Circuit Court judges. Herchmer was advised by the gentlemen of the bench that the pass system was illegal and that if the right of the police to enforce it was challenged in the courts, the police would surely lose. The commissioner at once informed the Indian Department that the police would no longer attempt to order Indians without passes back to their reserves. A

---

6   Public Archives of Saskatchewan, Diary of William Wallace Clarke, 1875.

7   PAC, RG 18, A-1, vol. 24, no. 667, Superintendent P.R. Neale to Herchmer, 17 July 1888.

8   PAC, RG 18, A-1, vol. 181, no. 163, Ft Macleod Monthly Report for November 1900.

9   PAC, RG 18, A-1, vol. 36, no. 817, Superintendent Steele to Herchmer, 12 August 1889.

10   PAC, RG 18, A-1, vol. 55, no. 586, Steele to Herchmer, 23 June 1891.

legal opinion from the government's law officers was also requested.[11] The Indian Department urged the police to continue enforcing the pass regulations on the rather peculiar grounds that the moral responsibilities of the Indian Department transcended treaty obligations.[12] The advice of the law officers was unequivocally opposed to continuation of the practice. A circular immediately went out from Regina directing all officers to refrain from ordering Indians back to the reserves.[13] When the question came up again in later years the position of the force remained the same.[14]

The police were no more inclined after 1885 than they had ever been to give credence to ranchers and settlers who tried to blame the Indians for every missing cow. Complaints of this nature when investigated usually proved to be without foundation.[15] The police also continued to restrain those officials whose zeal to civilize the Indians sometimes outweighed their common sense. Investigating a small fire at the school on the Blood Reserve near Ft Macleod in 1895, Superintendent Steele discovered that the principal of the school was in the habit of locking his pupils in their dormitory at night to prevent them from escaping and returning to their parents. The principal was ordered to cease doing so immediately and was informed that if a child ever died in a fire in such circumstances he would be tried for manslaughter.[16]

The same approach can be seen even more clearly in an incident which took place on a different reservation the same year. An Indian by the name of Standing Buffalo removed his child, a boy named Dominick, from the Industrial School at Qu'Appelle because the child was ill. The principal of the school summoned a Mounted Police constable and asked him to bring the child back, by force if necessary. He also sought to have Standing Buffalo arrested as an example to others on a charge of stealing the boy's clothes, which technically belonged to the government. The constable refused to take any action without consulting his superior officer.[17] The officer, Inspector Charles Constantine, declined both of the principal's requests. After citing some legal grounds for leaving the boy with his parents he went on to say: "Whether these reasons are good or not, it would have been an inhuman act to have taken the boy away, to say nothing of the criminality attached to it should the child have died after his having been taken out in such cold weather."[18] This settled the particular case but not the principle involved. The issue eventually reached the prime minister, with the police arguing that care must be exercised in enforcing the education regulations. New regulations must be introduced gradually, Herchmer wrote, with the preservation of peace and order taking precedence over a narrow interpretation of the rules. "In the

---

11   PAC, RG 18, A-1, vol. 218, no. 763, White to Herchmer, 20 May 1893.

12   Ibid., Hayter Reed to L. Vankoughnet (Deputy Superintendent of Indian Affairs), 5 June 1893.

13   Ibid., Steele to Herchmer, 19 June 1893.

14   Ibid., White to James A. Smart (Deputy Superintendent of Indian Affairs), 17 September 1901; and vol. 273, no. 303, Superintendent J.O. Wilson to Corporal Dubuque, 28 May 1904.

15   PAC, RG 18, A-1, vol. 73, no. 6; and vol. 84, no. 505.

16   PAC, RG 18, A-1, vol. 112, no. 665, Steele to Herchmer, 5 October 1895.

17   PAC, RG 18, A-1, vol. 103, no. 63, Father J. Hugonnard (Principal) to Indian Commissioner, 19 December 1894.

18   Ibid., Constantine to Superintendent Perry, 8 January 1895.

case of the boy Dominick, it appears that he really is sick, and may die, and yet we are called upon to arrest him and send him back to the school, where though no doubt he would receive better attendance and food, yet I think the parents' wishes should be considered in such a case."[19] The affair ended with the prime minister instructing the commissioner to use his discretion in cases of this nature.

In criminal cases involving Indians the police were quite as scrupulous as with any other group. Several instances exist of Indians suspected of murdering whites being released for lack of evidence.[20] When an Indian prisoner being held in a police guardroom managed to get his hands on a revolver and shoot himself, the sergeant responsible was reduced to the ranks and the constable actually guarding the prisoner received a month's hard labour.[21] Inevitably there were cases of discrimination against Indians which were not covered by the laws of the day. The police could not take direct action in such cases but they could and occasionally did bring informal pressure to bear, as in an incident at Calgary in 1898. The annual summer race meet was held that year at Springbank near the city. The committee in charge of organizing the races decided to exclude Indians from participation. Inspector J.O. Wilson reported:

> I protested on behalf of the Indians, whom I considered to be very unjustly treated, and a most short-sighted policy on the part of the stock owners. The bills did not bar Indians or anyone so I could not see how they could deter them. Public opinion, outside of the few horse owners who were no doubt afraid of being beaten, was with me in this matter.[22]

Wilson may well have been right about public opinion but the significant point was that he took the trouble to use his influence to bring it to bear.

However much their attitudes may have changed, the strategy of the police in dealing with the Indians remained constant. They consistently tried to demonstrate to the Indians that the actions of the police towards them were based on a rational system of laws which operated to the benefit of all. Superintendent Deane's approach to the problem of supervising the repatriation of a group of Canadian Crees from the United States illustrates the strategy perfectly. Some seven hundred Crees had been rounded up in Montana by the United States Army and put on trains to Canada. The Indian Department requested a police escort for the Indians on the grounds that the American officials considered it necessary to guard them with a troop of cavalry. Deane provided one man, Inspector Victor Williams, to perform this duty and sent him the following telegram:

> Accompany Indians here on train tomorrow. It is said they are inclined to be troublesome. Remember we have no right to coerce them and the law will hold us responsible for the abuse of its powers. Make no display of force. Do nothing to irritate them. Keep them from leaving the train if possible, but take no step from which you may have to recede. For these reasons I wish you to come without other police.[23]

---

19 Ibid., Herchmer to White, 22 February 1895.
20 PAC, RG 18, A-1, vol. 15, no. 28; and vol. 113, no. 8, Regina Monthly Report for July 1896.
21 PAC, RG 18, A-1, vol. 98, no. 679, Herchmer to White, 21 September 1894.
22 PAC, RG 18, A-1, vol. 143, no. 18, Calgary Monthly Report for July 1898.
23 PAC, RG 18, A-1, vol. 114, no. 25, Lethbridge Monthly Report for June 1896.

The inspector followed his instructions and conducted his charges to their destination without incident. In addition he spotted two suspected murderers in the group and arrested them. Deane, who was irritated by the attitude of the Indian Department to begin with, commented: "The Indians must be duller than we take them for, if they cannot appreciate the difference between moral coercion under the Union Jack and physical force under the Stars and Stripes."[24]

The Mounted Police employed some Indians and Métis as scouts and special constables. The name of the famous Métis scout, Jerry Potts, is known to anyone who has read anything of the history of the force. There were many others like him who served the police loyally for a pittance. These scouts and specials were strictly casual employees, even those like Jerry Potts who served continuously for twenty years or more. The police could not have done without these men and yet they received a fraction of the pay and none of the pensions or other privileges enjoyed by regular constables. In the early years scouts and interpreters were essential to maintain good relations with the Indians. In later years Indian special constables were hired to perform routine tasks during periods in which there was a shortage of regular constables.

Sir John A. Macdonald had originally intended to recruit substantial numbers of Indians and Métis into the force on the model of the British Army in India.[25] This plan was abandoned, presumably because of the Métis part in the 1870 rebellion. Nothing further was heard about hiring either group as permanent members of the police until 1891, when the Deputy Superintendent-General of Indian Affairs, Lawrence Vankoughnet, wrote to White and suggested that more Indians be employed by the police. He pointed out that the United States Army had successfully made use of Indians as soldiers.[26] White rejected the suggestion on the grounds that the police had found the Indians unwilling to stay with a job over an extended period of time. Hiring Indians would also mean establishing their families in the vicinity of posts. "The placing of a troop of Indians in the neighbourhood of a Police Post for drill and instruction, with their squaws, children, ponies, dogs and camp outfit, would be a source of much inconvenience and anxiety."[27] The matter was dropped and did not come up again.

During the South African War a situation arose which indicated that there were additional unstated reasons for White's lack of enthusiasm for the idea. When the police were recruiting in the North-West for the Canadian contingents and later for the South African Constabulary, a considerable number of Métis wanted to serve.[28] Herchmer asked White's opinion about enlisting them and received the following reply:

> This is a matter in which you must exercise your own discretion. You could not engage them as Half-Breeds, but any who are intelligent, educated and would pass as white

---

24 Ibid.
25 PAC, Macdonald Papers, vol. 516, Macdonald to William McDougall, 12 December 1869.
26 PAC, RG 18, A-1, vol. 61, no. 170, Vankoughnet to White, 12 December 1891.
27 Ibid., White to Vankoughnet, 18 February 1892.
28 PAC, RG 18, A-1, vol. 179, no. 106, Inspector F.J.A. Demers (Battleford) to Herchmer, 12 January 1900; vol. 180, no. 114, White to Herchmer, 29 December 1899; and vol. 207, no. 210, Prince Albert Monthly Report for January 1901.

men could be taken on the same as other applicants. It would be a mistake to accept men who would be known in the force as Half-Breeds; therefore only those who would be treated as equals by the rest of the Contingent should be engaged.[29]

The same considerations undoubtedly lay behind the reluctance of the police to recruit among the native peoples for their own service. Race was a factor to be considered because it correlated with the class ideas which were so important to the force.

Indian and Métis scouts and special constables continued to be used as the occasion demanded. They were unarmed and did not enjoy the same powers of arrest as regular constables.[30] On a few occasions Indians who were acquainted with or related to an Indian suspect were used by the police to detain or capture him so as to avoid arousing his suspicions. The murderer George Godin was captured in this way at Stony Plain in 1888 by four Indian special constables.[31] Bad Young Man (or Charcoal), a Blood who murdered one of his own tribe and then killed Sergeant Wilde of the police, was apprehended by his two brothers in 1897.[32] On rare occasions when the police were very shorthanded Indian special constables were used to carry out regular patrols and even detachment duty.[33] This was a last resort, however, undertaken with great reluctance because the police, like almost everyone else, believed that Indians were unreliable and because the public disliked the idea.

European immigrants evoked a different set of responses from the police. Those European settlers who took up individual homesteads were treated by the police as part of the majority, that is they received no special attention. Those who settled in groups or colonies as they were called at the time usually had a police detachment established in their community as soon as it was founded. If possible the police would select a man who spoke the language for this duty; if none were available an interpreter was hired.[34] Sometimes these detachments were set up as a result of pressure from other settlers in the surrounding districts, who frequently harboured dire suspicions about anyone with a foreign accent. If no such request was forthcoming the police would establish a detachment anyway, since they were not themselves immune from these prejudices. As the great influx of settlers was beginning in the 1890s Herchmer raised the question in a letter to White. "I would draw your attention to the very mixed nationalities of the other settlers now coming in, many of them from countries with very meagre ideas of right and wrong from our standpoint."[35]

The detachments in the various colonies proved to have very little to do in the way of actual law enforcement. With one exception the police found European immigrants less prone to break the law than the general population.[36] Reports on

---

29 PAC, RG 18, A-1, vol. 180, no. 114, White to Herchmer, 27 December 1899.

30 PAC, RG 18, A-1, vol. 261, no. 888, White to F. Bopp (German Consul at Ottawa), 28 December 1903.

31 PAC, RG 18, A-1, vol. 26, no. 48.

32 PAC, RG 18, A-1, vol. 127, no. 20.

33 PAC, RG 18, A-1, vol. 125, no. 605, Herchmer to White, 4 November 1896; and vol. 181, no. 63, Ft Macleod Monthly Report for May 1900.

34 PAC, RG 18, A-1, vol. 74, no. 68; vol. 126, no. 6; vol. 165, no. 193; vol. 167, no. 224; and vol. 257, no. 512.

35 PAC, RG 18, A-1, vol. 74, no. 68, Herchmer to White, 13 January 1893.

36 The exception was the Sons of Freedom sect of the Doukhobours, whose defiance of the law was religiously inspired and consisted of destroying their own property and parading in the nude.

German settlements were highly favourable.[37] The same was true of the Mennonites, who might have been suspect because of the resistance of some sects to public education. The Ukrainian settlers also impressed the police. Superintendent Sévère Gagnon, after visiting a Ukrainian settlement in Saskatchewan, reported that they were exceedingly poor and that many were having difficulty adapting to the farming techniques necessary on the prairies. "They are, however, frugal, industrious and certainly the best workers in the country. It is believed by many that they will eventually form the best settlers of the District. They are anxious to learn the English language."[38]

The fact that the police did establish detachments and get to know these groups at first hand proved a boon to all parties. In one case a settler near Qu'Appelle by the name of D. Henry Starr wrote an angry letter to the minister of the interior accusing some German colonists who lived nearby of stealing hay from him. Warming to his task, he went on to say that the Germans "have turned out to be the very worst and lowest class of people under the sun, and who are considered quite a nuisance, and ought to be banished from the country otherwise they will be the means of driving every respectable settler out of the place."[39] A corporal was dispatched at once to investigate and discovered that all Starr's ideas were based on hearsay; he had not talked to any of the Germans since their arrival in the community. After the corporal had finished his questioning Starr admitted that there was no shred of evidence to connect the Germans with the theft. In forwarding the report to Ottawa the officer in charge of the case appended his own views. "I might add that our experience of German settlers in the different parts of the North West points to the fact that they are law-abiding and good citizens and cause the police little trouble."[40]

A similar incident happened some years later at the Ukrainian settlement of Edna near Edmonton. The Member of Parliament for Edmonton, Frank Oliver, never one to be overly concerned with factual accuracy, wrote the police demanding that a detachment be established in the community at once. The English-speaking settlers were tired of the Ukrainians' thievery and would soon take the law into their own hands, Oliver said, adding that a smallpox epidemic had broken out in the community.[41] The police investigated at once. The smallpox epidemic turned out to be two cases of measles. No one could be found who had actually experienced theft from any source, but rumours of the larcenous propensities of the Ukrainians abounded. Inspector J.O. Wilson, who investigated the complaints, reported that both English-speaking and Ukrainian settlers were strongly in favour of a detachment being established. He urged that this be done at once to prevent rumour from getting out of hand in the future. For the Ukrainian settlers he had only praise as law-abiding and hard-working individuals.[42]

Police detachments established in new settlements like the one mentioned above spent the greater part of their time helping the settlers adjust to their new life. Many

---

37   PAC, RG 18, A-1, vol. 41, no. 339, report on a German colony near Medicine Hat.
38   PAC, RG 18, A-1, vol. 172, no. 426, Gagnon to Herchmer, 15 May 1899.
39   PAC, RG 18, A-1, vol. 97, no. 587, Starr to F.M. Daly (minister of the interior), 17 July 1894.
40   Ibid., Superintendent McIlree to White, 16 August 1894.
41   PAC, RG 18, A-1, vol. 172, no. 438, Frank Oliver to White, 1 and 8 June 1899.
42   Ibid., Wilson to Superintendent Griesbach, 21 June 1899.

of the new arrivals were inadequately equipped and the police distributed relief supplies.[43] On at least one notable occasion concern for the welfare of an immigrant community brought the police into conflict with the Department of the Interior, whose immigration agents were responsible for the well-being of new settlers. The incident began with a report in August 1897 from a Mounted Police corporal stationed at a Ukrainian settlement east of Edmonton. The corporal reported truly terrible conditions among the newly arrived settlers there. Many of them were starving, sick, and unable to find work so that they could buy tools and seed grain. The corporal asked for permission to issue relief supplies.[44] The report was forwarded to the Department of the Interior in Ottawa. The Department demanded an immediate explanation from the local immigration agent. The agent visited the settlement, reported no sickness or deprivation, and accused the police of encouraging idleness among the settlers by offering relief supplies.[45] After some months this report was forwarded to police headquarters along with a not very subtle suggestion that they should mind their own business.

The police, who had no particular axe to grind, were stung by the implied assertion that a member of the force had falsified his report and was intent upon subsidizing laziness. Inspector P.C.H. Primrose was sent to recheck the situation. He submitted a report which was a model of clarity and circumstantial detail, as opposed to that of the immigration agent which was couched entirely in generalities. The inspector's report, based on interviews with all thirty-five destitute families mentioned in Corporal Butler's original report, is one of the best descriptions anywhere of the difficulties encountered by immigrant groups in the harsh environment of the Canadian West. It leaves no room for doubt about the accuracy of the original police report.

Primrose discovered that the immigration agent, Sutter, had visited only a few of the more well-to-do families in the settlement. Sutter had suggested that those who claimed to be starving were hiding their food but Primrose rejected this idea. The houses he found were invariably one-room sod huts which were simply too small to hide anything. Only two of these huts had floors and only four had stoves. A majority of the families had only the light summer clothing they wore on their backs, their baggage having been lost on the long journey to Canada. None of the families had blankets, only one had meat, and the most food Primrose found in any house was three bags of flour. The inspector did not say so but his description of the physical appearance of the children makes it clear that many were suffering from severe malnutrition. As for the accusation of idleness, Primrose found that all men who were able had worked during the fall but most had not been paid by the farmers who employed them. If any further proof were needed about the deplorable conditions in the settlement, six people out of the group of thirty-five families had died since Corporal Butler's report four months earlier.[46] One would be happy to be able to relate that the Department of the Interior admitted its error and corrected all the

---

43 PAC, RG18, A-1, vol. 141, no. 545, White to Secretary of Department of the Interior, 5 October 1897.
44 PAC, RG 18, A-1, vol. 146, no. 96, Corporal Butler to Superintendent Griesbach, 28 August 1897.
45 Ibid., C.W. Sutter (immigration agent, Edmonton) to C.W. McCreary (Department of the Interior), 27 September 1897.
46 Ibid., Primrose to Superintendent Griesbach, 7 January 1898.

abuses, but this was not the case. Instead the police were ordered out of all Ukrainian settlements and did not get back in for several years.[47] Nevertheless, the mere existence of the police provided a valuable force for keeping nativist feelings among both government officials and the public in check.

It should be noted that the police attitudes described above applied to immigrants who settled on the land. Quite a different view of those in urban areas prevailed. In this period there was only one substantial urban group of European immigrants in the North-West Territories. Winnipeg was attracting thousands but it was outside the jurisdiction of the police. Only in Lethbridge, where there were large numbers of coal miners from eastern Europe, did recognizable immigrant groups exist in an urban setting. The miners were generally seen by the police as consisting of two groups: Hungarians and the blanket category of Slavs, or "Sclavs" as Superintendent Deane insisted on spelling it. These people were regarded by the police solely as a problem in law enforcement, without any of the sympathy present in dealings with their rural counterparts. It was taken for granted that the Hungarians and Slavs would live in crowded, filthy conditions, get drunk often, and occasionally murder each other.[48] Evidence was difficult to acquire in such cases because of the clannishness of these groups and their unwillingness to talk to outsiders. The police made no special effort to penetrate these barriers except in one instance when a rumour arose that a secret society, similar to the Mafia, existed among the Hungarians. A constable who spoke Magyar was brought in but failed to uncover any further details.[49]

Generally speaking, relations between the police and European immigrants were healthy. The presence of the police and their positive attitude had a calming effect on the majority of the population. At the minimum the police prevented outright conflict between ethnic groups. In a substantial number of cases they offered the kind of assistance which made adjustment easier. One group, however, was an exception to this rule. The police could neither understand nor effectively come to terms with the radical Sons of Freedom sect of the Doukhobours. Nude parades and farm burning in the name of religion had no place in the mental equipment of the average Mounted Policeman. When the Doukhobours failed to respond to the same approach that succeeded with other European groups the police were at a loss. They could not come up with any creative solution to the problem of the Doukhobours and fell back on mass arrests of all who violated existing laws.[50] After several of these, one optimistic officer wrote: "The Doukhobour question is now finally and satisfactorily settled and I fully believe that they will make excellent settlers."[51] What he was witnessing was the beginning, not the end, of a series of confrontations between the sect and the Mounted Police which was to last for almost seventy years.

The police reacted to settlers from the United States in much the same manner

---

47   The police did not have a detachment in this particular settlement again until 1901. PAC, RG 18, A-1, vol. 208, no. 213, Ft Saskatchewan Monthly Report for June 1901. The incident is described in more detail in Vladimir J. Kaye, *Early Ukrainian Settlements in Canada 1895-1900* (Toronto 1964) 322-37.

48   PAC, RG 18, A-1, vol. 49, no. 192, Lethbridge Monthly Report for February 1892.

49   PAC, RG 18, A-1, vol. 63, no. 247, Lethbridge Monthly Report for February 1892.

50   PAC, RG 18, A-1, vol. 295, no. 263.

51   PAC, RG 18, A-1, vol. 247, no. 101, Regina Monthly Report for February 1903 (Inspector A.R. Cuthbert).

as to European settlers but for different reasons. The prevailing attitudes to Americans were ambivalent. On the one hand they were regarded as the most desirable type of settler since they tended to be relatively well off and had no trouble adapting to the agricultural practices of the Canadian West.[52] On the other hand the police considered Americans to be even more in need of tutelage in the Canadian way of life than were Europeans. Americans were a more insidious threat simply because they adapted so easily. Although there is little evidence in the police records to support the belief, the police were convinced that all Americans were the potential bearers of anarchy, disorder, and violence. Commissioner Perry was merely expressing the view of the force as a whole when he wrote the following passage in a letter to White in 1903. "I suppose that the peace of the Territories may seem assured to those who are in the East, and even to the people of the Territories who are accustomed to it. They little know of the reckless class of American outlaws to the South of us."[53] This view prevailed in spite of many personal friendships between officers and Americans and constant friendly co-operation with United States law enforcement agencies. It was a fundamental part of the Canadian national myth and therefore not susceptible to rational analysis.[54]

The police arrived in the North-West with very definite ideas about Americans and American society. Early contacts were confined mainly to whisky traders and deserters from the United States Army; men who tended to reinforce the stereotypes. The police were constant and interested observers of the American scene across the border to the south. The only observations which registered, however, were those which provided opportunities to compare the quality of American life unfavourably with that of Canada. The police records are filled with lurid accounts of lynchings, mob violence, and general lawlessness garnered from American newspapers, hearsay, and observation of border towns. Sergeant G.W. Byrne, travelling in Montana on the trail of some cattle stolen in Canada, reported that he had been forced to pass himself off as a merchant because the town to which he traced the stolen cattle was controlled by a gang of thieves. "I might state here that the town of Culbertson consists of two stores, two gambling saloons, one boarding house and a couple of houses of ill fame. There are about 20 cowboys or horse thieves and gamblers who take turns watching our every movement, and immediately one of us leaves the town scouts are sent out in all directions to give the alarm."[55] Perhaps an even better illustration of police attitudes is to be found in the following comments by A. Bowen Perry, then a superintendent:

> The detachment stationed at Sterling, the new town on the Boundary on the Soo R'way did good service in keeping the peace. The track laying gang on the American side was accompanied by a number of whisky sellers, gamblers and prostitutes. S/Sgt. McGinnis' report, which I have forwarded you, relates that great disorder prevailed on the American side; serious rows, drunkenness and debauchery. On our side there was no trouble of any kind.[56]

---

52 PAC, RG 18, A-1, vol. 229, no. 156, Prince Albert Monthly Report for April 1902. Refers to American settlers as "the best class obtainable."

53 PAC, RG 18, A-1, vol. 274, no. 353, Perry to White, 17 October 1903.

54 The best discussion of this phenomenon is in S.F. Wise and Robert Craig Brown, *Canada Views the United States: Nineteenth Century Political Attitudes* (Seattle 1967).

55 PAC, RG 18, A-1, vol. 168, no. 241, Sergeant Byrne to Superintendent Howe, 12 March 1899.

56 PAC, RG 18, A-1, vol. 76, no. 161, Regina Monthly Report for August 1893.

It followed from these assumptions that if disorder existed in the North-West Territories it was probably the work of American settlers. The police were not slow to draw this conclusion and on several occasions attributed disturbances to Americans on no better evidence than the presence of American settlers in the neighbourhood. When an angry crowd of trial spectators at Carlyle voiced their disapproval of a liquor conviction by shouting, "To hell with the red coats," Superintendent J.O. Wilson offered the following explanation. "The settlers and residents of Carlyle and Arcola are chiefly Americans, a large proportion of them being single men, who are imbued with the American western idea of law and order, and consequently will have to be taught that they cannot do as they like on this side of the line."[57]

As Wilson's remarks imply, the remedy was as obvious to the police as the complaint. Commissioner Herchmer set forth the approach of the force to Canadian-izing the Americans in a letter to White in 1892:

> A very large immigration, as you are aware, took place last year into the Edmonton country, mostly from the Western States where law and order are not rigidly enforced, and I am credibly informed that the flow this year will greatly exceed all previous seasons, most of the immigrants being drawn from Oregon and Washington States, and it will be necessary to greatly increase our patrols in consequence as the opinion these people form of our administration of the laws on their first arrival, has the greatest possible effect on their future conduct, and inability on our part to impress them with the necessity of strictly obeying our laws, will, in my opinion, be certain to lead to heavy expenses later on in the administration of justice, the cost of which would greatly exceed that of laying a good moral foundation at the start, through the activity and vigilance of the police.[58]

The police reacted most strongly of all to the Mormon settlers who established themselves in southern Alberta in the late 1880s. It was one of the very few occasions upon which the actions of the police appear absurd in retrospect. No doubt it was the question of polygamy which aroused their animosity. Some of the reports indicate that part of the hostility derived from the fact that their religion made the Latter Day Saints more readily identifiable as Americans. When the Mormons arrived the police as was their custom checked out the new settlers. Superintendent Steele submitted a report on the Mormons which was so illogical that it can only be interpreted as the product of unvarnished prejudice. After confiding to Herchmer his suspicions that the Mormon settlers were continuing the practice of polygamy, Steele noted that the other settlers in the area disliked the new arrivals and continued:

> The intelligence of the Mormons is far below the average of the settlers of any country; there are some sharp, shrewd men among them at the head of affairs; but the remainder are, as a rule, steeped in ignorance and as perfect slaves to the Church and Elders as it is possible for any community to be.[59]

Without apparently realizing the contradiction, Steele then went on to state that the Mormons had the most prosperous and successful farms in the district.

After presenting this extraordinary collection of conflicting statements Steele suggested assigning a detective to spy on them. Herchmer was inclined to agree with Steele but fortunately cooler heads prevailed and White rejected the idea.[60] It is

---

57 PAC, RG 18, A-1, vol. 253, no. 304, Wilson to Assistant Commissioner McIlree, 28 February 1903.
58 PAC, RG 18, A-1, vol. 74, no. 68, Herchmer to White, 13 January 1893.
59 PAC, RG 18, A-1, vol. 41, no. 250, Steele to Herchmer, 4 December 1889.
60 Ibid., memo by White, 16 December 1899.

abundantly clear that Steele and Herchmer in this case were reflecting public opinion.[61] Public hostility was so much in evidence that a police corporal reporting on polygamy among the Latter Day Saints felt constrained to explain that he had obtained his information by winning the confidence of highly placed members of the church. "I mention these facts as outsiders have at different times made statements that I was unnecessarily friendly, and I wish no action of mine to be misconstrued with regard to Mormons or Mormonism."[62] Even Superintendent Deane, who got along well with the Mormons and regarded them as solid citizens, disliked the large role the church played in their life.[63]

The police continued to keep a wary eye on the Mormon settlements for years but that was the extent of their involvement. The Mormon communities generally had a member of the church as justice of the peace and ran their own affairs to a very large extent. When bad feeling between Mormons and other settlers surfaced in 1897 the latter asked a local magistrate for permission to carry guns. In spite of their suspicions the police quickly put an end to such notions. The settlers were warned that carrying firearms was illegal and would be punished with the utmost severity.[64] Perhaps because of public hostility the Mormons made a considerable display of celebrating Dominion Day every July first. The police regarded this phenomenon with curiosity since instead of making the Latter Day Saints less conspicuous it only made them more so. Canadians generally tended to be undemonstrative on the occasion. One officer commented: "It is strange how those Mormons start in to celebrate our natal day."[65] The police were more impressed by the fact that schools in Mormon communities made use of American textbooks, "wherein, of course, a hatred of everything English is inculcated."[66] This information was passed on to the Chairman of the Council of Public Instruction for the North-West Territories. Once the hierarchy of the Church of Jesus Christ of the Latter Day Saints suspended the practice of polygamy, public hostility died down but the police, at least until 1905, never accepted the Mormons as fully as they did other groups.

The final minority group to be discussed in this chapter, organized labour, presents a different set of problems than the ethnic minorities. Public attitudes toward labour have changed much more drastically in the last eighty years than toward any other minority. Nineteenth-century labour disputes are almost incomprehensible if approached with an assumption that people thought of them then as they do now. Attitudes to labour in the twentieth century have been polarized very strongly by a whole series of events. The Bolshevik Revolution in Russia and its repercussions elsewhere, for example, have planted the fear of class warfare among the middle and upper classes. On the other hand the successes of organized labour in raising the average standard of living in this century have convinced most union members and many others that the strike is almost entirely beneficial in its effects. These divergent views of labour and its place in society did not exist in nineteenth-century Canada

---

61   For unfavourable press reaction to the LDS see the Calgary *Herald*, 12 December 1889 and 5 January 1890; and the Ft Macleod *Gazette*, 6 February 1890.

62   PAC, RG 18, A-1, vol. 169, no. 305, Corporal Bolderson to Superintendent Deane, 11 March 1899.

63   PAC, RG 18, A-1, vol. 181, no. 163, Ft Macleod Monthly Report for September 1900.

64   PAC, RG 18, A-1, vol. 126, no. 3, Ft Macleod Monthly Report for January 1897.

65   PAC, RG 18, A-1, vol. 250, no. 177, Lethbridge Monthly Report for June 1903 (Inspector J.V. Begin).

66   PAC, RG 18, A-1, vol. 104, no. 131, Lethbridge Monthly Report for July 1895.

outside of a tiny handful of individuals. Instead the whole question of labour-management relations was subsumed under existing concepts of class. The key phrase in 1890 was not labour management relations but master-servant relations. This was the language of the law and of the public when they thought about the question at all.

Thus while the police spent much of their time dealing with problems which arose from labour disputes they did not think of it as a special problem apart from the other problems of maintaining peace and order. The police were not as they often were to be in the twentieth century, forced to commit themselves morally to one side or another. It did not occur to any of the parties involved in labour disputes that the police by intervening could be considered to be helping one class exploit another class. Only one incident which happened at the end of the period under discussion showed the direction in which events were moving. The police were effectively neutral in almost all labour disputes. They acted as honest brokers to the general satisfaction of both sides and as often took the part of labour as of management.

Organized labour was very weak in the Canadian North-West around the turn of the century. Unions were confined almost exclusively to two industries, coal mining and the railways. Even in these industries many workers were unorganized. Strikes were usually local affairs concerned with local grievances. Strike funds and industry-wide bargaining were far in the future. The laws heavily favoured management and barely permitted unions to exist. In the case of an essential service like the railway it was taken for granted that, although the railway unions might strike, they had no right to interfere with strikebreakers hired by the company. During a strike by CPR engineers in 1883 the Mounted Police not only guarded railway property but operated engines when necessary to enable the company to put trains together.[67] Deserting employment was an offence which companies could and sometimes did insist that the police prosecute.[68] Those workers who legally left their jobs because of dissatisfaction with working conditions sometimes faced prosecution for vagrancy.[69] The general attitude of the police was summed up in a report by Commissioner Perry on police operations in connection with a CPR strike in 1901. The police had stepped in twice to prevent violence between scabs and strikers, Perry explained in a letter to White, then offered this comment: "I know that it is difficult in such matters to please both parties. Without taking any part with the strikers it seems to me our duty to enable the railway company to continue its service."[70]

On the whole, however, the police preferred to act as mediators and to prevent disputes from developing into potentially violent situations. In Lethbridge in 1894 the Alberta Railway and Coal Company closed down the mines, locked out the miners, and announced that only one hundred and thirty out of five hundred and eighty would be rehired and these at lower wages. The situation was very tense until Superintendent Deane persuaded the company to offer free transport to Great Falls, Montana, for those out of work. Deane felt the company had handled the situation very badly. He talked to the miners and reported: "I mix freely with them and they will talk to me as one of themselves, in fact the only reliable information that Mr Galt

---

67   PAC, Diary of Inspector R. Burton Deane, 4 October to 30 December 1883.
68   PAC, RG 18, A-1, vol. 64, no. 248, Regina Monthly Reports for September and October 1892.
69   PAC, RG 18, A-1, vol. 113, no. 8, Regina Monthly Report for February 1896.
70   PAC, RG 18, A-1, vol. 217, no. 723, Perry to White, 28 August 1901.

[manager of the company] gets is from me. It is not always palatable, but I cannot help that."[71] The situation eased at once. In his years at Lethbridge Deane settled many similar disputes by the use of such informal procedures, as did other officers at other locations.[72]

Probably the best description of the approach of the police to labour problems is to be found in the reports on police supervision of the construction of the Crow's Nest Pass branch of the CPR in 1897 and 1898. Some five thousand men were employed on the project and the company requested police aid.[73] Two inspectors, G.E. Sanders and A.R. Cuthbert, were assigned to the task along with eight non-commissioned officers and constables. Since part of the construction was in British Columbia, arrangements were made with the government of that province to have the officers appointed magistrates in British Columbia.[74] Sanders and Cuthbert soon found themselves inundated by work. By December 1897 Inspector Sanders was handling twenty to thirty complaints a day in his capacity as magistrate. He was forced to stop dealing with most of them through the court and resort to less formal methods of settling disputes.[75]

Since almost all the complaints were from employees, the police spent much of their time trying to pressure the CPR and its sub-contractors into improving working conditions and behaving reasonably toward the men. Most of the workers had been hired in eastern Canada, many under false presences, as Inspector Sanders reported:

> There is no doubt whatever that a great number of these men would never have come out here had they known they had to pay their fare, which from Ottawa here at a cent a mile is $22.49. These men have families in the East and when they discover that after working six weeks or two months there is not a cent coming to them, or more probably they are in debt to the contractors, that they have no money to send to their families and that they have nothing themselves, they as a rule leave that particular employer and wander around destitute, without blankets or even boots in some cases, looking for other work, and people have had to supply them with food and in some instances I have had to do so, also giving them a night's lodging.
>
> Where the men have clearly understood their agreement in the East that they have had to pay their railway fare, we have endeavoured to make them stick to their contract. But where they were evidently brought up under false presences we have, as Magistrates, when the cases came up before us discharged them from their contracts.[76]

The police did their best to prevent the CPR and the contractors from using the law to defraud the workers. On many occasions a contractor would simply refuse to pay wages owed. The men would then sue and usually won a favourable judgement from the magistrate. What happened next in one typical case was described by Sanders. The contractor immediately appealed the magistrate's ruling and the men had to wait, out of work and penniless. "They could not hang around without money so we got another contractor, Mr. Buchanan, to employ them until Nov. 11."[77] The

---

71 PAC, RG 18, A-1, vol. 91, no. 148, Lethbridge Monthly Report for February 1894.
72 PAC, RG 18, A-1, vol. 127, no. 5; vol. 209, no. 235; vol. 225, no. 84.
73 PAC, RG 18, A-1, vol. 145, no. 56, G. Drinkwater (secretary of CPR) to White, 7 September 1897.
74 Ibid., White to Drinkwater, 14 September 1897.
75 PAC, RG 18, A-1, vol. 126, no. 3, Ft Macleod Monthly Report for December 1897.
76 PAC, RG 18, A-1, vol. 145, no. 56, Sanders to Superintendent Deane, 23 October 1897.
77 Ibid., Sanders to Deane, 30 October 1897.

CPR responded by pressuring Buchanan into firing them. Sanders was indignant. "This proceeding, after everything had been arranged amicably pending the Judge's decision, and after the decision of the Magistrate's court, was, to say the least, certainly foolish on the part of the CPR, and practically meant interference with the course of justice."[78] Sanders protested vigorously to the CPR officials, who grudgingly offered the men work:

> The Management of Construction have been given to understand that we recognize the difficulties we have to contend with in controlling such a large body of men and the great necessity on their part to retain the upper hand, but at the same time it has been pointed out that any injustice or attempt to interfere with the due course of the law would be stopped.[79]

In addition to adjudicating countless other disputes, the police checked and reported on shortcomings in other areas such as the provision of housing and medical care.[80] There were no strikes on the Crow's Nest Pass construction project, a fact which even the CPR construction boss admitted was due almost entirely to the tact and influence of the police.[81]

In 1905 the police encountered a situation which indicated that the old order in labour relations was passing. Unions were beginning to use the law to fight back. This meant that a whole new set of problems was appearing which would make the old approach used by the police obsolete. The incident began with a letter to a member of parliament from a solicitor, L.P. Eckstein, acting on behalf of District Eighteen of the United Mine Workers of America. Eckstein asked for an investigation into reports that the Mounted Police had summarily evicted sixteen men from houses owned by the West Canadian Coal Company.[82] The investigation requested was held immediately by the police.

According to the report of Corporal S.J. Kemby, who was involved in the incident, he had received a telephone call from the mine manager asking for police assistance. The manager explained that he intended to fire eleven men and feared violence. The corporal and a constable went to the mine. Once there they were informed by the manager that he planned to evict the men from their company houses on two hours' notice. The corporal replied that he would have nothing to do with the eviction proceedings but would accompany the manager while he was paying the men off in case violence should materialize. None did and the police left soon after.[83]

Copies of the report were sent to Eckstein and the union agreed to drop the matter. The lawyer expressed himself satisfied but added a further comment on the case:

> I suppose if the men had in the exercise of their lawful rights, refused to be thus ejected summarily by Williams, that the Police would have interfered. For my part, I know the record of the Police far too well to think that they would knowingly lend themselves to the commission of an act which was not lawful, and in this instance I

---

78   Ibid.
79   Ibid.
80   PAC, RG 18, A-1, vol. 143, no. 17, Ft Macleod Monthly Report for January 1898.
81   PAC, RG 18, A-1, vol. 156, no. 3, M.J. Haney to Herchmer, 31 October 1898.
82   PAC, RG 18, A-1, vol. 300, no. 517, L.P. Eckstein to W.A. Galliher, MP, 9 June 1905.
83   Ibid., Corporal S.J. Kemby to Inspector Primrose, 14 June 1905.

must advise my clients that the Police are wholly blameless insofar as intention to offend was concerned.[84]

Comptroller White was pleased by this ending to the affair but he also grasped the wider implications. Discussing the case with the member of parliament to whom the complaint had been made, he wrote:

> One of the most delicate parts of Police duty in the North West has been in deciding where their authority begins and ends. We have had many cases where efforts have been made to use the Police Force for the collection of debts recoverable by civil action. Also, as is apparent in the Lille case, an effort to use men in uniform, with all the semblance of the authority of the law, to awe those against whom proceedings have been taken.[85]

The reputation of the force had sustained it but the time would soon arrive when its disinterestedness would not be taken for granted.

The same could be said for all the techniques developed by the police to handle the problems created by minority groups. They were tailored to a society which had definite and strongly held beliefs about the place of minorities in the social order. Almost all these beliefs would be challenged in the decades after 1905. The genius of the Mounted Police lay precisely in the fact that they recognized the realities of their time and place and strove to meet them in a humane way. With few exceptions the police reacted to the difficulties they faced as human beings confronted by human problems. They could do so only because they were entirely confident of their own position in society.

NOTE

This chapter was first published in R.C. Macleod, *The NWMP and Law Enforcement 1873-1905* (Toronto: University of Toronto Press, 1976), pp. 143-161 and 194-198.

---

84 Ibid., Eckstein to Galliher, 24 June 1905.
85 Ibid.

TEN

The Miners and the Mounties: The Royal North-West Mounted Police and the 1906 Lethbridge Strike

William M. Baker

According to John Sewell, Canadian policemen "are talked about as either heroes or bums, and not much in between."[1] Such a depiction hides more than it reveals, because few segments of Canadian society consistently hold to either side of the dichotomy. Indeed, nearly every Canadian has ambivalent views of the police depending, for instance, on whether the police are handing that citizen a speeding ticket or rousting drug dealers loitering around his or her kids' school. It is true, as Talbot *et al.* claim, that "there are probably very few countries in the world where ... citizens have a better relationship with their police than Canada."[2] What other country is symbolized in a positive and humane light by a police force as Canada is by the RCMP?[3] Nevertheless, Canadians share with other peoples a deep-rooted, traditional fear of a body which has been granted a monopoly of the legal use of force against its citizens and have seen or heard of the abuse of that power.[4]

---

1 J. Sewell, *Police: Urban Policing in Canada* (Toronto 1985), 14. The term "police" itself is not easily defined and thus, as D.H. Bayley has put it "the boundaries of a history of the police are both ambiguous and arbitrary, depending on definitions of the word police" (Bayley, "Police: History," in S.H. Kadish, ed., *Encyclopedia of Crime and Justice* (New York 1983), 1120. As used in this paper the term refers to persons employed by the various levels of government and authorized by them to maintain order and enforce laws. Thus, the military is included, as well as more conventional policing forces. For other useful encyclopedia discussions of the term see M. Punch, "Police," in A. and J. Kuper, eds., *The Social Science Encyclopedia* (London 1985), 604-5; D.J. Bordua, "Police," in D.L. Sills, ed., *International Encyclopedia of the Social Sciences* (n.c. 1968), vol. 12, 174-81; B. Smith, "Police," and W.H. Hamilton and C.C. Rodee, "Police Power," and H.B. Davis, "Policing, Industrial," all in E.R.A. Seligman and A. Johnson, eds., *Encyclopedia of the Social Sciences* (New York 1934), XII, 183-96; and C.D. Shearing and P.C. Stenning, "Police," and D. Forcese, "Policing," both in J.H. Marsh, ed., *The Canadian Encyclopedia* (Edmonton 1985), III, 1439-41.

2 C.K.Talbot, C.H.S. Jayewardene and T.J. Juliani, *Canada's Constables: The Historical Development of Policing in Canada* (Ottawa 1985), v.

3 On the positive image of the Mounties, see K. Walden, *Visions of Order: The Canadian Mounties in Symbol and Myth* (Toronto 1982); R.C. Macleod, *The North-West Mounted Police and Law Enforcement 1873-1905* (Toronto 1976), ix; and C. Betke, "Pioneers and Police on the Canadian Prairies, 1885-1914," *Canadian Historical Association Historical Papers* (1980), 9-32.

4 Many sources comment on the fear aroused at the time of the introduction of police forces and

Perhaps this ambivalence is shared by academic historians in Canada, but despite the obvious importance of the police, historical assessments of Canadian society have devoted little attention to police history. Beyond the few studies of the Mounties, such as those by Macleod and Walden, academic historians have left police history a virtual *tabula rasa* in Canada. Indeed, the only reasonably comprehensive history of Canadian policing was prepared by three members of the University of Ottawa's Department of Criminology.[5]

The disinterest of Canadian historians in the police has meant that leading journals have carried few articles or reviews related to police history. Readers of *Canadian Historical Review, Labour/Le Travail, Histoire sociale/Social History, Urban History Review and Acadiensis* from 1981 to 1989 were presented with but three articles and one research note devoted wholly or significantly to Canadian police history, most by the same author.[6] Of a sample of seven books on police history which one might have expected to see evaluated in the above journals only two were reviewed.[7]

---

discuss the gradual reduction of this fear, but given the constant and frightening examples of the use of policing forces throughout the world, it is doubtful that fear of the police can ever be completely eradicated from the public consciousness. See T.A. Critchley, *A History of Police in England and Wales 900-1966* (London 1967), xiii; H. Pelling, *Popular Politics and Society in Late Victorian Britain* (London 1968), 69; J.H. Skolnick, *Justice Without Trial: Law Enforcement in Democratic Society* (New York 1966), 1; Walden, *Visions of Order*, 33 and 77; R.D. Storch, "The Policeman as Domestic Missionary: Urban Discipline and Popular Culture in Northern England, 1850-1880," *Journal of Social History*, 9 (1975-6), 481.

5 Talbot *et al.*, *Canada's Constables*. At first blush this work, which is based on the authors' *The Thin Blue Line: An Historical Perspective of Policing in Canada* (Ottawa 1983), appears to be an apologia. The authors received a contract from the Canadian Police College and the introduction to the earlier work contains the following: "it is to these early unsung heroes that this book is dedicated, for it is to their credit that the thin blue line still holds quite magnificently today" (v). Yet the content of the book is by no means uncritical of the police. Perhaps the preface was mere window-dressing to pacify the sponsor.

6 Greg Marquis seems to be one of the few Canadian historians actively pursuing the topic. His publications demonstrate not only an awareness of police historiography outside the country but also a fine sensitivity to the nuances of documentary evidence. See G. Marquis, "'A Machine of Oppression Under the Guise of the Law': The Saint John Police Establishment," *Acadiensis*, 16 (1986), 58-77; G. Marquis, "Working Men in Uniform: The Early Twentieth-century Toronto Police," *Histoire sociale/Social History*, 40 (1987), 259-77; and G. Marquis, "The Contours of Canadian Urban Justice, 1830-1875," *Urban History Review*, 15 (1987), 269-73. The other article was T. Thorner and N.B. Watson, "Keeper of the King's Peace: Colonel G.E. Sanders and the Calgary Police Magistrate's Court, 1911-1932," *Urban History Review*, 12 (1984), 45-55. Additional recent publications in other sources of direct relevance to Canadian police history are N. Rogers, "Serving Toronto the Good: The development of the city police force 1834-84," in V. Russell, ed., *Forging a Consensus: Historical Essays on Toronto* (Toronto 1984), 116-40; T.W. Acheson, *Saint John: The Making of a Colonial Urban Community* (Toronto 1985), 214-29; P. Craven, "Law and Ideology: The Toronto Police Court, 1850-1880," in D. Flaherty, ed., *Essays in the History of Canadian Law*, Volume II (Toronto 1982), 249-307; G. Marquis, "Police Unionism in Early Twentieth-Century Toronto," *Ontario History*, 81 (1989), 109-28; B. Rawling, "Technology and Innovation in the Toronto Police Force, 1875-1925," *Ontario History*, 81 (1989), 53-71; and G. Homel, "Denison's Court: Criminal Justice and the Police Court in Toronto, 1877-1921," *Ontario History*, 73 (1981), 171-84. The focus of many of these articles is on police courts rather than on the man on the beat.

7 The seven books were all published between 1981 and 1985. Six were relatively-prominent, foreign publications: V. Bailey, ed., *Policing and Punishment in Nineteenth Century Britain* (New Brunswick, N.J. 1981); E. Monkkonen, *Police in Urban America, 1860-1920* (New York 1981); S.L. Harring, *Policing a*

Not one of these journals reviewed Talbot *et al.*, *Canada's Constables*.[8] Equally remarkable is the fact that not even *Labour/Le Travail* reviewed Harring's blockbuster, *Policing a Class Society*.

Scholars approaching the history of relations of police and strikers from a police-centred focus have presented a dualistic interpretation of the police. Desmond Morton's influential 1970 *CHR* article[9] established that on numerous occasions the militia had been used for strike duty, and that "the reality of class conflict in Canadian society emerges from the study of aid to the civil power." (424) On the other hand, Morton's account notes that "dramatic incidents of labour strife in the United States had only the palest reflection in Canada," and that the "most violent clash between militiamen and strikers which took place at Valleyfield in October 1900" was really a pretty mild affair. (421) Even at the time of publication, Morton's statistics were problematical since they were simply raw totals of militia involvement, giving no sense of how usual it was for the militia to be involved in strikes, and providing no comparison with the frequency for other countries.[10] In summary, there was an interpretive ambiguity in Morton's article: on the one hand troops had been used to suppress strike agitation, an activity which served the interests of employers; on the other hand this was to be expected at the time and the degree of repression involved was minor.[11]

Class Society: The Experience of American Cities, 1865-1915 (New Brunswick, N.J. 1983); C. Emsley, *Policing and Its Context: 1750-1870* (London 1983); C. Steedman, *Policing the Victorian Community: The Formation of English Provincial Police Forces, 1856-80* (London 1984); R. Geary, *Policing Industrial Disputes: 1839-1985* (London 1985). The seventh was Talbot et al., *Canada's Constables* or their earlier *Thin Blue Line*. Of the seven, Steedman was reviewed by B. Curtis in *Histoire sociale/Social History*, 35 (1985), 193-4 and Geary was reviewed by R. Warburton in *L/LT*, 21 (1988), 293-4. This trend seems to be continuing for, to date, none of the journals has reviewed J. Morgan, *Conflict and Order: The Police and Labour Disputes in England and Wales, 1900-1939* (Oxford 1987). Neither the *CHR* nor *Acadiensis* has a regular review section of non-Canadian books, but both have periodic historiographical or review essays. J. Weaver's review essay "Staying on the Straight and Narrow: Recent Books on Violence, Crime, and the Question of Order in Nineteenth-century Urban America," *L/LT*, 8/9 (1981/82), 296-308, included an evaluation of two books concerning police history.

8   Sewell's *Police* was reviewed by J. Taylor in *Urban History Review*, 14 (1985), 213-4 but in none of the other periodicals.

9   D. Morton, "Aid to the Civil Power: The Canadian Militia in Support of Social Order," *CHR*, 51 (1970), 407-25.

10 It is unclear whether or not the strike involvement of policing authorities in Canada has been comparatively high. The 11 cases of military involvement during 1895-1904 and 17 during 1905-14 seem approximately equivalent in relative terms to the estimate of 118 cases of National Guard intervention in labour conflicts in the U.S.A. during 1885-95 cited in J.M. Cooper, *The Army and Civil Disorder: Federal Military Intervention in Labor Disputes, 1877-1900* (Westport, Conn. 1980), 13. On the other hand, the British military was only called out 24 times in the 39 years before 1908 (Geary, *Policing Industrial Disputes*, 17) whereas in Canada during the same period there were at least 32 military interventions in industrial disputes (J.J.B. Pariseau, *Disorders, Strikes and Disasters: Military Aid to the Civil Power in Canada, 1867-1933* (Ottawa 1973), 78-84).

11 Morton's and Terry Copp's continued involvement in both labour and military history is unusual amongst Canadian historians. Their text, *Working People: An Illustrated History of Canadian Labour* (Ottawa 1980), provides somewhat greater recognition of the role of the police than does B.D. Palmer's *Working-Class Experience: The Rise and Reconstitution of Canadian Labour, 1800-1980* (Toronto 1983). In the index to the Morton and Copp book there are 28 entries under "military forces in aid of the civil power," "police" (excluding "police unions") and "Royal Canadian Mounted Police."

This dualism is evident in the writing of other police historians. In his study of the Mounted Police to 1905, Rod Macleod argued that in most industrial disputes the police were "effectively neutral," operating as "honest brokers to the general satisfaction of both sides and as often took the part of labour as of management." Yet Macleod also asserted that the laws the police were expected to enforce "heavily favoured management and barely permitted unions to exist."[12] S.W. Horrall's article on the Mounties and 1919 demonstrates the covert infiltration and surveillance of labour organizations by the RNWMP, but also suggests that the police actually attempted to cool off the Red Scare hysteria rampant in Ottawa.[13] The survey of Canadian police history by Talbot et al.[14] evinces another type of duality. For these authors, local police forces were usually pro-labour, whereas the Mounties were usually anti-labour.[15] In general, then, the image emerging from the works of historians of Canadian policing agencies is that they occupied an ambiguous position in their relationship with labour.[16]

Recent pronouncements by leading Canadian labour and working-class historians contain few qualifications of the role played by the physical arm of the state. In his review of Craven's *"An Impartial Umpire": Industrial Relations and the Canadian State, 1900-1911*, Ian McKay castigated the author for ignoring the actual or implied state violence which underlay the government's industrial policy.[17] Elsewhere, McKay proclaimed that "Whatever William Lyon Mackenzie King's impenetrable doctrines

---

Palmer's index has six entries under the RCMP but omits the other categories. A non-academic article by Morton helps to clarify his attitude towards the police. In it he declares: "the basis of effective policing ... is the sense that police men and women are our neighbors, sharing our values and our confidence. They are not an army of occupation ... Supporting our local police is more than a bumper-sticker slogan ... It should start with ... human contact ... It should continue with a little hard reflection on the framework of law and punishment in which police officers carry out our responsibilities." The police, therefore, are 'us' — all of us — not 'them.' See D. Morton's column in *The United Church Observer*, New Series, 4, 8 (February 1986), 23.

12 Macleod, *NWMP*, 157.
13 S.W. Horrall, "The Royal North-West Mounted Police and Labour Unrest in Western Canada, 1919," *CHR*, 61 (1980), 169-90.
14 Talbot et al., *Canada's Constables*, 63-4, 116-21, 130-2, 267 and 280-1.
15 The phenomenon of local police being ineffective as an anti-strike force has been noted in both Britain and the United States. In both countries this ineffectiveness has been considered as an important contributor to the use of external policing forces and of centralized authority over policing in strikes. See Morgan, *Conflict and Order*, 148-228; B.C. Johnson, "Taking Care of Labour: The Police in American Politics," *Theory and Society*, 3 (1976), 89-117; H. Gutman, "Class, Status, and Community Power in Nineteenth-Century American Industrial Cities: Paterson, New Jersey: A Case Study" and "Two Lockouts in Pennsylvania 1873-1874," both in his *Work, Culture, and Society in Industrializing America* (New York 1977), 234-60 and 321-43. Harring argues that the examples cited by Johnson and Gutman were anomalies, largely inapplicable after the 1870s (see Harring, *Policing a Class Society*, 102-6). In the Canadian context, Sewell maintains that in 5 of the 6 cases dealt with in I. Abella, ed., *On Strike: Six Key Labour Struggles in Canada, 1919-1949* (Toronto 1974), local police sided with strikers (see Sewell, *Police*, 223).
16 The ambiguity is most explicitly examined in the studies by Marquis as cited earlier. An exception to this interpretation is L. and C. Brown, *An Unauthorized History of the RCMP* (Toronto 1973). They suggest that the Mounties were an absolutely reliable anti-strike force. A brief historiographical account of relations between the RCMP and labour is found in H.C. Klassen, "The Mounties and the Historians," in H.A. Dempsey, ed., *Men in Scarlet* (Calgary 1974), 183-5.
17 *L/LT*, 8/9 (1981/82), 369-70.

of conciliation amounted to, they barely concealed the crucial fact that, in defence of capitalism, the state was prepared to kill."[18] In their extremely valuable statistical study of Canadian strikes, Cruikshank and Kealey also have noted the importance of the state's "enthusiastic recourse to coercion." They further have asserted that "Workers remained aware of the state's potential for violence and behaved in a generally disciplined fashion."[19]

Such statements are useful in flagging the importance of the police in industrial disputes, but are insufficiently rigorous in their historical analysis. In his review of Craven, for example, McKay asks: "How can one write the history of industrial relations and the Canadian State and not once refer to the fact that from 1895 to 1904 the militia were called out 11 times (71 days) and no less than 17 times (1232 days) from 1905 to 1914?" What McKay does not note is that the militia were called out in but one of a hundred strikes and that there was no increase during the latter interval in the percentage of times the militia were called out compared to the number of strikes (1.07 per cent for 1895-1904; 1.06 per cent for 1905-1914).[20] There was, however, a significant increase in the days served by the militia in the latter period even when the increase of workers' strike days is taken into account.[21] As to the state being prepared to kill in defense of capitalism, one might ask what state, of any sort, has not been prepared to kill in defence of what it considered to be its vital interests. But that would merely be saying that other states are just as bad; in fact, the record of many other states and their policing forces have been considerably worse. The Canadian militia was, evidently, responsible for the death of one striker between 1867 and 1914,[22] and four other persons were killed in strike-related violence during this period.[23] In contrast, the period 1890 to 1909 saw more than 300 strike-related deaths in the United States;[24] 20 deaths and 600 injuries occurred in a single coal strike in France in 1907-08;[25] and two persons were killed by troops and over 200 injured in strike-related violence in Liverpool during 13-15 August 1911.[26] Canada may not have

---

18   I. McKay, "Strikes in the Maritimes, 1901-1914," *Acadiensis*, 13 (1983), 43. The policing force involved was the militia. McKay's source is, of course, Morton's *CHR* article.

19   D. Cruikshank and G.S. Kealey, "Strikes in Canada, 1891-1950," *L/LT*, 20 (1987), 96, 98-100.

20   Cruikshank and Kealey, "Strikes," 134. The estimates (98) of percentage of strikes involving military intervention is marginally lower.

21   The number of striker-days increased something like four-fold (estimated from Cruikshank and Kealey, "Strikes," 86; and McKay, "Strikes in the Maritimes," 16) whereas the number of days of militia involvement increased seventeen-fold.

22   D. Morton, "Aid to the Civil Power," 416, 421.

23   Three of the four were strikers killed, it appears, by company guards. The other was a company guard (see S.M. Jamieson, *Times of Trouble: Labour Unrest and Industrial Conflict in Canada, 1900-66* (Ottawa 1968), 94-5 and 112). On a statistical basis, therefore, one might say that strikers were as prepared as the state to kill in defence of vital interests. Employers were even more prepared. The statistics are derived from J.M. Torrance, *Public Violence in Canada, 1867-1982* (Kingston 1986), 243. It seems inconceivable that these figures are complete but they do indicate a low level of lethal strike violence. It appears that another 13 persons died in strike-related violence between 1914 and 1984 (see Torrance, *Public Violence*, 243-4).

24   Harring, *Policing a Class Society*, 101, 269-70.

25   Morgan, *Conflict and Order*, 280.

26   E. Wigham, *Strikes and the Government 1893-1974* (London 1976), 25. Troops opened fire again on August 17 at Llanelly in Wales killing two more persons (see ibid., 26). Infamous "Bloody Saturday"

been a "peaceable kingdom," but in comparative terms it witnessed but a modest degree of civic bloodshed;[27] not an insignificant fact since it stands to reason that there is a correlation between a low level of social violence and a low level of police violence.

The Cruikshank and Kealey assertion that workers, being aware of possible state violence, kept themselves on a tight leash is dubious, since it implies that higher levels of collective violence in other countries were the result of a weaker threat of state repression. It suggests that workers were not naturally peaceable, and that it was the threat of repression that kept the workers in line. It is often thought, however, that police intervention promotes outbreaks of violence. Indeed, this seems to be the implication of a statement later in their article that "collective violence occurred in 36 of the 46 cases of military intervention" ([100] — note that making the statement in reverse order presents a very different causational analysis). And what of the state's "enthusiastic recourse of coercion?" According to Cruikshank and Kealey, the percentage of total strikes with military intervention between 1891 and 1940 averaged 0.6 per cent over the five decades, never exceeding 1 per cent in any decade (98). The statistics are not conclusive, since they include instances when the military was put on alert but was not deployed. More importantly, however, they do not include intervention by other policing agencies, whether national, provincial, or municipal. The frequency of the utilization of the physical arm of the state in strikes is, therefore, considerably understated, but by how much is anyone's guess at this point. Such statistics will only become meaningful, however, when one has comparative data. How frequent was police involvement in strikes in the USA, Great Britain, and so forth? How prevalent was police involvement in other large social gatherings such as political rallies, rock concerts and hockey games?[28] It may be that in Canada the state enthusiastically resorted to coercion in strike situations but the case cannot be made on the basis of the data presented, namely that the military were involved in but one strike out of one hundred.

These examples are not meant to denigrate the work of individuals who are, after all, amongst the most prolific and insightful of Canadian historians. Rather, they demonstrate how easily taken for granted and easily dismissed are the police even by sensitive and sophisticated historians of Canadian labour. They, at least, pay some attention to the police and recognize their significance. Few other Canadian labour historians even bother with the police. Perhaps, however, this omission is an important statement of interpretation, for in leaving out the police, such historians are, in effect, saying that state violence was not much of a factor in Canada labour history.[29] While

---

of the Winnipeg General Strike saw one killed and 30 injured (see Palmer, *Working-Class Experience*, 176) while in the Regina Riot one policeman was killed and "scores of trekkers, citizens and policemen" were injured (see L. Brown, *When Freedom Was Lost: The Unemployed, the Agitator, and the State* (Montreal 1987), 195).

27 Torrance, *Public Violence*, 57-66.

28 As soon as this question is asked it becomes apparent that the mere presence of policing authorities in strike situations is not necessarily very instructive. It is interesting that despite a strike of more than 80,000 miners in the West Riding of Yorkshire in 1893 some 259 constables, nearly a quarter of the West Riding force, were sent to patrol the Doncaster Races (see Geary, *Policing Industrial Disputes*, 7 and 17).

29 It appears that labour historians in other countries also have given little attention to the police. For example, Morgan, *Conflict and Order*, 7, maintains that historians of British workers have dismissed the police as "a monolithic class enemy" or as "an irrelevance." If true, this seems curious since the

Canadian historians have paid scant attention to police/labour relations, outside the country it seems to be a burgeoning field, especially in Britain and the United States, the two countries with the greatest influence on Canadian policing.[30] The literature being produced is broad both in terms of coverage and approach, and is susceptible of categorization in a variety of ways. For purposes of examining police/labour relations, however, a rather crude distinction can be made between two conceptual frameworks. As M. Punch puts it: "Theories on the police differ widely: a Marxist would see them as pawns of ruling-class hegemony aimed at oppressing the working class, whereas a functionalist might emphasize the integrative role they play in promoting social solidarity."[31] The functionalist or pluralist perspective on the police is seldom articulated with much clarity or analytical rigour, being more an unstated premise,[32] but in essence this view considers that police serve society as a whole and that police enforcement of the law and maintenance of order is, on the whole, beneficial. This conceptual framework does not necessarily lead to an unsophisticated or uncritical examination of the police. The pluralist approach need not entail a belief that all social groups have an equal or just share of power or that social change will occur without conflict between competing groups. In the realm of police-labour relations, for example, many of the works in this genre, which include the bulk of Canadian police historiography, are highly critical of the police. Nevertheless, the perspective is fundamentally optimistic, maintaining that abuses of police power can be overcome by the vigilance of citizens in maintaining and developing their civil rights and their control over the police.

The second conceptual framework views the police as agents not of society as a whole but of the capitalist class. Police are the physical force which promotes and secures the conditions favourable for the accumulation of capital, particularly in keeping the working class under control. Again, this perspective need not lead to unsophisticated or even ungracious evaluations of the police. Practitioners of this type of police history usually acknowledge that in a democratic society the police are partially limited in their powers of repression because of the necessity to maintain some semblance of the legitimacy of the system. Nevertheless, the class-conflict approach is fundamentally antagonistic to the police and views the "law and order" enforced by the police as class-biased tools of domination.[33]

---

nature and operation of policing forces is surely an important mechanism for evaluating a society.

30 Useful entry points to the literature are the bibliographies in Morgan, *Conflict and Order*, and Harring, *Policing a Class Society*. Neither British nor American police historians make much use of the historiography of the other country. For example, Morgan lists neither Harring's book nor his earlier articles; Harring does not include two significant studies by R.D. Storch ("The Plague of Blue Locusts: Police Reform and Popular Resistance in Northern England, 1840-1857," *International Review of Social History*, 20 (1975), 61-90; and "The Policeman as Domestic Missionary: Urban Discipline and Popular Culture in Northern England, 1850-1880," *Journal of Social History*, 9 (1975-6), 481-509).

31 Punch, "Police," 605. Some analysts draw further sharp distinctions within each camp: on the one hand between functionalism and pluralism, with the latter being further divided into the "labelling perspective" and "conflict theory"; on the other hand, within the Marxist perspective, between instrumentalist and structuralist approaches. See S. Brickley and E. Comack, eds., *The Social Basis of Law in Canada* (Toronto 1986), 15-21.

32 Though not specifically addressing the role of police, a useful discussion of the liberal pluralist view of the state is presented in R.A. Dahl, *Pluralist Democracy in the United States: Conflict and Consent* (Chicago 1967).

33 Dividing police historiography into two camps may be a useful heuristic device, but it glosses over

Beyond conceptual frameworks, Anglo-American police historiography, taken as a whole, demonstrates that the nature, role, activities and characteristics of police forces have differed greatly from one another depending on location, time-period and circumstances. For example, a two-person police force in a rural area necessarily carried out its duties in a different manner than a large metropolitan force; indeed, even their duties differed markedly. In the 1970s, police were more technologically-sophisticated and more attuned to a bureaucratic ideal than they were a century before. Police in a society with a low level of lethal personal violence are likely to behave differently than those in a violence-prone society. Police forces also vary greatly in their degree of affinity with, and support from, the community or society in which they operate. Given these differences, and that police normally are agents of both service and repression, and given that even the term "law and order" is at times mutually exclusive, it is hardly surprising that there is no consensus among academics or the public on the police.[34] There is none because there is not, nor ever

---

many nuances and significant differences within each group. Within the pluralist perspective, for example, the range extends from conservatives to social democrats. Within the class-conflict perspective, a supposed example of a Marxist interpretation has argued that the police sided with the US working class (see Johnson, "Taking Care of Labour"). However, Harring, *Policing a Class Society*, 261-2, asserts that Johnson's work not only is severely deficient but also is definitely not a Marxist work. No less a figure than E.P. Thompson has argued that the rule of law was better than the rule of no law, that law could bind the rulers as well as the ruled, and that the ruled could, on occasion, use the law as a tool against the ruling class. See E.P. Thompson, *Whigs and Hunters: the Origin of the Black Act* (London 1975), 258-69.

34   These themes are discussed in many of the works already cited. In addition, from the large volume of scholarly works on the subject, the following items have been found useful in comprehending the range of interpretations of policing and its history: G.E. Berkley, *The Democratic Policeman* (Boston 1969); R.S. Bunyard, *Police: Organization and Command* (Plymouth, UK 1978); M.E. Cain, *Society and the Policeman's Role* (London 1973); I.A. Cameron, *Crime and Repression in the Auvergne and the Guyenne 1720-1790* (New York 1981); Centre for Research on Criminal Justice, *The Iron Fist and the Velvet Glove: An Analysis of the US Police* (Berkeley 1977); R.C. Cobb, *The Police and the People: French Popular Protest 1789-1820* (Oxford 1970); R. Lane, *Policing the City: Boston 1822-1885* (Cambridge, Mass. 1967); P.K. Manning, *Police Work: The Social Organization of Policing* (Cambridge, Mass. 1977); J.F. Richardson, *The New York Police, Colonial Times to 1901* (New York 1970); R. Sykes and E. Brent, *Policing: A Social Behaviorist Perspective* (New Brunswick, N.J. 1983); S. Walker, *A Critical History of Police Reform: The Emergence of Professionalism* (Lexington, Mass. 1977); S. Walker, *Popular Justice: A History of American Criminal Justice* (New York 1980); D. Philips, "'A Just Measure of Crime, Authority, Hunters and Blue Locusts': The 'Revisionist' Social History of Crime and the Law in Britain, 1780-1850," and S. Spitzer, "The Rationalization of Crime Control in Capitalist Society," both in S. Cohen and A. Scull, eds., *Social Control and the State: Historical and Comparative Essays* (Oxford 1983), 50-74 and 312-33; D. Humphries and D.F. Greenberg, "The Dialectics of Crime Control," and S.L. Harring, "Policing a Class Society: The Expansion of the Urban Police in the Late Nineteenth and Early Twentieth Centuries," and S. Spitzer, "The Political Economy of Policing," all in D.F. Greenberg, ed., *Crime and Capitalism: Readings in Marxist Criminology* (Palo Alto 1981), 209-54, 292-313 and 314-40; D.H. Bayley, "The Police and Political Development in Europe," in C. Tilly, ed., *The Formation of National States in Western Europe* (Princeton 1975), 328-79; S. Cohen, "Policing the Working-Class City," in B. Fine, et al., eds., *Capitalism and the Rule of Law: From Deviancy Theory to Marxism* (London 1979), 118-36; H. Hahn, "The Public and the Police: A Theoretical Perspective," in H. Hahn, ed., *Police in Urban Society* (Beverly Hills 1971), 9-33; R. Liebman and M. Polen, "Perspectives on Policing in Nineteenth-Century America," *Social Science History*, 2 (1978), 346-60; E. Monkkonen, "Toward a Dynamic Theory of Crime and the Police: A Criminal Justice System Perspective," *Historical Methods Newsletter*, 10 (1977), 157-65; E. Monkkonen, "From Cop History to Social History; The Significance of the Police in American History," *Journal of Social History*, 15 (1982), 575-91; C.D. Robinson, "Ideology as History:

will be, a definitive explanation of the nature and function of police forces. In his favourable review of Harring's book, John T. Cumbler concluded:

> It is amazing considering the evidence available that anyone will argue with this work, but it is clear that despite the depth of his research and the strength of his analysis, there are those who will not accept the conclusions of this work. Their rejection will be ideological not historical.[35]

Equally, however, and despite the excellence of Harring's work and the enormous stimulation it provides, acceptance of his conclusions would be just as "ideological not historical" as rejection. The historical record does not provide such clear answers either to current analysts or to contemporary participants and observers of events. Certainly, at least, the record of the Mounted Police during the Lethbridge coal-miners' strike of 1906 carried a mixed message, not least for the strikers themselves.

*****

The Lethbridge coalminers' strike began in March 1906.[36] The recently formed Local 574 of the United Mine Workers of America (UMWA) District 18 had proposed a contract to the coal company which would have given the Lethbridge miners parity with their unionized brethren in the Crowsnest Pass. Parity meant increased pay, shorter hours, a grievance procedure, and union recognition. The company, in 1906 properly termed the Alberta Railway and Irrigation Company (AR&I) but more popularly known as the Galt company after its founder, Sir Alexander Tilloch Galt, and his son and AR&I president, Elliott Torrance Galt, declined to bargain with an organized body of men as had been its practice for two decades. Its key management personnel — A.M. Nanton of Winnipeg, managing director; P.L. Naismith, general manager; and W.D. Hardie, mine superintendent — refused to negotiate and started

---

A Look at the Way Some English Police Historians Look at the Police," *Police Studies*, 2 (1979), 35-49; A. Silver, "The Demand for Order in Civil Society: A Review of Some Themes in the History of Urban Crime, Police and Riot," in D.J. Bordua, ed., *The Police: Six Sociological Essays* (New York 1967), 1-24; J.H. Skolnick, "Professional Police in a Free Society," in J.T. Curran et al., eds., *Police and Law Enforcement 1972* (New York 1973), 61-76; S. Spitzer and A. Scull, "Privatization and Capitalist Development: The Case of the Private Police," *Social Problems*, 25 (1977), 18-29; S. Spitzer and A. Scull, "Social Control in Historical Perspective: From Private to Public Responses to Crime," in D.F. Greenberg, ed., *Corrections and Punishment* (Beverly Hills 1977), 265-86; and R. Swift, "Urban Policing in Early Victorian England, 1835-86: A Reappraisal," *History*, 73 (1988), 211-37.

35 *Labor History*, 27, 1 (Winter 1985-6), 128. Cumbler was correct, of course, in believing that eminent police historians of a different ideological perspective would reject Harring's book out of hand. See, for example, Roger Lane's review in *Journal of American History*, 71 (1984-5), 650-1; and James Richardson's review in *American Historical Review*, 89 (1984), 1401. Wilbur Miller's review in *Journal of Social History*, 18 (1984-5), 490-1, is more evenhanded, and concludes that the book "is a must for historians and others interested in the impact of industrial capitalism on America." The present writer is in full agreement with this sentiment.

36 Relevant secondary sources on the strike include Craven, "An Impartial Umpire," 264-9; A.A. den Otter, *Civilizing the West: The Galts and the Development of Western Canada* (Edmonton 1982), 282-304; Jamieson, *Times of Trouble*, 127-8; Palmer, *Working-Class Experience*, 156-7; W.M. Baker, "The Miners and the Mediator: The 1906 Lethbridge Strike and Mackenzie King," *L/LT*, 11 (1983), 89-117; C.J. McMillan, "Trade Unionism in District 18, 1900-1925: A Case Study," MBA Thesis, University of Alberta 1969, 49-57; and A. Seager, "A Proletariat in Wild Rose Country: The Alberta Miners, 1905-1945," PhD Thesis, York University, 1982, 208-17.

to fire miners who had joined the union. As a consequence virtually all the miners, more than 500 in total, walked out.

The nine-month strike that followed was a significant test of strength. For the UMWA it was an opportunity to expand its recently-established foothold in the Crowsnest Pass. Accordingly, it provided considerable financial, organizational, and logistical aid to the Lethbridge strikers. For the well-established, locally-powerful and economically-diverse AR&I, involved in land development, irrigation projects and railways as well as coal mining, it was an occasion to halt the unionization drive which, it was perceived, would limit management's freedom of action and control. Consequently, the company simply dug in its heels and adopted a stance of sheer intransigence.

Neither party was able to defeat the other. The company reopened the mine in late May but the more than 200 inexperienced men working by October were never able to come close to acceptable production targets. Still, management remained confident that in the long term the company would emerge victorious, and thus remained steadfast in refusing to negotiate. The strikers, for their part, had succeeded in maintaining unity despite ethno-religious differences among themselves and had severely limited the availability of skilled miners.

What brought things to a conclusion was the fact that the public interest was involved since the strike hurt the local economy, and eventually contributed to a serious shortage of home-heating fuel on the prairies during the severe winter of 1906-7. Therefore, various representatives of the so-called public became involved, including the federal labour department in the person of W.L. Mackenzie King.[37] It was King's intervention that brought about a form of negotiation and a settlement of the strike in early December. Indeed, the outcome of the strike could be termed a victory for the strikers. They won a significant pay increase, a grievance procedure, and the right to belong to the union. The settlement was not a signed agreement with the union but even that was accomplished half a year later.

Such a bald summary ignores an important dimension of the strike: the supposedly high level of violence and the heavy involvement of the RNWMP. There were, in fact, two so-called riots, a half-dozen occasions when large groups of strikers and their families harassed strikebreakers, various instances of assault, charges of obstructing police officers, at least one case of arson, and no fewer than 13 separate explosions. As for the police presence, at one point shortly after the strike began, the Mounties had 34 officers and men on strike duty, 48 Mounties on call in Regina and Fort Macleod (amounting to over 10 per cent of the total RNWMP force at the time),[38] — and had sworn in a dozen special policemen. Given the manpower shortage, and that the suppression of crimes of violence against persons and property was the top priority for the police,[39] the RNWMP commitment to the Lethbridge strike was enormous, and indicates the Mounties' sense of apprehension. In fact, however, little seriously harmful violence occurred during the strike. Moreover, one might have anticipated that violence and police involvement in the strike quickly would have brought matters to a head — most likely to the detriment of the strikers. Yet not only

---

37 See Baker, "Miners and Mediator."
38 Talbot et al., *Canada's Constables*, 62-3.
39 T. Thorner, "The Not So Peaceable Kingdom: A Study of Crime in Southern Alberta, 1874-1905," MA thesis, University of Calgary, 1975, 45.

did the contest continue for months after the peak of both the violence and the police presence but also the strikers emerged triumphant at the end. On the face of it, at least, neither the violence nor the involvement of the RNWMP had harmed the strikers' cause. How and why had this occurred?

By 1906 the Mounties had been connected to the miners of Lethbridge for two decades. Indeed, the establishment of Division K (Lethbridge) owed much to the perceived need to be close by the "unruly" miners. Many of the day-to-day activities of the police related to the miners; the Mounties had also played a modest role in the industrial disputes of 1887, 1894, 1897, and 1903.[40] Even so, the rapid turnover of constables meant that few Mounties in 1906 had much experience either with Lethbridge miners or industrial conflict. Nor could they turn to their commander, J.O. Wilson, for expert guidance. He had joined the force in 1879 and had risen through the ranks because of his general competence. But he lacked experience with strikes, and had taken over the Lethbridge division only a month before the outbreak of the strike.[41]

No doubt there were strikers as recently arrived in Lethbridge as Wilson. Indeed, in that era the level of geographic mobility of the population throughout North America, certainly in Western Canadian cities, was high. Single, unattached miners were notorious for being on the move. Miners appearing before the Alberta Coal Commission of 1907, for example, had worked all over the world — Austria, France, England, Wales, Nova Scotia, South Africa, Australia, Pennsylvania, Montana — before landing in Southern Alberta.[42] What is noteworthy about Lethbridge miners, however, is not their considerable transience but the degree of their persistence. Approximately half the 1906 Lethbridge miners had settled in the city or environs, had purchased a town lot, built a modest house, and established a family. A number, precisely how many is impossible to determine, also had acquired homesteads and worked their farms in the summer when the Galt mines usually closed.[43] Clearly, the range of opportunities for miners and their children in Lethbridge was much greater than in most mining communities, including agriculture, commercial, service, industrial,

---

40 den Otter, *Civilizing the West*, 123 and 275-8; Glenbow Alberta Archives, R.B. Deane Papers, "Labour Troubles — A Lock-out of Miners"; and National Archives of Canada (NAC), RG18, Royal Canadian Mounted Police Papers (RCMP Papers), A1, vol. 91, file 148-94, Deane to Commissioner, 31 January, 2 and 28 February, 6, 9, 16, 30, and 31 March, 4 and 30 April 1894, and vol. 94, file 285-94, E.T. Galt to L.W. Herchmer, 15 March 1894; RCMP Papers, B1, vol. 1392. file 127-1897, Deane to Commissioner, 31 August 1897, vol. 1401, file 237-1897, vol. 261, file 790-03, J.V. Begin to Commissioner, 24 October 1903, Galt to F. White, telegram, 21 October and 23 October 1903, White to A.B. Perry, telegram, 22 October 1903, White to Galt, telegram, 22 October 1903, and vol. 250, file 177-03, Begin to Commissioner, 2 November 1903.

41 RCMP Papers, A1, vol. 96, file 413; vol. 249, file 131-03; and vol. 315, file 202-06, R. Belcher to Commissioner, 13 February 1906.

42 Provincial Archives of Alberta (PAA), Alberta Royal Commission on the Coal Mining Industry, 1907, Minutes of Evidence.

43 For example, Frank Sherman, President of UMWA District 18, took out a homestead near Taber, some 30 miles east of Lethbridge (Lethbridge *Herald*, 6 June 1907). A variety of sources, including Lethbridge assessment records and city directories, local histories such as West Lethbridge Book Society, *The Bend: A History of West Lethbridge* (Calgary 1982), and the Cummins Rural Directory Maps for Alberta, 1923 (available at NAC) provide strong evidence that many miners and/or their families became involved in farming or vice versa.

and even professional options.⁴⁴ Thus by 1906, many Lethbridge miners had passed the sojourning stage as their years of local residence turned into decades.⁴⁵ In short, there were a number of 1906 strikers who were well-acquainted with the community, with the history of industrial strife in Lethbridge and elsewhere, and with the standards, practices, and laws of the country. Indeed, such persons probably had a much better sense of the police than vice versa.

Of the several concentrations of miners in Lethbridge, the most important was in Stafford Village ("Number Three") because it was adjacent to the mine. Its population, mainly miners and their families, contained a large proportion of non-Anglos. This community, named after a former mine manager,⁴⁶ was not part of the city proper⁴⁷ and so was not under Lethbridge town police jurisdiction.⁴⁸ Stafford was within the RNWMP sphere of police authority. Its strategic location, just outside the entrance to the mine, meant that the village was both the scene of most of the disturbances that occurred during the strike, and where miners and Mounties came face to face.

*****

At the beginning of the strike Mounties and miners viewed each other with suspicion and apprehension. The gulf between the police and the strikers (especially that half termed "foreigners" — Russians, Poles, Ukrainians, Hungarians, Italians, and other eastern Europeans) was enormous. To the police, the "foreign" miners of Lethbridge were a troublesome, violent, treacherous, drunken, uncivilized lot of

---

44 For example, by the 1920s the male descendants of Michael Vaselenak Sr., a Slovak miner who had come to Lethbridge in 1887, had been occupied as farmers, a merchant, a machinist, a teacher and a lawyer (see *The Bend*, 217-22; and Glenbow Alberta Archives, Acc. 5390 (Uncatalogued), John Vaselenak Papers).

45 Some of the miners had been in the city for more than 15 years by 1906.

46 On William Stafford, the first mine manager, later mine inspector for the Territorial government, and who in 1891 had been petitioned by 200 miners to run for mayor of Lethbridge, see den Otter, *Civilizing the West*, 191-3 and passim.

47 Staffordville, as it was also known, emerged after Galt Mine No. 3 began production in 1892. This community was hived off from Lethbridge and possessed few of the amenities of the town. Moreover, its residents possessed no political rights in the municipality (nor did they pay Lethbridge taxes except for schools). Such exclusion was probably intentional and demonstrated that "foreign" miners were not really accepted as citizens. Stafford was not incorporated into Lethbridge until 1913 although its residents had long wanted annexation so that they could receive proper city services, such as water, and a political voice in municipal affairs (see A. Johnston and A.A. den Otter, *Lethbridge: A Centennial History* (Lethbridge 1985), 88; and A. Johnston et al., *Lethbridge: Its Coal Industry* (Lethbridge 1989), 35). Interestingly, the mayor of Lethbridge at the time of Stafford's incorporation was W.D.L. Hardie, who had been mine manager during the 1906 strike.

48 The Lethbridge police force consisted of but three men whose main function was to attempt to enforce municipal bylaws. Because the Mounted Police barracks were within the city, because the Mounties had provided municipal policing services in Lethbridge in the past, and because the Mounties were much more numerous and organized than the town policeman, the RNWMP were seen by townsfolk and the Mounties themselves as the real police force in Lethbridge [see den Otter, *Civilizing the West*, and J.H. Carpenter, *The Badge and the Blotter: A History of the Lethbridge Police* (Lethbridge 1975)]. During the 1906 strike itself, the city police played an insignificant role. Their presence was largely ignored by the Mounties as exemplified by Wilson's refusal to obey the order of the city police to get a license for his dog (Lethbridge Public Library, Police Daily Journals, vol. 5, 33, report of H.M. Parry, Chief Constable, 21 March 1906).

brutes who lived "in a piggish sort of way" and could only be kept in line by the use of force.[49] For the Mounties, then, strike duty promised to be a disagreeable assignment.[50] Nor were the strikers looking forward to being associated with the police. Their prior contact had usually been in circumstances in which the Mounties appeared as punitive enforcers of "middle-class" laws and morality. East European miners not only found few men of similar ethnic background in the force, but also remembered brutally repressive policing authorities in their homelands. In fact, each group desired minimal contact with the other, although it was thought in some quarters that the Mounties were a bulwark against the subversion of the country by "aliens," labour "agitators," and political radicals.[51] By and large, the Mounties neither had interfered with nor assisted the East European miners because, according to one of Wilson's predecessors, as long as "foreigners" did not disturb their neighbours, "it did not very much matter whether they damaged one anothers [sic] skulls or not."[52] English-speaking miners were not quite so distant from the police, and they shared rather similar views about the "foreigners" in their midst. Yet even they probably held less than positive views of the Mounties: "The middle class expects help from the police, the working class expects trouble."[53]

Given this initial precondition of reciprocal fears, anxiety, and opposition, it is not surprising that there was little contact between the two parties in the early days of the strike. In contrast, P.L. Naismith, AR&I general manager, having visited police headquarters to request protection for the mine property and working miners, explained the situation to Wilson. The recently-arrived Wilson accepted, in entirety, Naismith's evaluation of the situation: that the newly organized UMWA local was making unreasonable demands; that "serious trouble" was to be expected since "the men are very much worked up"; and that after a month or so "the men will have cooled down somewhat."[54] Wilson made no attempt to consult with union leaders either to express his concern about preserving order or to discern the temper of the

---

49 RCMP Papers, A1, vol. 21, file 373-88, R.B. Deane to Commissioner, 1 July and 1 August 1888, and vol. 101, file 37-95, J.H. McIllree to F. White, 4 January 1895, with extract from Deane's weekly report; Lethbridge *News*, 18 May 1906; and Deane Papers, "Labour troubles," 3.

50 During the Lethbridge strike, at least four constables deserted, while three others "committed breaches of discipline and asked to be dismissed at the expiration of their punishment" because the men found police duty at the mine "most distasteful." See RCMP Papers, A1, vol. 316, file 238-06, "Lethbridge — coal miners strike at — 1906," White to E.T. Galt, 19 July 1906. On the general problem of desertion from the force see Macleod, *North-West Mounted Police*, 83-4. It seems that the use in labour disputes of any policing force, whether municipal or national, militia or army, was not welcomed by the force itself since such activity threatened to damage efficiency, to drain morale, and to reduce public popularity (see L.W. Bentley, "Aid of the Civil Power: Social and Political Aspects 1904-1924," *Canadian Defense Quarterly*, 8, 1 (1978), 47; and G. Davidson-Smith, "The Military in Aid of the Civil Power: Limits in a Democratic Society," *Canadian Defense Quarterly*, 13, 4 (1984), 27-33).

51 Walden, *Visions of Order*, 129-35.

52 RCMP Papers, A1, vol. 21, file 373-88, Deane to Commissioner, 1 July 1888.

53 B. Jackson, *Working Class Community: Some General Notions Raised by a Series of Studies in Northern England* (New York 1968), 116. On the hostility of English workers to the police in the mid-19th century, see B. Weinberger, "The Police and the Public in Mid-Nineteenth Century Warwickshire," in Bailey, *Policing and Punishment*, 65-93.

54 Ibid., A1, vol. 316, file 238-06, Wilson to Commissioner, telegram, 27 February 1906. A number of the telegrams in this file, such as this one, were originally sent in cipher. See also ibid., B5, vol. 2478, file 57, Wilson to Commissioner, 27 February 1906.

strikers,[55] and he immediately requested reinforcements.[56] Detective-Sergeant G. Goodwin did attend a miners' meeting when strike action was debated. Such a gathering was bound to be excited, but Goodwin thought that it demonstrated "great unrest" and that the Hungarians and Slavs were "very rowdy."[57] In short, the meeting verified to the police that the strikers, especially the "foreign" element, posed a threat to peace and order.

Such a perception was reinforced as soon as the strike began on 8 March. That night there was an explosion outside the house of a non-union man. The blast was designed to frighten rather than injure, but it made Wilson most apprehensive. He viewed the strikers' possession of powder and dynamite, which they had purchased from the company for blasting, as a "grave source of danger." Consequently, he requested reinforcements and ordered continuous patrolling for a month in order to protect company property, "and also to allay the excitement among the Non-Union men caused by last night's explosion."[58]

A week later Wilson was still very anxious. The company had warned him to expect trouble on the weekend of 17-18 March, for this was when the strikers would be paid what was coming to them.[59] Moreover, Wilson understood that the strikers were heavily armed with revolvers and other weapons and that some had been soldiers.[60] He called for substantial reinforcements, believing that "my small force would not be much against five hundred men especially if crazed by drink." Contemplating what might happen, he believed that after reading the Riot Act, which he acknowledged would not be understood by many "foreign" strikers, he might have to give an order to fire. He said that he hoped it would not come to this, but made no attempt to reach out to the strikers in order to prevent a tragedy.[61] Rather, evidently viewing the strikers as the enemy, he wanted his force strengthened.

---

55 One can assert this with confidence since it is most unlikely that had such a consultation taken place it would have gone unrecorded in Wilson's reports.

56 Ibid., B5, vol. 2478, file 57, Wilson to Commissioner, 27 February 1906. The commissioner's office alerted the Fort Macleod division to be prepared to send men if required (see ibid., A1, vol. 316, file 238-06, McIllree to P.C.H. Primrose, 28 February 1906).

57 Ibid., A1, vol. 316, file 238-06, Goodwin to Wilson, 1 March 1906.

58 Ibid., Wilson to Commissioner, 9 March 1906. The one-month period may be another indication of the impact Naismith's initial evaluation had had on Wilson.

59 Ibid., Wilson to Commissioner, telegram, 14 March 1906. The Company's general manager sent a wire to RNWMP Comptroller Fred White requesting more police (see ibid., Naismith to White, telegram, 14 March 1906).

60 Ibid., E.H. Bolderson, "Crime Report — Strike at Lethbridge — Re Sale of Arms of Late in Lethbridge," 14 March 1906. Reports of arms appear to have been greatly exaggerated. None of the four firms dealing in arms in Lethbridge kept proper records and only two purchasers could be named. Ironically enough, at least one of these was a strikebreaker.

61 Ibid., B5, vol. 2478, file 57, Wilson to Commissioner, 14 March 1906. It is axiomatic that any police or military force desires to be present with ample strength or not at all rather than with numbers of questionable adequacy (see, for example, J. Foster, *Class Struggle and the Industrial Revolution: Early Industrial Capitalism in Three English Towns* (London 1974), 48-50). Wilson's failure to attempt to explain to the strikers in advance such things as the Riot Act, which he knew would not be comprehended in the heat of the moment, is in marked contrast to the present-day situation in Toronto where two policemen are permanently designated to explain the law to management and strikers in an attempt to prevent altercations (see Lethbridge *Herald*, 17 June 1981, E6).

A swift response came from the commissioner of the Mounties, A.B. Perry. He had already promised general manager Naismith that "everything possible will be done to protect your property,"[62] and now not only sent reinforcements, increasing Wilson's manpower to some 58 men available for strike duty, but also kept another 21 in readiness in Regina.[63] In addition, a plainclothes policeman, Constable Gorski, was planted amongst the East European miners.[64] Perry also advised closing bars to preserve peace, arranging to use fire hoses to prevent bloodshed, and swearing in special constables to augment the regular force. He further ordered Wilson to instruct the policemen "to act patiently and firmly" and to "take no side in the strike but ... protect Company's property from injury and any men who desire to work."[65]

Wilson followed all the suggestions. But the ostensible neutrality of the police was questionable, and not merely because the sending of reinforcements pleased the company. In the first place, when Wilson decided to place his main force in railway cars on the mine property,[66] it was understood that the company would provide accommodations and food. Secondly, Wilson acknowledged that his outlook and actions had been "guided to a large extent" by Naismith and W.D.L. Hardie, the mine manager. Finally, all eleven special constables were company employees.[67] In effect, Wilson was deputizing non-union miners at the request of company officials. He figured this was unexceptionable, because the Mounties were not paying them; nor were any "foreigners" sworn in. In fact, however, he was conferring significant legitimacy and legal authority upon men who were so far from being neutral that they might be called company guards.[68]

If the Mounties remained suspicious of and hostile to the strikers by mid-March, those sentiments were reciprocated. The strikers complained, for example, that the police had accompanied a company official who went into miners' homes to get strikers back to work. To union officials, this was a form of police intimidation, for the presence of Mounties might overawe "those foreigners who do not understand that this is a free country and that no man needs work if he don't wish to."[69] It

---

62   RCMP Papers, A1, vol. 316, file 238-06, Perry to Naismith, 14 March 1906.

63   Ibid., Perry to Comptroller, telegram, 15 March 1906. The reserve force in Regina was not sent.

64   Ibid., B5, vol. 2478, file 57, Perry to Wilson, 14 March 1906.

65   Ibid., A1, vol. 316, file 238-06, Perry to Wilson, telegram, 15 March 1906.

66   In part, this was because both hose and water were available there.

67   Ibid, Wilson to Commissioner, telegram, 15 March 1906; Wilson to Commissioner, 15 March 1906.

68   The RNWMP Comptroller questioned the arrangement but seemed satisfied with Wilson's response (see ibid., White to Perry, telegram, 23 March 1906; Wilson to Commissioner, 25 March 1906; and Perry to Comptroller, telegram, 25 March 1906). It is not clear exactly how much authority was granted special constables. A justice of the peace could appoint them for a period not extending beyond the end of the year and it appears that in a formal sense these "specials" held all the powers, privileges and duties of regular constables (see *The Ordinances of the North-West Territories, 1905* (a consolidation) (Edmonton 1907), chapter 33, An Ordinance respecting Constables). The situation in Montreal in the 1880s respecting special constables had been similar. See G.S. Kealey, ed., *Canada Investigates Industrialism: The Royal Commission on the Relations of Labor and Capital, 1889* (Toronto 1973), 229-30.

69   *Herald*, 15 March 1906. The UMWA District 18 solicitor had complained about a similar sort of police "presence" in a case of eviction from company housing in Lille nine months earlier. At that time, the Comptroller of the NWMP indicated that this had been an error of judgment. See R.C. Macleod, "The Problem of Law and Order in the Canadian West, 1870-1905," in L.G. Thomas, ed, *The Prairie West to 1905: A Canadian Sourcebook* (Toronto 1975), 212-5.

reinforced their view that the police had been brought in at the instigation and for the benefit of the company, rather than to preserve the peace which the strikers claimed they had no intention of breaching. The strikers publicly expressed their opposition to the police at a mass meeting on Saturday 10 March, when they passed a resolution protesting such police action and directed that copies be sent to the press and politicians.[70] By mid-March, the gulf between strikers and police was even wider than it had been at the beginning of the strike.

Several developments in mid-March narrowed this gap. Until then, the strikers had treated working miners going to and from the mine to concerts of rough music. They banged tin cans, blew horns and mouth organs, and waved flags.[71] Wilson decided to end these activities and to charge the leaders with intimidation despite his depiction of a procession on 15 March as "orderly and good natured."[72] Thus, when a crowd of about 50 gathered close to the mine shaft to "razz" the strikebreakers about 4 p.m. the next day, six Mounties warned them against following and intimidating. But as three strikebreakers made their way home from the mine, a crowd which grew to about 150 including women and children fell in behind the police, all of whom were mounted, and began to serenade the so-called scabs. Five Mounties pulled revolvers and "presented them to the persons forming the procession," while the sixth dismounted and made an arrest. The noise then ceased and strikers politely asked what wrong they were doing. A deal was then struck: the arrested striker would be released and the strikers would stop following the working miners. A side action flared up when the crowd, "apparently incited by some women," went after two other men, but this was quelled by the police and by several of the strikers who "went through the crowd and urged them to keep quiet." The crowd eventually dispersed and "men who appeared to be leaders" assured the police "that they will give the scabs no more trouble." True to their word, the strikers allowed the non-union men to go to work the next day without interference. During the incident, according to witnesses, no attempt was made by any member of the crowd to use violence against any person and no resistance "by word or gesture" was made to the police.[73]

Such behaviour did not go unnoticed by Wilson. In fact, he considered the drawing of arms an "error in judgement" and expected that union leaders would make "some capital" out of it. But the incident was also evidence that no extreme threat to law and order existed. The same lesson was apparent in other instances. There had been a gunshot on the 15th, but the culprit proved to be "an old Frenchman about 70 years old" who intended no harm and was released. Wilson

---

70 RCMP Papers, A1, vol. 316, file 238-06, Copy. Resolutions Passed by the Lethbridge Miners Union on March 10th 1906.

71 The symbolism of all this was important. The music was dissonant rather than harmonious, thus registering the disapproval of the strikers towards strikebreakers. The flags were threatening rather than celebratory: one was black, while another was white with "cure for scabs" written on it. For analysis of the import of such activities, see E.P. Thompson, "Rough Music: Le Charivari anglais," *Annales: E.S.C.*, 27 1972), 285-312; and B.D. Palmer, "Discordant Music: Charivaris and Whitecapping in Nineteenth-Century North America," *L/LT*, 3 (1978), 5-62.

72 RCMP Papers, A1, vol. 316, file 238-06, Wilson to Commissioner, 16 March 1906.

73 Ibid., Sergeant Major C.C. Raven to Wilson, 17 March 1906; William Gardiner's declaration, 17 March 1906; and John Harvie's declaration, 17 March 1906. The account given is pieced together from these sources. The chronology in Raven's report differs in that he claimed that pistols were not drawn until after he'd arrested the striker and the crowd started to rush him.

gained confidence not only because of the arrival of reinforcements on the evening of 16 March but also because actual experience had demonstrated that the strikers were not out to destroy lives and property. By 17 March, Wilson could understand even that the explosions which had occurred the two previous nights were symbolic demonstrations rather than genuine dangers.[74]

Events, or rather the lack of events, on 17 March consolidated Wilson's sense of assurance. That day was when Naismith and Wilson had feared that all hell would break loose. It did not. Indeed, for two weeks afterward almost complete tranquillity prevailed. As Wilson reported "the town people say that they never remember seeing the Village of Stafford so quiet and orderly."[75] Things were so peaceful that Wilson cut the RNWMP complement at the mine from 34 to 8 men.[76] While this was still an important commitment, since Wilson expected to have to keep the full contingent there for months, it was a significant reduction and caused Naismith real qualms.[77]

If Wilson was becoming less apprehensive, the strikers also seem to have been adapting to the presence of the police. The first ten days of the strike had not occasioned instances of police brutality. This interval also demonstrated that inappropriate police actions could be challenged by public complaints. In addition, the incident of 16 March had shown the strikers that they could make an agreement with the Mounties. In short, the strikers' actual experience modified their stereotype of the police. Indeed, by 17 March, it seemed appropriate to Frank Sherman, the President of UMWA District 18, to visit Wilson.

Sherman began by apologizing for his tardiness in consulting with the Mounties because he wanted to be cooperative and because he did not agree with the view held by many strikers that the police sided with the company.[78] He acquired information about the Riot Act and the law regarding intimidation in order to inform his men. Indeed, his stated intent was to designate about 50 union men, with badges, to maintain order amongst the strikers and for them to report any wrongdoing to the police.[79] He sought Wilson's assurance that access to bar-rooms would be restricted as he feared what might happen if booze flowed freely. He also questioned Wilson about a rumour that 150 Mounties were escorting strikebreakers to Lethbridge since such action would certainly create trouble.[80] Wilson was quick to deny the rumour, doubting that the company intended to commence operations in the near future.

---

74   Ibid., Wilson to Commissioner, 16 and 17 March 1906.

75   Ibid., Wilson to Commissioner, 20 March 1906. See also *Herald*, 29 March 1906.

76   RCMP Papers, A1, vol. 316, file 238-06, Wilson to Commissioner, 22 and 25 March and 1 April 1906; and R. Belcher to Commissioner, 29 March 1906. Wilson's monthly report for March stated that the police complement at the mine was two noncommissioned officers and six men (see ibid., A1, vol. 315, file 202-06, Wilson to Commissioner, 17 April 1906). The company put on several guards of their own (see ibid, A1, vol. 316, file 238-06, Wilson to Commissioner, 22 and 24 March 1906).

77   Ibid., Wilson to Commissioner, 22 March 1906 and Naismith to White, 23 March 1906.

78   Information on the meeting is contained in ibid., Wilson to Commissioner, 17 March 1906.

79   It does not appear that the strikers formally established their own security force, but it may be that some sort of informal system was developed.

80   In a letter to W.A. Galliher, M.P. for the Kootenay riding, Sherman had indicated that if the company attempted to import strikebreakers he could not guarantee what the strikers, who had been "very peaceful and well behaved" until then, would do (see ibid., Sherman to Galliher, 12 March 1906).

Sherman, undoubtedly relieved, explained that the union did not object to the company operating the pumps and maintaining its mine property.

The full significance of this discussion was not immediately obvious. Wilson's report indicated his suspicion of Sherman and his predilection to think ill of the strikers. In an earlier letter to his superior, Wilson had stated that the strikers should consult with him if they had any complaints,[81] yet when their representative requested an interview Wilson was "much surprised." Every comment the commanding officer made about Sherman's motives was negative. He did not even make much of the District 18 president's statement on allowing the pumps to operate,[82] despite the fact that the opposite was one of the company's key arguments in demanding police protection.[83] At no time did he express appreciation for Sherman's concern to maintain peace or for the steps the union was taking to preserve order.

Yet even at the time of the interview, several important developments were obvious. In the first place, Sherman's initiative in itself suggested the strikers' more moderate attitude toward the police. The interview enabled Sherman to present the strikers' viewpoint and to indicate their desire to preserve order, thereby making possible a more amiable relationship between the strikers and the police. Moreover, the exchange of information that took place was crucial: Sherman became informed about the details of relevant sections of the Criminal Code; Wilson learned about the desire and plans of the union to maintain peace; Wilson scotched the report about the alleged arrival of protected strikebreakers; Sherman indicated that the strikers had no qualms about the mine being kept in running order; Wilson explained that the police were bound to preserve property and protect working miners but did not intend to force the strikers back to work or defeat the strike. In short, this direct communication between the two parties allowed them to exchange valuable information and to relieve anxieties and animosities.[84]

Despite Wilson's initial suspicions, the most plausible explanation of Sherman's visit is that in his desire to further the strikers' cause, he was genuinely concerned to preserve peace, to stay within the law, to avoid conflict with the police, and to exchange information with the Mounties which would calm the situation. Wilson himself seems, gradually and partially, to have come to accept that explanation, for his evaluation of events shifted subtly after the interview. He reacted calmly to Constable Gorski's report that a number of "foreigners" said that Sherman had gone to the town of Taber to get arms for about 150 men and then "they were to form a ring about the Police Camp and prevent any scabs from going to work; the scabs were to be shot but not the Police." At the beginning of the strike, even just prior to his discussion with Sherman, Wilson might have found the report plausible. Now, however, he dismissed it: "How such stories could be circulated among the foreigners

---

81 Ibid., Wilson to Commissioner, 15 March 1906.
82 This was, in fact, the normal position adopted by the UMWA.
83 Ibid., Naismith to White, 23 March 1906.
84 As indicated earlier Wilson had made no attempt to confer with union leaders. He had entertained the idea in regard to the charge of police intimidation but decided against it. During the interview with Sherman on 17 March Wilson offered to go with him to explain the law and the role of the police to the strikers, but as Sherman did not seem overly enthused this was not done.

I am at a loss to know, but it shows how grossly ignorant they are to place any stock in such wild rumours."[85]

The calm which existed during the last two weeks of March had several sources. Wilson believed that the show of force by the police had been crucial.[86] This factor should not be discounted, but at the very least needs to be supplemented. In the first place most of the strikebreakers, some with families, had moved into railway cars at the mine.[87] This meant that the strikers were no longer confronted, twice daily, by a score of men[88] travelling between their houses and the mine, men who not only refused to accept the standards of the vast majority but also threatened to undercut the strength of the collectivity. From the strikers' perspective, those they called scabs had been sealed off, ostracized, almost imprisoned.[89] Certainly, this reduced the opportunities for the outbreak of violence. An even more important factor in explaining the tranquillity was the self-control exercised by the strikers. Actual experience demonstrated the absurdity of Naismith's and Wilson's notion that the strikers were a crazed and violent mob of "foreigners" who had no respect for the law and who could only be kept in line by force. In short, the evidence suggests that substantial violence was averted at least as much because the strikers were generally peaceable as because the police were present. Even if this were not the case, the strikers were anxious to avoid confrontations with the police because they well understood the harm that violent episodes would do to their cause, particularly with regard to public opinion.[90]

The factors helping to curb violence were of a long term nature and operated throughout the strike. They must be kept in mind when examining the series of incidents which occurred between 31 March and 4 April. In the first place, despite sensational press and police reports, the violence associated with these incidents actually was quite limited and verifies rather than contradicts the generalization that the strikers were, in the main, nonviolent and accepted police authority. Secondly, two major elements which had contributed to peace in the two weeks preceding — a lack of new strikebreakers and a lack of contact between strikers and strikebreakers — no longer prevailed by the end of March. Indeed, this was a crucial time both for the company and the strikers. A strike merely of a few weeks' duration was not terribly damaging for either side but by the end of March the significance of a lengthy struggle was becoming apparent. The striking miners had to face the issue of how they were to survive without pay. Company officials had to wonder how the mine ever could resume operations without its skilled work force. The simplest solution to both problems was for the men to return to work but as neither party would accept the

---

85   Ibid., Wilson to Commissioner, 19 March 1906. Wilson does not seem to have considered whether Gorski was getting "straight goods" or whether the miners knew that this newcomer was a spy of some sort and therefore fed him a line.

86   Ibid., Wilson to Commissioner, 19 March and 17 April 1906.

87   This was first reported by Wilson on 22 March but they may have been there for a couple of days by that time (see ibid., Wilson to Commissioner, 22 March 1906).

88   Naismith said about 30 men were working (see ibid, Naismith to White, 23 March 1906).

89   S.A.B. Crabb to Editor, n.d., in the *United Mine Workers Journal* (Indianapolis), 28 June 1906, (hereafter *UMW Journal*).

90   Gorski's report specified directly and Sherman's visit implied this realization by the strikers (see RCMP Papers, A1, vol. 316, file 238-06, Wilson to Commissioner, 17 March 1906).

other's terms for this to occur, the struggle narrowed at this juncture to the question of whether or not the strikers would go back to the mine.

A test of strength occurred on 31 March when a blacksmith/teamster decided to quit the strike and go back to work.[91] The strikers needed to demonstrate their disapproval of such action and to warn others that it was unacceptable, perhaps even dangerous, to follow his example. The company, in order to encourage others to follow suit, needed to show that this striker safely could return to work. Not surprisingly, mine manager Hardie turned to the Mounties to secure safe passage to the mine for the blacksmith and his belongings. Four Mounties were detailed for this duty, although they were instructed merely to prevent a breach of peace and not to assist in moving furniture. The ensuing events can be reconstructed from the somewhat-contradictory police reports. While a wagon was being loaded at the blacksmith's house, a crowd of between 20 and 50 "foreigners" gathered and began to hoot and yell. When the wagon started to pull away with the blacksmith walking behind it, and RNWMP Corporal Brewer walking behind him, the din escalated with much jeering, whistling, and beating of cans with sticks. Corporal Brewer told the crowd to stop making such a racket. He then grabbed a man who struggled to escape with the help of others in the crowd. During this tussle, Constable Kelly drew his pistol, believing that a man with a stick was about to hit Brewer. According to Kelly's account, he told the man that he would "hit him a crack" with his pistol. The strikers' own, more-plausible account is that Kelly threatened to shoot. In any case, the man dropped his stick and Kelly put his pistol away. Meanwhile, Brewer had lost his prisoner. The Mounties, obviously thinking that discretion was the better part of valour, turned and escorted the blacksmith and his possessions to the mine, with the crowd, still beating cans, following.

The aftermath of this incident is highly instructive. One could easily envisage Wilson calling for reinforcements, for instructing his men to bring charges of intimidation, disturbing the peace and illegal assembly against strikers who acted in this manner, and for taking a tough line. None of this transpired. Indeed, the Mounties were put on the defensive, not the strikers. Sherman had seized the initiative by phoning Wilson to complain "that the police had pulled their revolvers and threatened to shoot some men who were holding a procession." Wilson had not even heard about the incident from his own people at this point, but promised Sherman that he would make an immediate inquiry. Sherman's complaint shaped the entire nature of Wilson's investigation, which focused, in the event, on whether or not the police had been at fault rather than upon the actions of the crowd. In short, the accused became the police rather than the strikers.

Wilson's interviews with the Mounties involved in the incident did not substantiate the "threat to shoot" charge, but did clarify that such a threat, if made, was unacceptable. Indeed, the record demonstrated that the police had been warned frequently against even drawing firearms unless absolutely necessary. One of the difficulties, according to the commanding officer, was that the Mounties only had pistols — "under similar circumstances, if armed with clubs, they would draw them and use

---

91 Information related to the incident of 31 March comes from ibid., "Memorandum of evidence taken in complaint made by Mr. Sherman that a Constable did draw his pistol and threaten to blow out the brains of certain men at Stafford Village at about 2:00 p.m. of the 31 April [sic], 1906"; Wilson to Commissioner, 1 April, 1906; and Perry to Comptroller, 3 April 1906.

them instead of pistols." Wilson made other criticisms: 1) sending an escort was a mistake — a patrol should have been nearby to act if violence had threatened, but not a designated escort; 2) no arrests should have been attempted by a few Mounties when confronted with a large crowd of excited people; 3) the blacksmith should not have walked behind the wagon but have ridden it, thereby allowing the horses to trot off; and 4) "In this instance, I feel sure, had Corporal Brewer been a live man, of good judgement, he would have avoided any trouble, but unfortunately he is one of the slowest men I have ever seen." Wilson issued new orders to his men in accord with these findings, and also removed Kelly, though not Brewer, from strike duty.[92] Wilson also recognized that the company's effort to recruit workers posed a threat: "There is plenty of time yet for serious trouble in this strike if the Company attempts to hire individual men who wish to return to work, and if they attempt to put men to work in place of all the Union men there is sure to be trouble, and it will take a considerable force to handle the situation." It is clear, from Wilson's failure to call for reinforcements at this time and his disinclination to provide escorts for returning miners, that he preferred the RNWMP not be placed in the position of helping the company hire strikebreakers, even though Wilson acknowledged the company's right to hire non-union men. In other words, on the strikebreaker issue, Wilson sided with the strikers. It was not that he wanted to help the strikers win the struggle; rather, he was concerned with preserving order. Wilson was also responding to pressure applied by the strikers. Sherman not only had complained to Wilson about the "threat to shoot" but also had caused police actions in Lethbridge to become, once again, a matter of scrutiny in Ottawa.[93] Moreover, the threat of the union pressing charges against Kelly hung over Wilson's head for a week after the incident and led him to address Sherman in most courteous terms.[94]

It would be absurd to think that the Mounties suddenly had become partners with

---

92 It was not an unusual tactic of police forces to transfer unpopular policemen (see Emsley, *Policing and Its Context*, 156-7).

93 Sherman had telegraphed Alphonse Verville, the Labour M.P., with the strikers' version of the incident, claiming that "if this continues fear serious bloodshed," and directing Verville to take steps in Ottawa (RCMP Papers, A1, vol. 316, file 238-06, Sherman to Verville, copy of telegram, 31 March 1906). Verville was the newly elected M.P. for Maissonneuve and President of the Trades and Labour Congress of Canada. Earlier in the strike he had asked embarrassing questions in the House of Commons about police involvement (see ibid., copy of seven questions raised by Mr. Verville on 21 March 1906; ibid, Answers to Inquiry by Mr. Verville, M.P.; *Canada: House of Commons Debates, 1906* (Ottawa, 1906), 573-4 (26 March); and *Herald*, 29 March 1906). In regard to the 31 March incident, the RNWMP comptroller in Ottawa sought and received information from the commissioner (see RCMP Papers, A1, vol. 316, file 238-06, White to Perry, telegram, 2 April 1906; and Perry to White, telegram, 3 April 1906). At the same time Ralph Smith, the MP for Vancouver District, asked for copies of correspondence relating to the strike and the calling in of the Mounties [see *Debates, 1906*, 998 (2 April)]. These were returned without discussion on 6 April, 1906. The return was Sessional Paper No. 80 for 1906 but was not printed. Nonetheless the correspondence had been made public. Smith, Verville, or other parliamentarians or reporters could have raised the matter if they had considered that anything untoward had occurred. The fact that this did not happen should not blind one to the important fact that the police, once again, had come under public examination.

94 On this matter see RCMP Papers, A1, vol. 316, file 238-06, Wilson to Commissioner, 1 April 1906; Wilson to Sherman, 7 April 1906; and Sherman to Wilson, 8 April 1906. For a brief discussion of the dynamics of constables being judged on an alleged misconduct by senior officers of the same policing force, see Cain, *Society and the Policeman's Role*, 244-5.

the strikers. Nonetheless, Sherman's skilful tactics again had put the Mounties on the defensive, forcing them to justify their actions in public and in private, encouraging them to recognize that the company's attempts to hire jeopardized the peace they were trying to maintain, and compelling them to modify their crowdhandling tactics. This was quite an accomplishment in the wake of an incident in which the strikers could have been castigated as violent hooligans.

Demonstrations against non-union men had been a prominent feature of the strikers' prosecution of the strike from its inception. The results of the 31 March incident, including the revised tactics of the police, did nothing to diminish such activities. At noon on 3 April, a crowd composed mainly of women jeered at and threw snow at a strikebreaker who was attempting to move furniture from his house to the mine camp.[95] A couple of Mounties eventually moved in, but the women were not cowed and some altercations occurred. In fact, a union source boasted: "We have a Slav woman who went out and whipped one of the police to a standstill."[96] Only one man was arrested. The next day he received a 15-day jail sentence. Beyond this the strikers paid no legal consequences for harassing working miners. Undoubtedly, the story of the noontime confrontation was related at the supper tables of the strikers and fuelled their resolve to maintain pressure on their backsliding brethren.

Early on that evening of 3 April three working miners — Louis Albert, Andrew Robi, and Steve Ungvarie — went to fetch a dozen chickens and board up the windows of Ungvarie's house. Their noisy presence attracted a crowd of up to 300 men, women and children who jeered, whistled, and shouted threats at the threesome. Stones, bottles, bricks, and sundry items were flung in their direction. Two of the non-striking miners left the fenced yard with a tub of chickens and were allowed to proceed without injury, though chased by stones and threats. The third, Louis Albert, stopped to close the gate and with his left hand, in which he held a hatchet as well as a pair of boots, took a swipe at a youth who was bothering him. The response was immediate. One member of the crowd, Karl Theodorovics, hit the strikebreaker with a rock. Albert went down; the strikers moved in on him. At this point Sergeant Bolderson came to the rescue and put himself between Albert and the crowd. Bolderson was hit with flying stones but managed to protect the injured man and, with the assistance of a few more Mounties, to get him back to the safety of the mine property. The RNWMP halted the pursuing crowd and it gradually dispersed, though evidently in bad humour.[97]

---

95   Information on this incident is located in ibid., Wilson to Commissioner, 3 and 4 April 1906; and *News*, 6 April 1906. Material on this case is scanty, probably because it paled in significance beside the "riots" of the evenings of 3 and 4 April, and the reconstruction of events requires some speculation.

96   Peter Patterson to Editor, 6 May 1906, in *UMW Journal*, 17 May 1906. Constable Fitzgerald wanted her arrested for assault but Wilson "thought it better not to bother with women..."

97   Information on the events of the evening of 3 April is located in *Herald*, 5 April 1906; *News*, 6 April 1906; RCMP Papers, A1, vol. 238-06, Wilson to Commissioner, 4 April 1906; ibid., Bolderson, "Crime Report — Re. Riot on evening of Tuesday, 3 April, 1906," 6 April 1906; ibid, Wilson, "Crime Report — Re. assault on Louis Albert by Karl Theodorovics, causing actual bodily harm, on the 3rd of April, Inst. at Stafford Village," 10 April 1906; ibid, Wilson, "Crime Report — Re. Disturbance at Stafford Village, April 3rd 1906," 10 April 1906; Ibid, Bolderson, "Crime Report — Re. Strike at Lethbridge. Assault on Louis Albert," n.d.; and PAA, Acc. 78.235, Supreme Court Criminal — Fort Macleod, Box 11 (1-C-1) (henceforth Alberta Supreme Court Records), files 848 and 850-55.

Both altercations on 3 April tested Wilson's revised tactics: no police escorts; no pistols or even clubs drawn; no arrests in crowds. The results were not entirely satisfactory to Wilson, for one man had been wounded, Mounties had been attacked though not seriously injured, and the crowd had not been very manageable. For Wilson, even the policy of not drawing pistols seemed to have promoted violence, not suppressed it: "It has been circulated among them [the "foreigners"] that the Police cannot draw their arms[;] consequently their fears of our power has been lessened."[98] Indeed, the Mounted Police image of the strikers reverted somewhat towards its original view: a "mob" of "foreigners" who had been involved in a "riot."[99] Wilson's suspicion of the strikers revived: "the foreigners are by some means kept worked up."[100] Indeed, Wilson half-implied that a labour conspiracy was afoot since he mentioned that a Winnipeg strike[101] was having a bad effect on the one in Lethbridge, and also noted that the Taber miners nearby were expected to go on strike shortly.

Given his frame of mind, Wilson's response to the "riot" was predictable: the power of the police had to be demonstrated through greater vigilance, increased manpower, and judicial prosecution. Wilson's immediate reaction upon learning of the altercation had been to send eight mounted men to patrol the miners' village for several hours, and the following day he arranged to augment the contingent at the mine encampment. In addition, he asked the commissioner to increase his strength by 20 men. Finally, he pressed charges against nine men, convinced that convictions would "have a good effect."[102] In short, Wilson believed that a tougher stand was required to make the "foreigners" toe the line and to show everyone that punishment would be meted out to those who overstepped it.

From the strikers' perspective, police behaviour during both incidents on 3 April had been acceptable. No escorts had been provided for strikebreakers and the police had not used weapons to threaten the strikers. In reality the Mounties had allowed the strikers to do their job, for the police had not stopped the strikers from showing their displeasure with strikebreakers. Indeed, the Mounties had not prevented the strikers from demonstrating their physical power — something that would have deterred other strikers who may have been considering returning to the mine. The police had not even prevented the strikers from punishing a hatchet-wielding strikebreaker who, from their perspective, had attacked a defenseless boy. In other words, the Mounties had allowed the strikers to accomplish their primary goals without direct confrontation. But this was a reciprocal arrangement. The strikers had allowed Sergeant Bolderson to rescue Albert, and had halted when told by the police to stop following the strikebreakers. Moreover, despite Wilson's analysis, the strikers

---

98 RCMP Papers, A1, vol. 316, file 238-06, Wilson to Commissioner, 4 April 1906.

99 Ibid. Given the technical definition of "riot" in the Criminal Code (see *Canada: Revised Statutes, 1906*, chapter 146, section 88), this depiction of the incident was not incorrect, but was hardly the only term that might have been used. The charges against those eventually brought to trial were not for rioting but for unlawful assembly and disturbing the peace. Wilson's use of the terms "foreigner," "mob," and "riot" is a potent indicator of his emotional attitude and interpretive understanding.

100 RCMP Papers, A1, vol. 316, file 238-06, Wilson to Commissioner, 4 April 1906.

101 A brief description of the strike of Winnipeg street railway workers in March and April is given in Jamieson, *Times of Trouble*, 84-5.

102 RCMP Papers, A1, vol. 316, file 238-06, Wilson to Commissioner, 4 April 1906.

had not run amok but actually had shown considerable restraint. Nobody, not even Albert, had been seriously injured, and no property had been destroyed. Since protection of property and persons was the mandate of the police during the strike, the police had few grounds for complaint based on the actual behaviour of the strikers. The 3 April incidents demonstrated a kind of saw-off between the strikers and the Mounties. The strikers had been able to demonstrate their unwritten code of conduct, or law, while the police had been able to demonstrate theirs. The strikers accepted the line drawn by the Mounties, while the Mounties tacitly acknowledged the legitimacy, or at least the predictability, of strikers' demonstrations against strikebreakers.[103] A *modus vivendi* had been established between the two groups and their separate rules of law.

This *modus vivendi* was challenged but not, in the final analysis, overthrown by what the Mounties again called a "riot" at dusk on the following day, 4 April.[104] At about 7 p.m., three strikers and two working miners were carrying on a discussion near the boundary of the mine property. After they had evidently drifted onto company land, a Mountie went over to disperse the strikers. They started to move off, but then one of them, Sam Popovitch, stopped and, according to the policeman, acted as follows:

> [He] put up his fist and shook it at me and called me something in a loud voice; I at the same time was motioning them to move on. He then called in a loud voice ["]you God damned son of a bitch Policeman you no good["]; he repeated this twice and other things which I could not understand; he said also ["]me fix scab last night me fix Policeman to-night["]; he was all the time shaking his fist at me...[105]

The constable then attempted to arrest Popovitch but was impeded by the drunken Wasyl Weidok. The ruckus and calls for assistance on both sides quickly brought reinforcements, eventually resulting in a crowd of more than 200 strikers and family members, some carrying sticks or clubs, facing six policemen and two company night watchmen. And while people gathered, the evidently dull-witted Corporal Brewer pursued Weidok, who'd run off. Predictably, other strikers tried to rescue Weidok and Constable Fitzgerald had to come to Brewer's aid. It was at this point, when only 15 or so strikers were on hand, that the most intense fighting of the whole affair took place. Fitzgerald, who had not fared very well in his scuffle with a

---

103 Aside from Wilson's earlier report that problems could be expected if men left the strike and went back to work, Bolderson stated in his crime report that Ungvarie had that very day quit the strikers, as though that was sufficient explanation for the crowd gathering at Ungvarie's house. Actually, other evidence indicates that Ungvarie and the two others had been working for weeks, for the names of all three were on an anonymous letter of 18 March which threatened the working miners (see ibid, "David and Goliath" to Joseph Oros, 18 March, translated copy enclosed in Wilson to Commissioner, 24 March 1906).

104 Information on the incident of the evening of 4 April is to be found in *Herald*, 5 and 12 April 1906; *News*, 6 April 1906; RCMP Papers, A1, vol. 316, file 238-06, Wilson to Commissioner, 4, 5, 6, and 8 April 1906; ibid., Perry to Comptroller, telegram, 5 April 1906; ibid., "Re Disturbance at No. 3 Shaft Stafford Village on the night of 4th April, Evidence taken under oath," enclosed in Wilson to Commissioner, 5 April 1906; and Alberta Supreme Court Records, file 849. In the account which follows only direct quotations are given specific references.

105 RCMP Papers, A1, vol. 316, file 328-06, "Re. Disturbance ... 4th April ..." enclosed in Wilson to Commissioner, 5 April 1906. It is judicial records rather than RCMP Papers that provide the first name of Popovitch [see PAA, Acc. 69.210, Justices of Peace Files, Box 89/JP (Robert Belcher), Return for 1906].

woman the day before, was hit in the stomach as he stooped to remove one man's hand from the prisoner's legs. Fitzgerald then began to use his own club, with such force that he broke it, and felt compelled to draw his revolver. Two other Mounties also waded in with truncheons and hands and thrashed about in the growing crowd, which in turn was using sticks, throwing rocks, and yelling "scabs" and other epithets in several languages. The police managed to retain Popovitch and Weidok, and got them to the guard car; although fighting, rock-throwing, and yelling continued sporadically for a while, the crowd gradually scattered.[106] Indeed, union officials helped the police quiet and disperse the crowd.[107] Yet no authority was able to prevent the strikers from punishing the three strikebreakers who had been involved in the incident of 3 April and who had compounded their sins in the strikers' eyes by giving evidence to the police against some of the strikers involved. Despite police patrols, within hours the houses of those three working miners were dynamited or burned, though none were destroyed and, since they were vacant, nobody was injured.[108] It was hardly coincidental that no strikebreaker testified against the strikers involved in the episode of 4 April.

Understandably police testimony initially alleged that the affray of 4 April had been a serious matter. It had involved direct fighting between Mounties and strikers and to a man, the police characterized it as a riotous gathering. Several declared that they had feared someone would be killed. Yet it could be argued that the degree of actual violence was limited and the amount of restraint exercised by the strikers was considerable. No one received other than minor injuries; the strikers concentrated their "violence" on attempting to release Popovitch and Weidok rather than on attacking the police; some strikers had come armed with sticks but no firearms, knives, axes, iron pipes, or chains were in evidence, despite the earlier police reports that the strikers were well-armed; union officials had worked to calm the crowd; even the explosions were carefully targeted.

The police response to the 4 April events was dual in nature. On the one hand, the Mounties' initial explanation was that drunken "foreigners" had caused the confrontation and had only been held in check by force, although the assistance rendered by union officials was acknowledged. As a consequence of this view, Wilson requested 30 additional men, 10 of whom should be mounted, and 50 police truncheons. He posted extra sentries at the mine, and ordered constant mounted patrolling of the miners' village.

But on the other hand, the tough line towards the strikers was greatly softened by other instructions and actions, or lack of action. In the first place, Wilson ordered his men to "be careful not to appear overbearing" and to "remain strictly neutral between the Company and the Strikers." Moreover, Wilson tacitly acknowledged the fault of his men for the 4 April fiasco by reiterating proper arrest procedure: "Should the necessity for making an arrest arise, with any possibility of an attempt to rescue,

---

106 From the beginning of the incident to the dispersal of the crowd, about 30 minutes and certainly no more than 45 minutes had elapsed.
107 A number of the reports suggest that more than one union official was involved, but only one was identified, as secretary of the union, rather than by name. The secretary was S.A.B. Crabb.
108 There is no conclusive proof that the strikers were responsible but any other explanation seems unlikely.

it would be better to telephone to Barracks for a mounted party, should there not be sufficient men on duty at the time." Wilson was also at pains to give close instruction on the use of arms: "You are instructed to avoid bloodshed and arms are only to be used in self-defense. Should the necessity for drawing arms arise (which should only be done in very grave and serious cases) they will be used as clubs, except in case of self-defense when a man's life is threatened."[109] Secondly, he was in contact with union officials to try to defuse the situation. The third example of Wilson's gentler approach was his unruffled response to actual and threatened explosions. True, he did have miners' houses searched for explosives, but none turned up and he suspended the hunt. The police seemed to have understood and largely accepted both their inability to prevent explosions and the reason for and nature of the blasts — that is, that strikers were not bombing inhabited dwellings. Thus, when Wilson heard that there was a threat to blow up an inhabited house, he was skeptical: "I do not place much stock in this..."[110] The fourth and most interesting illustration of the more accommodating approach of the Mounties was the lack of arrests stemming from the disturbance of 4 April, aside from the "swearer" and the "drunk," both of whom received fines of $5 and costs.[111] Wilson noted in his report that he considered that Belcher had taken "a fair view of the case." The lightness of the sentences and Wilson's comment cast grave doubt on the severity of the "riot" itself. Only one other man was arrested, the same Karl Theodorovics who had hit Albert with a rock on 3 April. Perhaps more arrests were simply impossible because of inadequate identification of the "rioters" or because some strikers went into hiding. Both explanations were given; but even Wilson found these excuses of his men peculiar and, indeed, they are unsatisfying. After all, the incident was supposed to have been a "riot," a serious challenge to established authority. In such a situation, as one analyst has argued, "to come back empty-handed would be to admit impotence. If rioters could not be found, they had to be invented."[112] Indeed, something like that had occurred in the aftermath of the 3 April "riot" when nine charges had been laid — in one case against a man who had simply been there. Why the difference after the second "riot"? Surely it might have been considered part of a trend of escalating violence and therefore have fit the pattern whereby "repression of crime grew more severe as criminal activity increased."[113] If it is true that "the police will endeavour to prove their own thesis about the origins, motivations, and leadership of a riot by the type [and number] of people they arrest,"[114] it would follow that the Mounties, on reflection, did not consider the incident a fundamental challenge. Undoubtedly they came to see that the outbreak of conflict had been accidental and might have been avoided had the police ignored the provocation given by Popovitch. Even with the

---

109 RCMP Papers, A1, vol. 316, file 238-06, Wilson to Inspector Camies, 8 April, enclosed in Wilson to Commissioner, 8 April 1906. Before the fracas of 4 April ended, three Mounties and the two night watchmen had drawn their firearms.

110 Ibid., Wilson to Commissioner, 6 April 1906.

111 These cases were tried by Inspector Belcher of the RNWMP who was also a Justice of the Peace. It was not unusual for the force in its various guises to fill the roles of investigator, arrestor, prosecutor, judge, and jailer (see Macleod, "Problem of Law and Order," 137; and Walden, *Visions of Order*, 15).

112 Cobb, *Police and People*, 28.

113 G.R. Elton, "Introduction: Crime and the Historian," in J.S. Cockburn, ed., *Crime in England 1550-1800* (Princeton 1977), 9.

114 Cobb, *Police and People*, 28.

eruption, union leaders had worked to restore order, the strikers had backed off, and nobody had been seriously hurt. The lack of arrests indicated that the police on the spot, if not Wilson himself, were satisfied that the so-called "riot" had been an unintended outburst and was inconsequential in terms of origins, motivation and leadership. In other words, for the Mounties there was an essential innocence in the actions of the strikers.[115] Given this perception, multiple arrests might well have been considered unnecessary and perhaps counterproductive, likely to result in greater unrest, not less. This was not a prospect the police could take lightly, for they were quite aware of the potential physical power of the strikers. There were, therefore, two rational grounds for the Mounties restraining themselves both in terms of crowd management and in terms of arrests: the fear of physical harm; and, more importantly, the promotion of their mandate to preserve order and prevent property damage. To a degree, therefore, the police collaborated with the strikers, a situation that should not be considered strange or unusual: "For in any urban community there would always be a certain degree of complicity between the police and those the police considered potentially dangerous. There was always a great deal of give and take, a carefully measured mutual toleration (combined with wariness)."[116]

For the strikers there was also much to be gained by cooperating with the police. Violence, or its threat, was not without utility for the strikers just as it was for the police. But just as the police could be taken to task for their actions before the bar of public opinion, so too could the strikers. Violence, especially clashes with the police, most certainly harmed the cause of strikers in the public mind for it undermined the image the union wished to project of miners being inoffensive, decent people who deserved better treatment from employers. It was even a source of doubt and division within the strikers' own ranks, as can be seen from Sherman's rather disparaging comments about "foreigners"[117] and the attempts of union officials to control the crowds. Retaining unity amongst the strikers, an essential ingredient to the prosecution of the strike, would best be achieved by maintaining order and order would best be secured by working together with the police. This cooperation took place on two levels. Firstly, union officials played a role clearly visible to and welcomed by the police. The initiative of one executive member during the 4 April incident has already been mentioned. Other activities followed. On 6 April Wilson reported that "a very decent chap," an executive member of Local 574 named Holbrook, was doing everything he could to maintain order and had promised to assist Wilson in every way possible.[118] In addition, Sherman had returned to Lethbridge on 5 April,

---

115 For a discussion of the Mounties' use of discretion and turning the blind eye and deaf ear, see Walden, *Visions of Order*, 40.

116 Ibid., 18.

117 For example, at a Lethbridge Trades and Labour Council meeting in March, Sherman had stated that there was no danger of trouble from the strikers unless they were provoked by injustice "and then it is hard to say what these mixed nationalities will do" (see *Herald*, 15 March 1906). On 23 March 1906, the Winnipeg labour newspaper *The Voice* reported Sherman as stating in a public meeting that he "condemned the bringing of miners from central Europe, they being the most revolutionary Socialists and would yet make demands undreamed of by English laborers."

118 RCMP Papers, A1, vol. 316, file 238-06, Wilson to Commissioner, 6 April 1906. Very little is known about Holbrook. One assumes that the Jno. W. Holbrook who chaired the nominating meeting at which Sherman was selected as the Labor candidate in the Provincial byelection was the same individual (see *Herald*, 29 March 1906; and *News* 27 March 1906).

presumably an immediate response to the trouble. Evidently he encouraged the Mounties in the belief that Karl Theodorovics, the one extra man arrested for involvement in the 4 April incident, had been the principal instigator. At least, Wilson was informed that Sherman was glad Theodorovics had been arrested and that the UMWA lawyer would not defend him.[119] Moreover, it was at this time that Sherman renounced his intention of pursuing the charge against the Mounties in connection with the "threat to shoot" incident.

The strikers' cooperation with the police is also apparent in a much more subtle manoeuvre. Many of the supposed troublemakers disappeared from sight. Immediately after the 4 April dust-up a number of them went into hiding. But progressively many more strikers left town, especially bachelors who were considered to be both more volatile and more likely to quit the strike and go back to work. On both counts their departure promised to bring greater serenity and it appears that the union assisted them in leaving and in finding work elsewhere.[120] Although it would be foolish to think that the exodus was simply a matter of getting along with the police, as though considerations of financial need did not impel many strikers to seek work elsewhere, it did have the effect of assuaging the concerns of the Mounties.

The upshot of the 4 April incident was reinforcement of the *modus vivendi*. Both police and strikers were able to see that it was in their interest to avoid confrontation with each other. Both saw that there was a line upon which they could agree without subverting the fundamental goals of either party. There was nothing insidious in this. Neither party had cause for shame. On the contrary, both sides were acting quite rationally in furthering their own interests. They discovered that cooperation was the best means to achieve their separate ends.

It would be an exaggeration to say that after 4 April the relationship between Mounties and miners was placid and uneventful. During the following months there were sporadic incidents and alarms. Periodic explosions continued, such as one which was most unusual in that it destroyed the verandah of an inhabited house, though even this one injured nobody.[121] Various types of confrontations between

---

119 The lawyer did act in the case. An examination of the evidence presented at the trial does not indicate that Theodorovics was especially culpable. But as he'd been involved in the Albert case, he was fingered for the incident of the 4th; union and police officials alike seemed quite content to place the blame on his shoulders (see Alberta Supreme Court Records, file 849).

120 By 17 May, Inspector Camies, the officer in charge of the mine camp detachment, reported that nearly all the single miners had gone, leaving miners who were property owners, and presumably family men to carry on the strike (see RCMP Papers, A1, vol. 316, file 238-06, Camies to Wilson 17 May 1906; also ibid, Wilson to Commissioner, 6 May 1906). On 8 June 1906, *The Voice* reported that 300 strikers had gone to seek work elsewhere, leaving 220 in Lethbridge drawing strike pay. It may be that property-owning married men were both more placid and less likely to go strikebreaking than single miners, but this commonsense assumption should be given only provisional acceptance. In the case of the 1906 Lethbridge strike, at least, the evidence on this matter is certainly inconclusive. No hard evidence exists to verify union assistance to strikers leaving Lethbridge, but it seems probable — not only because it would reduce union expenditure on strike pay, but also because there are examples of similar activities by the union in dealing with miners who came to Lethbridge looking for work during the strike. Moreover, the *News* of 14 April 1906 reported that 75 strikers were about to leave for the mines in San Coulee, Montana.

121 RCMP Papers, A1, vol. 315, file 202-06, Wilson to Commissioner, 18 September 1906 (monthly report for August); ibid., vol. 316, file 238-06, W. Munday to Wilson, 13 August 1906 and Wilson to Commissioner, 14 August 1906; and Alberta Supreme Court Records, file 896.

strikers and non-union men continued, including one case in which union official Sherman phoned Wilson to inform him that trouble was brewing because some of the working miners were challenging the strikers.[122] Yet throughout the strike, police involvement did not prevent strikers from using a variety of mechanisms to dissuade potential strikebreakers from going to work.[123] And despite the various threatening episodes which took place during the nine-month strike, after 4 April the tension between strikers and police subsided.

For months, however, Wilson clung to the interpretation that the tranquillity which prevailed was due to a strengthened force of Mounties.[124] There were always enough incidents to make this view plausible, but there was something absurd about a position which used both storms and calms as arguments in favour of retaining a significant police presence. In fact it would be more credible to think that if the police contributed to the maintenance of peace and order it was more a result of delicate tactics than large numbers. Yet Wilson went so far as to assert that he'd have to keep the men sent from other divisions until the strike was over.[125] But eventually he had to back off. On the one hand the commanding officer of the Macleod Division clamoured to have his men returned.[126] On the other hand the usual discipline problems within the ranks were exacerbated by the inactivity and distastefulness of guard duty during the strike. The result was everything from desertion to imprisonment, to dismissal from the force.[127] By mid-May, Wilson had reduced the mine camp detachment to a half-dozen men.[128] Given the exodus of strikers from Lethbridge the number of Mounties and miners confronting each other had, therefore, significantly decreased by mid-May. Two months later the RNWMP Commissioner ordered Wilson to remove the remainder and to notify company officials that "owing to stress of work,

---

122 RCMP Papers, A1, vol. 316, file 238-06, Wilson to Commissioner, 15 April 1906; and ibid., B5, vol. 2478, file 57, Camies to Wilson, 14 April 1906. Sherman's action is one more indication that union leaders worked with the police to maintain the peace.

123 These techniques, ranging from threats of various degrees of seriousness to a train ticket out of town to a place where union work was available, continued throughout the strike and were relatively successful. Few of the original strikers went back to work and many incoming miners were dissuaded.

124 Ibid., A1, vol. 315, file 202-06, Wilson to Commissioner, 17 April 1906 (monthly report for March). See also ibid., A1, vol. 316, file 238-06, Wilson to Commissioner, 15 April and 2 May 1906.

125 Ibid., A1, vol. 316, file 238-06, Wilson to Commissioner, 19 April and 2 June 1906.

126 Ibid., B5, vol. 2478, file 57, Primrose to Commissioner, 22 April 1906.

127 Ibid., A1, vol. 316, file 238-06, Wilson to Commissioner, 19 May 1906, Wilson to Assistant Commissioner, telegram, 15 July 1906, and McIllree (Assistant Commissioner) to Comptroller, telegram, 16 July 1906; White to Galt, 19 July 1906; White to A.M. Nanton, 1 August 1906; and ibid., Al, vol. 315, file 202-06, Wilson to Commissioner, 20 June 1906 (monthly report for May), 24 July 1906 (monthly report for June) and 24 August 1906 (monthly report for July). Evidently, some Mounties did not find the duty repugnant. After his discharge, Sergeant G. Goodwin became a special constable at Coal Creek in the Crow's Nest Pass (*The Frank Ledger*, 8 August 1906), and Corporal Brewer did the same thing for the Lethbridge mine (*Herald*, 6 September 1906). The monthly reports of the Lethbridge commanding officers both before and after 1906 demonstrate that breaches of discipline were frequent and, therefore, not solely related to strike duty (see, for example, RCMP Papers, A1, vol. 63, file 247-92, Deane to Commissioner, 31 August 1892; and ibid., A1, vol. 334, file 184-07 (Wilson's monthly reports for 1907).

128 Ibid., Al, vol. 316, file 238-06, Wilson to Commissioner, 6, 17, 19, 21 May 1906; and Camies to Wilson, 17 May 1906, and Wilson to Naismith, 19 May 1906, both enclosed in Wilson to Commissioner, 19 May 1906.

we can no longer furnish these men for that duty."[129] The order was not carried out immediately since it coincided with one of the sporadic episodes and might have given the appearance of withdrawing under pressure, but by early September all Mounties, save one, had been removed from duty at the mine camp.[130] For the last three months of the strike, then, the Mounties' involvement was negligible. Contrary to the claims of the company and the fears of Wilson, the strikers did not take advantage of this situation to destroy company property or to beat working miners. Aside from a couple of minor disturbances, things were extremely quiet and non-violent right to the end of the strike at the beginning of December.[131]

*****

The first conclusion to be drawn from examining the relationship of police and strikers during the 1906 Lethbridge strike is that for both groups there were social boundaries to their behaviour. In part, those limits were established by society at large. The public expected police to act in an even-handed, neutral fashion within the context of the Criminal Code. Biased and aggressive police action towards peaceable strikers was not, therefore, acceptable. The public also considered that individuals had a right to work (or not work) if they wished. Thus it was not permissible for strikers to use violence, or its threat, to prevent a person from working.[132] Both police and strikers were hedged in by such public views and were entitled to take action to force the other party to accept them. But the boundaries to behaviour also included the lines drawn by the other social group. Through a multiplicity of mechanisms ranging from brute force to mild entreaties, police influenced strikers and vice versa.

The accommodation of strikers and police did not represent a true meeting of minds. RNWMP officers never developed much comprehension of the justification of the strike, expressing the wish more than once that the strikers would just go back to work. Wilson undoubtedly considered the miners an already-advantaged group of workers who were making excessive demands, especially since many were "foreigners." Certainly this would be the inference the Mounties would draw from their discovery that the average daily earnings of seven prominent strikers ranged between $2.80 and $5.03 for the six months prior to the strike, some four to eight times the $.60 per day received by a RNWMP recruit at the time.[133] Other invidious comparisons could have been drawn by the police. If miners complained of harsh treatment by the company,

---

129   Ibid., Perry to Wilson, telegram 17 July 1906. See also ibid., McIllree to Comptroller, 16 July 1906.

130   Ibid., Wilson to Commissioner, 17 (2 letters), 18 (letter and telegram), 24, 27 and 30 July, and 7 September 1906.

131   On the conclusion of the strike, see Baker, "Miners and Mediator."

132   The term "public" is not, of course, very precise. It refers to those, presumably a majority, who hold the dominant, commonly-accepted ideas or notions within a society.

133   S.W. Horrall, *The Pictorial History of the Royal Canadian Mounted Police* (Toronto 1973), 34. It was $.75 a day in 1873, reduced to $.40 in 1880, raised to $.60 in 1905 and to $.75 in 1912. However, the Mounties received food and lodging in addition to their pay and they had a pension plan. It is interesting that although there are few items in the Mounted Police papers related to the issues in dispute between management and labour during the strike, multiple copies of the list showing the strikers' pay were filed, though without comment or reference, in the Mounted Police papers. The company must have supplied the information, undoubtedly to shape the perceptions of the police.

ordinary Mounties might have responded that it was nothing compared to the authoritarian management procedures of the RNWMP whereby fines, jail sentences, and dismissals were quite normal practices.[134] If strikers argued the need to establish better economic conditions for their wives and children, Mounties might have noted that for most constables, marriage itself was unlikely both for financial reasons and because personnel were moved frequently. Clearly, Mounties had little sympathy for strikers. Yet there is little indication of strong police hostility toward the strikers once the initial negative stereotype had been overcome. Indeed, the Mounties did develop an independent judgement of what was required of them as witnessed, for example, by the decision in July, without consultation with company officials, to withdraw the force at the mine encampment.[135] It is true, of course, that the Mounties had accepted "direction" by company officials at the beginning and then retained a jaundiced view of the presumed violent proclivities of the "foreign" strikers. But then "it is the duty of the police to be two steps ahead of potential violence."[136] There were, moreover, other police activities which also demonstrated a lack of neutrality — but in favour of the strikers. Examples include the limited number of charges laid by the Mounties following the altercations of 3 and 4 April, and their unwillingness to provide escorts for working miners venturing out of the mine camp even though the police knew that the strikebreakers were at risk. The argument about the failure of the Mounties to act in a neutral fashion cuts both ways.

For their part, if the strikers ever saw the police as implacable opponents, their actions spoke differently. Of course they criticized RNWMP activity in the "police intimidation" case at the beginning of the strike and in the "threat to shoot" incident. Certainly strikers used abusive language toward the police, spread the rumour that the Mounties had corruptly and illegally secured a supply of beer and liquor for themselves,[137] and complained that the presence of the police was quite unnecessary.[138] But the hostility of strikers towards the police was actually quite muted and controlled. For the most part, the rank-and-file accepted the authority of the law enforcement officers. Little violence was directed against the police and at no time were highly lethal weapons such as knives and firearms used by strikers. Moreover, union leaders not only refrained from pressing very far their criticisms of police actions, but also cooperated with and assisted the Mounties in a variety of ways. In short, while the strikers were wary of the police and did not see them as allies, their actions indicate they did not view the Mounties as enemies. On occasion strikers even turned to the police to protect their rights: Theodorovics' complaint about being hit during the 4 April altercation was the most unusual case in point; Sherman's complaint about non-union men harassing the strikers on 14 April was another.[139]

During the strike each party learned things about the other that allowed for the

---

134 The RNWMP Act (57-58 V., c. 27) printed in *The Revised Statutes of Canada, 1906*, chapter 91, provides numerous examples of autocratic administration. Since the force was a quasi-military establishment such organization was hardly surprising.

135 RCMP Papers, A1, vol. 316, file 238-06, Perry to Wilson, telegram, 17 July 1906. See also ibid., McIllree to Comptroller, 16 July 1906.

136 Cobb, *Police and People*, 19.

137 Patterson to Editor, 6 May, in *UMW Journal*, 17 May 1906.

138 See, for example, ibid.; and Crabb to Editor, n.d. in *UMW Journal*, 28 June 1906.

139 Indeed, Sherman was forced to turn to the police in December for protection for his person and his house in Fernie (see *Frank Paper*, n.d., in *Herald*, 3 January 1907).

establishment and maintenance of the *modus vivendi*. The strikers discovered that the police were not out to repress them brutally, were not the simple agents of the coal company, and were committed to the concept of police neutrality. The Mounties found that the strikers were basically peaceful, were not out to kill or maim non-union men, not intent on destroying company property, not desirous of violating the Criminal Code, and not eager to have violent confrontations with the police. Moreover, both the strikers and the police discovered the many ways of influencing the other party to abide by the principles of "right not might." That the police influenced the strikers is not to be doubted. Yet it is especially important to emphasize that through the skilful use of a wide range of activities, the strikers were able to have an enormous impact on the behaviour of the police. For if the police approached a reasonable facsimile of neutrality during the strike, pressure from union members had done much to bring this about.

No single case study can provide a definitive answer to such a major question of interpretation as the role and function of police *vis-à-vis* workers during strikes.[140] Yet for a particular episode to hold broad significance it must be related to general considerations, just as the utility of a generalization must be based, in part, on its fit with specific occurrences. In regard to the striker/police relationship, the 1906 Lethbridge strike illustrates very clearly that drawing a definitive interpretive conclusion is extremely difficult. From the perspective of the participants no absolute lessons could be drawn. To the strikers, the police were not at all as bad as might have been feared but they were dangerous nonetheless. And, of course, the police could say the same about the strikers. If the development of class consciousness, or indeed of pluralist consciousness, is a matter of historical experience, then one might venture, given the negative stereotypes that existed at the beginning of the strike, that in general the pluralist rather than the class outlook was strengthened by the relationship between police and strikers in the 1906 strike. But even if strikers' attitudes towards the police improved during the strike it does not necessarily mean the non-existence of, or even a decrease in, class (or at least occupational) consciousness. In the first place the strike was merely one point along a continuum. The perspectives of individual workers towards the police would have been shaped by a multiplicity of events over a long period of time. Secondly, it could be argued by strikers that police behavior in 1906 had been determined by the solidarity of the vast majority of the mining community and the strikers' skilful use of a variety of tactics ranging from shows of force to public appeals. Of course, such an argument could be met by suggesting that if this were possible, then the socio-economic system clearly was capable of reformation, thus strengthening the ideas of gradualism and pluralism. But if the "lessons" of the strike were ambiguous, this was not entirely disadvantageous for the strikers. For in terms of strategy, why would they come down firmly and uniformly on one interpretation of the police? Workers kept open their options in other areas, such as whether they wanted to overthrow the capitalist order or whether they wanted a larger slice of the pie. Workers needed to retain a wide repertoire in order to maximize their power. Certainly, if they painted the police as inveterate enemies and acted accordingly then it would no doubt be a self-fulfilling prophecy. But they also needed to retain in their minds the possibility that the police were agents of capitalists for such skepticism made them less vulnerable to potential manipulation

---

140 Not, at least, without committing what D.H. Fischer calls the "telescopic fallacy." See his *Historians' Fallacies: Toward a Logic of Historical Thought* (New York 1970), 147-9.

and control. It seems that Canadian workers, as a body, kept open both options regarding the nature of the police, indeed of society and the state: the pluralist model and the class conflict model.

Perhaps modern academic analysts should do likewise. Taking the 1906 Lethbridge strike, for example, it is no easier now than it was then to draw interpretive conclusions about the relationship of strikers and police. Or, put another way, the conclusion to be drawn is that the relationship is vastly more complex than the simple dichotomy which has been posed. Stressing nuances and complexities is currently a growth industry in the field of labour history in Canada because the experience of past workers was neither one-dimensional nor straightforward, the 1906 Lethbridge strike being a perfect example of this reality. Thus for the case under examination the pluralist theory works; but the class conflict interpretation does as well. That this should be so is enormously frustrating and terribly inconclusive. One would like to be able to say that one theory is correct, the other quite wrong. But only if one wills it can one come to such a conclusion for the evidence will not substantiate it. The unfortunate academic is thus in the same boat as the object of the academics' study: the essential meaning of human affairs is not readily evident. Yet for all participants, then and now, the search for meaning is most instructive.

From the pluralist perspective, striker/police relations during the 1906 Lethbridge strike may be seen as demonstrating that the police did serve the public weal rather than the interest of the company; that the strikers were treated equitably by the police; that potential abuses of police power were checked by the efforts of the strikers to protect their civil rights; and that a non-elite social group was able to have an important influence on an essential appendage of the state. Moreover, the pluralist might also note that the intervention of the Mounties not only did not prevent the strikers from making significant gains in the end, but even might have made that success possible by preventing an alternate unfolding of events such as occurred in the same year at a lumber mill in Buckingham, Quebec. In that case company guards had been employed, three persons had been killed, the militia subsequently had been called in followed by regular troops, and the strike had been lost.[141] Indeed, using another comparison even the *Macleod Advance* noted the difference the Mounties meant: "While in the States when a strike is in progress an armed mob of Pinkertons and thugs are maintained ... in this country a dozen of these Mounted Police have always been found sufficient to keep law and order."[142]

Yet pluralists would have some answering to do to explain why the police were far from objective at the beginning of the strike, did not consult with the strikers, and had to be pushed hard to bring them into a more neutral position. Does this sound like a social structure which represents the interests of the various groups as a general rule or merely on occasion? Does it not seem that the structural influences largely

---

141 J.C. Hopkins, *The Canadian Annual Review of Public Affairs, 1906* (Toronto 1907), 288; and P.L. Lapointe, *Buckingham 1906* (Asticou 1973). Wilson noted the different patterns of the two strikes in RCMP Papers, A1, vol. 315, file 202-06, Wilson to Commissioner, 19 October (monthly report for September) 1906.

142 Macleod *Advance*, n.d., in *Herald*, 12 August 1906. The numerous Thiel detectives employed by the Winnipeg Street Railway Company during a strike in April 1906, had certainly exacerbated matters there (see Jamieson, *Times of Trouble*, 84, and the files of the *Voice*.) For a revealing debate on the use of Mounties or company guards, see RCMP Papers, B5, vol. 2478, file 57, Primrose to Commissioner, 22 April 1906; and Perry to Primrose, 26 April 1906.

favoured the elites rather than workers? The pluralist response, of course, is that social groups do not have equal power or influence in a society and that in a society in transition, structural elements such as the law will usually favour established groups rather than emerging ones. But, the pluralist would conclude, the 1906 strike demonstrates beyond doubt that change was possible for those who worked for it.

From the class-conflict perspective the relationship between strikers and police demonstrated that first and foremost the physical force of the state was available to the company and was used to restrict the activities of the strikers. The mere presence of uniformed police who protected the employer's property and strike-breakers showed that the Mounties were agents of the mine management. In other words, whether or not actual violence was used to repress strikers is not the point; the threat of physical suppression always existed if the strikers went beyond carefully circumscribed limits. It is also apparent that the police comprehended and sympathized with management's perspective more naturally than with the viewpoint of the striking miners, as evidenced by Naismith's tutoring of Wilson and the latter's neglect to consult with union officials at the beginning of the strike.

On the other hand, class-conflict theory does not easily accord with the substantial degree of neutrality the police attained over the course of the strike and the failure of the Mounties to seize the opportunity for significant repression afforded by the "riots" of 3 and 4 April. The explanation that can be provided is that in a democratic but class-divided society a process of "legitimation" occurs.[143] Agencies of the state such as the police must be seen to be neutral, objective, merely serving the public will rather than being seen to act as the instruments of the ruling class. Only in this manner can the state retain its legitimacy in the public mind and continue to promote the interests of the ruling class if not the special requirements of particular members of that class. Moreover, it might well be argued that legitimation could be practiced in the 1906 Lethbridge strike because it did not involve a major crisis in the relations of labour and capital. The stakes for the particular individuals and organizations involved were not absolutely crucial. The strikers were supported by the powerful UMWA, had other occupational options in the Lethbridge region, and seldom worked the mines in summer in any case. The company's interest focused more on profiting from its extensive land holdings than on coalmining. In fact, the strike was probably of more concern to the company because of its land than because of the mine itself, since bad publicity about shortages of home heating fuel deterred settlers. Moreover, both groups could be relatively optimistic about the long term. The company estimated it had sufficient coal reserves to last another century. Miners could look forward to acquiring land of their own, or at least to balancing their reliance on the mine with other economic endeavours. In short, unlike in other strike situations, neither side was wholly dependent on the mine or, indeed, absolutely required an immediate decision, a fact which may account for the protracted nature of the dispute. It may also explain not only the restricted degree of violence by both the police and the strikers, but also the relatively good relationship that was established between the two parties. The Mounties were, of course, under federal control. It should be noted, therefore, that federal interests were focused on the agricultural development of the prairies and thus had little concern for issues related to industrial

---

143 The nature and process of legitimation is discussed in R. Miliband, *The State in Capitalist Society: An Analysis of the Western System of Power* (London 1969), 161-236.

development.[144] Moreover, there is no evidence that Ottawa considered the Lethbridge strike to be much more than an isolated incident concerning a single mine out of hundreds — certainly nothing like the core of a broad upheaval which could be dangerous to the security and stability of the state. Thus, it could be argued that legitimation could be practiced because the company did not require abrupt, aggressive action by the police, because the strikers were not in a position which demanded an immediate resolution even if it meant violent challenges to police authority, and because the state was little concerned until the autumn when home-heating fuel shortages threatened.

Instructive as the concept of legitimation may be, pushed to the limit it becomes impossible to see where legitimation ends and a genuine legitimacy of a democratic society begins. It can become a type of paranoia in which every action by state agencies, no matter how noble and enlightened and progressive, is seen as an insidious snare for entrapping the unwary into an acceptance of social control. It would be silly to accept that things are necessarily as they seem on the surface, but it would be equally foolish to maintain that they are necessarily not as they seem. Put in other terms, at some point in attempting to appear to play fair one actually does play fair — even if one does not so intend.

Finally, it might be thought that viewing the 1906 Lethbridge strike as a point in time and place can help to resolve the interpretive debate. But even from this angle the message is ambivalent. One might claim that the relatively good relationship which was established between police and strikers during the strike was the wave of the future as competing groups in the society learned how to get along with each other for the mutual benefit of all. Equally, however, one might claim that the relationship between police and strikers in 1906 in Lethbridge was an anomaly, or at least at a point of transition, prior to the establishment of thoroughly repressive and controlling policing of strikes. Further detailed studies of the relations of police and strikers in other locations and times, along with additional statistical and comparative analyses, no doubt will shed much light on the historical pattern in Canada. But it is difficult to believe that the interpretive issue will ever be conclusively determined.

Perhaps, indeed, the pluralist theory when it admits differential power wielded by various social groups is not so far removed from class conflict theory when it acknowledges the legitimation process. Each formulation is afflicted by an Achilles' Heel which each must have in order to retain its credibility and utility, but which go far to transform or undercut the basic theories themselves. Certainly, an examination of striker/police relations during the 1906 Lethbridge strike makes it difficult to accept one construct over the other. Most of the strikers, and the Mounties for that matter, probably could not decide, either.

NOTE

This chapter was first published in *Labour/Le Travail* 27 (Spring 1991), 55-96. The author gratefully acknowledges the research support provided by the University of Lethbridge, the Social Sciences and Humanities Research Council of Canada, and the Alberta Historical Resources Foundation. To W.J.C. Cherwinski, M.R. Greenshields, J.D. Tagg, and several anonymous reviewers I express my appreciation for their helpful comments and suggestions.

---

144 A. Seager, "West Canadian Collieries and the Riddle of the Crow's Nest Pass," paper to the Canadian Historical Association, Quebec, 1989.

ELEVEN

The (Royal) North-West Mounted Police and Prostitution on the Canadian Prairies

S.W. Horrall

Prostitution was not the oldest profession to be practiced on the Canadian prairies, but it was a part of the vanguard of settlement. Calgary has the dubious honour of having the first brothel to be closed by the Mounted Police. In March 1884 Inspector S.B. Steele, JP, found Nina Dow and Nellie Swift guilty of keeping a "house of ill-fame." Steele gave them a choice of sentence — six months imprisonment, or leave town on the next train. They chose the train.[1]

Prostitution had arrived in the North West Territories a year or so earlier. As in the American West, the demimondaines were a part of the retinue of the railway construction crews. They flourished wherever there was a large body of unattached males. Their presence accompanied the laying of the track of the Canadian Pacific Railway, advancing westward with each new construction camp from Winnipeg, where they had existed as early as 1875.[2] Only a few months after the line reached Regina, a local newspaper complained of the number of brothels in the town north of the tracks.[3] After Nellie Swift was forced out of Calgary, she did what many of her colleagues would do. She moved on to the next construction camp at Laggan, where four months later she was convicted by Steele again and fined $50.[4] From the rail lines the women moved to the mining camps that followed, and they finally settled in the red light districts of the new urban communities. Prostitution was part of the process of settling and developing the Canadian West.

As the principal law enforcement agency in what is now Alberta and Saskatchewan, from the 1870s until the outbreak of World War I in 1914, the (R)NWMP became deeply involved in the policing and control of prostitution. During the early years the "social evil" presented little difficulty for police. With few settlers and fewer social

---

[1] Canada, *Sessional Papers*, 1884, no. 15, "Report of the Commissioner of the NWMP" (hereafter referred to as the *(R)NWMP Annual Report*), 54.

[2] *A Chronicle of the Canadian West: NWMP Annual Report, 1875* (Calgary: Historical Society of Alberta, 1975), 24.

[3] Regina *Leader*, 17 May 1883.

[4] *(R)NWMP Report*, 1884, 58.

institutions, the ascendant position of the Mounted Police enabled them to act in what they believed were the community's best interests. The course of action adopted by the Mounted Police to regulate prostitution was well-defined in a 1904 investigation into charges that Medicine Hat was threatened by a syphilis epidemic. Eventually, however, the dominant position of the Mounted Police was challenged as settlement increased and urban centres developed. Municipal councils, reform groups, the establishment of local police forces and the appearance of provincial governments created a more complex milieu in which the Mounted Police had to function. As with other forms of crime, the new conditions forced them reluctantly to change or modify their behaviour regarding prostitution.

From the time of their arrival on the prairies until World War I, officers of the Mounted Police, with no important exceptions, looked upon prostitution as a necessary evil which, given the basic urges of human nature, would never be eradicated.[5] In fact, they saw a positive benefit in allowing it to exist. Prostitution provided an outlet for those men who were unable to control themselves, and made them less likely to prey upon the respectable women in society. In other words, the prostitute's existence helped to protect their own wives and daughters. They did not favour its legalization, however.

The legalization of prostitution was fiercely debated from time to time during the latter part of the nineteenth century in both Europe and North America. In most European states it did attain a legal status usually under the supervision of the local police. One of the few exceptions was Britain. In 1864 the British Parliament adopted a measure which gave prostitution a quasi-legal status, but public reaction resulted in the measure's repeal in 1886. The British stuck to the Victorian double standard. Prostitution might be necessary and it might be impossible to suppress, but it would not be legalized. Canada and the United States followed the British pattern. An attempt in the 1870s to have it legitimized by Congress failed. Instead, respectable society and the legislative authorities of both countries turned a blind eye to the presence of prostitutes, leaving the police to devise some *modus operandi* for the control of their illegal but desirable activities.

At the annual meeting of the International Association of Chiefs of Police in 1907, Chief Kohler of the Cleveland Police Department outlined the three options open to law enforcement agencies.[6] The first was official acceptance. This, he stated, could not be the policy of any police administration whose avowed function was the maintenance of public decency. Another serious drawback for the police was that prostitution was usually accompanied by graft and official corruption. Official acceptance nevertheless was police practice in some parts of the United States. In 1897 New Orleans passed a law permitting prostitution in a part of the old French Quarter known as Storyville, the so-called "Storyville Option." The chief described the second course open to police as "suppression by crusade," which usually came as part of a "reform wave." When that method failed, as it invariably did, he continued, the police are blamed for being unsympathetic. Instead of rooting prostitution out, it scattered

---

5   The prostitution of Indian women which the Mounted Police regarded in quite a different light, is not examined here.

6   D.C. Dilworth, ed., *The Blue and the Brass* (Gaithersburg, Maryland: International Association of Chiefs of Police, 1976), 135.

it throughout the community making control more difficult. The third method, he explained, was the one most calculated "to produce the best possible results from a moral and police standpoint." The solution was the orderly supervision of prostitution by the police, who would suppress it as individual cases or circumstances warranted.

Few police chiefs in the United States or Canada, the officers of the Mounted Police included, would have disagreed with the principles laid down by Kohler. On the prairies the police took a pragmatic approach to the problem of control. The best means to assure prostitution's orderly supervision was to confine its activities to one area of the community, a place where prostitutes would not intrude on the life of the respectable classes. By segregation, the Mounted Police could easily maintain surveillance and keep the operators in line by occasional raids and fines. The majesty of the law would be upheld and the prostitutes would be reminded who was in control. Provided the police acted efficiently, there would be no public complaint.

Under Canadian criminal law it was an indictable offence to operate, to frequent or to be an inmate of a house of ill-fame. Upon conviction an offender was liable to a sentence of up to one year in prison.[7] The Mounted Police, however, usually treated these offences as misdemeanors and proceeded under the less severe provisions of Sections 238-239 of the Criminal Code relating to vagrancy.[8] These provisions defined as a vagrant anyone who:

(a) being a common prostitute wanders in the fields, public streets or highways and does not give a satisfactory account of herself;
(b) is a keeper or inmate of a bawdy house or house of ill-fame;
(c) is in the habit of frequenting such houses;
(d) supports himself by the avails of prostitution.

Upon conviction for vagrancy an offender was liable to a fine of up to $50, or imprisonment for up to six months, or both. There was no substantial change in the laws relating to prostitution until the Criminal Code was amended just prior to World War I in an effort to stiffen the penalties, particularly against procuring.

A house of ill-fame was defined as any "house, room, set of rooms or place of any kind kept for the purposes of prostitution or the practice of acts of indecency."[9] To convict keepers and inmates it was not necessary for the police to show that money changed hands, or that sexual acts actually took place. The law required only evidence that the house was resorted to by men and lewd conduct took place.[10] Likewise, the common prostitute, or street walker, was guilty if she was unable to give a satisfactory account of herself. Interestingly enough, it was quite common during this period for the police to charge the frequenters or customers. In part, this was due to the attitudes of the time. For a considerable section of society, no stigma was attached to visiting a brothel. Men did so openly in broad daylight, rather than furtively in the dark of night.

Until the early 1890s prostitution received little attention from the police. The records show only twelve convictions of inmates or keepers from 1874 until 1890, mostly associated with the railway construction camps.[11] In the male-dominated

---

7 Canada, Criminal Code, 1892, 55-56 Vic., C.29, ss. 228-229.
8 Ibid., ss. 238-239.
9 Ibid., s. 225.
10 *Canadian Criminal Cases* (abridgement 1892-1925) (Toronto: Carswell, 1926), 172.

frontier settlements prostitution appears to have been openly tolerated. The Mounted Police records reveal no complaints about its existence, and the police seem to have been concerned only that it did not become too unruly in its operation. The rank and file of the force were themselves some of the prostitutes' best customers, although the prostitutes were off limits to commissioned officers, who were clearly expected to identify with the respectable class in society and to act like gentlemen. With tongue in cheek the *Regina Leader* reported that the

> red-coat of the Mounted Policeman is seen flashing in and out from these dens at all hours. As no arrests have been made the character of these visits may easily be surmised![12]

The newspaper went on to report that those in authority in the force considered the houses a necessary evil. The paper did not criticize. Nicholas Flood Davin, the publisher, would probably have agreed with Kipling that "Single men in barracks don't grow into plaster saints."

The rank and file of the force was made up almost entirely of young single men under the age of thirty. There had been reports of them frequenting brothels as early as 1875.[13] Such activity was not considered a disciplinary offence, at least not a serious one. Commissioner Herchmer, nevertheless, was concerned about the venereal disease contracted by the men. A fervent guardian of the public purse, he felt that it was downright unreasonable that men should be off duty sick and receiving medical attention at government expense because of their own indiscretions.[14] As a result, a regulation was sanctioned that authorized deductions from the pay of such constables to cover the cost of their hospitalization.[15] Making men pay for treatment they needed because of their immoral behaviour was not a new idea. It had been tried as a deterrent by the British Army. There was one drawback — the men tended to hide their condition and instead of obtaining qualified medical attention, they sought instead unprofessional remedies. No instances of this problem, however, have come to light in the Mounted Police records.

Sometimes things did go a little too far. On the evening of 24 October 1888 three constables being transferred to Calgary the next day came into Edmonton to celebrate. On their way into the settlement of some six hundred souls, one of them dropped off at Nellie Webb's establishment, while the other two set out to paint the town red. Sometime later, quite drunk, these two also headed for Nellie's house. Nellie refused to let them in. According to her testimony later, they threatened to wreck the house and to kill her. Drunken customers were one of the hazards of being a prostitute, but Nellie Webb knew how to take care of herself. She got the .38 revolver she kept in the house and warned them that if they tried to break in, she would use it. When they started kicking the door down, she fired through the broken panels hitting Constable Cairney in the thigh, breaking his hip.[16]

---

11   *(R)NWMP Annual Reports*, 1874-1890.

12   Regina *Leader*, 17 May 1883.

13   *A Chronicle of the Canadian West*, 24.

14   Public Archives of Canada [PAC], Royal Canadian Mounted Police Records, RG 18, vol. 1065, Herchmer to White, 30 September 1887.

15   RG 18, vol. 2328, General order 384, August 1886.

16   Edmonton *Bulletin*, 27 October and 3 November 1888.

Nellie claimed she fired in self-defence. Nonetheless, Sergeant Davidson of the town detachment arrested her. She was charged with malicious shooting and released on $2,000 bail. The Mounted Police were not anxious to keep her in the cells as she was also the local midwife and her services were required at any moment.

The case against her never came to court. The most likely reason was that the constables were too drunk to testify reliably as to what happened. Instead, Nellie was convicted of keeping a house of ill-fame and fined $20 and costs.[17] Edmonton was too hot for her then, and like "The Outcasts of Poker Flat" she was forced to move on. She went south to Calgary and set up business again. Constable Cairney spent several weeks recovering in the barracks' hospital at Fort Saskatchewan; then he was dismissed.

The residents of Edmonton were used to drunkenness and brawling but the Nellie Webb incident went too far. Frank Oliver, the editor of the local newspaper, described it as "one of the most disgraceful affairs that has ever happened in Edmonton, through a set of men that are supposed to protect the citizens and their property."[18] He went on to place the real fault at the feet of those in charge of the Mounted Police. It was one sign that westerners were beginning to demand better moral standards from those who policed them.

About 1890 the Mounted Police started to develop a more systematic approach to the handling of prostitution. Behind the change was pressure from moral reformers, usually Protestant clergy. They were often the same groups or individuals who pressed for prohibition. If prostitution was illegal, they argued, it should not be allowed to exist. Apart from being immoral, it ruined innocent girls and it was the cause of disease and crime. The police themselves should set an example by not patronizing the houses. There were citizen groups, too, who objected to the presence of the brothels, perhaps because these houses affected property values and were a deterrent to settlement.

Conditions varied from place to place, but the NWMP evolved a fairly standard procedure for handling the matter. Once a complaint was made the house was raided and the women charged. Often they were given the alternative of a suspended sentence instead of a fine, if they promised to leave town. If they stayed and remained in business, the Mounted Police would raid them again from time to time and impose further fines. This system of licence by fine, which was common elsewhere, was from time to time practiced in most districts.

In response to public criticism, the police also established more control over the operation of the brothels and the lives of their inmates. The movements of the women were restricted. They were prevented from flaunting their profession in the face of the town's respectable women. In some cases they were also required to undergo periodic medical examinations. As for the houses, the police usually required them to be segregated to some area where they were out of sight and sound of the rest of the town. Under Herchmer disciplinary steps were also taken to make it clear that consorting with prostitutes was not acceptable behaviour for a member of the NWMP. In January 1891 Constable G.T. Emigh received fourteen days hard labour for walking the streets of Macleod with a prostitute after being repeatedly warned not to do so.[19]

---

17 Edmonton *Bulletin*, 10 November 1888.
18 Edmonton *Bulletin*, 3 November 1888.
19 RG 18, vol. 1217.

Mounted Police officers, however, did consider prostitution a necessary evil and, for a time, they were able to resist pressures to have it completely suppressed. Even when they closed houses and told the women to leave, they knew that the former residents would soon be replaced by another party of "soiled doves." In July 1889 the Mayor of Regina asked the Mounted Police to close a house on Lorne Street run by a Mrs. Turner.[20] (The territorial capital still had no police force of its own). The house was closed. The following year the police gave another group of the demimonde twenty four hours to leave town. The Regina *Leader* reported that they went bag and baggage.[21] Within a few weeks another contingent had arrived.[22] A group of citizens complained to the Mayor. Once again he called upon the sergeant at the town station. The women were arrested but later were released when they promised to leave Regina. No doubt further replacements soon followed.

With a population of almost four thousand in 1891, Calgary was the largest settlement in the territories. It was also rapidly becoming its prostitution capital. Early that year, the Mounted Police stepped up enforcement against the numerous houses which had been established just outside the town limits. The Calgary Herald applauded the Colonel's (Supt. J.H. McIllree) efforts to punish the "strumpets."[23] During that year, about thirty convictions were obtained against keepers and inmates.[24] Often the same women were charged every few months. For the first offence the fines were usually $20 for keeping a house of ill-fame and $5 for being an inmate. The alternative was imprisonment for a few days. Three men found guilty of being frequenters had to pay $1 and spend one day in jail. All those convicted in Calgary that year paid a fine.

One Calgary madam was a thorn in the side of the NWMP for some time, undermining morale and proving difficult to dislodge. Her name was Lottie Carkeek, alias Dutch Lottie, alias Lottie Diamond. Prostitutes frequently changed their names and seemed to prefer diminutive first names like Tilley, Trixie, Georgie, Lulu and Allie that had a friendly ring of familiarity. Occasionally they adopted a more ribald sobriquet; the two women who once functioned in the Empress Hotel in Moose Jaw were known as "Knockout Duffy" and "Pussy Jake."[25] In their tussle with Lottie Diamond, the Mounted Police ran into a problem they would find elsewhere — conflict with the local police.

Lottie first established a house of ill-fame in Calgary in 1888. She soon struck up an affair with Sergeant Sargent, the son of a Church of England missionary and a member of the local NWMP post. The liaison resulted in Sargent being disciplined and reduced to the rank of Constable. A short time later he obtained his discharge and married Lottie. The newlyweds moved to Vancouver, but Lottie must have tired of respectable life because in 1891 she returned to Calgary and started a business on the bank of the Elbow River, a short walk from the Mounted Police barracks.[26]

---

20 RG 18, vol. 1160, Mayor of Regina to Herchmer, 22 July 1889.
21 Regina *Leader*, 30 September 1890.
22 Ibid., 21 October 1890.
23 Calgary *Herald*, 22 January 1891.
24 *(R)NWMP Annual Report*, 1891, 156-160.
25 RG 18, vol. 1786, file 170.
26 RG 18, vol. 86, file 659-93.

In spite of being "old and withered in appearance," Lottie proved to have some unusual quality that NCOs of the Mounted Police could not resist. Within a few months one sergeant-major, two staff-sergeants and one sergeant had been reduced in rank for being intimately involved with her. In June 1892 Commissioner Herchmer was forced to order her house declared out of bounds to members of the NWMP.[27] The clandestine visits continued, however, and the Sergeants' Mess became bitterly divided between the "friends" of Lottie and those who wanted to see her closed down.

The personnel problem was solved by transferring a number of men to other districts, but moving Lottie was not so easy. In trying to do so the Mounted Police stepped on the toes of the Chief of the Calgary Police. Lottie's house was within the town limits. It lay, therefore, within the jurisdiction of the town force, although it would probably not have been illegal for the Mounted Police to act.

In June 1892 Inspector A.R. Cuthbert, who had replaced McIllree in command of the Calgary District, wrote to the Mayor asking him to take action against Lottie. The Mayor was sympathetic but Chief of Police English seemed slow to move. Cuthbert believed that he was protecting Lottie. The most likely explanation is that English was tolerating prostitution as the Mounted Police did.[28] In any event Cuthbert threatened to raid her house every night until she was driven out. This brought some action on the part of the town police, but not the results that Cuthbert hoped for. Lottie was charged with keeping a house of ill-fame and fined $50. By this time relations between the two police forces had soured, and Chief English was threatening a civil suit against Cuthbert for suggesting that he was protecting a prostitute.[29]

Prostitution also flourished in Lethbridge during the 1890s. The hundreds of men who worked in the nearby coal mines flocked into town on Saturday nights to enjoy themselves, thus providing a lure to prostitutes. The town was incorporated in 1891 and its first council quickly passed a bylaw aimed at closing the brothels. It was an abortive attempt, however. The newly-appointed town constable proved to be ineffective and the bylaw was considered *ultra vires*.[30] Nevertheless, two dedicated guardians of the town's morals kept prodding local authorities to act. Getting no response, one of them, the Reverend Charles McKillop, a Presbyterian minister, finally wrote to Herchmer asking him to remove the houses from the town.[31] McKillop, who was known locally as the "Fighting Parson," claimed that there had been twenty-six prostitutes in the community since he moved there in 1886.

He received no satisfaction from the Mounted Police, who had just taken over the policing of the town under an arrangement with the council. Deane, the commanding officer in Lethbridge, told Herchmer that McKillop and the Methodist minister, the Reverend Bates, had publically addressed the town council on the matter but got no satisfaction and "retired covered with ridicule."[32] Deane had no sympathy with their cause. He was a strong believer in tolerating prostitution under the strict control of

---

27 Ibid., vol. 3339, file 878.
28 Chief English remained head of the Calgary Police Department until 1909 when he fell victim to a crusade for moral reform.
29 RG 18, vol. 69, file 616.
30 J.H. Carpenter, *The Badge and the Blotter* (Lethbridge: Historical Society of Alberta, 1975).
31 RG 18, vol. 1269, file 220, McKillop to Herchmer, 12 June 1894.
32 Ibid., vol. 91, file 148, Monthly Report "K" Division, July 1894.

the police.[33] According to Deane, the two clergymen would have done better to pay more attention to the juvenile depravity among their own congregations as two of their respectable young ladies had recently been involved in love affairs with married men. The "professional ladies," said Deane, are "orderly, clean, and on the whole not bad looking."[34]

A few years later, at Macleod, Deane successfully thwarted another attempt to disturb the control of the police over prostitution. The Macleod Town Council asked him to close the establishments in the municipality. Deane knew that this action would result in the prostitutes scattering throughout the district, which would make supervision more difficult. He artfully responded, therefore, by telling the town fathers that if the houses in Macleod were closed, they would not be allowed to open elsewhere. In other words, he gave the councillors a choice of prostitution in the town under the eye of the police, or no prostitution at all. Under this threat, another council meeting was quickly called and it was decided to leave the matter to the discretion of the Mounted Police.[35]

One of the frequent accusations of those who wished to close brothels was that they were a major cause of the spread of venereal disease. In April 1904 the Deputy Attorney General in Regina received an anonymous letter which claimed that over one hundred new cases of syphilis had been treated by a doctor in Medicine Hat in the previous two months.[36] The cause of this epidemic, the letter claimed, was the local sporting houses. The Mounted Police investigation that followed revealed a good deal about their supervision of prostitution. It also raised the question of confidentiality in the relationship between medical practitioners and their patients.

Syphilis was first diagnosed among French soldiers in Naples in 1495. It was initially dubbed *morbus gallicus*, or the French disease. The name syphilis originated from an Italian poem of 1530 in which the gods inflict the disease upon a shepherd named Syphilis as a punishment. The origin of the great pox, as it was also called, is still in dispute.[37] Some claim that it existed in Europe before 1495, but was not identified. Others give Asia or Central America as its source. The French said that their troops contracted it in Naples from Spaniards who had been in contact with Columbus's crews. Clearly, nobody wanted the stigma of being associated with its spread. Its name, therefore, varied. The English and the Italians called it the French Pox. The French called it the Neapolitan Pox. The Turks called it the Christian Pox and the Chinese labelled it the Portugese Pox.

Its spread in Europe in the sixteenth century resulted in a reaction against prostitution. Brothels in London and Paris were closed and their business was driven underground. Another consequence of the appearance of syphilis at this time was the development of the first sheaths or condoms as a means of preventing infection. It would not be until the vulcanization of rubber in the nineteenth century, however, that these would be widely used.

There was no reliable medical cure for syphilis until 1910 when the German Nobel

---

33 (R)NWMP Annual Report, 1890, 51.
34 RG 18, vol. 91, file 148, Monthly Report "K" Division, July 1894.
35 Ibid., vol. 1416, file 120, Monthly Report "D" Division, September 1898.
36 RG 18, vol. 1533, file 7, Perry to C.O. "A" Division, 26 April 1904.
37 Vern L. Bullough, *The History of Prostitution* (New York: University Books, 1964), 132.

prize winner Paul Ehrlich developed an arsenical preparation known as salvarsan. The most common treatment in North America prior to this was the use of salts of mercury taken orally or by injection.[38] There was no guarantee that this provided a cure, however, as there was no dependable means of diagnosing the disease until Wasserman's development of the blood test in 1906. All the patient could do was wait and hope that the usually fatal tertiary stage of its progress, which could take years, did not appear.

The Deputy Attorney General forwarded the anonymous letter to Perry and asked him to investigate the claims. The Commissioner sent it on to the indomitable Deane who, by now, was in command of the Maple Creek District, which included Medicine Hat. Deane referred to Maple Creek as that "funny little Methodist-ridden place."[39] Perry told him to observe the usual practice. If the houses of ill-fame had become a nuisance, close them. Deane's initial reaction was that he did not believe there was any truth in the accusations. The only case he had heard of was that of one of the hotel clerks who was infected by an entirely unprofessional source.[40]

The NWMP maintained a four-man detachment in Medicine Hat in 1904. The town, with a population of about two thousand, was a busy divisional depot for the CPR. It was also close to the branch line to the Lethbridge coal mines. As a result, there were railway workers residing there, as well as miners and other travellers passing through the town. Deane called upon the officer in charge at Medicine Hat, Inspector C. Starnes, to carry out the investigations.

Starnes's first thought was that the letter was probably written by the Reverend Nicholl, a Church of England clergyman. Nicholl had complained earlier about a house and had asked that it be closed. Starnes had taken no action, however, as the house was in a quiet spot about two and one half miles from town and no one else seemed to support the minister. Given the nature of the new charge, the inspector began his investigation by interviewing the town's three doctors. They were co-operative to a point, and proved to be Starnes's main source of information. Dr. Smyth reported that he had treated only six cases of syphilis in Medicine Hat in the last year. He had traced three of these to the brothels. Dr. C.F. Smith informed Starnes that he had been practicing in the town for nine years and in all that time he had diagnosed only ten cases of syphilis. He believed that two of these originated from the houses. He had treated many cases of gonorrhea, but the sources in most cases were non-professional. Smith also stated that he was called to the house run by Stella Hattley quite frequently as she was very particular about the health of her inmates.

Dr. J.G. Calder's assessment varied from those of the other two medical men. He told Starnes that he had treated fifty cases in the last six months, more than he had seen in the previous sixteen years. He claimed to have traced the majority of cases back to the prostitutes. According to Calder, the inmates did not use proper antiseptic precautions. He accused the madams of allowing their women to get drunk and to neglect themselves. He had been asked to examine the prostitutes, he stated, but he had refused because many of them were either drunk or addicted to cocaine and

---

38 W.A.R. Thomson, *Black's Medical Dictionary* (London: Black, 1965), 867.
39 R. Burton Deane, *Mounted Police Life in Canada* (Toronto: Coles Publishing, 1973), 97.
40 RG 18, vol. 1533, file 7, Deane to Perry, 28 April 1904.

morphia. All three doctors steadfastly refused to reveal the names of their patients, claiming that such information was privileged.[41] Deane grumbled that the police could hardly be expected to do their job if vital information was held from them. But the Mounted Police did not challenge this claim to confidentiality, although the claim had no basis in law.

Meanwhile, two of the town's justices of the peace, Benson and Crosskill, had also written to the Attorney General's office complaining that the brothels were running wide open and that over one hundred cases of syphilis were at that moment being treated in Medicine Hat. Starnes spoke with Benson, who admitted writing the first anonymous letter. He told the inspector that his source of information was one of the town's doctors. Starnes had no doubt that the doctor in question was Calder. Starnes had the two houses raided and fined two keepers and ten inmates, as well as two Chinese cooks, and twelve customers.[42]

The epidemic clearly had been deliberately exaggerated, probably with the intent of closing the houses. Nevertheless, to what extent were the prostitutes of Medicine Hat a source of disease? Deane instructed Starnes to obtain a medical certificate for each girl, informing him that if any was diseased, she was to be told that she could not stay in business. The two madams, Stella Hattley and Marjorie Dale, were summoned to the police detachment. Starnes told them that they must have all their girls medically examined and that they should return next day with certified health statements for each one. He also got the madams to agree that the inmates would no longer be seen in the town. Instead, the madams would come to town once weekly to purchase necessities. In return, Starnes promised to do something about the drunken men who broke into their houses and damaged their possessions.[43] The next day the two women dutifully returned. Each had a certificate signed by Dr. Smith which asserted, in effect, that every prostitute was free from contagious disease. It was safer to pay in Medicine Hat than play around. The accusation that the local prostitutes were the source of a venereal disease epidemic appeared to be false, although it should be remembered that medical diagnosis at the time was not entirely dependable.

By June, Deane was able to tell the Commissioner that life in Medicine Hat had returned to normal. The prostitutes had been punished to remind them that their illegal activities would be tolerated only as long as they behaved themselves. Everyone was happy with the situation again, reported Deane, even the "kickers."[44] In Regina, the Deputy Attorney General expressed his satisfaction with the outcome although he was concerned about the difficulty of enforcing the liquor laws in Medicine Hat, a politically more sensitive issue.

The reports of venereal disease were not the only reason that the presence of

---

41 Ibid., Starnes to Deane, 30 April 1904. (Anyone who knowingly did not take steps to prevent the spread of a contagious disease could have been subject to charges under the Public Health Ordinances.) The Canadian Medical Association code of ethics of 1868 included a provision for confidentiality between patient and doctor based upon historic tradition. See C.D. Naylor, "The Canadian Medical Association's First Code of Ethics" in *Journal of Canadian Studies* 17, no. 4 (1982).
42 Ibid., Starnes to Deane, 9 May 1904.
43 Ibid., Starnes to Deane, 4 May 1904.
44 RG 18, vol. 1533, file 7, Deane to Perry, 16 June 1904.

prostitution in the community was no longer accepted by some citizens. The attempt to close the brothels was also sparked by the relaxation of police control over prostitution. The women had got out of hand. They had been allowed to visit the town where they were noisy, gaudily dressed, and flaunted their profession in the faces of "respectable" citizens. At the root of the problem was a serious staffing problem. With a constable's basic pay at sixty cents daily, the NWMP was experiencing considerable difficulty in recruiting enough men of good character and steady habits.[45] In 1904 alone just over 10 percent of the rank and file either were dismissed for serious breaches of discipline or they deserted. Of those who remained, the majority would not re-enlist when their period of service was complete because wages were low and there were few opportunities for advancement. As a result, most of the men on strength in these years were young and of short service.

The corporal and two constables at Medicine Hat who made up Inspector Starnes's detachment were unmarried, inexperienced men in their early twenties. The corporal had only three years service, while the constables had just a few months. As Deane said, they easily "succumbed to the temptations of the place," and discipline deteriorated. In March 1904 one of the constables was dismissed for theft. Early the following month, his replacement and the other constable deserted after becoming involved in some unpoliceman-like activity. They stole two horses and headed for the United States border. The corporal, meanwhile, had been drinking heavily and had struck up a liaison with one of the sporting women. When Deane heard that this woman had visited the barracks, he recalled the corporal to Maple Creek. Rather than face Deane's wrath, however, the corporal decided to join his comrades in Montana. His replacement, an experienced sergeant, soon straightened things out. As Deane reported later, the women had been permitted to come and go as they please, "but they are seldom seen in town now. When they do go, they dress and behave quietly. It is easy to keep them in order, if the non-commissioned officer is firm."[46]

After the inauguration of the provinces, the enforcement of the laws against prostitution by the NWMP entered a new phase. In 1906 an agreement between federal and provincial authorities placed the Mounted Police under the direction of the attorneys general of the new governments as far as the administration of criminal justice was concerned. During the colonial period, the police had a freer hand in determining their activities and, consequently, they dragged their heels with their new masters. Gradually, however, more and more control was exerted over the police.

The change saw a more determined movement for moral reform. This first appeared in 1904 in Winnipeg, where a long and vigorous campaign to remove social evil was to be fought. The Reverend C.W. Gordon (Ralph Connor), author of one of the early novels about the Mounted Police, denounced immorality amongst women from his pulpit in the city. Gordon and his reformers were not entirely successful, but they would try again, and what happened in Winnipeg would be repeated in many Alberta and Saskatchewan communities in the next decade.

Rapid urban growth also complicated the handling of prostitution for the Mounted Police. The force was relieved not only of responsibility for law enforcement in many

---

45 (R)NWMP Annual Report, 1904, 11.

46 Loc. cit.

settlements as they were transformed into incorporated municipalities, but existing towns and cities also expanded their police departments. As a result, the matter of jurisdiction became complicated and differences occurred over enforcement. In addition, there was a reaction among the prostitutes to the movement to put them out of business permanently. Some were neither willing to pay fines or to pack their bags and move on. Instead they fought back in the courts.

For a time the Mounted Police tried to follow their former practices with regard to prostitution, but it was soon evident that new influences were at work. In June 1904 the Calgary City Police closed three of the city's brothels. The former occupants moved across the Bow River into the village of Riverside and started to build new establishments. The residents of Riverside did not welcome them as three houses were operating in the village already. A petition was drawn up and sent to Superintendent Sanders, the officer commanding the Calgary District, asking him to close all the brothels. Sanders later told the Commissioner that at night it was not safe to cross the Langevin Bridge, which connected the village with Calgary, because numerous teams carrying customers travelled over it at breakneck speed. As a result of this danger and the petition, he closed the brothels and told the women to leave. Perry approved this action because local citizens had protested.[47]

In the spring of 1906 the Moose Jaw Council passed a resolution calling upon the Mounted Police to close the two houses of ill-fame just outside the city. The task was delegated to South African-born Corporal R.B.C. Mundy, who was later to become one of the force's outstanding detectives. Mundy was unable to find sufficient evidence to lay charges so he gave the prostitutes forty-eight hours to leave. He allowed the two madams to remain, however, as one owned the house she was using and the other had hers leased until the end of the month.[48] Later that year the possibility of conflict with the Edmonton City Police arose after its members raided houses of ill-fame outside the city limits. Inspector Worsley was concerned that a serious dispute might result between his men and those of the Edmonton force. He wanted to raise the matter with the chief of police but Commissioner Perry cautioned him against it.[49]

Venereal disease remained a problem. In Calgary, in February 1907, it was reported to Perry that diseased Japanese women were in business in houses on Nose Creek, a red light district across the river from Calgary and outside the city limits. The district was by now under the command of Superintendent R.B. Deane, a firm believer in the segregation and supervision of prostitution. Deane told his superior that, in addition to white women operating on Nose Creek, there were four Japanese houses with a total of twelve inmates. These, he informed the Commissioner, were medically examined every nine days, and all but one were free of disease. With regard to suppression, he continued, there is a "very pronounced body of opinion" that believed that the prostitutes were a necessary evil. If the houses were closed, the inmates would scatter all over the city, as they had done in Winnipeg, and there would be no control whatever.[50] When Deane's report reached Edmonton the Deputy

---

47 RG 18, vol. 1546, file 133, Sanders to Perry, 7 June 1904.
48 Ibid., vol. 1580, file 133, Mundy to C.O. "B" Division, 5 May 1906.
49 Ibid., Perry to Worsley, October 1906.
50 Ibid., vol. 1605, file 133, Deane to Perry, 28 February 1907.

Attorney General there was shocked to find that the mounted policeman had not closed the brothels. He wrote directly to Deane instructing him that "if such houses are known to exist, they exist contrary to the law of the land and this should not be permitted."[51] It was a sign of the provincial authorities changing attitude towards prostitution. Deane, however, seems to have quietly ignored this directive from his nominal superior. One can hear him muttering to himself and saying that he had been keeping law and order on the prairies for over twenty-five years and no jumped-up official in Edmonton was going to tell him how to go about it. In any case, Calgary citizens were happy with the arrangement, at least for the present.

The forces of change were growing, however. The fury of their attack would be concentrated in the larger urban centres where gambling, prostitution and illegal drinking appeared to be flourishing under the protection of the authorities. The municipal police forces and local police commissions would feel the brunt of this campaign. Accusations would be followed by public enquiries and police chiefs would be forced to resign. The Mounted Police were not to escape. The reformers were also active in the construction camp towns along the new rail lines and on the fringe of the municipalities where the Force still had jurisdiction.

In Calgary a Citizen's League was organized in autumn 1907. It brought charges against the police chief that the city's houses of ill-fame were being protected. Exerting pressure upon the Attorney General, the League succeeded in getting a judicial enquiry established to look into the accusations. Lawyers for the Citizen's League asked the Mounted Police to assist them in obtaining evidence against the chief by raiding the houses.[52] Deane balked at the suggestion. Relations between the two forces had not been good in the past. He did not now wish to be the means of its exposure. He fell back on an old excuse. He told the lawyers that the Mounted Police had no jurisdiction within the city limits. The representatives of the Citizen's League were not to be diverted from their objective, however. The Attorney General was contacted and he instructed Deane to raid the houses. It would be a familiar story in Alberta. When local police forces were under investigation or suspicion, the Mounted Police, or the provincial detectives in the Attorney General's department, would conduct enquiries.

Two years later, the Calgary reformers turned their attention to the brothels outside the city. The Presbyterian and Methodist ministers in the city's east end complained to Deane that the colony of sporting women on Nose Creek "was prejudicially affecting the morals and welfare of the community."[53] In company with his sergeant-major, Deane visited all the houses and told its madames that they must find another locality for their establishments. The houses were soon reoccupied by new prostitutes. Deane found that they were paying from $100 to $150 rent monthly. He suggested that the most effective way to deal with the trouble would be to make it unlawful for a person to rent a house for the purposes of prostitution.

Entwistle, Alberta, made the newspaper headlines as a place of vice and debauchery in May 1909. The source of the story was the Reverend J.J. Wright, the local Methodist

---

51 RG 18, vol. 1605, file 133, Deputy Attorney General, Alberta to Deane, 13 March 1907.
52 Provincial Archives of Alberta (PAA), Records of the Attorney General's Department, box 17, file 282.
53 (R)NWMP Annual Report, 1909, 31.

minister. In letters to the Edmonton newspapers Wright claimed that Entwistle was a wide-open town where gross immorality was rampant and that the Mounted Police did nothing about this state of affairs.[54] Another Methodist minister came to his support and, far away in Toronto, the editor of the *Globe* thundered against the inaction of the North West Mounted Police. Wright also complained directly to the Attorney General.

Entwistle was a centre for the construction camps on the Grand Trunk Pacific Railway. At weekends hundreds of men descended on the town looking for one diversion or another. They brought money and business profited. The citizens of Entwistle did not take kindly to the clergyman's public statements. In fact, they were very angry and a public indignation meeting was held to denounce Wright and to express support for the Mounted Police. A petition also was circulated and this was then sent to the Methodist Council calling for the removal of the clergyman from the town.

The Attorney General reacted by dispatching a Provincial Detective to Entwistle to crack down on the unlicensed liquor vendors and any other irregularities. Among other items, he unearthed a prostitute who was selling photographs of herself having sexual intercourse with an Irish prize-fighter named Kelly. Kelly managed to elude the police, but the prostitute was sentenced to six months imprisonment. "Dirty pictures" do not appear to have been common on the prairies at this time.

The NWMP reacted quickly too. The officer commanding the district ordered the NCO at Entwistle, Sergeant V.J. MacGillicuddy, to close all the brothels. Perry, meanwhile, arranged for Deane to hold an enquiry in the town concerning the accusations. Deane heard the testimony of a number of witnesses. A.J. Gayfer, chief engineer for the GTP testified that:

> compared with many other railway towns Entwistle has been a quiet town ... I have never known a construction town where prostitution, gambling and illegal selling of liquor did not go on.

MacGillicuddy stated that the prostitutes conducted themselves well and as "I considered that it was a necessary evil where there [*sic*] so many men passing through and as there were no complaints about it I let it run." Deane discovered that Wright, the Methodist minister, had formerly been a private detective. Apparently, he had gathered the evidence for his charges by sneaking around the town at night and peering in windows. Deane made it clear that he considered Wright a troublemaker who was upsetting the entire community using religion as a guise for his real intentions. Most of Entwistle's citizens would probably have agreed with Deane, who concluded his enquiry by finding that no blame could be attached to the Mounted Police.[55] There had been several brothels in the town but these had been raided periodically and the prostitutes had been charged. In coming down in favour of the old order Deane was refusing to accept the reformers' view that prostitution could no longer be controlled by a practice of raids and fines.

Even the intransigent Deane was eventually forced to accept that the pendulum was beginning to swing in another direction. In Calgary, reformers maintained pressure on him to take action on Nose Creek. Deane began replacing fines with

---

54 RG 18, vol. 376, file 386.
55 Ibid.

mandatory prison sentences in a number of cases where prostitutes were convicted. This reduced the number of brothels, but it also brought more determined resistance from the women.

One of the most intransigent was Diamond Dolly, a familiar figure in Calgary and one of the most notorious brothel operators of the period. Deane was determined to close her Nose Creek establishment. One reason was that this brothel had become an attraction for some of his own constables. During the early hours of 12 July 1910, the Sergeant Major had led a surprise raid on one of the houses where he found ten who had broken out of barracks. Two weeks later plans were laid to raid Diamond Dolly's house. A search warrant was obtained and at 5:00 A.M. on 26 July 1910 Corporal Denis Ryan and Constable Rosenkrantz (later Baron Rosenkrantz of Orumgaard, Denmark) raided the brothel. The keeper, Ray Mason, admitted them without any trouble. They found a woman in bed alone in one room and a man and woman in bed together in another room. The man claimed that the woman was sick and he was nursing her.

Subsequently, the keeper and the two women inmates were charged and convicted by Superintendent Deane and Inspector Duffus, JPs. All three were given prison sentences. To Deane's surprise however, an appeal was launched in the case of Mason, the keeper. To his even greater amazement, a few weeks later the District Court quashed the conviction, ruling that there was insufficient evidence. With typical sarcasm Deane warned the Moral Reform League that it was going to be difficult to suppress the social evil if, in future, unmarried men and women could go to bed together providing one was sick and the other a nurse.[56] Perry drew the case to the Attorney General's attention, complaining of his men's difficulty, and of the unreasonable demands of the moral reformers.[57]

Not everyone was prepared to knuckle down to the moral minority. In October 1911 a pimp named Joe Kelly set up a house with three girls north of Hardisty, Alberta. The CPR was building a branch line close by and, as a result, there were large numbers of construction workers about the town. Constable S.L. Warrior of Hardisty Detachment, who had already closed one brothel a month earlier, reported to his commanding officer with respect to the latest establishment that:

> the general opinion of this town is strongly in favour of a house of this kind owing to there being such a big bunch of railroaders here, but there are a few who will not stand for it and two complaints have come to me today.[58]

Before taking any action, Warrior requested that a plainclothesman be sent there to try and find what was going on. This task was given to D/Sgt. Tucker. He learned that Kelly had actually bought the house from the local JP, who had at one time considered going into partnership with the pimp. He also discovered that Kelly owed money to several merchants for furnishings and other items. The businessmen of Hardisty had no personal liking for Kelly, but they did have a vested interest in seeing that his brothel was not closed.

Nevertheless, the Mounted Police decided to close the house. A complaint had been made about it to the attorney general's office. Burbridge, the local JP, obviously

---

56 (R)NWMP Annual Report, 1910, 33.
57 PAA, Records of the Attorney General's Department, box 16, file 531.
58 RG 18, vol. 415, file 1911, Warrior to C.O. "G" Division, 30 October 1911.

could not be trusted, so arrangements were made for Inspector Worsley to come from Edmonton to hear the case. Once the towns-people knew what was afoot they drew up a petition calling on Worsley to give the brothelkeeper a fine instead of a prison sentence. Kelly couldn't pay his bills while he was in jail. The petition was signed by thirty residents, mostly merchants. Worsley, however, was not to be moved. He gave Kelly thirty days hard labour and a $50 fine. Warrior considered that "the moral standard of the majority of the residents of Hardisty was so low that they would sign a petition for the release of such a man as Kelly."[59]

On 20 February 1909 the Regina *Morning Leader* carried an article by a prominent United States district attorney exposing the growth of the white slave traffic in that country.[60] The crusade against white slavery was one more nail in the coffin of the toleration of prostitution by the Mounted Police. This exposé was printed at the request of the Moral and Social Reform Council of Canada who wished to alert Canadians to the danger of this vicious trade and to encourage them to agitate for tougher penalties against those responsible. The attack on white slavery was the latest crusade to sweep northwards across the border. The struggle to suppress the trade had started in Europe about two decades earlier. During the 1880s, the London *Pall Mall Gazette* had waged a vigorous campaign to expose the traffic in English girls being lured to Belgium, the principal centre for white slavery on the continent. In 1902 representatives of sixteen countries met in Paris to draft an international agreement for the suppression of the *Traite de Blanches*. The campaign in the United States started shortly after, and quickly gained ground there; in 1910 Congress passed the Mann Act which made it a criminal offence to transport women across state lines for immoral purposes. Three years later the Borden government reacted to Canadian public pressure to suppress white slavery by increasing the Criminal Code penalty for procuring.

The traffic in women for immoral purpose gave a new edge to the campaign against prostitution. It became difficult to argue for its toleration when, as reformers asserted, many of the women were tricked, drugged or lured into becoming prostitutes against their will. The view that some women freely chose to be prostitutes was not accepted. The inflammatory and exaggerated claims regarding the extent of the traffic captured public attention. A speaker at a WCTU Conference in Sherbrooke in 1911 said that fifteen hundred Canadian girls disappeared every year, most of them ending up in the Chicago brothels.[61] The previous year there had been shocking allegations of the traffic in several Canadian cities. What really caught the public's attention, however, was the claim in November 1910 by the Reverend Dr. J.G. Shearer, National Secretary of the Temperance and Moral Reform Council, that Winnipeg was the most vice ridden city in the country.[62] Writing in the Toronto *Globe*, Shearer accused Winnipeg's civic and police authorities of allowing some fifty brothels to operate in the city in a segregated area. Winnipeg, he charged, was a market place for white slavery. The Synod of the Presbyterian Church in Manitoba agreed with him. The outcry forced the provincial government to hold a judicial enquiry into prostitution in the city.

---

59 Ibid., Warrior to C.O. "G" Division, 13 December 1911.
60 Regina *Morning Leader*, 20 February 1909.
61 *Canadian Annual Review of Public Affairs* (Toronto: Copp Clark, 1911), 366.
62 Ibid., 1910, 569.

The police fraternity was sceptical of the reformers' claims. At the 1913 annual meeting of the Canadian Association of Chiefs of Police in Halifax, the country's top police expressed the view that the issue of white slavery had been exaggerated in the public mind. They went on to say that reports of thousands of Canadian girls being lured annually to the United States were misleading and unreliable.[63] White slavery was certainly not a subject which occupied the attention of the Mounted Police in Saskatchewan and Alberta. They received a few reports of its existence but, with one exception, they proved to be unfounded. The Mounted Police, however, did not escape some of the criticism of the reformers. It was no longer possible to defend prostitution as a necessary evil. The uncompromising crusaders would not listen to that argument. They wanted the brothels closed, even if the police had no evidence to do so. Under increasing pressure themselves, the attorneys general responded to the latest waves of reform.

One prostitute whose spirits had not been dampened by the ardour of the reformers was Rene Costa. She stormed into Perry's Regina office one day in July 1912 to make a bitter complaint. According to her, the Mounted Police at Swift Current had discriminated against her, and had prevented her from continuing to make a living. The substance of her complaint was that they had allowed two other prostitutes to build a house just outside the town, but had refused to let her do so. The response of the former gentleman cadet of the Royal Military College is not recorded. Orders quickly went to Swift Current Detachment, however, to close all brothels in the area.[64]

In November 1912 Shearer aimed his guns at Superintendent J.O. Wilson who was in charge of Lethbridge District. While on a tour of the west, Shearer had come across three houses of ill-fame outside Medicine Hat. He spoke to Wilson about closing them. Wilson objected, pointing out that he had no legal right to order the prostitutes out of their houses and that it was difficult to get evidence if they decided to fight conviction. Shearer, however, was not interested in legalities. He took the case to the Attorney General and the houses were subsequently closed on his orders.[65]

Dr. A.T. Moore, General Secretary of the Temperance and Moral Reform Department of the Methodist Church, was active in seeing that the police carried out their duties. Hearing of gambling and prostitution in the Macleod District, he fired off a letter from his Toronto office to Superintendent Primrose, complaining of his inaction. Primrose, something of a martinet, was not one to take criticism lightly. In reply, he told the eastern busybody that the reports were exaggerated. He also informed him that he "was firmly of the opinion that the laws are just as well enforced in Southern Alberta as they are in Toronto."[66] Actually, most of the places mentioned by Moore were incorporated towns where the Mounted Police had no jurisdiction. The reformers often neither understood the question of police jurisdiction nor considered it relevant. Moore continued to make charges of irregularities against the RNWMP.

As with the temperance movement, the crusade against prostitution reached its

---

63 Regina *Morning Leader*, 9 July 1913.
64 RG 18, vol. 1683, file 74.
65 Ibid., vol. 444, file 507.
66 Ibid.

peak in 1913. Thereafter the pressure from moral reformers tapered. The economic dislocation and the outbreak of war that followed deflected attention to other issues. They also brought new and more urgent duties for the Mounted Police that occupied more and more of its time. Nineteen sixteen marked the end of an era in the policing of the Canadian prairies. At the end of that year the federal-provincial contracts for the services of the RNWMP were terminated, and the enforcement of the Criminal Code in Alberta and Saskatchewan was taken over by provincial police forces.

The published reports of the Mounted Police annually record the number of convictions obtained against the keepers of houses of ill-fame and their inmates.[67] Starting in the 1880s the rate rises steadily, reaches a peak in the years 1906-13, and then begins to decline. Lack of other data, however, make it impossible to derive any meaningful conclusions from these figures. For example, they cannot be reliably related to the number of prostitutes who were active, or to the operations of other police forces. As the population of the prairies grew substantially during these years, it would be reasonable to assume that the number of prostitutes also grew, and that, consequently, there were more convictions. Unfortunately this is too simple. First, the growing population was not matched by a substantial increase in police. The amount of work and the duties grew, but the number of men remained much the same. Second, after 1900 the incorporation of numerous towns and cities resulted in the establishment of local police forces who took over from the Mounted Police in those areas where prostitutes were most likely to be active. A more likely explanation for the rise in convictions, particularly after 1900, is that they represent an increase in activity by the Mounted Police against a diminishing or fairly static number of prostitutes within their jurisdiction, in response to pressures from various social and political forces.

Mounted Police reports also reveal something about the prostitutes themselves and the nature of their business. They do not show clearly, however, to what extent the women were victims of socio-economic conditions or marital circumstances. More about their personal lives will be known when the 1891 and subsequent census returns are made public. No evidence links prostitution to organized crime. The Hardisty case was the only one uncovered where the brothel was operated by a male. According to Mounted Police records, pimps had a very small role in prostitution on the prairies. The basic economic unit appears to have been an independent group of women who occupied a house owned or rented by one to whom the rest paid a rent or percentage of their income for accommodation. The madam acted as manager or overseer. The establishment might also include a Chinese cook or houseboy. The price of service ranged from $3.00 to $10.00. It probably varied according to what they could induce from the customer. Leona Stanley, an inmate of Pearl Rogers's house on Wood Street in Lethbridge, complained because the police burst in upon her and a patron before she had time to collect her $3.00. She was fined $5.00.[68] Of the scores of cases documented in police files, not one was found where a prostitute was unable to pay her fine.

In Macleod, one brothel was run by two sisters named Jean and Addie Hughes, who led double lives. When they closed their Macleod business they returned to

---

67 (R)NWMP Annual Reports, 1874-1916.
68 J.H. Carpenter, *The Badge and the Blotter*, 29.

respectability on a fruit farm they owned in California. There they were known as Mrs. Herring and Mrs. Boyes. Prostitution, it seems, was a seasonable occupation.[69] It is difficult to imagine that the two fruit farmers were forced by dire economic need to operate a brothel in Alberta. Perhaps prostitution had been the means of their entering the respectable property-owning class.

There was another side to the prostitute's life. The possibility of becoming pregnant or contracting venereal disease was a constant hazard. Police files reveal nothing regarding birth control methods. There were also the problems of alcohol and drugs. One Japanese woman whom Deane noted as being diseased with syphilis was a particularly unfortunate case. She had only been in Calgary a few days when the Mounted Police discovered her condition. She had a small child with her and no money. Deane tried to get her admitted to Holy Cross Hospital, but the hospital would not take her. Deane asked CPR officials to pay her fare back to her home in California. The company was prepared to pay half of it, but no more. He then turned to the attorney general's office in Edmonton, enquiring as to whether she would qualify for deportation. In reply, the Deputy Attorney General instructed him to charge her under the Criminal Code and deport her if convicted. What finally happened the records do not say.[70]

Police records clearly identify prostitutes as belonging to a morally inferior class. It should be remembered, however, that the officers who wrote most of the reports considered themselves morally superior. They would have included many other westerners in the same class as prostitutes, including most of their own men. As for these men, their relationships with prostitutes could go beyond sexual contact. One who was familiar with the prostitutes of Macleod just after the turn of the century remembered them with admiration, noting that they came into town on Thursdays to shop and on those occasions you saw better dressed and more attractive women than on the other days of the week. The women, he continued, were constantly changing and most were American.[71] They sometimes assisted the police by passing on information about their customers. It was a tip from a prostitute that enabled the Mounted Police to solve the brutal murder of Tucker Peach in 1910. The police reports put the prostitute in her place, but their tone was still tolerant. They expressed disapproval, but not condemnation. They contain none of the abhorrence reserved for the male homosexual, who for the mounted policemen was the unspeakable social pariah of western society. After all, Nellie Webb was also Edmonton's midwife. From what we know of her, she fits the typical image of the dance hall girl of the western movies, with a tough exterior covering a heart of gold.

The Mounted Police took a realistic approach to the problem of policing prostitution, based upon their own experience. They believed that society could no more outlaw illicit sex than the consumption of alcohol. To control prostitution they adopted methods that were widely used throughout North America. Their action was based upon standards of behaviour that communities would accept. This was a familiar role for the Mounted Police who, as a colonizing instrument of the federal government, had considerable discretionary power in carrying out their duties. In their own field

---

69   RG 18, vol. 409, file 212.
70   RG 18, vol. 1605, file 133, Deputy Attorney General, Alberta to Deane, 13 March 1907.
71   Ex-S/Sgt. G.E. Blake, interview by S.W. Horrall., Calgary, 13 January 1969.

they became something of a ruling elite. As the example of Medicine Hat shows, their methods worked quite well, until moral reformers and others muddied the waters for their own narrow interests. Reluctantly, the Mounted Police bowed to the changing order. But their experience with prostitution was one more reason why the management of the force became disenchanted with the prospect of continuing to police the increasingly industrialized and urbanized self-governing provinces. The halcyon days were over. As Commissioner Perry was fond of saying, the Mounted Police is a "Frontier" police not a "Civil" police. He looked forward to the termination of the contracts for its services and a return to its original role in the new frontiers of the Yukon and the Arctic.

NOTE

This chapter was first published in *Prairie Forum* 10, no. 1 (Spring 1985): 105-127.

TWELVE

Abortion and Infanticide in Western Canada 1874 to 1916: A Criminal Case Study

William Beahen

Recent historical writing on the subject of abortion in Canada has put a positive light on the practice of terminating the lives of the unborn. Angus McLaren, in an article in the *Canadian Historical Review* entitled "Birth Control and Abortion in Canada, 1870-1920,"[1] says that in the late nineteenth and early twentieth centuries abortion in Canada was used mostly by married women as a second line of defence, (the first line being birth control) to limit the size of their families. A smaller number of unmarried women sought abortions, some of them disappointed when marriage prospects disappeared with pregnancy, and others more in the feminist spirit, choosing career over marriage and parenthood. Various methods to secure this end were available from traditional home remedies such as hot baths and violent exercise to abortifacient drugs advertised and sold at least in some parts of Canada. Those disappointed with results from these methods turned to unlicensed and licensed medical practitioners who performed surgical abortions. Much of the evidence used to support this view of abortion in Canada is drawn from reports concerning Toronto alone. With regard to the situation in western Canada a similar theme is present in a recently published history. Elaine Leslau Silverman, in an oral history of Alberta women, 1880 to 1930, presents hearsay evidence to support her contention that

> contraception and abortion were a major, and sometimes, subversive way for women to assert, even if only to themselves in a whisper, that they had selves that might exist apart from their generative function.[2]

This paper will present evidence of attempts by men and women to dispose of unwanted babies in the prairie west between 1874 and 1916. It deals with abortion and also with infanticide which in numbers was almost as significant a form of terminating human life, a fact so far ignored by the authors referred to above. In my view, there is nothing noble in these accounts but there is much pathos and

---

1 Angus McLaren, "Birth Control and Abortion in Canada, 1870-1920," *Canadian Historical Review*, September, 1978.
2 Elaine Leslau Silverman, *The Last Best West: Women on the Alberta Frontier, 1880-1930* (Montreal: Eden Press, 1984), p. 59.

sordidness. The cases of abortion and infanticide studied here were not bold assertions by women of a spirit of liberation. Instead, acting out of desperation and often ignorance, people rid themselves of children whose presence was an embarrassment and whose nurturing was perceived to be too great a burden. This taking of human life the law would not permit, even if the police and the courts were often inclined to compassion for the plight of the perpetrators.

A word of caution about the evidence presented: I drew from several sources as complete a list as possible of charges laid against individuals for crimes related to abortion and infanticide between 1874 and 1916 by the (Royal) North-West Mounted Police in their jurisdiction on the prairies. Through this period the (R)NWMP was the principal police force, but other municipal forces and provincial law enforcement agencies slowly evolved and may have handled other cases which are not dealt with here.

Some background on the history and organization of the Mounted Police on the prairies may be helpful. In 1874 the Canadian government sent the 300-man North-West Mounted Police force west to assert control over the vast hinterland recently acquired from the Hudson's Bay Company known as the North-West Territories. Arriving in the vanguard of settlement the Force was expected to prevent the violent conflict between settlers and Indians which had characterized the frontier experience in the United States. The area of the western prairie, approximating the present provinces of Alberta and Saskatchewan, was separated into several divisions and fortified headquarters were built in each one. For the most part the NWMP was successful in meeting its objectives in pacifying the native peoples. The American whiskey trade which had demoralized the Indians was terminated. Treaties were signed and tribes settled on reserves of land. Even Chief Sitting Bull and the Sioux, fresh from the annihilation of Custer and his men at Little Big Horn, were accommodated for several years in Canada by the Mounted Police. To some extent the NWMP must share in responsibility for the failure in government policy which preceded the North-West Rebellion. However, a case could be made that the Mounted Police prevented the spread of the Indian uprising beyond Big Bear and Poundmaker's Crees through their good relations with the other tribes.

In any case, the end of the rebellion and the completion of the Canadian Pacific Railway ushered in a new era for the Mounted Police. A trickle of white immigration to the west became a stream and then a river. Originally, it was intended that the NWMP would be replaced by local law enforcement agencies as settlement occurred. But new settlers were reluctant to assume this burden and demanded that the organized and efficient Mounted Police protect them. Even when the provinces of Alberta and Saskatchewan gained autonomy in 1905, they contracted the (after 1904 Royal) North-West Mounted Police to perform provincial police services. This lasted until 1916 when, stretched thin by security duties related to the war, the force gave up its contracts, and Alberta and Saskatchewan formed their own provincial police forces.[3] So it is fair to say that in the period 1890 to 1916 the Mounted Police was the principal police force in the west and that its primary duty was combatting crime.

---

3   As a matter of federal governmental policy, incorporated towns and cities in the North-West Territories were to organize their own police services and were not to be policed by the NWMP. However, by 1905, there were 21 incorporated towns and five incorporated cities and a total of only 47 municipal policemen. The largest police force was at Calgary, numbering six men. (R.C. Macleod,

Great was the variety and the volume of crime handled by the police. In 1905 the Mounted Police laid 4,647 charges in 70 different categories of offences against the Criminal Code, various federal acts and provincial and territorial ordinances. They obtained 3,767 convictions.[4] The amount of criminal work in the previous few years had increased considerably; for example, the number of convictions in 1900 was 936.[5] In 1905, aside from charges related to drunkenness, the most frequently investigated cases were assault (573) and theft (560). There were 23 cases of homicide or attempted homicide in 1905. The statistical high for criminal cases during the period 1874-1916 was in 1914, when the RNWMP laid 16,212 charges and obtained 13,701 convictions. There were 54 cases of homicide or attempted homicide that year.[6]

The purpose of these statistics is to establish that investigation of abortions, infanticides and related crimes was a statistically insignificant part of the duties of the Mounted Police. In the entire period under examination the Mounted Police only investigated 48 cases involving abortion or suspected abortion.[7] Out of these cases only 30 are known to have resulted in convictions for any crimes. Regarding infanticide, 39 cases were investigated, resulting in 20 convictions obtained. There will be more analysis of these figures later in the paper, but initially they indicate that abortion and infanticide were not major problems in prairie society. This must be asserted with reservation because one cannot deduce the number of unreported cases of any crime from the number of reported cases. This might be used to support the argument of those who believe that there was a successful underground conspiracy of women to promote and abet abortion in this period. However, the ignorance and desperation displayed by those caught in the act belies the assertion that the general populace was well informed on abortion. Certainly the fact that cases of infanticide were almost as common as cases of abortion indicates that abortive techniques and assistance were unavailable to these women. It must be noted, too, that, as far as we know, no abortion or infanticide cases came to the attention of police in the early days of the west. Whether this is a comment on the closed nature of native society or on the commitment by the Mounted Police of its resources to more pressing security problems is not known. But as white settlers increased, so did the number of police investigations into cases of abortion and infanticide. Of the 48 suspected abortions and 39 suspected infanticides, the Force investigated six abortions and five infanticides between 1874 and 1900 and 42 abortions and 34 infanticides between 1901 and 1916.

Under the Criminal Code of Canada passed by Parliament in 1892, there were two ways in which a person accused of being involved with an abortion could be charged: either for attempting to procure a miscarriage; or, for supplying a drug or an instrument intended for use to procure a miscarriage. If police failed to produce

---

The NWMP and Law Enforcement, 1873-1905 (Toronto: University of Toronto Press, 1976), pp. 50, 178; and A.F.J. Artibise, *Prairie Urban Development 1870-1930*, Canadian Historical Association Booklet No. 34 (Ottawa, 1981), pp. 33-35.)

4   Canada, Sessional Papers, *Annual Report of the Commissioner of the Royal North-West Mounted Police*, 1905, pp. 7-9 (Hereafter referred to as *Mounted Police Annual Report*).

5   *Mounted Police Annual Report*, 1900, p. 4.

6   Ibid., 1914, pp. 10-18.

7   Figures for abortion and infanticide and other crimes were derived from information on cases found in: *Mounted Police Annual Reports*; Record Group (RG) 18, RCMP records at the Public Archives of Canada; western Canadian newspapers.

convincing evidence against a practitioner of this crime, they could charge him or her with the more minor offence of practicing medicine without a licence. This paper will examine cases investigated under each one of these categories. For abortion the most serious charge which could be levelled was attempting to procure a miscarriage. Chapter 23, Section 272 of the Canadian Criminal Code for 1892 made liable for life imprisonment anyone who attempted to procure a miscarriage on a woman through drug or instrument whether she was pregnant or only believed to have been pregnant. Section 273 of the same act made the pregnant woman liable to seven years in prison who herself attempted, or permitted others to attempt to procure an abortion through drugs or instruments whether the woman was pregnant or only believed to have been pregnant.[8]

During the period 1874 to 1916, 44 persons were charged with one or the other of these offences and at least 16 persons were convicted. Of the remainder, 20 charges were either withdrawn by police, dismissed by the court at some point in the judicial process, or terminated by the acquittal of the accused. In eight other charges the outcome of the case is unknown. Not counting the last eight cases, this represents a conviction rate of 44.44%. For the period 1901 to 1916, when the Mounted Police presented and analyzed crime statistics in their annual reports, the conviction rate of 44% for abortion does not stand up well to overall conviction rates of 75% and 85%, routinely reported. However, it must be remembered that overall conviction rates cover hundreds of cases, like vagrancy and drunkenness, for which conviction was a virtual certainty. Calculating the conviction rate for homicide or attempted homicide for the years 1901 to 1916, for cases in which the outcome is recorded, the conviction rate is 44.06%, almost precisely the same as for abortion.

There were also lesser charges which could be pressed in cases where abortion was suspected. Chapter 29, Section 274 of the Canadian Criminal Code, made a person liable for 2 years in prison who unlawfully provided a drug or instrument to be used to procure the miscarriage of a woman whether or not she was pregnant in fact.[9] There were 17 of such cases recorded by the Mounted Police for this period, in which the outcome of 15 is known, 10 convictions, and five dismissed, withdrawn, or acquitted. This represented a conviction rate of 66.66%. Also, suspected abortionists were on four occasions charged with practicing medicine without a licence and all were convicted and paid fines of from $25.00 to $100.00.

An important point to be made at this juncture is that the focus of police attention in pursuing cases of abortion was on the person performing the abortion. It was not usual in abortion cases investigated by the Mounted Police to charge the woman having the abortion even though she was criminally liable. In the cases researched here, where the outcomes are known, none of the women who had abortions were convicted of any crime. The intent of the police was clearly to stop the work of those performing abortions and punish them for their crimes. Implicit in this process was the clear perception that women were victims when social circumstances persuaded them to turn to abortionists.

The difficulties of bringing an abortionist to justice in the frontier west were considerable. The case of Professor Andrew Campbell, alias Dr. Lovingheart of

---

8   Canada, *Sessional Papers*, 1892, "An Act Respecting the Criminal Code," 55-56 V.
9   Ibid.

Calgary, is a good example. Lovingheart was not a medical doctor, despite his self-bestowed title, and, although he was a man of property, various exploits made him notorious within the community. In 1892, the Mounted Police arrested Lovingheart for neglecting to provide for the welfare of a young employee who had run into bad weather on his way to purchase coal at Knee Hill mine 50 miles from Calgary and had died from starvation and exposure. Lovingheart was acquitted by Mounted Police Justice-of-the-Peace, Inspector A.R. Cuthbert, as the evidence indicated that the employee was irresponsible.[10] A few months later Lovingheart was in trouble again, this time charged with procuring an abortion.

The Calgary police suspected Lovingheart of being an abortionist and in early 1893 put him under surveillance. On April 15, the town police arrested him on a charge of aborting the fetus of one Maggie Stevenson by administering a noxious substance. The Calgary *Herald* reported that Lovingheart was quite overwhelmed by his situation, weeping incessantly in his cell for hours.[11] His situation soon brightened, when his able attorney, Senator James A. Lougheed, had him moved from the unsanitary town jail to the more habitable Mounted Police guardroom. Meanwhile, the police case disappeared when Maggie Stevenson skipped town. Lovingheart was released on bail on April 19. The case was revived on May 2, 1893 when the Mounted Police located Maggie Stevenson at Langden about to board a train out of the North-West Territories. Lovingheart was returned to custody only briefly, however, as Stevenson refused to identify him as the abortionist.[12]

Abortion on the western frontier was most graphically explored in the case of Fred Gibbs in 1894, in which Dr. Lovingheart's name once more appeared. Gibbs was arrested by the Mounted Police in Calgary on May 28, 1894, charged with administering a noxious drug to a young girl named Ida Morton in an attempt to procure a miscarriage. At the trial in July, a sordid story unfolded of Gibbs' family life. The common law wife of Mr. Gibbs, Alice Morton, had many years before left her legal husband and arranged for her little daughter to be raised by relatives in a respectable manner. Alice then led what was described in the press as a wild life, under assumed names, before taking up with Gibbs. Having achieved a degree of stability, Alice brought her daughter Ida to Calgary in 1890 to live in her house, where Gibbs posed as a boarder. Not long after the girl turned 16 years old she was seduced by her mother's lover. Gibbs forced the girl into a continuing sexual relationship, apparently through fear and guilt, which was kept secret from her mother. Finally, early in 1894 the girl became pregnant. Gibbs then obtained a bottle of noxious liquid, which he said he got from Dr. Lovingheart to precipitate an abortion. He poured the first dose and forced Ida to take the potion daily. He told her that if a miscarriage did not occur, Dr. Lovingheart had agreed to perform an abortion by operation for $50.00. However, mother got suspicious and daughter confessed her shame. The Mounted Police were called in and Staff Sergeant Brooke ordered a chemical analysis of the contents of the bottle. It was found to contain, in part, cantharides, which was believed to cause miscarriages. Gibbs was arrested.

---

10 *Mounted Police Annual Report*; Calgary *Herald*, November 21, 22 and 25, 1892.
11 Calgary *Herald*, April 19, [1893].
12 RG 18, Vol. 75, File 127-1893, Insp. A.R. Cuthbert's Monthly Report from Calgary, April, 1893; *Mounted Police Annual Report*, 1893, p. 200; Calgary *Herald*, May 3, 1893; Edmonton *Bulletin*, May 8, 1893.

Gibbs was represented by a well-known lawyer, J.P. Nolan, yet curiously little defence was offered at his trial. The defence attorney did not call any witnesses, and in addressing the jury, Judge Rouleau made much of the fact that Dr. Lovingheart was not called to the stand. The jury took less than an hour to find Gibbs guilty. Before sentencing, Gibbs made a long rambling statement claiming that the girl had wanted the abortion and that he had supplied her with what he thought was a harmless substance to prevent her from achieving her end through drastic means. In sentencing Gibbs, Judge Rouleau referred to the case as one of the most unpleasant he had presided over in 17 years on the bench. He commented that he had heard that abortion had become too common in Calgary and he intended to make an example of every case which came before him. Gibbs received nine years and six months in penitentiary for the abortion charge and six months additional for stealing a watch.[13]

As for Dr. Lovingheart, he managed to stay one step ahead of serious trouble with the law. On May 4, 1894 he was charged with practicing medicine without a licence. He appeared before Inspector Frank Harper the next day and was fined $ 25.00 and costs. He appealed the decision but lost. Later that fall he was again charged with attempting to procure an abortion and appeared before Judge Scott on November 23 and won an acquittal.[14] Dr. Lovingheart, alias Professor Campbell, left Calgary in a malodorous fashion in 1895. He apparently persuaded the parents of a 14-year-old girl to allow her to accompany him and his wife on a trip to the United States. When the trip was extended beyond the anticipated period, the parents contacted Calgary police. The girl had been allowed to write to her parents, so she was known to be in Washington, D.C. Chief English contacted the police in that city, who found the party in the back room of an isolated tenement. The girl told a lurid tale of Lovingheart's alternate threats to skin her alive and promises to buy her expensive presents, accompanied by frequent attempts to kiss her. She was returned to her parents but there is no record of charges laid against Lovingheart. The Calgary *Herald* commented obliquely "the doings of the 'Professor' while a resident here are well-known to the citizens of Calgary."[15]

After Lovingheart parted the scene, no backstreet abortionist of the same notoriety came to the attention of the Mounted Police for some time. In fact, no record has been found of any Mounted Police investigations into abortions between 1895 and 1904. After that, abortion cases became an annual occurrence. In May, 1910 a man in southern Alberta identified as Dr. Tucker was prosecuted at the behest of the Medical Association of Alberta for furnishing medicine without being registered as a medical practitioner. Upon conviction, he was fined $100.00. A month later a man by the same name in the same area was charged with giving drugs to procure an abortion, but it does not appear that this legal action succeeded in conviction.[16] In other cases abortions were performed by people who did not pretend to a conventional medical education.

In 1909, one of only two married women discovered in the Mounted Police reports to have sought abortions almost died from the experience. At the request of Mrs.

---

13   *Mounted Police Annual Report*, 1894, p. 231; Calgary *Herald*, July 6 and 10, 1894.
14   *Mounted Police Annual Report*, 1894, pp. 230, 233.
15   Calgary *Herald*, March 15, 1895.
16   RG 18, Vol. 2354, Crime Registers, Macleod District, pp. 16, 24, 32.

Freeman, at or near Paynton, Saskatchewan, Isabel Tetrault performed the abortion operation but peritonitis set in. A medical doctor was called, who had to perform a second operation to save her life. Isabel Tetrault was tried and convicted on the abortion charge and sentenced to three years in Edmonton Penitentiary. Ironically, Isabel's uncle Amédée Tetrault, with whom she lived, was convicted of a brutal murder and sentenced to death a month after his niece went to jail.

A husband and wife team practicing folk medicine in Rosthern, Saskatchewan were suspected of criminal activities in 1909. A married woman had gone to their home in March, 1909 and submitted to an operation "resembling abortion" which resulted in her death from blood poisoning. The corpse was then secretly buried in a cemetery nearby. Information on this reached police two months later and the body was exhumed and an inquest held. The coroner's jury found that the woman had died, following a probable abortion operation, due to the negligence of the folk-medical practitioners. The couple was tried in December, 1909 on charges of abortion and manslaughter. The judge charged the jury very strongly against the accused but the jury returned a verdict of not guilty. Thereafter, however, the police kept an eye on the pair and, in February, 1910, the woman was convicted of impersonating a doctor and fined $50.00. Her husband was fined $50.00 for a similar offence in September, 1910.[17]

Mounted Police surveillance of another suspected abortionist, Joseph Pritchard of Wapella, Saskatchewan, was rewarded in 1913. In 1912 a Sergeant Joyce heard a story that Pritchard had performed an abortion on a servant girl who had had sexual relations with her employer, a wealthy farmer. The Mounted Policeman had no concrete evidence in this case but he kept track of Pritchard's activities and on June 12, 1913, armed with a search warrant, he visited Pritchard, found his abortion instruments and charged him with two counts of procuring an abortion. Pritchard was found guilty and sentenced to four years in prison. After conviction Pritchard admitted to performing an abortion on the servant girl in 1912 and her employer was charged with procuring someone to perform an abortion. The outcome of this case is unknown.[18]

A notorious case of abortion in Red Deer Hill, Saskatchewan, resulted in the death of both mother and baby. Gladys Read, a 16-year-old girl, was driving a wagon home from her brother's place on the night of December 1, 1914, when she met a neighbour, Frank Inkster, on the road. He accepted her offer of a ride and then forced her to drive off the main road and raped her. Inkster promised Gladys that if she got pregnant he would marry her. This offer Gladys spurned, but by January, 1915, she knew that she was pregnant and she told Inkster. His solution was to obtain medicine to stimulate an abortion.

Inkster approached a doctor in Prince Albert wanting some medicine for his wife who, he said, was suffering from irregular and painful menstruations. The doctor wrote out a prescription for some capsules and a liquid. As Inkster was leaving the office he asked the doctor if the prescription was safe for a young girl whose period had not come on. The doctor's exact reply is not known but apparently he reassured Inkster in some way on this point. Gladys Read took the drugs for about a week but

---

17 *Mounted Police Annual Reports*, 1909, p. 115; 1910, p. 101.
18 Ibid., 1913, p. 183; 1914, pp. 57-58.

fell ill early in March. Her mother rushed her by sleigh to Victoria Hospital in Prince Albert. There Gladys made a statement to Police concerning the entire matter. The doctors found that a miscarriage had occurred, the fetus being expelled from the womb. However, the afterbirth had remained in the womb and septic infection had set in. The doctors tried to remove the poisonous tissue from the uterus but their efforts were unsuccessful and Gladys died on March 19, 1915.

As a result, Frank Inkster and the doctor were charged with manslaughter, procuring an abortion and supplying drugs to procure an abortion. Medical testimony at this trial was to the effect that the capsules taken by Gladys were made up of Apial, Ergatin, Oil of Savin and Aloin which were described as powerful uterine stimulants capable of causing a miscarriage. The liquid prescription was the drug Black How which served to stop bleeding and to act as a sedative. Two doctors testified that the capsules were a straight abortive prescription but, fortunately for the doctor being prosecuted, other doctors came forward to say that such a prescription might be given to a woman with menstrual problems if the patient were examined first. The doctor was found not guilty on all three charges by the jury, the verdicts described by the Mounted Police investigation as being for "reasons beyond comprehension."[19] Frank Inkster likewise was saved from the most serious consequences of his acts when, after debating for 27 hours, the jury would not agree on a verdict on the manslaughter charge. He was, however, found guilty on the two abortion charges and sentenced to five years in Prince Albert Penitentiary.[20]

A man who frequently posed as a doctor was charged on two counts of abortion in March, 1916. G.J. Grant had been a medical student in his native England but had not attained a degree. He had set up practice in Nottingham, England in 1902 as a ladies' specialist and was strongly suspected by local police of procuring abortions. In fact, one woman died in his office but he was not charged because an inquest found the cause of death to be a brain hemorrhage. In 1912 Grant, his wife, son and a young chambermaid, Marie Evans, immigrated to Canada, taking up residence on a rural property near Kantenville, Saskatchewan.

It was not long before police took notice of the new arrivals. There were two houses on the property, one for Grant's wife and son and another for Grant, Marie Evans and assorted other women who lived with him from time to time. Grant represented himself as a doctor, using M.D. after his name, and was believed to be performing abortions on women in the district. Finally, in 1916 the Mounted Police arrested him. Two women, one of them his employee Marie Evans, testified that he had performed abortions on them. A search of Grant's house turned up a number of drugs analyzed as abortifacient, a prescription pad, medical instruments suitable for performing abortions, erotic literature and Grant's correspondence, which showed him to be a man obsessed by sex. Marie Evans testified at the trial that Grant was the father of the child whom he had aborted and that her pregnancy had been so far advanced when the operation took place that the aborted fetus bore quite human features. On April 4 at Weyburn, Grant was convicted on both counts of abortion and sentenced to four years in prison. He was also given an additional six months for sending an indecent letter through the mail. The Mounted Police were disappointed that the

---

19   RG 18, Volume 486, File 279-1915, April 26, 1915, Report by S/Sgt. Prince, Prince Albert.
20   Ibid.

sentence was not more severe, particularly because, on his release from prison, he would likely return to his wife, whom he had regularly abused physically and morally, and resume the torment.[21]

The abortifacient drugs mentioned in the Inkster and Grant cases raise another question concerning nineteenth and early twentieth century abortions. Abortifacient drugs were obviously available in western Canada, at least to doctors or pseudo-doctors. McLaren's article on abortion in Canada states that abortifacient drugs were widely advertised in newspapers using oblique references to restoring female regularity.[22] A spot check of western newspapers for this period failed to confirm this contention. Advertisements did appear for pills and elixirs to help women with pain and distress during their menstrual cycles but these are more likely to have been harmless patent medicines than abortifacient drugs. One advertisement alone seemed to have some underlying message. In 1902, the Calgary *Herald* carried an advertisement for Doctor Pierce's Favorite Prescription which "establishes regularity, dries disagreeable drains, heals inflammation and ulceration and cures female weakness."[23] However, this notion was dispelled in another issue of the paper which advertised exactly the same product as a tonic for expectant mothers.[24] It appears that abortifacient drugs were not as easily available as some writers have contended.[25] This is confirmed to a degree by several cases of infanticide which occurred after women had unsuccessfully sought abortifacient drugs.

As mentioned above, the (R)NWMP laid charges in 39 cases of suspected infanticide, obtaining a total of 20 convictions for homicide, concealing a birth or neglecting to procure medical assistance. Murder or manslaughter in the death of a newborn infant was difficult to prove because it was necessary to establish that the infant had existence separate from the mother after birth.[26] Fifteen persons were charged with murder or manslaughter during this period with three convictions, 11 cases where charges were withdrawn or dismissed or acquittal won, and one case where the outcome is unknown. This is a conviction rate of 21.43%, which compares unfavourably with the overall conviction rate for homicide of 44.06% attained by the Mounted Police in the period 1901 to 1916. It was easier for police and prosecution to prove concealment of birth, a crime under Chapter 29, Section 240 of the 1892 Canadian Criminal Code, for disposing "of the dead body of any child in any manner with intent to conceal the fact that its mother was delivered of it, whether the child died before, or during, or after birth."[27] There were 30 persons charged with this crime with 16 convicted, 13 charges withdrawn, dismissed or acquitted, one outcome unknown. This is a conviction rate of 55.17%. More rarely, the Mounted Police charged persons with

---

21 RG 18, Volume 3270, File 1916-HQ-640-F-1.

22 McLaren, op. cit., pp. 329-330.

23 Calgary *Herald*, January 4, 1902, p. 4.

24 Ibid., January 8, 1902, p. 4.

25 The whole question of the role of drugs in inducing miscarriage in this era is still open to question. There is literature which states that nineteenth century medicine did not have effective abortifacient drugs except for women already prone to miscarriage. See James C. Mohr, *Abortion in America: The Origins and Evolution of National Policy, 1800-1900* (Toronto: Oxford University Press, 1978), p. 276.

26 Canada, *Sessional Papers*, 1892, "An Act Respecting the Criminal Code", 55-56 V., Chapter 29, Section 219.

27 Ibid., Section 240.

neglecting to procure proper medical assistance when a death of a newborn occurred.[28] There were five such charges laid with one conviction, three withdrawn, terminated or acquitted, and one outcome unknown.

Only one person was convicted of murder for infanticide in this period. Jesse Hammond murdered his newborn child of whom his sister-in-law was the mother. Hammond and his wife and her sister lived together on a farm near Wynyard, Saskatchewan. He and his sister-in-law established a sexual relationship which brought forth a child on August 22, 1911. Hammond abandoned the child on a pile of straw outdoors where it eventually died. On November 6, 1912, the two parented a second child, which was also disposed of. When Hammond was arrested in 1913, he made prosecution easy by confessing his misdeeds. Proving separate existence was no problem and Hammond was convicted of murder by judge and jury and sentenced to be hanged on August 14, 1913. The Minister of Justice was not entirely satisfied with the conduct of the trial and ordered a new trial for September, 1913, which, however, resulted in the same verdict and sentence. On December 13, 1913, just four days before he was to be hanged, Hammond's sentence was commuted by Order-in-Council to life imprisonment.[29]

A much more complicated case was the 1913 trial of three people for the murder of a newborn child in Eyebrow, Saskatchewan. Mrs. Maude Greenman was a well-to-do widow with five children living on a farm with her parents, Mr. and Mrs. Austin Foy. She became pregnant by her hired man, Patrick Kelly, an unreliable character whom the police considered may have been "half crazy."[30] Mrs. Greenman tried unsuccessfully to persuade Kelly to get some abortifacient medicine for her from a drug store in Moose Jaw. Kelly, meanwhile, sued Mrs. Greenman for unpaid wages and also had her charged with breach of promise to marry him. However, in the midst of litigation Kelly stole an overcoat and was sent to jail.

On March 25, 1913, Mrs. Greenman gave birth to a baby girl, assisted by a trained nurse, Mrs. Jane Caldwell. The event took place during the night and Mrs. Greenman was most anxious lest her other children and some visiting relatives hear the infant's cries, as they did not know that she had been pregnant. At the behest of the mother the nurse administered chloroform and laudanum to the infant to keep her quiet but without effect. After consultation with her parents, Maude Greenman pleaded with Jane Caldwell to get rid of her child for her. Reluctantly, Caldwell complied and, accompanied by Mr. Foy, she carried the child in freezing weather to an unheated meathouse on the property and placed her in a box on the floor. She checked her several times during the day until she was sure she was dead and then she buried her in the chicken coop.

This homicide came to the attention of the Mounted Police in a bizarre way. When Patrick Kelly was released from jail, he visited Maude Greenman on June 4, 1913, and threatened her with a revolver. She called for help over the rural telephone and brought forth the local Justice-of-the-Peace and two other men in an automobile who

---

28   Ibid., Section 239.
29   *Mounted Police Annual Report*, 1913, pp. 177-178; Department of Justice records, Public Archives of Canada, RG 13, C1, Volume 1483.
30   RG 18, Vol. 3247, File HQ-681-F-11, August 30, 1913, Report from Moose Jaw Subdistrict to Officer Commanding, Regina District.

chased Kelly, fleeing the scene in a buggy. Kelly fired some shots to ward off his pursuers, but they caught him. Just before being subdued Kelly pointed the revolver at the J.P.'s head and pulled the trigger. Luckily the hammer struck a defective cartridge. Kelly was charged with pulling the trigger of a firearm with intent. In the subsequent investigation, he told police how Maude Greenman had killed their child. A few days later Jane Caldwell and Austin Foy were arrested and charged with murder and Maude Greenman with conspiracy to commit murder. All were tried separately.

The stories of the three accused supported the main facts of the case but put a different complexion on each individual's responsibility for the crime. Maude Greenman denied that she was a party to the murder, contending that Jane Caldwell had been solely responsible. Caldwell confessed to her part in the crime but implicated Greenman and Foy as accomplices. A Dr. Snow, a former employer of Jane Caldwell, put an unusual medical angle on the affair. He claimed that Mrs. Caldwell suffered from a disease of the head and throat which affected her mind at times. Furthermore, he stated that Mrs. Caldwell was menstruating at the time of the offence, which clouded her judgment. Austin Foy claimed that when he helped put the baby in the meathouse he thought that she was already dead.[31] At the trials held at Moose Jaw in November, 1913, Maude Greenman and Jane Caldwell were found guilty of reduced charges of manslaughter and sentenced to ten years each in the penitentiary at Edmonton. Austin Foy was acquitted. Patrick Kelly was convicted at the same November sitting of the Alberta Supreme Court and sentenced to one year hard labour in prison.[32]

Several charges of murder failed due to the necessity to prove that the child had enjoyed a separate existence. Such was the case when a newly born infant was found dead in a slough near Melville, Saskatchewan in 1913. A comb belonging to an unmarried 16-year-old Austrian girl was found near the body. Police investigation revealed that on the night previous to the discovery of the corpse the girl had taken ill at a dance at a home near the slough and left with her mother. Subsequently, medical examination indicated that the girl had recently given birth to a child. The girl and her mother were both charged with murder, but the case fell apart at the trial because the crown could not produce indisputable medical evidence that the child had enjoyed separate existence.[33] The same verdict for exactly the same reason occurred in the case of a 20-year-old woman who gave birth to a child at Marquis, Saskatchewan in 1914. She had subsequently put the dead body in a suitcase, taken a train to Moose Jaw and checked the luggage into the parcel room at the train station. The story came to notice of the police when she sought attention from a local doctor.[34]

One of the most heart-rending cases of infanticide during this period concerned Ernestine Labelle, a 14-year-old girl who went free due to the public perception of her as a victim rather than a criminal. Ernestine came from Wittenberg, Alberta, and entered St. Joseph's Convent in Red Deer as a boarding student in September, 1915.

---

31 RG 18, Vol. 3247, File HQ-681-F-11, Criminal Case file — Greenman, Caldwell, Foy; Regina, *The Morning Leader*, June 14 and 18, 1913; *Regina Daily Standard*, June 14, 16 and 18, 1913.
32 *Mounted Police Annual Report*, 1914, pp. 58-59.
33 Ibid., 1913. pp. 24, 178.
34 Ibid., 1914, p. 59.

At the time of registration her father warned the sisters that she had missed several periods and had been ill. The sisters thought nothing of this because of the girl's age and because she was very well behaved. At 4 p.m. on February 25, 1916 Ernestine retired to the dormitory complaining of stomach pains. Between 2 and 4 a.m. on February 26, she gave birth to a daughter in the lavatory. At 8:30 a.m. a Sister Francis went to Ernestine's bed to see if she needed anything. She noticed blood stains on the floor and the bed clothes. The sister then went to the girl's locker to fetch a kimono for her and inside found the dead baby lying face down on the floor with a boot lace tied around her neck.

After Ernestine received medical attention she was charged with murder by the Mounted Police and kept in custody at Memorial Hospital in Red Deer. The girl gave a statement that her uncle Lionel had taken sexual advantage of her and made her pregnant. She also said that the baby had been born dead but "I was scared to leave him [sic] there to come alive so I tied the rope around his neck."[35] An autopsy was held on the baby and the medical examiner reported he found the lungs inflated, indicating the baby had breathed after birth. In his opinion the cause of death was strangulation from the boot lace which had been wound tightly twice around the neck. At the conclusion of the girl's trial in September, 1916, the judge in his address to the jury explained that it could bring in a verdict of murder or of concealment of birth. However, the jury found her not guilty on both counts. The judge would not comment on the murder verdict but felt compelled to say that he couldn't agree with the decision on concealment of birth. Corporal Hanna of the Mounted Police explained to divisional headquarters that:

> The verdict, which was undoubtedly a sympathetic one, was a popular one, as public feeling was very much in favour of the girl and against her uncle Lionel Labelle, who was the father of the child and the cause of getting her into trouble. It was felt that he, if anyone, should be the one to suffer.[36]

Lionel Labelle was charged with carnal knowledge of a girl under 14 years of age on March 6, 1916, and tried at the same sitting of the Supreme Court as Ernestine in September. The results of that trial were not available to the writer.

As pointed out earlier, the police and the Crown had more success winning convictions on the charges of concealment of birth than of infanticide. However, there was a consequent trade-off in the severity of sentences awarded for this crime. Of the 16 convictions obtained, the sentences are known for eight cases. Two were for the maximum of two years, one for 23 months, two for six months, one for one month hard labour, one for one day in jail with a $200 fine and one sentence was suspended. The heavier penalties are easily explained by the heinous nature of the offence but some of the lighter sentences seem strange.

In the case of the three more severe sentences, the circumstances indicated murder but the evidence was not strong enough to convict. All three cases involved illegitimate babies who were disposed of, in two cases by the mother and in one case by the common law husband of the mother with her complicity. The latter case is a good example of one where homicide could not be proven, yet the strongest punishment for a lesser charge was in order.

In 1916, Winnifred Van Sant, aged 28 years, a woman described by police as of

---

35 RG 18, Volume 3270, File HQ-678-K-1, Crime Report dated March 7, 1916.
36 Ibid., Crime Report dated September 30, 1916.

low mentality, lived in a filthy shack near Peace River, Alberta. She shared the accommodation with William Briggs, aged 55, recently released from the Mounted Police guardroom at Peace River where he had served time for theft. This arrangement was not a happy one for Winnifred, as Briggs frequently beat her. She also became pregnant, not by Briggs, but by the man who lived on a neighbouring farm with his wife and five children. Sometime in late 1916, Winnifred gave birth to a baby boy. Delivery was difficult, as the child was in the breech position, but despite Winnifred's pleas Briggs refused to summon help. After delivery, someone punctured the baby's head with a sharp object and buried it in a manure pile. In the next while, neighbours who had noticed Van Sant had been pregnant asked her about the baby but she denied that she had given birth. The Mounted Police were alerted, and upon visiting the place they located the corpse and elicited a confession from Van Sant.

Briggs and Van Sant were tried in Edmonton in January, 1917 for concealing and disposing of the body of a newly born child. The evidence in the case was strong so there was little question of acquittal. Yet pathologists found that while the baby's lungs had inflated, this was more probably due to gas absorbed from bacteria in the manure than to breathing. Thus they determined that the child had not had a separate existence. Judge Simmon, who presided without jury, told Briggs that the medical report had saved him from a charge of murder. Briggs was given two years in prison and Van Sant, who had been clearly dominated by Briggs, was given six months in jail. A pathetic footnote to this case was that after her trial Van Sant asked to serve her sentence at the Mounted Police guardroom at Macleod, where she had been held while awaiting trial. She declared that she had been happier there than at any time in the previous seven years.[37]

In at least two of the lighter sentences given for concealment of birth, cultural attitudes toward the death of an infant seemed to have been taken into account. This was the case for a woman in Claresholm convicted in 1907 of concealing the birth of a child and of neglecting to obtain medical assistance. The body of her child had been found under the floor boards of her house. The woman was German by birth and separated from her husband. Chief Justice A.L. Sifton let her off with a suspended sentence, explaining that it was "a custom amongst people of this class, not to obtain assistance in such cases."[38] The outcome was similar with an Indian woman from the Crooked Lake agency convicted of concealment of birth in 1915. Vitalene Le Rat confessed to strangling her infant daughter, who had been fathered by her brother. She was charged with murder but the jury brought in a verdict of guilty only of concealment and she was sentenced to six months in jail. The Mounted Police were satisfied, Superintendent McGibbon observing: "The fact of this woman being prosecuted for this serious offence will probably be a lesson to the Indians, who do not look upon the life of an infant as valuable."[39] Only the bare facts are known about the conviction of a mixed blood girl of Cumberland House for concealing the birth, but it could be speculated that cultural reasons were also behind the imposition of only a one-month sentence.[40] Details are sketchy on the remaining case, the conviction

---

37 RG 18, Volume 3272, File HQ-685-K-1, Criminal Case File.
38 *Mounted Police Annual Report*, 1907, p. 51.
39 Ibid., 1916, p. 37; RG 18, Vol. 3262, File HQ-681-F-8, Criminal Case File.
40 RG 18, Volume 107, File 224-1895, Monthly Report for March from Superintendent G.B. Moffatt, Commanding Officer, "F" Division, Prince Albert.

of a man, J. Flack, for concealing the birth. This resulted in a sentence of one day in jail and a $200 fine. The proceedings appear to have been poorly handled, from an inconclusive medical examination of the corpse to a strange sequence of charges, first against the father, then against the mother, his own stepchild, and then against the father again. Perhaps the light sentence was a reflection of some weakness in the case.[41]

Finally, of the five cases where charges were laid for neglecting to procure medical assistance in the birth of a child, the circumstances are known in only two. One of these was the case noted above of the German woman who was convicted of both concealing and neglecting and received a suspended sentence. In the other case, in late 1904 a woman living in Fort Macleod, whose marital status is unknown but who had a five-year-old girl living with her sister, became pregnant. She sought information on an abortifacient medicine from a friend without success. On July 22, 1905, she gave birth to the child on a secluded bank of the Old Man River not far from the Mounted Police barracks. Three days later the body was found on that spot and circumstantial evidence led the Mounted Police to the woman. She admitted that the child belonged to her. A coroner's examination revealed that the child had breathed after birth and the jury's verdict at the inquest was that the child died as a result of the neglect of the mother to secure medical treatment. A jury found the mother not guilty of this charge at the trial, perhaps out of sympathy for the woman's plight.[42]

Clearly, then, the reality of criminal abortion and infanticide in the prairie west during this period was a sad and sordid one. There is no sign of women asserting control of their generative functions as a step towards liberation. Nor is there a sign of any underground network of informed women and sympathetic men which operated outside the law helping women to escape the unreasonable demands of a male-dominated society that they bear unwanted children. Instead, where the circumstances are known, the cases which came to the attention of the Mounted Police were of people ridding themselves of the products of irregular relationships. At that time the law and society did not accept that the penalty for a conception of inconvenience was death to the fetus or to the infant. The police and the judicial system were conscientious in pursuing the criminal acts of abortion and infanticide. There was, however, a moderating factor in the bent of this pursuit. This was a recognition in individual cases that the mother was often a victim as well as the child, a fact that was reflected in leniency of treatment. Although there were occasional expressions of outrage by the judges, the policemen or the public at particularly cruel acts of abortion or infanticide, there was no sense of a moral urge for a crusade against such abuse. This is, I believe, because abortions and infanticides were isolated acts, seen as all too human failures, admittedly more common as the white population grew, but uncommon enough not to be any threat to social order on the prairies.

NOTE

This chapter was previously published in Canadian Catholic Historical Association, *Historical Studies*, 53 (1986), 53-70. The author thanks Allison Phillips, a McGill University student, who assisted with the research for this paper in the summer of 1985.

---

41 RG 18, Volume 126, File 2-1892, Monthly Report for October from Inspector J. Howe, Commanding Officer, "C" Division, Battleford.

42 Macleod *Gazette*, July 27, 1905 and November 16, 1905; RG 18, Volume 2453, Register of Cases — Macleod, 1904-1909.

SECTION D

Characteristics of the Force

THIRTEEN

Pioneers and Police on the Canadian Prairies, 1885-1914

Carl Betke

In the preface to his recent impressive historical analysis of the North-West Mounted Police, R.C. Macleod marvelled at the "consistent popularity" of the mounted police, "particularly in western Canada."[1] His book goes on to support the proposition that their popularity was based upon their success at maintaining law and order. Rather than follow the traditional emphasis on stories of spectacular individual heroism in quelling desperate Indians and criminals alike, Macleod has stressed the mounted police capacity for crime prevention in their military style, discipline, and prestige; their regular system of patrols; and their service to minimize active illegal expression of general or individual animosities against vulnerable minorities such as Indians and immigrants. That the incidence of crime was rare is obvious from the lists compiled in annual reports or from patrol reports.[2] Macleod's conclusion, that the peaceful situation was a result of the police presence, cannot altogether satisfactorily be demonstrated because the police were in the North-West Territories before almost all of the settlers, preventing any useful before-and-after contrast.

In any case, settlers did not, in the main, see any police heroics, whether or not their systematic patrols were effective deterrents to crime. It seems a sensible question to ask what the early settlers did see the police doing. There are at least two possible approaches to finding an answer: to study pioneer correspondence, reminiscences, and local histories; and to study the day-to-day reports of policemen in the rural West. A rapid glance through several local histories in search of references to North-West Mounted Policemen confirms the impression that they were for the most part not linked to dramatic criminal chases in community memories. What follows, then, is derived from the second approach, a study of police records for the period of rapid western settlement.

In a nation which reveres its police force, it is particularly important to probe the origins of the police image. At issue might be a conception of social order or the rule

---

1 R.C. Macleod, *The North-West Mounted Police and Law Enforcement 1873-1905* (Toronto: University of Toronto Press, 1976), p. ix.
2 Ibid., p. 46.

of law. If actual exploits did not create the reputation, then the nature of normal, peaceful service cannot be overlooked, dismissed, or reduced in significance. If the major impression the police created was of benevolent assistance in a host of important areas, that has implications for an assessment of the collective national character. Rather than a people riddled with criminal tendencies or overly acquiescent to repressive police authority, Canadians may have been a people particularly susceptible in their pioneer conditions (as were the Indians in their altered circumstances) to the first agents of government welfare. It can hardly be surprising that so mundane an appreciation would be expressed more colourfully in the popular literary imagination. But for the majority of original prairie settlers, there is striking evidence that the police may have been most noticeable for their visits, their assistance to those who were struggling or who felt alien in a strange, new land, their control of quarantine procedure during periods of disease epidemics, their veterinary contributions, or their usefulness in combatting the menace of prairie fires.

*****

The first factor in the esteem enjoyed by the North-West Mounted Police was their great visibility. This was not so much a function of numbers as of deployment. Indeed, after the excitement of the North-West Rebellion in 1885 temporarily boosted the establishment of the force to one thousand, its size actually declined, even though the Klondike gold rush in the Yukon drained off several hundred to the North for a few years around the turn of the century. The mounted policemen were well known because of their commitment to regular systematic patrols, summer and winter.

The patrol system of the police appears to have originated in response to escalating horse stealing in Canadian territory by American gangs after 1884.[3] In 1886 the previous custom of sporadic patrols was replaced by a much more rigorous programme, not without occasional reaction on the part of ranchers unaccustomed to mounted policemen roaming their lands and grazing police horses on their valuable grass.[4] Commissioner Lawrence Herchmer immediately saw a general value to patrols beyond only the border region, and had them extended throughout the West from the numerous, scattered, small police detachments. That Herchmer's primary objective was to prevent horse stealing and other crime by maintaining an obvious police presence and a fund of knowledge about settlement conditions cannot be doubted. Information on "the state of the country, condition of crops, presence of strangers, travellers met" was to be obtained casually, since, of course, the police had no special right to pry. The concentration on crime prevention was all the more notable in occasional admonitions to secrecy stressing, as one confidential order put it, that some "patrols are to be made at uncertain times, so that those intending to smuggle may not be able to make out plans to get through."[5] Just before the turn of the century, Commissioner Herchmer was fond of describing his "outpost and patrol system" as "the great cause of the absence of crime on our side" of the border, or of

---

3   Ibid., pp. 44-5; D.H. Breen, "The Mounted Police and the Ranching Frontier," in H.A. Dempsey, ed., *Men in Scarlet* (Calgary: Historical Society of Alberta/McClelland & Stewart West, ca. 1974), pp. 122-4.

4   Superintendent P.R. Neale to Commissioner Herchmer, 30 August 1887: Public Archives of Canada, Record Group 18, Records of the Royal Canadian Mounted Police (hereafter RG 18)-B1.

5   See File 511 for 1903, n.d.: RG 18-A1; Macleod, *The North-West Mounted Police*, pp. 45-9.

crediting it with convincing "foreigners that law and order must be respected in this country."[6]

It is equally clear, however, that patrol instructions included far more than the requirement to watch for "doubtful characters." The legendary Superintendent Sam Steele issued orders with quite a different emphasis at Macleod in 1889:

> You will collect all the information you can about the settlers in the vicinity of your Detachment; how many new ones have arrived during the past year, how much stock they have and of what kind, where they are settled, what crops good or bad are generally raised, quantity of hay put up, general feelings amongst them as to the fitness of the country for settlement, and if any have suggestions to make as to the revising of any of the Ordinances for the better Government of the District, their feelings on the Prairie Fire law and powers given under it...[7]

Even the "small flying patrols" of a commissioned or non-commissioned officer and two constables, the purpose of which in some cases was to provide a surprise factor in the watch for desperadoes, were often made to isolated ranches and settlements not covered by regular outpost patrols in order to ascertain the same ordinary details of the settlement process.[8] To some extent the continuation of this emphasis was dictated by periodic requests from the Department of the Interior for copies of patrol maps, for crop information to counter detrimental reports circulating in Britain and the United States on crop prospects in light of the growing season and weather, and for detailed information about numbers of settlers moving into and out of the North-West Territories. The last demand was ongoing, formalized after 1896 by the new Liberal minister of the Interior Clifford Sifton, who desired to know the details of sex, age, and location of origin or destination for the migrants.[9]

Whatever the purposes for patrol reports, the usual effect of the procedure was to provide regular visits to settlers that constituted the only alleviation of monotony not just for many pioneers, but also for the policemen themselves. Many patrol reports perfunctorily listed the observations required but, even among those that contain quite full descriptions of the experience, only occasional incidents broke the tedium of the ride. Difficulties for the police to handle were rarely registered; the police normally received "no complaints" and rode on. References to stray horses, stolen cattle, crop and stock conditions, dotted the thousands of patrol reports that were submitted throughout the Territories.[10] A rancher might complain of a

---

6   Canada, Sessional Papers, NWMP *Report* for 1890, p. 2; NWMP *Report*, 1898, pp. 134.

7   Steele to non-commissioned officer in charge of Porcupine Hills detachment, 14 October 1889: RG 18-C2.

8   Circular memorandum from NWMP Headquarters to Officers Commanding Divisions, 12 April 1890: RG 18-A1.

9   NWMP Comptroller Fred White to Herchmer, 13 October 1892 and 9 August 1897; and correspondence with Interior Department officials, 1894: RG 18-BI; Canada, Sessional Papers, Department of the Interior *Report*, 1891, part I, p. xxiv; Circular memorandum dated 1 June 1895, RG 18-C3; Superintendent A.R. Cuthbert, Battleford, to Sergeant Bird, Duck Lake, 1 June 1901: RG 18-C1.

10   See, for examples, Inspector V. Williams to Officer Commanding at Calgary, 29 July 1887; and diary report of Sergeant Dee, High River, for week ending 28 January 1893: RG 18-B1; Diary of Constable William Murray, North Fork of Sheep Creek (Calgary Division), for week ending 4 June 1891: RG 18-A1; Sergeant Saul Martin to Officer Commanding Prince Albert Division, 5 May 1892: RG 18-C1; Milk River Detachment Diary, 17 August 1895; and daily journal, St. Mary's Detachment, 14 September 1896: RG 18-C2; Diary of Medicine Lodge Detachment, 13 February 1900: RG 18-C1.

homesteader cutting hay on his land; a settler might report his important lumber stolen; the constable might notice poor grain yields and the possibility of future distress at next year's seeding time.[11] These were the limits of most policemen's excitement. Some remembered in their retirement that the frontier farming situation itself promoted very little criminal tendency. "You take when people had come in there and taken up land," reminisced one, "they were too busy to get into trouble." The settlers, pointed out another, "were all in a small way and they were all looking out for their own business — they were just quiet decent people." His detachment "was the easiest place to work you could ever want ... You kept riding your district, you were interested in people in it, you were welcome where you went — it wasn't regarded as police surveyals."[12] In the early years the welcome was conditioned by isolation; in later years it was fostered by the fund of police experience that made their advice good on farming conditions, soil, climate, and winter survival.[13]

The lack of incident is aptly illustrated by some senior officers' reprimands about patrol reports that came in "very scant and uninteresting." The assistant commissioner was moved to enjoin his divisional commander at Battleford in 1900 "not to let your detachments go to sleep, and have the reports sent in promptly." One commanding officer, Inspector Begin, responded to another such missive with the comment that "if nothing at all occurs, and there is [sic] no complaints, he [the patrolman] will have no information to give only regarding the weather, condition of cattle, state of trails and river and whether there are any American cattle in the sub-district or not, or whether any strangers are passing through..."[14] Not to report much was less serious than not to patrol properly. A commanding officer for a district might notice a paucity of families visited, or a concentration in one favoured direction, or failure to keep up patrolling on Sundays. The occasional complaint from settlers on this last deficiency before the turn of the century would bring a stern response. Superintendent Burton Deane at Macleod, on receiving one of these reports, wanted an immediate investigation by a detachment sergeant. "Send me a complete list of all the settlers in this section, and place against the name of each the date of the last visit paid by a police patrol."[15] Patrols, whether or not significant crime threatened, were not to be neglected, and the settlers evidently derived comfort from them.

After 1900, with the population multiplying rapidly, new conditions reduced the possibility of complete coverage. The development of towns apparently distracted

---

11 Constable A.W. Oaks, North Fork/Fish Creek Detachment, to Superintendent J.N. McIllree, Calgary, 27 August 1891: RG 18-A1; Patrol report of Constable J. Thornton, Ft. Qu'Appelle, 7 February 1895: RG 18-C3; Weekly report of Constable D.L. McClean, Willoughby, Prince Albert Division, 2 November 1895: RG 18-C1.

12 Transcripts of interviews by S.W. Horrall with G.J. Duncan, 17 January 1969, p. 36; and with G.H. Blake, 13 January 1969, p. 53: RCMP Historical Section, Ottawa; G.J. Duncan, "Retrospect," *Scarlet and Gold*, 1964; Macleod, *The North-West Mounted Police*, pp. 46 7.

13 S.B. Steele, *Forty Years in Canada* (Toronto: McClelland, Goodchild, Stewart, 1918), pp. 256-7; NWMP *Report*, 1888, p. 11; NWMP *Report*, 1901, pp. 3 and 85.

14 Assistant Commissioner, NWMP, to Officer Commanding Battleford Division, 21 February 1900; Begin to Commissioner Perry, n d., (1903): RG 18-B1.

15 Steele to Constable P—, 10 August 1889; and Deane to the sergeant in charge at Porcupine Detachment, 16 May 1898: RG 18-C2; Herchmer to Officer Commanding "B" Division, 13 February 1894: RG 18-B1; Circular memorandum to Officers Commanding Divisions, 9 November 1895: RG 18-C3.

patrolmen from proper attention to more isolated areas, causing civilian complaints that came to Commissioner A. Bowen Perry's attention. It was no part of the "mounted constabulary's" role to protect small towns, ordered Perry in 1901; his was not a "municipal body" but one intended to provide geographically broad protection. The retort by Superintendent Morris at Prince Albert in 1902, that unprecedented expansion of settlement made regular visits to all settlers an impossibility, did not prevent Perry from continuing to insist on patrol efficiency. Despite orders to officers inspecting detachments to detail patrol activities meticulously, Assistant Commissioner McIllree still observed in the Prince Albert district in 1910 a tendency of the detachment men to "hang around the town too much." Patrol slips, which had been regularly signed by settlers along the routes of patrols in the 1890s, were reinstated.[16]

The point is not so much the growing failure just before World War I to maintain the process for every last settler, as it is the insistence on making the effort, so that some proportion of the pioneers undoubtedly did continue to see mounted policemen from time to time. This was so even though the settlement frontier shifted northward. Extended northern patrols taking several weeks each were initiated, and a new division was created at Athabasca Landing. Here distances were greater and even local patrols were matters of at least several days' journey, but the substance of patrol reports was much the same as for those of the earlier settlements.[17] The pattern that had been well established on the prairies by the early 1890s would make the North the most notable scene of this particular part of the mounted police legend after the First World War.

*****

Rural patrols in a period of immigration encountered many ethnic minorities among the settlers, some quite alien to the Canadian experience. That most of them were treated well had little to do with any individual propensities among policemen for tolerance. It seems reasonable to suppose that most constables and officers would have expected newcomers to adopt the English-Canadian way of life according to its basic British traditions.[18] The requirement of tolerance was dictated first by the federal Department of Agriculture and after 1892 by the Department of the Interior in their capacities as colonizers of the Canadian prairie west. During both the Conservative and Liberal periods of government before and after 1896, the singular official demand was for immigrants who would enhance western agricultural production: "capitalists, farmers with capital, farm-labourers, and domestic servants," as Sir Charles Tupper put it in 1893. This was a businesslike economic venture, but one inseparable from the prevailing nationalist dream. The Deputy Minister of the Interior, A.M. Burgess, quoted Tupper again in 1896 on the priority that should be given to the proper filling of the "vacant lands" of Manitoba and the North-West Territories.[19]

---

16   RNWMP Standing General Orders, March 1901, p. 42: RCMP Headquarters, Ottawa; NWMP *Report*, 1902, part 1, p. 67; Circular memorandum #560, 18 February 1908: RG 18-B4; McIllree to Perry, 13 June 1910: RG 18-C1.

17   See, for example, patrol reports from "N" Division, 1911: RG 18-B1.

18   R.C. Macleod, "Canadianizing the West: The North-West Mounted Police as Agents of the National Policy, 1873-1905," in L.H. Thomas, ed., *Essays on Western History* (Edmonton: University of Alberta Press, 1976), pp. 99-110.

19   Department of the Interior *Reports*, 1894, part I, p. xxxiv; part III, p. 13; and 1896, part I, p. xxx.

The well-known emphasis of the new Liberal Minister of the Interior after 1896, Clifford Sifton, and of his Manitoba colleague, Deputy Minister James A. Smart, hardly needs comment. The department's policy, stated Smart at the turn of the century, "was based upon the assumption that it is highly desirable that at the earliest possible moment all the fertile lands of the West should be located, and the country enriched by the general production which will be sure to follow the settlement of a hardy class of settlers." Commerce, other industries, and the general citizen would benefit from "the consequent lightening of our national burdens, such as they are, by the presence of a great number of shoulders to carry them." Smart even transformed the oft-repeated term, "desirable class" of immigrants, into "desirable agriculturalists." This concentration on competent agriculturalists would sanction the acceptance of many East-European immigrants thought by many Canadians to be culturally marginal or unsuitable, and it would condition the response of the police as well.[20]

The combination of cultural preference with official economic objectives brought British, American, Scandinavian, and German settlers the best general acceptance (and the least ethnic reference) in police reports. They came with sufficient capital and farming knowledge (especially the Americans), were in most cases accounted thrifty and hard-working (notably the Germans and Scandinavians), and therefore brought themselves almost immediately to reasonably prosperous circumstances. In addition, they shared acceptable cultural values, emphasizing cleanliness and neatness, following similar Protestant religious traditions (for the most part) and, in striving for the comfortable life, accepting the virtue of self-sufficiency. Canadian laws were not very alien to the British and Americans; Germans and Scandinavians respected the authorities. When mounted police officers contrasted alleged American disorder with Canadian law and order, the object seems to have been more to enhance the prestige of the Canadian police force than to complain about lawless American immigrants.[21]

Alien habits, however, could also be overridden by evidence of economic success. There are several striking examples of this phenomenon. The Mennonites established self-contained communities which sometimes seemed exclusive and vaguely threatening. One Sergeant St. George regretted in 1890 the "immense power" of Mennonite elders: "… so long as they remain so these people will be what they are today — foreigners in language, customs and sentiments" among whom "the rising generation is growing up as ignorant of the language of the Dominion as those who came some eighteen years ago from Russia." But their prosperity, contentedness, and peacefulness overcame these criticisms. A new Mennonite settlement at Duck Lake in 1891 immediately showed promise of the traditional farming ability and good behaviour; the police therefore discounted critical reports about them by neighbours as a mere reaction to their isolationism.[22]

---

20 Canada, *Journals of the House of Commons*, 1900, Appendix No. 1, *Report of the Select Standing Committee on Agriculture and Colonization*, p. 308; Department of the Interior *Reports*, 1899, part I, p. ix; and 1901, pp. ii, xv; and for a clear presentation of Sifton's attitudes, see D.J. Hall, "Clifford Sifton: Immigration and Settlement Policy 1896-1905," in Howard Palmer, ed., *The Settlement of the West* (Calgary: University of Calgary/Comprint, 1977), pp. 60-85.

21 This is not the point made in, but seems a logical conclusion from, Macleod, *The North-West Mounted Police*, pp. 153-5; and Macleod, "Canadianizing the West," p. 108.

22 Department of the Interior *Report*, 1893, part I, p. 9; NWMP *Report*, 1890; Sergeant H.E. Bierd and Inspector Albert Hirot, Duck Lake, to Officer Commanding at Prince Albert, 22 June 1892: RG 18-C1;

When Mormons began arriving in southern Alberta in the late 1880s, the moral risk of their presence was at the outset discounted by the Interior Department in favour of their experience with irrigation, which would, it was thought, provide an example to far more settlers beyond themselves.[23] Though they quickly established themselves as major food provisioners for mounted police posts, especially at Lethbridge, yet Commissioner Herchmer and Superintendent Steele at Fort Macleod felt constrained to place police detachments among them on watch for titillating evidence of polygamy, their zeal compounded by the "distrust and contempt" of surrounding settlers for the Mormon newcomers.[24] Though Steele's men by 1890 produced a few reports of suspected polygamy, no one in Canadian officialdom appeared to take an interest. In fact, Department of the Interior Deputy Minister Burgess confided to the minister, Edgar Dewdney, his opinion that not only was "the evidence on which Mr. Steele's conclusions are based ... of the most flimsy and unsatisfactory character," but what Steele's reports indicated should be dismissed as merely "a low condition of morality among the Mormons ... a matter which it is beyond the power and province of the Government to deal with." Furthermore, "if the progress of a settlement is not the measure of both the intelligence and industry of the settlers, I confess that I do not know what can be," and the great potential value of Mormon irrigation projects had to be kept in mind. The government, and therefore the police, simply accepted a statement by local Mormon leader, Charles O. Card, denying polygamous activity.[25]

Subsequent attempts by Commissioner Herchmer to revive investigations by surveillance were discouraged by Fred White, North-West Mounted Police Comptroller in Ottawa, as "unnecessary irritations" to the Mormon people. Thereafter, police records concentrated on the admirable agricultural example shown by the Mormons (particularly in developing irrigation systems and mills) within a peaceful and law-abiding community life. Ironically, most of the police dealings with the Mormons were in the nature of defusing the ill-feeling held for them by neighbours, ostensibly because of sharp or doubtful business practices.[26] When a local constable heard and excitedly reported another embarrassing rumour of polygamous arrangements in 1899, Superintendent R. Burton Deane quickly undermined his enthusiasm: "the less interest we appear to take in the Mormons' customs the better."[27]

While the fascination with Mormons focused on but one aspect of their tradition, the picture presented by the Doukhobors, after more than seven thousand of them arrived in 1899 in what would eventually be east-central Saskatchewan, was much more completely strange to Canadians. It was not just a matter of clothing and

---

Superintendent S.V. Gagnon, Prince Albert, to Herchmer, 15 May 1899: RG 18-A1.

23 Department of the Interior *Report*, 1888; pp. xxi-xxii.

24 NWMP *Report*, 1888, pp. 22, 58; Steele to Herchmer, 25 August 1889: RG 18-C2; Steele to Herchmer, confidential, 4 December 1889: RG 18-A1.

25 Correspondence on southern Alberta Mormons in RG 18-A1 for 1890, including copy of a confidential letter from Burgess to Dewdney, 16 December 1889; and another from Card to Burgess, 22 February 1890. See also Macleod, *The North-West Mounted Police*, pp. 155-6.

26 Herchmer to White, 19 March 1890; White to Dewdney, 25 March 1890; and Steele to Herchmer, 1891: RG 18-A1; Excerpts about the Mormons in NWMP *Reports*, 1890-1897 and 1901.

27 February and March correspondence, 1899: RG 18-A1; Deane to Herchmer, 17 March 1899: RG 18-C2.

language, but also a religious understanding, which stressed noncompliance with those government regulations which might restrict their communal commitment (individual land ownership) or register their personal information (births, deaths, marriages).[28] Early efforts to resist these Canadian government requirements, and attempts to understand and follow the curious leadership of Peter Verigin, included a series of protest marches by ever diminishing proportions of the Doukhobor people. The first, in the late fall of 1902, involved nearly two thousand Doukhobors, unprepared with proper food or clothing to withstand the cold, who got as far as Minnedosa, Manitoba on foot before being turned back. Later Saskatchewan demonstrations rarely involved as many as one hundred, but their effect was dramatized by the highly embarrassing tactic of public nudity and by occasional violent internal clashes between those determined to maintain a communal lifestyle and the majority reconciled to individual homestead registration and other Canadian laws. The police attitude in all this was unbelievably patient, again not because of any exceptional sympathy for or insight into Doukhobor problems, but because the Department of the Interior desired to retain the remarkable agricultural finesse of these people. The troublesome few were most often escorted back home after their marches, only their most stubborn leaders occasionally being jailed briefly.[29]

The nature of the Interior Department's policy, with its ramifications for the police, was most clearly illustrated by the response to the thousands of Ukrainian immigrants who streamed into the North-West Territories after the mid 1890s. Immigration officials saw the "primitive" lifestyle and "generally ignorant" condition of a "very modest, thrifty and hard working" people to be the formula they were looking for to wring Canadian prosperity from the newcomers' struggles to survive. The same observations, however, led police officers to the conclusion that many would not only have to be fed, but would require assistance in the form of seed and cattle to begin their farming operations. The perspectives were strikingly different: the Department of the Interior expected Canada to benefit from the very desperation of the new alien settlers; the police could not imagine leaving so destitute a people on their own.[30]

The police received their education at the hands of the Interior Department at the Edna settlement north-east of Edmonton. During 1896, the police were providing limited assistance to destitute "Galician" pioneers there, mainly in the form of clothing in exchange for such work as clearing brush. When a police corporal with the aid of an interpreter reported extensive distress in August of 1897, immigration officials accused the police of meddling and of allowing themselves to be naively exploited by shrewd immigrants whose normal living conditions might easily appear as destitution to Canadian observers.[31] Following reception of a stiff reprimand to

---

28 See George Woodcock and Ivan Avakumovic, The Doukhobors (Toronto: Oxford University Press, 1968); Carl Betke, "The Mounted Police and the Doukhobors in Saskatchewan, 1899-1909," *Saskatchewan History*, XXVII (Winter 1974), pp. 3-5.

29 Betke, "The Mounted Police and the Doukhobors," pp. 4-12.

30 Department of the Interior *Report*, 1895-96, part IV, p. 120; NWMP *Report*, 1896, p. 12. For fuller treatments of the exploitive expectations of Canadian immigration policy, see Hall, "Clifford Sifton"; and Donald Avery, *"Dangerous Foreigners"* (Toronto: McClelland & Stewart, 1979).

31 Superintendent A.H. Griesbach to Herchmer, 2 November 1896; and A.M. Burgess to White, 12 November 1896: RG 18-A1; Assistant Commissioner, NWMP, to Griesbach, 10 December 1897: RG

leave the Ukrainian settlers to their own devices, the mounted police reduced their alleviation of distress, and concentrated on educating a people of alien habit to cope with the unusual dangers of prairie fires in the new land and with the quarantine approach to epidemic disease. In the meantime, of course, the police acquired a much more benevolent reputation among Ukrainian immigrants than did immigration officers.[32]

Subsequent mounted police reports reaching the Department of the Interior must have been gratifying, stressing as they did the commendable speed with which young Ukrainian men and women went out from their homesteads to work as railway construction navvies and domestic servants in order painfully to raise the money to launch successful farms. As early as 1902 they admired the fine buildings which were replacing the earliest huts of the Ukrainians. They were not to be moved by unfounded criticisms from English-speaking neighbours, who found the alien newcomers' lifestyle distasteful, even on the occasion when those complaints were registered through the Member of Parliament for the Edmonton area, Frank Oliver. Oliver claimed in 1899 that "Galicians" were responsible for rampant theft, but a special investigation by Inspector J.O. Wilson concluded that a fundamental anti-Galician prejudice underpinned the rumours.[33] The initial police dismay at the poor prospects of Ukrainian immigrants was transformed into a positive response first by Interior Department policy and then by evidence of agricultural success.

It was certainly not engendered by first impressions of Ukrainian social habits. Police reports early associated Ukrainians with violent acts, many of them in connection with their entertainments which allegedly featured heavy drinking. Confirmation for the police of the reputation for violent crime among the "Galicians" (generalized on occasions to apply to all East Europeans) was the incidence of murder arising from family quarrels. To commissioned officers of the police, the simple explanation in that era was that "some of these foreign races hold life very cheaply and will commit murder on slight provocation," particularly when, in 1912-13, mounting unemployment increased the "large floating population" mainly composed of out-of-work railroad construction navvies. Violence was, like the "shocking depravities" of "incest and defiling girls under 14," simply associated with ethnic character compounded by idleness in time of unemployment.[34] There was no calculation of the connection between the pressures leading to family quarrels on the one hand and the causes of transience among East-European job seekers on the other; even as there was no insight into the reasons why "foreign labourers" crowding into Edmonton in 1912 should be susceptible to the militant industrial unionism of the Industrial Workers of the World.[35] Though their understanding was not sophisticated, however, from

---

18-B1. See also the account in Macleod, *The North-West Mounted Police*, pp. 151-2.

32   Correspondence, August 1897 to February 1898: RG 18-A1; Telegrams between Superintendent S. Gagnon, Prince Albert, and Herchmer, 1 May 1899: RG 18-B1; Gagnon to Corporal St. Denis, Rosthern, 12 September 1899: RG 18-C1; RNWMP *Report*, 1911, p. 151.

33   Department of the Interior *Report*, 1902, part II, p. 119; Inspector S. Crosthwait to Officer Commanding at Fort Saskatchewan, 12 February 1902: RG 18-B1; Oliver to Fred White, 1 June 1899; and report of Inspector J.O. Wilson, 21 June 1899: RG 18-A1. See also the account in Macleod, *The North-West Mounted Police*, p. 151.

34   RNWMP *Reports*, 1907, p. 87; 1908, pp. 38, 103; 1909, pp. 67, 83, 87; 1910, p. 75; 1912, pp. 74-5, 157; 1913, p. 9.

first to last the police paid close attention, some of it kindly, to what they could only consider worrisome difficulties of adjustment by a most alien immigrant population. Perhaps the police constituted too much the first agency to be contacted about those problems ever to accept without reservation the Department of the Interior's complacent self-satisfaction with the remarkable agricultural advances made by East-European peasant immigrants against substantial economic and cultural odds.

The contrast which proves the economic basis of mounted police approval for certain alien immigrants is to be seen in their disparagement of those groups that were not only foreign, but agricultural failures to boot. A collection of "old country French" settlers who entered the St. Louis de Langevin district near Duck Lake from 1893 through 1895 never received police accolades for their farming ability. Inspector D'Arcy Strickland labelled them from the beginning "a very undesirable class of people" because they arrived "with little or no money and are quite unable to buy machinery or make improvements on their locations." Two years later, a pair of patrolling sergeants still did not consider them "a class intended to be much of an acquisition to the country" for, although they had built "very fair houses," yet "they had not the least idea of farming in this country." The superintendent commanding the Prince Albert district concluded that their previous experience did not suit them for frontier trials.[36] There were several unfavourable references to the lifestyle and lack of progress among Jewish settlers. Some Roumanian Jews at South Qu'Appelle in 1902 were characterized as a "lazy, dirty and lousy" people who would "not do a hands turn to help themselves." A neighbour attributed their troubles to the financial cheating of the New York agent for the colony but, whatever the reason, the combination of strangeness and ineptitude deprived them of police sympathy.[37] Interestingly enough, another group judged equally inept, the English Barr colonists, were nevertheless accounted desirable acquisitions whose survival should be ensured to encourage more of the same immigration.[38] Point of origin did count, but negatively only if accompanied by failure at the essential western business of farm production. The majority of settlers, therefore, were in good position to benefit from mounted police help.

*****

Although Clifford Sifton was eager to induce agriculturalists to settle in prairie Canada, he was loath to provide them much material assistance once they arrived, lest the result be a new nation of subsidized paupers.[39] This official reluctance to guarantee the welfare of farmers who ought to be independently establishing their own security and Canada's wealth left the North-West Mounted Police as the sole

---

35 RNWMP *Report*, 1912, p. 83.

36 Reports of Inspector D'A.E. Strickland, Duck Lake, 19 December 1893, 8 May and 2 June 1894; of Sergeant H. Keenan, Duck Lake, 22 June 1895; and of Sergeant I.W. Weeks patrolling to Fishing Lakes and Boucher, 28 September 1895: RG 18-C1; NWMP *Report*, 1895, p. 115.

37 NWMP *Report*, 1892, p. 49; Report of Constable G.T. Howdey, South Qu'Appelle, 17 May 1902: RG 18-A1; H. Bolocan to Laurier, June 1904: Public Archives of Canada, Sir Wilfrid Laurier Papers, microfilm C-813, pp. 8743-8.

38 White to Perry, 15 April 1903; to Interior Deputy Minister Smart, 25 August 1903; and to Perry, 6 and 20 November 1903: RG 18-A2.

39 Hall, "Clifford Sifton," pp. 74-5; and see Donald Avery, *"Dangerous Foreigners."*

agency available in the early settlement stages to supply at least the services which were deemed unavoidable. That the Department of the Interior conscientiously eschewed being soft on the pioneers actually helped to create a situation in which the police gained the glory along with the work. This can be understood by reference to urgent problems of great collective concern to prairie settlers: contagious animal diseases, contagious human diseases, destitution, and prairie fires.

Of crucial importance to western agriculturalists, whether homesteaders or cattle ranchers, was the veterinary service of the police, and the medical work performed had a far vaster significance for everyone whose domestic animals were thus protected from epidemic disease. Until 1896, when total responsibility for domestic animal health was given to the federal Department of Agriculture, both the Territorial and the Dominion governments relied heavily on police veterinarians, and on the force itself, to fend off potentially disastrous contagious diseases.[40] There were two branches of this work. One was quarantine and inspection of immigrant domestic animals at the Canadian-American border, and the other was identification and eradication of disease that appeared within the country despite border precautions.

At the particular locations (five after 1893) where cattle could legally enter Canada and be subjected to quarantine procedure, special police detachments, which might have removed some fifty men and four officers from regular duty, were required to labour on behalf of the Departments of Agriculture and the Interior. This peaceful cowboy work for policemen was justified on the basis of its lesser cost than the alternatives and at the same time its provision of an extra reserve force of police available for emergencies that might arise, say, with respect to Indians. Before the turn of the century, presiding veterinary surgeons were for the most part police personnel. In order for the quarantine system to work, of course, the police detachments undertook daily border patrols to ensure that it was evaded as little as possible. Department of Agriculture delight with the arrangements was matched by Commissioner Herchmer's unhappiness. At the Wood End quarantine station near Estevan, he complained in 1895, not only the police veterinarian but also most of the "police herders" were doing nothing other than quarantine work: their salaries might just as well be paid by the Department of Agriculture. Nevertheless, police stationed at those detachments continued to have far more contact with "lumpy jaw" (actinomycosis) in cattle and with "sheep scab" than with criminals.[41]

Rather than being reduced, the police role in both border quarantine and general detachment detection of animal diseases was formalized by the 1896 legislation consolidating the service under the federal Department of Agriculture. The Commissioner of the North-West Mounted Police became the chief veterinary official of the Department of Agriculture and his veterinary surgeons automatically became inspectors of contagious animal diseases. As for the involvement of the regular policemen, in 1897 the public was informed that "in all suspected cases of contagious diseases, such as Glanders among horses, Tuberculosis and Lumpy-Jaw among cattle, scab among

---

40   Franklin M. Loew and E.H. Wood, *Vet in the Saddle* (Saskatoon: Western Producer Prairie Books, 1978), pp. 26-8, 49-51, 88-93; Canada, Sessional Papers, Department of Agriculture *Report*, 1893, pp. xii-xiii; "A Precis of Orders in Council Relating to Cattle Quarantine Regulations" (Department of Agriculture, 30 January 1894) in Public Archives of Canada, John Lowe Papers.

41   John Lowe, "Report on Cattle Quarantine ... November 27, 1895," in John Lowe Papers; Department of Agriculture *Report*, 1896, pp. viii, 91.

sheep or Hog-cholera, the nearest Mounted Police Constable should at once be notified, when the necessary steps will be taken to prevent spread of the disease."[42] While the ultimate authorities were the Commissioner and his veterinary surgeons, first resort was to the multitude of constables on detachment. After several years of experience with this "excellent system," Agriculture officials found control of animal contagious diseases "performed much more economically and effectively than would be possible under any other arrangements" by a police force distinguished by its mobility and "knowledge of the country and its conditions."[43]

Even before the 1896 changes, however, regular detachment procedures became quite as systematic as border quarantines. All detachments were instructed to watch for diseases as part of normal patrol duty, no small order considering that Commissioner Perry's list of most significant diseases after the turn of the century included mange, tuberculosis, anthrax, actinomycosis, and eye disease among cattle; scab in sheep; swine plague and hog cholera in hogs; and glanders, typhoid fever, and *maladie du coît* in horses. Veterinarians, who could not possibly conduct this kind of close supervision alone, were therefore dependent on the perceptiveness of the policemen, even though on occasion settlers themselves were unwilling to trust a constable's judgement. The reason was simple: identification of disease meant at least a quarantine corral on the spot, and perhaps immediate destruction of animals, something settlers were unwilling to accept needlessly. They wanted a veterinarian's judgement in every case, something for which neither level of government would provide extra funds. Usually, though, neighbouring farmers who first reported such cases had good reason to appreciate police intervention, especially if the owners might "contend that their respective beasts are not afflicted with lumpy jaw and that the animals have either defective teeth or are suffering from the effects of a blow." As the prairie population multiplied after the turn of the century, the demands for inspection put an immense strain on the police capacity to prevent immigration of diseased stock or to deal with all outbreaks as quickly and effectively as formerly. In the circumstances, actual veterinary inspection continued to fall behind while regular police attention became even more vital.[44]

The veterinary experts would be brought in to make final diagnoses and prescriptions, accompanied on their journeys by the ever-present detachment policemen. Only the veterinarian could sometimes quell opposition to destruction of valuable animals. Destruction was always the ultimate answer in cases of anthrax (or "black leg"), and sometimes of glanders, mange, "lumpy jaw," and tuberculosis. Anthrax was so dreaded that settlers themselves could be entrusted with the recommended shooting and cremating procedure even though there was no government compensation forthcoming, but the others required judgements about the stage of disease advancement. It was police business to enforce the orders. Any attempt to treat rather

---

42   Loew and Wood, *Vet in the Saddle*, pp. 50-1; NWMP General Order 11602, referring to Privy Council Order of 22 October 1896: RCMP Headquarters, Ottawa; Circular Memorandum #237, 5 April 1897: RG 18-B4; Commissioner Herchmer's press release, 9 July 1897: RG 18-B2.

43   Department of Agriculture *Report*, 1904, p. 71.

44   Herchmer to Commissioner of Dominion Lands H.H. Smith, 25 October 1893; and report of Sergeant Blake, Graburn Detachment, 28 June 1895: RG 18-A1; Circular Memorandum by Inspector J.D. Moodie, Macleod, 20 March 1901: RG 18-C3; Constable H. Thompson to Officer Commanding at Prince Albert, 21 December 1897: RG 18-C1; Department of Agriculture *Reports*, 1901, pp. 114-7; and 1906, pp. 130-3, 196.

than destroy animals with contagious diseases still involved the order (and sometimes the supervision) for quarantine. After 1894 the designation of quarantine districts of several square miles gradually became a standard practice for dealing with widespread outbreaks. In 1904 and again in 1905, the government found yet another onerous task for the police: the compulsory chemical "dipping" of all North-West Territories cattle each fall. This was a major undertaking, necessitating separation of the untested from the tested by fencing and close quarantining.[45]

In 1899 Commissioner Herchmer expressed pleasure about the general lack of friction between the police and owners of diseased animals. Some early complaints in the Maple Creek area suggested very great interest indeed in this aspect of police assistance: these referred to alleged negligence by detachment policemen not responding quickly enough to requests for veterinary investigations, apparently with the result that disease spread. Obviously, the majority found the veterinary service of the police most valuable; even the occasional reluctance to cooperate was actually a sign that the system worked, for without the police presence it was those very people who would have constituted a danger to their neighbours. Contagious disease, in animals as well as in humans, was one of those conditions that could not but emphasize the cooperative element in the agrarian lifestyle. The mounted police were the available agents to foster that cooperation. But by 1906 the number of stock being imported or drifting into the country annually and the heavy demand for investigation of suspect maladies overstrained the manpower of the Royal North-West Mounted Police, so that the next year the police relinquished those and border quarantine duties to the relevant provincial and federal departments of agriculture.[46]

Before World War I, a fair number of contagious diseases constituted an ever present menace in western Canada to the settlers themselves, but escalation to epidemic proportions was unpredictable. When these emergencies arose, the police were valuable for establishing initial quarantine procedures until the proper authorities could take over (in early years, local boards of health; in later years, medical health officers). Even when others directed the operations, policemen were best able to enforce quarantines and to transport doctors or provisions.[47]

Eighteen ninety-seven was an epidemic year for diptheria and German measles (a deadly disease at the time); police assistance warranted special files on the subject. A good example of the standard procedure concerned an outbreak of diptheria in and near Saskatoon, at that time a tiny village. Sergeant George Will first reported the odd case being watched, then found himself in a dilemma, for according to custom he was expected to provide both quarantine control at Saskatoon and transportation for the police physician to the neighbouring settlement of Dundurn to check reports of diptheria there. Reinforcements were both sent and recruited for

---

45 Loew and Wood, *Vet in the Saddle*, pp. 106-7; Department of Agriculture *Reports*, 1892, part II, p. 49; 1905, p. 126; and 1906, p. 130; Telegram, Superintendent J. Cotton, Prince Albert, to Herchmer, 20 June 1892; Lowe to White, 21 July 1892; Robert Evans to Herchmer, 12 February 1894; and Perry to Herchmer, 15 February 1894: RG 18-B1; Lowe to White, 20 April 1894; and White to Herchmer, 24 April 1894: RG 18-A1; Circular memorandum #458, 16 March 1904: RG 18-B4.

46 See, for example, J.M. Cosgrave to Herchmer, 4 August 1893: RG 18-B1; Department of Agriculture *Reports*, 1906, pp. 132-3, 196; 1908.

47 See examples of smallpox, diptheria, and scarlet fever reports near Macleod, the Beaver Hills, and Battleford in RG 18-B1 for 1892 and 1897; NWMP *Report*, 1894, p. 109.

special constable duty. At infected houses Sergeant Will posted yellow flags and placards on the doors announcing "Diptheria." Notices at "conspicuous places" warned people to stay away from specified houses. No "ingress or egress" was allowed in an area defined by an eight-mile radius around Saskatoon. A less extensive quarantine procedure involving the service of a special constable was put in place at Dundurn. Sergeant Will drove the doctor around on visits to the sick; when the doctor was absent, Will himself conducted the visits to check the condition of the afflicted, to take them supplies, and to ensure that the quarantine was being observed. At the end, release from quarantine was accomplished with a final sulphur fumigation of the infected residences. Whether or not medical experts were present, the police were important to epidemic control procedures and in this case the force was absolutely essential to cover the period before a board of health was properly constituted.[48]

The spread of any contagious disease was in itself serious enough to deserve reprimands for sloppy enforcement of control procedures, but in some circumstances the importance of the police must have escalated considerably in the perceptions of those receiving their assistance. As Inspector A. Ross Cuthbert reported from Prince Albert in 1902:

> As you are aware a very large portion of the inhabitants of this District are very poor and to many of them enforced quarantine is tantamount to starvation unless assisted. There are at present upwards of thirty cases of smallpox, this has entailed in addition many persons being quarantined as suspects from contact with affected persons in the same house or camp, and the issue of necessary relief is becoming a very considerable item of expense.

That Cuthbert would have liked to saddle federal Agriculture Department agents (then responsible for health regulations) with the task of relief provision did not alter the fact that, in such emergencies, it was the police who were seen to act with kindness. In another similar case of smallpox, a police report indicated that of "26 persons ... quarantined for smallpox, 6 are sick, 25 [are] drawing relief."[49]

Clashes of jurisdiction serve to illustrate the continuing mounted police prominence in actual operations. In July of 1903, Commissioner Perry was still trying to obtain repayment of expenses incurred in May of 1902, when two special constables were placed at the disposal of a quarantine officer of the Dominion Immigration Branch to control a diptheria outbreak among newly arrived Roumanian Jews at South Qu'Appelle. The Territorial government refused to pay the bill, naturally, since the service was performed for immigrants. Yet the Department of the Interior also hesitated to accept responsibility. Before it was resolved, the issue finally involved Territorial MP Walter Scott, to whom Comptroller Fred White remarked in October 1903:

> It is only one of many instances where an emergency arises, the Police have to step in and do what is necessary, and then the other Departments squabble about paying little bills amounting to but a percentage of what the same service would have cost if performed through the proper Department.

White went on to cite the case of about a dozen "foreign immigrants" who were

---

48   Correspondence among Sergeant G. Will, Superintendent S. Gagnon at Prince Albert, and Herchmer, October 1897: RG 18-B1.

49   Cuthbert to Sergeant Bird, Duck Lake, 26 August 1902; and to Perry, 15 April and 31 August 1902; Superintendent W.S. Morris, Prince Albert, to Perry, 30 January 1903: RG 18-A1.

dropped off by the CPR at a wayside station with measles or some other contagious disease, which had already killed a child among them. A mounted policeman who happened to be present "acted the friend in need" and rented shelter. No other government department would reimburse the cost of the police, even though a failure of the policeman to act might easily have resulted in "several other deaths, and a lot of correspondence adverse to our Canadian Immigration system."[50]

The police response fulfilled an expectation among other officials which exasperated at least one commissioned officer, whose very objection betrayed the extent to which police assistance had become common practice. "I think I understand your views," wrote Superintendent P.C.H. Primrose to Commissioner Perry in 1907. "We are cheerfully to assist any branch of the Government if requested to do so, with a view to furthering the best interests of the country." But Primrose rebelled against what he perceived as the growing attitude that any official could

> say to the nearest Policeman 'Here you go and do this' and that it then becomes that policeman's duty to go and obey these orders ... Fancy asking us to go out and fumigate or assist in fumigating houses; that surely is no part of our duty, nor considering our duties to the general public is it fair to ask our assistance.

He resented that policemen might "be ordered around at will by any rural practitioner who may happen to be in charge of a case," and he thought Alberta communications sufficiently advanced to eliminate any necessity for temporary emergency police help in the absence of medical authorities.[51] At least until the war, however, police assistance of that sort proved unavoidable. Although they were described primarily as duties on behalf of the provincial health departments,[52] they must have confirmed an impression of the mounted police as first on the scene to prevent potentially catastrophic epidemics.

The most lasting impact of the police on the average settler's consciousness might have been made by the police response to the desperation caused for otherwise healthy and thriving immigrants by the sudden deprivations so characteristic of the pioneer experience. One major crop failure in the early stages of his business could cripple a farmer's capacity to recover in the next crop year. The main answer to this form of destitution was "seed grain relief" — that is, advances of seed grain to stimulate a revival of independent agricultural production — and in the early years, especially, the mounted police provided much of the identification and distribution. Failure to recover from economic setbacks or separate climatic disasters led to countless cases of the next level of want: the actual inability to secure sufficient food, fuel, or clothing. Here the requirement for relief was immediate, personal, and dramatic. Repeated hundreds of times, generous assistance through the agency of the mounted police could not help but enhance their reputation among the population at large. The effect was strengthened by two extreme winter-time episodes which brought epic proportions to the story of the mounted police battle against the elements on behalf of the new settlers.

For their relief service to agrarian immigrants, the police had been prepared by the extreme suffering and need of Indian peoples prior to the North-West Rebellion.

---

50   Perry to White, 3 July 1903; and White to Walter Scott, 13 October 1903: RG 18-A1.
51   Alberta Provincial Health Officer L.E.W. Irving to Superintendent P.C.H. Primrose, Macleod, 8 July 1907; and Primrose to Perry, 12 July 1907: RG 18-B2.
52   Ibid., vol. 50; RNWMP *Reports*, 1910, p. 80; and 1911, p. 87.

After the Rebellion, moreover, the police frequently reported and responded to the needs of "half-breeds" right up to the First World War. But the police did not take up this work simply out of the goodness of their own hearts. One of the prevalent attitudes about relief for any destitute people was expressed already in 1888 in a reference to "half-breed relief" by Superintendent (later to be Commissioner) Perry:

> Free issue of rations must, of course, be made, to prevent actual starvation, but where the Government thus act in a paternal manner great care must be exercised to prevent the recipient from deeming as a right what is given in pity...
>
> A free issue of rations does not promote industry nor encourage independence in any community. Its demoralizing effects spread rapidly, and too quickly taint those attempting to preserve their independence and self-respect.[53]

He went on to recommend that work be required in exchange for aid. Nor were the indigent welcomed into Canada by the police. In 1904 a Minnesota woman whose husband was crippled appeared at North Portal without money and seeking police assistance. She was informed that the mounted police had no authority to relieve destitute immigrants and that, if she did not return to the United States, she would be arrested as a vagrant.[54] Again, in the Medicine Hat region early in 1912, a corporal patrolling during extremely harsh and dangerous winter conditions avoided visiting a reportedly needy family because "it was also the unanimous opinion of every one that their improvidence was caused by utter laziness and that their dwelling was in a lousy condition." His superintendent noted in the margin that these were subjects the Immigration officials would on investigation likely deport.[55]

Charity was to be extended to the deserving; the police demonstrated no special talent for sympathy beyond the norm of the day, but frontier circumstances nevertheless ensured that this part of their work would be large. For one thing, as the commissioner noted about one case near Yorkton in 1892, unrelieved distress as a result of crop failures among American immigrants would be very poor advertising to the delegations from various states coming to estimate prospects. On this occasion, he recommended provision of temporary railway construction grading work, even if completion of a line was not projected for the area immediately.[56] Public works were recommended in other situations as well, but the more common practice was to assist those in dire circumstances by supplying essential food and fuel. One example involving a French immigrant family was designated "extreme destitution," warranting emergency relief on the grounds that the children were dying of starvation.[57] When, as in 1895, the Department of the Interior decided a more general policy of seed grain distribution was in order, the NWMP got the extra work, sometimes having to set up temporarily at points where no detachment existed. The police were reported to be far more efficient than those who previously had administered such programs.[58] During the winter of 1895-96, the general policy of relief was extended beyond seed

---

53 NWMP *Report*, 1888, p. 96.

54 Corporal H. Lett, Estevan, to Officer Commanding at Regina, 17 August 1904: RG 18-A1.

55 Corporal Wiedeman, Irvine Detachment, to Officer Commanding at Medicine Hat, 18 January 1912: RG 18-A1.

56 Herchmer to White, forwarded to Department of the Interior, n.d., (1892): RG 18-A1.

57 Strickland to Herchmer, 16 February, 2, 16 March 1895: RG 18-C1.

58 A.M. Burgess to White, 27 March 1895; and telegram, Herchmer to White, 31 March 1895; and Herchmer to White, 16 May 1895: RG 18-A1.

grain to such basic provisions as flour. In the two districts most affected, in the vicinities of Edmonton and Prince Albert, the amount of police time spent receiving, investigating, and satisfying immigrant claims scattered over wide regions left Commissioner Herchmer a trifle grumpy, for relief work superseded what he regarded as proper police work.[59]

The necessity for such a widespread relief policy dissipated after 1896, when some settlers at least were already actually able to pay back their advances.[60] Relief measures returned to the standard form of individual cases treated on their merits. After creation of the new provinces of Alberta and Saskatchewan in 1905, applications for relief provisions were directed to the federal Immigration Branch, to local rural municipalities where they existed, or to the provincial boards of health, according to each applicant's status as immigrant or resident of more than three years.[61] While those were the authorities and the sources of funds, the mounted police continued to do the work, filling in the appropriate application forms, then distributing the relevant items upon authorization. In emergencies, the police would often supply fuel (coal) or work until empowered by the proper agency to do more. With the elimination of great distances between farms during the immigration boom, and especially with the introduction of telephone communication, the traditional mounted police role showed signs of erosion just before the Great War. Settlers began to apply on their own, without waiting to be discovered; while the police detachments were still the points of contact, their patrols were no longer essential or possible in the same way as they had once been.[62] Nevertheless, Immigration authorities, at least, were still happy to receive general reports by district on the likelihood of destitution during impending winters.[63]

A pair of emergency actions in those later years, however, reinforced the impression of mounted police omnipresence to relieve suffering. The winter of 1906-07 was known for its "fuel famine," an extreme shortage of coal. In those places, mainly in Saskatchewan, where coal could not be obtained, settlers were forced to find and haul wood, not always an easy task for novices having to travel long distances in very cold weather and deep snow. Rumours of distress spread, often in newspapers. "A farmer named Radcliffe with his wife and three children have been found frozen to death," reported the Estevan *Evening Journal* in February. "Radcliffe was a homesteader, who came here for coal about a fortnight ago. A neighbour called at Radcliffe's during his absence and found his wife and children frozen solid and no fuel or wood in the house." But the police found this to be irresponsible conjecture: though isolated by a snowstorm, the family survived very well.[64] Although Commissioner Perry continued to be convinced that "the casualties resulted from want of knowledge of

---

59   See 1896 correspondence in RG 18-A1, Files 70 and 151.

60   Will to Officer Commanding at Prince Albert, 22 December 1896: RG 18-C1; Department of the Interior *Report*, 1899, p. xxi.

61   See examples in the thick file 132 of 1912: RG 18-B1. In the same file, see Perry to Commissioner of Public Health for Saskatchewan, 31 January 1912; and a circular memorandum by Perry, 28 February 1912.

62   A case of this sort appears in correspondence following an initial report by Constable H. Moorhead, Stirling Detachment, 27 March 1913: RG 18-B1.

63   Perry to Commissioner of Immigration, Winnipeg, 17 November 1913: Ibid.

64   Clipping from Estevan *Evening Journal*, 22 February 1907; and report of Sergeant H. Lett, Estevan, 24 February 1907: RG 18-A1.

the country, drunkenness, or other preventable causes,"[65] now and then frozen bodies were indeed found, and some settlers did experience considerable anxiety over the fuel problem. Many worried about their families should they lose their way in search of wood. In at least two cases, south of Battleford and near Moosomin, patrolling policemen reported available bush nearly exhausted for farmers coming for the green wood from some distance.[66]

The severity of the rumours was enough to stimulate action directed by the new minister of the Interior, Frank Oliver, "not only from the humane point of view," as Comptroller White put it, "but also to prevent reports being circulated injurious to Canadian Immigration interests."[67] At first Immigration officials concentrated on the region south of Battleford, where heavy snowfalls made trail breaking difficult. Fuel, seed grain (later), and other provisions were hauled to Tramping Lake some sixty miles south of Battleford. Mounted policemen patrolled the vicinity to record the extent of suffering and to advise settlers of the provisioning opportunity, then were authorized to carry out the actual distribution as well. On occasion, police constables themselves hauled provisions to families isolated and in distress.[68] As a precaution, the police were soon instructed to patrol every newly settled district in Alberta and Saskatchewan in search of any who might urgently require relief. Prime Minister Laurier himself was kept informed of the results. As it turned out, there was little exceptional suffering to be alleviated anywhere else, except at another new settlement region north of Swift Current.[69]

Though the extent of the problem proved not to be dismayingly widespread, the publicity was enormous, the reports came from mounted policemen, and the burden of work fell on their shoulders. A similar flurry of attention occurred in 1910-11, when exceptionally deep snowfalls in southern Alberta and Saskatchewan created difficulties for feeding stock and prevented many settlers from travelling at appropriate times to obtain food and fuel. By this time the federal immigration policy was to treat aid as an advance, repayable with 5 per cent interest per annum but, when urgency dictated immediate action, the police were to issue relief and work out financial responsibilities later. Patrols were made in terrible conditions, through snow drifted six or seven feet deep, constables frequently persevering despite dangerous exposure. One froze the skin of his legs to his pants during an errand of mercy, but most were more sensibly prepared.[70] "Settlers are great in the praise of a Government that will send patrols

---

65   Perry to White, 6 March 1907: RG 18-B10.

66   Inspector Generaux to Officer Commanding at Battleford, 24 December 1906: Inspector A.M. Jarvis to Officer Commanding at Regina, 11 February 1907; and a report of Saskatoon detachment on a found frozen body beginning to be eaten by wolves, 19 March 1907: RG 18-A1; W.D. Scott, Superintendent of Immigration, to Frank Oliver, 1 February 1907: RG 18-B10.

67   White to Perry, 5 February 1907: RG 18-A1.

68   Constable R.C. Bright reporting a Tramping Lake patrol, 19 December 1906; memorandum to Sergeant Adams, Regina, 1 February 1907; W.D. Scott to Oliver, 1 February 1907 and General Colonization Agent C.W. Speers, Battleford, to Assistant Commissioner McIllree, 17 February 1907: RG 18-B10; Constable W.H. Burke to Officer Commanding at Battleford, 8 January 1907: RG 18-A1.

69   White to Laurier, 8 February 1907; and telegram, Perry to White, 11 February 1907: Laurier Papers, microfilm C843, pp. 119475-6 and 119599.

70   See file on winter destitution in the vicinities of Lethbridge and Maple Creek: RG 18-B1. See another on relief issued during 1910-11; RG 18-A1, including Circular Memorandum #600 of Commissioner Perry, 27 January 1911; and a patrol report by Constable A.P. White, Pendant d'Oreille detachment,

throughout the District in such weather in order to prevent loss of life," reported Lethbridge police, "and freely state that they would be permitted to freeze to death in any other country before anyone would visit them..." Settlers from the United States in particular were most appreciative. This comment was forwarded to senior Immigration officials by Comptroller White, again "not as showing what the Mounted Police are doing, but as furnishing another link in your chain of evidence of the satisfactory manner in which immigrants are treated in our Canadian North West."[71] White here indicated not only the standard businesslike motivation for government compassion, but also the perception of settlers as to the agency that was most responsible for it.

The summertime problem of prairie fires proved that there were limits to the assistance which could be expected even from the mounted police. Prairie fires were of course less controllable hazards before the major settlement influx; hence the Territorial government was eager already in the 1880s to "secure more fully the services of the North West Mounted Police Force" to prevent and extinguish them. Police officers followed up with "the most stringent orders" both to assist in the suppression of prairie fires and to arrest their perpetrators.[72] The insistent demands made on the police to be the main force responsible for actually putting out the fires were aggravating because they were so impossible of fulfilment, though perhaps understandable among so widely scattered a populace. The investiture of police in charge of detachments as "fire guardians" as of 1889 gave them the added power and responsibility for turning out "all male persons within ten miles of a prairie fire" to proceed immediately to help extinguish it, but the spotlight was not removed from the mounted police when action was required, nor were dangerous practices among settlers effectively curtailed.[73] It would be years before settlers were sufficiently packed together on prairie land that the self interest of many would stimulate their own response to each fire that threatened their homesteads.

In the meantime, the mounted police were subjected to criticism on this account at a rate to which they were not otherwise accustomed. The terrific extent of damage a prairie fire could do flared tempers. The Calgary *Herald* in 1890 claimed that in one situation the police did "not appear to have stirred a finger until the fire had burnt itself out," even though the editor was persuaded that there were many mounted policemen "in barracks in Calgary not over-burdened with serious duties, and on the whole, passing life easily." A settler at Turnip Lake near Edmonton wondered in 1897 what these "paid servants of the government" were supported for if not to prevent destruction of his homestead by prompt attention to raging fires. The Battleford *Star*

---

4 February 1911.

71 Extract from monthly RNWMP report from Lethbridge for January 1911, enclosed with letter from White to W.D. Scott, 2 March 1911: RG 18-A1.

72 Copy of resolution of NWT Council, signed by A.E. Forget, Clerk of Council, 24 October 1887; Herchmer to Commanding Officers, 25 October 1887; and Lt. Gov. J. Royal to Herchmer, 17 August 1889: RG 18-B1; NWMP General Order #1863 in 1887: RG 18-B4; Perry to detachment commanders, "F" Division, 27 October 1887: RG 18-C1; Superintendent A.H. Griesbach to Corporal McLellan, Peace Hills, 27 August 1889: RG 18-C7.

73 See, for example, J.G. Gordon to Herchmer, 18 September 1888; and Inspector C. Constantine to Herchmer, 22 September 1888: RG 18-B1; North-West Territories, *Revised Ordinances*, 1888, chapter 20.

in 1899 excoriated a police force that waited on civilians to show the first initiative in stopping fires. These protests were of course uttered in the heat of the moment, sometimes without much foundation, and there were also balancing commendations, but they show that public expectations from this particular police force were very great.[74]

The police thought such expectations unrealistic if not grossly irresponsible. Commissioner Herchmer in 1893 outlined the differences between the police and the public understanding of the duties of fire guardians. For him they meant "to turn out all settlers in the locality when a fire is running, to put it out, and to investigate the cause of the fire, and lay information against the parties guilty of setting it, after first submitting the evidence to their Commanding Officers for consideration." The public in most areas (except in ranching regions) seemed to feel that "police should be scattered in small parties throughout the country, and that they should be employed in putting out the fires, and that the settlers should not be called upon, at any rate until the efforts of the police have failed." He cited examples of cases in which extensive police efforts to apprehend those responsible for setting them either failed (as neighbours were reluctant to testify unless they had suffered damage and were angry), or were nullified by fines of less than three dollars, often when serious damage had been done. An example of the result, complained Herchmer, was that settlers would carelessly burn stubble and, if the fires got out of control, "callously let them go believing that if found out it will be cheaper to be fined than to devote their time to putting them out." He saw no alternative to fixing fines at "deterrent sums," despite possible occasional injustices, with a view to enforcing greater settler vigilance and self-help.[75]

Eventually the police were relieved of a good deal of the pressure of coping with prairie fires, which had always been exaggerated by the necessity to handle concurrently a great deal of other business and by civilian fire guardians' unwillingness to discharge their duties because they were "either too lazy or too afraid of making enemies to do anything."[76] Under the jurisdiction of the provincial attorneys general, "Fire Commissioners" and an associated officialdom were established in 1912, and in the matter of investigation of "the cause, origin and circumstances of every fire ... by which property has been destroyed or damaged," the mounted police were not designated.[77] Simultaneously, a long-term aggravation, the exemption of the Canadian Pacific Railway from Territorial and provincial prairie fire ordinances, was eliminated by a 1912 order of the federal Board of Railway Commissioners that railways were required to plough fireguard strips at least sixteen feet wide on both sides of the railway track, except where utterly impracticable. No longer did the police have to beg railway

---

74 Clipping from Calgary *Herald*, 14 November 1890; Inspector A.E. Snyder, Edmonton, to Officer Commanding at Fort Saskatchewan, 29 May 1897, enclosing clipping from Edmonton *Bulletin* of 17 May; Clipping from Battleford *Star*, 12 May 1899; J.W. Ings of Rio Alto Ranche, Lineham, to Superintendent R.B. Deane, Calgary, ca. August 1910: RG 18-A1.

75 Herchmer to White, 13 January 1893: RG 18-A1.

76 Constable T.G. Coventry, Castor Detachment, to Superintendent A.R. Cuthbert, Edmonton, 25 April 1910 and Cuthbert's appended note: RG 18-B1; Constable W.C. Jackson, Kinistino, to Officer Commanding at Prince Albert, 24 September 1894; and Constable R. Beatty to Officer Commanding at Prince Albert, 3 April 1895: RG 18-C1.

77 *Statutes of Saskatchewan*, 2 Geo V (1912), Chap. 23, pp. 97-9: "The Fire Prevention Act."

officials to do something to prevent engine sparks from igniting the surrounding countryside.[78]

*****

Even in the sporadic criticism endured by the police about their inability to crush the fearful threat of prairie fires, a basic pioneer attitude to the mounted police stands out, though it was usually expressed more positively. They were there to provide settlement (one might even say colonization) services. Prairie fires were aspects of the environment, like climatic extremes, which were not susceptible to individual conquest. Collective responses coordinated by a government agency were hardly avoidable. The same approach was essential for combatting animal and human contagious diseases. Though they had not originally been placed in the prairie west to ensure anything more than legal security, in the absence of any other government initiative the mounted police temporarily filled the need for external aid beyond the settlers' own resources precisely when the settlers were most vulnerable: when they were first establishing themselves. The police therefore inadvertently provided an early example in a particular region of Canada of public responsibility for individual welfare, not to be confused with the judgemental condescension implicit in the old tradition of private charity. Though prime ministers and western parliamentary representatives frequently referred to these services in justification of the force's existence, the way this role was given legitimacy over several decades of pioneer experience undoubtedly made its greatest impact in the west. It is difficult to imagine how the mounted police could fail to earn the gratitude of those they served.

But if Department of the Interior officials left the basic welfare of the settlers to the police, they stubbornly maintained the criterion of agricultural progress as the foundation for estimations of immigrant suitability. Early mounted police scepticism about some foreigners was frequently overcome by this Interior Department preoccupation; later evidence of success stimulated natural admiration. The result was to place the policemen at the side of the alien sometimes against great economic and cultural odds. And for all settlers of whatever origin, the presence of a patrolling police force was the most obvious (sometimes the only) sign of that limited degree of government care that did exist for pioneers thrust into the imposing prairie frontier. It does seem appropriate to conclude that a significant factor contributing to the mounted police popularity in prairie Canada was the force's role in the first faint stirrings of the Canadian welfare state.

NOTE

This chapter was previously published in Canadian Historical Association, *Historical Papers 1980*, 9-32.

---

78 Correspondence involving one Walter Simpson of Greendyke, the Superintendent at Regina, and the Assistant Commissioner of the NWMP, and C.W. Milestone, CPR, Moose Jaw, 16-23 October 1901; and correspondence about railway matters, 1909-1912: RG 18-B1; Inspector Baker, Maple Creek, to White, 21 November 1901: RG 18-A1.

FOURTEEN

Fort Battleford and the Architecture of the North-West Mounted Police

Walter Hildebrandt

... the Gothic Revival was part of a distinctive epoch within architectural history which for want of a better name can be called "Victorian." The older idea of some "battle of styles"... is rapidly giving way to recognition that all of the different styles of the Victorian era — Greek Revival, Roman Revival, Gothic Revival, and so forth — have a common denominator [which is] the principle of borrowing forms from past styles because of their association with certain given ideas. Roman building types were revived primarily because of their association with ideas of republicanism and civic virtue, Greek for associations with permanence and wisdom, Moorish for exoticism, and so on — the choice in any given case being determined by what sort of symbolic imagery social circumstances seem to call for ... the primary function of Gothic Revival architecture was to create symbolic imagery...[1]

The major buildings of the North-West Mounted Police at Battleford, built between 1876 and 1900 and designed by the Department of Public Works in Ottawa, reflect the influence of Victorian architectural trends popular during the 19th century in Eastern Canada, Britain, and the United States. Among the earliest public buildings in the North-West, they were significant in that they stood as cynosures of the Anglo-Canadian elite then emerging as the dominant force in Western Canada. The sophistication of this new architecture must have provided a startling contrast on a frontier where previously log buildings had provided only the barest of shelter.

The role of the North-West Mounted Police in preparing the way for an Anglo-Canadian West has been well documented.[2] They were harbingers of a culture already entrenched in Ontario. This paramilitary police force entered into the legendary Whoop-Up Country, motivated by a more confident sense of mission than those traders and wolfers who, prior to the arrival of the police, freely roamed the territory. The mounties came as agents of the politicians and the imperial federationists determined to expand into what they perceived as the Great Lone Land.

---

1   Alan Gowans, "Introduction," to *A History of the Gothic Revival* (Charles Eastlake American Life Foundation, 1975), p. x.

2   R.C. Macleod, *The NWMP and Law Enforcement, 1873-1905* (Toronto: Univ. of Toronto Press, 1976), and Paul F. Sharp, *Whoop-Up Country, the Canadian-American West, 1865-1885* (Norman: Univ. of Oklahoma Press, l955).

Plate 1. Troops stationed inside the stockade during the 1885 Riel Rebellion: Victorian architecture of the Commanding Officer's Residence in the background (ca. 1885). Courtesy of the Saskatchewan Archives Board.

The police received enthusiastic support from members of the fledgling Western Canadian elite, who had recently arrived, primarily from Ontario. At Battleford perhaps the most prominent representative of this elite was P.G. Laurie, the founder of the *Saskatchewan Herald*.[3] Established in 1878, the *Herald* was the first newspaper published in the territories west of Winnipeg. Laurie was a supporter of Sir J.A. Macdonald and a member of the Canadian faction at Red River in 1869. From there he set out with a single-minded determination to establish an Anglo-Canadian society in the North-West and he saw the police as guarantors of safe settlements for that society. The police function as legal enforcers and administrators was broadly outlined in "An Act Respecting the Administration of Justice, and for the Establishment of a Police Force in the North-West Territories" (1873); an Act which gave them a formidable role in shaping the nature of Western Canadian society. Their imperialist function was given a more lasting and visible presence in the buildings designed for them by the Department of Public Works (see Plate 1).

Before the police buildings appeared at Battleford exhibiting the imperial style of the East, the police had already begun to impose the concepts of order in what Prime Minister Macdonald had characterized as that "fretful realm." Through distant

---

3 Walter Hildebrandt, "P.G. Laurie: The Aspirations of a Western Enthusiast," M.A. Thesis, Univ. of Saskatchewan, 1978.

perceptions of the vast North-Western frontier, Victorians believed that violent primitive savages vented their passions unchecked by conscience or religious and secular authority. In effect the police became the agents of a rational, progressive and peaceful order that the imperialists thought necessary if civilized people were to settle in the North-West.

Prior to construction of the buildings which helped to carry eastern culture to the frontier, the police relied on other symbols of order and authority to garner instant respect. The "mounted" policeman became the awe-inspiring image still widely treasured in Canada. On well-trained horses, clad in red tunics and carrying lances, the Mounties came as physical symbols of political and moral authority. The image had easily traceable roots in eastern Canada where tradition and order was paid greater deference than the individualism of the American frontier that was actively touted in the American east.[4] Little architecture based on "national styles" was found in the early towns of the American frontier where the image of the gunslinger-cum Marshal is still held dear in the popular culture of North America. In the Canadian North-West the heroic individual was a rare phenomenon. True there were men like Sam Steele and James Walsh, but in the overall analysis it was the symbolic impact of the idea of the force that gave them their authority. This is clear in the self-congratulatory accounts of Walsh's encounter with the Sioux:

> Several times a tragedy was narrowly averted by the presence of mind and bold bearing of the Inspector and his officers. On one occasion a large number of Sioux, followers of the redoubtable chief, Sitting Bull, skulked in the underbrush of the hillside and were ready for any excuse to fire upon the troopers below. In this critical moment the commander of the little garrison went bravely, tackled the old chief in person, and bluffed him so successfully that the band moved on without giving further trouble. On this occasion, by the way, Inspector Walsh literally carried his life in his hands. When he rode towards the Sioux camp he had on a short blue jacket with black braid, while his men were all wearing greatcoats. At the sight of the hated blue, the "American colour" to all Indians, the rifles of the "braves" went up instantly, covering the Inspector. Seeing his danger, one of the foremost troopers had the presence of mind to throw open his coat, revealing the scarlet tunic beneath, and in a moment the weapons dropped. These were the "Queen's soldiers"; all was well.[5]

The collective image of the force in red tunics made a greater impression than the individual Walsh, even though he was highly respected by the Sioux. Authoritarian symbolism became a useful tool of enforcement for the Mounted Police, and it was natural that the design of the structures that housed the garrisons should attempt to perpetuate the impact of these symbols.

The Victorian architecture of North-West Mounted Police buildings at Battleford embodied imperial styles and were symbols particularly important for Battleford which was chosen as the site for the Territorial capital. These structures were visible reminders of the society intended for the North-West. The predominant building style at Fort Battleford was an eastern derivative but the essential materials were local, a circumstance which necessitated the adaptation of techniques which were often crude and haphazard. For at least one of the significant Fort Battleford structures,

---

4   For a discussion of images of the mounted police in Canadian literature, see Dick Harrison's introduction to *Best Mounted Police Stories* (Edmonton: Univ. of Alberta Press, 1978).

5   A.L Hayden, *Riders of the Plains* (London, 1910), p. 49.

the shortage of milled lumber resulted in the use of log walls although the plans had called for the "balloon frame" construction that had become popular in other parts of North America by the mid-nineteenth century. At the same time environmental pressures often forced construction crews to cut corners to ensure completion of buildings before it became impossible to endure the outdoor weather.

Despite these problems, however, the buildings reflected trends remarkably similar to "national styles" being exhibited in public buildings elsewhere in Canada. Even though log construction was used in many of the earlier buildings, facade treatments covered unevenly dressed timber and crude joining techniques. Log construction was hidden by a neat shiplap exterior on both the Commanding Officer's Residence and the Officers' Quarters. Decorative details were added to convey an imposing impression on a frontier which previously had been dotted by structures that basically provided protection from the elements, with little concern for fashionable trends, much less a "national style."

Adaptation was required to cope with unanticipated environmental conditions, such as the extreme cold of winter and the heat and dust of summer. This was best reflected in the addition of porches over main entrances: "In a climate such as this, they [porches] are useful in winter and summer; in the latter season they furnish protection from the constant winds and sand storms that often accompany them..."[6] Funds for renovation were frequently requested from Ottawa in order to make buildings habitable. Invariably the requests fell on deaf ears, despite the often piteous pleas from the frontier where the unseasoned wood shrank, cracking the mud, and leaving gaps in the walls which allowed wind to whistle through the buildings. The consequences were sometimes severe. As one Commanding Officer at Battleford reported to the officials in Ottawa:

> I have the honor to make the following report regarding the [Commanding Officer's Residence] I occupy as quarters and which I consider unfit for such in their present state. During the past winter four stoves were kept going the whole time, the building was not any too warm. At night full pails of water frozed [sic] solid — there is no storm sash — many mornings I have seen my bed covered with snow and rain — one half of the building has no ceiling, only paper and cotton — parts of the logs are rotten and when soaked by rain throws a dampness and has an odour throughout the house. The moulding inside is in between the cotton and wall.[7]

As is evident, the inhabitants of the buildings at Fort Battleford had not been freed from the elements enough to be concerned over the aesthetic appeal of uncluttered structures; such concerns were still a luxury when the environment necessitated porches and patchwork for self-preservation.

In many cases buildings had to be extended even though funding for new structures was not forthcoming: the result was the appearance of lean-to additions which like porches were unforeseeable afterthoughts: makeshift extensions to otherwise completed buildings.

For the Victorians, architecture not only provided shelter, but served as a means of communication. Architectural forms were often chosen "for their symbolic

---

6   Public Archives of Canada, Royal Canadian Mounted Police Records, Record Group 18, vol. 1403, file 33, August 1, 1898.

7   PAC, RG 18, vol. 1165, file 28, June 8, 1890.

Plate 2. Government House at Battleford, built in 1876 by the same crews that built the North-West Mounted Police buildings. Courtesy of the Fort Battleford Library Collection.

implications rather than for their fitness for particular buildings needs."[8] Regionally, the structures erected at Battleford by the Department of Public Works were the first buildings after 1870 to depart from the simple log shelter and were built with a style and panache to convey messages of this vernal culture to newcomers. Government House at Battleford is an example of this more sophisticated style. (See Plate 2)

The "picturesque" structures occupied by the North-West Mounted Police were instrumental in disseminating Anglo-Canadian ideas to the West. Many immigrants may not have understood the concepts depicted by Victorian styles, but the culture represented by these buildings and the customs of the society they symbolized was firmly passed on by the police, while many waited to move from the so-called immigrant "sheds" provided for them on police property.

The buildings at Fort Battleford were constructed in the last quarter of the nineteenth century, at a time when the influences of Victorian architecture were strong in Canada. Two architects, Thomas Fuller, Sr., and Thomas Scott, shared responsibility for imposing the Gothic and Italianate style upon public building in Canada late in the century.[9] Both were born in Britain and both worked on the design and construction of the Parliament buildings — and both had lengthy careers in the

---

8   See Alan Gowans, *Building in Canada: An Architectural History of Canadian Life* (Toronto: Oxford Univ. Press, 1966).

9   Gowans, pp. 118-19; "Gothic was the style chosen for [the Parliament buildings]. That was no surprise; the architects hardly had an alternative. It was practically mandatory on them to express the country's close ties with Britain by taking as their model Westminster New Palace, home of the Mother of Parliaments in London."

Plate 3. Refurbished Commanding Officer's Residence. Note bay window and trefoil bargeboard design. Pinnacles at peak of gable have not been replaced (1976). Courtesy of Pat McCloskey, Parks Canada.

public service.[10] Fuller, whose tenure as Canada's chief architect lasted from 1881 to 1897, was particularly influential in determining the style for federally-financed buildings in Canada. His tenure ensured that Gothic and Italianate became dominant modes even for relatively insignificant wooden buildings such as those designed for the North-West Mounted Police.[11] The Commanding Officer's Residence at Fort Battleford built in 1876-77 and still standing, is clearly within the Gothic Style of the "Romantic Revival." Its vertical lines, originally crowned by a finial, vergeboards, pendants, bay window and "picturesque setting" make it typical of this style.[12] (See Plate 3)

---

10   For example, the Stratford Post Office. See Christopher Thomas's article, "Architectural Image for the Dominion: Scott, Fuller and the Stratford Post Office," *Journal of Canadian Art History*, 3 (Fall, 1976).

11   See, for example, the Walker Letterbooks, May 17, 1877 to Feb. 21, 1879, particularly the letter written by Inspector Walker to the Secretary of State, Dec.17, 1877. The original Walker Letterbooks are housed in the library at Fort Battleford. Correspondence between the federal government and officials at Fort Battleford shows that the architects in the Department of Public Works had a definite hand in dictating the shape these buildings on the frontier were to take.

12   This picturesque quality was not only to be achieved by the building but also by trees and landscaping. See A.J. Downing, *The Architecture of Country Houses* (1850; rpt. New York: Da Capo Press, 1968): "The picturesque is seen in, ideas of beauty manifested with something of rudeness, violence or difficulty. The effect of the whole is spirited and pleasing, but parts are not balanced, proportions are not perfect and details are made. We feel that at first glance of a picturesque object the idea of power is exorted, rather than the idea of beauty which it involves" (pp. 28-29). See also A.J. Davis, *Rural Residences* (New York, 1837); A.J. Downing, *Cottage Residences* (1842); and Henry Hudson Holly, *Country Seats* (1863) and *Modern Dwellings in Town and Country* (1878).

The Gothic revival was apparent not only in Canada but throughout North America. Its ambience followed the wake of widely-read pattern books of architects such as A.J. Downing and Hudson Holly. Downing is generally considered to be "the Gothic manner's chief herald in America..."[13] Originally a landscape gardener, his designs profoundly affected North American architecture. As a traveller through America in 1849-50 noted: "nobody, whether he be rich or poor, builds a house or lays out a garden without consulting Downing's works; every young couple who sets up housekeeping buys them."[14] Downing, like Holly, was strongly influenced by English architects and designers. Downing, however, cautioned against grotesque mimickry and urged builders to be cautious in choosing styles. As he pointedly wrote in a chapter entitled "The Real Meaning of Architecture," design had to be in harmony with the environment; it had to be in keeping with the purpose of the building, and with the social standing of the builder:

> So far as admiration of foreign style in Architecture arises from an admiration of truthful beauty of form or expression, it is noble and praise worthy. A villa in the style of a Persian palace (of which there is an example lately erected in Connecticut), with its original domes and minarets, equally unmeaning and unsuited to our life or climate, is an example of the former; as an English cottage, with its beautiful home expression and its thorough comfort and utility, evinced in steep roofs to shed snow and varied form to accommodate modern habits, is of the latter.[15]

Hudson Holly, another prominent American architect, in his essay entitled "Some Accounts of the History of Architecture," presented a more detailed explanation of the Gothic roots in America.[16] Holly was searching for a style which most appropriately suited the aspirations of the American people. He considered that the arts were a reflection of the character of a people and that architecture was a more conscious expression of the national character than any other art form. Holly rejected Greek styles as too impractical, and unsuited to the number of windows which he felt were necessary in contemporary buildings. The Roman styles were considered too horizontal, commemorating secular triumphs "but serving no loftier purpose." The Gothic, however, was closer to the style Holly would have liked for Americans,[17] because it embodied Christian principles as well as the British connection.

The religious emphasis was particularly important in revealing the "higher aspiration" of a Christian society. Christian spires were evidence to Holly of a more spiritual life than the concerns revealed by "heathen domes." Architecture could be used to "raise the eye above the level of mere human perfection, giving it a 'heaven-directed' aim."[18] Holly found further fault with the worldly architecture of the Greeks and Romans:

> Their lofty pillars seemed rather to spring from earth, than to rest "upon" it; and those windowless walls, which in the Heathen temple remained in stubborn solidity to exclude the light, were now pierced on all sides to admit the beams of divine day.[19]

---

13   John Mass, *The Gingerbread Age: A View of Victorian America* (New York: Rinehart, 1957).
14   Quoted by George Tatum in the "Introduction" to A.J. Downing, *The Architecture of Country Houses*.
15   *The Architecture of Country Houses*, p. 27.
16   Henry Hudson Holly, in *Holly's Country Seats*, p. 27.
17   Holly, p. 7.
18   Holly, p. 11.
19   Holly, p. 11.

Plate 4. *Refurbished interior of Commanding Officer's Residence (1976). Courtesy of Pat McCloskey, Parks Canada.*

Other details characterizing Christian traditions were included on Gothic structures. Trefoil designs represented the trinity and the trefoil pattern carved into the wooden bargeboard beneath the peak of the gable in the Commanding Officer's Quarters is a graphic depiction of "Carpenter's Gothic." Cruciform plans were used to symbolize the everlasting sacrifice, while pinnacles represented souls seeking their "'finial' in that heaven where alone the soul's consummation 'can' be sought."[20] Although the Commanding Officer's Residence was L shaped (as was Government House) instead of the cross shaped floor plan, it did originally display finials (or pinnacles) at the peak of each gable, and Government House does have a quadrefoil design beneath the peak of the gable.

The adaptation of the Gothic to domestic housing led to the introduction of a number of other features such as bay or oriel windows (which allowed for a feeling of closeness to nature), chimney stacks, roof ceilings and panelled wainscots around interior walls.[21] Both the Commanding Officer's Residence and Government House exhibited these additional features, the most outstanding of which was the elaborate bay window in the Commanding Officer's Residence. (See Plate 4)

Of course Greek revival was not totally excluded from public buildings in North America, nor was it categorically condemned. In fact as Hudson Holly stated:

> for ecclesiastical structures, colleges etc., the Gothic designs are rapidly superceding the Italian, while for public buildings for government, and other secular purposes, the Grecian is generally regarded as preferable...[22]

---

20   Holly, p. 11.
21   Holly, p. 19.
22   Holly, p. 19.

Plate 5. Commanding Officer's Residence and (right) Officers' Quarters in Second Empire style popular during mid to late nineteenth century (ca. 1925-30). Courtesy of Fort Battleford Library.

Details of the Greek revival are found in the pedimented window casings in both the Commanding Officer's Residence and in Government House. Classical details, however, dominated the appearance of Government House to a greater extent than the residence intended for the Superintendent of the North-West Mounted Police. The pillars on either side at the front door immediately attract the eye at Government House, while similar features on the Commanding Officer's Residence are less noticeable and give way to the overall picturesque impression of this residence.

The interior features of the Commanding Officer's Residence are consistent with those of other Victorian houses.[23] Immediately to the left of the front entrance is a large livingroom or parlour for public or official occasions. To the right, upon entering the front door, a stairway leads to the private section of the house, making the division between public and private areas of the house immediately apparent. At the back is the winter kitchen and servants diningroom while an ell containing the summer kitchen is attached to the rear of the house. The servant's stairway is another feature common in Victorian housing. The second storey contains three bedrooms and a small landing.

The Officers' Quarters, with its French-style mansard roof, decorative bargeboards, finials and dormer windows, is clearly within the Second Empire style popular during the mid to late nineteenth century. (See Plate 5) Even though this fashion originated in France, it was seen as a variation of the Italianate style because it corresponded to the heavy forms and elaborate ornamentation of this tradition.[24] It was the addition to the Louvre, commissioned by Napoleon III that brought Second Empire international recognition and most often "focused on notable, newly

---

23 Downing, p. 21ff.
24 George Hersey, "Replication Replicated on Notes on American Bastardy," *Perspector, the Yale Architectural Journal*, Nos. 9 and 10 (1965), p. 220.

constructed public buildings."[25] The style did not, however, make its way to North America directly from France, but through British architects who were designing public buildings in Britain after the Second Empire mode. It therefore became part of the broader Victorian architectural tradition in North America through this British connection. The Italianate was part of the "Romantic Revival" in Victorian architecture which swept North America during the latter part of the nineteenth century.[26] Pattern books of the nineteenth century show numerous examples of "French style roofs."[27] With finials on the dormers and fretted bargeboards complimented by surrounding evergreens, the Officers' Quarters portrays the "picturesque" quality that architects of the "Romantic Revival" tried to popularize. Internationally the Second Empire style enjoyed prominence until the 1870s.[28] The Officers' Quarters is a clear indication that the style was still appropriate for public buildings in Canada as late as 1885.

The Officers' Quarters took nearly four years to complete and serves as an example of a building whose construction was significantly influenced by local circumstances. A shortage of materials meant that the walls of the structure had to be built of logs instead of finished lumber. Although porches were initially not part of the building they were later added because of the effects extreme temperatures had on the building. An absence of skilled labour on the Canadian frontier in the 1880s frequently resulted in jerry-built construction as is evident in the trussing visible in the attic of the Officers' Quarters. But as the architectural historian Douglas Richardson has pointed out: "The handling of materials aware but abrupt — helps to identify those structures as part of the Canadian vernacular."[29]

Victorian details are also found scattered throughout other buildings at Fort Battleford where the cross shaped floor of the Surgeon's Residence and the gingerbread gables recall Victorian style. The Gothic arch on the Concert Hall (no longer standing) was an interesting sidelight on an otherwise ordinary building, and an example of late Victorian eclecticism could have been found in the original pagoda-style cupola on the Sick Horse Stable, although it has since been replaced. This scattering of detail is in itself illustrative of the derivative nature of western building, though the retention of "picturesque" features and asymmetrical designs in the face of the "classical revival" seems more suitable to the plains environment.

Although the buildings at Fort Battleford had to be adapted to their environment, the styles represented a transplanting of traditional British and eastern Canadian values. The North-West Mounted Police were Canada's Victorian constabulary whose federal image and national role was more than reinforced by the long arm of the design group of the Department of Public Works. They are a reminder of a culture that imposed structures and institutions on a frontier, leaving little room for the

---

25   Charles Lockwood, *Bricks and Brownstone, the New York Row House, 1783-1929, an Architectural and Social History* (Toronto: McGraw-Hill, 1972).

26   For a discussion of the layout of Victorian houses, see Clifford Clark, "Domestic Architecture as an Index to Social History: The Romantic Revival and the Cult of Domesticity in America, 1840-1870," *Journal of Interdisciplinary History* (Summer 1976).

27   For example, F.C. Hussey, *Victorian Home Building: A Transcendental View of 1875* (1875; rpt. Watkins Glen, N.Y.: American Life Foundation, 1976).

28   Lockwood, p. 225.

29   Douglas Richardson, "Canadian Architecture in the Victorian Era: The Spirit of the Place," *Canadian Collector*, 10 (Sept.-Oct. 1975).

emergence of an autochthonous architecture. The police, like the buildings they lived in, had to adapt to unfamiliar conditions. The resultant changes, however, were more a matter of degree than form and issued from a desire for self-preservation rather than from an empathy for problems faced by indigenous people of the North-West. Many of the policemen retired to settle in the west and helped to perpetuate the culture they had carried with them. An indigenous Western architecture of the late nineteenth century could hardly be expected to emerge from a sparsely-populated frontier where other more desperate attempts at self-expression — culminating in the so-called "rebellions" of 1869 and 1885 — were suppressed or ignored. In fact it might be argued that Western Canadians have still not shaken their cultural dependence on their British and American antecedents.

NOTE

This chapter was previously published in *Journal of Popular Culture* 14, no. 2 (fall 1980), 313-25.

FIFTEEN

Captain R. Burton Deane and Theatre on the Prairies, 1883-1901

William M. Baker

Historians of theatre in Canada have always credited military units as being amongst the earliest promoters of the dramatic arts in the country. Indeed, the opening sentence of Jesse Edgar Middleton's hoary account of the origins of theatre in Canada runs as follows: "British army officers have been inveterate devotees of private theatricals."[1] From that point the author proceeded to demonstrate the importance of the military in establishing drama in Canada. To Middleton, however, these efforts were mere dilettantism, a mechanism to "beguile the tedium of garrison duty."[2] In the final analysis he dismissed the contribution of the military as inconsequential compared to the appearance of professional stock companies. More recently, Natalie Rewa has maintained that although garrison productions were prevalent in the earliest theatrical performances by whites in Canada and fulfilled a social function, being one of the more amiable means of promoting the domination of British "civilization," "the British garrisons' encouragement of local amateur and touring professional theatre did not contribute significantly to Canadian theatre history."[3] Indeed, she maintains that with only minor exceptions, garrison theatricals became extinct after Confederation. Eugene Benson and Leonard W. Conolly agree with Middleton's view that the military became involved partly to relieve tedium. They also accept Rewa's contention that involvement of the military in theatre may have promoted its control of the society since the productions promoted good relations between the garrison and local inhabitants. However, Benson and Conolly claim that by the mid-nineteenth century the military had made "a substantial contribution to theatre in the Atlantic provinces [and presumably in the other British North American colonies], not only building theatres but equipping and staffing them. They had also encouraged and welcomed participation from local amateurs."[4] As for the quality of

---

1   J.E. Middleton, "The Theatre in Canada," in Vol XII of *Canada and Its Provinces*, ed by A. Shortt and A.G. Doughty (Toronto 1914), p. 651.

2   Ibid., p. 652.

3   N. Rewa, "Garrison Theatre," in *The Oxford Companion to Canadian Theatre*, ed by E. Benson and L.W. Conolly (Toronto 1989), p. 222.

4   E. Benson and L.W. Conolly, *English-Canadian Theatre* (Toronto 1987), p. 4.

both garrison and mixed productions, Benson and Conolly suggest that while there was a wide range, "the overall picture of amateur theatricals [including those with a connection to the military] in nineteenth-century Canada is not one of drunken incompetence but of enthusiasm, commitment, and no small degree of talent."[5] David Gardner also finds that the garrison productions, usually of comedies imported from England, were frequently of good quality and suggests that they often aided local charities and boosted community morale.[6]

This brief review of basic sources concerning the involvement of the military in the origins of "white" theatre in Canada suggests several issues of information and interpretation which might profitably be examined: 1) Did the tradition of military theatricals die after 1867? 2) What was the motivation of military personnel for becoming involved in drama? 3) Of what quality were these productions? and 4) What was the significance of military involvement in the origins of theatre in Canada? Although no single case study can answer all these questions in any definitive way, the example of Captain R. Burton Deane sheds some light on each one.

Deane was born in India in 1848, the son of a Church of England chaplain for the East India Company. Not long thereafter the family returned to England and settled in Suffolk where Deane's grandfather had at one time been a substantial landholder. Deane's father became the rector of a parish on the outskirts of Ipswich and Deane attended the prestigious local grammar school. Deane's social status may have been better than adequate but his financial backing must have been meagre, for in 1866 he joined the Royal Marines, a "non-purchase" corps, as a Lieutenant.[7] His most active service was with the Ashanti Expedition on the Gold Coast of Africa in 1873-74. In 1876 he became Adjutant of the Chatham Division and in 1881 was promoted to Captain. But this was horrendously slow progress. Deane had been caught in wholescale retrenchment in the Marines which resulted in virtually no upward mobility for junior officers for more than a decade. By 1882, realizing that mandatory retirement was but eight years away and that it would be difficult to support himself, his wife and five children on a restricted pension entitlement, Deane took an early retirement payout of £1,600 from the Marines and headed to Canada. He joined the quasi-military North West Mounted Police in 1883 as an Inspector and the following year was promoted to the rank of Superintendent. While in charge of the Regina Division in the mid-eighties Deane also acted as adjutant to the force and did much to establish its basic rules, regulations and routines. In 1888 he became the commanding officer of the Lethbridge Division. From then until his retirement back to England in 1914 he commanded one or more of the several divisions in the southern prairies. In 1916 he published *Mounted Police Life in Canada: A Record of Thirty-one Years' Service, 1883-1914*. He died in 1930 in Italy.

Only three references in Deane's book comment on his role in promoting theatre. In a single sentence he mentions that he organized a theatrical troupe in Regina,

---

5 Ibid., p. 8.

6 D. Gardner, "Little Theatre and Amateur Theatre," in *Oxford Companion*, p. 302. Additional information about the contributions of the military to theatre in Canada may be found in Section 1 of Richard Plant's entry on "Drama in English" in *Oxford Companion*, pp. 148-153.

7 At this time the usual practice in Britain was for gentlemen to purchase commissions as officers. One could be accepted in some branches of the service on the basis of competence and influence, but joining as a non-purchase officer was usually an indication of scarcity of funds.

"and we had considerable fun from our amateur attempts and from little dances that we occasionally gave." This was, he indicated, one of the ways in which they "beguiled the time."[8] Only half a sentence was devoted to remembering the pleasure given him during his days as commanding officer in Lethbridge by "our theatrical entertainments, which were always given for a local charity…"[9] Finally, there was a passing comment about his opening a performing hall in Lethbridge with a play.[10] It may seem, therefore, that Deane considered these activities as barely worth mention. It is likely, however, that it was not Deane who gave these activities short shrift in his recollections, but rather his publisher. The original manuscript Deane produced was reduced by about one-third prior to publication, and it would appear that the sixty-five page handwritten document entitled "Reminiscences of a Mounted Police Officer by Captain R. Burton Deane," presently held by Calgary's Glenbow Alberta Archives, formed a major portion of the excision.[11] Be that as it may, the "Reminiscences" provide a good deal of information on the where, when, how and why of Deane's involvement in theatre.[12]

For Deane, the story began in 1866 when he was a newly commissioned Second Lieutenant in the Royal Marines stationed on the southern coast of England near Portsmouth. The occasion was a visit to the barracks of a "Professor" Raymond, who wanted to acquire students wishing to take lessons in the "Cult of Mesmerism."[13] Deane signed up and claimed that he became quite a capable hypnotist. But he did not like a number of examples he witnessed of the power hypnotism gave the master over the subject: "I formed the conclusion that the practice of mesmerism or electro-biology, or whatever it may be called, is not desirable for amateurs in the general interests of mankind, and I therefore gave up the practice of it for good and all."[14] Deane's distaste for mesmerism left him with a problem:

> As I reasoned it out with myself, I could not play any musical instrument and I could not sing, so how was I going to make my contribution to the amusement of that "state of life to which it had pleased God to call me"?[15]

The answer Deane found, the activity that eventually led him into theatre, was sleight

---

8 R.B. Deane, *Mounted Police Life in Canada: A Record of Thirty-one Years' Service* (London 1916: reprint by Coles Publishing Company 1973), p. 37.

9 Ibid., p. 44.

10 Ibid., p. 69.

11 A file of Deane's letters to his publishing agent, The Authors' Syndicate Ltd., is housed in the National Archives of Canada under reference file MG28, I, vol 259. These letters do not specify the exact material that was cut out, but the title of the material in the Glenbow Archives under reference file M311 is an important clue because Deane's correspondence with the agent reveal that the ultimate title for the book was not the one he preferred and had been working with for four years. It would also make sense that the British publisher, Cassell and Company, would have considered material about Deane's card tricks, theatrical involvement, and cricket days, of little interest either to a British or Canadian audience. On the other hand, there is a reference in the "Remiscences" on page 53 that seems to indicate that they were written after 1916, the publication date of Deane's book.

12 The "Reminiscences" provide the bulk of the information in what follows. To provide specific page references for all details would be pedantic and, therefore, only quotations from the "Reminiscences" or information deriving from other sources will be footnoted.

13 "Reminiscences," p. 1.

14 Ibid., p. 4.

15 Ibid., p. 5.

of hand. And the motive, from the outset, was to provide a bit of inexpensive entertainment for his own socially elite class.

It was the mesmerist Raymond who piqued Deane's interest in the performance of card tricks. During a recess in a lesson in hypnotism, Raymond picked up a deck of cards and proceeded to execute a trick. Deane was hooked and asked the "Professor" to give him some lessons. Raymond agreed, with the warning that much practice would be required, and that under no circumstances was Deane to attempt any tricks before other people for at least six months. Deane practiced diligently with cards and coins before making his public debut at a banquet in the summer of 1867 following a cricket match, a game in which he was sufficiently skilled to have been selected to the team representing the Portsmouth Division. His first successful coin trick at the dining table led to numerous card tricks in the ante room. Deane's performance went very smoothly: "I amused the company and acquired the confidence which never left me."[16]

By the time he joined the HMS *Warrior* for a tour of duty in 1869 Deane had advanced beyond informal performances in the officers' mess. For example, he gave a show in Portugal for the benefit of the Church of England Sunday School, for which he not only received accolades in the Portuguese press but also a dinner invitation from the British Ambassador to Portugal. Needless to say, Deane performed a few tricks at that august affair as well. During the cruise on the *Warrior*, Deane further developed his skills with the assistance of shipmate Lieutenant Hill. In June 1871, the two conjurers provided an evening of magic at the Theatre Royal in Gibraltar for the benefit of the Sailors' Home in that place, a charity under the patronage of Vice Admiral Wellesley and the officers of the fleet.

Deane's "Reminiscences" indicate that he gave numerous public exhibitions of sleight of hand for charitable purposes in addition to being a willing entertainer at dinner parties and on other social occasions. It is also apparent from Deane's writings that much of the skill in sleight of hand depends on the ability of the magician to talk through the trick. Verbal patter was not only part of the mechanism of the trick, for it frequently distracted the audience from what the entertainer was doing with the hands, but it was also a large part of what made the performance entertaining and amazing. Even when the magician was in difficulty, rhetoric could buy time. The conjurer had to become as quick-witted as quick-fingered, and as confident in public speaking as in the technical performance of the tricks. Thus, magic performances were not dissimilar to other types of theatrical entertainment, and as Deane seems to have become proficient at the various requirements of the craft, it was a natural step for him to become involved in the theatre.

In 1876 Deane was appointed Adjutant of the Chatham Division of the Royal Marines. In this post for the ensuing five years he was located at the headquarters close to London on the first bay on the sea south of the outlet of the River Thames. As an adjutant he quickly demonstrated his organizational and administrative capabilities and, given his interest and experience in providing entertainments, it was not too remarkable that he was made manager of the theatre on the grounds of the barracks. The theatre itself was newly built, the old one having posed a fire hazard, and was called The Globe by the outgoing manager.[17] The first task Deane faced was to

---

16   Ibid., p. 12.
17   As Deane explained it, the name derived from combining three items: Shakespeare's statement "All

provide basic scenery, for what remained from the old theatre was useless. Chatham's proximity to London and, presumably, Deane's ability to make the right connections, resulted in the hiring of a scene painter from no less than Covent Garden to come to the barracks for a week's work: "Between us we got through quite a lot, as he sketched out for me work that I could continue after he had left."[18]

Deane's "Reminiscences" do not provide a complete list of the plays he produced and acted in at The Globe. One was Charles Dance's *Wonderful Woman* which, according to Deane, received favourable notice in *The World* of 24 November, 1880. Indeed, Deane claimed that complimentary reviews appeared from time to time in other British journals such as *Truth* and *Figaro*. Deane's greatest sense of triumph at The Globe was his production of Oliver Goldsmith's *She Stoops to Conquer*. The *Rochester Observer*, a local community newspaper, found that although the audience took time to warm to the production it was so well performed by Deane and the rest of the cast, with good costumes and scenery along with a fine band, that the audience was won over to enthusiastic appreciation.[19] Deane's productions were amateur, but hardly seem unskilled or unsophisticated. Nor were they merely and exclusively by and for the military. "My Company was gathered from quite an extensive clientele; officers and ladies from the Garrison at large; residents from Rochester and its surroundings; anybody who could act and would act, (preferably liked acting) was welcome at 'The Globe'."[20]

The use of the theatre to integrate community and barracks was also evident in Deane's inauguration of dances at The Globe. The new floor was good, the building was easily warmed, the divisional band was supplemented with strings, and with Deane selecting music programmes which included numerous waltzes to meet the demand of the times, the weekly dances soon attracted the best dancers of both sexes in the neighbourhood. Deane not only utilized local actors and provided entertainment at the barracks' theatre for the community, but also contributed to theatre off the base. In collaboration with Mr. Stephen Aveling, a knowlegeable local actor who was Deane's principal theatrical consultant, he produced two plays at the Theatre Royal in Rochester: *Honey Moon* by Jonathan Tobin and *Wife's Secret* by George William Lovell. Deane's own acting performance in the first won plaudits from the critic in the *Rochester Observer*.

By the time Deane left England for Canada in 1882 his experience with theatre was substantial. He had been a performer of illusions, an actor, a producer, a director, a theatre manager, a scenery maker, and a make-up artist. He had done everything from selecting plays, to acquiring a cast, to painting sets and ensuring that the floors were polished. Moreover, his experience had not been gained at some remote and

---

the world's a stage"; the equation of the world with the globe; and the fact that the crest of the Royal Marines is the globe. Deane's predecessor as manager was a Captain Sweny who, according to Deane, was a skilled amateur actor with lengthy experience in managing the barracks' theatre; so long, in fact, that he could not avoid foreign service and he therefore turned over the reins of The Globe to Deane.

18   Ibid., p. 28.
19   The newspaper critique was quoted by Deane in ibid., pp. 27-28. Although it has not been possible to check the original newspapers in England, one may place confidence in the accuracy of Deane's quotations since the "Reminiscences" are entirely correct in quoting Canadian papers.
20   Ibid., p. 28.

isolated village but on the very doorstep of London, and his performances and productions over a period of fifteen years had taken place before audiences containing both military and lay members of the social elite who, no doubt, were capable of being discriminating and demanding.[21] That his cast members had or were to have social prominence is incidentally demonstrated in the story Deane told from his Chatham days of having to replace one of the main actors in J. Sterling Coyne's *Nothing Venture, Nothing Win*. The man, a Lieutenant, had the character down beautifully but simply could not remember his lines and at the dress rehearsal he was a complete disaster. Fortuitously, the next day at Sunday service Deane recognized the man sitting in the pew in front of him — an individual who Deane knew had played the lead in the same play when stationed in Montreal with the Royal Welsh Fusiliers. Deane convinced him to take the lead in his production, switched himself from the lead to the part supposed to have been played by the poor soul who could not recall the right words, and called an emergency rehearsal. The result of this stroke of extraordinary luck and of Deane's quick and decisive action in seizing the opportunity presented by fortune was a successful production. The replaced actor, who was more relieved than offended, became Lieutenant General H. St. G. Schomberg, CB while the man who stepped into the lead was Captain G.W.A. Fitzgeorge, son of the Duke of Cambridge and at the time Private Secretary to Mr. Hugh Childers, Secretary of State for War. As this tale indicates, Deane was accustomed to interactions with the socially prominent in his theatrical activities. Deane combined, therefore, two of the three traditions which have been identified as the foundation of amateur theatre in Canada: productions sponsored and promoted by military garrisons on the one hand, and by high society on the other.[22] Deane may have been an amateur but it is quite obvious that he was very well versed in many aspects of theatrical production. He brought that expertise with him to the Canadian Prairies as a Mounted Police officer.[23]

By the autumn of 1883 the Deane family had settled down in their comfortable quarters at the Mounted Police barracks a couple of miles out of Regina, the newly created capital of the North-West Territories.[24] Deane found his official duties

---

21 The "Reminiscences" give an example of a particularly tenacious sceptic, an Admiral Warren, of one of Deane's card tricks on pages 18 to 22. Deane's account suggests that he handled Warren's scrutiny with aplomb.

22 Gardner, "Little Theatre...," p. 301. The other tradition enumerated by Gardner is theatre for pedagogic purposes.

23 The "Reminiscences" say nothing about performing magic tricks in Canada but he had done so on the voyage over and had given the ship's captain a lesson on a "money and hat" trick (Glenbow Alberta Archives, M313, R. Burton Deane's Diary). It is likely that he continued to practice legerdemain until he broke his wrist in Toronto in 1883 and although the wrist healed well, the splint that was applied curled his fingers over a rod. In the process of time his fingers gradually stiffened and curled one after the other so that by the end of the century he could not even play cricket let alone do card tricks.

24 The North-West Territories consisted of all of western Canada except for the then tiny province of Manitoba and of British Columbia. For the history of Regina consult J.W. Brennan (ed), *Regina Before Yesterday: A Visual History 1882 to 1945* (Regina 1978); J.W. Brennan, *Regina: An Illustrated History* (Toronto 1989); E.J. Drake, *Regina: The Queen City* (Toronto 1955); and W.A. Riddell, *Regina from Pile O' Bones to Queen City of the Plains* (Burlington 1981). On the history of theatre in Regina see the section in E.R. Stuart's *The History of Prairie Theatre* (Toronto 1984); P.B. O'Neill's "Regina's Golden Age of Theatre: Her Playhouses and Players," *Saskatchewan History*, XXVIII, 1 (Winter 1975), pp. 29-37; and Section I of O'Neill's entry on "Theatre in Saskatchewan" in the *Oxford Companion*, p. 487. All are useful but none provides much information on the very earliest productions of the 1880s.

relatively straightforward for he was charged with the development of Standing Orders and other rules and regulations that would bring a greater sense of order to the "armed mob" of Mounted Policemen. With his experience in the Marines, especially as the adjutant of a division of over 3500 men, he found it "child's play ... to draft regulations for a little force of 500 men..."[25] Deane's "Reminiscences" relate that the winter of 1883-84 brought such unfamiliar pleasures as sleighing, snowshoeing and tobogganing. Temperatures of minus 40 degrees and white-out blizzards were dangerous, but were accepted with the fortitude expected of a soldier and a man. In short, the Deanes were able "to make life more than bearable..."[26] Following the Christmas festivities, plans were made for an evening's entertainment. It was to consist of a play produced by Deane and, as he styled it, a "nigger minstrel show" developed by the enlisted men.[27]

There was, unsurprisingly, no theatre at the barracks and it was left to Deane to find an acceptable location. The building normally used for warehousing and quartermaster's stores was the only possibility and there Deane constructed the stage, proscenium, drop-curtain and set. While this was proceeding, Deane commenced rehearsals. The play he had selected was "the well known farce 'Ici on parle français'."[28] He cast himself as the Frenchman in Thomas J. Williams' play, since he already knew the part, and relied on enlisted men and the wives of officers for the other main characters. As the performance night approached Deane feared a disaster like the one narrowly avoided several years earlier in Chatham, for one of the leads was in deep water and sinking rapidly. But there was no miraculous option this time. Deane plastered make-up on the man and when he appeared on stage his appearance immediately drew a laugh. To the great relief of Deane and the rest of the cast, "this set him on his feet and put heart into him, and he played his part uncommonly well."[29] Deane's own performance was lauded in the Regina *Leader*: "Captain Deane as Victor Dubois looked the bewildered eager and susceptible Frenchman to the life, indeed so excellent was his acting that only for the playbill his most intimate friends would not have known him."[30] The reviewer, in all likelihood, was the *Leader*'s founder and editor, Nicholas Flood Davin, the Irish-born journalist, poet, politician and lawyer; a man with extensive international experience, a wonderful orator, and one who himself had tried his hand at playwriting a few years earlier.[31] The *Leader* maintained

---

25 Deane, *Mounted Police Life*, p. 3.

26 "Reminiscences," p. 33.

27 Ibid. Both the term "nigger" and the concept of a minstrel show were common in the 1880s and even three decades later when Deane wrote his "Reminiscences." Such stereotypes were evident at the turn of the century in the series of cartoons published by the Montreal *Star* under the title "Songs of the By-town Coons." It depicted prominent federal politicians (at one time Ottawa had been called Bytown) in blackface, playing and singing songs which were printed alongside the caricature. Needless to say, the songs used idiomatic language supposedly typical of Afro-Americans. In a sense, the 1884 Regina presentation of the minstrel show coupled with the play represented, in turn, the influence of the United States and Britain on Canadian culture.

28 "Reminiscences," p. 34.

29 Ibid., pp. 36-37.

30 Regina *Leader*, 24 Jan. 1884.

31 Davin's play *The Fair Grit* (1876) was a satirical farce about Canadian politics according to Benson and Conolly, *English-Canadian Theatre*, p. 18. On Davin see C.B. Koester, *Mr. Davin, M.P.: A Biography of Nicholas Flood Davin* (Saskatoon, 1980), especially pp. 175-192. In addition, Ken Mitchell has written

that the performance "left little or nothing to be desired" and hoped that the evening's entertainment was a "harbinger of many such nights of pleasant art effort and innocent amusement."[32] But this production, one of the earliest but not the first in the North-West Territories,[33] did not lead to a steady stream of performances.

In April 1884, Deane was promoted to Superintendent and Adjutant of the force, a job which put him in charge of organizing and administering the Commissioner's office. It was a formidable task to bring order to the near chaos that existed there, as well as being the Commanding Officer of the Headquarters Division during the Riel Rebellion. Consequently, Deane had no time for the production of plays for over two years. It was not the case, however, that his thoughts were completely divorced from the theatre. During the Rebellion, Deane was authorized to construct increased prison accommodation to secure suspected rebels. He added some cells to the existing guardroom and erected a spacious addition:

> At the south end of this building a room was partitioned off for the use of the Guard who would have to look after the prisoners, while they would be housed in a double row of roofless cells that ran down the centre of the building. The walls of the cells were about 8 feet high and were so constructed that they could be easily removed without causing any damage to the floor. A platform athwart the cell column at its northern end enabled a sentry, with moccassined [sic] feet, to overlook the cells without disturbing their occupants. I had it in view that, when the building should be no longer required for prison purposes, it would form a very useful Concert Hall, in which church services as well as concerts &c. could be held and the room at the south end would require nothing more than a partition to convert it into dressing rooms for ladies and gentlemen.[34]

It was not until November 1886, that Deane was able to put on another play. The fund-raising evening, which attracted Lieutenant-Governor Dewdney and his wife,[35] in aid of Saint Paul's Church began with a concert by vocalists from Winnipeg, followed by Deane's selection, the brief comedy *Dearest Mama, my Mother-in-Law* by "Walter Gordon," a pen name of William Aylmer Gowing. The entertainment was put on in the Regina Town Hall and Deane's cast was a mixed crew of townsfolk and residents of the barracks, the same formula that he had developed back in Chatham. During the performance a humorous insertion was made alluding to the infamous liquor prohibition law in the North-West Territories, a comment that convulsed the house.

---

a play about this talented and complex character entitled *Davin: The Politician* (1979). See also R. Plant, "Davin, Nicholas Flood," in *Oxford Companion*, p. 132.

32 Regina *Leader*, 24 Jan. 1884.

33 It would be very difficult to establish the date of the first theatrical production in the North-West Territories even if one restricted it to presentations by the white community. Stuart's *History of Prairie Theatre* and John Orrell's *Fallen Empires: The Lost Theatres of Edmonton* (Edmonton 1981) both cite performances in the 1880s, while a Mounted Policeman stationed at Fort Macleod reported a December, 1877 presentation by the Drama Club (H.A. Dempsey, ed, *William Parker: Mounted Policeman* (Calgary 1973), p. 132). However, it would not be surprising to discover that an even earlier dramatic presentation had taken place at a location such as Fort Walsh, the main Mounted Police quarters in the 1870s.

34 "Reminiscences," pp. 41-42.

35 The account in the Regina *Leader*, 16 Nov. 1886, reported that Dewdney had suggested that the performance be repeated in aid of the Territorial Hospital and that Deane had agreed. Whether this took place is not known.

In February 1887, Deane presented a dual offering at the barracks: a repeat of *Ici on parle français* and *Chimney Corner* by "Henry Thornton Craven," the pen name of Henry Thornton. As had been his practice from the first, Deane sent Police horses and sleighs into Regina to transport townspeople to the barracks over two miles distant. This procedure guaranteed an audience in anything but the most impossible of winter weather. Once again the cast was a mixture of town and barracks, and their efforts were well received.[36] The same was true of William Schwenk Gilbert's *Engaged* which was presented, along with John Maddison Morton's *Steeple Chase*, for two nights in January 1888. Deane had come across Gilbert's play in Toronto while on a recruiting drive and enjoying some leave a few months earlier and he had immediately bought up a supply of the books. He was delighted with the cast he was able to gather in Regina and considered the play one of the most successful he ever produced.[37] As had been the case with some previous productions Deane was aided on this occasion by an experienced theatre man named Tim Dunne,[38] who played a small role in the play but was of great help in preparing sets. The final performance of Deane and his "Company" before a Regina audience was on 22 February 1888, when they played a double bill: *Sweethearts* also by Gilbert, and *Turkish Bath* by Francis C. Burnand.[39]

Even assuming that he presented no other plays in Regina, Deane's accomplishments were not inconsiderable. At the very least, during his five years in Regina he had produced, and almost always took a lead in, eight plays, one of which was a repeat. He had constructed a theatre of sorts, stage fittings, and a variety of sets. He had gathered what seems to have been competent cast members, a number of whom were in several of his productions. In no sense did he find the Regina personnel inferior to those he had encountered in Chatham/Rochester. He even mentioned, without any mocking overtones, that one of the actresses had intended to go on the English stage. Productions in Regina seem to have been of equal quality to those he had presented at Chatham. Deane had used a mixed cast of personnel from town and barracks in both Chatham and Regina and he did not rate the productions in the Prairie community as deficient. On the contrary, he considered that the Regina performance of *Engaged* was one of his greatest triumphs in the theatre. Indeed, these early performances seem to have been of commendable quality. The location may have been frontier, but persons like Deane brought to it the knowledge, experience and skills of the English cultural metropolis. Deane was transferred from Regina to the command of the Lethbridge Division in 1888. For the next fourteen years the

---

36 The production was reviewed in Regina *Leader*, 1 March 1887. The report stated that Deane's performance as Peter Probity in *Chimney Corner* repeatedly brought down the house, while in his repeat role of Victor Dubois in the second play Deane gave "a capital picture of the typical stage Frenchman with his broken English and monkey like gestures."

37 The Regina *Leader*, 31 Jan. 1888, had much praise for the performance. Deane himself played the leading role of Cheviot Hill in *Engaged*. One unique feature of the cast was that Mrs. Deane played a small role, evidently the only occasion that she appeared in one of Deane's productions.

38 Aside from Deane's allusion to Dunne's expertise, Stuart's *Prairie Theatre*, p. 47, refers to a T.H. Dunne (surely the same man) as an "active Dramatic Club member" in Calgary in 1884.

39 See review in Regina *Leader*, 28 Feb. 1888. Once again Deane took the male lead in the Gilbert play, the part of Harry Spreadbrow. The *Leader* was generally positive about the production but did note that "a word of praise must be awarded to the prompter, whose office on this occasion could not be called a sinecure."

Deanes resided in Lethbridge and thoroughly enjoyed the experience.[40] But he brought more than his family with him. Two leading members of his Regina troupe, Inspector and Mrs. White Fraser, were also transferred. Moreover, Tim Dunne joined the gathering in Lethbridge when he received his discharge from the Mounties. In fact, Deane was instrumental in getting Dunne a permanent position with the major employer in Lethbridge, the Alberta Railway and Coal Company.

Deane had barely settled before his theatrical skills were called into demand, evidently by C.F. Conybeare, KC, who requested that Deane prepare a dramatic entertainment in aid of the fund to buy pews for the new Anglican church.[41] Deane agreed in a minute to present a short play, provided that "local ladies and gentlemen would contribute some music for the first half of the evening."[42] This was easily arranged, but according to Deane's "Reminiscences," the program had to wait until the stage could be readied, even though previous performances had gone off at the barracks quite well. Nevertheless, as in Regina, Deane modified one of the buildings at the barracks:

> The Division mess room was a fine big room opening through double doors into a spacious kitchen. It was easy to construct proscenium and stage fittings in a more or less permanent form and to leave a passageway about eight feet wide through the stage without in the least interfering with the ordinary purposes of the rooms.[43]

On the stage the wife of the manager of the Union Bank, "an accomplished musician with a sweet voice," presented a fine program of music "ably supported" by several others.[44] Deane, along with Mr. and Mrs. White Fraser, performed the three-character little comedy *Cut off with a Shilling* by S. Theyre Smith. Their efforts were much

---

40 On the history of Lethbridge see A. Johnston and A. den Otter, *Lethbridge: A Centennial History* (Lethbridge 1985); and A. den Otter, *Civilizing the West: The Galts and the Development of Western Canada* (Edmonton 1982).

41 Deane's "Reminiscences" appear to be incorrect in several specifics concerning this matter. It is true that Deane produced *Cut off With a Shilling* in August, 1888, as a benefit for St. Augustine's, but the performance for the pew fund took place in December 1889, in response to a request Conybeare had made seven months earlier (Lethbridge *News*, 1 May, 6 Nov. and 4 Dec. 1889). It seems likely, therefore, that the modifications to the mess room described below probably took place in the summer of 1889 rather than in 1888.

42 "Reminiscences," p. 46. This was not the first entertainment at the barracks and assisted by the Mounties, in aid of St. Augustine's church. In April 1887, the band from the Fort Macleod Division and one Sergeant Monjean, a capable violinist, had lent their support (Lethbridge *News*, 27 Apr. 1887). Other denominations, most particularly the Presbyterians, also used barracks' facilities for fund-raising concerts (ibid., 22 Dec. 1887). Indeed the barracks had even been the site of earlier dramatic performances. The 1887 Christmas entertainment of the Presbyterians had included a scene from *School for Scandal* (ibid.), while the one in support of St. Augustine's ended off with the farce *Martyr to Science*, which "provoked hilarious mirth" amongst the audience (ibid., 14 and 22 Dec. 1887). In January 1888, it was announced that a dramatic club had been formed at the barracks and that it was expected to put on a production before long (ibid., 26 Jan. 1888), but no record of a performance by this group, prior to Deane's arrival, has been uncovered. There was, however, an entertainment in April 1888, which included three scenes from *Bluebeard* and two from *Bohemian Girl* (ibid., 19 Apr. 1888). Frequently, dances lasting into the early hours followed the performances. In any case, it is quite evident that Lethbridge had not waited for Deane before beginning its theatrical endeavours.

43 "Reminiscences," p. 46.

44 Ibid., p. 47.

appreciated. The Lethbridge *News* vowed that it was the best entertainment ever given in the town and had attracted an overflow crowd: "The acting of Capt. Deane and Mr. and Mrs. White Fraser was pronounced by competent critiques to be equal to many professionals."[45] The evening netted the church fund some $100, no mean sum in those days and the equivalent of $5000 in 1993. A similar concert/play presentation was engineered sixteen months later with Deane selecting *Dearest Mama* for the occasion. The event was lauded by the local newspaper as "one of the most pleasing entertainments the people of the West have had the good fortune to patronize" and Deane's acting was complimented as "simply splendid."[46] In-between these projects in aid of the Anglican Church, Deane staged a repeat of his Regina productions of *Chimney Corner* and *Ici on parle français*. The beneficiary of two consecutive evenings of performance was the acquisitions fund for the recreation room at the barracks. Once again, Deane and Mrs. White Fraser were specially commended by the critic for acting in both plays "as though in the manner born."[47]

These offerings were but a prelude to a more challenging enterprise in March, 1890 — a fully costumed production of Dance's comic drama *Wonderful Woman*. For the production Tim Dunne provided valuable assistance to Deane both off and on stage, while the cast, composed of a preponderance of townsfolk, proved more than satisfactory. The reviewer for the Lethbridge *News* was mightily impressed:

> For amateurs, it was an exceedingly ambitious undertaking to place a drama of the nature of "The Wonderful Woman" before a critical audience — and such, strange to say, is frequently found in the west — yet, when it became known that it was under the direction of a gentleman who bears more than a local reputation, none doubted its success.
>
> The plot of the above piece is laid in the time of Louis XIV. The costumes are, therefore, picturesque; the manner stiff; the dialogue stilted, and the humor frequently ponderous, yet it was amusing to note how quickly, from the "dress circle" to "gods," every stroke of wit was appreciated.
>
> The scenery, painted by local artists, was pretty and effective, the tapestried chamber in Madam Bertrand's house being particularly well executed.
>
> The part of the Marquis of Frontignac was taken by Capt. Deane, and, it is needless to say, was admirably done. Enconiums have long since been exhausted in describing that gentleman's excellencies as an actor, and we were glad to see that his efforts of producing the first dress play in the Territories met with the encouragement it so richly deserved.[48]

To receive such a response must have been most satisfying, but what really interested Deane about this production was the process of providing costumes for the characters:

> I procured the necessary wigs in Chicago, and, for the rest, I.G. Baker & Co., of St. Louis, had had in the town since its inception a general store which was able to supply

---

45 Lethbridge *News*, 22 Aug. 1888. "Critiques" is an obsolete form of "critics." The *News* also was complimentary about the decorations and fittings of the stage.

46 Ibid., 4 Dec. 1889.

47 Ibid., 21 Nov. 1888.

48 Ibid., 19 March 1890. This account went on to provide complimentary evaluations of the performances of the rest of the cast members. It is difficult to know the validity of its being the first dress play in the Territories, for the claim would seem to depend on the elaborateness of the costumes. In any case Deane repeated the assertion in the "Reminiscences."

us with velveteens and such other finery as was needed to make our costumes. The making of the costumes was easy — there was resident in Lethbridge at the time an old lady named Mrs. Kean, wife of a Church warden, one of the old unconquerable breed of Canadian pioneers to whom difficulties were but flies to be "swatted," and she, with a pattern in one hand and a pair of scissors in the other, was not to be beaten by anything that required to be cut out. We procured, and where we could not procure, we invented patterns, and there was no lack of willing workers to complete the job. The costumes were as well turned out as any I had ever hired.[49]

Deane was well-satisfied with the entire effort, not only with the dress play but also with the performance of *Betsey Baker* which concluded the evening's entertainment: "to me the most agreeable feature was the fraternal spirit that animated the whole Company. We all pulled together like a happy family."[50]

Deane was quite willing, therefore, to take the show the thirty-two miles to Fort Macleod for a third performance, all of which were in aid of the Presbyterian Church.[51] Three four-horse teams hauling wagons carried the Company: one for the ladies, one for the men, and the last for the scenery and properties:

At the Kipp Crossing of the Old Man's River the ice gave a disgruntled crack as the leading waggon [sic] reached the further shore, and no one was surprised when its immediate successor broke through into the water which we knew was not deep. Police horses, however, were well accustomed to such little interludes as that, and the property waggon lost no time in rejoining its companions on the opposite bank.[52]

The citizens of Fort Macleod repaid the troupe with a full house — for Deane's reputation for fine theatricals was well-known — an appreciative audience, a most enthusiastic report in the town newspaper, and a splendid banquet following the performance.[53]

Deane's "Reminiscences" provide little detail after this point. They merely indicate that various plays and concerts continued, frequently in support of worthy causes in Lethbridge and on occasion involving Deane's two daughters.[54] By late 1891 the Alberta Railway and Coal Company had erected a substantial building containing a

---

49   "Reminiscences," pp. 48-49.

50   Ibid., p, 49. The Lethbridge *News*, 19 March 1890, considered that the concluding farce "suffered very much from following so closely its ambitious predecessor," though it maintained that the performers themselves did a good job.

51   On this occasion, however, *Betsey Baker* was replaced by *Cut off With a Shilling* as the accompaniment to the main feature. It was anticipated that in spite of healthy audiences the heavy costs of the production would not leave a lot for the Presbyterian fund (Lethbridge *News*, 19 March 1890).

52   "Reminiscences," p. 50. Deane reported that one of the cast members, the lawyer C.C. McCaul, KC, made some sketches of this episode that were later published in the *London Sporting and Dramatic News*.

53   Macleod *Gazette*, 27 March 1890. The reporter made the following assessment of Deane's acting: "There was not much scope for his well known talent for acting, and his faithful rendering of the character was, therefore, all the more creditable."

54   In January 1889, both daughters participated in a Sunday School concert. One played the piano while the other acted in a little play and sang a part in Gilbert and Sullivan's *Three Little Maids from School* from *The Mikado* (Lethbridge *News*, 16 Jan. 1889). The pianist also participated in the December 1889 entertainment on the same occasion that *Dearest Mama* was performed (Lethbridge *News*, 4 Dec. 1889). One of Deane's daughters played a small role in *Wonderful Woman* in 1890 (see Macleod *Gazette*, 27 March 1890). Both Misses Deane also performed in an 1891 concert at the barracks in aid of the Protestant Cemetary Fencing Fund (see Lethbridge *News*, 16 Jan. 1891).

large auditorium which provided an alternative to the barracks' mess room for the staging of plays and concerts. Deane aided its construction by offering a benefit performance of *Ici on parle français* in September 1891, and then inaugurated the facility in December 1891, with the dual presentation of John Oxenford's *Porter's Knot* and James Kenney's operatic farce *Illustrious Stranger*.[55] In 1892 he became a member of the executive committee of a newly created musical and dramatic club in the city.[56] Two months later, in the Company Hall, he produced Henry James Byron's *Not Such a Fool as He Looks*, and himself played the role of the honourable, if confused and innocent, Sir Simon Simple. While the Lethbridge *News* praised the quality of the production, its report indicated slender attendance for the two evenings of presentation.[57] However, the turnout for a December 1894 musical and dramatic entertainment was much better, in spite of a terrible wind, and $80 was raised for St. Augustine's Anglican Church. For the occasion Deane produced and took a major role in Charles James Mathews' comedy *Who killed Cock Robin?*[58] Deane was significantly less active in theatre after that point. He had filled an important gap in local theatre but had no vested interest in remaining dominant in the field when others were able to take over. Thus as the 1890s wore on, his theatricals were superceded by other local amateur groups and by touring professional companies, although variety nights in aid of worthy causes continued at the barracks with Deane's full approval.

During the 90s Deane was given the chance to present a play written by a Lethbridge citizen and with a local setting. As the plays Deane produced were invariably British imports having little local flavour — except for occasional inserts such as the reference to the liquor law added to the 1886 Regina production of *Dearest Mama*[59] — this might have seemed a golden opportunity. But to Deane it was merely an amusing anecdote for, as he explained, there were problems with the proposal made by the author:

> He had christened it "The Mirage" ... and said it had to do with a murder which had been committed on the prairie and which had been discovered by means of a mirage, that is to say by its reflection in the sky! Describing the surroundings and details at considerable length he said that the murder would turn out to have been committed by the local superintendent of police, and he wanted me to play the villain.[60]

The prospect of portraying himself in such light no doubt was anathema to Deane, but what he told the author was that the staging of a mirage would be terribly difficult and he'd need time to think it over. The writer, an official with the Coal Company, was sufficiently discouraged that he never troubled Deane again. It would not have done for an actual Mounted Police officer to play the role of a murdering Mountie, but it would have been uncharacteristic for Deane to have played a genuine villain in any case.

According to Deane's "Reminiscences," his own participation in theatre entirely

---

55 Lethbridge *News*, 16 Sept. and 30 Dec. 1891.
56 Ibid., 2 March 1892.
57 Ibid., 11 May 1892.
58 Ibid., 5 Dec. 1894.
59 The Lethbridge *News*, 19 March 1890, indicated that there were some "local hits" in the production of *Betsey Baker*. In its evaluation of the 1892 production of *Illustrious Stranger*, the *News* found the local jokes an interruption and "tiresome" (see ibid., 30 Dec. 1891).
60 "Reminiscences," pp. 52-53.

ceased after 1897 when he was given charge of the large force of Mounted Policemen stationed at Fort Macleod, in addition to continued superintendency of the Lethbridge Division. The burden of these extensive duties, which required him to spend part of each week in each location, made it difficult for Deane to mount theatrical productions. But in his "Reminiscences" he had forgotten his theatrical swan song in Lethbridge. In April 1901 he participated in yet another evening of amateur entertainment on behalf of St. Augustine's. For this, his final production of *Dearest Mama*, Deane enlisted the talents of his daughter and "some of the most prominent amateurs of Lethbridge." The *News* found the presentation worthy of the highest praise and Deane's performance as most commendable.[61] But that seems to have been the end of Deane's theatrical activities. He was transferred to the Maple Creek Division in 1902 and subsequently to the Calgary Division in 1906, but Deane did not resume his involvement in theatre. In later years, however, he recalled his lengthy involvement in magical and theatrical entertainment with fondness and as worthy of being recorded. The modern-day historian of pioneer theatre in Saskatchewan and Alberta can only be grateful that he left behind those recollections in his "Reminiscences."

Let us now return to the four questions itemized at the beginning of this paper. In the first place it is clear that the role of the military in promoting dramatic productions after Confederation was continued in the pioneer west by the North West Mounted Police, a body modelled very much on military principles and practices. Deane may have been the most prominent example of the extension of the tradition but certainly he was not the only one. Indeed, one can hardly examine the record of the force in any locale of the North-West Territories without encountering some involvement in theatrical activities.

No doubt the motivations of military personnel were complex, including boredom and a desire to improve and cement community-police relations. Deane's involvement certainly was successful in regard to the latter objective. When an 1891 production in Lethbridge was delayed because of Deane's illness, the local newspaper voiced its concern for the welfare of "that popular gentleman,"[62] and although his good standing was due to more than his theatrical activities, they helped. So attached to Deane was the Lethbridge community that when his transfer was ordered in 1891, an aggressive and successful campaign was undertaken by its leading citizens to retain him.[63] But it would be erroneous to think that Deane's motivation was different from that of other actors and producers. One simply cannot comprehend the amount of time, expertise, and energy he devoted to the stage over so many years without crediting him both with a sense of responsibility to do his part to provide for the enlightenment and entertainment of his social peers and with a sheer love for and devotion to the theatre.

The matter of the quality of Deane's productions may be divided into two parts: the plays themselves and their performance. We know that Deane produced fourteen different plays in Canada. Thirteen of them had initially been performed in London between 1849 and 1877 at such theatres as the Lyceum, the Adelphi, the Olympic, Theatre Royal (Haymarket), the Princess, and the Prince of Wales.[64] Few of the plays

---

61 *News*, 11 Apr. 1901. The evening raised the rather disappointing sum of about $55.
62 Ibid., 23 Dec. 1891.
63 Deane, *Mounted Police Life*, p. 61.
64 Information on each one of these plays is contained in Allardyce Nicoll's monumental *A History of*

have left much of an imprint on the annals of the history of English theatre and, aside from W.S. Gilbert, the authors of the plays are not well-known today. But a cursory examination of the literature on English theatre in the third quarter of the nineteenth century suggests that Deane frequently used the better work of some quite popular and prolific writers of the time.[65] For, not only Gilbert, but Dance (*Wonderful Woman*), Morton (*Betsey Baker*), Byron (*Not Such a Fool as He Looks*), and Burnand (*Turkish Bath*) were all notable figures in English theatrical circles at the time. Deane's selections were also representative of English theatre of the period both in their emphasis on comedy and farce, and in their concentration on gender relations and on the characteristics, manners and foibles of leading social classes. In short, Deane's selections, though limited in both number and type, were not dissimilar to the fare that one might have expected for respectable audiences in the substantial county towns of England and what did appear in the major centres in Canada.[66]

If the plays themselves were not enormously different in quality to those appearing in older and more populous centres, an evaluation of Deane's productions is more difficult. The critiques appearing in local newspapers were overwhelmingly complimentary but this might have been a form of local boosterism expressing local pride more than critical judgement. While one must accept that these newspapers did not wish to discourage the participants by harsh criticism, it is also clear that they believed that the ability to evaluate productions was a mark of sophistication and culture. Therefore, they were not beyond pointing out deficiencies. For example, of one performer in *Porter's Knot*, the Lethbridge *News* stated that "his emotions had not that freedom and grace which characterizes a good actor."[67] The constant references in the press to the excellence of Deane's productions ought, therefore, to be given a good deal of credence, especially since the performances by other groups did not usually receive the same praise.[68] Then too, Deane's own evaluation did not denigrate

---

English Drama 1660-1900 in six volumes (Cambridge, 1923-1959). Unless used as part of a quotation, titles of plays produced by Deane are given in this paper as Nicoll has them, including capitalization. The fourteenth play was *Illustrious Stranger* which was first produced in 1827.

65 Of the numerous sources available the most helpful to the author in providing background to nineteenth century English theatre and of comedies/farces, one of the period's dominant genres, have been, aside from Nicoll, the following: E.J. Burton, *The Student's Guide to British Theatre and Drama* (London 1963); M. Booth, *Prefaces to English Nineteenth-Century Theatre* (Manchester n.d.); J.O. Bailey, *British Plays of the Nineteenth Century* (New York 1966); E. Reynolds, *Early Victorian Drama (1830-1870)* (New York 1965; reprint of 1936 publication); A.H. Thorndike, *English Comedy* (New York 1965; reprint of 1929 publication); A. Bermel, *Farce: A History From Aristophanes to Woody Allen* (New York 1982); J.M. Davis, *Farce* (Bristol 1978); N.W. Sawyer, *The Comedy of Manners from Sheridan to Maugham* (New York 1961; reprint of 1931 publication); and G. Powell, *The Victorian Theatre 1792-1914: A Survey* (London 1978; 2nd edition).

66 For example, *Ici on parle français* appears three times in M.M. Brown and N. Rewa, "Ottawa Calendar of Performance in the 1870s," *Theatre History in Canada*, 4:2 (Fall 1983) 134-191; *Chimney Corner* receives five entries in the index of M.E. Smith, *Too Soon the Curtain Fell: A History of Theatre in Saint John 1789-1900* (Fredericton 1981); *Betsey Baker* was one of the plays the son-in-law of Queen Victoria and Canadian Governor General, Lord Lorne, attended in Ottawa in 1882 (see J. Noonan, "Lord Lorne Goes to the Theatre, 1878-1883," *Theatre History in Canada*, 11:1 (Spring 1990) 36); and Deane's "Reminiscences" show that in 1887 there was a production of *Engaged* in Toronto.

67 Lethbridge *News*, 30 Dec. 1891.

68 A performance by one group in 1900 received the following comment in the Lethbridge *News*, 23 Aug. 1900: "Those who were not present did not miss much of a treat."

his Canadian productions in comparison with those he had undertaken in England. His casts, though amateur, usually contained a number of able and experienced actors. Indeed, the sophistication and breadth of both performers and audiences in the Territories were considerable. This may have been a frontier, but it included persons such as the previously-mentioned Nicholas Flood Davin, who had arrived in Regina via Cork, London, Paris, Belfast and Toronto; Francis Dickens, Mounted Policeman and son of novelist Charles Dickens; Charles Mair, the Shakespeare-quoting immigration agent and author of the 1886 Canadian drama *Tecumseh*; and Rev. A.M. Gordon, better known as Ralph Connor, who learned of the lumber shanties he wrote about in his novels on Glengarry from the "fighting parson" of Lethbridge, Rev. Charles McKillop.[69] The point is not that any of these persons necessarily saw any of Deane's productions — although it is a good bet that at least Davin, Mair, and McKillop did — rather, it is that the west was littered with people of extraordinary breadth, knowledge and talent. The Regina and Lethbridge audiences attending Deane's productions included individuals of wide-ranging experience who would not easily accept effusive newspaper reviews that were blatantly uncritical. The composition of the audience was seldom reported in newspaper accounts, but it is certain that the elite attended Deane's productions. Clearly, the promoters of the entertainments and the cast members included leaders — or their spouses or children — of the political, judicial, religious, and business sectors. This is best illustrated by the 31 January 1888 issue of the Regina *Leader* which reported that "His Honor Lieut. Gov. and Mrs. Dewdney with His Lordship Bishop Pinkham and Mr. Justice and Mrs. Wetmore were present" at Deane's production of *Engaged*. It would seem, therefore, that what the newspapers wrote about the high quality of Deane's work must not be regarded as lacking in substance. On the other hand, of course, the question of what constituted a "good" show might be raised, for the special need of people in pioneer communities to establish the basics of "civilization" may well have influenced their evaluation of the quality of the productions. Yet their views differ little from the evaluation of Deane's productions by audiences and critics in Rochester/Chatham on the doorstep to London back in England. In all likelihood, and even if one applies quite demanding criteria, Deane's work was of a high standard.

Of what significance was the military's role in establishing theatre in the North-West Territories, as seen in the case of R.B. Deane? Firstly, one must note that the paramilitary Mounties were instrumental in early theatrical productions and other types of dramatic and musical entertainments in practically every community in which they were established. The Mounties not only provided the performers and production crew but also the facilities and an important portion of the audience. It is true that the force benefitted by using such congenial means to establish positive relations with local citizens, especially the elite, but the communities were greatly enriched as well. Deane's productions, for example, provided an outlet for local amateur performers, supported charities, and provided a connection with the culture of such a dominant centre of the English-speaking world as London, where most of

---

69   On Dickens see the semi-fictional work by Eric Nicol, *Dickens of the Mounted* (Toronto 1989). Concerning Mair see N. Shrive, *Charles Mair: Literary Nationalist* (Toronto 1965). The information about Gordon's indebtedness to McKillop appears in J.D. Higginbotham, *When The West Was Young* (Toronto 1933), 156-158. McKillop was one of the best boxers and wrestlers in the community and was not reticent to demonstrate his prowess.

the plays Deane presented were originally performed. Regina and Lethbridge might have had their cow dung and vacant vistas but they also had William Schwenck Gilbert and John Maddison Morton. Moreover, Deane's activities formed a base for the evolution of amateur groups and even the touring professional companies that appeared in places like Lethbridge during the 1890s.[70]

Finally, an examination of the importance of Deane's productions must pay brief attention to the social function of theatrical offerings within a community. In part, as has been indicated, Deane's plays kept those who formed the new elite groups in frontier Prairie towns in touch with the culture of the English metropolis. A superficial examination might suggest that this was an alien import because the activities of the leading social classes in England, which formed the core of the plays Deane produced, might seem to be of little relevance to life in newly-established pioneer communities. Yet there were social issues raised in the plays which were of concern even in these Prairie centres. Two examples must suffice. The first is the very matter of social class. In Victorian England, of course, social classes were in flux as the landed aristocracy was having to make room for the plutocracy and both groups were being pushed by an increasingly large number of "respectable" middle class citizens.[71] In pioneer western towns there was also a jostling for social dominance, but here society was particularly imbued with democratic and utilitarian values. Worth to the community, not accident of birth, was the basis of social leadership in the west. Audiences were no doubt amused by the pretensions and foibles of the gentry in *Engaged* in which Cheviot Hill, the character played by Deane, goes about proposing marriage to every woman he meets but also proves himself to be a thorough-going miser. All the other characters in the play also demonstate that whatever class they emanate from, their prime motivation is greed and their sense of honour entirely dubious. The question of class was also examined in *Not Such a Fool as He Looks*. Here, Sir Simon Simple, played by Deane, is "a sympathetically conceived aristocratic fool whose heart is as pure as gold..."[72] As the play progresses Simple discovers that his lineage is not aristocratic but, as he first thinks, lower class, only to find out that his blood parents are actually of the middle class, though not married to one another. Thus, whatever dignity Simple possesses, and whatever course his life takes, are due not to his status of birth but to his own innate character and are under his own direction. These plays, and others like them, therefore presented Prairie elites with images of personalities and actions that should be avoided if they were to be the true, useful leaders of their community.

A second social issue of particular relevance on the Prairies was the matter of gender relations.[73] The Canadian West, like other pioneer societies, was one which

---

70   It is hardly coincidental that Deane's productions petered out in the 90s at the same time as a number of touring companies placed Lethbridge on their itinerary. On occasion these groups used the theatre at the barracks (see Lethbridge *News*, 6 Jan. 1891).

71   Of the numerous works on the social history of Victorian England, three are particularly rich in analyzing the internal concerns and dynamics of the society: W.E. Houghton, *The Victorian Frame of Mind 1830-1870* (New Haven 1957); H. Perkin, *The Origins of Modern English Society 1780-1880* (London 1969); and F.M.L. Thompson, *The Rise of Respectable Society: A Social History of Victorian Britain* (London 1988).

72   Nicoll, *English Drama*, V, 112.

73   There is an enormous literature on the topic. Readers might begin with Peter Gay's *The Bourgeois*

was dominated by males, or so it seemed. The prime economic activities of ranching, mining, construction, and farming attracted single males to the area and resulted in an enormous imbalance in male-female ratios. In 1901, for example, there were 2 single males in Lethbridge for every single female.[74] In a territory where there were limited opportunities for men to meet eligible women it was a dilemma for males to know how to relate to females. But this was not so different from middle and upper class males in England who, like Deane, attended segregated schools[75] and then joined the military. Dances at the barracks were one answer, but plays which explored male-female relations were another. In Act I of *Sweethearts*, Spreadbrow, played by Deane, is desperately in love with a woman who appears to be coolly aloof to him. In the second act they meet again thirty years later, but Spreadbrow has virtually forgotten his former attraction, while the woman, far from being indifferent, has carried the torch for him for three decades. By showing the absurdity of the relationship at both points in time, the play thus carried the message that both men and women should avoid the nonsense of romantic sentimentalism and the playing of games in male-female relationships. Moreover, *Illustrious Stranger* and *Not Such a Fool as He Looks* demonstrated the determination and dignity of women who had the right and the ability to determine for themselves how they would lead their lives and to whom they would give their hearts. Indeed, in Deane's productions it was the males who tended to be the fools while the females were more frequently depicted as being controlled, intelligent and rational. While the characterization of women in these plays was hardly an advanced position, at least it was not the gross misrepresentation that found currency in male enclaves where women were seen as a separate species, beyond comprehension, to be dominated and used, as well as protected, indulged and ultimately elevated. Any modification of this stereotype was all to the good, especially since Prairie women were daily demonstrating their enormous contribution to the development of pioneer communities, in activities quite as essential as those of males.

In the final analysis, therefore, Deane's involvement in theatre was an important

---

Experience: Victoria to Freud (2 vols: New York 1984) including the bibliographical essays at the end of each volume. Note also the following: E. Helsinger and R. Sheets (eds), *The Woman Question: Society and Literature in Britain and America, 1837-1883* (3 vols: London 1983); M. Vicinus (ed), *Suffer and Be Still: Women in the Victorian Age* (London 1972); M. Vicinus (ed), *A Widening Sphere: Changing Roles of Victorian Women* (London 1977); B. Harrison, *Separate Spheres: The Opposition to Women's Suffrage in Britain* (London 1978); R. Cook and W. Mitchinson (eds), *The Proper Sphere: Women's Place in Canadian Society* (Toronto 1976); B. Light and J. Parr (eds), *Canadian Women on the Move, 1867-1920* (Toronto 1983); E.L. Silverman, *The Last Best West: Women on the Alberta Frontier 1880-1930* (Montreal 1984); P.N. Stearns, *Be A Man! Males in Modern Society* (New York 1979); and J.A. Mangan and J. Walvin (eds), *Manliness and Morality: Middleclass Masculinity in Britain and America, 1800-1940* (New York 1987).

74 Canada: Census of 1901, I, 132-133. Prostitution flourished under such circumstances (see J.H. Gray, *Red Lights on the Prairies* (Toronto 1971)). In his capacity as Mounted Police officer, Deane preferred to control rather than attempt to eradicate red-light districts.

75 The classic depiction of the boys school for the privileged, *Tom Brown's Schooldays* by Thomas Hughes, was published in 1859 when Deane himself was a schoolboy. There is, of course, an interesting contrast between the virtues taught in Hughes' work — of being religious, defending the weak, working hard, being forthright and honest, and of nobility depending on actions rather than birth or wealth — and the characteristics of the males in the plays Deane produced. See also J. Chandos, *Boys Together: English Public Schools 1800-1864* (New Haven 1984).

component of his overall contribution to the development of white society in the Prairies. This Mounted Police officer cannot be seen simply in terms of bringing murderers, cattle smugglers and sundry miscreants to heel. The breadth of his activities was extensive, including stints filling in for Anglican clergymen, organizing and playing on cricket teams, and experimenting with the growing of vegetables and trees on the barren plains. But theatre was one of his great loves and to it he brought much expertise and skill. Dramatic offerings preceded Deane's arrival and survived his retirement from the stage, but the contributions made by this military man to the development of theatre on the Prairies in the 1880s and 1890s were significant and are entirely worthy of recognition by historians of theatre in Canada. Equally, the case of Deane demonstrates that further detailed examination of the role of the military in the establishment of theatre in Canada promises to be richly rewarding.

NOTE

This chapter was previously published in *Theatre Research in Canada/Recherches Théâtrales au Canada*, 14, no. 1 (spring 1993), 31-59. Illustrations in the original have been omitted. The author gratefully acknowledges the research assistance provided by the University of Lethbridge, the Social Sciences Research Council of Canada and the Alberta Historical Resources Foundation. To my U. of L. colleagues George Mann, Martin Oordt, Ches Skinner and David Spinks I express my appreciation for their helpful comments, interest and support.

SIXTEEN

Character

Keith Walden

The nineteenth century was an age of heroes. Of course, the ideal of a man striving for righteousness in a world of evil and danger has a universal appeal, and since fundamental human virtues remain relatively constant there has always been a similarity in the depiction of romantic heroes. But the nineteenth century found the hero especially attractive because he represented a release from many of the problems of modernity, including overly developed reflective thought, and increasing social regulation and fragmentation. The twentieth century inherited these concerns, and though there has been some tendency in recent years, especially in serious literature, to reject the traditional figure in favour of the anti-hero, the hero remains an important ideal, a symbol of "wholeness, unself-conscious passion and the ability to act."[1]

The nineteenth century desired heroes, and one of those it found and cultivated was the Mounted Policeman. As was usually the case, once granted this status, the Mountie became a convenient peg on which to hang a whole cluster of attributes associated with his type. The character of the policeman, at one level, was entirely predictable; all the requisite virtues of the hero were there. At another level, however, the characterization of the Mountie was not as cut and dried, for the preoccupations of the era that embraced him led to an emphasis of particular qualities within the conventional spectrum of heroic character. The search for assurances of order, progress, and morality were clearly reflected in descriptions of the policeman, so that while he conformed completely to the traditions of the centuries-old romantic genre, he was also indisputably a symbol of the age that spawned him.

It would be wrong to conclude that because the heroic image was conventional, no thought went into the characterization of the policeman. To the society that focused so much attention on the force, character was exceptionally important, a fact attested to by the existence of masses of books, pamphlets, and articles that taught how to develop it, and described those who already had it. Small wonder! The notion of character was essential to those who wanted to achieve both a moral and a social

---

1   Walter Reed, *Meditations on the Hero: A Study of the Romantic Hero in Nineteenth-Century Fiction* (New Haven and London: Yale University Press, 1974), p. 5.

order on the one hand, and a freely developed self on the other.[2] It was central to the liberal-democratic ethos of the age. Democracy theoretically freed individuals from traditional class restraints, but it also forced them to accept responsibility for their own position in society. If everyone had an equal chance at salvation, justice, and opportunity, then inequality could only be explained by differences in character. Accidents of birth and background did not determine a man's fate; innate abilities did. This message provided hope for those at the bottom of the social heap and ideological security for those at the top. The rich could not be blamed for the unfortunate position of others. Success, status, and happiness lay within the reach of all. Those who doubted had only to look at the example of the Mounted Policeman.

Composition of the Force

"In every sense of the word," declared the *Times* of London a mere six years after the founding of the force, "the Canadian Northwest Mounted Police has been a corps d'elite." The *Times* might have been surprised to know that some residents of the Canadian West, not so enamoured with the Mounted, were beginning to point to instances of improper police conduct, including drunkenness, consorting with prostitutes, mismanagement, and corruption. The *Times* might have been shocked to learn that of the first men recruited by the force, two were blind in one eye, five had acute heart disease, and others suffered from tuberculosis, syphilis, varicose veins, and a leg fracture, all of which conditions had existed prior to enlistment.[3] But it did not know, nor did most people. The judgment of the *Times* was representative of the popular consensus.

The members of the force have always been considered a special group, exceptional in their characters and abilities. Not just anyone, it was felt, could join; entry was difficult. "The North Western Buck," observed one admirer, "is always a picked man." In part, this was credited to a supply of applicants that always exceeded the demand; the force could pick and choose among "exceptionally fine material." But merely outshining other candidates was no guarantee of acceptance into the corps. Those admitted, one novelist told his readers in 1923, had to prove themselves worthy by a variety of tests, and once enrolled had to live up to the traditions of the force or they would be fired. "Only men of sterling qualities and almost physical perfection are permitted to join," insisted another.[4] The force, in other words, did not simply choose the best available. It chose only if it could get the best.

---

2   Warren Susman, "'Personality' and the Making of Twentieth-Century Culture" in John Higham and Paul Conkin, eds., *New Directions in American Intellectual History* (Baltimore and London: Johns Hopkins University Press, 1980), p. 214. Susman argues that in the late nineteenth century ideas about character began to change. In earlier decades, the notion involved an emphasis on qualities of service that promoted communal ends. By the 1890s the vision of self-sacrifice was beginning to be displaced by a vision of self-realization. Character, in the age of mass society, began to involve the development of "personality," of traits that would allow the individual to stand out and be noticed. While Susman is persuasive that some change was taking place, his case is probably a bit overstated. It seems likely that older notions were augmented rather than completely superseded by the new ones. In any event, the Mountie clearly encompassed both.

3   The *Times*, August 22, 1879; E.C. Morgan, "The Northwest Mounted Police: Internal Problems and Public Criticism, 1874-1883," *Saskatchewan History*, xxvi (1973), pp. 42, 61.

4   E.B. Osborn, "Warden of the West," *Cornhill Magazine*, n.s. viii (1900), p.775; the *Times*, August 22, 1879; F. Haydn Dimmock, *The Man From Freezing Point* (London: C. Arthur Pearson, 1923), p. 169; William Campbell, *Arctic Patrols* (Milwaukee: The Bruce Publishing Co., 1936), p. 329.

Occasionally, it was admitted, an unworthy prospect did manage to get through the screening process. Even the staunchest defenders of the police acknowledged that some misfits were taken in. However, these were soon discovered. According to R.G. MacBeth, Presbyterian minister, historian, and fervent admirer of the force, there was "an intangible but real atmosphere in the corps which in some quiet but definite fashion, eliminated any man who did not measure up to the mark which the members felt they ought to reach." There was, he assured his readers, no overt discrimination. Rather the unfortunate recruit would feel uncomfortable and leave quickly of his own accord. Charles Mair, on the other hand, maintained that the other policemen were not so passive. If a "hard character" crept into the force, Mair suggested, "he fared ill with his fellows, and speedily betook himself to other employment." Some mistakes were inevitable; the force was, after all, human, and it was bound to contain some weaklings, and incompetents. These were clearly exceptions though, and "the percentage of such [was] minute, as [was] the scope of error by comparison with the size and complexity of operations."[5] There were very few people in the police, it was believed, who did not belong.

The force, as its strict entrance requirements showed, was an exclusive organization, composed of highly select men. But while it was clearly an elite group, its membership was based on merit, not privilege. In fact, as many writers took pains to suggest, the backgrounds of its members were extremely diverse, for as long as recruits met its high standards, the force did not care where they came from. According to Agnes Deans Cameron, a Vancouver school teacher and author, more individuality went into the makeup of the Mounted Police than any other organization of its kind. It was "a combination of all sorts of men drawn together by the winds of heaven." The point was made by A.R. Douglas in his poem "Riders Four":

> There was Texas, he of the forty-five,
> Who could live on grass if need be,
> There was Jones who had last served before the mast
> On a whaler in the North Sea.
> And Jackson, gentleman of ease,
> With a castle in the old land,
> Who had hied away from the life so gay,
> On a bet, to be a cowhand.[6]

Such variety, while dispelling fears of unwarranted favouritism, also created a glamorous cosmopolitan image which did the force no harm.

There was one sort of diversity that was not frequently mentioned, however, and that involved race. The Mounted Police seemed to be composed almost exclusively of Anglo-Saxons and Celts. In the novels, this impression was universal. Fictional Mountie heroes had English names like Yorke, Passmore and Grey, Scottish names like MacRae, Cameron and MacLean, or Irish ones like Shannon and Clancy. Rarely in fiction was mention made of a French-Canadian policeman and almost never was

---

5   R.G. MacBeth, *Policing the Plains* (London: Hodder and Stoughton, n.d.), p. 37; MacBeth, "The Fame of the Mounted," *Scarlet and Gold* (1926), p. 73; Charles Mair, "A Tribute to the Royal North West Mounted Police," *Scarlet and Gold* (1919), p. 45; Frank Spalding, *Stop the Musical Ride, I Want Off* (Victoria: Gray's, 1972), p. 106.

6   Agnes Deans Cameron, "The Riders of the Plains," *Cornhill Magazine*, n.s. xxxiv (1913), p. 90; A.R. Douglas, "Riders Four," *Scarlet and Gold* (1922), p. 95.

there mention of policemen descended from the racial stock of continental Europe. The same was not true of villians. In the non-fiction, policemen with names like Griesback, Brisebois, Gagnon, Bazowski, Zaneth and Wendt occasionally appeared but did not stand out greatly in relief. Here too an impression was given that the force was quintessentially Anglo-Saxon. A few writers stated explicitly that "more often than not the Mounted Policeman is English-born" or that many troopers were "smart young fellows from the old country and eastern Canada,"[7] but as with the novels, the racial impression was implanted mainly through negative evidence. The contribution of French Canadians or "alien" races to the force was almost never discussed.

This sort of depiction was understandable in the late nineteenth and early twentieth centuries when Social Darwinist notions of race were influential. Most people of British background believed that the Anglo-Saxon race was innately superior, especially with respect to justice and organization. This helped them to explain why the force was so successful, and helped them as well to see a close connection between its triumphs and their own qualities. It also provided a comforting assurance that the development of the Canadian frontier was in the secure hands of the best race. By the 1940s, Social Darwinist racial theories had been largely discredited, but surprisingly little new emphasis was placed on the contribution to the force of some of the other elements in the Canadian mosaic. Perhaps there was a tendency to assume that even if other ethnic groups were not less intelligent or cultured, Anglo-Saxons were still socially superior. To maintain their elite status, the police also had to retain their charter-group roots.

Although foreigners were almost completely excluded from the popular conception of the force, care was taken to demonstrate the close cooperation within it of those men derived from British stock. In Harold Bindloss's novel of 1907, *Winston of the Prairie*, for example, Trooper Shannon, "an Irishman from the bush of Ontario" worked side by side with Trooper Payne, "English and a scion of a somewhat distinguished family in the old country…" Bindloss, who seems to have been inclined toward notions of Imperial Federation, perhaps emphasized this sort of collaboration because it provided a vivid example of the possibilities of a united empire, but other writers who did not share his outlook made similar portrayals. Samuel A. White, writing in the 1940s long after Imperial Federation had become a dead issue, brought together "Constable Driscoll from Prince Albert, a ruddy son of Erin," "Constable Fowler, a wiry Englishman out of the home dragoons," Constable Fraser, a Scottish trooper possessed of "a gleam like the flash of his own land's claymores" and Constable Stout, rugged, powerful, and Canadian born. Similarly Joseph Holliday, writing in the 1950s, matched his hero, Dale Thompson, with Terrence Sweeney, a young chap with "a strongly Irish look about him." In such a cooperative atmosphere even Americans, as long as they came from the proper stock, could be allowed into the force. Laurie York Erskine's creation, Corporal Renfrew, was American born, and so was Jack O'Brien's Constable Bradley.[8]

The emphasis on the diverse origins of the police helps to explain the popularity

---

7   Osborn, p.775; S.B. Steele, *Forty Years in Canada* (Toronto: H. Jenkins, 1915), p. 96.

8   H. Bindloss, *Winston of the Prairie* (New York: F.A. Stokes, 1907), pp. 22-23; Samuel A. White, *North West Crossing* (New York: Phoenix Press, 1944), pp. 117-20; Joe Holliday, *Dale of the Mounted* (Toronto: T. Allen, 1951), p. 25; Jack O'Brien, *Corporal Corey of the Royal Canadian Mounted* (Philadelphia and Toronto: Winston, 1936); Laurie York Erskine, *Renfrew Rides North* (New York: D. Appleton, 1931).

of the force outside of Canada. Since it was composed of all elements within the English-speaking community, each of those separate groups could identify more closely with the characters portrayed. For Britons and Americans the force was not necessarily a foreign preserve; it could be seen as an extension of their own cultures. Moreover, the fact that the force linked not simply different ethnic and national groups, but also the old world and the new, made it exciting and much more resonant with imaginative possibilities. The interaction of elements representing Europe and America was of interest on both sides of the Atlantic.

Members of the police, it was continually asserted, did not come from any particular class. They represented the full spectrum of society from the top to the bottom. However, what gave the force so much distinctiveness and exclusivity in the popular view was the fact that most men in it were extremely well bred. "The troopers were all men of good birth or instincts," wrote the novelist R.W. Campbell, and they represented the best blood of Canada, Britain, and America. John Mackie, who had served in the force, was equally insistent that "a very large percentage of the men belonging to the rank and file were gentlemen." His character, Sergeant Yorke, for example,

> like many more in his position seemed born for better things. Even now although his face was unshaven, although the stump of an old briar pipe protruded from between his lips, and his seedy old buffalo coat was buttoned up to his chin, one could see at a glance that Harry Yorke was a gentleman.[9]

This high quality of breeding and conduct apparently shone through during the rigours of a patrol.

Evident even at the worst of times, the refinement of the policeman was usually patently obvious. The Mountie was scrupulous about his appearance. Sergeant Silk, though in charge of a remote outpost where there were no neighbours to see him, "was as particular over his toilet as if he were preparing for a parade." "Dandy" Dorrance, on patrol in the wilderness, was "as immaculate as if he had just stepped out on the parade ground for inspection." The police, it was regularly asserted, were by habit "bandbox neat from clinking spur to forage cap balanced on its traditional three hairs." Of course, such neatness carried the possible implication that the Mountie never did anything rigorous. One observer asked of Sergeant Silk, pointing out that the policeman was just a bit too tidy and too consciously elegant, "Do you suppose that a dandy such as he is could do any real good in a scrimmage?" The questioner's companion provided him with the appropriate answer:

> The man you're looking at isn't always dressed as if he had just come out of a bandbox to parade his elegance and his good figure on a railroad platform. If he is clean and tidy now, it is because he hates slovenliness of any kind...[10]

He assured his friend that on occasion the Sergeant looked quite different.

Even more revealing of Mounted Police refinement than appearance were the skills and interests of individual policemen. Many had a wide knowledge of music.

---

9 Captain R.W. Campbell, *A Policeman from Eton* (London: J.M. Murray, 1923), pp. 4-5, 21; John Mackie, *Sinners Twain* (London: T. Fisher Unwin, 1895), pp. 27-28.

10 Robert Leighton, *The White Man's Trail* (London: C.A. Pearson, n.d.), p. 61; A. deHerries Smith, *Drums of the North* (New York: Macaulay, 1928), p. 198; Cameron, p. 92; Leighton, *Sergeant Silk, the Prairie Scout* (Cleveland: The World Syndicate Publishing Co., 1929), pp. 98-100.

Corporal Brown in the novel *Mountie on Trial* played the piano beautifully. The Inspector in William Lacey Amy's *The Lone Trail* was a connoisseur of the classics. Even Sergeant Benton, who usually played down his cultural interests, when asked if he was fond of reading and music replied:

> Aye! You just bet I am! ... I've read, and played, and sung every chance I've got — wherever I've been. Fond! — well, I should say I am. I fancy if it hadn't been for *that*, I'd have gone to the devil long ago.

Love of art and dancing was also widely evident.[11]

Proof of police gentility was especially obvious in the ability of the Mountie to conduct himself among the social elite, indeed in the very willingness of that elite to include him in their company. Sergeant Silk, invited to join a Colonel and a titled millionaire who were making the same rail journey, acted and was treated as their equal. Sergeant Floyd Morgan was on a first-name basis with the Governor of the Red River Colony. King of the Mounted vacationed with the president of a railroad. Occasionally these social abilities were even useful in combatting crime. In the oft-recounted Spanish Consul case, for example, a police sergeant impersonated a rich American businessman to infiltrate a smuggling ring which included the Spanish consul in Montreal:

> The Spanish consul looked at his prospective customer with satisfaction. Here was a man of obvious cleverness and wealth. He admired the immaculate haircut and fingernails, the expensively tailored suit that the American wore with such casual ease ... Here was a man accustomed to power, he thought.[12]

If his interaction with high society was relatively rare, it was because the Mountie had more important things to do, not because he was vulgar or boorish.

Professor R.C. Macleod, who has examined the social composition of the force up to 1905, suggests that although most rank-and-file policemen were recruited from the lower-middle class, they entertained exaggerated notions of their social status. This was due to their position in a force which had great prestige in western Canadian society and perhaps, as well, to a sense that their fortunes as a class were on the rise. Officers encouraged this view, since it helped to bolster the authority of their men.[13] It would seem, however, that the emphasis on the refinement of the police derived less from an understanding of the early aspirations of the force and more from preconceived notions.

For one thing, English-speaking societies have traditionally had a suspicion of standing armies and police forces, partly because they have often been composed of social dregs. The Mounted Police were clearly different. They were not thugs recruited from the streets of slums, nor were they mere mercenaries interested only

---

11   Oscar Olson, *Mountie on Trial* (Toronto: Ryerson, 1953), p. 2; William Lacey Amy [Luke Allan], *The Lone Trail* (London: H. Jenkins, 1922), p. 272; Ralph Kendall, *Benton of the Royal Mounted* (New York: John Lane Co., 1918), p. 278.

12   Leighton, *Sergeant Silk*, p. 100; Samuel A. White, *Morgan of the Mounted* (New York: Phoenix Press, 1939), p. 113; Zane Grey, *King of the Royal Mounted and the Ghost Guns of Roaring River* (Racine: Whitman, 1946), p. 248; Irvin Block, *The Real Book About the Mounties* (Garden City: Garden City Books, 1952), pp. 151-55.

13   Roderick Charles Macleod, *The North-West Mounted Police and Law Enforcement, 1873-1905* (Toronto: University of Toronto Press, 1976), pp. 85-87.

in a job. Respectable births and obvious refinement went a long way to prove this, especially to those influenced by the Social Darwinist ideas that good breeding and lineage were usually indications of moral and intellectual fitness. Moreover, the hero of romance almost always possesses refined and genteel qualities. These indicate his allegiance to the higher ideals of society, and it is his willingness to serve these ideals that makes him a hero.

So important was the belief in the well-bred nature of the force that assertions were continually made to the effect that some members were born of noble blood. According to the popular image, the force was a haven for young aristocrats. Declared one writer just after the turn of the century, "Dukes, earls and baronets galore have chased Indians and cattle-thieves, garbed in the scarlet tunic and blue trousers …" Some sixty years later, Charles Rivett-Carnac, an ex-Commissioner, still thought it significant to point out that the force included some of the younger sons of English aristocracy. Mountie novels were full of nobility. Constable Fate Westward was the son of Sir Edwin Kirkwaller. Inspector Weston was the future Earl of Erremount. Constable Bart Chester was related to Lord Sanford. Constable "Bunny" Rushmore was more properly known as Sir James Rushmore. Constable Montague was the Earl of Falkney and Dunleith. Less common in the ranks but still significant, it seemed, were offspring of the rich. The hero of Walter Liggett's novel, *The Frozen Frontier*, for example, had joined the force to prove himself at the urging of his father, a Wall Street millionaire.[14]

These origins did not count for much within the force itself. John Temple, his obituary declared, "had never told his fellow constables that he was a baronet. This isn't done in the Royal North-West Mounted Police." Policemen were modest, of course, but even if his associates had known, what did it matter? There were probably others of equal or greater rank who retained their secret. Besides, if every policeman was "in essence an aristocrat," the actual fact of noble birth was meaningless. More importantly, noble birth would not help a policeman do his duty. A Trooper like John Temple, it was asserted, "proves his real nobility when he rides into trouble … Men who make good in that force must be men when shorn of title and influence." In the police, as the Reverend MacBeth put it, "genuine manhood was the only hallmark allowed as a standard."[15]

Despite protestations that aristocratic birth was immaterial, many people clearly felt it was significant. Since only a very unusual force could attract this calibre of recruits, it certainly indicated that the police were no ordinary group of men. Perhaps as well, emphasis on the nobility of individual policemen helped shore up the contention that the privileged classes actually did a great deal to maintain their societies. This was not merely a self-serving attempt by the conservative establishment

---

14 L.R. Freeman, "The North West Mounted Police," *Overland Monthly*, March, 1904, p. 222; Charles Rivett-Carnac, *Pursuit in the Wilderness* (Boston, Toronto: Little, Brown, 1965), p. 136; Harwood Steele, *The Ninth Circle* (Toronto: McClelland and Stewart, 1927), p. 269; T. Lund, *The Vanished Prospector* (London: T. Werner-Laurie, 1937), p. 77; Samuel A. White, *Called Northwest* (London, 1944), p. 20; Robert Leighton, *The Red Patrol* (London: Jarrold and Sons, 1915), p. 116; Muriel Denison, *Susannah: A Little Girl with the Mounties* (New York: Dodd, Mead, 1937), pp. 253-54; Walter Liggett, *The Frozen Frontier* (New York: Macaulay, 1927), pp. 20-21.

15 "John Temple, Baronet," *Scarlet and Gold* (1920), p. 87; Alan Phillips, *The Living Legend* (Boston, Toronto: Little, Brown, 1957), p. 43; MacBeth, *Policing the Plains*, p. 37.

to deceive the public. Some people in the nineteenth century and after, though they were not aristocrats, and in fact were desirous of curtailing the political power of the aristocracy, "wanted no less to preserve the legitimate influence of its 'great and good qualities' in the democratic society that was emerging."[16] As the willingness to make sacrifices for the general good seemed to erode under the pressure of acquisitive materialism, the ideal of service and altruism — qualities which had supposedly characterized the old elite — seemed especially valuable.

The concern about nobility in the force is interesting for another reason. As Joseph Campbell, Otto Rank, Lord Raglan and others have pointed out, one of the distinguishing characteristics of many myths is the hero's noble birth.[17] Often the hero shuns his privileged background to prove his worthiness; often he is deprived of his rightful heritage and must win it back by mastering tests or overcoming various obstacles. The plots of many novels dealing with the force involved these very themes. The aristocratic background of some of the force's members was important because it suggested at an almost subconscious level that the Mountie, of which the aristocratic constable was a representative type, was a true romantic hero.

It was never suggested that everyone in the force was titled. Such a claim, besides being preposterous, would have carried connotations of unearned privilege and exclusivity. On the other hand, by suggesting that only some policemen were of genteel background, the democratic image of the corps was reinforced, for the presence of nobility led to some interesting anomalies. As Agnes Cameron explained, "many a constable if transferred to a state function in London would have to take precedence of every officer in the detachment."[18] In London it would have been a problem; in Canada and in the Mounted Police it was not. In the force merit, not birth, was the basis of respect. Rank was seen in a proper perspective, and the diverse origins of its members proved this. Moreover, the ability of those policemen to cooperate in an effective and efficient organization was a reassuring symbol of the class cooperation that could build a better society.

The force was democratic yet exclusive, egalitarian yet elitist. It was composed of men who were diverse in background and experience, and yet basically similar in character and abilities. It brought together the genteel aristocrat and the rugged yeoman. It combined the traditional values of the old world with the driving energy of the new, and suggested that these could combine in harmony with each other. The famous scarlet tunic was truly appropriate, for its colour symbolized both the rare nobility of those who wore it and the common element of blood which flowed through the veins of all humanity. Here, surely, was a mystical, powerful, and happy union.

Authority

What distinguished the Mounted Policeman was not where he came from or what

---

16   Walter E. Houghton, *The Victorian Frame of Mind* (New Haven and London: Yale University Press, 1969), pp. 283-84; see also E.D. Baltzell, *The Protestant Establishment: Aristocracy and Caste in America* (New York: Random House, 1966).

17   See Joseph Campbell, *The Hero With a Thousand Faces* (Princeton: Princeton University Press, 1972), p. 319; Otto Rank, *The Myth of the Birth of the Hero and Other Writings* (New York: Vintage, 1964), p. 65; Fitzroy Richard Somerset Lord Raglan, *The Hero: A Study in Tradition, Myth and Drama* (London: Watts, 1949), p. 178.

18   Cameron, p. 90.

he did before joining the force. Rather, it was his character. The set of qualities and virtues he possessed set him apart from other men and fitted him for his job. Although there was no uniform agreement on the specific attributes that were essential, there was general concurrence that a combination of endowments was vital. It was not enough to be strong or intelligent. For William Fraser, "a combination of sinew, strength, endurance, brain, and a fair moral tone" was necessary to be a policeman. To L.V. Kelly, the outstanding characteristics were "tact, and courage, and an endless patience and persistence." Douglas Spettigue insisted on strength, courage, and initiative, while Morris Longstreth added discipline to this list.[19] Clearly, it was only the "all round man" who was acceptable. Such men were obviously rare, and therefore this emphasis on the depth as well as strength of character helped to indicate why the force was so exclusive.

Although a combination of characteristics was vital to succeed in the force, some qualities were emphasized more than others. Foremost among them was authority. The Mountie, it was believed, no matter how difficult the situation, acted with a calm, unhesitating assurance that flowed from great reserves of inner power. He could impose his will on those around him with ease. There was no consensus as to whether an individual possessed such authority before he was recruited into the force, or whether it derived from the fact of his membership and the nature of his training. But this was not an important dispute; what was important and undeniable was that the Mountie had it in abundance.

The authority of the Mounted Policeman was extraordinary. According to the novelist Bertrand W. Sinclair, "'In the Queen's name,' out of the mouth of an unarmed redcoat, with one hand lightly on your shoulder, carries more weight than a smoking gun." "They seldom raised their voices," wrote Pierre Berton, "almost never drew a gun, and rarely had to give an order twice." Mounted Policemen kept order even when confronted by forces which were stronger or more numerous. One journalist, writing at the turn of the century, expressed his astonishment at "what a wholesome influence is exerted on the rougher elements of a district by the presence of even a single constable." William Lacey Amy offered a fictionalized account of this phenomenon by describing how a single policeman confronted the leader of a gang of visiting American desperadoes. The Sergeant

> planted himself squarely on braced feet before the lounging man and ran cold eyes over him. He was thirty pounds lighter, a mere slip in his tight scarlet tunic. But it was the larger man's eyes flickered as he straightened away from the counter.[20]

Needless to say, the troublemakers left town forthwith.

The mere possession of such authority by the individual policeman significantly lessened the need for any exercise of coercive force, but if force had to be applied its effectiveness was soon apparent. In the novel *Corporal Corey*, for example, Jack

---

19   W.A. Fraser, "Soldier Police of the Canadian Northwest," *Canadian Magazine*, xiv (1900), p. 370; L.V. Kelly, "Canada's Famous Mounted Police," *Scarlet and Gold* (1920), p. 38; Douglas Spettigue, *The Friendly Force* (Toronto, New York, London: Longmans, Green, 1960), p. 26; T.M. Longstreth, *The Scarlet Force: The Making of the Mounted Police* (Toronto: Macmillan, 1953), p. 11.

20   Bertrand W. Sinclair, *Raw Gold* (Chicago and New York: M.A. Donohue, 1908), p. 172; Pierre Berton, *Klondike* (Toronto: McClelland and Stewart, 1972), p. 267; B.J. Ramage, "The Canadian Mounted Police," *Sewanee Review*, viii (1900), p. 296; William Lacey Amy [Luke Allan], *Blue Pete: Detective* (London: H. Jenkins, 1928), p. 54.

O'Brien described how a squad of troopers was sent to quell an outbreak of labour violence. Using only riding crops, the Mounties marched through the crowd of strikers:

> It seemed almost incredible that such a small group of men could so completely turn a drunk-maddened mob into a thoroughly cowed and leaderless mass. In twenty minutes it was all over.[21]

With or without physical force, the police always imposed their will.

Naturally, authority carried a danger of its misuse. The Mounties might be, as one fictional villain put it, "a bunch of overbearing, swaggering nincompoops who think they are the cream of the universe."[22] What guarantee was there that the police would not twist the law to their own purposes, or ignore it, or use their personal and legal power to oppress ordinary citizens? That guarantee was their possession of a number of other qualities which held in check any tendency to abuse their power.

Patience and courtesy were also Mountie characteristics. John Macoun, writing in 1882, went so far as to suggest that on no occasion had any member of the force lost his temper under trying circumstances. These virtues were inspired, not by any patronizing forbearance, but by a sincere respect for each individual. One "famous old Mountie" explained how he had developed these qualities: "'Denny,' said my mother to me, 'always remember that all people make mistakes. You can be very sure of yourself, but never refuse to listen. The other fellow may be right'."[23] Knowledge of fallibility inspired genuine consideration, not simply formal courtesy, and where there was genuine consideration, authoritarian behaviour was not likely to take root.

Another reassuring virtue was modesty. According to many writers, among the greatest of the unwritten laws which governed the police was the injunction not to boast of their deeds. As an editorial in the first issue of the *RCMP Quarterly* put it:

> For sixty years, aside from the annual report, an official reticence has been one of the cardinal rules of the Force. It was sufficient to know that a job had been satisfactorily done.

Even the annual reports, however, were not much help. To anyone who knew the police well, claimed A.L. Haydon, the reports were amusing for what they left unsaid, "as if the writer had definite instructions to give no more than the barest facts, or as if he feared the imputation of a desire to show off." From this it could be assumed that many members of the force did not receive the recognition that their efforts deserved. Indeed, it became problematic to explain how any detailed stories of police exploits emerged from this shell of reticence. Fortunately, it was revealed, an outsider occasionally was able to see them at work, to win their confidence, and hear their stories. Such a man was R.G. MacBeth, who informed his readers that "as I am not one of their number I do not feel bound by their rule of silence."[24] Undoubtedly, some exciting and inspiring tales were not passed on to the public, but it was reassuring to know that the authority of the Mounted Policeman was not exercised to gratify his ego.

---

21   O'Brien, pp. 121-22.

22   T. Lund, *Robbery at Portage Bend* (London: T. Werner Laurie, 1933), p. 39.

23   John Macoun, *Manitoba and the Great Northwest* (Guelph: The World Publishing Co., 1882), p. 575; Richard L. Neuberger, *Royal Canadian Mounted Police* (New York: Random House, 1953), p. 175.

24   "Editorial," *Royal Canadian Mounted Police Quarterly*, I (1933), p. 6; A.L. Haydon, *The Riders of the Plains: A Record of the Royal North West Mounted Police of Canada, 1873-1910* (Toronto: Copp Clark, 1912; reprint ed., Edmonton: Hurtig, 1973), p. 281; R.G. MacBeth, "Editorial," *Scarlet and Gold* (1919), p. 5.

A much more important quality than these was the Mountie's sense of morality. The very motto of the force, "Uphold the Right," was an unequivocal admonishment to do what was ethically sound, not just what was legally correct. To a large extent this attribute could be taken for granted, since the law and those who administered it were normally felt to be moral, but explicit assurances were not lacking. "These men must be clean and strong morally, mentally, physically," declared William Campbell. "One cannot be strong and healthy if dirty — this applies to morals as well as to the mind and body." The hero of Harwood Steele's novel, *Spirit of Iron*, demonstrated the moral purity of a Mountie who refused to take advantage of an Indian maiden, resisted the advances of the wife of a fellow officer, and avoided using any underhanded tactics. Perhaps rural dwellers especially appreciated the degree of morality in the force after hearing Commissioner Perry's remark, repeated by the Reverend MacBeth, that his men could be let loose in London with complete assurance that not one would succumb to the temptations of a large exciting city.[25] If men could resist the sinful enticements of the world's largest and most glamorous metropolis, they were indeed imbued with a finely tuned moral sense.

An emphasis on morality was predictable. In a world that seemed to be dominated by chance and selfish materialism, a desire for moral stability was understandable. This impulse helps to account for the continuing popular interest in romance, where virtue is unambiguous and triumphant. These romantically inspired expectations would have been especially credible to many Anglo-Saxons in the late nineteenth century and beyond who believed that morality was one of the distinctive characteristics of their race.[26] Who could doubt that the Mountie possessed it?

Closely allied to morality was integrity. The police, it was asserted, always performed their duties to the best of their abilities and upheld the spirit as well as the letter of the law. In the vernacular of the late nineteenth century, the Mounted Police were "straight."

> No officer or constable is permitted to deride the law or seek notoriety out of "a cheap offence" or a "manufactured crime." An empty police court and a blank charge-sheet are considered evidence of efficiency and diplomacy.

No one understood this integrity more than criminals. According to Bishop Pinkham, the troopers were held "in full respect and in absolute confidence by all and by none more than by those whom they have to arrest and hold." The point was confirmed in the many novels and stories whose Mountie heroes, faced with long treks back to civilization with villains captured in the wilderness, refused to shoot their prisoners in order to lighten their loads. This "moral prestige" greatly contributed to Mounted Police success; people knew they would be dealt with honestly and fairly by the force. Crowfoot realized this, supposedly, when he declared that Colonel Macleod never lied, and that his tribe would follow the policeman's advice to sign Treaty Seven with the government.[27] And so, while the integrity of the police ensured they would not

---

25 William Campbell, p. 329; Harwood Steele, *Spirit of Iron: An Authentic Novel of the North-West Mounted Police* (Toronto: McClelland and Stewart, 1923), pp. 60-64, 241; MacBeth, "The Scarlet and Gold Men" in MacBeth, ed., *Trail Makers Boys' Annual* (1920), p. 32.

26 Richard Faber, *The Vision and the Need: Late Victorian Imperialist Aims* (London: Faber, 1966), p. 122.

27 Major-General A.C. Macdonnell, "Scarlet and Gold," *Scarlet and Gold* (1919), p. 13; Captain R.W Campbell, *Spud Tamson Out West* (Edinburgh: W. and R. Chambers, n.d.), pp. 108-9; Bishop Pinkham, "A Tribute to the RNWMP," *Scarlet and Gold* (1919), p. 21; Longstreth, pp. 82-83.

abuse their authority, it also greatly increased the effectiveness of that authority when it faced disorder.

An important aspect of this integrity was the force's incorruptibility. One of Ralph Connor's creations exemplified the quality perfectly:

> Money was still easy in the town, and had Sergeant Crisp been minded, for the mere closing of his eyes or turning of his back upon occasion he might have retired early from the Force with a competency. Unhappily for Sergeant Crisp, however, there stood in the pathway of his fortune the awkward fact of his conscience and his oath of service.

If money could not sway men like Sergeant Crisp, neither could "popular clamour." The upholding of the unpopular prohibition laws in the West was proof of this. Even when others grafted, it was confidently asserted, the police did not.[28]

Although the force was incorruptible and unswerving in its duty, its actions were governed by discretion and a sense of proportion, and these qualities also helped to balance the authority it possessed. One western pioneer recounted how a starving man had killed some prairie chickens out of season to feed his family. When he discovered the crime, the policeman did nothing:

> Though the majesty of the law was personified in Red Coat Billy, a human heart beat beneath his red coat, and he had not read about Nelson's blind eye at the battle of the Baltic for nothing.[29]

In many fictional works as well, an important element of the plot was a policeman's decision to ignore what, strictly speaking, was crime, because of a realization that the perpetrator was essentially innocent and no purpose would be served by bringing the full force of the law against him. This seeming conflict between their discretion and their incorruptibility was reconciled in part by their morality. Discretion, it was made clear, was never used for personal advantage, and because the policeman had a firm sense of right and wrong, the blind eye would only be turned when warranted. But, if it was warranted, it would be employed: the police were not interested in arbitrary exercises of authority.

Impartiality was another aspect of police integrity, a further manifestation of their incorruptibility. "We see that every man gets a fair show," said one officer in Ralph Connor's *Corporal Cameron*. Neither friendship nor hatred could change this. Once he had investigated a particular circumstance a Mountie might take sides to aid an innocent party, but as long as the issue was in doubt, he was scrupulously impartial. In Samuel White's *Northwest Law*, for example, the policeman who was sent to investigate a robbery at a local ranch was a former railway clerk, who had himself been victimized by a hold up. In both crimes, the major suspect was the owner of the ranch. Nevertheless,

> the Sergeant knew that his versatile, able Constable Milton Slade could carry the Mounted Police authority onto Three Torches ranchland without anything personal in it, without the lenience of good neighborliness or the antagonism of bad.[30]

---

28   Charles William Gordon [Ralph Connor], *The Patrol of the Sundance Trail* (Toronto: Westminster Co., 1914), p. 96; L. Douthwaite, *The Royal Canadian Mounted Police* (London and Glasgow: Blackie, 1939), preface; J.G.A. Creighton, "The Northwest Mounted Police of Canada," *Scribner's Magazine*, xiv (1893), pp. 415-16; W.H.P. Jarvis, *The Great Gold Rush* (Toronto: Macmillan, 1913), pp. 55, 61.

29   H.B. Adshead, *Pioneer Tales and Other Human Stories* (Calgary: Alberta Job Press, 1929), p. 37.

30   Charles William Gordon [Ralph Connor], *Corporal Cameron of the North West Mounted Police* (New York:

Again, such fairness mitigated fears that police authority would be abused, and also helped to explain why that authority was so effective.

One reason why the force was able to sustain its impartiality, according to many observers, was its freedom from political influence. "Politics" they claimed, "plays no part in its administration of justice." There were two aspects to this nonpartisanship. First, the force did not use its authority to further political causes. In a novel by Oscar Olson published in 1953, the police rebuffed a small-town politician's attempt to use the force's power to discredit his opponents. Instead, the reeve and his council received a lecture on the nature of democracy. Second, the force brooked no political interference in its internal affairs, and refused to be intimidated by the threat of appeals to higher political authorities. Politicians could make the law, but no one could interfere with its enforcement. In Harold Bindloss's novel *Prescott of Saskatchewan*, one dissatisfied citizen warned the local officer that he would "apply to Ottawa." "A look of weariness crept into the officer's face. 'You have my sympathy, Mr. Jerryngham, but you can't be allowed to interfere with the Northwest Police'."[31] The force in the popular mind, did not play politics, nor did it allow politicians to play with the force.

The relationship between the Mounted Police and politicians was more complex than most writers indicated. Although the police could retain some immunity in local politics, they could not escape the clutches of the federal government. In the nineteenth century, in particular, patronage was rife in politics, and since the force was set up by the government, the police could hardly evade it. The appointment of many officers and men to the force was the result of influence rather than merit. Indeed, in the early years the commissioned officers of the force tended to reflect the religious, ethnic, and regional splits of the country in much the same way as cabinet appointments. Moreover, as agents of government policy, particularly in remote areas, the police were sometimes drawn into political quarrels, and since they were responsible to and dependent on the government, it seems only reasonable to expect that in many day-to-day activities some political considerations did govern their conduct.[32] Finally, inasmuch as the force has always had difficulty distinguishing between political dissent and subversion, it actively discriminated against a number of political groups. To assert, as many writers have, that the force was free from political partisanship is a distortion. No institution in a society can be divorced from politics.

Some novelists who wrote about the force did recognize this fact. The politically appointed officer was a relatively common fictional type. John Mackie described one such beast in *Sinners Twain*:

> his whole facial expression might be summed up in three words — red, round and vulgar. Indeed, he enjoyed the sobriquet of "Pudding-face Jamie," from the supposed

---

Hodder and Stoughton, George H. Doran, 1912), p. 382; S.A. White, *Northwest Law* (New York: Phoenix Press. 1942), p. 32.

31 W. Leo Murphy, *Trail's Ends: A Tale of the Royal Canadian Mounted Police in the Catholic Land of Evangeline* (St. Naziannz, Wisc.: Society of the Divine Savior, 1944), p. 33; Olson, p. 174; H. Bindloss, *Prescott of Saskatchewan* (New York: Grosset and Dunlap, 1913), pp. 217-18.

32 Stan W. Horrall, *The Pictorial History of the Royal Canadian Mounted Police* (Toronto, Montreal: McGraw-Hill Ryerson, 1973), p. 84; Macleod, pp. 92-101; William Robert Morrison, "The Mounted Police on Canada's Northern Frontier, 1895-1940," unpublished Ph.D. thesis, University of Western Ontario, 1973, p. 9.

resemblance of the facial features aforesaid to that popular but homely article of diet. He had at one time been a private holding some subordinate "staff job" in the force, but, having the necessary influence at his back, had secured a commission ... true to the old adage regarding the putting of a beggar on horseback, when he tasted power he rode roughshod over the unfortunates under him.[33]

Novelists who used such characters made it clear that these men were incompetent, dishonest, or both; that they were universally disliked by their fellows; and, that they were an exception to the general calibre of officers. Invariably, they were discovered and punished. By acknowledging the existence of political appointees, and then by qualifying so completely their presence, these writers reinforced the general impression that the corps was by and large free from political influence. In both fiction and non-fiction, the reader was assured that political considerations would not cause, at least not for long, the police to abuse their authority.

Authority was an important aspect of the Mounted Police character. Although there was some theoretical danger of absolutism and repressiveness, it was unlikely that these would be a problem because of the exemplary character of policemen. Here was an important symbol of the possibility of reconciling society's need for some sort of regulation with the desire for basic rights and individual freedom.

The emphasis on the authority of the Mounted Policeman is not surprising. Interest in the force developed in the late Victorian period when the western mind was "a wasteland strewn with blasted articles of faith." As suitable convictions on which to base authority became more and more elusive, the desire for authority became correspondingly stronger.[34] This longing has not abated in the twentieth century. In fact, the advent of a highly complex technological civilization, in which small disruptions can have widespread paralytic effects, has probably increased it. The symbol of the Mounted Policeman could not fill the void left by a disintegrating world view. It could, however, provide a needed reassurance that even if cosmic or divine certitude was not possible, some fundamentally moral authority could exist. It might be simply the will and determination of one individual policeman, but even this provided comfort for many.

Courage, Strength, Discipline and Efficiency

The possession of authority includes the ability to enforce it when necessary. Four qualities attributed to the Mounties helped to explain why the policeman could impose his will if circumstances required it. These were courage, strength, discipline, and efficiency. Some were traditional virtues ascribed to any romantic hero; others were rooted in the historical context which produced the force itself. All of them, however, marked the Mounted Policeman as a man of action. As a man who could fruitfully exert himself in the world, he was an inspiration to many who were immobilized by the uncertainties and complexities of modern society.

By the conventions of romance, the policeman could be assumed to possess courage. For readers not familiar with those age-old formulas, many writers took care to point out the obvious. Harold Bindloss wrote, "courage and endurance still command respect in the new Northwest, and that both the lads possessed them was made evident by the fact that they were troopers of the Northwest Police." Most

---

33 Mackie, pp. 26-27.
34 Richard D. Altick, *Victorian People and Ideas* (New York: Norton, 1973), pp. 236-37.

observers seemed to feel that Mounted Police courage, however axiomatic, was a special type. Harwood Steele called it "lone-hand courage." Lone-hand courage was not like "grandstand courage ... exemplified in the matador, who risks his life with the crowded arena to cheer him." Instead, it was "the courage of those who dare and endure, with no hope of reward and with no one to see."[35] This courage came from the inside, and could be summoned when there was no one else to impress. The many stories of individual policemen venturing into the lonely wilderness to bring criminals to justice demonstrated time and again its existence.

Lone-hand courage was calm and deliberate. No one knew this better than the villain in a Hiram Cody novel who warned a friend that the Mountie would "stroll into a gang of cutthroats as cool as ye please, pick his man, snap on the irons, an' walk out." "It takes nerve to do that," was the comment of his listener. The police were well aware of the risks they ran. Sometimes their composure was a facade. Ralph Connor described how the police were successful during the 1885 Rebellion in "presenting even in their most desperate moments such a front of resolute self-confidence to the Indians, and refusing to give any sign by look or word or act of the terrific anxiety they carried beneath their gay scarlet coats."[36] This conduct, undertaken in full consideration of the danger and not merely in an unthinking fit of anger or exuberance, demonstrated the authentic nature of police courage.

While bluff was occasionally used in exceptional circumstances, normally it was completely unnecessary. The police generally went about their business confident that if trouble did arise, they would be strong enough to handle it. Officers of the force, declared Reverend MacBeth, were "almost invariably men of outstanding strength," for weaklings could not survive the strenuous life of the plains and the mountains. Almost all writers agreed that what distinguished the strength possessed by the men of the force was "tremendous power of endurance" and "unflinching stamina." The extent of these qualities was often conveyed through descriptions of the arduous demands of police life. Sergeant Prior, for example,

> was hollow-eyed from overwork and long hours of duty but directly from a long ride eastward to assist in a prairie fire fight, he had come across to the double LF as soon as he had got in touch with Inspector Barker ... For thirty hours he had scarcely been off his feet, and in the last three days a dozen hours of sleep had sufficed him. It was all in the day's work of a Mounted Policeman.

Although they grew fatigued at times, most Mounties revelled in the swirl of "ceaseless activity" and yearned for it in quieter times.[37]

The notion of endurance suggested a controlled, unwavering strength that would not falter. It was a more intelligent kind of strength than, say, brute force. If, as many in western society were beginning to believe, the unending task of ordering and controlling the world was an obligation of men rather than God,[38] this was exactly

---

35   Bindloss, Winston, p. 22; Harwood Steele, *To Effect An Arrest* (Toronto: Ryerson, 1947), p. 50.

36   H.A. Cody, *The Long Patrol: A Tale of the Mounted Police* (Toronto: Briggs, 1912), p. 54; Charles William Gordon [Ralph Connor], *Sun Dance Trail*, p. 266.

37   R.G. MacBeth "The Story of the Royal North West Mounted Police," *Scarlet and Gold* (1919), p. 8; R.G. MacBeth, "The Scarlet and Gold Men," p. 32; William Lacey Amy [Luke Allan], *The Westerner* (London: H. Jenkin, n.d.), p. 175; Milton Richards, *Dick Kent and the Malemute Mail* (Akron: A.L. Burt, 1927), p. 38.

38   Houghton, pp. 217, 334.

the kind of strength that was necessary. Many wanted to believe that the Mountie possessed it.

Physical strength was a highly desirable quality then, but by itself and in combination with authority, it could conceivably get out of hand. It might be used without forethought, or inappropriately. How was a man of enormous strength, especially one who could sanction his excesses under the mantle of the law, to be controlled? In the case of the Mounted Police, it was the individual Mountie who would control himself. This self-control was possible because he possessed discipline. "Discipline," said Jack O'Brien, "is vitally necessary to the success of any organized enterprise. Armies or police would be lost without it." From the very beginning this realization had guided the force. The first Commissioner, Colonel French, it was claimed, had concentrated on "building up that rigorous discipline that has remained the pride of the force."

> French had the needful vision to see that an immense country ... could be policed by a small body of men if they were disciplined, trained, equipped and well fed. Courage and endurance would be required, but discipline was the prime essential.

However crucial, discipline was not something that came easily. Most men, as Captain R.W. Campbell put it, were "ever at war with orders." Part of the process of becoming a Mounted Policeman was learning to accept orders and to carry them out without thought of self. Many novels dealt with this theme of transformation. The hero of Norman Plummer's *The Long Arm*, for example, had some initial trouble obliterating "the effects of his carefree and spoilt youth," but once on patrol he discovered the value of his training.[39] Indeed, if discipline had to be learned, there was nothing like service in the force to teach it.

Harwood Steele's story, "The Martinet," provided a vivid example of this teaching and its ultimate value. The hero of the tale, aging Inspector Praed, was extremely hard on his men, and as a consequence was unpopular. One day his patrol was ambushed by an insane Doukhobor. While remaining under cover himself, he ordered the two men with him to attack. When they failed to subdue the lunatic and more men arrived, he repeated the orders from the safety of his shelter. The newcomers despised his cowardice, but they obeyed, not because they wanted to but because they had to. When they failed as well it was Praed himself who finally advanced resolutely toward the madman, disarmed him and took him alive. As Praed marched forward, his men realized he was seriously wounded. He had not been cowering in terror; he had, instead, been nursing his resources to ensure that the necessary job was done.[40]

Praed taught his men some important lessons. He showed them that only through mastery of self could others be mastered. He demontrated, by refusing to kill his quarry, the highest level of self-control. He proved the value of following orders without question. Here was a man whose strength, courage, and authority were not dangerous, because he had enormous amounts of discipline to control them. He could be trusted with his great power and, having learned his lesson, so could his men.

---

39 O'Brien, p. 87; Spettigue, p. 5; Longstreth, p. 11; Campbell, *A Policeman From Eton*, p. 18; Norman M. Plummer, *The Long Arm* (Toronto: Nelson, n.d.) pp. 184, 210.

40 Steele, *To Effect An Arrest*, pp. 63-77.

Perhaps the most conclusive proof of Mounted Police discipline, as Praed's conduct suggested, was a refusal to use firearms except as a last resort. The police, it was frequently asserted, had a very simple rule: never fire first. Colonel James Macleod himself had started this tradition when he insisted on riding directly up to the gates of Fort Whoop-Up to order the surrender of what he thought was a mob of defiant whisky traders spoiling for a fight. Luckily, the fort was almost empty. Sergeant Denton, in one of Luke Allan's novels, was not so fortunate. After cornering a vicious rustler, Denton was mortally wounded when he approached in the open to make the arrest. He knew the danger, but he also knew the Mountie tradition. Of course, there were times when violence was unavoidable, and when the Mountie did pull his gun he used it effectively, though his intent was normally to wound rather than kill.[41] Discipline taught a higher purpose than self-preservation.

Because he was disciplined, the policeman could channel his energies in the most productive way, and this helped to account for another valuable quality of the force — efficiency. One impressed novelist wrote of "the almost uncanny efficiency of these officers. Not any single or particular officer, but each and every one of them." Police efficiency was a particular kind. It was, as the *Times* put it, "quiet efficiency." The force did its work "silently, unostentatiously and efficiently," maintained A.L. Haydon, and Roger Pocock claimed its greatest boast was "that it is scarcely ever mentioned in the newspaper."[42]

The most conclusive manifestation of police efficiency was the fact that they did not fail. Bishop Pinkham attributed this success to a continual willingness and ability to discharge their duty. Others asserted that failure was simply not tolerated. Those who slipped up, if they were still alive, resigned and made way for better men. Whether inspired by fear or dedication, the words "can't" and "fail" were thought to be stricken from the vocabulary of the force. Some writers did admit that occasionally criminals got away, but usually this admission was so qualified that it lost its sting. One of William Lacey Amy's fictional policemen, for example, confessed "now and then [some] one does escape ... and now and then we let him." Alan Phillips told the story of two tax delinquents who died just before they were caught. When the law was beaten by the grim reaper, little harm was done to the reputation of the force.[43]

One explanation for the efficiency of the police was their authority, but the quality of persistence was also key. The Mounties, claimed one admirer, follow criminals "to the ends of the earth":

> ... follow through blizzard, the heat or the rain,
> Over the mountains across the bleak plain,
> On through the night ever onward will go,
> Far up the barrens, where Arctic lights glow.
> Northward or southward, to east or to west,
> The Red Riders follow the trail of their quest.

---

41   William Lacey Amy [Luke Allan], *Blue Pete: Half Breed* (New York: James A. McCann, 1921), pp. 32-34; Fraser, p. 367.

42   E.H. Williams, *Red Plume of the Royal Northwest Mounted* (New York and London: Harper and Bros., 1928), p. 4; the *London Times*, September 11, 1957; Haydon, p. xxiii; Roger Pocock, "The Riders of the Plains," *Chambers Journal*, Sixth Series, i (1898), p. 13.

43   Pinkham, p. 21; F. Haydn Dimmock, *Dupree's Tenderfoot* (Bath: Venture Books, 1949), p. 113; Macdonnell, p. 13; William Lacey Amy [Luke Allan], *The Tenderfoot* (London, H.Jenkins, 1939), p. 155; Alan Phillips, "Look What They've Done to the Mounties," *Maclean's*, July 1, 1954, p. 55.

The previously mentioned exploits of Inspector Praed also vividly exemplified this perseverance. Praed demonstrated "the tremendous moral force of a tenacity which persists despite failure after failure and of a steady, passive, unhurried advance into the wide open jaws of death."[44] Given such determination it was no wonder that the police were so effective.

Efficiency is a virtue closely associated with the industrial age. In Victorian times it was one of the most admired qualities of the machine, and individuals were often urged to emulate mechanical principles by doing as much as possible, as cheaply as possible, through regulated and disciplined effort.[45] The notion became one of the mainstays of the idea of progress: if only waste could be eliminated, so much could be achieved. In the twentieth century, efficiency has provided the major rationalization for the unhindered advance of technology and automation. It has been an extremely powerful concept. As beings who were efficient, then, the Mounted Police were fulfilling one of the most important canons of the period.

Courage, strength, discipline, and efficiency were all qualities that allowed a person to function productively and harmoniously in the world. They provided a capacity to take action in a sensible and responsible fashion, and those who possessed them have been highly regarded. Every society, of course, esteems its men of action who pit themselves against the world and get things done. These are the annals of heroes. But for western society from the mid-nineteenth century on, the ability to act was particularly attractive.

Sensitivity about action came from two sources. On the one hand, in an era of material progress, the results of action were increasingly apparent. Through concerted effort, it seemed, the quality of all human life could be improved. The machine was a particularly important symbol, for it suggested that almost infinite reservoirs of creative energy were available to free people from drudgery and fatigue. The dream that action could be both more effective and more pleasurable naturally created a longing to grasp the possibilities.

However, while the desire to take action was growing, the confidence to do so was being undermined. The erosion of Christianity, which had been the ultimate source of authority for all activity, and the absence of anything to replace it, was creating for many a block between thinking and doing. Since there was no longer a firm standard of values, it was more difficult to know which actions should be undertaken and which avoided. If mistakes were made, and the power of the machine was harnessed for the wrong purposes, the results would be disastrous; the perception of some that machines enslaved rather than liberated was not heartening. Doubt and confusion sometimes led to a despair that perhaps nothing was worth doing. Sometimes it led to compulsive activities designed to stave off troubling thoughts. Neither response was very comforting.

The symbol of the Mounted Policeman as a man of action helped relieve some of this frustration and despondency, and indeed, suggested they were unnecessary. Positive, controlled action could be used to improve the condition of humanity, even if its sanction came from this world rather than a higher one. In helping to free people from doubts about activity, the policeman helped them to believe that action might overcome the causes of their anxiety. He was a neat solution to a troubling double bind.

---

44 A.R. Douglas, "Riders in Red," *Scarlet and Gold* (1922), p. 95; "The Riders of the Plains," *Scarlet and Gold* (1919), p. 187; Steele, *To Effect an Arrest*, pp. 75-76.

45 Altick, p. 109.

Hearts and Minds

Courage, strength, efficiency, discipline — these have been four of the major virtues of industrial society. But, as even the Victorians realized, they possessed a danger, one which was manifest in an incident in Harold Bindloss's novel, *Delilah of the Snows*. A young trooper was ordered to march toward a barricade erected by a group of rebelling miners. Onlookers could see that "he had no great liking for his task, but beyond the fact that he was holding himself unusually straight, and looking steadfastly in front of him, he showed no sign of it." The miners warned him to stop:

> The trooper did not stop, nor did he answer. If he had his misgivings as a human being, he was also a part of the great system by which his nation's work is done and its prestige maintained; and he went on with his stiff measured strides which suggested the movements of an automaton.[46]

The movements of an automaton! Here was the rub.

A machine-like response did have some advantages. It allowed the Mounted Policeman to take action instantly without wasting valuable time trying to decide what to do or how to do it. In some situations this could mean the difference between life and death. In one novel, for example, the mind of the Mountie hero who dived into a raging river to save the heroine, "had become a machine, solving an ever changing equation which had as its factors the length of time for the current to bear the girl to a point in the river below him, the time of his own fall, and the probable distance he would have to cover in the water to reach her." It was a problem, declared the author, that an engineer with a slide rule might have spent many minutes on.[47] In other cases, such as the one Bindloss described, it enabled the policeman to undertake tasks of exceptional danger.

But the idea of the automaton had negative connotations as well. At one extreme it could imply a certain vacuous unconcern. Was Constable Milt Slade, who "imbibed all the divisional lectures on duties, filled any vacancy in various districts and let the commandants mostly shape his future career," a versatile and enthusiastic policeman, or was his malleability an indication that he could not think for himself? When Slade finally swung into action, his initiative became apparent, but until then his demeanour could have been misinterpreted. At the other extreme, robot efficiency could imply a cruel indifference to human emotion. A policeman in a more recent Canadian novel, for example, was described as "hard-faced, inquisitorial, the barely human symbol of an inhuman irresistible force."[48] This was a man who was deliberately aggressive, hoping to win promotion by his display of zeal. Sympathetic emotion stood in his way, and so he completely suppressed it.

What glory was there in Mounted Police courage, endurance, and discipline if they were the product of an unthinking brain or an unfeeling heart? A machine is useful but not heroic. To be truly admirable, the Mountie had to be more than a robot. It had to be made clear that he was a feeling, thinking human being, alive to the world and sensitive to others. To this end, he was credited with a number of significant attributes.

---

46   Harold Bindloss, *Delilah of the Snows* (New York: F.A. Stokes Co., 1907), p. 279.
47   Grey, pp. 117-18.
48   White, *Northwest Law*, p. 33; Edward McCourt, *Walk Through the Valley* (Toronto: McClelland and Stewart, 1958), p. 183.

For one thing, it was suggested that the police as individuals had typical human weaknesses. Sergeant Blue, hero of Robert Stead's poem, "The Squad of One," was

> ... a so-so kind of guy;
> He swore a bit, and he lied a bit,
> and he boozed a bit on the sly...[49]

These faults did not interfere with the performance of his duty, though. When a gang of dangerous toughs arrived in his district, Sergeant Blue calmly and efficiently captured them, and singlehandedly at that.

Another indication of the essential humanity of the policeman was his compassion. Underneath the official exterior was what Ralph Kendall described as "a great brutal heart." Ralph Connor went so far as to lecture Theodore Roosevelt about this quality. "Those laddies," he said, "are rather like dry nurses to the whole community," and he told the President of Sergeant Bagley who, instead of arresting a bootlegger he had caught red-handed, urged him to return to Scotland to avoid falling more deeply into the clutches of crime. Bagley realized that the man was not fundamentally a bad chap, merely one who had gone astray. Mercy and compassion would set him straight again.[50]

Connor's analogy between Mountie and nurse was typical. Not only was the Mounted Policeman a good Samaritan, he also frequently exhibited what was described as an almost feminine tenderness and concern. One of John Mackie's policemen "held the head of Black Jim as tenderly as any woman would have done and did everything that lay in his power to render easy the position of the wounded man." Robert Leighton's character, Sergeant Silk, nursed a prisoner through his sickness "just like a woman." Robert Service's Clancy, bringing a lunatic back to civilization, "clothed him and nursed him as a mother nurses a child." Such tenderness in no way implied a diminution of manliness for, according to Captain Ernest Chambers, "your bravest man is always your best nurse."[51]

This sensitivity was evident not just in the care of the sick. It was an integral part of the police character. In his innermost soul, for example, Ellis Benton "hid an almost womanish tenderness, coupled with a sensitive artistic temperament." Similarly, under the surface, one of Bertram Sinclair's heroes "was sensitive as a girl, one could wound him with a word or a look."[52] A Jungian psychologist might claim that this was a manifestation of an archetypal anima figure, but the general reader probably realized that these were men capable of caring and feeling, not cold and unthinking machines, immune to the nobler sentiments of life.

At times, it seemed impossible to reconcile the dictates of duty with the desire for compassion. When this happened, some policemen found a way to cope. Sergeant Silk, who came across a band of starving Indians camped illegally, was obliged to

---

49   R.J.C. Stead, *Why Don't They Cheer?* (London: T.F. Unwin, 1918), p. 112.

50   Kendall, *Benton*, pp. 229-30; Charles William Gordon [Ralph Connor], *Postscript to Adventure: The Autobiography of Ralph Connor* (New York: Farrar and Rinehart, 1938), p. 157.

51   John Mackie, *The Devil's Playground* (London: T.F. Unwin, 1894), p. 151; Robert Leighton, *Rattlesnake Ranch* (London: C.A. Pearson, 1912), pp. 108-9; Robert Service, *Collected Poems of Robert Service* (New York: Dodd, Mead, 1959), p. 155; Captain E.J. Chambers, *The Royal Northwest Mounted Police* (Montreal: Mortimer Press, 1908, reprint ed., Toronto: Coles, 1972), p. 156.

52   Kendall, p. 17; Sinclair, p. 60.

refuse them aid and to order them to move. On duty "his heart [was] buttoned up under his tunic." Off duty, however, he returned with food and other provisions. His heart had been unfettered. The co-existence of concern and compassion with unfeeling authority created a paradox that made the police intriguing. As Gilbert Parker's halfbreed character, Pierre, put it, "In one hand the soft glove of kindness, in the other voila! the cold glove of steel."[53] It was indeed a mystery, but no one doubted that the Mounted Policeman could encompass both extremes of duty.

The policeman was capable of thinking as well as feeling, and this provided another reassurance that he was not simply an automaton. The *Globe* as early as 1880 declared:

> It would be hard to find in any regular army a regiment of equal intelligence ... Their character is exemplified in the barrack rooms, when one will hear at all times intelligent and gentlemanly conversation taking the place of the low boisterous language usually heard in such places.

In the following years the nature of the evidence might have changed, but the basic judgment remained constant. The intelligence of the Mounted Policeman was rarely portrayed as a flashing brilliance. There were exceptions like Sergeant Silk, whose intellectual range and depth were extraordinary. He could, for example, diagnose what was wrong with a locomotive simply from the sound, and set fractured bones with "the skill and tenderness of a surgeon." Mounted Policemen, however, were not geniuses. They were instead possessed of "good judgment" and "shrewd common sense."[54] Theirs was a practical kind of intelligence which gave them uncommon insight into the nature of the world.

They had two skills in particular which demonstrated this quality. First, like John Mackie's hero, Sergeant Passmore, they "somehow seemed to know everything" that was going on around them. The possession of this sort of knowledge was accounted for in several ways. It was claimed that the police made a habit of investigating all newcomers to their various districts. As Luke Allan's Inspector Barker put it: "We look you all up when you show signs of settling among us. I could tell you things about you that you never imagined anyone but yourself would ever know." Another factor was the ability of the police to observe. "Unceasing vigilance" was considered a standing directive to all Mounties, and nothing apparently escaped their glance. On top of this, they had the knack of seeming to be everywhere at once. Sergeant Benton for one "seemed to possess endless disguises and hiding places and never to sleep." His "disquieting presence, supremely indifferent to weather conditions or darkness," upset any criminal calculation as to his whereabouts and doings. When all these skills and qualities were put together, it meant that the police had an incredible knowledge of the vast hinterland they controlled, and this realization thwarted many potential criminals. As one would-be villain in a Blue Pete novel complained: "... and how can we hide it from the Mounties? They'll hear of this, they're sure to. They know everything that goes on, damn them."[55]

---

53 Leighton, *White Man's Trail*, pp. 228-30; Gilbert Parker, *Pierre and his People* (Toronto: Copp Clark, 1897), p. 85.

54 The *Globe* (Toronto), April 17, 1880; Robert Leighton, *Sergeant Silk, The Prairie Scout* (Cleveland: The World Syndicate Puhlishing Co., 1929), pp. 23, 36; J.B. Kennedy, "Scarlet of the Mounted," *The Mentor*, 16 (March, 1928), p. 6.

55 John Mackie, *The Rising of the Red Men* (London: Jarrold, n.d.), p. 18; William Lacey Amy [Luke

Not only could the police observe external qualities, they could read internal ones. They were said to be excellent judges of character. One citizen in a novel by Captain Lund described their ability this way:

> They had a way of looking a fellow over, as if they was reading right to the bottom of his mind. And they give you a feelin', as if they had read any move a feller was goin' to do before he had properly figured it out for himself, and that they had also made up their minds how to block any game that might be coming...

This understanding naturally operated within the force as well as without, and the ability of Mounted Police officers to judge the capacities of their men was uncanny. Samuel White's Sergeant Stewart was perhaps the most amazing in this regard. He understood both his men and the animals they rode so well "that he possessed the unique gift of fitting man to horse, or maybe horse to man, as the individual case might be."[56] This insight was another reason why it was safe for the Mountie to exercise compassion in certain cases, even to the extent of ignoring the strict letter of the law. He was not compromising his integrity; he was reacting to the true character of those with whom he dealt. Because he could see into them so well, he knew when mercy was warranted.

The essence of Mounted Police intelligence, then, was not a cold intellect or an obsession with pure facts; rather, it was a shrewd appreciation of how the world operated and what sorts of actions would be effective. In an age that defined progress as an ability to manipulate the environment, an emphasis on such intelligence was only natural. The possession of that understanding, however, gave the police extraordinary control over people and things. They were not automatons. If anything, they did the directing.

The most conclusive evidence that the Mounted Police were thinking beings was their "high degree of initiative." Because the Mountie was on his own so much of the time, more so than any other policeman, he could not fall back on others for advice. "It was useless and not expected," declared Captain Campbell, "to phone for higher direction when faced with a crisis." An existence like that of Inspector Stanley Fyles, in which "scarcely a day passed but that some strenuous emergency arose demanding quick thought and quicker action," made it absolutely essential that he possess the "ability to decide for himself when there is no one near to tell him what to do."[57] Since such circumstances were normal for members of the force, it was obvious that the Mounted Policeman was not a creature of mindless discipline.

Paradoxically, it was this enormous freedom of action that made discipline so necessary. Only the man of "complete and final self-control"[58] could be trusted to handle a dangerous situation by himself. Without initiative, discipline was mindless; without discipline, initiative was bound to be foolhardy and doomed to failure. Each one required the other.

Allan], *Blue Pete: Rebel* (London: H. Jenkins, 1940), p. 64; Macdonnell, p. 13; Kendall, p. 231; William Lacey Amy [Luke Allan], *The Vengeance of Blue Pete* (London: H. Jenkins, 1939), p. 179.

56   T. Lund, *The Lone Trail Omnibus: Weston of the North West Mounted Police* (London: T.W. Laurie, 1936), p. 15; White, *Northwest Crossing*, p. 119.

57   Macdonnell, p. 13; Campbell, *Spud Tamson Out West*, pp. 108-9; Ridgwell Cullum, *The Law Breakers* (Toronto: Chapman and Hall, 1914), p 18; Spettigue, p. 26.

58   Spettigue, p. 28.

Given his intelligence, compassion, and initiative, the Mountie clearly was "a head, not an automaton nor a flunky." Being a member of the force did not require a man to stop feeling or thinking for himself. In fact, it confronted him with problems which heightened the ordinary necessity to do these very things. At least, this is what admirers of the force wanted to believe. In a society that was becoming increasingly industrialized, coordinated, and compartmentalized, a self-possessed hero had tremendous appeal. The enormous potential of the machine had been grasped, but so had a stark awareness of wage slavery, industrial depersonalization, monotony, and bleak routine. The hero provided a reassurance that the individual still counted, that self-reliance was possible, and that human beings could choose their own destinies.[59] The Mounted Policeman was an especially appealing symbol, for he suggested that one could submit to regimentation and direction without sacrificing individuality. He exemplified, in a sense, the Christian precept that freedom came with submission to authority, and if that authority no longer resided with God, there were human agencies to replace Him.

Motivation

The qualities possessed by the Mounted Police were, by and large, conventional qualities attributed to any successful person. The Mountie could have excelled at almost anything he wished to undertake. Why did he join the police then? Why did he stay with the force when its service was so exacting?

One fact about the policeman's motivation was clear. He was not in the force for money. The Mountie was "unspoiled by the greed of men"; he asked for "neither riches nor gain." The most conclusive proof of this was the Klondike experience of the force. Here, it was said, men had worked hard and faithfully, without a single desertion to blemish their record, in some of the world's most unpleasant conditions. While others around them sought and found fortunes, the police toiled for little more than a dollar a day. They could be trusted to escort tons of other people's gold out of the Yukon without any fear that they would be tempted to abscond with the riches. "Possibly," declared Reverend MacBeth, "there is nothing finer in history."[60]

Obviously, this lack of interest in material things was not from laziness. Far from it. The work was much harder than any ordinary job, and it was done willingly. As one admirer of the force put it: "These men demonstrate fairly convincingly the old Socialist thesis that people do not need promise of riches to brave danger, endure hardships, and to do great deeds." Nor did the policeman denigrate money because he was not capable of holding a high-paying job. Constable Stewart Fuller turned down the vice-presidency of Boswick Golds. Constable Sam Acton rejected a job selling a newly invented amphibious cargo carrier even though it would "make him richer than he'd ever be as a Mountie." Nor did any member of the force perform half-heartedly because he was not being paid his full worth. As Sam Steele emphasized, "no member of the force worked any less conscientiously on account of there being

---

59 W.M. Tait, "Stories of the Redcoat Riders," *Canadian Magazine*, xlix (Oct., 1917), p. 512; Houghton, p. 337; Altick, p. 245.

60 S.W. Skilling, "The R.C.M.P.," *The Royal Canadian Mounted Police Quarterly*, 10 (1942), p. 192; MacBeth, "The Scarlet and Gold Men," p. 37.

no prospect of individual reward."[61] The policeman served in the force, it was made clear, in spite of, not because of, the money.

That the police were described as being so disinterested in wealth is not surprising. It provided reassurance that their integrity and honesty could not be compromised, and that they would enforce the law fairly and without favour. It was a proof of heroic character. But beyond this, to an age fearful that traditional morals and standards of value were being destroyed by insensitive greed, such a depiction was very attractive. The Mounted Police were a symbol that not all people had succumbed to corrupting and grasping tendencies. Old virtues had not disappeared.

If the police did not act from material considerations, what did motivate them? Occasionally such things as the healthy outdoor life, comradeship with the other men, or honour were mentioned. But the two most commonly attributed motivations were adventure and duty. These two factors induced men to join the ranks and to put up with the rigours of police life.

Adventure, according to T.M. Longstreth, was the godfather of the force:

> In those days nearly a century ago there were few amusements that came ready made ... So when restless young men of Ontario, Quebec and the Maritime Provinces saw advertisements in the newspapers of this new sort of authorized adventure, many dropped what they were doing and hurried to enlist.

Although society developed new diversions over the years, the old impulse did not die. Men joined the force because they looked for thrills and excitement. "Dandy" Dorrance had an "adventurous nature that kept him always on the edge of things." He might have had a comfortable job at headquarters but that wasn't his style. "He was no company clerk." Corporal Downey was just the same. His father tried to make a storekeeper out of him until the local banker pointed out, "the wild country's in his blood, an' you can't change it." One of Constable Beresford's colleagues, a titled chap who could have done something else with his life, had become a policeman "because he was a wild ass of the desert and his ears heard only the call of adventure."[62]

Even without these explicit insistences, almost all popular materials dealing with the force conveyed a strong sense of adventure. Novels had an adventure format that made it clear the policeman enjoyed the succession of trials which confronted him. The fictional Mountie was never pushed out the door; he strode out, braced for the excitement. In non-fiction as well, a heavy emphasis on the "case" approach duplicated the format of novels and created the same impression. Lip service was paid to the importance of routine duties and mundane tasks, but it was the exciting, action-filled adventure that seemed to be the norm of police existence.

The idea that adventure was a major force propelling the Mounted Policeman was somewhat worrying, however. While it suggested that he had energy and enthusiasm, it provided no guarantee of restraint. Would common sense or the public welfare be abandoned for the excitement of selfish pleasure? The answer, of course, was no. The Mountie was also a creature of duty.

---

61   Neuberger, p. 92; Samuel A. White, *Northwest Wagons* (New York: Phoenix Press, 1941), p. 254; T.M. Longstreth, *Mountie in a Jeep* (Toronto: Macmillan, 1949), p. 22; S.B. Steele, p. 88.

62   Longstreth, *Scarlet Force*, pp. 8-9; deHerries Smith, p. 198; J.B. Hendryx, *Downey of the Mounted* (New York: Putnam's, 1926), p. 54; W.M. Raine, *Man-Size* (Toronto, Boston, New York: Houghton Miffin, 1922), p. 245.

A sense of duty was one of the most distinctive features of the Mounted Police character. On this, all observers agreed. The police, it was said, were "fearless and faithful in the discharge of duty." They exhibited "unflinching execution of duty" and "absolute devotion." For Ralph Connor's Sergeant Crisp, "Duty was supreme." The one purpose of Sergeant Silk's existence was "to do his duty with efficiency." One writer went so far as to suggest that devotion to duty by every man of the force "has been almost a religion."[63] There was no doubt in the minds of admirers that duty was a primary motivation of the policeman.

One indication of the seriousness of the Mountie's dedication to duty, suggested many writers, was the fact that all crimes were investigated, not just obvious or important ones. Corporal Metcalfe, for example, who discovered an unidentified body in rural Saskatchewan,

> could have saved himself and the state plenty of trouble and expense if he had adopted the verdict of the neighbourhood and said: "Some poor bohunk got lost in a blizzard and froze to death, and that's all there is to that!"

He did not, however. Through patient investigation, he proved the man had been murdered, and went on to find the killer. Another proof was the fact that the police would go anywhere and do anything to accomplish their work, whatever the conditions. "To these gallant riders," declared Ralph Connor, "all trails stood open at all seasons of the year, no matter what snow might fall or blizzard blow, so long as duty called them forth." Nor could discomfort or fear for personal safety turn them away. When a policeman on patrol in Ottwell Binn's novel, *A Hazard of the Snows*, discovered a red flag indicating smallpox, "he was under no illusion as to the risk which a halt would involve. But it was his duty to investigate; to do what he could for any sick man in this solitary land." As Reverend MacBeth put it, "their refusal to count the odds against them when duty is to be done has been absolutely proven again and again."[64]

Even more remarkable than the refusal of the policeman to succumb to physical obstacles to duty, was his seeming reluctance to be moved by emotional ones. By its very nature, duty entailed isolation and loneliness. Its true test came when the Mountie's actions threatened the few important human relationships he did have. No one demonstrated more fortitude than James B. Hendryx's creation, Corporal Downey. Immediately after meeting Margot, the love of his life, Downey was ordered to undertake an arduous patrol. "You care more for your old policing than you do for me," declared the petulant heroine, trying to persuade him to stay. "That is not true," replied Downey. "But I do care more for duty than I do for anything. You will see that I am right when you think about it. You could not love a man who was a quitter."[65] As soon as Downey returned from his patrol — the most difficult ever performed by a rookie policeman — he was informed he would have to go out again.

---

63 Pinkham, p. 21; Hon. N.W. Rowell, "Royal North West Mounted Police," *Scarlet and Gold* (1919), p. 6; Frank Yeigh, "True Stories Worth Telling" in MacBeth, ed., *Trail Makers Boys' Annual*, p. 221; Charles William Gordon [Ralph Connor], *The Prospector* (Toronto: Westminster, 1904), p. 345; Leighton, *Sergeant Silk*, p. 100; L.V. Kelly, p. 37.

64 John Cobham, "Skeleton in the Willows," *Canadian Magazine*, lxxii (May, 1936), pp. 7, 52; Gordon [Ralph Connor], *Patrol*, p. 234; Ottwell Binns, *A Hazard of the Snows* (London, Melbourne: Ward, Lock, 1921), pp. 223-24; MacBeth, *Policing the Plains*, p. 10.

65 J.B. Hendryx, *Downey of the Mounted* (New York: Putnam's, 1926), p. 108.

He complied instantly. When he finally returned to Margot after two or three years, she had already married.

For nineteen years Downey bore his sorrow, refusing promotion and refusing to leave the North. One day, searching for a thief, he saw a girl who was an exact double of the young Margot. It was her cousin. Downey's hopes, raised to new heights, turned to despair when he realized the criminal he was after was her father. What could he do? He had no recourse but to bear up and do his duty. When he came across the man unexpectedly, there was a gunfight and the criminal was killed. Downey returned to confront his inevitable rejection. This time, miraculously, the woman understood the dictates of duty. "What else could you do?" she said simply. "That would not change the obligation to do one's duty — it would make it harder, that's all."[66] Downey's story had a happy ending, but there was no guarantee that this would always be the case, and the many fictional Mounted Policemen who put their closest emotional relationships on the line indicated to the public just how strongly they were committed to duty.

Duty was the prime motivating factor of the policeman, but what or whom was that duty felt toward? Just what agency or institution or being was the policeman ultimately serving? On occasion it was suggested that the duty was owed to God. The story "Wading In" by A.R. Douglas, for example, described how a young missionary in the West joined the force to achieve God's ends more effectively. For some British and Canadian imperialists, duty implied upholding "the integrity and honour of the Empire," which in turn was often seen as an agency dedicated to the advancement of human progress. Others insisted that the primary obligation was to the force itself. After a man had put in several years in the Mounted, claimed William Brockie, "the welfare and prestige of the force as a whole comes before all else." The desire to uphold the traditions of the force was a plausible explanation of why a man would perform so well once he had joined, but it did not indicate as satisfactorily why he would accept such an onerous burden to begin with. Some observers suggested that ultimately the notion of duty rested with the self. It arose from "pride in their own accomplishments" as much as from the traditions they revered. Devotion to duty was essential to self-fulfillment. As Alan Phillips stated: "perhaps, in the end, this is what man really wants: to be used to the full, to be tried to the utmost, to be free only to realize all that he is."[67] The policeman had this opportunity. By accepting the constraints of duty, he could reach his true potential.

In general, however, there was a vague understanding of the sources of duty. "Your greatest reward," explained one fictional policeman to a potential recruit, "will be the satisfaction of knowing that you have strived to do your duty." "We do our duty," said Sergeant Silk, "That is enough."[68] By leaving the notion of duty open, the readers could assume that the force served whatever they felt was deserving of such devotion. Its unspecified grounds allowed almost anyone to accept the notion of duty, and this

---

66 Ibid., p. 250.
67 A.R. Douglas, "Wading In," *Scarlet and Gold* (1925), pp. 40-41; Jarvis, p. 92; W. Brockie, *Tales of the Mounted* (Toronto: Ryerson, 1949), p. 48; New York *Times*, November 4, 1934; Phillips, *Living Legend*, p. 328.
68 Milton Richard, *Dick Kent, Fur Trader* (Akron and New York: A.L. Burt, 1927), pp. 203-4; Leighton, *Red Patrol*, p. 270.

may help explain why so many non-Canadians could identify with the police. The vagueness also suggests some confusion as to the ultimate source of authority. As the basic assumptions of western society began to be questioned, there may have been a greater hesitation to specify first causes. Indeed, this uncertainty may have resulted in even firmer exhortations to perform allotted tasks, without questioning the wherefore and why. As long as everyone did their job, order could be maintained through the exercise of human will. If that order were questioned, however, there was no telling what sort of chaos might be unleashed.

Duty is an essential requirement for any hero. A hero performs acts that are socially useful or redeeming in a deliberate or consistent way. Necessarily, some sense of commitment to society is involved. But an age that demanded an increasingly disciplined work force, and that insisted on an often soul-destroying fragmentation of tasks, must have seen duty as an especially significant notion. The Mountie, a symbolic hero of the industrialized Anglo-Saxon world, explicitly dedicated to maintaining the order of that world, had to have a highly developed sense of duty.

Mounted Police motivation, then, was explained in the main by adventure and duty. The policeman served because he wanted excitement and because he wanted to serve society. There is, it would seem, something contradictory here. The self-gratification implied by adventure jars with the idea of denial implicit in duty. The symbol of the Mountie was able to reconcile the two poles, indicating the possibility of finding excitement and enjoyment within the confines of society, and at the same time, suggesting that a commitment to duty did not mean the acceptance of a life of sterile dullness. Duty itself could be an adventure.

The Individual and the Group

The Mounted Policeman was an individual, as his adventuresome spirit, intelligence, and initiative all indicated in unmistakable terms. The police succeeded not "by force of numbers but by individual acts of heroism and tact." No matter what he did or where he was, the Mountie stood out from ordinary men. But although an individual, he was also part of a group. "Paradoxically," noted one writer, "from the moment a man joins the force he is pressured to conform, to obey, to submit to authority." He was a member of an organization that demanded everything he had to give. His willingness to give it was shown by his extraordinary esprit de corps. "Year by year," claimed one observer, "the morale, the 'esprit de corps', remains at the same high level that has marked the force from its inception." So strong was this spirit that it persisted long after the completion of service.[69]

Members of the force saw each other as more than just employees of the same organization, and perhaps the most effective explanation of this powerful bond was embedded in the relationship between the two basic stereotypes of Mounted Policemen. The predominant type was the young hero. Despite their possession of the authority and discipline of mature adults, rank and file Mounties were usually described as "young men, mere youths," "lads," even "boy policemen." Jack London's portrait was typical:

> He was a stalwart young fellow, broad-shouldered, deep-chested, legs cleanly built and stretched wide apart ... His eyes were cool and grey and steady, and he carried himself with the peculiar confidence of power that is bred of blood and tradition.

---

69 Block, p. 38; Phillips, *Living Legend*, p. 43; Hendryx, p. 63; Fraser, p. 373.

> His splendid masculinity was emphasized by his excessive boyishness — he was a mere lad — and his smooth cheek promised a blush as willingly as the cheek of a maid.[70]

Wise and strong for his years, yet there was something about him not entirely formed.

The second stereotype was the elderly, experienced officer. In novels, these figures were often distinguished by silvery hair and penetrating eyes, which saw through everything. Although sometimes brisk and gruff on the surface, and prone to idiosyncracies, they were deeply venerated by their men. Ellis Benton and his comrades would fume and curse at the "numerous erratic bursts of temper and little eccentricities" of their commanding officer, and yet, he recalled, "how we learned to trust and respect that irascible but kindly old aristocratic face." The nickname of Benton's superintendent was "father."[71]

Officers supposedly did take a very paternal interest in their men. Sometimes they appeared to be almost indifferent to the accomplishment of the difficult tasks they set. "Good work rarely receives commendations," wrote William Brockie, "it is taken for granted that a man selected for a certain job will do it." The reticence to bestow praise, however, was not a sign of insensitivity. The superintendent in *Benton of the Royal Mounted* was "secretly pleased" with the conduct of his extraordinary sergeant but "evinced little sign of his satisfaction." "Praise men up — spoil 'em! Let 'em think it's their ordinary course of duty," was his customary maxim.[72] Silence masked a deep appreciation of what his men achieved.

The genuine concern of officers for their men was apparent in almost all popular materials dealing with the force. They were fair and just and refrained completely from "a spirit of petty bullying which too often is found in military service." More importantly, they always put the welfare of their men above their own comfort and safety. When Colonel Macleod made a dangerous winter ride to the United States through a blizzard to get pay and supplies, declared Morris Longstreth, he "instituted another pattern to become familiar in the Mounted Police, the pattern where an officer shares the hardships and faces the dangers with his men."[73] Those who followed faithfully kept the tradition intact.

This willingness to share the burdens of duty created a curious paradox around the notion of rank. While rank was obviously important and unavoidable in the force, the nature of police activities often undercut it completely. "A mighty leveller is the northern trail," declared Hiram Cody. "Here each stands for what he is, and his sole worth lies in himself." Ralph Connor agreed:

> When officer and man ride side by side through rain and shine, through burning heat and frost "forty below," when they eat out of the same pan and sleep in the same "dug-out," when they stand back to back in the midst of a horde of howling savages, rank comes to mean little and manhood much.

Those who commanded, it was stressed, relied "more upon the force and influence of their individuality than any mere supremacy which rank gave them."[74] It was a curious corps in which rank was at the same time denied and affirmed.

---

70   G.B. McClellan, "Introduction to the New Edition" in Haydon, pp. xv-xvi; Bindloss, *Winston*, p. 22; Cameron, p. 92; Jack London, *Best Stories of Jack London* (New York: Garden City Books, 1953), p. 52.

71   Kendall, p. 25.

72   Brockie, p. 101; Kendall, p. 31.

73   Gordon [Ralph Connor], *Corporal Cameron*, p. 401; Longstreth, *Scarlet Force*, pp. 56-57.

The influence of the Mounted Police officers on their men was profound, almost mystical. It transcended the mere imperative of direct orders and came to reside in the innermost core of their being, until in moments of crisis, it surfaced. One fictional Mountie, compelled to make an arrest which would cause great pain to someone he cared for, recalled the image of his superintendent. He remembered "the kindly eyes of the stern, gray-haired man, his fatherly smile," and then he did his duty. Even more striking was Dick Kent's experience. Dick was struggling single-handedly and without much success to quell a rebellion in an Indian village.

> Then suddenly his gaze seemed to waver. The crowd became a blur — a shadowy something before his eyes. In their place rose up the stern figure of Inspector Cameron — the worn, austere face, the steel-gray eyes, the decisive chin. Again Dick threw up his arm. A strange calmness pervaded him.[75]

Suddenly he was surrounded by an irresistible aura of authority, and the riotous Indians quickly submitted.

The kind of effect that Inspector Cameron had on Dick Kent went far beyond conventional authority. In fact, Cameron and those like him conformed to one of the major archetypes — the "wise old man." According to C.G. Jung, this figure represents "the superior master and teacher, the archetype of the spirit, who symbolizes the preexistent meaning hidden in the chaos of life."[76] He possesses the secret that there is, indeed, order beneath the chaos, and a knowledge of how to make that order manifest and possible. He is the confidant, the guide, and the helper of the hero. At a deep subconscious level, the popular image of the relationship between the Mountie and his officer often described the traditional relationship between the hero and his cosmic ally. This invested the officer with an authority that could not be questioned, an authority symbolized by rank but legitimized by something far beyond it. It was the authority of a father passing on the secrets of existence to a son, who one day would teach the same lessons to his son.

Paternalism reigned both within and without the force. One manifestation of this was the relationship between members of the force and their animals. The police, it was asserted, knew how to win the trust and affection of their dogs and horses. Sergeant Thorne earned the confidence of Silver Chief by refusing to beat the dog when it bit him. Sergeant Reilly tamed his bronco by exhibiting the kindness and calm assurance of "a firm parent toward a naughty but quite harmless child." Even though the force depended upon animals in its work, this sort of treatment was due to much more than pragmatic necessity. Sergeant Fones and his horse not only understood each other; "perhaps they loved each other." Roger Pocock recounted how one of his companions was found dead after a blizzard, his buffalo coat spread under the saddle "to ease and warm the horse at the expense of the rider." Of course, the best proof of affection was the conduct of the animals themselves, and the dog described by Major George Bruce demonstrated a typical willingness to face danger in aid of his master. It went for help when its trainer fell into an old bear trap, and then returned to attack a wolf about to pounce on the immobilized policeman. The

---

74 Cody, p. 10; Gordon [Ralph Connor], *Corporal Cameron*, p. 401; Mackie, *Sinners Twain*, p. 190.
75 J.B. Hendryx, "Delhanty of the Mounted," *Scarlet and Gold* (1922), p. 34; Richards, *Dick Kent and the Malemute Mail*, p. 216.
76 C.G. Jung, *The Collected Works of C.G. Jung*, Vol. 9, Part I, *The Archetypes and the Collective Unconscious* (London: Routledge and Kegan Paul, 1959), p. 35.

wounds the dog sustained were so severe it had to be shot.[77] Such devotion and courage could only be inspired by love, and the fact that such love was given by unreasoning, intuitive beasts was a sure sign that police concern for their animals was genuine.

Even more impressive was their "fatherly, gentle" treatment of the native peoples. The police were "ready always to help the Indians, to protect them from fraud, to keep away the whiskey peddler, to be to them as friends and brothers." In the North, declared the New York *Times* in 1931, the Mountie sometimes exhausted himself to "save the lives of those who have been given into his protection." Police paternalism was not restricted to Indians. The force demonstrated the same concern for newly arrived European settlers in the West, for the gold seekers who flocked to the Klondike, and for explorers in the Arctic. "Their influence," concluded MacBeth, "was felt constantly on the pulse of the growing country which, like a boisterous growing boy, needed restraint and guidance in reaching the fullness of its power."[78] Given the almost feudal concern of the police for the welfare of those in their charge, and given as well their strength, courage, discipline, and high sense of duty and refinement, it was inevitable that the police would be described in chivalric terms. To R.G. MacBeth, the force was a "unique body of knights of our modern day." Alan Phillips declared that "not since the days of King Arthur has there been such a chivalrous character" as the Mountie. The policeman was the "knight errant of order"; his actions were the "deeds of chivalry." For Harwood Steele the truth of the metaphor was all the more obvious, since his own father had been knighted, in large measure for services with the force. In a novel based loosely on his father's life, Steele made the point emphatically. The true love and wife-to-be of the hero, Hector, told him:

> you're the first real *man* I've ever met. Oh, it isn't just that nice red coat — though that goes to my head like champagne ... Every girl has dreams, too. "Someday," I dreamt, "I'll meet a real, real, man — brave, strong, chivalrous, with great, yes, great ideals — a fairy Prince, a knight of the Round Table." They say they don't live now — Oh, but they do! Perhaps the armour's gone but they are knights and Princes just the same.[79]

Chivalry was not dead, nor were its ideals.

---

77 John S. O'Brien, *Silver Chief, Dog of the North* (New York: Winston, 1933), p. 84; Harwood Steele, *To Effect an Arrest*, p. 6; Parker, p. 9; Pocock, *Tales of Western Life* (Ottawa: C.W. Mitchell, 1888), pp. 112-13; Major George Bruce, "Natuck: Experiences in the Life of Dr. H.G. Esmonde," *Blackwood's* 255 (Feb. 1944), pp. 105-10.

78 H. Steele, *Ninth Circle*, p. 54; Gordon [Ralph Connor], *Sun Dance Trail*, p. 205; Russell Owen, "Canada's Wardens of the Frozen North," *New York Times Magazine*, August 23, 1931, pp. 14, 20; H. Steele, "Policing the Arctic," *Scarlet and Gold* (1926), p. 16; MacBeth, *Policing the Plains*, pp. 40-41. According to Prof. R.C. Macleod, the relationship of the police to the Indians, especially after 1885, was a paternal one, although it became increasingly coercive. However, when the force moved north and encountered the Yukon Indians, who did not resemble the "noble redskins" of the plains, this paternalism became a contemptuous sort. This distinction in attitude was never suggested in the popular literature dealing with the force. See R.C. Macleod, "The North West Mounted Police, 1873-1905: Law Enforcement and the Social Order in the Canadian North-West," Ph.D. thesis, Duke University, 1972, p. 168; W.R. Morrison, "Native Peoples of the Northern Frontier" in Hugh A. Dempsey, *Men in Scarlet* (Calgary: Historical Society of Alberta/McClelland and Stewart, n.d.), pp. 77-94.

79 R.G. MacBeth, "The Fame of the Mounted," *Scarlet and Gold* (1926), p. 73; Phillips, *The Living Legend*, p. 8; J.M. Gibbon, "The Mountie," *Scarlet and Gold* (1938), p. 17; Evelyn D. Adams, "Prairie Ballad," *Scarlet and Gold* (1923), p. 88; Harwood Steele, *Spirit of Iron*, pp. 136-37.

The identification of the Mounted Policeman with the knight was extremely apt. The knight was one of the most conventional romantic heroes, and knighthood suggested the qualities attributed to the Mountie: the possession of strength, courage, and discipline. The knight embodied the authority and integrity that were so central to police character, reflecting the refinement and gentility, and the exclusive character of the corps. Knighthood rested on the interplay of adventure and duty, as did the policeman's devotion to the force. It symbolized the merging of the self into a corporate whole, without a loss of individual identity or freedom of action, harking back to a time when the ruling passion of a man's life was honour and service, not money. The policeman was not an anachronism — his efficiency testified to that. He was the heir of a glorious old tradition, which might have been faltering, but with its high aspirations and selfless ideals still exerting a catholic appeal.

The qualities attributed to the Mounted Policeman were unusual in degree but not in kind. His character conformed to a preconceived ideal, an ideal derived from the realm of myth and romance where chivalric imagery is extraordinarily constant.[80] Thus, there was something timeless about the Mountie. The appeal of his character transcended national boundaries and specific epochs. He was part of the universal realm of all archetypes.

But, at the same time, his portrayal reflected many of the concerns that confronted western society in the late nineteenth and twentieth centuries. Through the symbol of the Mountie, many of the conflicting desires and aspirations of the period were reconciled. He provided hope that society would not founder in a welter of contradictory impulses, and hope that, ultimately, satisfying answers would be found to the questions causing tremendous anxiety in an age of rapid and profound change.

In particular, the character of the Mounted Policeman provided a symbolic reassurance on two important questions. First, it addressed for many the crisis of authority associated with increasing doubts about the traditional Christian world view. Even if the old cosmology seemed to be losing some of its power, the symbol of the Mountie suggested that humanity itself could summon the necessary authority to stave off chaos. Even if the divinely enforced system of values was being fundamentally challenged, people could be strong enough to establish and preserve their own ethical code. Order would be enforced and morality maintained by an elite based on merit, which could preserve the aristocratic obligation of duty without contravening the democracy it served.

Second, the symbol of the Mountie addressed the problem of the individual in mass society. It suggested that individuals did not have to become meaningless and insignificant, but could exert themselves in the world and affect the destiny of both themselves and others. They could reconcile their own aspirations with the requirements of society, and could find work that was adventurous and challenging and yet, at the same time, useful and necessary. Even those of lowly background could earn fame, distinction, and honour. The future did not hold out a spectre of bleak monotony for the individual. It held out all the glory of the past.

NOTE

This chapter was previously published in Keith Walden, *Visions of Order: The Canadian Mounties in Symbol and Myth* (Toronto: Butterworth & Co., 1982), pp. 27-69.

---

80   Gillian Beer, *The Romance*, (London: Methuen, 1977), p. 16.

SECTION E

Crisis and Change

SEVENTEEN

Malczewski's List: A Case Study of Royal North-West Mounted Police-Immigrant Relations

Steve Hewitt

Stephen Malczewski had a problem. A naturalized Canadian of Polish birth and a lawyer by profession, the resident of Canora, Saskatchewan had heard repeated tales of corruption on the part of members of the Royal North-West Mounted Police (RNWMP), the forerunner of the Royal Canadian Mounted Police. Some Mounties were allegedly extorting money from immigrant farmers in the period immediately following the First World War. Through the intervention of Malczewski, dozens of allegations were investigated in 1919 and 1920, and one Mountie was prosecuted on bribery charges. These events would reveal a great deal about Mounted Police and immigrant attitudes toward each other and also demonstrate the often fearful and fragile nature of an immigrant's existence in Canada.

The roots of the problem in police-immigrant relations in Canora at the end of 1919 stretched back to the advent of the Liberal government of Sir Wilfrid Laurier in 1896 and the appointment of Clifford Sifton as Minister of Interior, the individual responsible for immigration. Sifton fostered an aggressive governmental policy which sought immigrants he deemed suitable for rural life in Western Canada. He gave a simple description of his ideal immigrant: "... a stalwart peasant in a sheep-skin coat, born on the soil, whose forefathers have been farmers for ten generations, with a stout wife and a half-dozen children, is good quality."[1] Sifton believed that this type of individual came from Eastern Europe. Consequently, for the first time the immigration of Ukrainians, Russians, and Poles, many of whom homesteaded, was encouraged.[2]

Ukrainians, like several other minority groups, received their share of bigoted treatment from nativist elements amongst the dominant Anglo-Canadian majority.[3] With the advent of the First World War, the situation grew far worse. Of the 170,000

---

1 Robert Craig Brown and Ramsey Cook, *Canada 1896-1921: A Nation Transformed* (Toronto: McClelland and Stewart Ltd., 1974), 63.
2 Gerald Friesen, *The Canadian Prairies: A History* (Toronto: University of Toronto Press, 1987), 245-6.
3 For an excellent study of nativism see Howard Palmer's *Patterns of Prejudice: Nativism in Alberta* (Toronto: McClelland and Stewart, Ltd., 1982).

Ukrainians living in Canada, most were originally inhabitants of the provinces of Galicia and Bukovyna in the Austro-Hungarian Empire, one of Canada's main antagonists in the war.[4] As a result, Ukrainians, many of whom were labelled "Galicians" and "Ruthenians," found themselves classified as "enemy aliens" by the Canadian government. The Conservative government of Prime Minister Robert Borden introduced several measures to deal with this alleged enemy. In October of 1914, an Order in Council required certain classes of "enemy aliens" to register at government offices, to report monthly, to carry government-issued identification, and to acquire special papers for travelling.[5] On the prairies, registration centres supervised by the Mounted Police were set up. This measure seemed designed with urban immigrants in mind: the centres were established in major cities and enemy aliens within twenty miles of these cities were required to report. A large number of rural Ukrainians outside of these areas thus escaped reporting.[6] By 1917, however, many Ukrainian-Canadians were stripped of their right to vote in the federal election, and approximately 6,000 were interned by the Canadian government.[7] Because of the many government regulations, the police had regular contact with numerous immigrants. In Saskatchewan and Alberta, 173,568 citizens of German and Austrian backgrounds were investigated during the war.[8] In Manitoba alone, between April and September of 1919, 75,000 enemy aliens made monthly reports to the Mounted Police.[9] The potential for an abuse of police authority was clearly present.

The nature of the RNWMP contributed to problems with immigrants. The Mounted Police had become a powerful Canadian institution, especially in western Canada, since its creation in 1873. Originally designed to pacify a large rural frontier, its mission changed along with a changing Canada. The twentieth century brought rapid urban growth to the nation and it was urban problems that increasingly dominated the Mountie agenda. One primarily urban problem was industrial strife. Fresh in the mind of the Mounted Police Commissioner A. Bowen Perry was the most dramatic example of a labour disturbance: the 1919 Winnipeg General Strike. The leaders of this event had been inaccurately labelled as "enemy aliens."[10] There was, however, a certain degree of industrial radicalism among immigrant workers, and it was this image of Eastern Europeans that was increasingly held by the Canadian state and its institutions.

The Force had traditionally experienced good relations with rural immigrants, in part because the latter group tended to be property owners and thus fairly

---

4 Frances Swyripa and John Herd Thompson, "Introduction," in *Loyalties in Conflict: Ukrainians in Canada During the Great War*, Frances Swyripa and John Herd Thompson, eds. (Edmonton: Canadian Institute of Ukrainian Studies, 1983), vii.

5 Peter Melnycky, "The Internment of Ukrainians in Canada," *Loyalties in Conflict*, 2-3.

6 Orest T. Martynowych, *Ukrainians in Canada: The Formative Period, 1891-1924* (Edmonton: Canadian Institute of Ukrainian Studies Press, 1991), 326.

7 Melnycky, 1; John Herd Thompson, "The Enemy Alien and the Canadian Government Election of 1917," *Loyalties in Conflict*, 25.

8 William and Nora Kelly, *The Royal Canadian Mounted Police: A Century of History* (Edmonton: Hurtig Publishers, 1973), 146.

9 "Report of the Royal North-West Mounted Police for the Year Ended September 30, 1919," *Sessional Papers*, No. 28 (1920), 13.

10 Friesen, 363.

conservative.[11] In 1899, one Mountie officer described the members of a Ukrainian settlement in Saskatchewan as "frugal, industrious and certainly the best workers in the country. It is believed by many that they will eventually form the best settlers in the district. They are anxious to learn the English language."[12] As the last comment suggests, a hierarchy of ethnic groups existed in western Canada, and Ukrainians were nowhere near the pinnacle. That position was reserved for Anglo-Saxons, from whom the RNWMP traditionally recruited a large number of members, especially to fill the officer ranks.[13] Many of these individuals reflected a society that was replete with class divisions. This class hierarchy aided the hardening of racial attitudes during the Victorian era because inequality seemed inherent in society. In other words, if the concept of a lower class was accepted then it was not a great leap in logic to believe that there were racial and ethnic groups beneath one's own.[14] Ignorance, fear, and suspicion characterized the attitudes of the Canadian state towards ethnic minorities during the First World War and its aftermath. The official RNWMP response to events in Canora in 1919 and 1920 reflected these characteristics.

In December of 1919, over a year after the war had ended, Malczewski responded to complaints of RNWMP injustice by putting pen to paper and writing a lengthy letter to J.A. Calder, a Member of Parliament from Saskatchewan and the federal Minister of Immigration and Colonization. The letter criticized several aspects of police activity:

> Since the Parliament passed the new Naturalization Act a lot of Poles and Ruthenians and generally foreigners from different countries apply for naturalization papers... The rule is to examine these applicants and make them as miserable and unpleasant as [the police] possibly can ... What more [sic] they intimidate this people and make them pay some amount of money for the examination ... the Constables are becoming a proper nuisance. Prosecutions every day for not registering, bothering on the trains for certificates, summonses to the Court for not having any papers, etc. The Justices of the Peace do not know what the Act is, and dont [sic] want to do in most cases, and the poor *Galicians pay, suffer abuse,* loses his time and what is most important, *gets so antagonized to the country and the laws of the country, that he thinks of leaving it by the first opportunity.* This Galician that had done the hardest work in the Northern part of the Province, the pioneers [sic] work, and is law-abiding, is always abused, because he cannot talk English and is too frightened to resist the abuse.[15] [Emphasis his]

---

11   R.C. Macleod, *The North-West Mounted Police and Law Enforcement 1873-1905* (Toronto: University of Toronto Press 1976), 150-61.

12   Ibid., 150.

13   Ibid., 73-88.

14   Douglas Lorimer, *Colour, Class and the Victorians: English Attitudes to the Negro in the Mid-Nineteenth Century* (New York: Leicester University Press, 1978), 106-7.

15   National Archives of Canada (NAC), Record Group (RG) 18, Royal Canadian Mounted Police (RCMP) Documents, Volume 591, Files 1055-1059, Malczewski to Calder, 18 December 1919. (Quotes in this paper appear in their original form. No attempt has been made to correct spelling or grammatical errors.) In 1919 the Canadian government passed a Naturalization Act that mirrored the policy proposed by the 1917 Imperial Conference. One of the main points was a ten year moratorium on the naturalization of enemy alien immigrants. The Liberal opposition pointed out that this would cause considerable confusion when dealing with groups such as Ukrainians, a minority group in the former Austro-Hungary Empire. Joseph A. Boudreau, "The Enemy Alien Problem In Canada, 1914-1921," Ph.D. diss., University of California, Los Angeles, 1965, 182-3.

Malczewski had a special familiarity with many of the allegations because, for a fee, he assisted immigrants on matters of naturalization. The role he played was similar to the *padrone* or "ethnic entrepreneur" written about extensively by historian Robert F. Harney. Harney offers this relevant description of *padronism*:

> It was protection that the *padrone* offered, protection against undue delay, protection against fraud by others, protection against all the dangers of an unknown world, of a world where the labourer could not cope for himself because of lack of education, lack of language skills, and lack of time to stand and fight when his cash supply was threatened.[16]

These were all roles Malczewski played. He was also not above using the events for his own personal advantage. For example, in a January 1920 letter to Saskatchewan Attorney-General W.F.A. Turgeon dealing with the allegations, Malczewski concluded with a request that he be appointed as a Justice of the Peace.[17]

Malczewski had also written to the Attorney-General back in December before his letter to the Minister of Immigration. In that letter he lodged an official complaint against Constable L.W. Preece of the Kamsack Detachment of the RNWMP. He alleged that Preece had charged a local farmer, Anton Kryschuk, five dollars for naturalization documents.[18]

At this point events became even more complicated because Preece, on hearing about the complaint, approached Malczewski and, in the latter's words, "promised me never again to treat this people bad…"[19] According to the same source, the Constable also mentioned his military service and his fear of losing his job. Malczewski, sufficiently sympathetic, wired Turgeon to request that Preece's name be removed from the original complaint. He still wished, however, to "make a general complaint against the behaviour of [the RNWMP] and if it is necessary I can furnish you with affidavits from a dozen of men of being forced to pay certain amounts of money to the RNWMP officers when examined for naturalization affairs."[20] Turgeon, however, had already forwarded Malczewski's initial letter to A. Bowen Perry, the Mounted Police Commissioner.

Not surprisingly, the first reaction of the Mounted Police to Malczewski's complaint was to investigate him. After all, this was a police force whose Assistant Commissioner at the time once underlined the words "Russian Jew" and wrote "NO" in the margin of a letter that offered the services of an individual of that background.[21] In fact, there was little effort made to hide Mounted Police attitudes toward ethnic minorities. Commissioner Perry's annual report on the RNWMP for 1919 stated:

> During the war … all foreigners received the most considerate treatment as long as they obeyed the laws of the country and pursued their ordinary avocations. The returned soldiers found them filling their jobs and enjoying prosperity. In Winnipeg,

---

16　Robert F. Harney, "Montreal's King of Labour: A Case Study of Padronism," *Labour/Le Travail*, Vol. 4 (1979), 73.

17　Saskatchewan Archives Board (SAB), M3, File 1.j., Box 22, W.F.A. Turgeon Papers, Malczewski to Turgeon, 14 January 1920.

18　NAC, RG18, Vol. 591, Files 1055-1059, Report of Sergeant R. Minces, 24 December 1919.

19　Ibid., Malczewski to Turgeon, 17 December 1919.

20　Ibid.

21　NAC, RG 18, Vol. 2169, file 16/18, Letter to Asst. Commissioner Routledge, 3 April 1919.

Calgary, Medicine Hat and other points, the resentment of the soldiers found expression in small disturbances provoked by the indiscreet acts and words of these people, who, as a body, have shown little appreciation of the just and fair treatment meted out to them by the people of this country. They have shown themselves ready to follow and support the extremists who play upon their ignorance and appeal to their national prejudices and sympathy for the central powers. Bolshevism finds a fertile field among them and is assiduously cultivated by the ardent agitator.

The assimilation of our large alien population is of the greatest importance and it demands wise and sympathetic action and constant attention.[22]

On 30 December 1919, Commissioner Perry received a report which described Malczewski's ethnic background and included the opinion of a Canora lawyer that the people of the town viewed him as a German agent. The report also noted that a Mounted Police Sergeant had failed to discover anything substantial on Malczewski other than his "considerable influence amongst the foreign element handling all naturalization applications for which he charges twelve to forty dollars and apparently poses as leader…"[23]

By 9 January, the case appeared to be closed. On that day, Inspector A.B. Allard, commander of the Southern Saskatchewan Detachment of the Mounted Police, Depot Division, informed the Commissioner that

the allegation made by Malczewski is false, no reason can be deduced, other than that of spite, either personally against Const Preece or against the Force generally, caused probably by the fact that he has induced many aliens to apply for Naturalization, so that he can charge them a sum of $12 to $40.00 as a fee. [A]fter collecting such a large fee it is hardly to his liking to have a policeman run his applicant up for failing to report, and he probably finds a falling off on the part of the Aliens to seek naturalization when they know, that they will likely draw attention to the fact that they have been avoiding the necessity of reporting.[24]

Allard based his dismissal of the complaint on the Mountie interview with Kryschuk, who had allegedly paid Preece the five dollars. The farmer said the money was for a livery bill. The investigating Mountie thus repudiated the allegation and noted that "Malczewski has for some time been under observation, and a number of reports have been rendered regarding him during the last few years. It is significant that as soon as Malczewski made the complaint he at once took steps to stop it."[25]

Five days after Allard labelled the complaint as "false," Preece was brought up on three separate charges of accepting bribes, including the one that had sparked Malczewski's initial letter to the Saskatchewan Attorney-General. An additional investigation by a Mounted Policeman had turned up other bribery allegations and inconsistencies in Preece's reports, and the charges were laid.[26]

The trial began on 14 January 1920. The prosecutor and Justice of the Peace were one and the same person: A.B. Allard. In fact, Allard, previously confident of the erroneous nature of the original accusation, also had another job as the officer commanding the RNWMP's Southern Saskatchewan Detatchment. His judicial role

---

22 "Report of the Royal North West Mounted Police for the Year Ended September 30, 1919," 14.
23 NAC, RG 18, Vol. 591, Files 1055-1059, Report to the Commissioner, 30 December 1919.
24 Ibid., Allard to Perry, 9 January 1920.
25 Ibid., Report to Allard, 7 January 1920.
26 Ibid., "Court Transcript: Testimony of Const. P.A. Jansen," 16 January 1920.

demonstrated the tremendous power enjoyed by the Mounted Police in western Canada. Mountie officers had served as Justices for less serious crimes since the creation of the Force. At that time, bureaucratic structures were not yet in place on the newly acquired frontier, thus police officers were called upon to fill additional positions. This procedure continued in smaller centres such as Canora well into the twentieth century.[27] Undoubtedly, RNWMP officers serving as Justices inhibited complaints against the Force, especially by immigrants, many of whom brought negative views of police with them when they came to Canada,[28] and who, once in their new country, found themselves labelled as "enemy aliens" and stripped of many of their rights.

Constable Preece's accusers took the stand first. Malczewski reiterated his earlier allegation. Under oath, Anton Kryschuk offered a rather different version from his previous description of the events in question:

> I am talking to Constable Preece about my case and I told him that my father and mother had naturalization papers before I was under 18 years, but I am not sure. He said I will give you a parole sheet and he made out a parole sheet, and he asked me if I was rich, and I told him if a man has good hands and good feet and he could see well I would not call him poor. He told me that Five Dollars won't bust me and he said if I stuck you on a case it would cost you more and I told him he would do without a case, and I gave him the Five Dollars...[29]

He informed Allard that he had lied previously because he "did not want to put Constable Preece in trouble..."[30] Sam Jarmicki was the next witness. He too admitted to paying Preece a bribe:

> Constable Preece came to my place on the 7th of last month ... He asked me if I report every month and I told him I never report. He asked me for my card and I said I have none. I am a farmer. He said you have to go to town and report. He sit down after while he said I will make you a parole card, then he made a parole card and I asked him if I had to pay something he said yes. I then gave him two dollars and he give me one dollar back...[31]

Two Mounties, including Preece's immediate superior, testified to some discrepancies in the accused policeman's reports.[32]

The man on trial was confident enough not to question any of the witnesses. Consequently, it was his word against his immigrant accusers. At the conclusion of the prosecution's case, Preece took the stand. He denied two of the charges, including the allegation that he had received money from Kryschuk; he did admit, however, to issuing a parole certificate to Kryschuk and later asking him to destroy

---

27   Macleod, 35-6.

28   Greg Marquis, *Policing Canada's Century: A History of the Canadian Association of Chiefs of Police* (Toronto: University of Toronto Press, 1993), 152. Cortlandt Starnes, Perry's successor, specifically voiced the notion that immigrant attitudes toward the police might have been poisoned by the policing environment in the country of their birth.

29   NAC, RG 18, Vol. 591, Files 1055-1059, "Court Transcript: Testimony of Anton Kryschuk," 15 January 1920.

30   Ibid., 15 January 1920.

31   "Testimony of Sam Jarmicki," 16 January 1920.

32   Ibid., "Testimony of Const. P.A. Jansen and Sgt. W.G. Pearce," 17 January 1920.

the document because it was not needed. The next day, the embattled Mountie told the court that he had received a dollar as a "present" from Sam Jarmicki.[33]

In the end, Preece's word was good enough for Justice of the Peace Allard. He acquitted Preece on two of the charges because the Inspector "experienced great difficulty, in finding out when these witnesses in giving evidence, were speaking the truth…"[34] Allard did, however, convict Preece on the third charge, the only one he had admitted to: accepting a one dollar bribe. Allard fined him fifteen dollars and returned him to active duty.[35]

Allegations of Mounted Police corruption involving immigrants did not, however, end with these acquittals. On 16 January, just after Preece's trial had started, Malczewski mailed the Commissioner a list of forty-one immigrants who he claimed had paid bribes of some sort. Malczewski's covering letter explained why all the allegations were suddenly coming to light:

> It appears to me that certain officers of your force abused their authority by taking money from the applicants for naturalization while interviewing them as required by the act … Up until the end of October last year there were not prosecutions but only certain amounts of money paid to the officer interviewing the applicant. This was not so bad and while it was not right the men did not want to have any trouble with an investigation and when I asked them, whether I should take the matter with proper authorities, they always told me not to do anything as they did not mind to pay the few dollars and be done with it.
>
> But since the regular force started to do their duties in this district, nearly all men that applied for naturalization were fined before Justice of Peace. Then the complaints started to come in such lots, that I thought the best to ask Ottawa to do something…[36]

The response of Canora-area immigrants was in keeping with Harney's analysis of *padronism*. He notes that while migrant Italian workers were not averse to paying tribute to a *padrone*, they became angry when the padrone failed to provide the services he had been paid to supply.[37]

Specifically singled out by the various complainants were Preece as well as a former member of the Force. Once again, Mounties investigated the allegations. And, once more, local residents presented damning testimony. Several farmers alleged that a Mounted Policeman requested reimbursement for the expense of his trip to their farm. Most of those making accusations were not interviewed by the Mounties, however, and of those that were, all but a few denied making any complaint against the police (see Table One).[38]

Still, the allegations did not end. This time another individual informed his local Member of the Legislative Assembly (MLA) of alleged illegalities. In turn, the MLA made an official complaint to the Commissioner. A Mounted Policeman again conducted interviews with complainants and the same result occurred: the accusations

---

33 Ibid., "Testimony of Const. L.W. Preece," 18 January 1920.
34 Ibid., Allard to Perry, 2 February 1920.
35 Ibid., "Decision of A.B. Allard," 2 February 1920.
36 NAC, RCMP Records, Vol. 591, Files 1055-1059, Malczewski to Perry, 16 January 1920.
37 Harney, 74.
38 NAC, RCMP Records, Vol. 591, Files 1055-1059, Allard to Perry, including interviews, 2 February 1920.

Table One
Malczewski's List

Name	Address	Alleged Amount	Result
Metro Maydanyk	Ormside, SK	$10.00	Unknown
Wasyl Suknacki	Ormside, SK	Unknown	Not under oath, denies allegation
Andrew Tymochko	Ormside, SK	Unknown	Unknown Not under oath, denies allegation
Stach Antonishyn	Ormside, SK	Unknown	Unknown Under oath, denies allegation
John Baymack	Ormside, SK	$10.00	Not under oath, denies allegation
Nykola Baytalan	Ormside, SK	$10.00	Under oath, alleges being made to pay $2.50 to Mountie driver
Joseph Juzwak	Ormside, SK	$10.00	Not under oath, denies allegation
Wasyl Doroshi	Ormside, SK	$10.00	Not under oath, denies allegation
Joseph Magdy	Ormside, SK	Unknown	Unknown Under oath, denies allegation
W. Radwanski	Glenn Elder, SK	$3.00	Unknown
Mike Kostyniuk	Glenn Elder, SK	$3.00	Unknown
John Szczur	Glenn Elder, SK	$3.00	Unknown
Henry Sakaluk	Glenn Elder, SK	$3.00	Unknown
Geo. Czerniawski	Glenn Elder, SK	$3.00	Unknown
John Ewaschuk	Glenn Elder, SK	$3.00	Unknown
Mike Balicki	Glenn Elder, SK	$3.00	Unknown
Jim Cherwonicki	Glenn Elder, SK	$3.00	Unknown
Mike Kuzmeniuk	Glenn Elder, SK	$3.00	Unknown
Harry Kostyniuk	Glenn Elder, SK	$3.00	Unknown
Stephen Kliszcz	Glenn Elder, SK	$3.00	Unknown
Alex Sandak	Glenn Elder, SK	$3.00	Unknown
John Diaduk	Glenn Elder, SK	$3.00	Unknown
George Presniak	Glenn Elder, SK	$3.00	Unknown
Miron Jalowicki	Glenn Elder, SK	$3.00	Unknown
Johan Tokar	Glenn Elder, SK	$3.00	Unknown
Metro Chahorski	Glenn Elder, SK	$3.00	Unknown
John Fedyk	Glenn Elder, SK	$3.00	Unknown
Stephen Nahirniak	Glenn Elder, SK	$3.00	Unknown
Anton Kucharyshyn	Glenn Elder, SK	$3.00	Unknown
John Demetriuk	Glenn Elder, SK	$3.00	Unknown
John Kostyniuk	Glenn Elder, SK	$3.00	Unknown
Dominik Medloski	Sturgis, SK	$3.00	Unknown
Andrew Kutny	Canora, SK	$3.00	Unknown
Sam Jarmicki	Ormside, SK	$10.00	Unknown
Zydor Jaremski	Ormside, SK	$10.00	Unknown
Teodor Juzwak	Ormside, SK	$10.00	Unknown
Tom Tymoczko	Stenen, SK	Unknown	Unknown
Andrew Michajluk	Sturgis, SK	$10.00	Allegation dismissed: "one man's word against another's"
Nykola Piwusz	Sturgis, SK	Unknown	Legally fined
John Ratushniak	Canora, SK	Unknown	Unknown
John Popek	Canora, SK	Unknown	Unknown

Source: Names and figures are from NAC, RCMP Records, Malczewski to Commissioner Perry, 16 January 1920. Results are from ibid., Allard to Commissioner Perry, 2 February 1920.

were dismissed. In this case, there appears to have been a genuine misunderstanding, as individuals fined by the police found their fines cancelled by a Justice of the Peace. It was not properly explained to the men involved that the government had revoked the Order in Council between the time the fines were levied and the time that court appearances were made to pay the required amount.[39] This incident clearly demonstrates a lack of communication between police and immigrants.

Of the allegations made over a three month period, only one conviction occurred. Several factors explain this. While the Mounted Police did investigate the complaints, an ethnocentric bias hampered the fairness of both the examination and the eventual trial. Accusations from "enemy aliens," especially ones who did not always have an efficient grasp of the English language, did not carry much weight with Anglo-Canadian Mounties. In addition, the immigrant farmers themselves seemed unwilling to pursue the matter beyond grumbling to Malczewski. Such hesitation on the part of newcomers to an occasionally hostile nation, however, is understandable. These men came to Canada not to challenge the status quo, but to create a better life for themselves and their families. It was far easier (and perhaps more rational) to comply with a policeman's demand for money. One farmer explained his compliance this way: "I am not a naturalized British subject, and I was afraid that they might take my land away that is why I paid up the $10.00 as soon as I could…"[40] The fear of deportation also pervaded immigrant communities at the end of the war. A June 1919 amendment to Section 41 of the Immigration Act, ostensibly to deal with those involved with the Winnipeg General Strike, created broad criteria to deem an immigrant prohibited and thus deportable. The changes even allowed naturalized citizens to be "denaturalized" and expelled.[41]

Making an allegation of corruption against the Mounted Police would also have filled most native-born Canadians with trepidation. As historian Douglas Owram has noted, the Mounties

> were often depicted as the law itself … Once the police came to symbolize the abstract concept of rule by law they were endowed with greater power and authority than could have been obtained through mere cunning or the crude use of force. In essence the individual policeman, though praised for his attributes, was subordinated to the much more powerful tradition of British law and British justice. The scarlet coat of the North West Mounted Police had been deliberately chosen in order to evoke the British tradition. Thus the myth of the police became in reality a part of the tradition of law in British society … The man and the abstract concept merged into a symbol that few dared to challenge.[42]

Combine that powerful symbolism with a negative image of the police that many

---

39 Ibid., Allard to Perry, 23 February 1920.

40 Ibid., Testimony of John Zyckzkowski, 20 January 1920. Near the end of the war the Great War Veteran's Edmonton convention passed a resolution calling for the confiscation of all lands granted to immigrants from enemy countries. This measure justifiably terrified Ukrainians in northern Alberta. Two members of the Alberta legislature, including one who was Ukrainian-Canadian himself, received Prime Minister Borden's personal assurance that the government was not contemplating such a policy. Boudreau, 171-2.

41 Barbara Roberts, *Whence They Came: Deportations from Canada, 1900-1935* (Ottawa: University of Ottawa, 1988), 84-5.

42 Doug Owram, *Promise of Eden: The Canadian Expanionist Movement and the Idea of the West, 1856-1900* (Toronto: University of Toronto Press, 1992), 140.

immigrants brought with them from their home countries and it is perhaps surprising that any allegations surfaced at all.[43] The intervention of Stephen Malczewski ensured that the complaints were heard. For him his reason for acting was simple: "It was getting bad and I could not stand any longer the abuse."[44]

NOTE

This chapter was first published in *Saskatchewan History*, 46, no. 1 (spring 1994), 35-41. Illustrations in the original have been omitted. The author extends his special thanks to Dr. W.A. Waiser for his helpful comments.

---

43 Similar events occurred in Moose Jaw in 1914. See Melnycky, "The Internment of Ukrainians in Canada," 4.

44 SAB, Turgeon Papers, Malczewski to Turgeon, 14 January 1920.

EIGHTEEN

The Royal North-West Mounted Police and Labour Unrest in Western Canada, 1919

S.W. Horrall

During the early morning hours of 17 June 1919 eight leaders[1] of the Winnipeg General Strike were arrested by members of the RNWMP and charged that as officials of the One Big Union they had conspired together to replace constituted authority with a soviet form of government.[2] Although a royal commission which investigated the causes of the strike[3] found no evidence of any seditious conspiracy, nor any connection between the strike and the OBU,[4] seven of the eight accused were eventually convicted by the courts of trying to "overthrow" the state.[5]

The verdict touched off a controversy which still continues. "Strike or Revolution?" asked Masters in his pioneering study of the labour dispute. Most historians now accept his conclusion, with varying refinements, that it was not an incipient revolution but "an effort to secure the principle of collective bargaining."[6] Nonetheless, it was widely believed at the time that the OBU represented a revolutionary challenge to established authority. Borden, in his memoirs, described the strike as an attempt to supersede the existing government with one based upon "absurd conceptions of what had been accomplished in Russia."[7]

What evidence did the prime minister have for such a view? Although a full study of the role of the federal security agencies has yet to appear, it is generally accepted that the government's action was influenced by information it obtained from a number of intelligence sources. Rodney has emphasized the reports of "Moscow Money" being diverted to Canada for revolutionary purposes as reason for the position of the authorities.[8] Others have turned to the intelligence reports of the

---

1   R.B. Russell, W. Pritchard, J. Queen, A.A. Heaps, G. Armstrong, R.E. Bray, W. Ivens, and R.J. Jones.
2   D.C. Masters, *The Winnipeg General Strike* (Toronto 1950), 115.
3   "Report of the Royal Commission ... upon the causes and effects of the General Strike ... H.A. Robson, KC, commissioner," 1919, 3.
4   Ibid., 13.
5   W.J. Tremeear, ed., *Canadian Criminal Cases*, XXXIII (Toronto 1938), 12.
6   Masters, *Winnipeg General Strike*, 134.
7   H. Borden, ed., *R.L. Borden: His Memoirs* (Toronto 1938), 972.
8   W. Rodney, *Soldiers of the International* (Toronto 1968), 26.

Dominion Police, RNWMP, and the Department of Militia to explain its response, although McCormack has shown that there was very little co-ordination in their investigations and their findings were often contradictory.[9]

As the responsible federal police force in western Canada in 1919 the Royal North-West Mounted Police was perhaps the most important of these security agencies. McNaught and Bercuson have suggested that the intelligence reports of the RNWMP supported the official view that the strike was revolutionary in nature.[10] This seems a reasonable conclusion considering that it was the members and secret agents of the Mounted Police who provided the backbone of the evidence that led to the conviction of the strike leaders.

It is a view that has been perpetuated by the writers of quasi-official histories of the force which, although too often preoccupied with justifying its ways to man, have been widely read in their time. Longstreth wrote colourfully of "Red wisdom" journeying from "sweat shop to sweat shop," and the spread of "Russian venom" by "Muscovite emmissaries."[11] Fetherstonhaugh was more explicit, describing the strike as "No ordinary fight for higher wages or improved working conditions ... but a campaign to impose upon the people a dictatorship by the One Big Union."[12] More recently the Kellys, ignoring the historical scholarship of the last quarter century, have claimed that the strike leaders "were plotting to overthrow the government, by force if necessary."[13]

How true is this interpretation of the intelligence role of the RNWMP during those critical months that led up to the breaking of the strike? What steps did that force take to organize a secret service and how did it operate? Did the Mounties see bolsheviks and caches of arms behind every tree? Did they advise the government that the One Big Union and the Winnipeg strike were all a part of a plot to kick it off Parliament Hill? For so convinced was Borden of the revolutionary nature of the labour unrest that following the strike he quickly took steps to use the legendary frontier force as the nucleus for a new nation-wide, centrally controlled, federal security organization — the Royal Canadian Mounted Police.

The Mounted Police was initiated into the world of secret agents and espionage in 1914 when it became a part of the intelligence network organized under the Dominion Police to protect national security. As the provincial police force in Alberta and Saskatchewan it spent the early years of the war investigating the rumoured plots of German spies and enforcing the various regulations under the War Measures Act which were aimed at restricting the activities of the large enemy alien population on the prairies.

As the war drew to a close the RNWMP began to direct its attention to radical labour organizations like the Industrial Workers of the World. These security investigations were gradually curtailed, however, following the termination of the contracts for provincial policing in 1917 and the government's decision to allow

---

9   R. McCormack, *Reformers, Rebels, and Revolutionaries* (Toronto 1977), 178.

10   K.McNaught and D.J. Bercuson, *The Winnipeg Strike: 1919* (Toronto 1974), 91.

11   T.M. Longstreth, *The Silent Force* (New York 1927), 290.

12   R.C. Fetherstonhaugh, *The Royal Canadian Mounted Police* (New York 1938), 179.

13   N. and W. Kelly, *The Royal Canadian Mounted Police: A Century of History* (Edmonton 1973), 151.

members of the force to volunteer for overseas military service.[14] By the fall of 1918 over eighty police posts had been closed in Alberta and Saskatchewan, and the transfer of men to the Canadian army had reduced the Mounted Police to little more than a border patrol.

Just when it looked as if the Mounted Police was about to disappear into the pages of history an important intelligence-gathering role was suddenly thrust upon it. Behind the change was the federal government's dogged belief that a sinister conspiracy lay at the root of the growing number of strikes and industrial disputes that occurred in 1918. Reports from the Dominion Police and the Department of Militia on the labour situation were contradictory.[15] As a result Borden asked an old political colleague, C.H. Cahan, later director of public safety, to investigate the revolutionary propaganda prevalent in the country.[16] Cahan submitted the results of his enquiry to the minister of justice in September. It was not the Germans or the IWW, he reported, that were behind the unrest, but the Bolsheviks. If there was any doubt about these findings they must have been dispelled when Borden learned from British intelligence sources in December 1918 that the Soviet government intended to launch a propaganda campaign in North America.[17]

Among the measures taken to meet this perceived threat was a reorganization of the federal security and intelligence system in western Canada. Hitherto the Dominion Police had had nation-wide responsibility for the enforcement of federal laws and the security provisions of the War Measures Act. On 12 December 1918 this responsibility was geographically cut in half.[18] The RNWMP took over from the Dominion Police from the Lakehead to the Pacific, leaving the operations of the latter force confined to eastern Canada. In addition, the strength of the Mounted Police was increased to twelve hundred men.

One of the principal thrusts of this reorganization was the desire to ensure that there was an adequate mobile force in the west to meet any civil disturbance. N.W. Rowell, the minister in charge of the Mounted Police, was at pains to inform the provincial governments later in the new year that the force was available to assist them should any disorders occur.[19] With many of the municipal police forces already unionized, the government had already taken steps to ensure that the Mounties themselves could not be affected by the unrest by passing an order-in-council which prevented them from joining or associating in any way with any union or association of employees.[20]

Another result of this change was that it created two secret services where formerly there had been only one. The RNWMP reported to the president of the Privy Council, the Dominion Police to the minister of justice. No provision was made for any overall direction of their operations or analysis of their intelligence. Cahan, the director of

---

14 Canada, *Sessional Papers*, Report of the Commissioner of the RNWMP for 1918, 7-8.
15 R. McCormack, *Reformers, Rebels and Revolutionaries* (Toronto 1977), 441-2.
16 Public Archives of Canada [PAC], Borden Papers, 56642, Borden to Cahan, 19 May 1918.
17 Borden Papers, 60920, Borden to White, 2 Dec. 1918, telegram.
18 PC Order 3087, 2 Dec. 1918.
19 RCMP Headquarters, Ottawa, RCMP Records, G-2-6, Rowell to the attorneys-general of BC, Alberta, Saskatchewan, and Manitoba, 16 May 1919.
20 PC Order 2213, 7 Oct. 1918.

public safety, was supposed to advise the government on security matters but he resigned early in 1919. Lacking centralized control, each departmental intelligence service more or less went its own way, each carrying out its own investigations, sometimes tripping over each others' toes in the process, and each drawing up its own assessment of conditions. They tried to keep each other informed of the results of their work by circulating the reports of their agents among the five or six key ministers and their senior advisers in Ottawa. It was not the best of security systems at a time when the country needed reliable intelligence and analysis of what was happening and was likely to happen. Added to this, the effective leader of the government, Sir Robert Borden, was in Europe from November 1918 to May 1919 attending the Peace Conference.

Since October 1917 the minister responsible for the RNWMP had been Newton Wesley Rowell. A onetime leader of the Liberal party in Ontario, he had broken with his party over the conscription issue and joined Borden's Union Government. Rowell quickly set about organizing an effective secret service and laying down guidelines for its operation. Following the transfer of responsibility to the Mounted Police in December 1918 he had taken steps to secure the return of the Mounted Police cavalry squadrons serving overseas.[21] Early in the new year he informed his deputy minister, A.A. Maclean, the comptroller or administrative head of the force, of the priorities he wished given to secret service duties: "It is most important that this branch of the service should receive most careful consideration and that an efficient service should be maintained so that the government would be kept thoroughly advised of what is going on in the principal centres where I.W.W. or other revolutionary agitators might be at work."[22]

Rowell did not share the opinion of the hardliners among officials in Ottawa on the extent of the Bolshevik conspiracy and the measures needed to confront it.[23] He was conciliatory in his attitude towards labour and opposed to a repressive policy.[24] This was apparent in his assessment of the labour unrest, and the operational guidelines he brought to the attention of A.A. Maclean. Most of the leaders of organized labour, he informed Maclean, were opposed to Bolshevik propaganda. The ordinary workers who appear to express approval of revolutionary doctrine do so, he continued, without clearly understanding its real nature or what is actually happening in Russia. In Rowell's view, their ignorance had to be met with education. Finally, he identified a "small minority," largely of "foreign birth," who had imbibed the doctrines of class war and believed in revolution to achieve their ends. "Take care," he warned the comptroller, that where prosecutions are begun they are only taken up against this final group.[25]

As soon as he was informed of the minister's policy, Commissioner Perry of the RNWMP took steps to draft operational directives for the guidance of his divisional commanders. In the first of these he outlined the main threat to security and the legal action which was to be taken against those behind it. The objects of security

---

21 Borden Papers, 49413, White to Borden, 16 Dec. 1918, telegram.
22 RCMP Records, G-2-6, Rowell to Maclean, 4 Jan. 1919.
23 McCormack, Reformers, *Rebels and Revolutionaries*, 445.
24 M. Prang, *N.W. Rowell: Ontario Nationalist* (Toronto 1975), 267.
25 RCMP Records, G-2-6, Rowell to Maclean, 20 Jan. 1919.

investigations, he informed his field officers, were to be those individuals and organizations that espouse the pernicious doctrines of Bolshevism. He identified the main centres of radical activity as Winnipeg, Edmonton, and Vancouver. All those suspected of revolutionary activities, he ordered, were to be watched and a careful record kept of all their public utterances. In addition, the divisions were to keep themselves informed on all radical publications in their area. Legal proceedings, he instructed, were to be taken up where possible under the various wartime regulations and the sections of the Criminal Code dealing with sedition. Perry also requested that each commanding officer forward a summary of the secret service activities in his district to Headquarters every month.[26]

In his second memorandum the commissioner drew the attention of his immediate subordinates to the need to create an efficient detective service of carefully selected men who could operate without drawing suspicion on themselves. Their primary task was to penetrate all labour organizations in their district, identifying which groups and which leaders favoured revolutionary action. Finally, Perry demonstrated that he had well and truly grasped the fundamental objectives of any intelligence service. "It must be borne in mind," he stated, "that the only information which is of any value in connection with Bolshevism is the valuable and first hand information of what is going to happen before it occurs in sufficient time to permit arrangements being made to offset any intended disturbance."[27]

The new duties required a considerable amount of reorganization. Men had to be transferred to Manitoba and British Columbia, and accommodation found there for new divisional headquarters and detachments. Funds had to be found to support the new operations. During the war Perry had employed individuals from time to time to assist him with the administration of secret service investigations. With the expansion of responsibilities some of this work was now taken over by a new department at Headquarters in Regina known as the Criminal Investigation Branch.[28] Its first head was Assistant Commissioner W.H. Routledge. CIB became responsible for all correspondence and instructions regarding criminal and security matters between Headquarters and the field divisions. The change resulted in a significant delegation of the commissioner's authority, although during 1919 Perry continued to exercise close personal control over all secret service duties.

One of the commissioner's immediate problems was lack of personnel. In December 1918 he had only eight secret agents and a half dozen detectives in his entire command.[29] Most of the agents employed during the war to investigate enemy aliens had been discharged. Several of his most experienced detectives were overseas with the cavalry squadrons. While he awaited their return he requested immediate authority to hire twenty additional agents. Perry estimated the cost of the new secret service operations during the coming fiscal year at $87,500. This sum included salaries for the agents at $125 per month, their expenses, and the pay of informants. The government readily agreed to his request and the funds were made available in February 1919 from the War Appropriation.[30]

---

26   Ibid., B-1, 958, Circular Memorandum 807, 6 Jan. 1919.
27   Ibid., Circular Memorandum 807A, 6 Jan. 1919.
28   Ibid., General Order No. 13176, 2 Feb. 1919.
29   Ibid., G-2-6, Perry to Maclean, 14 Jan. 1919.
30   PC Order 363, 20 Feb. 1919.

Procuring suitable men to operate undercover at such short notice was not easy. As the officer in charge of the Crow's Nest Pass District wrote after turning down a clean-cut Anglo-Saxon applicant: "What we need is men who can speak several Slavic languages, and do the work of a coal miner."[31] At the end of February the commanding officer in Winnipeg was still without suitable men who had the language requirements to investigate the unions in the Fort William area.[32] Not surprisingly, many of the agents and many of the regular members who were recruited to work undercover were of central eastern European origin.

One of the most successful of these was Detective Constable F.W. Zaneth. Born in Italy, Zaneth (Zanetti) emigrated as a boy with his family to Moose Jaw where they eventually became naturalized British subjects. Later the family moved to the United States, but the young Zaneth returned and joined the RNWMP in 1917. In the spring of the following year he was sent to Drumheller to investigate the radicals believed to be behind the coal strike there. Like many other agents he had no prior experience or training. His success depended largely upon his own initiative. A factor in his favour was his ability to speak several languages. If he succeeded in infiltrating the union and providing useful intelligence, he would be kept on. If not, he would be withdrawn and transferred back to regular police work.

Zaneth did so well that Perry sent him back to Drumheller in September 1918, posing as Harry Blask, a member of the IWW from the United States. He soon gained the confidence of the union leaders and was initiated into the "secret grip" and other clandestine practices. In December he moved to Calgary where he became an organizer for the Socialist Party of Canada, and an acquaintance of most of the leading radicals in Alberta. A month later he attended the conference of the Alberta Federation of Labour in Medicine Hat. In March 1919 he was a delegate at the all-important Western Labour Conference in Calgary that spawned the One Big Union. Zaneth was one of Perry's prime sources of intelligence during the critical months that led up to the strike in Winnipeg. He was also to be the star witness for the prosecution in the trial of the strike leaders.[33]

To many of the labour organizations the secret agents and detectives of the RNWMP were police spies or agent provocateurs, a despicable group of men who carried out what they believed were dishonest and unlawful assignments simply for money. Elaborate precautions were often taken to prevent them from penetrating unions and political parties. In Winnipeg Superintendent Starnes reported that his agents had to operate with great care, as members of the Socialist Party of Canada suspected every stranger of being a police spy.[34] The commanding officer in Vancouver, meanwhile, reported that the radicals had formed their own counter-intelligence service called the "Holy of Holies," which had his offices under constant surveillance and attempted to follow his men whenever they left the building.[35]

By one means or another the Mounted Police were able to evade these precautions skilfully. In Calgary, for example, some IWW sympathizers suspected that there was

---

31   RCMP Records, B-1, 955, Junget to Spalding, 21 Jan. 1919.
32   Ibid., Starnes to Perry, 27 Feb. 1919.
33   Ibid., SF, 0-284.
34   Ibid., B-2, 20, Starnes to Perry, 15 April 1919.
35   Ibid., B-1, 930, Horrigan to Perry, Feb. 1919.

a "stool pigeon" in their midst. It was decided that he had to be unmasked. The object of their anger, D/Constable Zaneth (Harry Blask), who was present, heartily endorsed their resolve to do away with the "son of a bitch." To allay any suspicion from falling upon himself Zaneth made an excuse to travel to Regina. Once there, Perry arranged for him to be arrested under the Wartime Regulations as an alien travelling without a permit. He was subsequently brought to court, fined, and released. The local press gave considerable prominence to the case, which didn't go unnoticed in Calgary. As a result Zaneth was able to return to that city without any doubt in the minds of his fellow radicals that he was anything other than a union organizer.[36]

A more serious threat to the intelligence network occurred in Vancouver. Two secret agents of the Mounted Police had infiltrated the Russian Workers Union, one of the organizations declared illegal on Cahan's recommendation in September 1918. In June of the following year fourteen of its members were arrested and deportation proceedings were started against them based upon the evidence supplied by the two agents. Shortly after their arrest friends of the Russians brought charges of perjury against the Mounted Police agents, contending that the testimony they gave at the deportation hearings was completely false. The case dragged on through the courts, attracting a great deal of publicity as the identity of the two men was revealed. Perry anxiously awaited the outcome. If they were convicted, the whole secret agent system would be endangered. The credibility of the force's agents was at stake. In addition, no intelligence organization was likely to succeed unless the agents it employed could be sure that their anonymity would be protected, even after they had left its service. Fortunately for the commissioner they were finally acquitted.[37]

The decision to re-organize the secret service in Western Canada was not without its critics. Opposition centred on the transfer of duties in British Columbia, where M.J. Reid, an official of the Immigration Department, had acted for several years as agent for both the Dominion Police and British Intelligence. Reid had built up an organization of secret agents and informers who were investigating radical labour unions as well as Chinese and Hindu nationalist groups. Cahan objected strongly to the reorganization. He felt that it was ridiculous to replace Reid, who had years of experience in security on the west coast, with the Mounted Police who had none.[38] Cahan was supported in his view by two influential Conservative members of parliament, H.H. Stevens and J.A. Calder.[39]

Pressure was brought to bear upon Perry to retain Reid's services in the same manner that he had been employed by the Dominion Police. With the apparent support of Rowell, the commissioner dug in his heels and refused to agree to any modification of the policy to place federal security matters in the west under the direct control of the RNWMP. For one thing Perry's staff in Vancouver had already gathered intelligence on Reid which led him to believe that he could not be trusted.[40] While Ottawa considered the subject, Reid dragged his feet, finding one excuse after another for not turning over his files to the officer commanding the Mounted Police

---

36 Ibid., SF, 0-284, Pennefather to Perry, 26 July 1919.
37 Ibid., A-1, 589.
38 Ibid., A-1, 1919, Cahan to deputy minister of justice, 9 Jan. 1919.
39 Ibid., G-2-6, Stevens to Rowell, 20 Feb. 1919.
40 Ibid., Horrigan to Perry, 24 Jan. 1919.

in Vancouver. Perry, meanwhile, took steps to reinforce his position. Upon his prompting the comptroller wrote to the heads of the other security agencies in Ottawa, informing them that henceforth any enquiries on security matters in British Columbia should be directed to the RNWMP. Perry also moved to have British Intelligence authorities informed that the Mounted Police had taken over from Reid, and that in future they should communicate with his office, if they required any investigation carried out.[41] The commissioner was determined to put an end, in western Canada at least, to the disjointed kind of security system that had existed. In the end Cahan and Stevens failed to get their way, which was perhaps one reason why the former eventually resigned as director of public safety.

In spite of the difficulties, by April 1919 the RNWMP had organized a highly successful covert intelligence operation in western Canada. Secret agents or detectives had managed to penetrate every important radical organization, some of them occupying executive positions in which they had the confidence of the leadership. Their reports gave a detailed account of the activities of the radicals, as well as a verbatim record of their public speeches. It is in these that one finds the problem of language which Bercuson and McNaught have noted.[42] Union agitators are frequently described as "Reds" or "Bolsheviks," their speeches as "Revolutionary." One suspects that these descriptions reflect not only the prejudices of the agents and informers, but also the universal difficulty encountered with the rhetoric of the radicals. Baxter has shown the diversity of opinion at the time as to the meaning of phrases like "Russian Revolution" and "Bolshevism."[43]

It was this kind of undigested intelligence that the crown used to prosecute its case against the strike leaders. Although some of this raw material found its way to Ottawa, it did not form the primary means by which the Mounted Police informed its minister on conditions in the west. In each division the agents' reports were analyzed by the commanding officer who used them to draw up his own monthly assessment of the situation in his area. These, as Perry had ordered, were forwarded to the CIB at Headquarters in Regina. From there copies were sent, often with additional assessments by the commissioner, to the comptroller in Ottawa who circulated them among the departments concerned. In this manner the government was being kept fully informed, as Rowell had requested.

The first of these monthly reports, which were for February, began to reach Regina early in March. It was clear from the beginning that the industrial areas were the ones which would give cause for concern. The commanding officer in Prince Albert, for example, in his report for March informed the commissioner that there was little in the way of radical activity among the unions, and no evidence of any sinister agency at work. A month later he expressed the view that the OBU would get little support in his area.[44] From the Maple Creek district, meanwhile, it was repeatedly reported that investigations had revealed nothing in the way of labour unrest, nor were they expected to as the area was largely rural and there were no organized unions.[45]

---

41   Ibid., Maclean to Rowell, 24 Feb. 1919.
42   McNaught and Bercuson, *Winnipeg Strike: 1919*, 43.
43   T.C. Baxter, "Selected Aspects of Canada Public Opinion on the Russian Revolution and its Impact in Canada, 1917-19" (MA thesis, University of Western Ontario, 1973).
44   RCMP Records, B-1, West to Perry, 5 May 1919.
45   Ibid., Demers to Perry, 12 April 1919.

Of more concern were the Lethbridge and Fort Macleod Divisions which had large mining industries in their areas. By March agents from Fort Macleod had already established themselves among the mining unions in the Crow's Nest Pass. They reported that a number of revolutionary speeches had been made, and that most of the agitators were Russians connected with the Russian Social Democratic party in Winnipeg. The commanding officer estimated that 90 per cent of the miners supported the radicals, and that a serious strike could result if they did not get their demands.[46]

In Lethbridge the February report indicated that the miners in the district were not as radical as those in the Crow's Nest Pass, and that there appeared no organized attempt to make trouble. These conditions changed after the March meeting of the Western Labour Conference in Calgary, and its decision to organize the One Big Union. The reports for April, May, and June highlight the effect of this event. The influx of OBU propaganda was noted as well as the presence of OBU spokesmen who were holding meetings at the various mines. The commanding officer believed that the OBU was gaining considerable support, especially amongst the "foreign element," and that a strike was possible, but nothing more sinister than this.[47]

From Edmonton the reports followed much the same pattern. There, however, considerable attention was paid to the activities of Joe Knight, the organizer for the Socialist Party of Canada. In June the sympathetic strike was reported as "orderly." A month later, at the behest of the crown prosecutor in Winnipeg, Knight's home, as well as the Trades and Labour Council office, was raided and material seized and forwarded to that city to be used in the trial of the strike leaders.[48]

One of the earliest areas of concern was British Columbia, where the Mounted Police had to start its security organization from scratch. What with the size of the province, the lack of staff, and Reid's obstruction, the commanding officer encountered some delay in establishing agents in all the industrial areas, especially outside the Lower Mainland.[49] By the end of March this situation appears to have been rectified and agents had penetrated most of the radical labour groups. As elsewhere, discontent appears to have quickly polarized in support of the OBU following the Calgary conference. In the March report the British Columbia Federation of Labour was stated to be all in favour of the new organization and the use of a general strike as a means of securing economic change. As a result, particular attention was paid to the activities of Kavanagh and Naylor, two OBU organizers. Superintendent Horrigan, the commanding officer, predicted the possibility of a general strike occurring, probably in June. His reports, however, were more concerned with the likelihood of trouble from the returned soldiers and the small "anarchial" organizations like the Russian Workers Union than they were in the OBU.[50]

As the OBU emerged as the catalyst of western discontent, attention naturally focused on the reports of the Western Labour Conference in Calgary's Paget Hall, from 13 to 15 March. This gathering was attended by two Mounted Police agents,

---

46   Ibid., Tucker to Perry, 28 Feb. 1919.
47   Ibid., Pennefather to Perry, 8 May 1919.
48   Ibid., Wroughton to Perry, 6 Aug. 1919.
49   Ibid., B-2, 70, Horrigan to Perry, 24 Feb. 1919.
50   Ibid., B-1, 930, Horrigan to Perry, 4 April 1919.

D/Constable Zaneth and Agent No. 10, who Perry described as having "for many years taken an active part in the Industrial Workers of the World and kindred associations, and is therefore peculiarly competent to discuss the leaders in such movements and their aims and objectives."[51] No. 10 was alarmed by the events which took place at the conference. The radicals, he reported, largely members ot the Socialist Party of Canada, had gained control and their resolutions had all been accepted. The ultimate aim of this leadership, he continued, was the overthrow of the existing "social order." To achieve this, they intended to unite organized labour in the west into One Big Union, and under the rallying cry of the "Six Hour Day" pull off a general strike about 1 June. Publicly, he stated, these leaders, who he identified as Knight, Kavanagh, Midgely, Pritchard, Naylor, and Johns, declare that they intend to reach their objective within legal bounds, but privately, he continued, their hope is that the strike will precipitate such drastic action by extreme individuals or groups as to lead to a breakdown of civil order which they can then exploit.

No. 10 had some recommendations which he believed would prevent this from happening. First of all, he suggested that the leadership of the present labour organizations should be strengthened as they were by no means unanimous in their support for the OBU. Following this, some progressive reforms in the area of wages, unemployment, and minimum working hours should be undertaken by the government. His most startling suggestion, however, was that the leaders should be illegally detained and held in secret custody until the danger period had passed. This he considered necessary if the government was to avoid going "down to defeat."[52]

None of the other intelligence reports of the Mounted Police had suggested anything quite like this. It was just the kind of evidence the hardliners in Ottawa would seize on to support their position. The officer in charge of the CIB in Regina recognized that it needed careful analysis before being forwarded east. He believed that No. 10's assessment of the situation was "considerably 'over drawn'," based upon the mistaken view that the radical leaders "had actually accomplished something, and the masses were ready to do their will." The aims of these individuals for a change in the social order are only "far fetched dreams," he wrote in his forwarding note to Perry, and unlikely to be accepted by the general public once they are shown in their true light. After all, he continued, the labour organizations seem to be "split" over the question of support for the One Big Union. "I have refrained from forwarding No. 10's report to Ottawa," he informed the commissioner, "as I concluded that you would wish to express your personal opinion with regard to the situation."[53]

Perry's subsequent comments on the proposed OBU were probably the most judicious and accurate assessment of conditions in the west that one can find among the plethora of intelligence reports to reach Ottawa. Avoiding inflammatory references to revolutionaries and Bolsheviks, he clearly identified that what he meant by "reds" were socialist "agitators." The commissioner agreed that the ultimate aim of the OBU was a fundamental change in the social and economic order of the country, but nothing would be done to achieve this, he informed the comptroller, until the five-man organization committee appointed at the conference had had an opportunity to gain the support of a majority of the union members in the western provinces.

---

51   Borden Papers, 56825, Perry to Maclean, 2 April 1919.

52   Ibid., 56831-5, Report of Agent No. 10 re Inter-provincial Labour Convention, Calgary, March 1919.

53   Ibid., 56830, Notes for Commissioner's Perusal re Report of Agent No. 10, nd.

Perry's analysis was largely based upon an extraordinary meeting that he had with three members of that committee — Midgely, Pritchard, and Kavanagh — shortly after the Calgary conference. At this face-to-face encounter there appears to have been a frank discussion between the head of security in the west and the union leaders concerning their aims and objectives. Perry described them afterwards as "Revolutionary Socialists," able and determined men who sought to bring about a change in social and economic conditions, but were "opposed to force or violence." Their immediate objective, they informed him, was to perfect the organization of the OBU following which they would call a general strike to demand a six-hour working day. This, they believed, would occur sometime in June.

"I am not prepared to say that they are aiming at a revolution," wrote Perry, but they are "influencing a section of labour in the west, and unchaining forces which, even if they so desire, some day they would be unable to control." There was a "possibility" of a revolution, the commissioner believed, if the strike was to lead to a breakdown of civil order which could be exploited by extremists. He identified Vancouver and Victoria as the most dangerous points, and suggested that the naval forces there be strengthened as a precaution. Perry concluded his analysis with a number of recommendations which were to go largely unheeded by government leaders in the weeks ahead. Above all, he warned against interfering with the organization of the OBU, prosecuting its leaders, or preventing them from publicly expressing their opinions. Such action, he continued, would only antagonize the larger and more moderate element of the labour movement who were sensitive about their civil liberties. Finally, he urged, measures must be adopted to provide employment for the returned soldiers.[54] He did not identify the existence of any sinister plot to overthrow the goverment by force, either by the western radicals or foreign agents.

Perry's report reached the comptroller's office in Ottawa by 12 April, on which day a copy was forwarded to White, the acting prime minister.[55] Government leaders, it appears, were already in a near state of panic over the situation in British Columbia. On 16 April White cabled Borden in Paris expressing the cabinet's alarm over plans "being laid for a revolutionary movement" among the "workers and soldiers there." Fearing serious disturbances, White asked Borden to arrange "for a British cruiser to be sent to Vancouver or Victoria.[56]

Understandably, Borden, who was in the throes of asserting Canada's sovereign status at the Peace Conference, balked at the suggestion. Assistance from the British government, he replied, should only be solicited "as a last resort." Why not, he suggested, use the RNWMP with its strength increased if necessary?[57] Plans began to increase the strength of the Mounted Police to 2500 men, but White was still not satisfied. He cabled Borden again a few days later on account of the "serious conditions in British Columbia and projected revolution movement about June first," again urging the despatch of a British warship.[58] The source of this intelligence, he informed Borden, was the comptroller of the RNWMP and the Militia Department.

---

54   Ibid., 56825-8, Perry to Maclean, 2 April 1919.
55   Ibid., 56824, Maclean to White, 12 April 1919.
56   Ibid., 60923, White to Borden, 16 April 1919, telegram.
57   Ibid., 60924, Borden to White, 18 April 1919, telegram.
58   Ibid., 60926, White to Borden, 28 April 1919, telegram.

The RNWMP source that White referred to was most likely a "Memorandum on Revolutionary Tendencies in Western Canada" drawn up by the assistant comptroller of the force, C.F. Hamilton, early in April. Hamilton had only recently returned to his position with the Mounted Police after serving during the war as deputy chief censor for Canada. His assessment reflected the views of the hardliners in Ottawa like Cahan, and it differed both in tone and substance from those of Perry and his officers.

Hamilton identified the existence of a sinister organization which was under the control of a "central directing body somewhere in Canada." Its influence could be seen not only in the OBU but in many other radical groups. The ultimate aim, he reported, of those behind it was the subversion of the existing social and political institutions and the establishment of a "Soviet Government" based upon the "Dictatorship of the proletariat." Although the "weapons and explosives" they had were insufficient for serious fighting, a "revolution by force of arms," he advised, "was conceivable under existing conditions."[59]

Within a few days of White's last cable to Borden regarding the situation in British Columbia, government leaders in Ottawa began to turn their attention more and more to events which were taking place in Winnipeg. On 1 May in that city workers in the buildings and metal trades walked off their jobs over demands for wage increases and the refusal of employers to bargain collectively. Two weeks later they were joined by some 30,000 other workers and the Winnipeg General Strike had begun.

The commanding officer of the RNWMP in Manitoba was Superintendent Cortlandt Starnes, who was later to succeed Perry as commissioner. Throughout the months that led up to the breaking of the strike, Starnes never identified it as anything other than a labour dispute.[60] He did not connect it to the OBU, although many of his agents' reports, which were also forwarded to Ottawa, did contain alarming rumours of events in Winnipeg and accounts of the inflammatory statements of the strike leaders.

As in the case of British Columbia, the Mounted Police had no existing organization in Winnipeg. This resulted in some delay, but by the end of March Starnes was able to report that his agents had penetrated the three main areas of radical activity, the Socialist Party of Canada, the Ukrainian Social Democratic party, and the socialist organizations among the Finns at the Lakehead.[61] Early in April Starnes was optimistic about the labour scene in the city, and his assessment gave no hint of the bitter conflict that was to occur a month later. The Socialist Party of Canada, he reported, had been working hard to win the support of the returned soldiers, but was having little success. As to the possibility of a strike, he expressed the view that many of the unions had just received wage increases "and danger of a large scale strike has been averted."[62] A month later conditions had changed. The effect of the Calgary conference was once again evident. There has been much discussion, he reported, in union circles over the OBU and all appear to be in favour of it. He also warned that

---

59   PAC, RG 24, vol. 3985, file NSC 1055-2-21, Memorandum on Revolutionary Tendencies in Western Canada, contained in Gwatkin to Stephens, 12 April 1919.

60   See, for example, Canada, *Sessional Papers*, Report of Commissioner of RNWMP, 1919, 11-12.

61   RCMP Records, B-1, 929, Starnes to Perry, 22 March 1919.

62   Ibid., Starnes to Perry, 9 April 1919.

the dispute between the workers in the building and metal trades would likely lead to a "sympathetic strike involving all the unions in the city."[63]

In spite of Starnes' reports, officials in Ottawa continued to see the strike as a seditious conspiracy. On 21 May 1919 two federal cabinet ministers, Meighen and Robertson, arrived in Winnipeg to try to bring an end to the general strike. Like the Citizens Committee and others, they already regarded the strike as an attempt at revolution.[64] As the crisis heightened, in the weeks which followed, this conviction among government leaders would grow until steps were finally taken to break the strike. Incredible as it may seem, however, Starnes was still reporting on 10 June that "Indications are that the backbone of the strike is broken, and it should only be a matter of a few days before the majority of the strikers are back at work."[65] He also informed his superiors that his agents had found no trace of any outside support for the strike. Seven days later, with the cabinet's approval, the strike leaders were arrested and charged with trying to overthrow the state.[66]

In the months that had preceded the arrests the Mounted Police had developed an effective intelligence service. All suspected organizations were successfully penetrated and enough information obtained to give reliable indication of their aims and the plans of their leaders. To obtain this intelligence the RNWMP had established a body of paid informers and undercover agents who had covertly infiltrated the various groups posing as fellow radicals. In selecting these agents the police had shown a willingness to recruit individuals of a suitable cultural or linguistic background, and to maintain them, if necessary, in their double role for months or even years at a time. These were professional developments which were to be important for the future.

A systematic means of reporting and analyzing the results of undercover operations had also been established. The agents submitted regular lengthy accounts of their investigations and the information supplied by their informers. These were evaluated by local area commanders, who used them to draw up monthly reports on the conditions in their districts. These in turn were forwarded to CIB at Headquarters in Regina for yet further analysis and comment.

Where this system seems to have fallen down was in Ottawa. It appears to have been the practice to forward to the comptroller's office not only the monthly reports and the additional assessments of Commissioner Perry, but also the grass roots material provided by the undercover agents. These were often heavily laden with the alarming and inflammatory statements of the radical leaders. They were recorded verbatim with the intention that they could be used later, if criminal charges were laid. What the agents reported could differ markedly from the conclusions and assessments of their commanding officers. These would be based upon the information provided by several agents working independently of each other.

In Ottawa there was no central body responsible for evaluating the material forwarded by the various security forces, resolving any contradictions in it, and

---

63 Ibid., Starnes to Perry, 9 May 1919.
64 McNaught and Bercuson. *Winnipeg Strike: 1919*, 57.
65 RCMP Records, H-V-1, vol. 2, Starnes to Perry, 10 June 1919.
66 McNaught and Bercuson, *Winnipeg Strike: 1919*, 79.

advising the cabinet on conditions. All the comptroller could do was to circulate copies of such reports as he felt necessary, or important, to other department heads and ministers. They in turn reciprocated in a similar manner. No overall analysis of the information received on the situation in the west seems to have been attempted. Instead, government leaders were faced with a miscellaneous collection of material that at times must have been understandably alarming and confusing.

Apart from Hamilton's unsubstantiated claims, there had been nothing in the reports of the RNWMP during the months prior to the breaking-up of the strike which revealed a revolutionary plot. Perry had expressed his concern over the possibility of disorder, if strikes and demonstrations should get out of hand, but he had not identified caches of arms, secret armies drilling, or foreign agents hatching a conspiracy.

Government leaders, nevertheless, stuck to the sinister-plot theory expounded by Cahan in the fall of 1918. One cannot be precise about why Borden and some of his colleagues continued to take the position they did. It is possible that they were affected to some degree by the widespread fear of red revolution that gripped the country. The strikes in the United States, revolutions in Europe, the rhetoric of the radicals and the conduct of the strikers may have helped to reinforce their convictions. There were also intelligence reports from other sources which usually conflicted markedly with those of the Mounted Police. It was reported by Chambers, the chief censor, for example, that a prominent Ukrainian socialist in Winnipeg was actually an ambassador of the Soviet government.[67] Meighen, the acting minister of justice, learned from a member of the Manitoba legislature that the Ukrainians in his province had guns and ammunition ready for a revolution.[68]

There was also Cahan's dogged belief in a Bolshevik conspiracy. The former director of public safety told Borden, on the latter's return from Europe, that the OBU intended to "kick the Government off Parliament Hill."[69] This conclusion was supported by reports received by the Directorate of Military Intelligence in Ottawa. The commander of the military forces in Winnipeg stated the "Evidence so far searched proves conclusively Bolshevik money from United States has been received; also Strike Committee working closely with supporters 'One Big Union.' No doubt seriousness of conspiracy throughout West."[70]

It is strange that the largest and best organized security force in western Canada, whose agents had penetrated the senior levels of the most radical organizations, should have had such little impact in Ottawa. Perhaps it fits the familiar pattern of miscalculation and ignorance on the part of Ottawa with regard to western conditions. How far did officials in Ottawa select those intelligence reports which suited their own preconceptions of the situation there? How far did they still see the prairies as a violent uncivilized frontier, albeit populated with radical foreigners rather than savage Indians, which had to be firmly dealt with?

---

67 D. Avery, "The Radical Alien and the Winnipeg General Strike," in C. Berger and R. Cook, eds., *The West and the Nation* (Toronto 1976), 218.
68 Ibid., 219.
69 Borden Papers, 61631, Cahan to Borden, 28 May 1919.
70 Ibid., 62009, general officer commanding Military District No. 10 to adjutant-general of militia, 18 June 1919.

Borden's obscure role is yet another factor in the whole affair. We know from the warning he cabled in December 1918 of Soviet plans to launch a propaganda campaign in North America that he had access to British intelligence sources. It appears that during his months in Paris these same sources continued to inform him on matters relating to Canada, and that after his return he regularly received a digest of a special weekly intelligence report prepared by the British Intelligence Service for the British cabinet.[71] What these reports told him, and how they affected his decisions regarding events in Winnipeg, remains a mystery. It is possible, however, that the British may have been deliberately selective in the nature of the information they made available to Borden in the hope of promoting anti-Soviet feelings in Ottawa which would strengthen Canadian support for measures like the allied intervention in Siberia.

The Winnipeg General Strike does seem to have brought one thing home to Borden — that the country's secret service system was inadequate. When the responsibility for security had been geographically divided in December 1918 between the RNWMP and the Dominion Police, Sir Percy Sherwood, the chief commissioner of police, had retired. During the war years Sherwood had established a high profile as the head of the nation's security forces. His departure left a vacuum that his interim replacement, A.J. Cawdron, could not fill, and it also appears to have disrupted the close intelligence liaison between the Dominion Police and Scotland Yard's Special Branch.[72]

The lack of leadership was brought to Borden's attention by the premier of Ontario who informed him that the chief of the Toronto Police Department had complained that "at this very difficult and crucial time there is really no head to the organization of the Secret Service of the Dominion."[73] Borden readily agreed that a successor had to be found for Sherwood, and his comment in reply that "until my return I supposed that this had received attention" indicated a lack of direction on security matters within the cabinet itself during his prolonged absence.[74]

Obviously concerned about any recurrence of industrial unrest or general strikes, the prime minister proceeded to bring about a radical change in the federal system of security and policing. On 5 August 1919 he held discussions on the subject with Perry in Ottawa. As a consequence the commissioner, who had already decided views on the deficiencies of the existing security system, drew up recommendations for a new federal police force.[75]

Perry's primary criticism was the division in ministerial responsibility; the Mounted Police reported to the president of the Privy Council, the Dominion Police to the minister of justice. His first recommendation, therefore, called for the two forces to be brought under one department without delay. This he suggested could be accomplished in two ways:

---

71   Ibid., 60930, colonial secretary to governor general, 27 May 1919, telegram.
72   Ibid., 60940, colonial secretary to governor general, 4 June 1919.
73   Ibid., 60947, Sir William Hearst, premier of Ontario, to Borden, 5 June 1919.
74   Ibid., 60954, Borden to Hearst, 6 June 1919.
75   Ibid., 50763, Perry to Borden, 7 Aug. 1919.

(a) by bringing them under one minister, leaving each with its existing area of jurisdiction, and its own executive head;

(b) by amalgamating the two forces into one, which might take the form of absorption of one by another.

In considering the merits of these two choices, he drew Borden's attention to the differences between the RNWMP and the Dominion Police. The first, he pointed out, was subject to military-type training, strict discipline, and was also armed. As well as being peace officers, he continued, its members were prohibited by law from becoming unionized. Perry was also careful to note that it had experienced detectives, commissioned officers who had a recognized social status and a reputation that was respected throughout the country.

The Dominion Police, in contrast, was organized like a municipal force. It was not armed, had no military training, and its discipline could only be enforced by a civil court. Because of its size, about 140 men as compared to the Mounted Police strength of 2500, it had to rely on other agencies to assist it in carrying out its duties. Here thought Perry was the basic weakness of any federal police service established under the Dominion Police. The latter agency depended upon the public, the assistance of the municipal police forces, and the employment of agents from private detective firms, about half of whom were American, to operate its secret service. It could not provide the basis for a federal police and security institution which was truly national in organization, sentiment, and direction.

Perry also believed that it was no longer possible to depend upon the ordinary citizen as a source of intelligence. During the war Canadians had been patriotically united in the cause to defeat Germany. But the war was over and the public was divided over the issues facing the country. As for the municipal police forces, they were no longer reliable either. Many of them had become unionized. In Winnipeg and Vancouver they had participated in the recent strikes. In the United States there had also been some serious labour disputes involving city forces. In London, England, even the Bobbies had gone on strike. Municipal forces, argued the commissioner, could not be depended on where industrial disputes were concerned. The government must have a force which would stand by the civil authorities when a breakdown in public order occurred.

Perry reserved his final criticism for the Dominion Police practice of hiring private investigators. The federal force had not developed its own body of experienced detectives. Some believe, he stated, that the detectives provided by such companies as the Pinkertons were the best in the world. This, he continued, had not been his experience. The country's secret service investigations should not be conducted by Americans, but by detectives who were "Canadian in nationality and sentiment." In concluding his memorandum Perry recommended that the best interests of the nation would be served by extending the jurisdiction of the RNWMP to all of Canada.[76]

The commissioner's recommendations became the blue print for a new federal police force. After some discussion with Rowell, the president of the Privy Council, Borden took steps to implement the proposals. On 10 November 1919 the RNWMP

---

76 Ibid.

Act was amended.[77] The legislation provided for the absorption of the Dominion Police and its duties by the western force. The Headquarters of the new body was to be located in Ottawa, and it would be answerable to one cabinet minister for its "control and management." It was to be responsible for federal law enforcement and national security throughout Canada. In keeping with its new role the RNWMP was to be renamed the Royal Canadian Mounted Police. To head the force the government named Perry. As a young man he had been one of the first graduates from the Royal Military College of Canada. Later he served as an officer with the NWMP during the North-West Rebellion. Laurier had promoted him to the office of commissioner in 1900 when the Boer War gave the government an opportunity to rid itself of his troublesome predecessor. Now, at the age of sixty, he prepared to take on the task of organizing the new body when the legislation came into effect on 1 February 1920.

Canada's secret service dated back to the days of Confederation when John A. Macdonald employed a number of agents under the umbrella of the Dominion Police to ferret out the plots of the Fenians. Thereafter, the Secret Service Section, as it came to be called, saw only flurries of activity prior to 1914. With the outbreak of war the dominion was faced with the biggest security problem in its history. At issue was the possibility of espionage and sabotage by the large population, mainly in western Canada, of enemy aliens. To meet this threat the government secured passage of the War Measures Act and organized a highly decentralized intelligence network which, although co-ordinated to a degree by the Dominion Police, relied upon municipal forces, officials in a number of federal government departments, and private detective agencies to carry out its investigations. The threat from the German and Austrian settlers, however, proved to be a hollow one, and the wartime security system was never severely tested.

In the industrial dislocation of the postwar period Ottawa thought it saw a far more serious threat to its authority. Its response was the establishment of a non-civilian centralized federal police and security force. The change contrasted with developments in the same area among its closest allies, Great Britain and the United States. In Washington and London responsibility for security and intelligence was to remain divided among a variety of government departments. It also reflected the growing influence of the federal government in the life and affairs of the nation. With the War Measures Act Ottawa showed that it was prepared to assume powers unto itself when questions involving the security of the country arose. With the creation of the RCMP it gave itself a capability of enforcing that authority. These developments were to provide the means for future action in times of national emergency. As a model for the new organization, the government turned back to the country's frontier experience, selecting a semi-military police force which had been founded half a century before to bring order to the western plains, an institution whose origins lay in the traditions of British colonial rule.

The change made the federal government the number one police power in the nation. It was not without its critics. There was concern that the RCMP would infringe upon the rights of the provinces under the BNA Act to administer justice. Prior to 1920 the enforcement of federal statutes was largely left to local police forces. As a result, Ottawa proceeded to tred softly throughout the 1920s, maintaining little more

---

77 *Statutes of Canada*, 1919 (2nd Session), 10 Geo. v, c 28.

than a token federal police presence in provinces like British Columbia and Quebec. In Parliament, meanwhile, J.S. Woodsworth, who saw the RCMP as an authoritarian threat to civil liberties, would persist for years without success in trying to reverse Borden's decision. One of the most important developments, however, of the reorganization of 1920 was that it paved the way later for federal-provincial contracts for the RCMP as a provincial and municipal police force, eventually giving Canada a unique system of law enforcement in all but two of its provinces. Finally, of course, it is no exaggeration to say that the Royal Canadian Mounted Police is but one more offspring of the Winnipeg General Strike.

NOTE

This chapter was previously published in *Canadian Historical Review*, LXI, no. 2 (June 1980), 169-190.

NINETEEN

The Surveillance State: The Origins of Domestic Intelligence and Counter-subversion in Canada, 1914-1921

Gregory S. Kealey

The groundwork laid in those early years formed the foundation of the present security and intelligence branch of the Force, a service which, in my opinion, and in the opinion of professionals in other countries, must rate with the best and most experienced counter-intelligence organizations in the world. (Commissioner C.W. Harvison, Royal Canadian Mounted Police, retired, 1967)

Such proud and confident words were commonplace in the years before the ugly revelations of the MacDonald Commission and the more speculative but equally embarrassing allegations concerning James Bennett and the death, during RCMP Security Service interrogation, of the former Canadian Ambassador to the Soviet Union, John Watkins.[1] Perhaps more surprisingly, Commissioner Harvison's certainty has been reflected to a considerable degree in the few serious works on the history of the RCMP. To a large degree the lack of historical scholarship on the RCMP has resulted from the paucity of sources. The RCMP and its successor agency, the Canadian Security Intelligence Service (CSIS), except for some minor and later much-regretted openness in the early 1960s, have deservedly earned a reputation among archivists and historians for inaccessibility.[2] The Access to Information Act of 1983 and the National Archives Act of 1985, however, have brought some relief from the problems of the past. Thus, the time has arrived for a re-examination of the origins of the RCMP, especially its security service, and for a reconsideration of the role the Canadian state has played in the area of surveillance and counter-subversion in the twentieth century.[3] This article is a first effort at such revision.

---

1   The literature on these episodes is growing but the best accounts remain John Sawatsky, *Men in the Shadows: The RCMP Security Service* (Toronto, 1980) and his *For Services Rendered: Leslie James Bennett and the RCMP Security Service* (Toronto, 1982); Jeff Sallot, *Nobody Said No: The Real Story About How the Mounties Always Get their Man* (Toronto, 1979) and Robert Dion, *Crimes of the Secret Police* (Montreal, 1982). On Watkins, see William Kaplan and Dean Beebe (eds.), *Moscow Dispatches* (Toronto, 1988).

2   One examination of the history of the RCMP and the National Archives is my "The RCMP, the CSIS, the PAC, and Access to Information: A Curious Tale," *Labour/Le Travail* (*L/LT*), 21 (1988), pp. 199-226. Further information is provided in *L/LT* 24 (1989), pp. 6-9.

3   Two works that deserve special mention for their attention to such questions are Donald Avery,

With the notable exception of intelligence work commissioned by Sir John A. Macdonald against the Fenians in the 1860s and 1870s and continuing co-operation with the British government concerning Irish and Indian nationalists before the First World War, the Canadian state had almost no security and intelligence capacity in 1914.[4] The Dominion Police had certain security functions, such as the guarding of public buildings, as part of its mandate, but it was an extremely small and poorly funded force. The outbreak of the First World War was the occasion of the first systematic political concern in this area, but, as so often in Canada during that war, the development of an appropriate governmental response was halting, indecisive and often confused. Nevertheless, the necessity of policing the long border with the initially neutral United States with its large population of German and Irish immigrants and of solving the domestic problem of a large immigrant community from the enemy nations demanded the Borden government's attention.[5] Similarly, the need for secrecy about the war effort demanded the development of policies governing the censorship of all forms of communication.[6] Last, but certainly not least, opposition to the war and, more specifically, to conscription demanded the development of yet heavier repressive responses. This final problem loomed ever greater on the government's agenda after the passage of the Military Service Act and as labour impatience with the war effort manifested itself in the labour revolt of 1917-20.[7]

The major historical account to date of the emergence of the RCMP is an 1980 article by S.W. Horrall, the head of the Historical Section of the Force.[8] Working with the advantage of access to documents then unavailable to other historians, Horrall

---

"Dangerous Foreigners": European Immigrant Workers and Labour Radicalism in Canada, 1896-1932 (Toronto, 1979) and A. Ross McCormack, *Reformers, Rebels, and Revolutionaries: The Western Canadian Radical Movement, 1899-1919* (Toronto, 1977). As their subtitles suggest, their major focus is not state repression. Nevertheless, both authors opened up these questions, and McCormack actually received some unmerited attention from the RCMP SS as a result. For a brief version of this story see the transcript of my "National Security vs. the Public's Right to Know," *CBC Ideas*, 18 Feb. 1989.

4   On the Fenian experience see Jeff Keshen, "Cloak and Dagger: Canada West's Secret Police, 1864-1867," *Ontario History*, 79 (1987), pp. 353-81 and Wayne Crockett, "The Uses and Abuses of the Secret Service Fund: The Political Dimensions of Police Work in Canada, 1864-1877," MA thesis, Queen's University, 1982. On Indian Nationalists in Canada, see Hugh Johnston, "The Surveillance of Indian Nationalists in North America, 1908-1918," *BC Studies*, 78 (1988), pp. 3-27 and his *The Voyage of the Komagata Maru: The Sikh Challenge to Canada's Colour Bar* (New Delhi, 1979). Also see Richard Popplewell, "The Surveillance of Indian 'Seditionists' in North America, 1905-1915," in Christopher Andrew and Jeremy Noakes (eds.), *Intelligence and International Relations, 1900-1945* (Exeter, 1987), pp. 49-76.

5   Part of this story is told in Martin Kitchen, "The German Invasion of Canada in the First World War," *International History Review*, 7 (1985), pp. 245-60.

6   The efforts of Colonels C.F. Hamilton and E.C. Chambers, the Deputy Chief Censor and Chief Press Censor respectively, are peripheral to this article but will be covered in subsequent work. The former was primarily responsible for cables; the latter for newspapers and other publications. In addition the Deputy Postmaster-General was responsible for mail censorship. Thus three departments — Militia, Secretary of State, and Post Office — shared censorship responsibilities.

7   The events culminating in the Amherst, Toronto, and Winnipeg General Strikes and the subsequent wave of sympathy strikes have been frequently described and need not detain us here. For example, see my "1919: The Canadian Labour Revolt," *L/LT*, 13 (1984), pp. 11-44.

8   S.W. Horrall, "The Royal North-West Mounted Police and Labour Unrest in Western Canada, 1919," *Canadian Historical Review*, 61 (1980), pp. 169-90.

wrote a compelling essay which quite correctly attributed the revival of a moribund RNWMP and the subsequent birth of the new RCMP to the Canadian labour revolt. The article, however, is quite concerned to justify the role of the Mounties throughout 1919 and argues that the quality of their advice to the politicians transcended what the Borden government was receiving from the rest of its confusing array of intelligence sources. Indeed, the reader is left with the general impression that not only was Canada much better for the creation of the new force with its potential for systematic counter-subversion work but also that the excessive state response in Winnipeg might have been avoided if the wise counsel of RNWMP Commissioner A.B. Perry had been followed by Borden. Without doubt Horrall's defence of the Force is a liberal one; indeed RCMP internal documentation obtained through the Access process shows that the Security Service was furious with Horrall's article because it identified documentary sources that other historians then sought.[9] Nevertheless there are considerable problems with Horrall's argument and, more importantly, with the additional evidence that is not presented concerning the precise nature of RCMP surveillance systems and techniques. Moreover, the account has a Whiggish quality, understandable from the Force's official historian, which fails to raise larger questions about the emergence of a para-military, federal police force with primary responsibilities for domestic intelligence and counter-subversion.

The Dominion Police and the RNWMP, 1914-17

In 1914 the Dominion Police (DP) received the responsibility for security matters. Given the extremely limited size of the DP, these new duties were largely delegated to the country's other police forces under DP co-ordination. In the case of the RNWMP, this gave the Force security responsibilities in the Yukon and North-West Territories and in Alberta and Saskatchewan, where they served as provincial police under contracts entered into by those provinces upon their creation in 1905. In Central Canada and the East such responsibilities were carried out by the Dominion Police where they existed and through municipal and provincial police forces. In addition, the DP hired detective agencies to provide extra undercover investigative capacities. For example, the Thiel Detective Service's Montreal Office billed the Canadian government for just over $17,000 in September 1916 for an array of investigations throughout Canada and in the United States. Among duties performed by Thiel detectives were "keeping in touch with anti-British sentiment at various points in the U.S. and with the workings of the inner circles of the German and Austrian secret societies in which we have confidential and reliable operatives," investigating the irregular purchase of horses for the military in Nova Scotia, and "special secret service precautions for the suppression of vices at the various camps."[10] Such dependence on private, foreign companies must have given some pause to government officials. As we shall see, it certainly became an issue after the war.

In the early years of the war the new RNWMP duties primarily involved the registration and internment of enemy aliens, and securing the border. In addition,

---

9   These documents were part of the material removed from the National Archives in 1971. Most, but not all, of these documents were returned in 1982 and now form part of RG18 again. For details see Kealey, "A Curious Tale."

10 National Archives of Canada (hereafter NAC), Sir George Foster Papers, MG 27 II D9, Vol. 76, file 122, E.R. Carrington, Vice-President, Thiel Detective Services, Montreal to Blount, 12 Aug. 1916.

Commissioner Perry availed himself of the new security concerns to hire the Force's first secret agents. In late August 1914 the Comptroller authorized Perry to "employ men for special service to gather information with reference to the movements, disposition, etc., of foreign settlers." Such agents were to be paid from war funds, administered by the Chief Commissioner of the DP, not from the normal RNWMP budget.[11] No systematic account of the work of these first secret agents has as yet turned up, but random reports include detailed descriptions of Crows Nest Pass coal strikes in 1915, a generalized report that secret agents detected "a very strong undercurrent of feeling against conscription" in July 1916, accounts of the anti-war and pro-labour activities of Edmonton politician and soon-to-be-Mayor, Joseph Clarke, in 1917, and numerous accounts of Quebec resistance to the Military Service Act.[12]

By summer 1916 RNWMP Commissioner A.B. Perry was expressing considerable concern to the Prime Minister that the Force could not be expected to continue to carry out its provincial policing duties in Alberta and Saskatchewan as well as its new security responsibilities:

> Owing to the wide distribution and paucity, the Mounted Police cannot be looked upon as defensive; their energies are absorbed in their various civil duties. To render it of more service in meeting war conditions its members would have to be largely increased, its ordinary police duties taken over by the different provinces, and its distribution revised.

Perry went on to recommend exactly that to the Prime Minister: "In the public interest ... during the period of the war the Force, except in the North-West and Yukon Territories should be relieved of police duties and its services be utilized for Federal Service only."[13] Perry's recommendation was accepted and Alberta and Saskatchewan created provincial police forces in 1917. By then, however, Perry's intentions had shifted. He now argued not for an increased domestic role but rather that the Force be allowed to join the Canadian Expeditionary Force as a cavalry unit.[14] Neither British nor Canadian Generals greeted this offer with enthusiasm. The British pointed out that cavalry had little utility in Europe and General Gwatkin worried about the large alien population of the Prairie provinces and of potential labour unrest in British Columbia.[15] While this debate played itself out, the RNWMP declined in size as many members retired from the Force to enlist in the CEF. Given that Perry himself openly argued that the Force had "largely finished the work for which it was called into existence," the future of the RNWMP did not look bright. Indeed one member of the RNWMP in those years recalls that there was "a prevalent rumour throughout the entire Force during my early years of service that the RNWMP would soon be disbanded."[16]

---

11 NAC, RCMP Records, RG 18, 83-84/321, file G-26-22, Comptroller to Commissioner, 25 July 1914 and Memorandum re Secret Agents by G.T. Hann, 14 Feb. 1949.
12 Ibid., Vol. 490, file 433-15; Vol. 524, file 38-17. For more on the RNWMP interest in Joseph Clarke, see NAC, Department of Justice Records, RG 13, Vol. 216, file 1962/1917, Deputy Minister of Justice to Chief Commissioner Dominion Police, 21 Nov. 1917.
13 NAC, Borden Papers, MG 26 H, Vol. 216, file RLB 1281, Perry to Borden, 11 Oct. 1916.
14 Ibid., Vol. 218, file RLB 1374, Perry to Borden, 11 June 1917.
15 Ibid., Gwatkin[?] Memo, 19 June 1917; Perry to Borden, 23 June 1917; Borden to Perry, 3 July 1917; Borden to Kemp, 21 Jan. 1918; and Kemp to Borden, 26 Feb 1918.
16 Vernon A.M. Kemp, *Scarlet and Stetson: The RNWMP on the Prairies* (Toronto, 1964), pp. 7-8.

In the end the Force was allowed to play a military role and on 30 May 1918 a cavalry draft of 12 officers and 726 NCOs and men left for Europe. In addition, when the Borden government allowed itself to be coerced by the British into sending Canadian troops to Russia, the RNWMP again provided men, specifically five officers and 181 other ranks for Siberia. As a result by early December 1918 the RNWMP establishment had fallen to a total of 303 in the whole of Canada.[17]

Renewed labour militancy changed all of that, but the choice of the RNWMP as the appropriate government agency to carry out the task of domestic intelligence was anything but certain. Earlier in 1918 Labour Minister Gideon Robertson had written to a number of cabinet colleagues to warn them that the American legal assault on the Industrial Workers of the World (IWW) raised the spectre of yet another invasion of the Canadian border from the south, albeit on this occasion by radicals, not Germans. "Inasmuch as the policies and purposes of the IWW are vicious in their character and intent" and "undoubtedly detrimental to the preservation of industrial peace," he recommended that agents be put on their trail and that the Post Office should seize any IWW propaganda in circulation through the mails. "Stern measures" taken early might discourage others from proceeding to Canada. Such action, he argued, was "offered on behalf of and in the interests of the bona fide labour organizations of Canada who are at the present time trying to co-operate with the Government."[18]

Almost simultaneously, and undoubtedly more to the point, Sir Joseph Flavelle, Chairman of the Imperial Munitions Board in Canada, also warned Borden of the IWW threat and called for an investigation by Sir Percy Sherwood, Chief Commissioner of the DP.[19] The subsequent DP search provides insight into the methodology of the state security apparatus in early 1918. Albert Cawdron, Sherwood's Assistant and Acting Commissioner for part of 1918, consulted the Chief Constables of the major urban police forces, the Superintendents of the various provincial forces, Perry of the RNWMP, the Immigration Department, the Canadian Pacific Railway's Department of Investigation, and the Pinkerton Detective Agency in New York. From all these agencies he sought a report on the IWW in general and comments on how best to deal with the IWW in Canada. In addition he commissioned the Thiel Company in Chicago and a Toronto firm, the Employers' Detective Agency, to report on the Wobblies. For further work he proposed hiring "the private agency that we think has the inside track of these people at present, with operatives working amongst them, in order that we might learn of any Headquarters ... and get first hand information of their doings." Money spent to learn their plans now, he added, will save thousands later by stopping this "very dangerous, socialistic, and perhaps murderous lot" before they get started here.[20]

Somewhat anti-climactically Cawdron reported two weeks later that "the sum total of the reports is that we have nothing to fear from them at the present time." But the IWW was now replaced, or confused at least in Cawdron's report, by the Ukrainian

---

17 RG 18, Vol. 1930, Comptroller A.A. McLean, Memorandum on an increase of the Force from 1,000 to 2,000 men, 10 Dec. 1918. On the Siberian Draft, see also Vol. 1929.
18 Borden Papers, Vol. 104, file Oc519, Robertson to Rowell, et al., 20 Feb. 1918.
19 Ibid., Flavelle to Borden, 22 Feb. 1918.
20 Ibid., Cawdron to Minister of Justice, 5 March 1918.

Social Democratic Party (USDP). The Acting Chief Commissioner reported proudly that he had "a special man on the inside with a view to learning if they have any plans for the present year."[21] Subsequent reports from Cawdron, however, indicated additional concerns, especially in Ontario and Quebec. These reports almost universally focused on immigrant workers and their organizations such as the USDP, the Russian Workers Union, and the Finnish Organization. The reports varied dramatically in tone and in strategic suggestions, but alarm was clearly mounting in the business community and among police and military officials.[22]

The Rise and Fall of C.H. Cahan, May 1918-January 1919

As a result of the conflicting information and advice the government was receiving, Prime Minister Borden, immediately before his departure for England, wrote to C.H. Cahan, a Montreal lawyer with British Secret Service ties, to enlist his aid.[23] Cahan had written to Borden a few days before offering his services to the Canadian war effort. Unfortunately, Borden's response and subsequent request were ambiguous at best. He described "certain evidence pointing pretty distinctly to a propaganda in various parts of the country which raises a suspicion that it is being carried on by German agents or with German support." After seeking Cahan's advice on establishing "some effective organization to investigate the whole subject," he concluded by enclosing a secret American document regarding such an "organization of a more or less voluntary character" under the control of the Department of Justice. While somewhat unclear, it would seem that Borden was considering a Canadian equivalent to the American Protective League.[24] Cahan, however, as we shall see, had other ideas.

---

21 Ibid., 19 March 1918.

22 Ibid., Cawdron to Minister of Justice, 21 March 1918; Temiskaming Mine Managers to Hon. Frank Cochrane, 22 March 1918; R. Allen, Special Agent, Hollinger Consolidated Gold Mines, Timmins, to Sherwood, 8 April 1918; Davis, Military Intelligence to Mewburn, 17 April 1918; Sherwood to Acland, Department of Labour, 9 May 1918.

23 Charles Hazlitt Cahan (1861-1944), b. Yarmouth, NS, 31 Oct. 1861. Educated Dalhousie University (BA 1886; LLB. 1890) and called to NS Bar 1893 (KC 1907). Practised law in Halifax, Mexico, and Montreal. Represented Shelbourne 1890-94 in the NS Legislative Assembly; Leader of Conservative opposition. In 1925 elected to represent a Toronto riding in the House of Commons and in 1927 unsuccessfully contested Conservative Party leadership at the Winnipeg convention. Secretary of State in Bennett government, 1930-35. Defeated 1940 General Election. He held LL.Ds from Dalhousie and the University of Montreal. See W.S. Wallace, *MacMillan Dictionary of Canadian Biography* (Toronto, 1963); *Canadian Parliamentary Companion; Canadian Who's Who*, 1936-37.

As for Cahan's British Secret Service ties, I have been unable to locate much evidence. He refers to "some three years I have been in touch with the British Secret Service in the United States" in his letter of 20 July 1918 to Minister of Justice Doherty, Borden Papers, Vol. 104, file OC19. In addition, he appears to have had some connection with the investigation of the January 1917 explosion at the Kingsland, NJ, plant of Canadian Car and Foundry. See Jules Witcover, *Sabotage at Black Tom: Imperial Germany's Secret War in America, 1914-1917* (Chapel Hill, 1989), pp. 184-96.

24 Ibid., Cahan to Borden, 11 May 1918; Borden to Cahan, 19 May 1918. On the American Protective League, see Julian F. Jaffe, *Crusade Against Radicalism: New York During the Red Scare, 1914-1924* (Pt. Washington, New York, 1972), pp. 49-50; Robert Justin Goldstein, *Political Repression in Modern America, 1870 to the Present* (Boston, 1978), pp. 109-13. More detailed studies are Joan M. Jensen, *The Price of Vigilance* (Chicago, 1968) and Emerson Hough, *The Web: The Authorized History of the American Protective League* (Chicago, 1919).

In June Chief Commissioner Sherwood provided Minister of Justice Doherty with a final report on the IWW. "After a thorough and exhaustive investigation," he wrote, "no trace can be found of any activity on the part of the IWW in this country." He noted a renewal of SDP activity but found nothing sinister there, but rather an organization for "the improvement of workers' conditions and the securing of better pay." Meanwhile, a few "aliens" had been interned to ensure that they did not become agitators, close censorship of the mail had been undertaken, and "a plan adopted for keeping in touch with the situation was approved of at a conference of experienced police officials held in Ottawa." Finally, the staff of the DP had been augmented by the seconding to Ottawa of Toronto Detective Wallace, an experienced political operative.[25]

Sherwood's confident report to Doherty was called into question one month later when Cahan filed his first report to the same minister. While Cahan found little to worry about among German or Austrian Canadians, he did note "considerable mental unrest among the peoples of Slavic origin in Canada, Russian, Ukrainian, and Austrian, which is directly attributable to the dissemination in Canada of the Socialistic doctrines, espoused by the Russian Revolutionary element, and more recently by the Bolsheviki Party in Russia." These problems had nothing to do with German activities in Canada and therefore an organization like the American Protective League would serve little purpose. Indeed, he argued that in Canada such an organization would almost certainly degenerate into warring parties of French and English. But more serious even than the slavic unrest:

> There is apparently wide-spread unrest and discontent throughout Canada, which finds expression in labor agitation and strikes, in attempts to avoid the Military Service Act, in mutterings against food prices, in criticism of the treatment of returned soldiers, in the prevalent suspicion that discrimination is shown in the collection of federal taxes, and in general discontent with the administration of the federal departments.

This general disaffection Cahan attributed to war-weariness and he recommended renewed efforts "to overcome existing unrest and disatisfaction." Most importantly, however, he promoted an expansion of the work of the Dominion Police and an elaboration of their co-operation with other police agencies.[26]

This eloquent document might be termed the opening round in Canada's Red Scare. Cahan, unlike Cawdron and Sherwood, pinpointed the subversive threat as Bolshevism in Canada and identified the immigrant communities as the locus of concern. Moreover, the unrest he described in July 1918 grew rapidly that summer. In late August Cahan wrote Borden to prompt him to consider his recommendations to Doherty and went a bit further calling specifically for increased co-operation between an expanded DP and both Military Police and Immigration authorities.[27]

---

25 Ibid., Sherwood to Minister of Justice, 16 June 1918. Wallace proved to be a useful ally of Cahan in promoting repressive measures. For example, see his letter to Sherwood of 30 July 1918 in RG 13, Vol. 229, file 2471/1918. "Anarchy or Bolshevism or whatever name it may be called is spreading and the agitators are gaining confidence."

26 Ibid., Cahan to Minister of Justice, 20 July 1918. See also RG 13, Vol. 229, file 2471/1918, Sherwood to Cahan, 22 July 1918; and Cahan to Doherty, 24 July 1918. Sherwood, somewhat defensively, commented that "An extension of the establishment may be necessary for I have endeavoured to be as economical as possible and for that reason have utilized free help as much as possible."

27 Ibid., Cahan to Borden, 27 Aug. 1918 and Borden to Cahan, 29 Aug. 1918.

Cahan next filed his final report with the Minister of Justice. This 17-page document articulated much more fully Cahan's campaign of repression, much of which was to be implemented by the Union government in autumn 1918. He first surveyed the alien registration and internment programme and generally applauded its successful implementation by the Chief Commissioner of the DP. He further commended the August 1918 extension of this registration to *all* enemy aliens over the age of 16 but recommended its additional expansion to cover Russians, Ukrainians, and Finns. The rationale, of course, derived from his earlier observations concerning the growth of Bolshevik propaganda in Canada:

> The Russians, Ukrainians, and Finns, who are employed in the mines, factories, and other industries of Canada, are now being thoroughly saturated with the socialistic doctrines which have been proclaimed by the Bolsheviki faction of Russia ... For several years before the outbreak of the war, the industrial centres of Canada were literally deluged with these publications; and, at the present time, I have before me a mass of this literature, filled with the most pernicious and seditious teaching, which is even now, in large quantities, being secretly circulated in Canada.

Identifying the guilty organizations as the Social Democratic Party of Canada, the Ukrainian Revolutionary Group, the Russian Revolutionary Group, and others unspecified, he noted their presence throughout Ontario and in Quebec, Manitoba, and Alberta. Membership in these groups was estimated at over 1000 in Toronto and from 150 to 175 in Hamilton, Winnipeg, Sault Ste. Marie, Timmins and Copper Cliff. Compulsory registration and monthly reporting would make them "amenable to local police supervision." Moreover, such close supervision "puts these aliens on their guard against personal misconduct, and the Government is thereby enabled to exercise a salutary restraining influence upon individuals who would otherwise prove obstreperous."

Cahan then turned to the subject of revolutionary propaganda. After citing various examples ranging from Jack London through the revolutionary new year's greetings of one Felix Connosevitch of Brantford, to the Constitution of the SDP, he recommended the "most stringent measures to curtail the importation, publication, and distribution of such doctrines, at least until the termination of the present war; and to prohibit during the same period, the oral advocacy of such doctrines at public or private meetings." More specifically he suggested the banning of the IWW, the Workers International Industrial Union (the Detroit IWW), the SDP, the USDP, the Ukrainian Revolutionary Group, the Russian Revolutionary Group, and "any other society or organization inculcating the same doctrines or teachings." Membership in or attendance at any meeting of such groups would be a criminal offence, punishable by imprisonment only, as would the public or private advocacy of their doctrines or teachings. In addition, he proposed that no newspaper, magazine or journal be permitted to publish in any language except English or French without receipt of a federal licence. Similarly no pamphlet, leaflet or poster should be published in any foreign language without prior submission in translation to the Press Censor for a certificate of approval. Finally, he promoted the wide extension of peace officers' rights to search, confiscate and destroy such materials.

Cahan next considered enforcement mechanisms. Noting that enforcement of the various security provisions of the War Measures Act were fragmented through numerous government departments under various ministers, he suggested centralization for efficiency. He cited quite favourably the American example of an Attorney General with a Department of Justice governing widely dispersed District Attorneys and with a Federal police and investigative capacity. He concluded that a similar pattern should be followed in Canada and that the Department of Justice should be given primary responsibility for the enforcement of War Measures Act regulations. Noting that many of those powers such as enforcement of the MSA were currently held by military authorities, he argued that they were at times "aggressive and arbitrary and seldom trained in the administration of law" and that this "often unnecessarily irritated and displeased the Canadian civilian population." The solution he offered was a new Public Safety Branch of the Department of Justice which was to be filled in a non-partisan fashion but by individuals "in cordial sympathy with the war aims of the government." Even if the government did not choose to establish this new agency, he called for the rapid expansion of the DP to allow the Chief Commissioner "to ensure that the regulations for the registration and supervision of all aliens are strictly enforced."[28]

The government moved very quickly in the aftermath of Cahan's report. Within a week they passed two new Orders-in-Council to implement his recommendations regarding the banning of various socialist, ethnic and labour organizations and their publications.[29] In late September Cahan began meeting with Doherty and his Deputy Minister to plan implementation of the rest of his report. In the process he began to map out a larger role for himself. Increasing emphasis was placed on the Public Safety Branch, which he now volunteered to direct. In addition the war-time justification for such a federal effort also began to slip into longer-range plans:

> Personally, I am disposed to believe that until demobilization is completed, and perhaps thereafter until the industrial unrest, which grows out of the war, is entirely dissipated, it will be necessary for the federal authority to maintain a strong and effective organization, in the Department of Justice, for the enforcement of federal laws. In my opinion, if we are to preserve a United Canadian nation, we will not, for a long time, be in a position to revert to the old policy of laisser faire, and leave the haphazard enforcement of federal laws to provincial and municipal authorities.

The aims of the organization remained much the same, although he now placed additional emphasis on its central role in co-ordinating all governmental activities in this area, and most particularly in directing prosecution and investigation. It is well worth noting that, throughout the Cahan documents, the RNWMP is almost never mentioned and the few allusions are only to their northern role.[30]

The Public Safety Branch was established by Order-in-Council on 2 October 1918 "for the effective administration of the laws, orders, and regulations enacted for the preservation of public order and safety during the continuance of the war, and more particularly to administer and enforce the orders and regulations sanctioned as war measures." Cahan became its first and only Director.[31]

In November Cahan provided a detailed and ambitious organizational plan for his new PSB. In addition to a central office staff including an Assistant Director (he proposed to appoint his son), his plan included a Bureau of Investigation of five

---

28 Ibid., Cahan to Minister of Justice, 14 Sept. 1918.
29 A convenient location of the text of these Orders-in-Council is Frances Swyripa and John Thompson (eds.), *Loyalties in Conflict: Ukrainians in Canada During the Great War* (Edmonton, 1983), pp. 190-6.
30 RG 13, 86-87/361, file 166/1919, Cahan to Doherty, 26 Sept. 1918.
31 Ibid., Cahan to Doherty, 1 Oct. 1918 and Minister of Justice to Governor General in Council, 2 Oct. 1918.

secret service agents "thoroughly qualified and competent and always available for special service." Working directly under the Director they were to receive $3000 per annum plus expenses which was extremely high pay by civil service standards. In addition he proposed a total reorganization of the Dominion Police. The country was to be divided into 10 Districts, each with a Commissioner of Police, three detectives, and between seven and 15 constables. For the entire nation he proposed a force of 24 detectives and 92 constables. He also proposed a reserve force of Dominion Police of 100 men, a third to be stationed in each of Nova Scotia, Quebec/Ontario, and British Columbia. This reserve force was intended for "the suppression of disorder where strikes, riots, etc., are anticipated or may arise." He priced this reorganization at about $300,000 in salaries per annum. Implementation of his scheme "would create a force of Dominion Police sufficient to preserve public order and safety throughout Canada during the period of demobilization, without the necessity of involving the frequent aid of the military forces."[32]

Cahan had reached the height of his influence with the Canadian government. His career as Canada's leading anti-Bolshevik declined precipitously thereafter. In many ways Cahan's political failure created the space for the RNWMP's uncertain path towards a new role as Canada's central domestic intelligence agency. A second fortuitous personnel change, however, also played a major part in the RNWMP's ascendancy. Sir Percy Sherwood, the Chief Commissioner of the DP, decided for health reasons to resign at the age of 65.[33] His Assistant, Albert Cawdron, became Acting Chief Commissioner but was never granted the full position.[34] Finally, and admittedly more speculative, is the course taken by Newton Rowell, the President of the Privy Council, and probably the most important Liberal in Borden's Union Government. As President of the Privy Council, Rowell's ministry included the RNWMP. Indeed in September 1918 when the new repressive PC Orders were being passed and the Public Safety Branch created, Rowell was on a tour of western Canada. A major purpose of his trip was consultation with Commissioner Perry on the future of the RNWMP.[35] No doubt the unanimous accolades that the Force received throughout Rowell's tour did much to reinforce for him the possibilities of redefining its role.

On his return to Ottawa he became embroiled in a Cabinet struggle over the PC Orders passed in his absence. He had no general objections to the repressive measures instituted but he did feel that the legislation had gone too far by including the Social Democratic Party of Canada on the list of specifically banned organizations. Rowell wrote to Doherty on 18 October to register his dissent, which was based on the opposition that the measure was generating in the labour community. He also

---

32   RG 13, Vol. 229, file 2472/1918, Cahan to Doherty, 7 Nov. 1918.
33   RG 13, Vol. 228, file 2297/1918, Sherwood to Minister of Justice, 12 Oct. 1918; and Minister of Justice to Governor General, 4 Dec. 1918. Sherwood was granted a six-month leave of absence in honour of his 37 years as Chief Commissioner and then allowed to retire.
34   RG 13, Vol. 232, file 397/1919. Cawdron received the endorsement of the Chief Constables Association of Canada. He was eventually nominated for the post by Meighen on 1 May 1919, but events outstripped the appointment. He transferred to the new RCMP as a Superintendent on 1 Feb. 1920 and retired in 1924. For his complicated pension difficulties, see RG 13, 86-87/361, file 1701/1924.
35   Margaret Prang, *N.W. Rowell* (Toronto, 1975), pp. 266-8.

noted that no doubt the SDP's presence on the list was simply an oversight in the drafting of the legislation. Cahan, however, refused to compromise. Instead he raised the stakes considerably by writing directly to Borden to complain of interference and to suggest, albeit subtly, that the objecting ministers were simply bowing to Red pressure. After outlining at length the "most insidious propaganda" efforts of the SDP, he argued at length against the deletion of the SDP from the Order, or at the very least a delay until the current prosecutions could be completed. In his more public submission to his minister for use in Cabinet, Cahan warned that any repeal would "be hailed by those followers of the red flag, who are the chief exponents of German propaganda throughout Canada, as an indication that they are at liberty in Canada to undermine, without restraint, the very foundation of our social, industrial, and political system." After detailing his charges at length, he concluded that the SDP was not a "political party in the ordinary meaning of those words. It is the Party of Red Revolution, advocating submission to German might, subversion of all constitutional government, robbery of personal property, and the accomplishment of its avowed aims by sabotage and general strikes." Again indicating his lack of trust in his minister, he sent this brief directly to Borden and offered to supply him with various examples of SDP propaganda if it would help.[36]

Rowell, with strong support from Thomas Crerar, won the day on this issue in Cabinet with his argument that the SDP was a recognized political labour party which had existed for 10 years without previous interference. In classic liberal terms he argued that as such the task was "to combat their ideas in public argument or propaganda." "A policy of repression," he argued, was "not only contrary to the public interest, but will alienate from government the support of the progressive elements in the community, who, while out of sympathy with the SDP programme, still insist on freedom of thought and freedom of speech on social and economic questions."[37] Crerar insisted that the SDP did not advocate violence and thus should not come under the ban. There was "no justification whatsoever," he argued, describing Cahan's attack on the SDP as "the very negation of the first principles of democracy."[38] While the SDP was removed from the list, the ban on the other organizations remained.

Coterminous with this debate a co-ordinated series of police raids took place across Ontario. For example, the Chief Constable of Sault Ste. Marie reported that raids against "social revolutionaries" on 19 October had led to 10 arrests and subsequent convictions with fines as high as $4000 or sentences of as long as five years.[39] Chief Grassett of the Toronto Police Force also reported similar success on 20 October. His raids had netted 41 members of the Chinese National League and

---

36 Borden Papers, Vol. 104, file Oc519, Rowell to Doherty, 18 Oct. 1918; Cahan to Borden, 21 Oct. 1918; Cahan to Borden, 22 Oct. 1918; and Cahan to Doherty, 22 Oct. 1918. See also Prang, *Rowell*, pp. 267-8.

37 Ibid., Rowell to Borden, 29 Oct. 1918. Crerar's position throughout these debates showed his increasing discomfort at the repression of civil liberties. See Crerar Papers, Queen's University Archives, Kingston, Ont., esp. F. J. Dixon to Crerar, 12 Oct. 1918; Crerar to Dixon, 25 Oct. 1918; Dixon to Crerar, 9 Nov. 1918; Crerar to Dixon, 15 Nov. 1918; and Dixon to Crerar, 3 Dec. 1918.

38 Ibid., Vol. 245, file RLB 2848, Borden to Crerar, 4 Nov. 1918 and Crerar, Memorandum, 1 Nov. 1918.

39 RG 13, Vol. 223, file 1026/1918, extract from letter of Chief Constable, 30 Oct. 1918.

23 members of the Russian Social Democratic Party, the Ukrainian Socialist Party, and the Finnish Socialist Party, as well as a vast array of prohibited literature.[40]

Cahan later, somewhat disingenuously given his plea to Borden, denied responsibility for the SDP prosecutions in Ontario under the Order-in-Council. This initial setback in Cabinet did not prevent Cahan from promoting further schemes. In his effort to create a replica of the Bureau of Investigation in the United States Department of Justice, he proposed a force of secret agents under his supervision:

> The Director of Public Safety should have available an adequate number of investigators to probe very thoroughly the sources of enemy propaganda in this country, the violations of law due to the advocates of social and political revolution, and the general social and industrial unrest throughout Canada, so that the Government of Canada may always be kept thoroughly informed of the actual existing conditions, and so that offences against existing laws may be effectively prosecuted.[41]

He even knew where he could recruit such agents, namely from the military groups then enforcing the Military Service Act and from Military and Naval Intelligence. To reinforce his argument he cited the recent assassination in Victoria of Tan Hui Ling, Minister of the Interior in the Chinese government, by Chung Wong, an activist in the Chinese Nationalist League.[42] He also drew a grim picture of the activities of "social revolutionists" throughout Canada's industrial districts. His recommendation then was to reorganize the Public Safety Branch and the Dominion Police to allow the hiring of secret agents without the Cabinet's direct approval of the expense. Here he again used the American example and concluded:

> I am convinced that even upon the declaration of peace, the Dominion Government can only ensure the maintenance of law and order throughout Canada by preparing now to control all the disturbing elements in this country; and, therefore, I earnestly invite the attention of the government to this matter, now, when possible future events may, in anticipation, be fully provided for.[43]

Cahan lost this battle as well. No agents were authorized to be employed under his control. Moreover, his request that his son, Charles Hazlitt Cahan, be appointed as his Assistant Director, was flatly rejected "as inappropriate" by the Cabinet. But, as was prefigured in the SDP case, his major offence was his refusal to play by the established rules of public service. As an important Tory politician in his own right, he simply failed to work through appropriate ministerial channels. Justice Minister Doherty's patience finally ran out when, in November, he read in the press announcements of policy directions emanating from the Director of the Public Safety Branch that he, let alone the Cabinet, had never approved. He warned Cahan to "be careful in the future to see that similar announcements are not made without having been authorized by the Minister." Nevertheless, Cahan continued to lobby for support from other Ministers. For example, his frustration with his lack of progress in Justice led him to correspond with General Mewburn, the Minister of Militia and Defence,

---

40 Ibid., Vol. 227, file 2021/1919, Grassett to Sherwood, 20 Oct. 1918.

41 Ibid., 86-87/361, file 166/1919, Cahan to Doherty, 29 Oct. 1918.

42 For additional information on the assassination and suicide, see Borden Papers Vol. 243, pt. 2, file RLB 2732, Cahan to Doherty, 16 Oct. 1918 and Borden to Cahan, 22 Oct. 1918. Cahan also proposed to offer a reward for further information in this case but Meighen as Acting Minister of Justice rejected the idea. See RG 13, Vol. 231, file 139/1919, Deputy Minister of Justice to Cahan, 16 Jan. 1919.

43 RG 13, 86-87/361, file 166/1919, Cahan to Doherty, 29 Oct. 1918.

to gain support for his efforts. When even this failed, he appealed to the acting Prime Minister, Sir Thomas White.[44]

It appears that his special pleading with White failed for he offered his resignation in early January and the Public Safety Branch was abolished, by PC 104 of 16 January 1919.[45] Thus ended a brief Canadian flirtation with a security solution akin to that of the United States, which had remained Cahan's model throughout. One is tempted to speculate that if Cahan had possessed only a minute portion of the political/bureaucratic talents of the young J. Edgar Hoover the outcome might have been quite different.[46]

The Re-emergence of the RNWMP, 1919

Cahan and his solutions went into eclipse, but the problem of labour unrest and socialist activity that they were intended to address remained. While in its phase of repressive mobilization in September and October 1918, the government had passed two other Orders-in-Council. The first, which received relatively little attention or protest, slammed the door shut on police unionism in the federal sector before it commenced. PC 2213 of 7 October 1918 forbade any member of the DP or RNWMP from "becoming a member of or in any wise associated with any trade union organization or any society or association connected or affiliated therewith" under threat of immediate dismissal.[47] The perceived threat that this action preempted was the potential spread of police unionism to the federal sector. Most municipal police forces in major Canadian urban centres were organizing in the summer and fall of 1918 and police strikes broke out in Toronto and Montreal that winter. Not surprisingly the subject of police unionism proved extremely controversial. The Borden government, on this occasion, spoke clearly and decisively.[48]

The other Order-in-Council, PC 2525 of 18 September 1918, banned strikes for the duration of the war.[49] A wave of public controversy and vigorous protest from the labour leadership combined with rank-and-file refusal to cease strike activities led the Borden government to withdraw the Order before actually using its punitive provisions. Cahan with his usual enthusiasm volunteered his Public Safety Branch to commence prosecution under the new Order-in-Council, but the Department indicated that they would handle the matter without his aid.[50]

---

44   Ibid., Cahan to White, 15 Nov. 1918; Doherty to Newcombe, 15 Nov. 1918; Doherty to Cahan, 15 Nov. 1918; and Cahan to Meighen, 18 Nov. 1918.

45   Ibid., Deputy Minister of Justice to Undersecretary of State for External Affairs, 2 Jan. 1919; and PC 104, 16 Jan. 1919.

46   On the career of the young Hoover, see Richard Gid Powers, *Secrecy and Power: The Life of J. Edgar Hoover* (New York, 1987), esp. Chs. 3-6; and Athan G. Theoharis and John Stuart Cox, *The Boss: J. Edgar Hoover and the Great American Inquisition* (Philadelphia, 1988), esp. Chs. 2-4.

47   RG 18, 83-84/321, file G-270-2, PC 2213, 7 Oct. 1918. See also RG 13, Vol. 227, file 1950/1918, Sherwood to Deputy Minister of Justice, 21 Aug. 1918. It was Sherwood not Perry who took the initiative on this question.

48   The best study of this phenomenon in the Canadian context is Greg Marquis, "Police Unionism in Early Twentieth-Century Toronto," *Ontario History*, 81 (1989), pp. 109-28. For a more general, albeit brief discussion, see my "The Labour Movement, the Peace Question, and State Repression, 1917-1920," *Geschichte der Arbeiterbewegung/ITH-Tagungsberichte*, 24 (1987), pp. 221-40.

49   RG 13, Vol. 228, file 2229/1918.

50   RG 13, Vol. 227, file 2017/1918, Cahan to Deputy Minister of Justice, 16 Oct. 1918; and DMJ to Cahan, 18 Oct. 1918.

In late October, as we have seen, Rowell began to explore with Commissioner Perry the post-war role of the Force and its relationship to the future of the Dominion Police. Perry drew up three possible scenarios for his minister. First, the Force could be greatly reduced in strength and police the Yukon and North-West Territories. Second, the Force could simply become part of the permanent military establishment. Third, the RNWMP could be amalgamated and consolidated with all Departmental law enforcement agencies to form a new Canadian Constabulary. After offering the options, Perry commented on each. The first, he felt, would need no more than 100 men and was simply not worth the trouble. The second, he recognized, had always been the assumed destiny of the Force, but he now wondered if the Force's experience was not more useful on the civilian side of Canadian life. Therefore, he recommended his third option, and suggested that such a constabulary could police the Territories, Indian reserves, the CNR, and the Dominion Parks; fulfil the functions of the Dominion Police, including the secret service; deal with customs and revenue service matters; enforce all federal laws; and, perhaps, serve as penitentiary guards.[51]

Another factor in the considerations before the government was the inappropriateness of any peacetime use of the military to continue to enforce the Military Service Act, especially in the pursuit of defaulters and deserters. Arthur Meighen, the Acting Minister of Justice, proposed to Borden and Doherty, both then absent in Europe, that such enforcement must be turned over to the Dominion Police and that for this and "other purposes" it was time to amalgamate the DP and the RNWMP under the President of the Privy Council. Sherwood's recent resignation as Chief Commissioner of the DP made such an action timely. Given that Perry, after almost 20 years as Commissioner of the RNWMP, was unlikely to agree to any subordinate role, Meighen suggested him to lead such a new force.

Borden and Doherty, however, objected to the merger. Somewhat out of touch, Borden doubted that Perry would accept such an amalgamation because of the Force's semi-military background and its "proud traditions." He still assumed, incorrectly as we have seen, that Perry would prefer to become part of the permanent military force. To resolve the problem of enforcement of the MSA Borden suggested giving the RNWMP the role as part of their mandate on a Canada-wide basis. Both men also objected strongly to the idea of a permanent police force reporting to the President of the Privy Council because any such force should be under the Department of Justice.[52]

Thus, the reorganization, which came in December 1918 to take effect in the new year, was not as dramatic as it might have been. As a first step, the country was simply split in two at the Lakehead. The RNWMP became the federal police force with responsibility for all federal law enforcement west of the twin cities of Port Arthur and Fort William. The Dominion Police maintained their position east of the imaginary line. Duties included enforcing all the Orders-in-Council under the War Measures Act and, more ominously, aiding and assisting the civil powers to preserve law and order. The authorized size of the force was increased to 1200, although Perry had sought 2000. The first priority for reaching that recruiting objective was to get

---

51 RG 18, Vol. 1927, file 150, McLean to Perry, 28 Oct. 1918 and Perry to McLean, 30 Oct. 1918.
52 Borden Papers, Vol. 246, file RLB 2854, Meighen to Borden and Doherty, 3 Dec. 1918; and Borden to Meighen, 11 Dec. 1918.

the A Squadron of the Canadian Corps back to Canada and to find the other former members of the Force in the CEF and assign them to A Squadron for the purpose of bringing them home as a high priority.[53]

The RNWMP now had a greater jurisdiction and more authority than at any time in its history. Commissioner Perry turned to the massive task before him with considerable energy. Faced with a significant manpower shortage, Perry recalled the RNWMP on loan to the DP for MSA enforcement in Quebec.[54] He then proceeded to take over the various DP operations in the west, incorporating the DP officers into the Force. The total strength of the DP in the west had amounted to only 154 men so further recruitment was necessary.[55]

The question of the secret service dimensions of the task arose immediately. Rowell sought information from McLean as to DP activities in the west in this area and instructed his officials:

> It is important that this branch of the Service should receive most careful consideration and that an efficient service should be maintained so that the Government would be kept thoroughly advised of what is going on in the principal centres where IWW or other revolutionary agitators might be at work.[56]

The fact that Rowell had to ask about secret service arrangements in the west is instructive, especially when it became clear that the RNWMP did not know the answer either outside Alberta and Saskatchewan where they already had such jurisdiction and where only two secret agents were in place before the expansion.[57] They knew vaguely of the operations of Immigration agent Malcolm J. Reid in British Columbia but only through further inquiry did they discover that all other DP activity in this area in Manitoba and British Columbia was handled by co-operation with municipal and provincial police forces.[58] Further evidence of the total disarray in government security policy was the letter written in late February by Comptroller McLean to the Director of the Public Safety Branch offering the Force's full co-operation in the area of counter-subversion. Apparently, almost two months after Cahan's demise and the termination of the PSB, the RNWMP remained uninformed.[59]

Moreover, despite his imminent removal, Cahan continued to lobby in early January against the government's new direction. The obsequious and ubiquitous Malcolm J. Reid was unhappy about the rise of the RNWMP in the west. Despite direct orders from Cawdron, he refused to turn over his extensive security files to the Mounties. In this resistance, he was fully supported by Cahan, who wrote to Deputy Minister Newcombe:

> It seems to me the most extraordinary thing imaginable that the RNWMP should proceed to intervene and take over all this confidential and legal investigation carried

---

53   Ibid., Vol. 1930, PC 3076, 12 Dec. 1918 and Memorandum of A.A. McLean, 10 Dec. 1918.
54   RG 18, 83-84/321, file G-2-6, McLean to Sherwood, 16 Dec. 1918.
55   Ibid., Cawdron to McLean, 3 Jan. 1919; Spalding, OC Calgary to Perry, 11 Jan. 1919; Cawdron to Reid, 11 Jan. 1919; Cawdron to McLean, 13 Jan. 1919; Perry to Mclean, 14 Jan. 1919.
56   Ibid., Rowell to McLean, 11 Jan. 1919.
57   RG 18, 83-84/321, file 2-6-1951, Perry to Comptroller, 14 Jan. 1919; and Comptroller to Commissioner, 22 Jan. 1919.
58   Ibid., McLean to Rowell, 14 Jan. 1919; Perry to McLean, 14 Jan. 1919; McLean to Perry, 22 Jan. 1919.
59   Ibid., McLean to Cahan, 24 Feb. 1919.

on by the Department of Justice without a word to this Department. Such action would seriously interfere with the administration of justice and place officials of the RNWMP in charge who lack every qualification for carrying on the work.[60]

While this struggle remained unresolved for some months, Perry eventually prevailed despite Reid's enlisting the support of Unionist MPs J.A. Calder and H.H. Stevens. The Mounties got the files and, in this case, successfully resisted getting the man, who McLean tersely described as "not a satisfactory official."[61]

Further evidence of the rough transfer of authority was apparent in the relationship between the RNWMP and the various other police forces in their half of the country. Whereas the DP had heavily utilized municipal and provincial police, Perry from the start carefully protected his mandate. In a most telling letter, he refused more co-operation offered by the Edmonton Police Commission:

> With regard to men operating in Alberta and your request that the Officer Commanding the Alberta Provincial Police in that section may be advised, I assume you refer to secret agents. Secret agents are operating in every part of Alberta and especially in the cities and industrial areas. Their identity is often not known to our Officer Commanding Districts and seldom are these agents known to each other. I do not think that there can be any danger of overlapping in their work as the information obtained by a special agent is generally fragmentary and cannot always be relied on. The more sources of information we have, the more likely we are to arrive at the truth.

Perhaps even more surprisingly, Perry also established a further principle that would govern later RCMP security work as well:

> An incident recently occurred in the Crows Nest Pass where a constable of the Alberta Provincial Police quite properly, no doubt, arrested one of our Agents. This may occur at any time. I have instructed our Agents not to disclose their identity, but to accept whatever may happen. You will recognize the necessity of this. An arrest and punishment may often strengthen his position and secure the confidence of the element he is investigating.[62]

The question of the justification of the use of *agents provocateurs* that immediately arises from this quotation was not addressed in any of the security materials that I have seen to date.

The recruitment of secret agents in a serious fashion began early in January 1919. Perry circularized all his Officers Commanding (OC) with two key memos. The first discussed the Bolshevik threat in general and the second issued more specific guidelines to detectives and secret agents. Proceeding from the premise that "the pernicious doctrines of Bolshevism" were spreading rapidly throughout the world and in Canada, he drew his officers' attention particularly to Winnipeg, Edmonton and Vancouver and to the foreign settlements scattered through the Prairies, which he noted were especially "susceptible to Bolshevik teaching and propaganda." Officers Commanding were "to take steps to see that careful and constant supervision is

---

60   Ibid., Vol. 1003, Cahan to Newcombe, 9 Jan. 1919.
61   Ibid., Stevens to Calder, 18 March 1919; Perry to McLean, 10 April 1919; and McLean to Rowell, 15 April 1919. See also Horrall, "The RNWMP," 177, however, the speculation that this case led to Cahan's resignation is clearly not sustainable. The Reid case arose after Cahan's fate was decided. See also Vol. 1930, McLean to Rowell, 24 Feb. 1919.
62   Ibid., Vol. 2169, file 16/3, Perry to Lieut. Col. Primrose, 20 Feb. 1919.

maintained over these foreign settlements with a view to detecting the least indication of Bolshevik tendencies and doctrines." Socialists all over the west, he continued, regarded the Bolsheviks "as champions of workers everywhere" and that "serious unrest" was an obvious possibility. Therefore, "our duty is to prevent the efforts of misguided persons to subvert and undermine the settled Government of Canada." OCs were to keep informed and "energetically deal with all unlawful and pernicious propaganda." To do so they should "take steps to select some good, trustworthy men ... as secret agents and submit their names, records, and qualifications for my approval." He also urged them to survey all radical pamphlets and publications and, if appropriate, to prosecute under Section 174 of the Criminal Code. Similarly, they were to record all questionable public speeches if they expected any seditious or treasonable content and particularly to watch street meetings. All this, of course, was to be done in such a way as "not to arouse suspicion or cause antagonism." In conclusion, he reiterated, "The Government relies upon the RNWMP to keep it early advised of any development toward social unrest. It is extremely important that such unrest should not be permitted to develop into a menace to good order and public safety."[63]

A second memo of the same date outlines the job expected of the undercover detectives and secret agents. They were to become "fully acquainted with all labour and other organizations in their respective districts." Each organization "should be carefully investigated with a view to determining" its purpose and object, its proclivity to Bolshevik influence, any current Bolshevik tendencies, or its Bolshevik nature. Not surprisingly, organizations in the last three categories "must receive careful and constant attention." Particular attention was to be addressed to "the officials and leaders of these organizations" who "must be carefully investigated and studied regarding their ways, habits, and antecedents." All such information was to be scrupulously recorded and the subsequent files would provide "a complete history of these men and their doings to date." Lest anyone had missed his point, Perry reiterated that "particular attention must be paid to the different labour unions in their district" because "this class of organization is particularly susceptible to Bolshevik teaching." He concluded by cautioning that great care needed to be taken to ensure the reliability of such sources.[64]

Thus from January 1919 the Security apparatus of the RNWMP targeted labour as its primary focus. Let us turn now to an examination of the devices developed by the RNWMP to carry out its surveillance and counter-subversion functions.

As the Perry memo cited above suggests, the Commissioner attached considerable importance to the development of Personal History Files (PHF). The register of these files consists of a file number, an individual's name, place of residence, and an occasional additional comment. The files themselves are filled with all information gathered by the Force by any means concerning the individual. To date only a few

---

63 Ibid., Vol. 599, file 1328, Perry to OCs, 6 Jan. 1919, Circular Memo. No. 807. See also RG 13, Vol. 231, file 113/1919, Perry to DMJ, 14 Jan. 1919, with the enclosure of Memos 807 and 807A. Given the general lack of co-ordination of security matters and the fact that the RNWMP reported to Rowell not Doherty, the forwarding of these memos is of some interest, especially because it only went to Rowell at the same time. For evidence of this see RG 18, Vol. 2441, Register Entry 58/1919, date 14 Jan. 1919.

64 Ibid., Perry to OCs, 6 Jan. 1919, Circular Memo No. 807A.

of these files have found their way into the Archives (Emma Goldman, Camillien Houde) but others can now be acquired from the Canadian Security Intelligence Service through the Access to Information legislation. The first Register can be found in the NAC and subsequent partial lists have been acquired by Access requests to CSIS.[65]

Assistant Commissioner W.H. Routledge, the first head of the Criminal Investigation Branch, followed up on Perry's initial memo to set up the new system in late February 1919. Routledge wrote the Officers Commanding instructing them personally to supervise the preparation of these files. Such files were to include the following information: "Names and usual descriptive particulars. A photograph if it is at all possible to obtain one without arousing suspicion. Date of arrival in Canada; if naturalized or not; married or single; family; home address; present occupation; particular associations affiliated with and standing in same; present locality of activities; points where he is known to have been in any way active; details of any police records which he may have had; degree of intelligence and education and all other possible information which would assist in compiling a complete record of the man."[66] Initially, these files were to be opened only upon the request of the CIB office, but two weeks later the instructions were modified to demand that the local OC should compile a PHF on "any prominent agitator coming under your notice ... but great care must be taken not to arouse the suspicions of the party being thus reported on."[67]

The Register available in the Archives covers the period from its conception in 1919 to the end of 1924. In those six years 2590 files were opened. These files concerned 2525 individuals once duplicates were removed. A subsequent access request to CSIS for the subsequent registers to the end of 1929 succeeded in gaining a massively exempted list which indicated that in the following five years another 2216 individual files were opened. In other words, on average 437 Canadians had files opened on them annually from 1919 to 1929.[68]

The lists lend themselves to relatively limited statistical analysis, but Table 1 shows the geographic breakdown for the first 2590 files. (The CSIS list had no geographical information for the 54 individuals whose names had not been deleted or could be identified by cross-referencing with subject files.) As may be seen, British Columbia and Alberta are significantly overrepresented, Saskatchewan and Manitoba somewhat, and the rest of the country is badly underrepresented. To some degree at least this is partially a statistical artifact of the initial western-only jurisdiction of the RNWMP. For example, the first Toronto file is number 1225 and the first Montreal file is number 1254, which suggests that almost half of the total files were generated before 1 February 1920 when the new Royal Canadian Mounted Police (RCMP) took over

---

65 These lists are published in Gregory S. Kealey and Reg Whitaker (eds.), *RCMP Security Bulletins: The Early Years, 1919-29* (St. John's, 1992).

66 Ibid., Vol. 2380, Memorandum CIB No. 10, Routledge to Officers Commanding, 28 Feb. 1919.

67 Ibid., Circular Memorandum CIB No. 10A, Routledge to OCs, 14 March 1919.

68 RG 18, Vol. 2448, Register of Bolsheviks, 1919-1924. My access request to CSIS was 87-A-41. The initial CSIS response was very restricted and after a complaint to the Information Commissioner a fuller response was supplied. Such examples simultaneously show the utility of complaints and the subsequent investigation process and the ongoing problems with the legislation. The rate in the two periods was almost identical, 432 versus 443, although given that the opening of files should be heavier initially this suggests some intensification over the period.

Table 1 "Agitators" by Location, 1919-24		
Number on List		2590
Number Names (after adjustments)		2525
Number Places Listed		2287
A. Geographic Breakdown of Provinces		
	No. of Agitators	% Agitators	% Canadian Population 1921
British Columbia	775	33.9	6.0
Alberta	477	20.9	6.7
Saskatchewan	286	12.5	8.6
Ontario	276	12.1	33.4
Manitoba	253	11.1	6.9
Quebec	158	6.9	26.9
Nova Scotia	15	1.0	6.0
Prince Edward Island	1	—	1.0
Yukon	1	—	—
New Brunswick	0	—	4.4
USA	24	1.0	
Other Foreign	5	.2	
Unknown	16	.7	
	2287	100.3	
B. Geographic Breakdown by City >50		
	No. of Agitators	% Agitators	
Vancouver	427	34.4	
Winnipeg	194	15.7	
Montreal	156	12.6	
Edmonton	118	10.0	
Toronto	80	6.5	
Calgary	74	6.0	
Regina	73	5.9	
Ft. William	65	5.2	
Saskatoon	53	4.3	
	1240	100.6	
Source: RG18, Vol. 2248, Register of Bolsheviks.		

national jurisdiction. Other scattered information which can be gleaned from the list is the presence of 68 women, one of whom, Alli Koivisto, is quaintly described as "an agitatress." In addition, the list includes 23 clergy (Ivens, Irvine, Smith, Woodsworth, and Bland are the most prominent), 14 doctors, six military, and five elected officials (John Queen of Winnipeg and Mayor Joseph Clarke of Edmonton, for example). The unfortunately rather random marginalia identifies nine IWW and six OBU members, as well as an array of less predictable entries such as English harvester, Jewish lecturer, Esperanto teacher, Hindu wrestler, and perhaps most intriguing, "ex-RCMP."[69]

---

[69] A complete list of these files is published in Kealey and Whitaker (eds.), *RCMP Security Bulletins, 1919-1929*.

Table 2 Number Subject Files Opened by Year, 1919-29		
Year	Number	% of Total
1919	3429	51.1
1920	299	4.4
1921	689	10.2
1922	789	11.7
1923	435	6.4
1924	344	5.1
1925	268	4.0
1926	178	2.6
1927	89	1.3
1928	126	1.9
1929	81	1.2
Total	6767	99.9

Source: CSIS, Register of Bolshevik Subject Files, Access Requests, 86-A-10, 87-A-125, and 88-A-91.

The second data series compiled by the new security section of the Force was a set of subject files on radicalism. The register of these files was obtained from CSIS by means of three access requests.[70] The rate at which these files were compiled seems quite uneven. As Table 2 illustrates, the Force opened the first 3459 subject files in 1919 or slightly over half of the total for the 11-year period. In the first four years fully 80 per cent of the total for the entire period were opened. While this is partially dictated simply by the cumulative nature of the development of a filing system, it probably also indicates a combination of a slowing of radical activities late in the decade and a similar decline in RCMP activity. A comprehensive analysis of this data and a careful cross-tabulation of the data in each set are yet to be completed. Nevertheless, it should be readily apparent that the surveillance entered into by the RNWMP from January 1919 was of a different order from what had gone before.[71]

Another significant change in RNWMP practice in early 1919 also took place because of the new security demands. Each Division OC's customary monthly report was no longer to contain any allusions to "matters which have been dealt with by secret investigation." As the old monthly reports were not confidential, "in future, commencing on first February 1919," each OC should file a "CONFIDENTIAL Report" monthly, "giving a summary of the secret investigation work and opinions of the OCs as to general conditions with regard to labour, industrial disputes, and socialistic and anarchical activities in triplicate."[72] Many of these reports survive in the archives for the years 1919 and 1920 but all attempts to locate the rest of this material for the rest of that decade have failed so far.[73]

A few examples of material culled from these reports will indicate the style of security operations in early 1919. The OC Edmonton, for example, reported in late January 1919 that they were keeping SPC leader Joe Knight under careful watch. He also worried about the problem of recruiting secret agents:

> I have been endeavoring during the month to engage some special agents with a view of getting definite information with regard to alien propaganda and socialistic

---

70 CSIS, 86-A-10 (1920); 87-A-125 (1921-1929); 88-A-91 (1919).

71 This list is also published in Kealey and Whitaker, *RCMP Security Bulletins, 1919-1929*. A third important list of files concerns prohibited publications which will also be published.

72 RG 18, Vol. 2380, Circular Memo No. 809, Perry to OCs, 10 Feb. 1919.

73 Various access requests to both CSIS and the RCMP so far have only turned up the non-confidential monthly reports and even those have had material severed from them at some point in the past. These materials are the subject of a series of ongoing complaints to the Information Commissioner. I should add that the RCMP Access Section in Ottawa and in St. John's went out of their way to make the material still held by the Force readily available to me.

matters. This I have found exceedingly difficult; the right class of man is very hard to get. I have engaged temporarily a returned soldier, W.P. Walker, who has been highly recommended and I think he will make good.[74]

A report from Vancouver two months later showed the progress that the OCs were making in recruiting agents:

> As cases have cropped up for investigation agents have been engaged; it is a difficult matter, however, to ensure efficient work in a new district like this, when one does not know the people on whom it is necessary to rely on for information and investigation and too the number must be kept in bounds. Up to date Messrs. Devitt, Spain, Eccles, Jones, Roth, Hall, Davies, Wilkie, and Lawrence have been engaged, all of whom are either ex-members of the Force or are returned soldiers or both. Special Agent Eccles was sent up to work through the camps in the Grand Trunk Pacific as per your instructions and I hope shortly to be able to supply you with some good information.[75]

Horrigan, the OC Vancouver, also contributed an eloquent, albeit somewhat purple, account of the Vancouver General Sympathetic Strike:

> Nevertheless, there was, as it were, a dangerous volcano constantly threatening; or I might say, it was as if it only required a spark to start a conflagration. The atmosphere, so to speak, was charged, ominous, and extremely dispiriting. One felt trouble in the air. Everywhere the strikers lined the streets, their glances bespeaking a sinister intent — depraved, vicious-looking men — the very dregs and refuse of the strikers, seeming to track our every move and action. Certainly, there were fanatics, who, in spite of the official mandate of the strike committee not to create any disturbance would have lost no opportunity, in an unguarded moment, to wreck our buildings in an attempt to destroy, or at least severely cripple, the police; men who, having no aptitude or propensity but for depredation and bloodshed, would have hailed with delight an opportunity of unrestricted license.[76]

Clearly, even the reassurance of secret agents' reports did not eliminate the fear engendered by the class struggle.

This is not the place to enter into a re-evaluation of the RNWMP role in the Winnipeg General Strike, but I think it is worth noting that S.W. Horrall's congratulatory tone about the quality of RNWMP intelligence is partial at best.[77] For example, the Force made available to Acting Prime Minister Sir Thomas White the report of Secret Agent No. 10 on the Calgary Convention. This agent was identified by Perry as having "for many years taken an active part in the IWW and kindred associations, and is therefore peculiarly competent to discuss the leaders in such movements and their aims and objectives." This agent is almost certainly Robert Gosden who enjoys the unique privilege of turning up both as a RNWMP Secret Agent and as the subject of a RNWMP Personal History File. Gosden is an interesting contrast to the heroic stories of F.W. Zaneth and John Leopold, the RNWMP undercover agents who fill the hagiographical accounts of the Force's brave battle with communism. Gosden was born in England in 1881 and emigrated to Canada

---

74 RG 18, Vol. 1931, OC Edmonton to Perry, 31 Jan. 1919. For additional examples, see the appendices to Kealey, "A Curious Tale." For a list of RNWMP secret agents identified to date from these documents, see Appendix 1.
75 Ibid., Horrigan to Perry, 13 March 1919.
76 Ibid., Vol. 1956, Vancouver Confidential Report, Horrigan to Perry, 10 July 1919.
77 Horrall, "RNWMP and Labour Unrest," pp. 184-8.

after fighting in the Boer War. He was apparently present in some capacity in the great pre-war coal strike in Nova Scotia and was heavily involved in a 1911 Prince Rupert IWW navvies' strike in which he was charged with attempted murder and served time. Later he was active in IWW free speech fights in California and was deported to Canada. In 1916 he became involved in a massive political scandal in which he was accused of aiding in electoral fraud, a charge he later admitted to. Hired by the RNWMP as an agent in 1919, he worked in the Crows Nest Pass and attended the Calgary Convention as a police agent.[78]

Gosden's report on Calgary went to the Prime Minister, admittedly with a few cautionary covering notes. After an astute consideration of the aims of the SPC leadership, Gosden outlined an intriguing proposal for a type of psychological warfare against those individuals. Based on his notion that their "one weakness consists of the fact that they lack the physical courage of their convictions and they possess the fear of the consequence of their acts," he suggested some subtle police terrorism:

> Immediately pick them up one at a time, in such a way that they will automatically disappear from their friends and their activities. They should be picked up secretly and should be safely placed in custody secretly. After one or two of these leaders had been picked up at various points in a mysterious manner, and disappeared just as mysteriously, the unseen hand would so intimidate the weaker and lesser lights that the agitation would automatically die down; where they were kept in custody no record should be kept on the books.

He was unsure what should be done with them afterwards, except that they should definitely not be granted a public trial. "This may not be in strict accordance with technical law, but this organization of men is taking advantage of the technical weaknesses of law to organize right under the nose of the authorities, the most drastic form of social revolution that one can conceive of," he added.

He spelled out his scheme in even more detail, expounding at length on its psychological advantages. Moreover, he attempted to answer the obvious legalistic objections by emphasizing the fragility of the government's control:

> The present condition of things, in a social sense, is so ripe for change that given a free hand for three months, and the government of the day will go down to utter defeat and the utter annihilation of its personnel. There is no half-way measures can be taken ... this is the only way ... All precedents and policies of the authorities must be swept aside to meet this newer and more subtle form of revolutionary activity.

Gosden also suggested a series of ameliorative reforms to accompany his plan of repression.[79]

No doubt other historians reading this report have dismissed Gosden's advice as the rantings of a madman. And perhaps he was, but the significance of the report is that it was deemed important enough to be sent to the acting Prime Minister. Also

---

78 For much of the detail on Gosden's pre-secret agent career I am grateful to Mark Leier.
79 Borden Papers, Vol. 104, file Oc519(A)1, McLean to White, 12 April 1919 with enclosures: Perry to McLean, 2 April 1919; Notes for Commissioner's Perusal of SA No. 10 Report on the Calgary Convention; and Report of SA No. 10, 19 March 1919. See also Crerar Papers, "Re: Interprovincial Labor Convention, Calgary," 19 March 1919; Perry to McLean, 2 April 1919 and "Notes for Commissioner's Perusal."

intriguing is the fact that the Department of Justice was asked in March 1919 to prepare a legal opinion on the holding of trials in private.[80]

Equally interesting and again unquestioned in any documents I have seen was the very early decision "to endeavour to have one or two of our agents become members (and, if possible, secure executive positions) of these various organizations." Indeed, in his summary report in the aftermath of the Winnipeg General Strike, Perry proudly announced that "at the present time, we have operatives who are members of practically every known organization in the west, which has been in any way connected with or influenced by the present wave of Bolshevik and socialistic propaganda." In this summary Perry indicates that as of June 1919 he had 30 detectives and 35 secret agents at work in the west. The largest concentrations of these were in Southern Alberta (six and nine), British Columbia (five and ten), and Manitoba (five and seven).[81]

The Dominion Police: The Beginning of the End, 1919

The documentation on the activities of the RNWMP until the spring of 1919 is extensive and has been reviewed at least in part elsewhere. It is important to remember that security responsibilities for Canada east of the Lakehead remained with the Dominion Police. Their activities have received far less attention. Indeed, the emphasis in the literature on *western* radicalism in 1919 is at least partially an artifact of the more readily available documentation on the RNWMP.

Cahan, shortly before his departure, demonstrated that he had some similar organizational ideas to Perry by compiling "A List of the Chief Agitators in Canada." His list of approximately 337 names focused primarily on the IWW and individuals prosecuted for transgressing the various anti-socialist Orders-in-Council.[82] (For a sample, see Appendix 2.) Thus, this list, unlike that of the RNWMP, was heavily dominated by Ontario radicals. Similarly, a list of those prosecuted under the 1918 anti-radical Orders-in-Council shows a wide range of sentencing patterns (Table 3) and a significant Ontario presence (Table 4a and 4b).[83] Such convictions, however, also illustrate a difference in philosophical approach between the DP and the RNWMP. The former sought to prosecute and to convict; the latter played a more calculated waiting game. One early articulation of this strategy came in McLean's explanation to Rowell why a prosecution was not being pursued:

> The policy carried out by the Commissioner is not to prosecute isolated cases wherefrom little benefit is derived, but to gather all possible data which will prove of the utmost value in the event of a general outbreak in any particular district.[84]

In a later variant of this argument, Perry himself explained that the policy of "no isolated prosecutions" "eliminated the danger of uncovering our agents ... and our channels of information were kept open at a very critical time." Moreover, he argued,

---

80 Department of Justice, Access Request A-8800018, file 641/1919.
81 Borden Papers, Vol. 96, Pt. 1, file Oc485, McLean to Yates, 7 Aug. 1919 enclosing Perry to McLean, 30 June 1919.
82 RG 13, Vol. 231, file 132/1919, Cahan to Doherty, 17 Jan. 1919. This list is available in Kealey and Whitaker (eds.), *RCMP Security Bulletins: The Early Years*.
83 RG 18, Vol. 2380, Routledge to OCs, CIB No. 104, 16 Aug. 1919.
84 RG 18, Vol. 847, Comptroller to Rowell, 25 Feb. 1919.

Table 3
Sentences for "Bolshevik Propaganda" or Membership in Prohibited Organization

Fines (144)	
under $10:	20
$11-50:	29
$51-100:	29
$101-500:	56
over $500:	10
Jail (35)	
interned:	15
under 1 year:	8
1-2 years:	10
3-5 years:	2
Jail and Fine (10)	
$500 + 1 month:	2
$500 + 6 months:	2
$500 + 2 years:	2
$500 + 3 years:	1
$1000 + 3 months:	2
$4000 + 5 years:	1
Suspended Sentence:	20
Dismissed:	5
Total:	214

Source: NAC, RG 18, Vol. 2380, Routledge to OCs, CIB No. 104, 16 Aug. 1919.

Table 4
A. Geographical Distribution of Charges by Province

	Number	%
Quebec	3	1
Ontario	154	73
Manitoba	1	0.5
Saskatchewan	23	11
Alberta	13	6
British Columbia	15	7
Unknown	1	0.5
	210*	99

* varies from Table 3 owing to multiple convictions versus some individuals.

B. Geographical Distribution by City (5 or more only)

Toronto, Ont.	27	Cobalt, Ont.	8
Windsor, Ont.	21	Kamsack, Sask.	7
Timmins, Ont.	20	Medicine Hat, Alta.	7
Vancouver, B.C.	15	Regina, Sask.	7
Sudbury, Ont.	15	Tisdale, Sask.	6
London, Ont.	13	Brantford, Ont.	5
Sault Ste. Marie, Ont.	11	Copper Cliff, Ont.	5
Hamilton, Ont.			

Source: NAC, RG 18, Vol. 2380, Routledge to OCs, CIB No. 104, 16 Aug. 1919.

"the movement must be viewed from a national standpoint, and that when action was taken it should be carried out simul- taneously throughout the country."[85]

The decision to make the RNWMP the dominant partner in the new federal police force created by the merger of the Force and the DP remains to be explored elsewhere. Suffice it to say that Cahan's failure did nothing to improve the position of the DP. Perhaps more surprisingly, much of Cahan's organizational structure for a revamped DP was present in the new RCMP that took over nationwide security responsibilities on 1 February 1920. The structure of the security component of the CIB changed only in the sense that it now covered the entire country. In effect very little would change in the next decade. Canada's security and intelligence system had been put in place and only the fine tuning of the internal relationship with Military Intelligence and of the external relationship with British and American security agencies remained to be worked out with the Force's removal to its new national headquarters in Ottawa.[86]

NOTE

This chapter was previously published in *Intelligence and National Security*, 7 no. 3 (1992), 179-210. This research was supported by the Social Sciences and Humanities Research Council of Canada. I would like to thank Drs. Linda Kealey, Stuart Pierson and Reg Whitaker for their helpful comments. A version of this paper was presented at the Law and Society Conference at the University of Victoria, Victoria, British Columbia, in May 1990.

---

85   Borden Papers, Vol. 96, Pt. 1, file Oc485, Perry to McLean, 30 June 1919.

86   The entire question of the relationship of military intelligence to the police has been left for another paper. Suffice it to say that the role of the military in this realm went far beyond anything I have seen in the literature to date and that it continued well after the end of the war. Similarly the question of co-operation with British and American intelligence merits a separate paper.

Appendix 1
RNWMP/RCMP Secret Agents, 1919-1920

1. F.E. Riethodorf, SA # 50 aka Frederick Edwards (RG18, v.573 + v.1916, f.49/5)
2. Roth, SA # 6 (RG18, v.589, f.892)
3. Dourasoff, SA # 14
4. John Jones, SA # 58, Vancouver (v.592, f.1073)
5. A.B. Smith, SA # 61, Victoria
6. F.H. Colam (v.599, f.1335)
7. F.W. Zaneth (v.829)
8. George C. Evans
9. R. M. Gosden
10. Devitt, Vancouver
11. W.P. Walker, Edmonton (v.1931)
12. Eccles, Vancouver
13. Spain, Vancouver
14. Orton Hall, Vancouver
15. Davies, Vancouver
16. Wilkie, Vancouver
17. Lawrence, Vancouver
18. Kobus (v.1932)
19. Kyzlick
20. Harry Daskaluk, SA # 21
21. Gore Kaburagi (v.1933) or Goro Karbarugi (v.2175)
22. John Leopold (v.1958, f.159/7)
23. T.E. Ryan
24. John Veloskie (v.2175)
25. Julius Chmichlewski

Appendix 2
Chief Agitators in Canada

"A"

Aho, Arthur	Address unknown. Alleged I.W.W. worker in B.C.
Ainger, Frank	Address unknown, Alleged I.W.W. worker in B.C.
Aldridge, F.	Box 531, Prince Rupert, B.C. Secy. Longshoremen's Union. Subscriber to "Solidarity."
Anderson, Nels	Address unknown, Alleged I.W.W. worker in B.C.
Alpatoff, B.	143 Powell St., Vancouver, B.C. Arrested on October 19th, 1918, charged with attending illegal meeting and with having objectionable matter in his possession. Pleaded guilty to charge of attending meeting and fined $10.00 on Dec. 23, 1918. Other charge withdrawn.
Ahlqvist, John	Toronto, Ont. Charged in October 1918 with having objectionable literature in his possession. Arrested at Sudbury, Ont.
Ajola, John	Sudbury, Ont. Charged in October 1918 with having objectionable literature in his possession.

Source: RG 13, vol. 231, file 132/1919.

EPILOGUE

From RNWMP to RCMP:
The Power of Myth and the Reality of Transformation

Steve Hewitt

In due course 200 very dissatisfied and wild-eyed Crees, with 450 horses, were rounded up and started northwards, with a strong force of United States cavalry in attendance. They were met at the Boundary Line by three Mounted Policemen, one corporal and two troopers.

The American commanding officer looked at them with a surprised air.

"Where's your escort for these Indians?" he asked.

"We're here," answered the corporal.

"Yes, yes, I see. But where is your regiment?"

"I guess it's here all right," said the corporal. "The other fellow's looking after the breakfast things."

"But are there only four of you then?"

"That's so, Colonel, but you see we wear the Queen's scarlet."[1]

This wonderful tale from A.L. Haydon's *Riders of the Plains* is merely one of many such stories involving the famous Royal North-West Mounted Police.[2] Heroic young men, clad in their scarlet tunics, battling all sorts of nefarious ruffians with only the lonely prairie and its accompanying evocative sky as a constant companion. These were the Mounties of legend, the Mounties of myth, the Mounties who became the world's most famous police force. As a news story on the copyrighting of the Mountie symbol by the Walt Disney Company noted, the force had attained an unheard of level of fame (in Canadian terms): "The Mountie is probably Canada's most enduring symbol, perhaps the most identifiable of all things Canadian."[3]

That myth can be found in countless books about the Mounted Police, both of the fiction and non-fiction variety. The historical literature on the Mounted Police

---

1   A.L. Haydon, *Riders of the Plains: A Record of the Royal North-West Mounted Police of Canada, 1873-1910* (1910; Edmonton: Hurtig, 1971), 85.

2   Originally called the North-West Mounted Police, the prefix "Royal" was added after members of the Mounted Police fought as a unit in the Boer War.

3   "Canadian Mounties Copyrighting," *Clari.World.Americas.Canada*, 13 February 1995.

displays similar extremes as other works on the police. The trend of scholarship resembles a movement from the general, celebratory and simplistic, to critical studies of complexities, contradictions, and sophistication. The works in the former category, however, could be listed in the dozens. Counting the studies in the latter group is much less time-consuming. Much of the early work on the force is hagiographic in nature, glorious fiction disguised as factual history. Works such as A.L. Haydon's *Riders of the Plains*, John Peter Turner's *The North-West Mounted Police, 1873-1893*, and R.G. MacBeth's *Policing the Plains* are packed with anecdotes of heroic young Englishmen confronting and confounding criminals, earning the respect of Natives, protecting the people, and doing it all with quiet confidence and competence.[4] This sort of work dominated literature on the force until the 1970s. Even the semi-official history of the force, published in 1973, the centenary of its creation, tended towards celebration of sensational cases and heroic individuals.[5] A recent popular work on the Mounted Police, *The Great Adventure: How the Mounties Conquered the West*, written in the style copyrighted by Pierre Berton and Peter C. Newman, suggests that which is old might be new once again.[6] Collectively the concentration of these various works on the nineteenth century did much to create the images of the Mounted Police that remain dominant even in the 1990s. There is an obvious irony to this emphasis in that so much of what is associated with the Mounted Police is based on a long disappeared era — in fact, one that no longer existed in western Canada by the beginning of the First World War in 1914.

The old frontier was on the verge of change when the first redcoats marched west in 1874. Within a few years the "national policy" of Prime Minister John A. Macdonald would begin the process of creating a new society in western Canada.[7] The fundamental change, however, began with the arrival into power of Wilfrid Laurier and the Liberals in 1896. Laurier, as it has been frequently noted, declared that the twentieth century would be Canada's. His government worked to ensure the accuracy of the prophecy. Western Canada played an important role in its plans. This hinterland region was to be the great breadbasket for the rest of the nation and the world. Immigrants were the key factor in constructing this new Canada. Under the influence of cabinet minister Clifford Sifton, massive immigration to Canada began, including the entrance of non-traditional immigrants. Sifton sought "men in sheepskin coats" — hardy peasants who knew how to make a farm work because it was in their blood and the blood of countless generations before them. Those he deemed

---

4 Haydon, *Riders of the Plains*; John Peter Turner, *The North-West Mounted Police, 1873-1893*, 2 vols. (Ottawa: Edmond Cloutier, 1950); and R.B. MacBeth, *Policing the Plains: Being the Real-Life Record of the Famous Royal North-West Mounted Police* (London: Hodder and Stoughton, 1921). Also see Cecil Edward Denny, *The Law Marches West* (Toronto: J.M. Dent, 1939); Ronald Atkin, *Maintain the Right: The Early History of the North-West Mounted Police* (London: Macmillan, 1973); R.C. Fetherstonhaugh, *The Royal Canadian Mounted Police* (New York: Carrick and Evans, 1938); and Louis Charles Douthwaite, *The Royal Canadian Mounted Police* (London: Blackie, 1939).

5 Nora and William Kelly, *The Royal Canadian Mounted Police: A Century of History, 1873-1973* (Edmonton: Hurtig Publishers, 1973).

6 David Cruise and Alison Griffiths, *The Great Adventure: How the Mounties Conquered the West* (Toronto: Penguin Books, 1996).

7 R.C. Macleod, "Canadianizing the West: The North-West Mounted Police as Agents of the National Policy, 1873-1905," in R. Douglas Francis and Howard Palmer (eds.), *The Prairie West: Historical Readings* (Edmonton: Pica Pica Press, 1995), 225-28.

unsuited for life in western Canada — urban unskilled workers, American Blacks, Asians, and southern Europeans — were discouraged from entering. While Britain and the United States continued to be the main sources for new Canadians, for the first time eastern and central Europeans began to arrive in sizable numbers. The population of Canada as a whole increased by 64 percent between 1901 and 1921.[8]

The newcomers arrived in a nation undergoing rapid change; they were part of the transformation, but it extended beyond them. Urbanization had come to the Prairies. Whereas there had been no cities on the Prairies when the Mounties appeared, in 1911 there were twelve with populations over 5,000, including Winnipeg which had nearly 150,000 residents.[9] In 1921 Canada became 50 percent urban for the first time. This urban component, despite the wishes of Sifton, included a growing industrial proletariat, a reflection of the increasing importance of industrialization and manufacturing to the economy of Canada. In the West the workers of the new factories, railways, and mines were often eastern and central Europeans who could not make a successful career at farming or who had been brought in by business interests as industrial labourers in the first place.[10]

Rapid change created friction. The presence of non-Anglo-Canadians, or "foreigners" as they were derogatorily labelled, generated hostility from entrenched ethnic groups, particularly those of a British background. Reformers, such as J.S. Woodsworth, called for the "Canadianization" of the newcomers.[11] Others, such as federal cabinet minister Frank Oliver, wanted to stop immigration from non-northern European sources. The numbers of non-British immigrants, especially eastern and central European navvies, increased, however, until the start of the Great War when virtually all immigration ended.

Organized labour was also on the rise: its numbers grew five-fold between 1900 and 1914.[12] While this trend was worrisome to many businessmen, those who belonged to unions tended to be the skilled workers who often had a decidedly conservative perspective. The unskilled, including a large number of non-British labourers, were left to fend for themselves. Industrial disputes often occurred. Many degenerated into violent clashes between strikers and the militia or police. Once the war began, labour peace quickly ensued in the initial excitement and patriotism of the conflict. This respite, however, lasted only until 1917 when a new militancy emerged in what one historian has called the "Canadian labour revolt."[13] The high

---

8   Robert Craig Brown and Ramsay Cook, *Canada, 1896-1921: A Nation Transformed* (Toronto: McClelland and Stewart, 1991 (1974)), 50-64.

9   Alan F.J. Artibise, "Boosterism and the Development of Prairie Cities, 1871-1913," in R. Douglas Francis and Howard Palmer (eds.), *The Prairie West: Historical Readings* (Edmonton: Pica Pica Press, 1992), 515.

10 Donald Avery, *"Dangerous Foreigners": European Immigrant Workers and Labour Radicalism in Canada, 1896-1932* (Toronto: McClelland and Stewart, 1979).

11 Brown and Cook, *Canada, 1896-1921*, 72. For example, see J.S. Woodsworth, *Strangers Within Our Gates Or Coming Canadians* (1909; Toronto: University of Toronto Press, 1972); and Ralph Connor, *The Foreigner: A Tale of Saskatchewan* (Toronto: Westminster, 1909).

12 Brown and Cook, *Canada, 1896-1921*, 113-14.

13 Gregory S. Kealey, "The Canadian Labour Revolt of 1919," in Bryan D. Palmer (ed.), *The Character of Class Struggle: Essays in Canadian Working-Class History, 1850-1985* (Toronto: McClelland and Stewart Ltd., 1986), 90-114.

cost of the war in the form of rampant inflation and the enormous loss of life fuelled the discontent on the part of Canadian labour. Conscription only made matters worse; workers might have to go off and die in France while business leaders such as Joseph Flavelle grew wealthy supplying the war effort. The number of strikes in Canada, which had declined precipitously in the first two years of the war, rose rapidly in its last years.

Even more disturbing to those in power than the growth of unionism and labour strength was the appearance of radicalism. Organized labour tended to be supporters of the traditional parties. Some workers, nonetheless, especially non-British ones, began to listen to appeals from more radical sources. Socialist parties appeared in Canada at the turn of the century although these organizations frequently fought amongst themselves over issues of policy and doctrine, diminishing their threat to the status quo of capitalism.[14] The 1917 Russian Revolution proved inspirational to many radicals in Canada and horribly worrisome to the Canadian political and economic elite. In the realm of political ideologies, as in so many other ways, by the early twentieth century Canada was a very different place than it had been in 1874.[15]

The frontier had clearly changed, but the main images associated with the Mounties had not. The Mounted Police myth, which has lingered on for most of the current century, has dominated the way the police have been viewed, especially by the general public. The myth has many of the trappings of a religion. There is the creation story (the march west), the prophets (the early commissioners and heroic individual Mounties), and the gospel writers (early authors about the Mounties). Historian Keith Walden has effectively described the process behind the generation of the Mountie myth:

> [b]ecause every human creation is inherently mythic, and every society agrees on some basic points about the nature of reality, the popular image of the Mounted Police may be viewed in terms of myth. When Britons, Americans, and English Canadians looked at the Mounted Police they collectively ignored certain aspects of the force, downplayed others, and emphasized those qualities and characteristics that to them seemed important. They thought they were describing a self-evident reality, but they were not. Instead they described what they wanted to see.[16]

What they wanted to see was very much a nineteenth-century creation. Essentially, this script suggests that the force kept the frontier orderly and safe for settlers. While undoubtedly a very powerful organization, especially in the context of the times, it did not abuse that power. Instead heroic Mounties dispensed frontier law in a very public fashion as they policed the prairie region of Canada. These horsemen maintained a degree of professionalism and neutrality that won them the support of citizens on the Prairies and made them the envy of police forces around the world. There was both a practical and a mythic aspect to this piece of Mountie history that has been well documented by both academic and popular historians. The script remains as entrenched in the 1990s as it was in the 1910s.

---

14 Ibid., 94.
15 Brown and Cook, *Canada, 1896-1921*, 122-25.
16 Keith Walden, *Visions of Order: The Canadian Mounties in Symbol and Myth* (Toronto: Butterworths, 1982), 11. See also Dick Harrison, "The Mounted Police in Fiction," in Hugh A. Dempsey (ed.), *Men in Scarlet* (Calgary: McClelland and Stewart West, [1975?]), 163-74.

In the era of the RCMP the images of the RNWMP continue to dominate. Such a trend was evident in two popular histories about the force written at the end of the 1930s. Huge sections of the books are devoted to policing on the new frontier, the Arctic. In *The Royal Canadian Mounted Police*, Louis Charles Douthwaite devotes 19 percent of his book to the Mounted Police's experience in the Arctic, including 68 percent of the material covering the years 1920 to 1939.[17] R.C. Fetherstonhaugh's *The Royal Canadian Mounted Police*, published in 1938, has material on the same period including chapters with titles that give away their obvious Arctic-based content: "Murders in the Arctic," "Northern Achievements, 1929," and "Further Achievements in the North."[18] In part this emphasis on the Mounties' northern activities in the interwar period is simply a reflection of the source materials available to the authors — namely, the annual Mounted Police reports that also contain considerable amounts of information on policing experiences in the North. There is, however, a deeper symbolic explanation for the attention to the Mounties' movement north. The old prairie frontier had vanished. In the North a new equivalent twentieth-century frontier had been discovered, one free of all of the problems associated with the modern industrial and urban world that the Mounties were increasingly facing elsewhere in Canada.

In the 1970s the RCMP participated directly in the veneration of the past as the force celebrated its centennial. William Kelly, a former assistant commissioner, and his wife Nora produced a full-length history of the men in scarlet. In style, *The Royal Canadian Mounted Police: A Century of History*, differed little from the histories written in the 1930s.[19] In the 1990s popular culture has had another fling with the Mounties. Television shows such as *Bordertown* and *Due South* have offered portrayals of Mounted Policemen where even if, as in the case of the latter, the setting was not of the nineteenth century the caricature of the Mountie certainly was. A recent set of historical moments recreated for the television generation, the Heritage Minute series, chose nineteenth-century Mountie Sam Steele as the subject of its profile. As this piece is being written CBC Saskatchewan is running television commercials inviting citizens to join in the celebration of the 125th anniversary of the Mounted Police by watching a performance of the musical ride.

Why the staying power of such tales of frontier policing?[20] These images are

---

17   Douthwaite, *The Royal Canadian Mounted Police*.

18   Fetherstonhaugh, *The Royal Canadian Mounted Police*.

19   N. and W. Kelly, *The Royal Canadian Mounted Police*.

20   Even the "dirty tricks" scandal in the 1970s did not carry much weight with those outside the Canadian political, media, and legal establishment. Despite story after story of Mounted Police illegalities a Gallop Poll found that fewer than 20 percent of Canadians believed that the Mounted Police was too powerful. More than two-thirds of those interviewed also did not want the Mounted Police subjected to any interference in their policing activities. Finally, some respondents believed that the RCMP should receive even more powers (see Walden, *Visions of Order*, 2). To Lorne and Caroline Brown such results were further evidence "that old myths die hard ... It is obvious that more people must be educated to the fact that the recent revelations of police activity reflect what and who the police represent *and have always represented* in Canada. It is only when people see the present events [the RCMP "dirty tricks" scandal] in historical perspective that they can begin to understand the repressive apparatus of the state in this country and then begin to devise strategies to defend themselves against it" (see Lorne and Caroline Brown, *An Unauthorized History of the RCMP* (Toronto: James Lorimer and Company, 1978 [1973], v. — emphasis in the original quotation). For a more

reassuring since continuity is suggested; they also recreate an image of the Prairies that was long vanished, even by the early twentieth century. Much of the social reform rhetoric that was popular by the 1920s, especially among agrarian movements, idealized the rural life, the countryside, while at the same time vilifying the city and what it represented: corruption, immorality, heterogeneity, crime, dirt, depravity, and poverty.[21] The old prairies were, with the notable exception of Métis and Indian peoples, virtually an Anglo-Saxon homogenous society in a rural setting. The bridge between the old and new societies was the reassuring Mounted Policeman; he represented continuity and stability in an era of rapid change.

For those interested in the Mounted Police, the nineteenth century was also a time of purity. In this constructed past there was no 1931 Estevan riot, no 1935 Regina Riot, no "dirty tricks" campaign of the 1970s, no turbans of the 1980s, and no Airbus of the 1990s.[22] In the old era, or so the story goes, the Mounties always caught their man, and they did so in their regulation uniform and without concern for political ties or wealth. The RNWMP images recreate a once glorious past; the realities of RCMP policing smack of the dangers and depravities of modernity.

There are practical reasons that the nineteenth-century symbols of the Mounted Police have resonated so long. Many of the early chroniclers wrote when that period was still fresh in the collective memory of the Canadian public. Then there are the available sources. Little material that fundamentally documented the transformation of the Mounted Police during the First World War was available to researchers until the 1980s.[23] Instead, writers interested in the Mounted Police had to rely on a carefully controlled public record, specifically the memoirs of those who served and the annual

---

recent study of the Mountie myth, see Michael Dawson, "'That Nice Red Coat Goes to My Head Like Champagne': Popular Images of the Mountie, 1880-1960," unpublished paper presented at the annual meeting of the Canadian Historical Association, June 1996.

21 See Richard Allen, *The Social Passion: Religion and Social Reform in Canada, 1914-28* (Toronto: University of Toronto Press, 1973), and David C. Jones, "'There Is Some Power About the Land': The Western Agrarian Press and Country Life Ideology," in R. Douglas Francis and Howard Palmer (eds.), *The Prairie West: Historical Readings* (Edmonton: Pica Pica Press, 1992), 455-74.

22 There are several sources for the Mountie role in these events. On Estevan see S.D. Hanson, "Estevan 1931," in Irving Abella (ed.), *On Strike: Six Key Labour Struggles in Canadian History* (Toronto: James Lorimer & Company, 1975), 33-77; and Steve Hewitt, "September 1931: A Re-Interpretation of the RCMP's Handling of the Estevan Strike and Riot," *Labour/Le Travail* 39 (1997): 159-78. On the Mounted Police role in Regina see Michael Lonardo, "Under a Watchful Eye: A Case Study of Police Surveillance During the 1930s," *Labour/Le Travail* 5 (1995): 11-41; Victor Howard, *"We Were the Salt of the Earth": The On-to-Ottawa Trek and the Regina Riot* (Regina: Canadian Plains Research Center, 1985), and Steven Roy Hewitt, "'Old Myths Die Hard': The Transformation of the Mounted Police in Alberta and Saskatchewan, 1914-1939," Ph.D. Dissertation, University of Saskatchewan, 1997, 207-60. On the "dirty tricks" campaign, see John Sawatsky, *Men in Shadows: The RCMP Security Service* (Toronto: Doubleday Canada, Ltd., 1980); Jeff Sallot, *Nobody Said No: The Real Story About How the Mounties Always Get Their Man* (Toronto: James Lorimer and Company, 1979); and Robert Dion, *Crimes of the Secret Police* (Montreal: Black Rose Books, 1982). Finally, for information about RCMP investigation of white collar crime in general and the Airbus affair in particular see Paul Palango, *Above the Law* (Toronto: McClelland and Stewart, 1994).

23 For a description of the controversy surrounding RCMP records at the National Archives of Canada see Gregory S. Kealey, "The Royal Canadian Mounted Police, the Canadian Security Intelligence Service, the Public Archives of Canada, and Access to Information: A Curious Tale," *Labour/Le Travail* 21 (1988): 199-226.

Mounted Police reports. While useful, some of these sources tended to emphasize the more colourful episodes of the force while neglecting the nuts and bolts of the Mounted Police structures and operations.[24]

Because the myth of the Mounted Police has lasted so long and remained so constant it suggests a continuity about its subject where, in fact, continuity does not exist. The force changed dramatically during the First World War. It was transformed or, perhaps more accurately, updated in order to allow Mounted Policemen to deal with twentieth-century policing priorities instead of nineteenth-century ones. R.C. Macleod, the pre-eminent historian of the early Mounted Police, has suggested that the First World War "fundamentally altered" the nature of the RNWMP.[25] That fundamental alteration involved the creation of a security/intelligence role; it was an era of Mounted Police history that would last until 1984 when, because of illegal activities in the 1970s, the Canadian Security Intelligence Service replaced the RCMP Security Service.

The nature of the transformation and the reasons behind it are intertwined. At various points in their history members of the Mounted Police have faced challenges to their future. The period in question was the occasion when the Mounties encountered their greatest threat and, in response, underwent their most dramatic change. To save itself the Mounted Police re-invented or transformed at least part of its purpose. It assumed security intelligence activities that initially overlapped with, and often overshadowed, its regular policing role. These two roles effectively turned the RCMP into a double-headed creature: the public Mounted Police with a public policing presence in various communities across Canada, and an invisible institution with a mandate to spy, infiltrate organizations, encourage informants, open mail, and act as "agent provocateurs" — all the classic characteristics of a secret police, an institution reviled in countries all over the world. Several categories of people received special scrutiny by the secret RCMP: members of certain ethnic groups, organized labour, and radicals, primarily of the political left. For various reasons, individuals who belonged, or were perceived to belong, to these groups were labelled as threats to the Canadian state and its institutions, including the national police force. The RCMP created a sticky web of interconnections — ethnic minorities had to be monitored because they brought the alien seed of Bolshevism to Canada; they also threatened to undermine the Anglo-Canadian character of the nation, turning it into a mongrelized country. Certain kinds of crimes became ethnic ones; these generally involved particular types of cultural activities, such as the use of opium by the Chinese or homemade alcohol by Ukrainians, that the state deemed immoral and hence a criminal activity. Such "immoral" activities, it was feared, could have a

---

24 See, for example, Charles Rivett-Carnac, *Pursuit in the Wilderness* (Toronto: Little, Brown and Company, 1965); Donovan T. Saul (ed.), *Red Serge and Stetsons: A Hundred Years of Mountie Memories* (Victoria: Horsdal and Schubert, 1993); and Donovan T. Saul (ed.), *The Way it Was: Fifty Years of RCMP Memories* (Victoria: RCMP's Veterans Association, Victoria Division, 1990). Historian Greg Marquis has commented on the apparent contradiction that "despite the federal institution's high profile in popular history, we know little of its activities in the twentieth century, when it invaded the fields of provincial and municipal policing" (see Greg Marquis, *Policing Canada's Century: A History of the Canadian Association of Chiefs of Police* (Toronto: University of Toronto Press, 1993), 5).

25 R.C. Macleod, *The North-West Mounted Police, 1873-1919* (Ottawa: The Canadian Historical Association, 1978), 18.

negative impact on the "white" population of Canada. Communists, a large number of whom happened to be non-British, had to be watched because they inspired labour and ethnic unrest. Workers had to be spied upon because they were responsive to Communist propaganda, and their members included ethnic minorities who were prone to violence and radicalism. Alone, these groups, while troublesome, did not appear to pose nearly the same threat; it was the perception of their many interconnections that made them seem dangerous. Over sixty years, the web stretched outward from these groups to entangle students and academics, women's groups, homosexuals, and countless other organizations and individuals.[26]

It was during the First World War that the development of full-time Mounted Police security functions occurred. At the beginning of the conflict, the Dominion Police was the main security intelligence force in Canada. Because of that force's limited size, however, at various points it was forced to recruit American private detectives to gather information.[27] In the case of the Mounties, they started their first extensive foray into secret service work with the outbreak of war in 1914. This type of activity occurred in Alberta and Saskatchewan where the RNWMP hired secret agents to keep watch on enemy alien groups in the two provinces. When it became obvious by 1915 that these communities posed no major security risks the force discharged many of these same agents.[28] In 1916 and 1917, however, problems relating to conscription were evident among the non-Anglo-Saxon population in the West. Agents were taken on or rehired and sent out to gather information.[29] Radicalism and labour unrest also increased as the war dragged on. By 1918, Commissioner A.B. Perry had already written a memo that set forth future options for the RNWMP, including the one that would be selected — amalgamation with the Dominion Police.[30] Then, at the beginning of 1919, in a series of memoranda, Perry put into place the framework of a Mountie secret service that would operate until the 1980s.[31] The following year, the Mounties absorbed the Dominion Police, their main rival for the affections of the security state. When the next war occurred in 1939, the Mounted Police role in security intelligence and security operations was unchallenged. Members of the force helped draft the Defence of Canada Regulations and the Mounted Police rounded up Communists and other enemies of Canada in

---

26   For information on campaigns against these groups see Paul Axelrod, "Spying on the Young in Depression and War: Students, Youth Groups and the RCMP," *Labour/Le Travail* 35 (1995): 43-63; Gary Kinsman, "'Character Weaknesses' and 'Fruit Machines': Towards an Analysis of The Anti-Homosexual Security Campaign in the Canadian Civil Service," *Labour/Le Travail* 35 (1995): 133-61; and Steve Hewitt, "Spying 101: The RCMP's Secret Activities at the University of Saskatchewan, 1920-1971," *Saskatchewan History* 47, no. 2 (1995): 20-31.

27   Carl Betke and S.W. Horrall, *Canada's Security Service: An Historical Outline, 1864-1966*, vol. 1 (Ottawa: RCMP Historical Section, 1978), 351.

28   Bill Waiser, *Park Prisoners: The Untold Story of Western Canada's National Parks, 1915-1946* (Saskatoon: Fifth House Books, 1995), 6.

29   Hewitt, "'Old Myths Die Hard'," 108.

30   National Archives of Canada (NA), Government Archives Division, Records of the Royal Canadian Mounted Police, Record Group (RG) 18, vol. 572, file 52-19, Perry to McLean, RNWMP Comptroller, 30 October 1918.

31   Ibid., vol. 599, file 1309-1335, Circular Memo #807, Re: Bolshevism, 6 January 1919; ibid., Circular Memorandum No. 807A, "RE: Detectives and Bolshevism," 6 January 1919; and ibid., Circular Memo No. 807B, 5 February 1919.

the aftermath of the opening of hostilities.[32] This security role that would involve RCMP resources, both human and financial, for over sixty years was largely a hidden one. Occasionally arrests would be made, but the very nature of the work involved secrecy and clandestine activities, activities strongly at odds with the older Mountie tradition of public policing activities that were so actively associated with those famous uniforms.

The intelligence activities, of course, are but one aspect of the post-RNWMP era. Considerable debate has ensued as to their importance.[33] Other Mountie duties, however, changed as well. Removed from regular policing duties for all of Canada, with the exception of the North, until the force replaced the Saskatchewan Provincial Police in 1928, the Mounted Police increasingly served a bureaucratic role for the federal government.[34] Naturalization investigations, enforcement of the Opium and Narcotic Drug Act, the Noxious Weeds Act, and the Migratory Birds Act, increasingly occupied the attention of the members of the newly created Mounted Police. With the exception of drug enforcement, it is difficult to build a myth around such activities. Counting birds is not the subject of major Hollywood movie productions by directors such as Cecil B. DeMille.[35] Battling crime, which Mounties returned to as a full-time occupation across Canada in the 1930s, with the notable exceptions of British Columbia, Ontario, and Quebec, would seem to have been a potential source for a RCMP myth to replace the RNWMP one. Increasingly, however, crime fighting was being bureaucratized and brought into the scientific age with new methods of policing. Commissioner J.H. MacBrien, who oversaw the rapid increase in the size of the force in the 1930s, also began the process of modernizing policing methods. In his annual reports, graphs and pie charts based on statistical analysis of crime fighting began to appear at the expense of highlighting a new round of heroes to replace the likes of Sam Steele. Indeed, the most famous or infamous Mountie in the interwar period was John Leopold, the Bohemian-born, five foot four Mountie who infiltrated the Communist Party of Canada in the 1920s and then testified against some of its senior members in the 1931 trial of the "Toronto 8."[36] No one has written any odes

---

32   Daniel Robinson, "Planning for the 'Most Serious Contingency': Alien Internment, Arbitrary Detention, and the Canadian State, 1938-39," *Journal of Canadian Studies* 28, no. 2, (1993): 5-20.

33   R.C. Macleod, "The RCMP and Provincial Policing," in R.C. Macleod and David Schneiderman (eds.), *Police Powers in Canada: The Evolution and Practice of Authority* (Toronto: University of Toronto Press, 1994), 44-56; Marquis, *Policing Canada's Century*, 5. For a spirited debate on the subject see R.C. Macleod, "How They 'Got Their Man'," *Literary Review of Canada* 5, no. 8 (1996): 19-21; Reg Whitaker and Greg Kealey, "Letter to the Editor," *Literary Review of Canada* 5, no. 10 (1996) and Macleod's response to the letter that appears on the same page.

34   Macleod, "The RCMP and Provincial Policing," 44-56.

35   *North West Mounted Police*, a movie directed and produced by Cecil B. DeMille, was released in 1940. It loosely, and the emphasis is on loosely, chronicled the events surrounding the 1885 North-West Rebellion. For more information on the film see Harry Medved and Randy Dreyfuss, *The 50 Worst Films of All Time* (New York: Warner Brothers, 1978), 164-69. See also Pierre Berton, *Hollywood's Canada: The Americanization of Our National Image* (Toronto: McClelland and Stewart, 1975), 109-66; and Bernard A. Drew, *Lawmen in Scarlet: An Annotated Guide to Royal Canadian Mounted Police in Print and Performance* (Metuchen, N.J.: The Scarecrow Press, 1990).

36   John Herd Thompson, with Allen Seager, *Canada 1922-1939: Decades of Discord* (Toronto: McClelland and Stewart Ltd., 1985), 228-29.

to Leopold, an individual whose background put him at odds with all of the dominant images of the Mounties.[37]

Even the most enduring symbol of the Mounted Police in the modern age, the musical ride, is a nineteenth-century artifact.[38] By the end of the First World War, horses were only useful in urban centres for crowd control. Their employment in rural areas lingered on into the interwar period. During a one-month period in late 1919, for example, Constable Carlson of the Short Creek Detachment in Saskatchewan travelled 375 miles on the back of a horse. Even in rural areas, however, technology of the new century had begun to displace the tradition of the previous one. In 1919 the North Portal, Saskatchewan, Mountie detachment was already using the railway, an "auto cycle" and automobiles as part of their policing duties.[39]

There is one final important reason why the images of the old Mounted Police linger on with those of the new: they benefit the RCMP and thus the force has a very strong interest in propagating them. There is not a police force in the world that would not want to be associated with values of heroism, honesty, and incredible competency that seem cornerstones of the nineteenth-century North-West Mounted Police. Popularity, however, is only part of the reason why the Mounted Police have perpetuated these images and continue, along with the Walt Disney Company, to closely guard their sanctity. Popularity also means power. Those who might criticize the force for various indiscretions face a very difficult task since they are battling not just a police force but a national symbol or perhaps even the nation itself. Michael Dawson has aptly described this equation: "the Force attempted to make its experiences, ideals, and aims seem as being identical to those of the 'nation', and thus of the entire population."[40] Doug Owram has also noted the important symbolism of at least one aspect of the Mountie image:

> The scarlet coat of the North West Mounted Police had been deliberately chosen in order to evoke the British tradition. Thus the myth of the police became in reality a part of the tradition of law in British society ... The man and the abstract concept merged into a symbol that few dared to challenge.[41]

Such connections work to the Mounted Police's advantage in numerous ways. At the end of the First World War those nineteenth-century images helped the force

---

37 Leopold eventually reached the position of superintendent. Even with his fame, however, he faced regular challenges by the guards at police headquarters in Ottawa because he was, in the words of the official historians of the RCMP Security Service, "foreign looking" (see Betke and Horrall, *Canada's Security Service*, vol. 1, 449).

38 The major parts of the musical ride (display riding and music) were developed in the nineteenth century. In 1904 it became a form of public entertainment (see S.W. Horrall, *A Pictorial History of the Royal Canadian Mounted Police* (Toronto: McGraw-Hill Ryerson, 1973), 156-63; and S.W. Horrall, "Lady Dewdney's Own: The Beginnings of the RCMP Musical Ride," *RCMP Quarterly* 49, summer 1984, 46-51).

39 NA, Royal Canadian Mounted Police Records, RG 18, vol. 1933, file 3, pt. 8, "Patrols made at the Short Creek Detachment from Oct. 23, 1919 to Nov. 25, 1919"; and ibid., "List of Patrols, made from North Portal Detachment, between the 24th September & the 24 October 1919."

40 John Michael Fraser Dawson, "Re-Weaving the Tapestry of Order: The Royal Canadian Mounted Police's 1973 Centennial and the Renovation of Historical Narrative," M.A. thesis, Queen's University, 1995, 17.

41 Doug Owram, *Promise of Eden: The Canadian Expansionist Movement and the Idea of the West, 1856-1900* (Toronto: University of Toronto Press, 1992), 140.

triumph over its Dominion Police foe; similarly in the 1920s, although they discussed it, the Liberal government of William Lyon Mackenzie King did not eliminate or even substantially reduce the power of the Mounted Police. Because the Mounted Police were perceived to have had such a positive past most people gave them the benefit of the doubt whenever things went wrong; their mythic past proved their good intentions. To use a simple analogy, the view of the Canadian public and power brokers was to overlook the sins of the child because they knew the parents and the parents were good people.

To the RCMP past makes perfect. For years the Mounted Police have employed a staff historian to produce various pieces for an internal and external audience. Those in command have long worried about portrayals of their institution. Generating myth has been a tradition within the Mounted Police. Thus, in urging that the name of the force should be retained, Commissioner Perry was attempting to cash in on the reputation of the old body. He may have lost that battle, but the new name — Royal Canadian Mounted Police — was as close to the old as possible while still recognizing the organization's new geographical scope.[42] In December 1919 *Scarlet and Gold*, a publication of the RNWMP Veterans Association, made its appearance. Edited by R.G. MacBeth, one of the force's early chroniclers, the 114-page magazine was replete with tales of the old Mounted Police and their nineteenth-century policing adventures. What was missing was almost any reference to the policing environment in 1919. One brief comment about the Winnipeg General Strike was made (and not by name), while only scattered references to the change the force was undergoing appear.[43] This publication was supplemented in 1933 by the first issue of the *RCMP Quarterly*. Its creation coincided with the sixtieth anniversary of the birth of its subject matter. In that first issue, and in those that have followed, veneration of the past played an important role. Leading off was Prime Minister R.B. Bennett who praised the force and cited its exemplary past. Even more significant was the first editorial which reiterated the intertwining of the history of the Mounted Police with that of Canada:

> Throughout the years the activities and accomplishments of the Force have been inextricably interwoven with the development of the country it serves. The expansion of Canada's interest, whether in the Yukon, along the Mackenzie to the Arctic Ocean, on Hudson Bay, or in the remote islands of the Eastern Arctic, has been preceded by the Force's presence, a presence which, unfailingly, established the principles of British justice at each new frontier, and ensured its unwavering application for all who followed behind.[44]

"Historical article" led the list of departments to be included in the new publication. In the first issue appears "Reminiscences of One of the Originals," a profile of one of the original Mounties. Two aspects of the publication, however, point to the reality of the new Mounted Police as opposed to its nineteenth-century mythic version. On the editorial board was Col. C.F. Hamilton whose regular job was as the head of the small unit that would eventually become the RCMP Security Service. The other contradiction to the imagined Mounties appeared on page 37: the obituary of Inspector J.L. Sampson who died, the writer noted, while helping to quell a

---

42   Horrall, *Pictorial History*, 181.
43   *Scarlet and Gold* 1, no. 1 (December 1919): 11, 41, 110.
44   "Editorial," *RCMP Quarterly* 1, no. 1 (July 1933): 6.

"disturbance." That "disturbance" was in fact the Saskatoon relief camp riot, an event primarily provoked by a headquarters' decision in Regina to remove relief camp agitators.[45] The problems of the modern age — massive unemployment, urban squalor, radicalism, absence of a social safety net, state repression — combined in Saskatoon as in countless other Depression venues to demonstrate once again that members of the RCMP were policing a very different era from their RNWMP predecessors.

Technology, urbanization, immigration, and industrialization, among many other factors, had all converged to change and transform both the force and the environment that its members policed. Rapid change does not just transform; it also disrupts, and it even frightens. Hence the comfort that can be derived from a well-known and mythic past. The RNWMP and the trappings that came with them offered all of that and in a very familiar setting, the wide-open Prairies. The RNWMP became an anchor. On the other hand, the RCMP and their new policing activities serve as a reminder of the discontinuity and realities of the new Canada.[46]

The power of the nineteenth-century Mountie, however, strikes an even more fundamental chord among many Canadians. Who would not want to be as that version has been portrayed: courageous, honest, competent, forthright, a defender of the weak, an enemy of the corrupt. The "honest broker" is also an image Canadians seek to project to the outside world. The twentieth-century Mountie, with a mixed record that has included incompetence, violence, and illegal activities, conflicts with how citizens of this country wish to see themselves. Is it at all surprising that the image of Dudley Do-right would triumph over that of Robert Samson, the Mountie blown up by a bomb that he was planting outside the house of a Montreal business executive.[47] There is a line from the movie "Nixon" which effectively captures the intricate relationship between Canada and its national police force. Near the end of the movie Richard Nixon is gazing forlornly at the portrait of his arch-nemesis, John F. Kennedy. "When they [the American people] see you, they see what they want to be," utters the discredited president. "When they see me, they see what they are."[48] So it was with the RNWMP and RCMP. One represented a past and an institution that never really was. The other represented an institution and a past that many would like to forget.

---

45   For more on the Saskatoon relief camp riot, including the RCMP role in it, see Glenn Makahonuk, "The Saskatoon Relief Camp Riot of May 8, 1933: An Expression of Class Conflict," *Saskatchewan History* 37, no. 2 (1984): 55-72; and Hewitt, "'Old Myths Die Hard'," 247-49.

46   The clash between old and new can be seen in the battle over allowing Sikh Mounties to wear their turbans while on duty. The leadership of the RCMP favoured the adjustment because of the need for the force to reflect and be able to police a multicultural Canada. RCMP veterans and many westerners opposed any change to the American-style headgear. See *Western Report*, 14 February 1994, 26.

47   Sallot, *Nobody Said No*, 94-95.

48   Oliver Stone, "Screenplay for the movie *Nixon*," 1996. Jack Ramsay, a former Mountie who was openly critical of his former employer in the 1970s, offered a variation of the Nixon lament: "I want people to know what the Mounted Police have become, instead of constantly being reminded of what they used to be" (as quoted in Edward Mann and John Alan Lee, *RCMP vs. the People: Inside Canada's Security Service* (Don Mills, Ont., 1979), 129).

Permissions

William M. Baker, "Captain R. Burton Deane and Theatre on the Prairies, 1883-1901," is reprinted courtesy of *Theatre Research in Canada/Recherches Théâtrales au Canada*.

William Beahen, "Abortion and Infanticide in Western Canada, 1874-1916," is reprinted courtesy of the Canadian Catholic Historical Association.

William Beahen, "Mob Law Could Not Prevail," is reprinted courtesy of the author.

Carl Betke, "Pioneers and Police on the Canadian Prairies, 1885-1914," is reprinted courtesy of the Canadian Historical Association.

Hugh Dempsey, "The Wild Ones," is reprinted with permission from *The Amazing Death of Calf Shirt and Other Blackfoot Stories: Three Hundred Years of Blackfoot History*. Copyright 1994 by Hugh A. Dempsey. Fifth House Publishers. Calgary, Canada.

Steve Hewitt, "Malczewski's List: A Case Study of Royal North-West Mounted Police-Immigrant Relations," is reprinted courtesy of the author.

S.W. Horrall, "The Royal North-West Mounted Police and Labour Unrest in Western Canada, 1919," is reprinted by permission of the University of Toronto Press Incorporated.

G.S. Kealey, "The Surveillance State: The Origins of Domestic Intelligence and Counter-Subversion in Canada, 1914-21," is reprinted courtesy of *Intelligence and National Security*.

R.C. Macleod, "Crime and Criminals in the North-West Territories, 1873-1905," is reprinted by permission of the University of Toronto Press Incorporated.

R.C. Macleod, "The NWMP and Minority Groups," is reprinted by permission of the University of Toronto Press Incorporated.

Anna-Maria Mavromichalis, "Tar and Feathers: The Mounted Police and Frontier Justice," is reprinted courtesy of the author.

B.J. Mayfield, "The Interlude: The North-West Mounted Police and the Blackfoot Peoples, 1874-1877," is reprinted courtesy of the author.

Keith Walden, "Character," is reprinted courtesy of the author.